MANAGERIAL EPIDEMIOLOGY

PRINCIPLES & APPLICATIONS

AMIR A. KHALIQ

PhD, MBBS, MSc, MSHS
University of Oklahoma, College of Public Health

JONES & BARTLETT
LEARNING

World Headquarters
Jones & Bartlett Learning
5 Wall Street
Burlington, MA 01803
978-443-5000
info@jblearning.com
www.jblearning.com

Jones & Bartlett Learning books and products are available through most bookstores and online booksellers. To contact Jones & Bartlett Learning directly, call 800-832-0034, fax 978-443-8000, or visit our website, www.jblearning.com.

Production Credits
VP, Executive Publisher: David D. Cella
Director of Product Management: Michael Brown
Product Manager: Sophie Fleck Teague
Product Specialist: Danielle Bessette
Production Editor: Kelly Sylvester
Composition: codeMantra U.S. LLC
Senior Marketing Manager: Susanne Walker
Manufacturing and Inventory Control Supervisor: Amy Bacus

Cover Design: Kristin E. Parker
Rights & Media Specialist: Merideth Tumasz
Media Development Editor: Shannon Sheehan
Cover Image (Title Page, Chapter Opener):
    © Monsitj/Getty Images, dem10/Getty Images
Printing and Binding: Hess Print Solutions
Cover Printing: Hess Print Solutions

Library of Congress Cataloging-in-Publication Data
Names: Khaliq, Amir, author.
Title: Managerial epidemiology: principles and applications / Amir Khaliq.
Description: Burlington, MA: Jones & Bartlett Learning, [2020] | Includes bibliographical references.
Identifiers: LCCN 2017052910 | ISBN 9781284082173 (paperback)
Subjects: | MESH: Epidemiologic Methods | Epidemiology—organization & administration | Health Services Administration
Classification: LCC RA651 | NLM WA 950 | DDC 614.4—dc23
LC record available at https://lccn.loc.gov/2017052910

6048

Printed in the United States of America
22 21 20 19 18   10 9 8 7 6 5 4 3 2 1

To:

Namir, the embodiment of all my hopes and dreams.

Shirin, my East and West and my Sunday rest.*

My parents, to whom the debt of my gratitude shall remain forever unpaid.

*Borrowed from a poem by W. H. Auden

Contents

About the Author viii

Preface...................................ix

Chapter 1 Epidemiology for Evidence-Based Management 1

1.1 Introduction 2
1.2 Epidemiology.............................2
1.3 Management 2
1.4 Decision-Making Process....................3
1.5 Evidence-Based Management.................4
1.6 Epidemiology and Evidence-Based Management 5
1.7 Managerial Epidemiology 5
1.8 Scenario for Application of Managerial Epidemiology...............................6
1.9 Sources of Epidemiologic Data 7
Case Study 1.1: Impact of Administrative Decisions on Patient Outcomes 7
Case Study 1.2: Epidemiologic Patterns That Can Guide Policy Decisions..............10
1.10 Summary 12
References 13

Chapter 2 Determinants of Individual and Population Health.............. 15

2.1 Introduction 16
2.2 Definition of *Health* 16
2.3 Definition of a Population 17
2.4 What Is Population Health?...................17
2.5 Population Health Model Versus Medical Care Model........................18
2.6 Link Between Physical and Mental Health 18
2.7 Determinants of Health 19
2.8 Genetic Makeup as a Determinant of Health ...20

2.9 Socioeconomic Determinants of Health 22
2.10 Race as a Determinant of Health.............27
Case Study 2.1: Effect of Education on Health 28
Case Study 2.2: Effect of Socioeconomic Status on Health 31
2.11 Summary 34
References 34

Chapter 3 Assessment of Personal and Population Health.............. 37

3.1 Introduction 38
3.2 Definition of Disease, Disability, and Death ...38
3.3 Assessment of Personal Health 42
3.4 Assessment of Physiologic Health 43
3.5 Assessment of Mental Health and Psychosocial Development...................43
3.6 Assessment of Functioning and Disability 44
3.7 Self-Assessment of Health and Well-Being 45
3.8 Assessment of Community Health............46
3.9 Assessment of Burden of Disease and Summary Measures of Population Health.....48
3.10 Classification of Diseases and Procedures.....50
3.11 Reportable/Notifiable Diseases 52
Exercise 3.1 53
Case Study 3.1: Assessment of Burden of Disease...54
Case Study 3.2: Influence of Gender and Age on Disability After Stroke 55
3.12 Summary 56
References 56

Chapter 4 Epidemiologic Measures of Population Health.............. 59

4.1 Introduction 60
4.2 Types of Statistics Reported in Population Health...........................60

4.3 Measures of Disease Frequency
        in a Population...............................62

4.4 Measures of the Frequency of
        Death in a Population......................66

4.5 Other Commonly Reported Statistics.........71

4.6 Adjustment or Standardization of Rates 75

Exercises 4.1.......................................80

Case Study 4.1: Example of Cumulative Incidence ..80

Case Study 4.2: Example of a Prevalence Study.....81

4.7 Summary....................................82

References..82

Chapter 5 Descriptive Epidemiology 85

5.1 Introduction................................86

5.2 Person......................................86

5.3 Place.......................................92

5.4 Time.......................................95

5.5 Types of Epidemiologic Investigations........96

5.6 Descriptive Epidemiologic Studies............97

Case Study 5.1: Example of a Case Series Report....98

Case Study 5.2: Example of a
        Cross-Sectional Study.....................100

Case Study 5.3: Example of a
        Cross-Sectional Study.....................101

5.7 Summary...................................102

References.......................................102

Chapter 6 Behavioral Epidemiology....... 105

6.1 Introduction...............................106

6.2 Behavioral Epidemiology....................106

6.3 Epidemiology of Physical Activity...........107

6.4 Epidemiology of Smoking...................108

6.5 Epidemiology of Obesity and
        Poor Nutrition...........................110

6.6 Epidemiology of Alcohol and
        Substance Abuse 112

6.7 Epidemiology of Cardiovascular Disease.... 114

6.8 Epidemiology of Diabetes...................115

6.9 Patient Incentives to Promote
        Healthy Behavior.........................115

6.10 Incentives for Providers....................116

Case Study 6.1: Behavioral Factors and
        Risk of Gestational Diabetes...............117

Case Study 6.2: Body Mass Index, Waist
        Circumference, and Risk of Mortality........ 118

6.11 Summary 120

References 120

Chapter 7 Infectious Disease Epidemiology... 125

7.1 Introduction 126

7.2 Infectious Diseases in the United States 127

7.3 Global Burden of Infectious Diseases 127

7.4 Emergence of New and Resurgence of
        Previously Known Infectious Diseases 129

7.5 The Infectious Disease Triad 130

7.6 Important Definitions Related
        to Infectious Diseases 131

7.7 Infectious Disease Outbreaks
        or Epidemics.............................. 134

7.8 Outbreak Investigation.................... 135

7.9 Example of an Outbreak Investigation 136

7.10 Zika Virus Outbreak 2015 138

7.11 Ebola Virus Outbreak: West Africa 2014 140

Case Study 7.1: California Measles Outbreak 2014... 141

Case Study 7.2: Ohio Botulism Outbreak 2015 142

7.12 Summary 142

References 143

Chapter 8 Injury Epidemiology 145

8.1 Introduction 146

8.2 Nature, Distribution, and Impact
        of Injuries in the United States.............. 146

8.3 Epidemiology of Intentional Injuries
        in the United States 147

8.4 Epidemiology of Road Traffic Injuries
        and Death in the United States............. 150

8.5 Epidemiology of Traumatic Brain
        Injury in the United States.................. 151

8.6 Epidemiology of Burns in
        the United States.......................... 153

8.7 Economic Impact of Injuries in
        the United States.......................... 155

8.8 The U.S. National Violent Death
        Reporting System (NVDRS)................. 155

8.9 The U.S. National Electronic Injury
        Surveillance System....................... 157

8.10 Global Injury Epidemiology 157

8.11 Example of a Study of Injury
        Epidemiology. 163

Case Study 8.1 Hospital-Based Injury Surveillance. . . 167

Case Study 8.2 Unintentional Firearm Deaths. 168

8.12 Summary 169

References 169

**Chapter 9   Epidemiology and
                        Measurement of Quality 173**

9.1 Introduction 174

9.2 Definition and Goals of Healthcare
        Quality. 174

9.3 Determinants of Healthcare Quality 175

9.4 Distribution of Healthcare Quality
        (Person, Place, Time). 176

9.5 Severity of Disease and
        Assessment of Quality. 183

9.6 Use of Checklists in Quality
        Improvement 184

9.7 Physician Quality Reporting System 184

9.8 Hospital Quality Reporting
        System—Hospital Compare. 185

9.9 Hospital Readmission Reduction Program . . 185

9.10 Institute for Healthcare
        Improvement—Triple Aim 186

9.11 Example of a Quality Assessment Study 186

Case Study 9.1: Reasons for Postsurgical
        Hospital Readmissions 189

Case Study 9.2: Impact of a Rapid
        Response System on Inpatient Mortality
        and Length of Stay 189

9.12 Summary 191

References 191

**Chapter 10   Community Health Needs
                          Assessment 195**

10.1 Introduction 196

10.2 Determinants of Healthcare Needs. 196

10.3 Need Versus Demand. 200

10.4 Definition and Scope of a Community
        Health Needs Assessment. 201

10.5 Requirements of the U.S.
        Affordable Care Act 202

10.6 Methods and Process of Needs
        Assessment. 202

10.7 Planning for a Community
        Health Needs Assessment. 205

10.8 Nature and Type of Data for a
        Community Health Needs Assessment. 205

10.9 Sources of Data for a CHNA 208

10.10 Priority Setting for Healthcare Needs 209

10.11 Community Health Needs Assessment
        After a Disaster. 209

10.12 Assessment of Unmet Healthcare
        Needs—Market Analysis 209

10.13 Estimation of Future Healthcare Needs 210

10.14 Forecasting Methods. 211

Case Study 10.1: Healthcare Needs of
        the Homeless 214

Case Study 10.2: Impact of Unmet
        Healthcare Needs 217

10.15 Summary 220

References 220

**Chapter 11   Healthcare Planning
                          and Marketing. 223**

11.1 Introduction 224

11.2 Definition and Purpose of Planning 225

11.3 Determinants of Geographic
        Markets and Service Areas 225

11.4 Estimation of Geographic Markets
        and Service Areas. 226

11.5 Estimation of Service Area and
        Market Share: Hospital Administrator
        Perspective. 227

11.6 Estimation of a Geographic Market:
        Policy Maker Perspective. 228

11.7 Measuring the Level of Competition
        in a Geographic Market 230

11.8 Priority Setting and the Role
        of "Healthy People" Reports 230

11.9 Small Area Health Planning 231

11.10 Facility Location Planning 233

11.11 Certificate of Need Programs. 234

11.12 Designation of Health Professional
        Shortage Areas 234

11.13 Determinants of Access to
        Health Services 237

11.14 Sources of Epidemiologic Data............ 238

11.15 Healthcare Marketing 239

Exercise 11.1..................................... 241

Exercise 11.2..................................... 241

Case Study 11.1: Example of Regional
       Market Analysis 242

Case Study 11.2: Planning for Mental
       Health Services 244

11.16 Summary 246

References 247

Chapter 12 Prevention, Detection, and Monitoring of Disease..... 249

12.1 Introduction 250

12.2 The Nature, Scope, and Levels
      of Prevention 250

12.3 Screening................................ 255

12.4 Surveillance.............................. 266

Exercise 12.1..................................... 271

Exercise 12.2..................................... 271

Case Study 12.1: Nosocomial Infection
       Surveillance............................. 271

Case Study 12.2: Screening for Colorectal Cancer... 272

12. 5 Summary................................ 273

References 274

Chapter 13 Basic Statistical Concepts and Tests 277

13.1 Introduction 278

13.2 Examples 278

13.3 Basic Statistical Concepts 281

13.4 Statistical Tests for Comparison of Groups... 286

Exercise 13.1..................................... 287

Exercise 13.2..................................... 287

13.5 Summary 288

Chapter 14 Observational Studies 289

14.1 Introduction.............................. 290

14.2 Observational Studies..................... 290

14.3 Ecological Studies........................ 291

14.4 Example of an Ecological Study 292

14.5 Cohort Studies............................ 293

14.6 Example of a Prospective Cohort Study ... 300

14.7 Example of a Retrospective Cohort Study... 302

14.8 Case-Control Studies...................... 303

14.9 Example of a Case-Control Study.......... 307

14.10 Risk Factor and Exposure in Cohort
       and Case-Control Studies 309

14.11 Comparison of Cohort and Case-Control
       Study Design 310

14.12 Association and Causality 310

14.13 Bias..................................... 312

14.14 Confounding 313

Case Study 14.1: An Ecological Study............. 315

Case Study 14.2: Prospective Cohort Study....... 316

Case Study 14.3: Retrospective Cohort Study..... 317

Case Study 14.4: Case-Control Study 318

14. 15 Summary 321

References 321

Chapter 15 Experimental Studies......... 323

15.1 Introduction 324

15.2 Experimental or Interventional
      Study Design 325

15.3 Categorization of Experimental Studies ... 327

15.4 Randomized Controlled Trials
      or Clinical Trials 328

15.5 Example of a Randomized Clinical Trial 330

15.6 Community Trials 331

15.7 Example of a Community Trial............. 331

15.8 Natural Experiments 332

15.9 Factorial Trials........................... 333

Case Study 15.1: Randomized Control
       Trial – Chlorhexidine Bathing in ICUs
       to Prevent HAIs 334

15.10 Summary 335

References 336

List of Acronyms 337

Glossary 341

Index 351

About the Author

Amir A. Khaliq is a Professor of Health Administration and Policy at the University of Oklahoma Health Sciences Center, College of Public Health, where he has taught courses in Managerial Epidemiology, Operations Research, Decision Analysis, and Comparative International Health Systems since 2000. He was trained as a physician in Pakistan and received MSc in Community Health and MS in Health Services degrees from the Universities of London and California. He earned a PhD in Health Administration from the University of Toronto.

Preface

Many academic programs offering a degree in health administration include a course on managerial epidemiology in their curriculum. The content of these courses, understandably, differs from one program to another. The diversity in the content of managerial epidemiology courses across programs reflects the diversity of opinions about the scope and nature of the field called *managerial epidemiology*. Increasingly, program directors and instructors favor content that combines elements of traditional introductory epidemiology courses with traditional population health courses. The desire to combine concepts, methods, and skills from epidemiology and population health is not accidental but reflects two important realities. First, the whole idea of managerial epidemiology is to extend the boundaries of epidemiology from an investigation of the determinants and distribution of disease and injury to the examination of the determinants and distribution of health outcomes in populations. Second, because of the changes taking place in our thinking about health and healthcare delivery, there is a growing need for healthcare managers to acquire epidemiologic skills on one hand and develop an understanding of the concepts and methods related to population health on the other. As such, managerial epidemiology must include the application of information regarding the determinants and distribution of disease and injury to health promotion, disease prevention, and planning of health services. This text presents a combination of materials from epidemiology and population health with the view that future healthcare managers need to have a good grasp of various aspects of population health as well as a foundational understanding of the epidemiologic principles and methods. The need for a new text in managerial epidemiology is evident from the dearth of existing textbooks on this subject.

Chapter 1 in the text is foundational in nature and sets the stage for in-depth discussions in succeeding chapters on the determinants and distribution of health in individuals and populations, assessment of population health status, and methods for community health needs assessment. The chapter prepares the reader for these discussions by introducing the underlying concepts of epidemiology, management, and evidence-based management.

Chapters 2–5 focus on the determinants, assessment, and measurement of health in individuals and populations and the characterization of health and disease in terms of person, place, and time. Chapter 2 explains the holistic concept of health and the population model of health as opposed to the traditional medical model. The chapter also provides a detailed discussion of genetic, socioeconomic, and racial or ethnic determinants of health. Chapter 3 deals with the complex concepts of disease, death, and disability and various approaches to assess the health and well-being of individuals and populations. Chapter 4 discusses various measures of morbidity and mortality and different types of summary statistics reported in literature as indicators of population health status. The chapter includes clear and concise definitions for a number of epidemiologic concepts necessary to measure the health status and distribution of diseases in populations. Chapter 5 discusses the demographic, geographic, and temporal characterization and reporting of health problems in terms of person, place, and time. The chapter also includes a discussion of different types of descriptive epidemiologic investigations in the way of case reports and cross-sectional studies.

Chapters 6–9 focus on the determinants of health in relation to lifestyle and personal behavior, the distribution of infections and injuries in populations, and assessment of quality of care delivered by the healthcare system. The materials presented in these chapters represent different dimensions of population health. Chapter 6 deals with health problems related to lifestyles and personal behavior, including sedentary lifestyle, substance abuse, and the impact of lifestyles on the prevalence of cardiovascular disease and diabetes in different populations. Chapter 7 engages in a detailed discussion of infectious disease epidemiology in the United States and worldwide, including the problem of emerging infectious diseases and antimicrobial drug resistance in microorganisms. Chapter 8 discusses the epidemiology of various kinds of injuries and provides national and international data on violence, drownings, and burns. Chapter 9 explains the relationship of the structure and processes of care with health outcomes and various methods of monitoring and reporting ambulatory and inpatient quality of care. The chapter also includes a discussion of the impact of severity of disease and case mix on health outcomes and indicators of healthcare quality.

Chapters 10 and 11 are designed to equip future healthcare managers with the tools and skills necessary for community health needs assessment and planning for adequate delivery of services. The chapters include various methods for estimating primary and secondary service areas, determination of the size of a geographic market, level of competition in a geographic market, and estimation of market share held by various providers. Chapter 11 describes different approaches toward healthcare planning, setting priorities, determining levels of access, and designation of health professional shortage areas by the U.S. Health Resources and Services Administration.

Chapters 12–15 deal with the concepts of prevention, monitoring, surveillance, and reporting of diseases that pose serious public health threats and the technical aspect of designing and conducting various kinds of epidemiologic investigations. Chapter 13 serves as a convenient resource for brushing up on basic quantitative and statistical concepts. Chapters 14 and 15 provide comprehensive information on the design, comparative suitability, and technical challenges of observational and experimental epidemiologic investigations. Chapter 14 discusses the importance, intricacies, and comparative advantages of prospective and retrospective cohort and case-control studies. Chapter 15 provides a discussion of the frequency and relevance of experimental epidemiologic investigations in the form of randomized controlled trials and the practical aspects of conducting experimental studies.

The content and case studies in various chapters are organized in a manner suitable to meet the needs of a diverse body of students and are drawn from a vast body of literature. The author hopes this text will make a meaningful contribution to the field of managerial epidemiology and serve as a valuable resource worthy of the time and attention of students and instructors in health administration programs.

Amir A. Khaliq

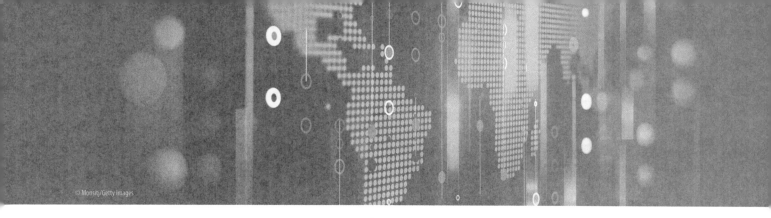

© Monsiti/Getty Images

CHAPTER 1

Epidemiology for Evidence-Based Management

CHAPTER OUTLINE

1.1 Introduction
1.2 Epidemiology
1.3 Management
1.4 Decision-Making Process
1.5 Evidence-Based Management
1.6 Epidemiology and Evidence-Based Management
1.7 Managerial Epidemiology

1.8 Scenario for Application of Managerial Epidemiology
1.9 Sources of Epidemiologic Data
Case Study 1.1 – Impact of Administrative Decisions on Patient Outcomes
Case Study 1.2 – Epidemiologic Patterns that Can Guide Policy Decisions
1.10 Summary

1

▶ 1.1 Introduction

Good management involves decisions that are guided by both quantitative and qualitative evidence. By its very nature, effective healthcare management requires the collection of appropriate data and application of decision-support tools from different disciplines. The purpose of *managerial epidemiology* is to familiarize both aspiring and practicing healthcare managers with the tools available from the fields of epidemiology and management and give them the ability to make a concerted use of these tools for efficient and informed decision making. The combined use of techniques from epidemiology and management is the foundation of the emerging field of **evidence-based management (EBM)**. Before discussing the application of epidemiologic methods in healthcare management, it is important to remind ourselves of the nature of the two disciplines called *epidemiology* and *management*. In the following sections, we introduce the terminology and basic principles of epidemiology and management and then explain how EBM can use the quantitative evidence generated by epidemiologic investigations. Two case studies at the end of the chapter demonstrate how epidemiologic evidence can be used for effective healthcare management and policy formulation.

▶ 1.2 Epidemiology

Porta[1] defines **epidemiology** as "The study of the occurrence and distribution of health-related events, states, and processes in specified populations, including the study of the determinants influencing such processes, and the application of this knowledge to control relevant health problems." A less-comprehensive older definition states that epidemiology is "the study of the distribution and determinants of diseases and injuries in human populations."[2] The implication of both definitions is that diseases and their causes are distributed neither randomly nor evenly across populations. Understanding the distribution of diseases across populations, time, and space can give us valuable information about their causes, and this information can be used to develop prevention and control strategies. Recognizing that diseases differentially afflict dwellers of different regions or people of different colors, creeds, and sexes has been an important element in our quest to live a healthier and longer life.

The field of epidemiology has experienced tremendous growth and methodologic sophistication in the last few decades. The scope of epidemiologic investigations now spans from genetics to social sciences, from forensic medicine to veterinary medicine, and from pharmaceuticals to plant diseases. Concurrent with these developments, more refined analytic and statistical techniques have been developed to address issues resulting from the complexities of study design. Easy availability of vast amounts of clinical, public health, demographic, and socioeconomic data from a variety of sources that can be integrated and analyzed within minutes with the help of relatively inexpensive powerful computers has enormously increased the number of epidemiologic investigations being conducted. Every year, thousands of research articles based on epidemiologic investigations are being published in dozens if not hundreds of conventional and open-access journals from every corner of the world.

There is a mutually supportive and symbiotic relationship between the practice of medicine and epidemiology. Epidemiology is *population medicine* in that it deals with the identification, investigation, and control of diseases in populations. The same is done at the individual level by those who practice medicine—namely physicians.[2] Clinical medicine benefits from the knowledge of the frequency of a disease in a given population obtained through epidemiologic investigations. Conversely, epidemiologic investigations rely on accurate identification of diseases in individuals by physicians. Although epidemiologic information is essential for better practice of medicine and formulation of control strategies, assessment of the incidence and prevalence of disease in a population is entirely dependent on accurate diagnosis and reporting of disease by clinicians.[2] For example, community-level strategies for the prevention and control of AIDS or delivery of medical and social services to Alzheimer's disease patients require data regarding the frequency and distribution of these diseases in the population. Such data can only become available through accurate diagnosis and reporting by physicians.

▶ 1.3 Management

Management can be defined as "The act, manner, or practice of managing, supervising, or controlling."[3] Another way to describe management is that it involves "getting results through the work of others for the benefit of the client."[4] In either case, management involves the use of organizational resources and handling of processes, situations, and relations. A number of theoretical models have been developed to explain what managers do and how they do it.[4-6] Management of healthcare organizations such as hospitals, clinics, and nursing homes poses challenges that are different from those of other organizations. Healthcare management requires knowledge of healthcare policy, regulatory environment, and insurance. Additionally, it requires an understanding of issues related to access, utilization, and biomedical ethics, as well as analytic skills to use epidemiologic data for decision making. Researchers explore how healthcare managers carry out their responsibilities and make decisions, and what factors explain different styles of management. For practitioners, management means attaining efficiency, improving quality, motivating staff, and achieving organizational goals. As practitioners, healthcare managers have to learn the principles of leadership, motivation, financial management, and quality improvement. They have to employ "soft power" and diplomatic skills, as well as "hard" analytic skills.[7]

The purpose of management is to specify, communicate, and achieve the goals and objectives of the organization in a consistent manner while providing a harmonious work environment for employees. Researchers have identified three main goals of healthcare management:[8] first, manage the financial affairs of the organization to ensure financial stability; second, provide highest quality services through efficient use of resources; and third, maintain high moral and ethical standards while serving competing or divergent interests of stakeholders. The success of an organization in achieving these goals is a direct measure of the success of its managers. Given the challenging economic, political, and social environment in which healthcare organizations operate, some of these goals can be in conflict with one another. For example, the necessity of attaining monetary success can compel managers to forego desirable social objectives, such as delivery of discounted care to socially marginalized populations.

While specific duties of managers inevitably vary from one organization to another or from one department to another, these duties are conventionally categorized into planning, coordination, directing, and control functions. Such a categorization is helpful in developing a framework in which appropriate empirical data or evidence can be used to understand managerial functions and to make a case for rational decision making. In practice, these roles merge and mix during the daily process of decision making and problem solving. Managers transition back and forth into these roles without compartmentalizing their work into these conceptual domains. In carrying out all these managerial functions, the use of data and empirical evidence can make the difference between an effective and ineffective manger.

Mintzberg[9] challenges the "planning, organizing, coordinating, and controlling" model of managerial functions developed in the earlier part of the 20th century and offers "interpersonal, informational, entrepreneurial, and decisional" activities as the main functions of managers. The interpersonal role involves leadership through motivation and mentoring. The informational role involves collection and dissemination of information and serving as a spokesperson for a department or the organization. As entrepreneurs, mangers set goals and objectives for their departments or organizations, and as "disturbance handlers," they resolve conflicts and solve problems.

In the "art" and "science" of management, the scientific component relies on systematic analysis of data and use of evidence, whereas the art of management requires creative thinking and innovation to solve a given problem.[5] The unique blend of art and science employed by a person creates his or her management style. Clearly, the management style of a person is also a function of individual characteristics, values, experience, analytic skills, and the level of authority enjoyed in the organization. Strong quantitative skills are essential for problem solving and finding the best solutions. Analytical tools are especially useful for solving problems that are discrete in nature and lend themselves to quantitative analysis. Although managers frequently encounter problems that are ambiguous or multidimensional, off-the-cuff decision making without quantitative analysis and empirical evidence can be very detrimental to the goals of an organization. The element of art in decision making is meant only to supplement the scientific approach toward decision making rather than replace it. Based on quantitative data, a good understanding of the demographic characteristics of the community, demand for services, and evolving patterns of morbidity and mortality are critically important for excellence in healthcare management.

▶ 1.4 Decision-Making Process

According to management theory, managerial decisions vary in complexity and can be divided into two main categories: *programmed* and *nonprogrammed* decisions.[10] **Programmed decisions** address problems that are encountered frequently and are repetitive in nature. In dealing with these problems, managers do not need to find new solutions. Because of the familiarity of managers with such problems, rules and procedures usually exist to resolve them. The level of risk associated with such decisions is minimal because of successful past application of similar decisions. **Nonprogrammed decisions**, on the other hand, are unprecedented and demand innovative solutions. In both programmed and nonprogrammed situations, managers are expected to adopt a rational and systematic approach to problem solving and decision making.

Researchers have also identified four different approaches toward decision making.[10] The underlying premise in all these approaches is that important decisions are complex, and individuals are constrained in their ability to make sound decisions because of their inability to simultaneously process multiple dimensions of a complex problem.[11] The first of these approaches focuses on the application of operations research or management science methods such as linear programming, Bayesian probabilities, and simulation modeling. The second approach emphasizes that decisions are not made individually by top managers such as the chief executive officer, but through an alliance and coalition-building process involving multiple participants. A collective or participatory process is primarily needed for clarifying the nature and importance of the problem and for negotiations among internal stakeholders to determine organizational priorities. The third model posits that decisions are made in multiple steps through an incremental process in which a series of smaller decisions finally lead to the culminating decision. According to this model, the process of arriving at a decision evolves over time and goes through the stages of *identification*, *development*, and *selection*. The fourth model, known as the "garbage can" model, characterizes the decision-making process to be highly chaotic, nonlinear, and fluid.[12] This model applies to organizational environments characterized by a high level of uncertainty in which participants come and go, and the emergence of ideas, problems, and solutions is independent or even a random event. As a result, in the garbage can model, solutions may be offered or implemented when a problem does not even exist, choices may be made that do not solve a problem, or people may stop trying to solve the problem, either because they become used to it or no suitable solutions exist.

The use of any of these decision making models depends on the characteristics of the organization as well as the specific situation or problem that calls for a decision. Therefore, approaches toward decision making vary across different organizations as well as within the same organization at different occasions.

▶ 1.5 Evidence-Based Management

In conjunction with the development of electronic health records, two other developments that have altered the practice of medicine in the last couple of decades are (1) emphasis on **evidence-based practice (EBP)**

of medicine and, (2) focus on the whole person rather than episodic treatment of "cases" of diseases. The demand for evidence-based decisions in the practice of medicine stems from studies showing that, in the past, only about 15% of physicians' decisions were based on evidence.[13] Following these developments in the practice of medicine, two similar developments occurred in health services management: (1) a growing emphasis on EBM and (2) a focus on population health. EBM simply means using data or statistical evidence to guide managerial decisions. Statistical evidence allows managers to make better decisions by rank-ordering priorities based on empirical evidence and following a systematic process in which steps are taken sequentially to arrive at the final decision. EBP is often used as an umbrella term instead of discipline-specific terms such as *evidence-based medicine*, *evidence-based nursing*, and *evidence-based management*. EBP is defined as "making decisions through conscientious, explicit and judicious use of the best available evidence from multiple sources."[14]

A variety of approaches, ranging from role modeling to teachable moments of the lived experiences of mentors, are recommended for teaching EBM. McAlearney and Kovner[15] have suggested the following six steps for EBM: first, framing a question for which an answer can be found; second, finding the data or evidence to answer the question; third, assessing the validity of the evidence; fourth, aligning the evidence to the specific circumstances of the organization; fifth, determining whether the evidence is adequate to guide the decision; and sixth, determining whether the organization can take action on the basis of the available evidence.

In contrast to clinical decisions, which are usually made by individuals in a relatively short timeframe, important managerial decisions are made by teams or groups of individuals through a consultative process over weeks and months.[16] The results of these decisions can take years to become clear. As such, there is enough time to collect data from various sources to guide important managerial decisions. Electronic resources and decision-support technologies can be used to identify, assess, and evaluate quantitative and/or qualitative evidence in the pursuit of EBM. Barends et al.[14] argue that the nature of "evidence" in EBP does not strictly translate into quantitative data, but rather should be interpreted as *information* that may be quantitative, qualitative, or descriptive in nature and that may come from a variety of sources. They argue that six misconceptions exist regarding the nature of evidence in EBM: (1) it "ignores the practitioner's professional experience"; (2) it "is all about numbers and statistics"; (3) "managers need to make decisions quickly and don't have the time for EBM"; (4) "each organization is unique, so the usefulness of scientific evidence is limited"; (5) "if you do not have high-quality evidence, you cannot do anything"; and (6) "good-quality evidence gives you the answers to the problem." In their opinion, these myths are completely unfounded and should not be allowed to get in the way of EBM.

According to McVey et al.,[17] "Evidence Based Management (EBM) is about removing emotion, opinion, bias, and personal experience from decision-making." Similarly, Pfeffer and Sutton[13] argue that "gut feeling" and obsolete "best practices" have no place in decision making. They contend that instead of using empirical evidence generated by research studies, typically managers use the following six substitutes for best evidence: (1) obsolete knowledge, (2) personal experience, (3) specialist skills, (4) hype, (5) dogma, and (6) mindless mimicry of top performers.[13] Rather than using obsolete knowledge, hype, or dogma, Pfeffer and Sutton have developed the following guiding principles for the practice of EBM (http://evidence-basedmanagement.com/):

1. Face the facts and build a culture in which people are encouraged to tell the truth, even if it is unpleasant.
2. Be committed to "fact-based" decision making, which means being committed to getting the best evidence and using it to guide actions.
3. Treat your organization as an unfinished prototype—encourage experimentation and "learning by doing."
4. Look for the risks and drawbacks in what people recommend—even the best medicine has side effects.
5. Avoid basing decisions on untested but strongly held beliefs, what you have done in the past, or uncritical "benchmarking" of what winners do.

▶ 1.6 Epidemiology and Evidence-Based Management

The origins of various approaches to incorporating epidemiologic data into the healthcare management and decision-making process can be traced back to the techniques developed at the Central University of Venezuela in the early 1960s. These techniques were later refined by the U.S. Institute of Medicine by using data on the frequency and duration of disease in various age groups. In EBM, priority problems are identified and rank-ordered by combining data on disease frequency, severity, lethality, and responsiveness to treatment in mathematical algorithms and developing an index or a composite score for each disease. Recent efforts in using epidemiologic data for healthcare planning and setting priorities have relied on the estimation of years of potential life lost (YPLL) due to a disease. Calculation of YPLL in a population takes into account life expectancy at various ages and premature deaths due to one disease or another in a population. The disease or condition responsible for the most number of YPLL is usually ranked as the number one priority.

Epidemiologic data are also valuable in evaluating the comparative impact of various services, strategies, and technologies. Such an assessment involves comparison of population health statistics, such as infant mortality or teen pregnancy rates, before and after the implementation of new strategies and services. The outcome of interest or the measure of impact in such studies can be the reduction in disease-specific disability, mortality, or YPLL that can be directly attributed to the new strategy or intervention.

▶ 1.7 Managerial Epidemiology

Managerial epidemiology is defined in various ways. Fos and Fine[18] defined it as "the study of the distribution and determinant of health and diseases, including injuries and accidents, in specified populations and the application of the study to the promotion of health, prevention, and control of disease, the design of healthcare services to meet population needs, and the elaboration of health policy." Fleming et al.[19,20] defined it as "the application of the tools and principles of epidemiology to the decision-making process within healthcare settings." Accordingly, managerial epidemiology entails the use of epidemiologic tools in designing health services and formulating health policy to meet the needs of target populations. Because epidemiologic investigations provide critical information to managers and planners regarding the burden of disease in populations and potential demand for health services, it is "virtually impossible to develop a comprehensive strategic plan without incorporating estimates of the prevalence of disease."[20] Rohrer[21] posited that managerial epidemiology involves planning for populations rather than individuals, planning for prevention rather than treatment, and planning for health rather than disease. He argued that managers are primarily concerned with issues related to cost, quality, and access; therefore, managerial epidemiology needs to draw from clinical epidemiology, the study of the determinants and impact of clinical decisions. Managerial epidemiology can do so by assessing the value of therapeutic and preventive interventions in relation to their costs, quality, and impact on access to health services. Inclusion of clinical variables in studies related to the cost and quality of care can be useful in addressing managerial concerns. The most direct application of clinical epidemiology to address a managerial concern is in the improvement of healthcare quality through reduction of healthcare-associated complications, morbidity, and mortality.[20]

▶ 1.8 Scenario for Application of Managerial Epidemiology

The management of Blue Sky Health, a hypothetical healthcare system that operates several urban and rural inpatient facilities and community-based outpatient clinics in St. Louis, Missouri, is interested in adding a full-service infertility treatment center to its portfolio. Blue Sky wishes to have this center go into operation by early 2020 in the Doctor's Plaza building adjacent to its main hospital in South St. Louis.

For planning and marketing the proposed infertility treatment center, Blue Sky would like to conduct a feasibility study in the fall of 2018. Mark Plato, the vice president for planning and marketing, has developed a list of epidemiologic questions he would like the feasibility study to address. These questions must be addressed before developing amortized projections of fixed and variable costs and determination of a fee structure to achieve a reasonable return on investment and a steady revenue stream. He believes the study proposal must also identify methods for primary data collection and a list of secondary data sources. Plato, who had taken a course in managerial epidemiology at Lyceum University, realizes that many of the questions in the feasibility study can be answered with the help of concepts, methods, and techniques described in the chapters of a good managerial epidemiology textbook. The following is a partial list of questions Mark Plato thinks he needs to have answered by the feasibility study.

1. How common is infertility, and what are the geographic, demographic, and socioeconomic characteristics of the affected population (i.e., what is the epidemiology of infertility)?

2. If epidemiologic data were not available to answer the above question, what kinds of investigations would be necessary to collect data regarding the demographic and socioeconomic characteristics of the target population?

3. What evidence exists regarding the success of treatment procedures such as artificial insemination and in-vitro fertilization, where did that evidence come from, and how good is that evidence?

4. What are the size, boundaries, and socioeconomic characteristics of the geographic market that would be served by the proposed center?

5. What is the projected volume of assisted reproductive services that Blue Sky can expect to provide every year?

6. Who are the competitors for infertility treatment services in this geographic market, and what is the current distribution of market shares among those providers?

7. What is the projected number of deliveries resulting from infertility treatment services and the volume of obstetric services that Blue Sky can expect to provide at its facilities?

8. What volume of patients and fee structure for various procedures would be necessary to make the proposed center financially viable?

Through a cursory examination of available literature, Mark Plato has collected the following epidemiologic information.

Currently 7.5 million American women aged 15–44 years—that is, 12.3% of women in this age group—have impaired ability to get pregnant or carry a baby to term. Nearly 6.9 million of them—that is, 11.3% of women aged 15–44—have used some form of infertility services.[22] Since 2003, there has been a 65% increase in in-vitro fertilization (IVF) in the United States. Every year, approximately 50,000 babies—about 1.6% of all babies born in the country—are born through IVF. In 2013, about 175,000 cycles of IVF were completed in the United States.[23] In a survey, 55% of those who had experienced infertility reported it to be more stressful than unemployment, and 61% reported it to be more stressful than divorce. Approximately 58% of respondents indicated that because of cost and lack of coverage by insurance companies as an essential health benefit, they would forgo infertility treatment.[24] Without assisted reproductive technology, fertile 30-year-old American women each month only have a 20% chance of conceiving.[25,26] About 61% of single-embryo transfers and 65% of two-embryo transfers result in a live birth. Nearly 30% of all IVF pregnancies and 46% of two-embryo transfers result in a twin delivery. Births through assisted reproductive technology (ART) pose greater risk for both mother and child than a normal pregnancy. For example, women who deliver through ART are much more likely to have multiple births than women who conceive naturally. In 2013, more than 160,000 ART procedures were performed at 467 infertility clinics in the United States, with a use rate of approximately 2,520 procedures per million women aged 15–44 years. These procedures involved more than 135,000 embryo transfers and resulted in more than 65,000 pregnancies, with about 66,700 live-born infants.[27] The total cost for one embryo transfer was estimated to be approximately $48,500, and $90,500 for two-embryo transfers.[24]

With the help of tools and methods described in the following chapters and infertility-related epidemiologic information provided in the preceding paragraphs, the student can find answers to Mark Plato's questions. Naturally, some assumptions about the size of the geographic market and the number of competitors in the service area of Blue Sky will have to be made. At the completion of the course for which this text is being used, the student is encouraged to undertake this task and create multiple estimates by changing assumptions regarding population density, socioeconomic characteristics of the population, cost and coverage of fertility services by insurance companies, and the size of the service area.

▶ 1.9 Sources of Epidemiologic Data

A wide variety of demographic, epidemiologic, and socioeconomic data are available on the Internet. As is often the case with the sources of secondary data, the type and quality of available data varies from one source to another or from one agency to the next. However, cross-sectional and longitudinal data from these and other sources can be successfully integrated and analyzed to guide managerial decisions. In the United States, some of the most common and useful sources of epidemiologic and demographic data include the following:

1. U.S. Census Bureau – Census Data (http://www.census.gov/2010census/data/)
2. National Center for Health Statistics – National Vital Statistics System (https://www.cdc.gov/nchs/nvss/index.htm)
3. National Health Interview Survey (NHIS) (http://www.cdc.gov/nchs/nhis/index.htm)
4. National Survey of Children's Health (NSCH) (http://www.nschdata.org/)
5. Health Resources and Services Administration – Maternal and Child Health Bureau (http://mchb.hrsa.gov/)
6. Centers for Disease Control and Prevention – Behavioral Risk Factor Surveillance System (BRFSS) (http://www.cdc.gov/brfss/)
7. U.S. Census Bureau – American Community Survey (https://www.census.gov/programs-surveys/acs/)
8. Harvard University's Maternal and Child Health (MCH) Data Connect – A catalog of more than 150 sources of data (https://dataverse.harvard.edu/dataverse/dataconnect)
9. Cornell University's National Data Archive on Child Abuse and Neglect (http://www.ndacan.cornell.edu/)
10. U.S. Bureau of Labor Statistics – Injuries, Illnesses, and Fatalities (http://www.bls.gov/iif/)
11. Centers for Disease Control and Prevention – National Center for Injury Prevention and Control (https://www.cdc.gov/injury/)

🔎 CASE STUDY 1.1: Impact of Administrative Decisions on Patient Outcomes

Modified from: Yarnell CJ, Shadowitz S, Redelmeier, DA. Hospital readmissions following physician call system change: a comparison of concentrated and distributed schedules. Am J Med. 2016;129(7):706–714. Copyright © 2016 with permission from Elsevier.

The physician call schedule is an important determinant of the quality of care at a hospital. However, it also presents a paradox between two conflicting variables: (1) physician sustainability (i.e., a physician cannot be available at all times) and (2) continuity of care (i.e., patients prefer to interact with the same physician throughout their hospital stay). In a

(continues)

recent study, Yarnell et al. examined the impact of changes in the physician call schedule at an academic tertiary care hospital by comparing patient readmission rates before and after a change in the call system.

On January 1, 2009, Sunnybrook Health Sciences Center in Toronto, Canada, transitioned from the old "concentrated" (or "bolus") call schedule system for all general medicine inpatient physician teams to a new "distributed" (or "drip") system. The main feature of the old system was that one team was on call every fourth day and managed all admissions in that 24-hour period. The main feature of the new system was that admissions were distributed over all teams every day. The new system entailed a host of additional changes. For example, a different member from each team was on call each day, and one member from each team was absent postcall each day. The schedule of rotating attending faculty remained unchanged. The change from the concentrated to the distributed call system was intended to improve quality and continuity of care by having at least one team member from a given team be present each day. The general internal medicine service at Sunnybrook comprised four teams—each with an attending physician, a senior resident, two or three first-year residents, and two or three medical students. Each team was responsible for 15–25 patients.

The researchers identified all consecutive adult patients who were originally admitted through the Emergency Department at Sunnybrook hospital and were later discharged from internal medicine teams during the 10-year period (January 2004 through December 2013) and examined whether each patient was readmitted for any reason within 28 days following discharge. Patients discharged for a surgical, obstetric, or psychiatric diagnosis were excluded from the study.

The study reported that during the 10-year period, 89,697 patients were discharged from the general internal medicine service, of whom 10,001 (11%) were readmitted within 28 days following discharge, and 4,280 died. The risk of readmission increased by 26% after the change in the physician call system (from 9.7% readmission rate before the change in call system to 12.2% after the change; P < .001). Using a computer algorithm (LACE score), the risk of readmission was adjusted for patient characteristics such as predischarge length of stay in the hospital, total number of Emergency Department visits in the preceding 6 months, and the Charlson comorbidity index—a composite measure of the overall effect of all other coexisting medical conditions or diseases a patient might have. To assess whether increased readmission rates at Sunnybrook were related to the change in the physician call system, Sunnybrook's readmission rates were compared with readmission rates at a similar nearby hospital (North York General Hospital) during the same interval. North York General Hospital is similar to Sunnybrook in all other respects, except it did not experience a change in the physician call system.

Before the call system change, a total of 37,982 patients were discharged, of whom 1,643 died and 3,675 were readmitted within 28 days after discharge. After the call system change, a total of 51,715 patients were discharged of whom 2,386, died and 6,326 were readmitted within 28 days after discharge. The results showed that, even after adjusting for extraneous factors, increased risk of readmission after the change in the physician call system persisted across all patient age groups and medical diagnoses. The overall negative impact of change in the physician call system was estimated to be about 7,240 additional patient days in the hospital. However, no increased risk of patient deaths was found to be associated with increased hospital readmissions and change in physician call schedule. **TABLE 1.1** provides data and assessment of the relative risk of readmission or death within 28 days of discharge before and after the call system change.

Questions

Question 1. What was the purpose of this study?

Question 2. How does the study relate to managerial decisions?

Question 3. What were the overall findings of the study?

Question 4. What impact, if any, did the management's decision to change the physician call system have on the quality of care?

Question 5. How did the investigators ensure that their findings regarding the impact of the physician call system were not tainted by extraneous factors, such as the characteristics of the hospital?

Question 6. Based on the data presented in Table 1.1, after the change in the call system, how much higher or lower was the overall risk of readmission or death within 28 days following discharge? Explain your answer with the help of data shown in Table 1.1.

Question 7. Based on the data presented in Table 1.1, after the change in the call system, how much higher or lower was the risk of readmission or death within 28 days following discharge for men and for those with congestive heart failure? Explain your answer with the help of data shown in Table 1.1.

TABLE 1.1 Readmissions or Deaths Within 28 Days Following Discharge

Characteristic	Before Call System Change	After Call System Change	Relative Risk (95% CI)
Total	5,318 (14%)	8,712 (17%)	1.20 (1.17–1.24)
Age in Years			
18–49	802 (9%)	1,215 (11%)	1.31 (1.21–1.43)
50–64	910 (12%)	1,729 (16%)	1.29 (1.20–1.39)
65–79	1,651 (16%)	2,605 (18%)	1.17 (1.10–1.23)
80 or older	1,955 (18%)	3,163 (20%)	1.10 (1.05–1.16)
Sex			
Female	2,624 (14%)	4,206 (17%)	1.16 (1.11–1.22)
Male	2,694 (14%)	4,506 (17%)	1.24 (1.19–1.30)
*Medical Diagnosis**			
Congestive heart failure	919 (23%)	1,286 (25%)	1.10 (1.02–1.19)
Ischemic heart disease	1,067 (16%)	1,306 (17%)	1.08 (0.99–1.18)
Influenza or pneumonia	537 (18%)	786 (20%)	1.11 (1.01–1.23)
Renal failure	671 (22%)	997 (24%)	1.08 (0.99–1.18)
Fall or fracture	307 (6%)	394 (7%)	1.24 (1.08–1.44)
Stroke or delirium	396 (11%)	746 (16%)	1.36 (1.21–1.52)
Duration of Admission in Days			
0–2	973 (11%)	1,942 (13%)	1.21 (1.13–1.31)
3–5	1,310 (13%)	2,167 (15%)	1.21 (1.14–1.29)
6–10	1,190 (14%)	2,035 (19%)	1.32 (1.24–1.41)
11 or more	1,845 (18%)	2,568 (22%)	1.20 (1.14–1.27)

* Selected list, not comprehensive. 1 patient may have had more than 1 diagnosis.

Reprinted from: Yarnell CJ, Shadowitz S, Redelmeier DA. Hospital readmissions following physician call system change: a comparison of concentrated and distributed schedules. Am J Med. 2016;129(7):706–714. Copyright © 2016 with permission from Elsevier.

🔍 CASE STUDY 1.2: Epidemiologic Patterns That Can Guide Policy Decisions

Modified from: Anglemyer A, Miller ML, Buttrey S, Whitaker L. Rates and predictors of violent suicide within military. Ann Intern Med. 2016; 165(3):167–174.

Suicide rates have increased globally in the last half-century, and suicide now ranks as one of the leading causes of death among those between the ages of 15 and 44 years. In the U.S. military, the suicide rate nearly doubled between 2001 and 2011.

In a recent study, Anglemyer et al. calculated suicide rates per 100,000 active duty enlisted (nonofficer) U.S. military personnel from 2005 to 2011. The purpose of the study was to examine suicide rates in different years across different branches of the military and identify personnel at the highest risk. For mortality statistics and demographics, the researchers used data from the Suicide Data Repository, which combines data from the U.S. Centers for Disease Control and Prevention and the Military Mortality Database. To obtain the count of enlisted personnel in each branch of the military in each of the study years, researchers used data from the military. The study did not include suicides committed outside the United States. Altogether, 1,455 active duty enlisted personnel in the U.S. Army, Air Force, Marine Corps, and Navy committed suicide during the study period. With 29.44 and 29.15 suicides per 100,000 individuals in 2009 and 2010, respectively, the rates were highest among Army personnel (see **FIGURE 1.1**). The rates were lowest in the Air Force and Navy in 2005 (9.95 and 9.79, respectively). More than 95% of suicides were committed by men. Only 1 female Marine and 9 female Navy personnel committed suicide. Of the 1,455 total suicides, 1,416 were among nontrainees **(TABLE 1.2)**. As shown in Table 1.2, about 60% of nontrainee suicides occurred in the lower ranks of enlisted personnel (E1 to E4). In the Navy and Air Force, less than 50% of suicides were in lower ranks, but in the Army, about 66.9% were in lower enlisted ranks. More than 75% of suicides in all branches were among white enlisted personnel.

Questions

Question 1. What percentage of suicides in the Marine Corps was among lower rank (E1 to E4) enlisted personnel?

Question 2. What percentage of suicides occurred in white Marines?

Question 3. Across various branches, was there much difference in the percentage of suicide by marital status?

Question 4. Across various branches, was there much difference in the percentage of suicides among those who were never married?

Question 5. What percentage of all suicides occurred in service members who only had a high school diploma?

Question 6. What was the overall number and percentage of female suicides across all branches of the military?

Question 7. Across all branches, what was the overall number and percentage of suicides among those who had education higher than a high school diploma?

Question 8. Based on the data presented in Table 1.2, what, if any, effect do education and rank have on the overall risk of suicide in the military and across various branches?

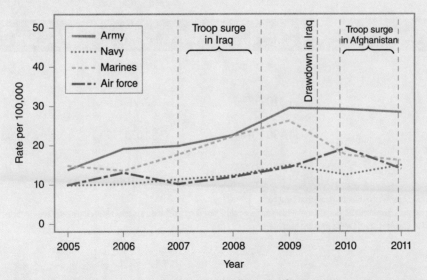

FIGURE 1.1 Suicide rates per 100,000 persons (2005 to 2011), by branch of service.

TABLE 1.2 Characteristics of Suicides Among Active Duty Military Personnel, 2005–2011*				
Characteristic	**Navy (n = 226)**	**Army (n = 744)**	**Air Force (n = 236)**	**Marines (n = 210)**
Median age (IQR), yrs.	26 (23–32)	25 (22–30)	26 (22–32)	22 (20–25)
Sex				
Female	9 (4.0)	37 (5.0)	13 (5.5)	1 (<1.0)
Male	217 (96.0)	707 (95.0)	223 (94.5)	209 (99.5)
Rank				
E1	5 (2.2)	53 (7.1)	4 (1.7)	11 (5.2)
E2	3 (1.3)	73 (9.8)	7 (3.0)	32 (15.2)
E3	26 (11.5)	140 (18.8)	43 (18.2)	77 (36.7)
E4	67 (29.6)	232 (31.2)	63 (26.7)	30 (14.3)
E5	64 (28.3)	120 (16.1)	59 (25.0)	39 (18.6)
E6	45 (19.9)	63 (8.5)	35 (14.8)	14 (6.7)
E7	12 (5.3)	48 (6.5)	22 (9.3)	6 (2.9)
E8	2 (<1.0)	12 (1.6)	3 (1.3)	0 (0)
E9	2 (<1.0)	3 (<1.0)	0 (0)	1 (<1.0)
Race				
White	160 (70.8)	560 (75.3)	172 (72.9)	179 (85.2)
African American	33 (14.6)	104 (14.0)	34 (14.4)	14 (6.7)
Asian/Pacific Islander	11 (4.9)	33 (4.4)	6 (2.5)	4 (1.9)
American Indian/Alaska Native	8 (3.5)	13 (1.7)	6 (2.5)	1 (<1.0)
Missing	14 (6.2)	34 (4.6)	18 (7.6)	12 (5.7)
Marital Status				
Never married	108 (47.8)	347 (46.6)	82 (34.7)	106 (50.5)
Married	118 (52.2)	353 (47.4)	127 (53.8)	96 (45.7)
Divorced/separated/widowed	0 (0)	43 (5.8)	27 (11.4)	8 (3.8)
Missing	0 (0)	1 (<1.0)	0 (0)	0 (0)

(continues)

TABLE 1.2 Characteristics of Suicides Among Active Duty Military Personnel, 2005–2011* _(continued)_

Highest Level of Education				
No high school diploma	22 (9.7)	153 (20.6)	0 (0)	21 (10.0)
High school diploma	181 (80.1)	482 (64.8)	197 (83.5)	179 (85.2)
Some college	9 (4.0)	31 (4.2)	0 (0)	3 (1.4)
Associate degree	4 (1.8)	32 (4.3)	31 (13.1)	5 (2.4)
Bachelor's or graduate degree	7 (3.1)	22 (3.0)	8 (3.4)	1 (<1.0)
Missing	3 (1.3)	24 (3.2)	0 (0)	1 (<1.0)
Religion				
Catholic	32 (14.2)	125 (16.8)	41 (17.4)	44 (21.0)
Protestant	77 (34.1)	296 (39.8)	124 (52.5)	84 (40.0)
Other religion	7 (3.1)	38 (5.1)	9 (3.8)	10 (4.8)
No religion	103 (45.6)	196 (26.3)	54 (22.9)	48 (22.9)
Missing	7 (3.1)	89 (12.0)	8 (3.4)	24 (11.4)

* _Values are numbers (percentages) unless otherwise indicated. Percentages may not sum to 100 due to rounding._
Modified from: Anglemyer A, Miller ML, Buttrey S, Whitaker L. Rates and predictors of violent suicide within military. Ann Intern Med. 2016;165(3):167–174. Copyright © 2016 American College of Physicians. All Rights Reserved. Reprinted with permission of American College of Physicians, Inc.

▶ 1.10 Summary

The materials presented in this chapter introduce the student to the fields of management and epidemiology and bridge the two disciplines by discussing how qualitative and quantitative data can be used to set priorities and make evidence-based decisions. There is growing emphasis on the need for managers to make decisions that are informed by evidence rather than by personal preferences or anecdotal information. We also explain in this chapter what is meant by EBM and how epidemiologic data that are readily available from a variety of sources can be used by healthcare managers. It is important that managers find a balance between the art and science of management—the art of management relates to negotiation, compromise, and appreciation of the interests of various stakeholders, whereas the science of management relates to setting priorities,

allocating resources, and convincing stakeholders based on empirical evidence. Such evidence may be derived from economic, market, and demographic data in the service area or may be generated through targeted epidemiologic investigations.

In Case Study 1.1, Yarnell et al.[28] show the impact of change in physician scheduling on hospital readmissions. This study demonstrates how epidemiologic studies can reveal the positive or negative impact of administrative decisions and can provide evidence to support a change in policy. In Case Study 1.2, Anglemyer et al.[29] provide comparative information on suicide rates in different branches of the U.S. military for different years. These kinds of studies generate data that reveal the characteristics of high-risk individuals. Such data can be used by public and private sector agencies for developing training programs and marketing resource centers for suicide prevention.

References

1. Porta M, editor. A dictionary of epidemiology. 6th ed. New York: Oxford University Press; 2014 [cited 2017 Jul 20]. Available from: http://irea.ir/files/site1/pages/dictionary.pdf

2. Mausner JS, Kramer S. Mausner & Bahn epidemiology: an introductory text. Philadelphia: WB Saunders; 1985.

3. Webster's new world college dictionary [Internet]. 5th ed. Boston: Houghton Mifflin Harcourt; 2016. Management [cited 2017 Jul 20]. Available from: http://websters.yourdictionary.com/

4. Shenhar AJ, Renier J. How to define management: a modular approach. Manage Dev Rev. 1996;9(1):25–31.

5. Mintzberg H. The manager's job: folklore and fact. Harv Bus Rev. 1990;68(2):47–63.

6. Leavitt HJ. Corporate pathfinders. Homewood, IL: Dow Jones-Irwin; 1986.

7. Liebler JG, McConnell CR. Management principles for health professionals. 4th ed. Sudbury, MA: Jones and Bartlett Publishers; 2004.

8. Haddock CC, Chapman RC, McLean RA. Careers in healthcare management: how to find your path and follow it. Chicago: Health Administration Press; 2002.

9. Mintzberg H. Managers not MBAs. San Francisco: Berrett-Koehler Publishers; 2004.

10. Daft RL. Organization theory and design. 3rd ed. St. Paul, MN: West Publishing Company; 1989.

11. Simon HA. Theories of bounded rationality. In: McGuire CB, Radner R, editors. Decision and organization. Amsterdam: North-Holland Publishing Company, 1972; p. 161–176 [cited 2017 Jul 20]. Available from: http://innovbfa.viabloga.com/files/Herbert_Simon___theories_of_bounded_rationality___1972.pdf And also from: http://pages.stern.nyu.edu/~rradner/publishedpapers/100BoundedCostlyRat.pdf

12. Cohen MD, March JG, Olsen JP. A garbage can model of organizational choice. Admin Sci Q. 1972;17(1):1–25.

13. Pfeffer J, Sutton RI. Evidence-based management. Harv Bus Rev. 2006 [cited 2017 Jul 20]. Available from: https://hbr.org/2006/01/evidence-based-management

14. Barends E, Rousseau DM, Briner RB. Evidence-based management: the basic principles. Amsterdam: Center for Evidence-Based Management; 2014.

15. McAlearney AS, Kovner AR. Health services management: Cases, readings, and commentary. 10th ed. Chicago: Health Administration Press; 2013.

16. Walsh K, Gundall TG. Evidence-based management: from theory to practice in health care. Milbank Q. 2001;79(3):429–456.

17. McVey L, Fazzino K, Palmucci J. Evidence-based management in healthcare. 2012. White paper [cited 2016 Mar 18]. Available from: http://healthleadersmedia.com/content/276574.pdf

18. Fos PJ, Fine DJ. Managerial epidemiology for health care organizations. San Francisco: Jossey-Bass; 2005.

19. Fleming ST, Scutchfield FD, Tucker TC. Managerial epidemiology. Chicago: Health Administration Press; 2000.

20. Fleming ST. Managerial epidemiology: it's about time. J Prim Care Community Health. 2013;4(2):148–149.

21. Rohrer JE. Managerial epidemiology (editorial). J Prim Care Community Health. 2013;4(2):82.

22. Centers for Disease Control and Prevention. Infertility. 2016 [cited 2017 Jun 29]. Available from: https://www.cdc.gov/nchs/fastats/infertility.htm

23. Society for Assisted Reproductive Technology. Clinic summary report. 2015 [cited 2017 Jun 29]. Available from: https://www.sartcorsonline.com/rptCSR_PublicMultYear.aspx?ClinicPKID=0

24. Reproductive Medicine Associates of New Jersey. Infertility in America: 2015 survey and report [cited 2017 Jun 29]. Available from: http://www.rmanj.com/wp-content/uploads/2015/04/RMANJ_Infertility-In-America-SurveyReport-_04152015.pdf

25. American Society for Reproductive Medicine. Age and fertility: a guide for patients–2012 [cited 2017 Jul 20]. Available from: http://www.care4ba.com/uploads/Age_and_Fertility_ASRM.pdf

26. Centers for Disease Control and Prevention, American Society for Reproductive Medicine, Society for Assisted Reproductive Technology. 2012 assisted reproductive technology fertility clinic success rates report. Atlanta: U.S. Department of Health and Human Services; 2014.

27. Sunderam S, Kissin DM, Crawford SB, et al. Assisted reproductive technology surveillance: United States, 2013. MMWR Morb Mortal Wkly Rep. 2015;64(SS11):1–25.

28. Yarnell CJ, Shadowitz S, Redelmeier DA. Hospital readmissions following physician call system change: a comparison of concentrated and distributed schedules. Am J Med. 2016;129(7):706–714.

29. Anglemyer A, Miller ML, Buttrey S, Whitaker L. Suicide rates and methods in active duty military personnel, 2005 to 2011: a cohort study. Ann Intern Med. 2016;165(3):167–174.

CHAPTER 2

Determinants of Individual and Population Health

LEARNING OBJECTIVES

Having mastered the materials in this chapter, the student will be able to:

1. Define health and explain different perspectives on defining health, as well as the complexities involved in assessing health status.
2. Explain how a population is defined from different perspectives and by different stakeholders.
3. Explain the difference between the medical care model and the population health model of healthcare delivery, and the tensions between the two.
4. Explain what different determinants of health are, how they interact with one another, and how they affect the overall health of individuals and populations.

CHAPTER OUTLINE

2.1 Introduction
2.2 Definition of *Health*
2.3 Definition of a Population
2.4 What Is Population Health?
2.5 Population Health Model Versus Medical Care Model
2.6 Link Between Physical and Mental Health
2.7 Determinants of Health
2.8 Genetic Makeup as a Determinant of Health

2.9 Socioeconomic Determinants of Health
2.9.1 Income as a Determinant of Health
2.9.2 Education as a Determinant of Health
2.9.3 Occupational Status as a Determinant of Health
2.10 Race as a Determinant of Health
Case Study 2.1 – Effect of Education on Health
Case Study 2.2 – Effect of Socioeconomic Status on Health
2.11 Summary

▶ 2.1 Introduction

The principles of *integrated healthcare delivery*, *patient-centered care*, and *accountable care* require healthcare providers and managers to think in terms of the whole person rather than a case or *episode* of a disease or a medical event in a person's life. Healthcare providers and managers need to move away from the traditional way of thinking about health and health care that narrowly focuses on treating or managing an episode of disease and meeting the medical care needs of individuals. Rather, they must develop a holistic understanding of the word *health* and fully appreciate the context in which disease or sickness occurs. People experience "poor health" not necessarily because they are afflicted with a malady, but because they do not have the circumstances, resources, and education to lead a healthy and meaningful life.

Healthcare managers need to understand why people get sick in the first place and why they do not seek or receive the right care from an appropriate provider in a timely manner—that is, they need to understand the context in which health care is needed, sought, and given. In this regard, *context* means understanding the relationship between health and socioeconomic conditions in which people are born, live, work, and die. They have to appreciate that health of individuals and communities is directly linked to education, income, and occupation. This chapter is designed to help future healthcare mangers attain such an understanding.

▶ 2.2 Definition of *Health*

Signed on July 22, 1946, by the representatives of 61 states and formally adopted by the World Health Organization (WHO) on April 7, 1948, the constitution of the WHO defines **health** as "a state of complete physical, mental, and social well-being and not merely the absence of disease or infirmity." Though officially unchanged since 1948, the definition was expanded in the 1980s by the leadership of the WHO to include "the ability to lead a socially and economically productive life."[1] The idealistic and unattainable nature of this definition has often been criticized by pragmatists who point toward the fact that health is an elastic concept that can only be assessed indirectly by looking for the presence or absence of disease and disability.[2,3] For the same reason, no direct measure exists to assess a person's "state of complete physical, mental, and social well-being." Many in the healthcare field find the WHO's definition of health to be of limited value and raise the question as to who makes a determination of another person's well-being, as a person can fully enjoy a state of well-being that may be considered unhealthy by someone else. An alternative definition offered by Taber's Cyclopedic Medical Dictionary[4] states that health is "A condition in which all functions of the body and mind are normally active." By implication, this definition recognizes that individuals are constantly responding to external stimuli or stressors that result in a person's overall condition being in a state of flux from day to day, or even from hour to hour. Consequently, the health status of a person cannot be viewed as a static condition; rather, it is a dynamic and ever-changing state on a continuum, with optimum physical, mental, and social functionality constituting the starting point of the continuum, and total loss of functionality being the other end. Given the impermanence or transient nature of one's overall condition, Dubos[5] has suggested that the goal of society is not for everyone to achieve "an ideal state of well-being through complete elimination of disease," but to enable everyone in the society to live a reasonably comfortable and rewarding life.

Because it is impossible for anyone to attain a perfect state of physical, mental, and social well-being, and it is equally difficult for scientists to devise methods for appropriately measuring the health status of individuals and communities, the only practical approach is to measure the level of disease, disability, and death as a proxy measure of health. Measurement of disease, disability, and death in a population at different times or in different populations at any given time allows social scientists to make comparative statements regarding improvement or deterioration in the health status of a population or disparities in the health status of different populations.

▶ 2.3 Definition of a Population

A **population** can be defined from a variety of perspectives. Taber's Cyclopedic Medical Dictionary[6] defines *population* as "1. All people, plants, or animals inhabiting a specified area. 2. The group of people from which a research sample is drawn."

From this perspective, the measurement and reporting of the total number of individuals or the number of people in a group, class, or race are tied to the specification of a geographically defined entity such as the world, a country, or a province. Naturally, any geographically defined entity can be, and usually is, further divided into smaller geographic units such as states, provinces, counties, census tracts, and postal codes. Additionally, the population of any geographically defined entity such as a country or province can be further divided into subgroups on the bases of characteristic such as gender, age, color, ethnicity, education, or religion. It is important to note that no population, even at the smallest geographic level, is perfectly homogenous with respect to any given characteristic such as age, gender, or education.

Because no population is static in time or space, in addition to the specification of a geographic area, the characteristics of a population or its subgroups cannot be discussed without the specification of a period, interval, or date. Hence, any discussion of a population necessitates specification of both a geographic boundary and a period or point in time. For example, we could discuss global population at the end of the 20th century, or the total population of blacks in the United States on December 31, 2017. Similarly, from an epidemiologic perspective, we could discuss the demographic characteristics of a population, such as age and gender distribution of whites in the United States, or birth and death rates per 1,000 Hispanics in the United States at the end of 2017.

Attributes such as age, sex, education, average income, or employment rates in a population are known to be associated with health status and use of health services. In population health studies, the basic unit of analysis and comparison of statistics is usually determined by the objectives of the study. For global and national policy initiatives such as disease control and vaccination or screening strategies, comparisons are made at the country level, whereas allocation of resources within a country or state may require analysis and comparison of data at a district or county level. For example, strategies to reduce teen pregnancy or health promotion initiatives to increase physical activity may require comparisons of teen pregnancy rates and levels of physical activity in various groups at the county level.

In the context of health services planning or healthcare delivery, a population may be defined from the perspective of a healthcare provider, insurer, or payer. For example, a hospital administrator may define *service area*, *service population*, or *catchment population* of the hospital in terms of zip codes and relative proportion of clients in those zip codes served by the hospital. Likewise, an insurance company may define population in terms of the "geographic market" it operates in and its "market share" of the privately insured sector of the population. A healthcare planner or economist, on the other hand, might define a population as the number of Medicaid- or Medicare-eligible individuals in a geographic area. In the United States, America's Health Rankings (http://www.americashealthrankings.org/), a joint initiative of the American Public Health Association and United Health, provides useful state-level comparative health information through its annual reports and issue briefs. The County Health Rankings & Roadmap (http://www.countyhealthrankings.org/), a program of the Robert Wood Johnson Foundation, provides state-by-state county-level data on various health indicators.

▶ 2.4 What Is Population Health?

Population health is generally considered as the field of study that examines the health status of populations or groups of individuals. However, there is considerable confusion and debate about the definition and scope of the term *population health*. Some believe that the term relates exclusively to an understanding and measurement of factors such as demographic characteristics, lifestyles and behaviors, genetic makeup, and availability of services that affect the health status of the population. Others put it squarely in the realm of the assessment and measurement of health status or health outcomes,[7] and still others take it as the conceptual framework for understanding why some populations are healthier in comparison with others.[8,9] This definition includes understanding the health outcomes and their distribution within a population or a group of individuals.[7] There is growing emphasis on disease prevention and health promotion by policy makers, third-party payers, and agencies such as the Centers for Medicare and Medicaid Services. As a result, healthcare managers and providers are becoming increasingly aware of the need for a holistic model of healthcare delivery to achieve population health outcomes and community-based goals, such as those listed in Healthy People 2020.

▶ 2.5 Population Health Model Versus Medical Care Model

Historically, healthcare systems all over the world were based on a *medical care model* that put a greater premium on reinstating health through treatment and rehabilitation than maintaining and promoting health by focusing on behavioral and socioeconomic determinants of health. The medical care establishment had focused in the past on meeting the needs of the sick rather than keeping people healthy. In most instances, it continues to do so even today. The medical care model neither was designed for nor rewards community-level investigation and management of factors that lead to ill health and death. Even at the individual level, the focus of healthcare systems all over the world remains, preeminently, on treatment and rehabilitation rather than disease prevention and health promotion. Up until the last few years, healthcare systems in most countries, including the United States, had largely remained disengaged from the epidemics of obesity, smoking, substance abuse, and teen pregnancy that ultimately led to high levels of morbidity and mortality both locally and nationally.

The *population health model*, on the other hand, focuses on developing a safe and health-friendly built environment promoting healthy nutrition through informative labeling of food products, discouraging the availability and consumption of sugary drinks, promoting the availability of opportunities for a physically active life, and providing preventive medical care in the form of vaccinations, periodic screenings, and lifestyle counseling. In contrast to the medical care model, the population health model is neither commonly understood nor fully appreciated by the practitioners of the medical care model. Though the population health model appeals to common sense, the scientific link between socioeconomic factors (such as poverty or lack of education) and health, despite overwhelming empirical evidence, is often regarded by the practitioner community as unproven or beyond the scope of their influence. Research on the effects of stress and anxiety on cardiovascular, endocrine, and neural systems has shown a definite link between

hypertension, heart disease, stroke, diabetes, and other disorders, and socioeconomic factors. The pathophysiologic effects of different gradients of these stresses are also well established.

In contrast to the population health model, the medical care model focuses on disease and injury at the individual level and is reactionary rather than preemptive in nature. It comes into action only after the most distal effects of genetic, behavioral, or socioeconomic determinants have become clinically detectable.

▶ 2.6 Link Between Physical and Mental Health

There is ample evidence that **mental health** and physical health are interconnected, and the relationship between the two is bidirectional—that is, both affect each other.[10] For example, chronic physical problems, especially those accompanied by chronic pain and loss of function, can also lead to chronic mental health problems, such as depression. Studies have shown that people living with chronic physical problems experience anxiety and depression at twice the rate of the general population. In fact, nearly 50% of patients with chronic pain have been shown to suffer from depression and are reported to be at greater risk of suicidal ideation and suicidal attempts, and have a higher suicide completion rate than the general population.[11-13] **FIGURE 2.1** shows the prevalence of depression in patients suffering from some common chronic physical disorders. It shows, for example, that 27% of patients with diabetes and more than half of Parkinson's disease patients suffer from depression.

Conversely, mental health disorders increase the likelihood of developing a wide range of physical ailments through psychosomatic pathways. Patients with serious mental disorders are known to be at increased risk of asthma, chronic bronchitis, and chronic obstructive pulmonary disease. Psychiatric problems commonly alter eating and sleeping patterns and affect hormonal balance. Stressful life conditions, traumatic experiences, and lack of social support can lead to poor eating habits, lack of physical activity, and alcohol abuse, thus increasing the risk of both physical and mental disorders. Further, the side effects of medication for psychiatric disorders can also result in weight gain and cardiac arrhythmias.[10] As discussed later in this chapter, similar to the association between socioeconomic factors and physical disorders such as hypertension and diabetes, socioeconomic factors are also known to be associated

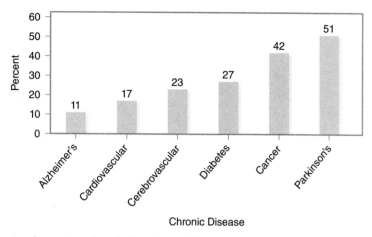

FIGURE 2.1 Prevalence of major depressive disorder in chronic disease.

Reproduced from: Centers for Disease Control and Prevention (CDC), National Center for Chronic Disease Prevention and Health Promotion, Division of Population Health. Mental health and chronic diseases. Issue brief no. 2. October 2012. Accessed on July 21, 2017. https://www.cdc.gov/workplacehealthpromotion/tools-resources/pdfs/issue-brief-no-2-mental-health-and-chronic-disease.pdf

with mental health conditions such as anxiety, panic attacks, and depression.

▶ 2.7 Determinants of Health

Health is maintained by the internal regulatory mechanisms of an individual. Therefore, a disease is nothing but the manifestation of a failure of biological functions and internal regulatory mechanisms of the body.[14] A host of variables collectively known as the **determinants of health** can disrupt the internal regulatory mechanisms and biological functions. These variables include both psychological and social factors. As such, determinants of health can be defined as both external and internal factors that directly or indirectly affect the health of individuals and populations. Gradients in these factors and their cumulative or interactive effects ultimately determine whether someone gets sick or remains healthy.[15-17] Over the years, a number of hypotheses have been offered regarding the biologic mechanisms through which various social factors such as education, marital status, social networks, and employment exert influence on the homeostasis or physiologic equilibrium.[16,17]

Historical data have provided convincing evidence that improvements in health and life expectancy observed in Europe in the 18th and 19th centuries were largely the result of rising standards of living and sanitary reforms.[17] In due course, this evidence led to the proposition that health status of a population is closely linked to the physical, social, and economic conditions of the population. Social scientists have investigated pathways through which emotional and psychological states of individuals bring about physiological changes that lead to diseases of different bodily systems.

The term *determinants of health* refers to extrinsic or intrinsic factors that, in a relatively short or long span of time, can affect the health status of individuals. The presence of these factors in varying degrees or their complete absence can make a person sick or can help a sick person recover to normal health. For example, the presence of toxins or pollutants of one kind or another in the air we breathe can make us sick. The nature and degree of the impact of such pollutants on one's health can depend on a variety of factors, including the nature of the agent and the amount present in the air. As an example, consumption of food rich in trans-fatty acids can increase the risk of coronary heart disease or death. However, the risk of coronary heart disease depends on the amount of trans-fatty acids in food consumed every day, as well as the length of time, in terms of month and years, of consuming food containing trans-fatty acids. Conversely, the term *determinants of disease* refers to extrinsic factors, such as microorganisms and chemicals in the environment, or intrinsic factors, such as genetic mutations, that can make us sick. The presence of a certain amount of substances such as minerals, vitamins, fats, and amino acids in our diet is essential for us to remain healthy. Deficiency or excess of these substances over a period of time (chronic deficiency) can make us sick.

A vast body of research conducted over the last few decades provides irrefutable evidence of the effects of genetic, behavioral, socioeconomic, environmental, and healthcare-access-related factors on the health status of individuals throughout the course of one's life, and the interactive or integrative nature of these factors.[18] In the United States since

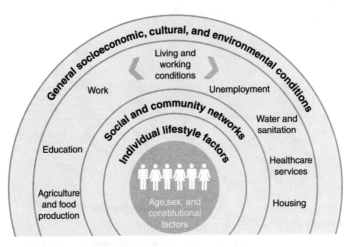

FIGURE 2.2 A guide to thinking about the determinants of population health.

2008, the Robert Wood Johnson Foundation's Commission to Build a Healthier America has issued a number of reports on how factors outside the healthcare system affect people's prospects to live a long and healthy life. For example, the Commission reported that in 2013, children born to mothers in Arlington and Fairfax Counties, as compared with those born just a few miles away to mothers in Washington, DC, could expect to live 6 or 7 years longer. Even more startling is the finding that average life expectancy for babies born to mothers across neighborhoods in New Orleans can vary by as much as 25 years.

The degree to which various factors, alone or in combination with other variables, influence the health status of an individual is often uncertain and difficult to estimate. However, understanding the role of various determinants is necessary to address disparities in the health status of different populations.[16] Some believe that the effect of isolated social factors accounts for only a small amount of variation in the health status of different individuals.[14] They suggest that the cumulative effect of multiple interactive factors, often referred to as the *allostatic load*, is what triggers the sequence of events that ultimately lead to an adverse health outcome.[19] Based on a review of literature from 1977 to 1993, McGinnis and Foege,[20] in a seminal article, concluded that close to 50% of all deaths in the United States resulted from a few nonmedical factors, of which smoking and diet topped the list. Subsequent assessments by the Institute of Medicine[21] and by the Centers for Disease Control and Prevention not only confirmed the findings reported by McGinnis and Foege but also increased the estimation to 70% of all deaths in the United

States and considerably broadened the list of such nonmedical factors.[22]

Tarlov[23] has developed a conceptual framework that classifies various determinant of health into the following five categories: (1) genetic and biologic factors, including age, gender, and race or ethnicity; (2) lifestyles and personal behaviors such as smoking, alcohol use, and sexual behavior; (3) socioeconomic characteristics such as education, income, and social network; (4) physical environment, such as housing, sanitation, and air quality; and (5) degree of access to and quality of health services. **FIGURE 2.2** provides a schematic representation of various determinants of health and their relative importance from core biologic and genetic factors to more peripheral environmental and social factors that directly or indirectly affect health—whether independently or through interaction with other socioenvironmental factors.

▶ 2.8 Genetic Makeup as a Determinant of Health

The list of physical and mental disorders that have been linked to a person's genetic makeup is long.[24-26] The 2010 revision of the Nosology and Classification of Genetic Skeletal Disorders by the Nosology Group of the International Skeletal Dysplasia Society listed 456 such conditions in 40 groups on the bases of molecular, biochemical, and/or radiological criteria.[25] It would not be surprising if future research shows that, aside from infectious and nutritional deficiency disorders such as those resulting from the deficiency of vitamins or minerals in diet, most other diseases have a genetic etiologic component. Even for some of the infectious and deficiency disorders, variance in susceptibility or severity of clinical condition may very well have a genetic explanation.

There is abundant evidence that variations in patients' responses to medication, the rate at which drugs are metabolized, the frequency and severity of side effects, and appropriate dose regimens for different individuals are all related to genetic variations.[27] In fact, between 20% and 95% of variation in metabolism, disposal, and effects of drugs may be the result of genetic variation.[28] For example, some patients with cystic fibrosis, a hereditary lung disorder, have a genetic mutation that allows them to benefit greatly from the drug Kalydeco (ivacaftor), which was developed specifically to target this mutation. Cystic fibrosis patients who do not have this mutation do not respond to the same medication.[29] With the identification of a growing number of oncogenes and the development of drugs that specifically target these genes, cancer care is becoming increasingly customized, personal, and precise. Scientists can now create the genetic profile of a tumor through advanced genomic testing and develop treatment options that are customized for individual patients.

Getting a person's genome sequenced through advanced genomic testing can give useful insights into a person's risk of various diseases and reveal the probability of passing genetic mutations or variants to their children. For example, knowing that a patient carries gene variants that predispose him or her to the risk of sudden death from abnormal heart rhythms such as long QT syndrome can allow preemptive interventional measures. As another example, about 1 in 10,000 to 1 in 15,000 children born in the United States have phenylketonuria (PKU)—a disease caused by an inherited genetic mutation. Untreated PKU can lead to a severe intellectual developmental deficit in children. With early detection through a simple screening test, the disorder can be treated through a strict diet regimen low in phenylalanine, an essential amino acid found in plant proteins.

With the exception of a few diseases, such as Huntington's disease or cystic fibrosis, most genetically linked diseases are not purely determined by the presence or absence of a single genetic mutation or marker.[14] For example, the presence of BRCA1 and BRCA2 mutations is a strong predictor of lifetime risk of breast and ovarian cancer in women. However, empirical evidence shows that only a small proportion of women who develop breast cancer have this mutation. Conversely, not all women with these mutations develop breast cancer—in fact, about 13% to 40% of women with BRCA1 and BRCA2 gene mutations do not develop breast cancer over the course of their lives, and even fewer develop ovarian cancer. Clearly, these mutations are neither a sufficient cause nor the only predictors of breast cancer—that is, there are factors other than the presence of BRCA1 and BRCA2 mutations that predispose women to breast cancer. For example, early onset of menarche, later age of having first child, not breastfeeding, and low fertility are known to increase the risk of breast cancer.[30] In fact, some of these observations now explain why breast cancer was commonly known as the "nuns' disease" or "spinster's disease." Further, there also exist factors that facilitate or suppress the effects or expression of genetic mutations.[14]

The observation that some individuals who are exposed to an environmental, dietary, chemical, or other biological insult develop a disease whereas others do not prompted inquiries into the effect of interactions among genes and the environment. These inquiries and research into DNA repair pathways have shown that there are genetic mutations that can exert a protective effect against risk factors such as carcinogens in tobacco smoke. Most scientists now seem to agree that few diseases are caused purely or exclusively by genes rather than an interaction of genes with the environment that leads to genetic mutations.[31] A number of studies, including some on obesity, sickle cell anemia, and functioning of immune systems, have provided ample evidence to show that the occurrence of diseases and severity of their symptoms are strongly influenced by the interaction of social and genetic factors.[31]

Aside from diseases, such as sickle cell anemia and cystic fibrosis, that result from simple Mendelian inheritance, most genetically linked diseases either occur due to the interaction of multiple genes (gene–gene interaction) or interaction of genes with environmental factors (gene–environment interaction). Variation in the distribution and severity of a disease such as lung cancer results from the combined effect of (1) variation across individuals in exposure to environmental factors—for example, different levels of exposure to tobacco smoke (**environmental heterogeneity**), and (2) variation in the genetic makeup of individuals (**genetic heterogeneity**). The unique combination of the extent of exposure to environmental factors and the personal genetic makeup of an individual (etiologic heterogeneity) not only determines whether a person will develop a disease in the first place, but also affects the level of severity and outcome of the disease.

Genetic variation from one individual to another and within the same individual at different stages of life likely affects all aspects of cellular, biochemical, metabolic, physiologic, and morphologic functions of the individual and responses to environmental, behavioral, and socioeconomic conditions. Because most diseases have a multifactorial etiology, it is virtually impossible to predict with certainty the likelihood of developing a disease as well as its course, progression, and outcome.[31]

▶ 2.9 Socioeconomic Determinants of Health

To better understand the nature and full spectrum of factors that can affect a person or a community's health, it is critically important to raise the question, "Is there truly such a thing as **socioeconomic determinants of health**?" and, if the answer is affirmative, then ask, "How do these factors affect health?"[14] Surveys of self-reported health status by middle-aged individuals in England and the United States have shown a strong negative association between socioeconomic status and diabetes, hypertension, heart disease, myocardial infarction, stroke, lung disease, and cancer in both countries.[32,33] Health disparities were found to be greatest for those at the bottom of socioeconomic status, measured in terms of years of schooling and household income. In both countries, biological markers of disease also showed the same exact patterns of association with the hierarchy of socioeconomic status.[32] Longitudinal studies of the relationship between poor childhood conditions and adult health behaviors and psychosocial characteristics have revealed that men whose parents were poor grew up to have low education levels, hold blue-collar jobs, and demonstrate poor health behaviors.[34] These findings lend further support to the previously observed relationship between health and indicators of social deprivation such as poverty, lack of education, poor nutrition, and certain environmental conditions.

The mechanisms or pathways that link a socioeconomic variable to health outcomes are distinct from those that link other variables such as genetic makeup or quality of care with health outcomes. For example, educational disparities can be linked to gradients in morbidity and mortality through unhealthy lifestyle choices such as smoking, poor nutrition, and obesity. The mechanisms linking income disparity and poverty to gradients in morbidity and mortality, on the other hand, are defined by the ability to afford better housing, food, and clothing, and greater access to health care. Higher income is also associated with positive psychological factors such as a sense of security and control over one's life, decisions, and environment.[31]

Generating convincing evidence of the health effects of socioeconomic and environmental factors is difficult for a number of reasons, including the challenge of bridging the realm of biology with the realm of sociology. It is known that stressful life events such as unemployment, divorce, or death of a loved one set the stage for unhealthy behavioral choices such as smoking and excessive alcohol consumption. However, the neurochemical or neurobiologic pathways through which socioeconomic factors exert influence on the risk of morbidity and mortality are not yet understood. One problem that social scientists encounter is that data regarding stressful life events and socioeconomic variables are gathered at the population level, whereas diseases occur at the individual level.

A number of studies have related endocrine, neural, and physiologic changes in the body to a wide range of stress factors in personal, social, and working environments. More important, these studies have shown that individuals with certain psychosocial and behavioral characteristics, such as introversion, emotional lability, and self-indulgence, are more prone to diseases or illness, including allergies, asthma, and gastrointestinal irritability. In short, such individuals are much more vulnerable to a range of health problems, from reproductive and gynecologic problems to bacterial and viral infections.[35]

Though neuroendocrine and biochemical pathways are not clear, there is compelling evidence of physiologic changes in human body in response to social stressors. Increased heart rate, perspiration, dilatation of blood vessels in the skin and muscles, and changes in the gastrointestinal and urinary systems have been noted during and after stressful events.[17,35,36] The direct and indirect relationships between stressors and health outcomes are complex. The direct effect is in the form of psychophysiologic changes that lead to increased blood lipid levels, abdominal obesity, high blood pressure, insulin resistance, and increased levels of C-reactive protein. These changes lead to increased risk of heart disease, stroke, and diabetes.[36] The indirect effects of a stressful environment or life situation occur in the form of unhealthy coping strategies such as smoking, substance abuse, alcohol dependence, and the secondary effects of mood alterations and insomnia resulting from stress.[37,38]

In two longitudinal studies known as Whitehall I and Whitehall II, which involved studying British civil servants, Marmot and colleagues[39-40] collected extensive longitudinal data from more than 27,000 individuals. Demographic, socioeconomic, and health-related data were collected in multiple phases from British civil servants of different ranks and income levels over a period of more than four decades. Follow-up with participants in the Whitehall II study has continued since 1985. The results of these studies have shown that individuals at the lowest rank and income level were 3.5 times more likely to die than those at the top. Further, the inverse relationship between social standing and mortality held strong at all levels of comparison. The inverse relationship also remained consistent for specific causes of death, such as heart disease, stroke, suicide, and lung cancer. Moreover, the difference in mortality between different ranks remained even after adjusting for differences in risk factors such as smoking and having high blood pressure and high cholesterol.

Marmot and his colleagues[39,41] discovered that the blood pressure of those at the top of the hierarchy was much lower at home after returning from work, whereas it was higher and remained higher for much longer among those at the lowest ranks.[42] Other studies on the effects of stress factors such as job loss, bankruptcy, social isolation, and discrimination have shown similar negative effects of stress on cardiovascular, endocrine, neural, and immunologic systems and increased risk of death and disease.[43,44] Socioeconomic factors such as income, education, employment, and social support are sometimes called the "upstream" factors because they directly affect "downstream" living conditions, including housing, nutrition, lifestyle, and levels of stress.[7,18] Clearly, a particular socioeconomic variable may not be independently sufficient to affect health outcomes, but in concert with other factors, it can set the stage for better or poorer health outcomes. From a health policy standpoint, it is important to bear in mind the interactive nature of the effects of socioeconomic factors and devise longitudinal interventions that simultaneously target multiple factors.

An interesting research finding is that women of higher socioeconomic standing are at a greater risk of breast cancer. However, the increased risk of breast cancer among women of higher socioeconomic standing is partly explained by reproductive factors, such as age at menarche, age of mother at first childbirth, and low fertility. Additionally, women of higher socioeconomic standing enjoy a much better chance of surviving breast cancer because of earlier detection and greater access to effective treatment.[45-47] It is worth repeating that breast cancer was historically known as the "nuns' disease" because of the known fact that nuns experienced much higher rates of breast cancer than did other women. Now it is understood that pathophysiologic pathways of breast cancer are directly linked to hormonal levels in the body. Hormonal changes related to pregnancy, fertility rates, and lactation confer a degree of protection against breast cancer.[46,47]

2.9.1 Income as a Determinant of Health

Accurate measurement of income is difficult for a variety of reasons, including the challenge of specifying the reporting time frame, sources of income, and units of measurement; determining whether reported income is for an individual or a household; and clarification regarding gross or disposable income.[31] Nonetheless, a large number of studies have documented a positive correlation between income and health status. Poverty affects the health and development of individuals from embryonic stages all the way to old age. This happens through interactive effects of exposure to environmental elements, poor nutrition, inadequate housing, lack of access to sanitation and safe drinking water, lack of access to good education, and lack of access to age-appropriate disease-preventive and curative health services.[31]

Results from the Panel Study of Income Dynamics, the longest running longitudinal U.S. household survey, which began in 1968, have shown a 3.6-fold mortality risk difference between working-age adults in the top posttax family income bracket of >$70,000 (in 1984 dollars) and those in the bottom income category of <$15,000 per year.[48] Similar to the effects of different levels of education attainment on health, the relationship between better health and higher income displays a gradient with successively higher levels of income. This gradient is steepest at lower income levels and plateaus at income levels that are twice the median income.[31] Further, the relationship between income and health is reciprocal in nature—that is, those in better health have better prospects of making more money, and those with higher income can afford, and display, healthier lifestyles.[49] In fact, poor health, one of the most common causes of job loss, results in a spiral of worsening economic deprivation and deteriorating psychosocial health. The hypothesized causal pathways of the income–health relationship are based on the greater ability of more affluent people to buy goods and services and having greater sense of security or peace of mind.[31]

FIGURE 2.3 provides a conceptual model of how parents' income can shape families' options for higher standards of living and children's prospects for better education, employment, and future income, as well as health status during the course of their entire life. The 2014 Robert Wood Johnson Foundation report titled "Time to Act: Investing in the Health of Our Children and Communities" suggests that "parents' income can affect children's chances for health by shaping options for living conditions and educational chances, which in turn shape their income and living conditions as adults." As shown in **FIGURE 2.4**, income gradients have a marked effect on health status within and across racial or ethnic groups. For instance, among blacks, only 6.8% of those with family income equal to or greater than 400% of federal

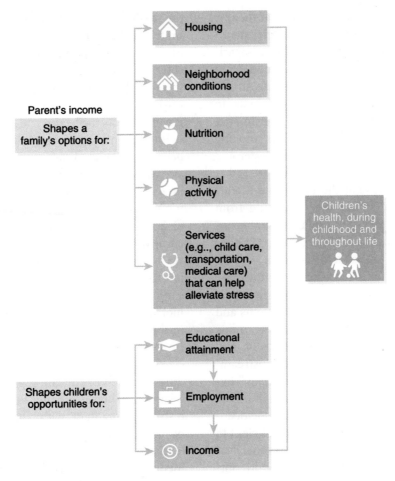

FIGURE 2.3 Parents' income can affect a child's chances for health throughout life.

poverty level in 2010 reported being in poor or fair health, as opposed to 23.9% of those in the family income bracket of less than 100% of the federal poverty limit.

2.9.2 Education as a Determinant of Health

Educational attainment in terms of the number of years of education has consistently been a good predictor of future health behaviors and health outcomes, including future morbidity and mortality not only of individuals themselves, but their children as well. Increasing levels of infant mortality have been observed with successively lower levels of educational attainment of mothers—that is, a gradient exists in the association of health outcomes and educational attainment.[31] The "totality of evidence" in this regard suggests a direct causal link between education and health outcomes. Part of the evidence comes from "natural experiments" that occurred in the form of United States legislation, passed in different localities at different times, making school

education compulsory; as schooling progressively became compulsory, health outcomes improved successively.[50] Randomized trials of preschool education also have been linked with reduced teen pregnancy rates when these children became adolescents and young adults.[51] The hypothesized causal pathways to explain the relationship between higher levels of schooling and future health outcomes include adoption of healthy lifestyles due to awareness, acquisition of health-related knowledge ("health literacy"), and better ability to "navigate the healthcare system."[31]

In a meta-analysis of 47 different studies that examined the health effects of sedentary time independent of all other factors, Biswas et al.[52] found that greater sedentary time was positively associated with increased risk of "all-cause mortality," cardiovascular disease incidence and mortality, cancer incidence and mortality, and incidence of type 2 diabetes. The greatest effect of sedentary time was on increased risk of type 2 diabetes. With regard to increased risk of cancer, specific associations of sedentary time were identified with colorectal, breast, endometrial, and epithelial ovarian cancer.

FIGURE 2.5 shows the effect of different levels of education on life expectancy. According to the data from the U.S. National Center for Health Statistics on which this figure in the Robert Wood Johnson Foundation 2014 report is based, on average, 25-year-old college graduates have a life expectancy 8 or 9 years longer than their counterparts who did not finish high school. Similarly, education is also linked with better health across racial or ethnic groups. As shown in **FIGURE 2.6**, across all racial groups, 42% to 50.7% of those 25- to

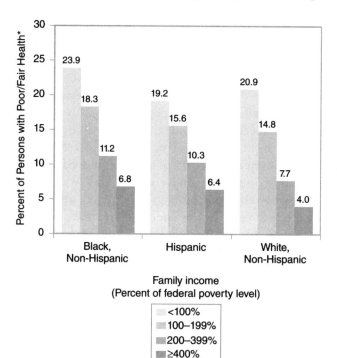

FIGURE 2.4 Income is linked with health across racial and ethnic groups.

* Age-adjusted. Based on self-report and measured as poor, fair, good, very good, or excellent.
Reproduced with permission from: Robert Wood Johnson Foundation. Time to act: investing in the health of our children and communities. Copyright © 2014 Robert Wood Johnson Foundation Commission to Build a Healthier America.

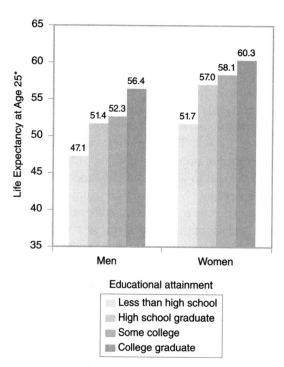

FIGURE 2.5 More education, longer life.

* This chart describes the number of years that adults in different education groups can expect to live beyond age 25. For example, a 25-year-old man with a high school diploma can expect to live 51.4 additional years and reach an age of 76.4 years.
Reproduced with permission from: Robert Wood Johnson Foundation. Time to act: investing in the health of our children and communities. Copyright © 2014 Robert Wood Johnson Foundation Commission to Build a Healthier America.

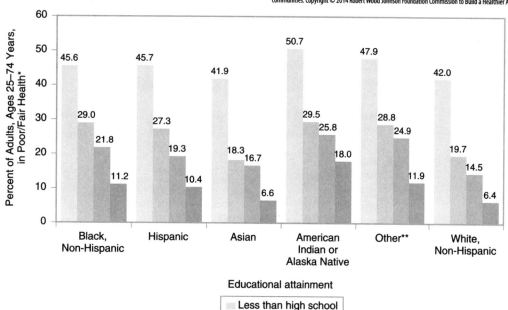

FIGURE 2.6 Education is linked with health across racial or ethnic groups.

* Age-adjusted. Based on self-report and measured as poor, fair, good, very good, or excellent.
** Defined as any other or more than one racial or ethnic group, including any group with fewer than 3 percent of surveyed adults nationally in 2008–20.
Reproduced with permission from: Robert Wood Johnson Foundation. Time to act: investing in the health of our children and communities. Copyright © 2014 Robert Wood Johnson Foundation Commission to Build a Healthier America.

74-year-olds who had less than a high school education reported being in poor health, whereas only 6.4% to 11.2% of those with a college degree reported being in poor health.

2.9.3 Occupational Status as a Determinant of Health

Occupational status is one of the legs of a three-legged stool called "socioeconomic status"; income and education constitute the other two legs. Broadly, occupational status represents the level of authority, prestige, money, and power not just in the labor market, but in the overall society as well. There are three different aspects to the relevance of occupational status with health status. First, the extent to which an occupation exposes a person to the risk of physical injury, including injury from falls and exposure to heat, cold, or chemical toxins. The second consists of the psychosocial aspects of a person's work environment, including the degree of job security, level of stress, and latitude in decision making. The third aspect of the relationship between occupational status and health relates to prestige and symbols of power that have an impact on the emotional and psychological health of the individual.[31]

A number of theoretical and methodological frameworks have been developed to measure occupational status.[53] For example, one way of classifying occupational status is based on manual versus nonmanual (blue-collar vs. white-collar) work.[54] Historically, blue-collar jobs, or manual work, have been associated with low prestige, power, and money, and greater health hazards. Cross-sectional and longitudinal studies on the conditions of mineworkers, construction workers, and factory workers support this assertion. An alternative approach to the classification of occupational status is Duncan's Socioeconomic Index (SEI).[55,56] Duncan's SEI combines subjective measurements of prestige with objective measurements of income and education. Higher scores on SEI have been linked with lower scores on self-reported physical, mental, and social health.[40] Similar to the effects of income and education on health, the relationship between occupational status and health is also bidirectional—that is, poor health poses a serious hindrance to achieving upward social mobility through attainment of higher occupational status.

Conversely, low occupational status can lead to poor physical, mental, and social health.[31] **FIGURE 2.7** shows differences in life expectancy for

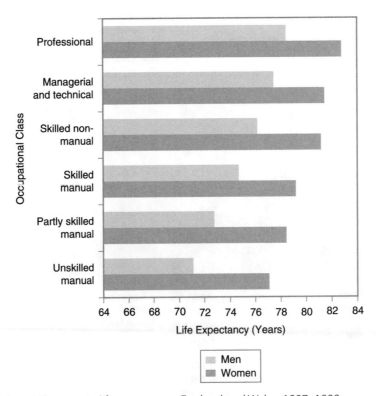

FIGURE 2.7 Occupational class differences in life expectancy, England and Wales, 1997–1999.

Original Source, Donkin A, Goldblatt P, Lynch K. Inequalities in life expectancy by social class 1972–1999. Health Statistics Quarterly. 2002;15:5–15. Secondary Source: World Health Organization: Europe. Social determinants of health: the solid facts. 2nd edition. Wilkinson R, Marmot M. (eds). 2003. http://www.euro.who.int/__data/assets/pdf_file/0005/98438/e81384.pdf © World Health Organization. 2003.

men and women in different occupational classes in England and Wales between 1997 and 1999. Although women in each occupational class have a longer life expectancy than men, both men and women in "unskilled manual" occupations, on average, have a life expectancy 6–8 years shorter than those in the "professional" class. The life expectancy gradient from one occupational class to the next consistently favors those in the successively upper occupational stratum.

▶ 2.10 Race as a Determinant of Health

In literature, the terms *race* and *ethnicity* are frequently used interchangeably and capture common geographic origins, ancestry, language, traditions, and cultural norms of a group of people.[18] In social science research, racial categorization has been used to reflect oppression, social inequality, and lack of opportunity for one group as compared with another.[57]

Rather than any evidence of intrinsic differences in biochemical, physiologic, or genetic makeup, the construct of **race** is based on the pigmentation of skin and other physical traits, as well as geographic distribution of people: African, Hispanic, Caucasian, Native American, Asian, Pacific Islander, and so on. Historically, racial categorization was largely used to imply differences in genetic makeup. However, genetic profile data unequivocally show that there is far greater genetic variation within racial groups (particularly among Africans) than exists between different racial groups such as Africans versus Caucasians. "Although race is still used as a label, the original concept of race as a genetically distinct subspecies of humans has been rejected through modern genetic information. . . . It is more appropriate to reconceptualize the old genetics of race into a more accurate genetics of ancestry."[31]

Outside of genetic predisposition to certain diseases, such as sickle cell anemia or thalassemia, the problem with employing race as a determinant of health is that it is a social construct for which we have no knowledge of how or whether, in and of itself, race predisposes a group of people to better or poorer health.[14] The only empirical evidence we have is that of a statistical association between race and disease prevalence or health outcomes such as hypertension or diabetes, or survival rates from various cancers. However, these associations cannot be isolated from, and can be explained on the bases of, gradients in socioeconomic factors. The cumulative effect and hemodynamic responses to the stress of social isolation, unemployment, poverty, and resentment of one's circumstances provide the physiologic bases of gradients in hypertension and diabetes.[19] Passive coping strategies to the stress of social isolation and other socioeconomic stressors also set the stage for poor behavioral choices, including excessive eating, drinking, and use of illicit drugs. The long-term health effects of these choices ultimately lead to obesity, diabetes, heart disease, psychiatric problems, and violence.[58]

Significant disparities in health and health care exist in the U.S. healthcare system between different racial groups. A disparity in health refers to differences in the burden of disease, death, and disability, whereas a disparity in health care relates to differences between groups in terms of access to services, quality of care received, and health outcomes for the same services and procedures. Minority individuals continue to have less access to health care, receive poorer quality care, and have worse health outcomes as compared with the white population. Although some of these disparities are explained by differences in the socioeconomic status of white and minority populations, notable disparities persist within the same socioeconomic strata in the same geographic districts. Black, Hispanic, Native, and Asian Americans, for example, face greater barriers to access, receive fewer services such as coronary artery bypass graft or perinatal care, and have worse outcomes for the same procedures as compared with their white counterparts of the same education and income levels. These disparities cost the nation approximately $35 billion in excess health care, $10 billion in lost productivity, and $200 billion in premature deaths every year.[59] Some of the differences in access and use of services are also linked to a historic distrust in minority population of government and healthcare providers. Designation by the federal government of various groups, such as people of color, the elderly, women, and children, as "priority population" attempts to reduce disparities in both health and health care.

In the chapter entitled *Descriptive Epidemiology*, we provide more information on the epidemiologic importance of genetically linked disorders found more commonly in various groups, such as African Americans or Ashkenazi Jewish women, and the categorization of various racial groups by the U.S. Census Bureau.

⌕ CASE STUDY 2.1: Effect of Education on Health

Extracted from: Rogers RG, Everett BG, Zajacova A, Hummer RA. Educational degrees and adult mortality risk in the United States. Biodemography and Social Biology. 2010;56(1):80–99.

In this 2010 study published in the journal *Biodemography and Social Biology*, Rogers et al. estimated the risk of mortality in U.S. adults aged 25 years or older by educational levels. The authors used the 1997–2002 National Health Interview Survey Linked Mortality Files and Cox proportional hazards modeling statistical analyses to estimate the risk of mortality for individuals with different levels of educational attainment. The study included data on 184,499 individuals 25 years or older who had participated in the National Health Interview Survey. The National Death Index matching criteria showed that 8,994 of these individuals had died since the survey. Based on the date of birth, the survey participants were divided into four cohorts: Good Warriors (born between 1909 and 1928), Lucky Few (born between 1929 and 1945), Baby Boom (born between 1946 and 1964), and Generation X (born between 1965 and 1982). **TABLES 2.1**, and **2.2**, present some of the results of the study. In Tables 2.1 and 2.2, a hazard ratio of 1.0 indicates that there is no relationship between the variable of interest, such as sex, race, or marital status, and the risk of mortality. A hazard ratio of greater than 1.0 suggests a heightened risk of mortality in comparison with the reference category. For example, a hazard ratio of 1.26 would suggest that the specific variable (e.g., having only a bachelor's degree) is associated with a 26% increased risk of mortality during the follow up period as compared with the reference category. Conversely, a hazard ratio of less than 1.0 means a reduced risk of mortality in comparison with the reference group. The statistical models developed in this study controlled for the effects of race/ethnicity on the risk of mortality (Model 1 in Table 2.1 and all models in Table 2.2) as well as the effect of marital status (Model 2 in Table 2.1 and all models in Table 2.2). The authors concluded that in comparison to adults who had a professional degree, those with a bachelor's degree, those with some college education, those with a high school diploma, and those with GED or ≤12 years of schooling were 26%, 65%, 80%, and 95%, respectively, more likely to die during the follow-up period. The heightened risk of mortality with lower educational attainment varied by gender and age cohort.

Questions

Question 1. In Table 2.1, as compared with those with a high school diploma, how much higher or lower is the risk of mortality for those with less than 12 years of education? What about those with a professional degree?

Question 2. In Table 2.1, as compared with Generation X, were the Good Warriors at a higher or lower risk of mortality? Explain your answer.

Question 3. In Table 2.2, as compared with those with a high school diploma, how much higher or lower is the risk of mortality for the Baby Boom and Generation X cohorts with fewer than 12 years of education? What is the risk of mortality for Baby Boom and Generation X individuals with a MA/PhD/professional degree?

TABLE 2.1 Hazard Ratios of Educational Degrees and Mortality Risk, U.S. Adults Aged 25 and Older, 1997–2002

	Model 1		Model 2	
	H.R.	**S.E.**	**H.R.**	**S.E.**
Education (High school diploma; reference category)				
Less than 12	1.21 ***	(0.04)	1.18 ***	(0.04)
Grade 12	1.07	(0.08)	1.09	(0.08)
GED	1.11	(0.08)	1.09	(0.08)
Some college	0.92 *	(0.03)	0.92 *	(0.03)
AA	0.80 ***	(0.04)	0.80 ***	(0.04)
BA	0.70 ***	(0.03)	0.70 ***	(0.03)

MA	0.59 ***	(0.05)	0.59 ***	(0.05)
Prof. degree (MD, DDS, JD, DVM)	0.55 ***	(0.07)	0.56 ***	(0.07)
PhD	0.60 ***	(0.08)	0.61 ***	(0.08)
Sociodemographic				
Male	1.58 ***	(0.04)	1.69 ***	(0.01)
Cohort (Generation X, born 1965–1982; reference category)				
Baby Boom, born 1946–1964	1.14	(0.31)	1.17	(0.30)
Lucky Few, born 1929–1945	1.11	(0.34)	1.12	(0.33)
Good Warriors, born 1909–1928	1.14	(0.36)	1.16	(0.34)
Race/Ethnicity (Non-Hispanic white; reference category)				
Non-Hispanic black	1.34 ***	(0.05)	1.26 ***	(0.05)
Hispanic	0.90	(0.06)	0.89†	(0.06)
Other	1.06	(0.07)	1.05	(0.07)
Marital Status (Married; reference category)				
Widowed			1.26 ***	(0.04)
Divorced/separated			1.48 ***	(0.06)
Never married			1.64 ***	(0.07)

Model 1 controlled for race/ethnicity; Model 2 controlled for both race/ethnicity and marital status.
†$p \leq .10.$ *$p \leq .05.$ **$p \leq .01.$ ***$p \leq .001.$
Abbreviations: H.R. = hazard ratio; S.E. = standard error.

Modified from: Rogers RG, Everett BG, Zajacova A, Hummer RA. Educational degrees and adult mortality risk in the United States. Biodemography and Social Biology. 2010;56(1):80–99.
Reprinted by permission of the Society of Biodemography & Social Biology, www.biodemog.org, Taylor & Francis Ltd.

TABLE 2.2 Hazard Ratios of Educational Degrees and Mortality Risk by Cohort and Sex, U.S. Adults Aged 25 and Older, 1997–2002

	Good Warriors (born 1909–1928)		Lucky Few (born 1929–1945)		Baby Boom & Gen X (born 1946–1982)	
	H.R.	S.E.	H.R.	S.E.	H.R.	S.E.
Males						
N	9,988		19,327		56,767	
Died during follow-up	2,495		1,391		764	

(continues)

TABLE 2.2 Hazard Ratios of Educational Degrees and Mortality Risk by Cohort and Sex, U.S. Adults Aged 25 and Older, 1997–2002 *(continued)*

	Good Warriors (born 1909–1928)		Lucky Few (born 1929–1945)		Baby Boom & Gen X (born 1946–1982)	
	H.R.	S.E.	H.R.	S.E.	H.R.	S.E.
Education (High school diplomo used as reference group)						
Less than 12	1.18 **	(0.06)	1.40 ***	(0.10)	1.51 ***	(0.19)
Grade 12	1.15	(0.15)	1.35†	(0.24)	0.97	(0.25)
GED	1.17	(0.17)	1.34 *	(0.18)	1.41 *	(0.25)
Some college	0.95	(0.07)	0.98	(0.09)	0.90	(0.10)
AA	0.80 *	(0.09)	0.96	(0.13)	0.84	(0.12)
BA	0.75 **	(0.07)	0.64 ***	(0.08)	0.46 ***	(0.06)
MA/PhD/Prof. degree	0.69 ***	(0.07)	0.56 ***	(0.10)	0.31 ***	(0.07)
Race/Ethnicity (Non-Hispanic white used as reference group)						
Non-Hispanic black	0.98	(0.07)	1.20 *	(0.12)	1.53 ***	(0.16)
Hispanic	0.76 *	(0.10)	0.89	(0.16)	1.37 *	(0.19)
Other	0.94	(0.14)	0.93	(0.21)	1.59 *	(0.30)
Marital Status (Married used as reference group)						
Widowed	1.19 ***	(0.06)	1.46 **	(0.17)	3.29 ***	(1.07)
Divorced/separated	1.29 *	(0.14)	1.68 ***	(0.13)	1.90 ***	(0.20)
Never married	1.16	(0.13)	2.01 ***	(0.23)	2.44 ***	(0.25)
Females						
N	14,472		21,573		62,372	
Died during follow-up	2,698		1,059		587	
Education (High school diploma used as reference group)						
Less than 12	1.10 *	(0.06)	1.47 ***	(0.13)	1.44 *	(0.23)
Grade 12	1.00	(0.13)	0.87	(0.18)	1.55 *	(0.33)
GED	0.52 *	(0.15)	1.04	(0.24)	1.03	(0.27)

Some college	0.95	(0.07)	0.79 *	(0.09)	1.00	(0.13)
AA	0.85	(0.09)	0.71 *	(0.11)	0.73†	(0.13)
BA	0.89	(0.08)	0.91	(0.12)	0.66 **	(0.13)
MA/PhD/Prof. degree	0.82	(0.11)	0.60 **	(0.11)	0.56 **	(0.12)
Race/Ethnicity (Non-Hispanic white used as reference group)						
Non-Hispanic black	1.14 *	(0.07)	1.47 ***	(0.13)	1.55 ***	(0.17)
Hispanic	0.87	(0.12)	0.56 **	(0.11)	1.02	(0.19)
Other	0.81	(0.16)	1.24	(0.24)	1.09	(0.26)
Marital Status (Married used as reference group)						
Widowed	1.23 ***	(0.06)	1.26 **	(0.10)	1.34	(0.37)
Divorced/separated	1.20†	(0.12)	1.34 **	(0.12)	1.75 ***	(0.19)
Never married	1.28 *	(0.14)	1.64 ***	(0.23)	1.55 **	(0.22)

†$p \leq .10$; *$p \leq .05$; **$p \leq .01$; ***$p \leq .001$.
Abbreviations: H.R. = hazard ratio; S.E. = standard error.

Modified from: Rogers RG, Everett BG, Zajacova A, Hummer RA. Educational degrees and adult mortality risk in the United States. Biodemography and Social Biology. 2010;56(1):80–99. Reprinted by permission of the Society of Biodemography & Social Biology, www.biodemog.org, Taylor & Francis Ltd.

🔍 CASE STUDY 2.2: Effect of Socioeconomic Status on Health

Extracted from: Banks J, Marmot M, Oldfield Z, Smith PJ. Disease and disadvantage in the United States and in England. JAMA. 2006;295(17):2037–2045.

In a 2006 seminal study, Banks et al. examined the relative health status of older individuals in England and the United States in relation to their socioeconomic status. The researchers used 2002 data from the U.S. Health and Retirement Survey (n=4,386) and the English Longitudinal Study of Aging (n=3,681) as representative samples of individuals aged 55 to 64 years in both countries. They supplemented their analysis with samples of individuals aged 40 to 70 years from the 1999–2002 waves of National Health and Nutrition Examination Survey (n=2,097) and the 2003 wave of the Health Survey from England (n=5,526). To ensure integrity of results untainted by health status difference among white, black, and Hispanic populations, the study was limited to only non-Hispanic white populations in the two countries. Age and health behavior–adjusted self-reported prevalence of diabetes, hypertension, heart disease, stroke, myocardial infarction, lung disease, and cancer were used as indicators of health status. These indicators were compared across different education and income groups in the two countries.

   Overall, the results showed that the U.S. middle-aged population was less healthy than the comparable English population. Within each country, a clear negative socioeconomic gradient for self-reported health status was observed. Adjusting for risky health behaviors such as smoking, being overweight, being obese, and abusing alcohol, health status disparities were greatest for those at the bottom of the education and income hierarchy. Diabetes was noted to be twice as high in the U.S. population of 55- to 64-year-old individuals as compared with the same-age English population. As only one fifth of the difference in the health status of the two populations was explained by a difference in health-related behaviors of the two populations, the difference in health status was deemed real and unexplained by differences in health-related behaviors. Similarly, average levels of C-reactive protein were 20% higher, and average levels of high-density lipoprotein cholesterol were 14% lower, in the U.S. population of 55- to 64-year-olds.

(continues)

TABLE 2.3 shows the percentage of 55- to 64-year-olds in each education and income category in the two countries who reported being smokers, drinking heavily, and being overweight or obese. **TABLE 2.4** shows that in both countries, even after adjusting for health-related personal behaviors such as smoking, abusing alcohol, and being obese, for all diseases, with the exception of cancer, a steep negative health gradient existed between different educational and income groups, with less educated and low-income individuals being worse off than their more educated and economically well-off counterparts.

Questions

Question 1. Based on the data presented in Table 2.3, across different education and income categories, were there any consistent patterns in the distribution of risk factors in the populations of the two countries? Explain your answer.

Question 2. Based on the data presented in Table 2.3, were middle-income Americans more or less obese than middle-income English 55- to 64-year-olds? How confident can one be in making this assertion? Explain your answer.

Questions 3. Based on the data presented in Table 2.3, were "current smoker" patterns across low-, medium-, and high-education groups different between the English and American 55- to 64-year-olds? Explain your answer.

Question 4. Based on the data presented in Table 2.4, what conclusions can you draw about the occurrence of stroke across education and income categories in the English and American populations?

Question 5. Based on the data presented in Table 2.4, what conclusions can you draw about the occurrence of cancer across education and income categories in the English and American populations?

TABLE 2.3 Prevalence of Self-Reported Risk Factors in England and the United States, Ages 55–64 Years*

Self-Reported Risk Factor	England				United States			
	Low	Medium	High	Total	Low	Medium	High	Total
Years of schooling, percent distribution								
Current smoker	28.6	18.2	13.3	21.9	24.9[†]	20.5	11.4	20.1
Ever smoked	69.1	64.0	62.6	66.1	64.5[‡]	65.0	54.8[‡]	61.9[‡]
Obese	26.5	20.9	18.6	23.0	33.6[‡]	34.5[‡]	24.0[‡]	31.1[‡]
Overweight	38.8	42.4	43.2	40.9	38.2	37.8	40.5[‡]	38.8
Heavy drinker	21.8	32.8	42.2	30.0	10.6[‡]	13.2[‡]	21.9[‡]	14.4[‡]
Income, percent distribution								
Current smoker	28.6	22.2	15.2	21.9	26.9	21.8	11.6[†]	20.1
Ever smoked	69.1	65.8	63.4	66.1	66.1	62.6	56.9[‡]	61.9[‡]
Obese	25.3	23.2	20.5	23.0	35.6[‡]	32.9[‡]	24.8[†]	31.1[‡]
Overweight	38.9	41.8	42.1	40.9	35.8	39.0	41.4	38.8
Heavy drinker	22.6	26.2	40.6	29.9	8.7[‡]	14.3[‡]	20.2[‡]	14.1[‡]

*Extracted from: English data are from first wave of English Longitudinal Survey of Aging, and U.S. data are from the 2002 wave of the Health and Retirement Survey. See Table 2.4 for sample sizes and definitions of income and education groups. All data are weighted.
[†]P<.01 for comparison of United States and England
[‡]P<.05 for comparison of United States and England

TABLE 2.4 Adjusted Self-Reported Health by Education and Income in England and the United States, Ages 55–64 Years*

Self-reported Disease	England				United States			
	Low	Medium	High	Total	Low	Medium	High	Total
Years of schooling, percent distribution								
Diabetes	7.7	6.2	7.4	7.2	13.9[†]	11.9[†]	10.6[‡]	12.5[†]
Hypertension	37.6	32.9	32.5	35.1	46.0[†]	40.2[†]	38.0[‡]	42.4[†]
All heart disease	12.2	8.3	7.9	10.1	17.1[†]	14.9[†]	11.9	15.1[†]
Myocardial infarction	4.8	4.0	3.3	4.2	6.7[‡]	4.2	4.3	5.4[‡]
Stroke	2.7	2.3	1.8	2.3	4.7[†]	4.1[‡]	2.0	3.8[†]
Lung disease	7.7	5.4	4.3	6.2	10.4[†]	7.9[‡]	4.4	8.1[†]
Cancer	4.9	5.3	6.5	5.4	8.8[†]	9.7[†]	10.5[†]	9.5[†]
Income, percent distribution								
Diabetes	8.1	7.7	6.0	7.2	16.8[†]	11.4[†]	9.2[†]	12.5[†]
Hypertension	37.9	35.8	31.6	35.1	46.1[†]	42.8[†]	38.2[†]	42.4[†]
All heart disease	14.3	9.1	6.9	10.1	20.2[†]	13.1[†]	12.1[†]	15.1[†]
Myocardial infarction	6.7	3.3	2.5	4.2	8.6	4.3	3.3	5.4[‡]
Stroke	3.5	1.9	1.6	2.3	5.8[‡]	3.7[†]	1.8	3.8[†]
Lung disease	7.6	6.3	4.8	6.2	12.3[†]	7.0	5.1	8.1[†]
Cancer	5.7	5.1	5.5	5.4	9.3[†]	9.8[†]	9.5[†]	9.5[†]

*Ordinary Least Squares regression models adjusted to reflect what health conditions would be if all individuals in both countries had the same level of behavioral risk factors as the average American in that age group. Regression coefficients are country specific.

Extracted from: English data are from the first wave of the English Longitudinal Survey of Aging, and U.S. data are from the 2002 wave of the Health and Retirement Survey. See Table 2.1 for sample sizes and definitions of income and education groups. All data are weighted.

[†]P<.01 for comparison of United States and England
[‡]P<.05 for comparison of United States and England

▶ 2.11 Summary

There are important philosophic and practical differences in defining health and practical challenges in assessing the health status of individuals, communities, and populations. One area in which there is general agreement is that the health of a person at any given time and over the span of a lifetime is the result of complex interactions among genes, personal behavior, and socioeconomic factors, including education, income, and occupation. Although our genetic makeup increases or decreases the risk of various diseases, few diseases are purely and exclusively the result of inherited genes or genetic mutations. There is increasing evidence that environmental and psychosocial stimuli trigger genetic changes or responses. The environment in which people are born, live, and work plays a large role in determining whether they are healthy or sick. Consistent empirical evidence from all over the world shows that people at the lowest levels of the socioeconomic hierarchy have the poorest health indicators. Adequate access to a medical care system is critical for relief from suffering and restoration of health. However, the availability and appropriate utilization of a comprehensive healthcare system that prevents the occurrence of diseases through education, timely vaccinations, periodic medical screenings, and sustained health promotion through optimal behavior modification and lifestyle choices is far more important. Access to and availability of balanced and nutritious food, good education, adequate housing, nonhazardous work environments, minimally stressful psychosocial conditions, and a supportive social network offer the best prospects for optimal individual, familial, and communal life.

References

1. Mahler H. The meaning of "Health for all by the year 2000." World Health Forum. 1981;2(1):5–22.

2. Mausner JS, Kramer S. Mausner & Bahn epidemiology: an introductory text. Philadelphia: WB Saunders; 1985.

3. Doll R. Health and the environment in the 1990s. Am J Public Health. 1992;82(41):933–941.

4. Venes D, editor. Health. Taber's cyclopedic medical dictionary [Internet]. 23rd ed. Philadelphia: FA Davis; 2017. [cited 2018 Jan 31]. Available from: http://online.statref.com/document.aspx?FxId=57&DocID=1&SessionID=2769A56UTKLRUNOP#H&1&ChaptersTab&q3e-xiOOz5Orb7ImA-4AgA%3d%3d&p37&57

5. Dubos R. Man, medicine, and environment. New York, NY: Pall Mall Press; 1968.

6. Venes D, editor. Population. Taber's cyclopedic medical dictionary [Internet]. 23rd ed. Philadelphia: FA Davis; 2017. [cited 2018 Jan 31]. Available from: http://online.statref.com/document.aspx?FxId=57&DocID=1&SessionID=2769A56UTKLRUNOP - H&4&ChaptersTab&DRDN53sgZjVGAm9ON9vT1g==&&57

7. Kindig D, Stoddard G. What is population health? Am J Public Health. 2003;93(3):380–383.

8. Evans RG, Barer ML, Marmor TR. Why are some people healthy and others not? The determinants of the health of populations. Hawthorne, NY: Aldine De Gruyter; 1994 [cited 2017 Jul 21]. Available from: http://books.google.com/books?id=nuvrg2AWCT0C&source=gbs_navlinks_s

9. Young TK. Population health: concepts and methods. New York: Oxford University Press; 1998.

10. Canadian Mental Health Association. The relationship between mental health, mental illness and chronic physical conditions. 2008 [cited 2017 Jul 21]. Available from: http://ontario.cmha.ca/public_policy/the-relationship-between-mental-health-mental-illness-and-chronic-physical-conditions/

11. Ruoff GE. Depression in the patient with chronic pain. J Fam Pract. 1996;43:S25–S33.

12. Fishbain DA. Current research on chronic pain and suicide. Am J Public Health. 1996;86(9):1320–1321.

13. Tang NK, Crane C. Suicidality in chronic pain: a review of the prevalence, risk factors and psychological links. Psychol Med. 2006;36(5):575–586.

14. Thisted RA. Are there social determinants of health and disease? Perspect Biol Med. 2003;46(3 suppl):S65–S73.

15. Raphael D. Social determinants of health: an overview of key issues and themes. In: Raphael D, editor. Social determinants of health: Canadian perspectives. Toronto, Canada: Canadian Scholar's Press; 2009. p. 2–19.

16. Brennan-Ramirez LK, Baker EA, Metzler M, editors. Centers for Disease Control and Prevention. Promoting health equity: a resource to help communities address social determinants of health. Atlanta: Department of Health and Human Services; 2008 [cited 2017 Jul 21]. Available from: https://stacks.cdc.gov/view/cdc/11130/

17. Locker D. Social determinants of health and disease. In: Scambler G, editor. Sociology as applied to medicine. 6th ed. Edinburgh, UK: Saunders/Elsevier; 2008 [cited 2018 July 3]. Available from: https://books.google.com/books?id=oiGpQ-m-8VoC&printsec=frontcover&dq=Sociology+as+applied+to+medicine+by+Graham+Scambler&hl=en&sa=X&ved=0ahUKEwiLu7KamIPcAhUBjq0KHUb9DOwQ6AEIKTAA#v=onepage&q=Sociology%20as%20applied%20to%20medicine%20by%20Graham%20Scambler&f=false

18. Williams DR, Mohammed SA, Leavell J, Collins C. Race, socioeconomic status, and health: complexities, ongoing challenges, and research opportunities. Ann N Y Acad Sci. 2010:1186:69–101.

19. Cacioppo JT, Hawkley LC. Social isolation and health, with an emphasis on underlying mechanisms. Perspect Biol Med. 2003;46(3) suppl:S39–S52.

20. McGinnis JM, Foege WH. Actual causes of death in the United States. JAMA. 1993;270:2207–2212.

21. Institute of Medicine of the National Academies. The future of the public's health in the 21st century. Washington DC: National Academies Press; 2003.

22. Mokdad AH, Marks JS, Stroup DF, Gerberding JL. Actual causes of death in the United States, 2000. JAMA. 2004;291(10):1238–1245. Corrected in Letters, Mokdad AH. JAMA. 2005;293(3):293–294.

23. Tarlov AR. Public policy framework for improving population health. Ann N Y Acad Sci. 1999;896:281–293.

24. National Institutes of Health, National Human Genome Research Institute. Specific genetic disorders. 2017 [cited 2017 Jul 21]. Available from: http://www.genome.gov/10001204

25. Warman ML, Cormier-Daire V, Hall C, et al. Nosology and classification of genetic skeletal disorders: 2010 revision. Am J Med Genet A. 2010;155:943–968.

26. Baird PA, Anderson TW, Newcombe HB, Lowry BR. Genetic disorders in children and young adults: a population study. Am J Hum Genet. 1988;42:677–693.

27. Evans WE, McLeod HL. Pharmacogenomics—drug disposition, drug targets, and side effects. N Engl J Med. 2003;348:538–549 [cited 2018 July 3]. Available from: http://www.nejm.org/doi/pdf/10.1056/NEJMra020526

28. Kalow W. Genetic factors that cause variability in human drug metabolism. In: Pacifici GM, Pelkonen O, editors. Interindividual variability in human drug metabolism. New York: Taylor & Francis; 2001 [cited 2017 Jul 21]. Available from: https://books.google.com/books?id=mNKWjla41qUC&pg=PA129&lpg=PA129&dq=interindividual+variability+in+human+drug+metabolism&source=bl&ots=BZbzBOTMj_&sig=3y6BpEIOj08gY9XaQC4pFcpjYcE&hl=en&sa=X&ei=SKEiVdCkDdb8oQSx2ICQDw&ved=0CDoQ6AEwAw#v=onepage&q=interindividual%20variability%20in%20human%20drug%20metabolism&f=false

29. Whiting P, Al M, Burgers L, et al. Ivacaftor for the treatment of patients with cystic fibrosis and the G551D mutation: a systematic review and cost-effectiveness analysis. Health Technol Assess. 2014;18(18). DOI: 10.3310/hta18180

30. Antoniou A, Pharoah P, Narod S, et al. Average risks of breast and ovarian cancer associated with BRCA1 or BRCA2 mutations detected in case series unselected for family history: a combined analysis of 22 studies. Am J Hum Genet. 2003;72(5):1117–1130.

31. Institute of Medicine. Hernandez LM, Blazer DG, editors. Genes, behavior, and the social environment: moving beyond the nature/nurture debate. Washington DC: National Academies Press; 2006 [cited 2017 Jul 21]. Available from: http://www.ncbi.nlm.nih.gov/books/NBK19929/pdf/TOC.pdf

32. Banks J, Marmot M, Oldfield Z, Smith PJ. Disease and disadvantage in the United States and in England. JAMA. 2006;295(17):2037–2045.

33. Donkin A, Goldblatt P, Lynch K. Inequalities in life expectancy by social class, 1972–1999. Health Stat Q. 2002; Autumn 15:5–15.

34. Lynch JW, Kaplan GA, Salonen JT. Why do poor people behave poorly? Variation in adult health behaviours and psychosocial characteristics by stages of the socioeconomic lifecourse. Soc Sci Med. 1997;44(6):809–819.

35. Thurlow HJ. General susceptibility to illness: a selective review. Can Med Assoc J. 1967;97:1397–1404.

36. Brunner E, Marmot M. Social organization, stress, and health. In: Marmot M, Wilkinson RG, editors. Social determinants of health. Oxford, UK: Oxford University Press; 1999. p. 6–30.

37. Chandola T, Brunner E. Marmot M. Chronic stress at work and the metabolic syndrome: prospective study. BMJ. 2006;332:521–525 [cited 2018 July 3]. Available from: http://www.bmj.com/content/bmj/332/7540/521.full.pdf

38. Najman J. Theories of disease causation and the concept of general susceptibility: a review. Soc Sci Med. 1980;14A:231–237.

39. Marmot MG, Rose G, Shipley M. Hamilton PJ. Employment grade and coronary heart disease in British civil servants. J Epidemiol Community Health. 1978;32(4):244–249.

40. Marmot MG, Smith GD, Stansfeld S, et al. Health inequalities among British civil servants: the Whitehall II study. Lancet. 1991;337:1387–1393.

41. Kuper H, Marmot M. Job strain, job demand, decision latitude, and risk of coronary heart disease within the Whitehall II study. J Epidemiol Community Health. 2003;57(2):147–153.

42. Marmot M, Ryff CD, Bumpass LL, Shipley M, Marks NF. Social inequalities in health: next questions and converging evidence. Soc Sci Med. 1997;44(6):901–910.

43. Russo P. Population health. In: Kovner AR, Knickman JR, editors. Health care delivery in the United States. New York: Springer; 2011. p. 79–98.

44. Sullivan DG, von Wachter T. Job displacement and mortality: an analysis using administrative data. Q J Econ. 2009;124(3):1265–1306.

45. Lagerlund M, Belocco R, Karlsson P, Tejler G, Lambe M. Socio-economic factors and breast cancer survival: a population-based cohort study (Sweden). Cancer Causes Control. 2005;16(4):419–430.

46. Woods LM, Rachet B, Coleman MP. Origins of socio-economic inequalities in cancer survival: a review. Ann Oncol. 2006;17:5–19.

47. Beral V, Bull D, Doll R, et al. Collaborative Group on Hormonal Factors in Breast Cancer. Breast cancer and breastfeeding: collaborative reanalysis of individual data from 47 epidemiologic studies in 30 countries, including 50302 women with breast cancer and 96973 women without the disease. Lancet. 2002;360(9328):187–195.

48. Duncan DJ, Daly MC, McDonough P, Williams DR. Optimal indicators of socioeconomic status of health research. Am J Public Health. 2002;92(7):1151–1157.

49. Case A, Paxson C. Parental behavior and child health. Health Aff. 2002;21(2):164–178.

50. Lleras-Muney A. The relationship between education and adult mortality in the United States. Rev Econ Stud. 2005;72(1):189–221. [cited 2017 Jul 21]. Available from: http://www.econ.ucla.edu/alleras/research/papers/mortality revision2.pdf

51. Schweinhart LJ, Montie J, Xiang Z, Barnett WS, Belfield CR, Nores M. Lifetime effects: The High/Scope Perry Preschool study through age 40. Ypsilanti, MI: High/Scope Press; 2005. [cited 2018 Apr 19]. Available from: http://www.highscope.org/file/Research/PerryProject/specialsummary_rev2011_02_2.pdf

52. Biswas A, Oh PI, Faulkner GE, et al. Sedentary time and its association with risk for disease incidence, mortality, and hospitalization in adults: a systematic review and meta-analysis. Ann Intern Med. 2015;162(2):123–132.

53. Berkman L, Macintyre S. The measurement of social class in health studies: old measures and new formulations. In: Kogevinas M, Pearce N, Susser M, Boffetta P, editors. Social inequalities and cancer. IARC Scientific Publications Number 138. Lyon, France: International Agency for Research on Cancer; 1997. [cited 2018 Apr 19]. Available from: http://www.iarc.fr/en/publications/pdfs-online/epi/sp138/sp138-chap4.pdf

54. U.S. Bureau of the Census. Methodology and scores of socioeconomic status. Working Paper No. 15. Washington DC: U.S. Government Printing Office; 1963. [cited 2018 Apr 19]. Available from: https://books.google.com/books?id=bj7ODlJynhMC&pg=PA1&lpg=PA1&dq=methodology+and+scores+of+socioeconomic+status&source=bl&ots=cPN8LO-q1O&sig=jKIjgnd_4wj2TlbYLxcaHDRALH4&hl=en&sa=X&ei=lg0bVYjhPMqwogSz14CQDg&ved=0CDIQ6AEwAg#v=onepage&q=methodology%20and%20scores%20of%20socioeconomic%20status&f=false

55. Hodge RW. The measurement of occupational status. Soc Sci Res. 1981;10:396–415. [cited 2018 Apr 19]. Available from: http://ac.els-cdn.com/0049089X81900120/1-s2.0-0049089X81900120-main.pdf?_tid=baf29138-d7f2-11e4-98ea-00000aab0f6c&acdnat=1427840004_ecace1969913d8f31a3dafcd3a0fde63

56. Burgard S, Stewart J, Schwartz J. Occupational status. In: Social Environment Notebook. MacArthur Network on SES and Health. San Francisco, CA: University of California; 2003.

57. American Sociological Association. The importance of collecting data and doing social scientific research on race. Washington DC: American Sociological Association; 2003. [cited 2018 Apr 19]. Available from: http://www.asanet.org/sites/default/files/savvy/images/press/docs/pdf/asa_race_statement.pdf

58. Sampson RJ. The neighborhood context of wellbeing. Perspect Biol Med. 2003;46 suppl:S53–S64.

59. Ayanian JZ. The cost of racial disparities in health care. N Engl J Med. 2016 [cited 2017 Jun 22]. Available from: http://images.nejm.org/editorial/supplementary/2015/hbr08-ayanian.pdf

CHAPTER 3

Assessment of Personal and Population Health

LEARNING OBJECTIVES

Having mastered the materials in this chapter, the student will be able to:

1. Explain different methods of assessing personal and population health.
2. Explain different methods of assessing levels of functioning and disability.
3. Explain different methods of measuring the burden of disease in a population.
4. Explain different systems of classification of diseases.
5. Use available secondary data to estimate the burden of disease in a population.

CHAPTER OUTLINE

3.1 Introduction
3.2 Definition of Disease, Disability, and Death
3.3 Assessment of Personal Health
3.4 Assessment of Physiologic Health
3.5 Assessment of Mental Health and Psychosocial Development
3.6 Assessment of Functioning and Disability
3.7 Self-Assessment of Health and Well-Being
3.8 Assessment of Community Health
3.9 Assessment of Burden of Disease and Summary Measures of Population Health
    3.9.1 Disability-Adjusted Life Years
    3.9.2 Quality-Adjusted Life Years

3.10 Classification of Diseases and Procedures
    3.10.1 International Classification of Diseases
    3.10.2 Current Procedural Terminology (CPT) Codes
3.11 Reportable/Notifiable Diseases
Case Study 3.1 – Assessment of Burden of Disease
Case Study 3.2 – Influence of Gender and Age on Disability after Stroke
3.12 Summary
Exercise 3.1

▶ 3.1 Introduction

Healthcare managers frequently have to deal with issues related to the assessment of health status, disability, and the burden of death, disease, and disability in the communities they serve.

In this chapter, we will discuss the fundamental concepts of disease, disability, and death, and the challenges of assessing the burden of disease in a population. We will also grapple with the difficulties inherent in defining the boundaries between being healthy and being sick, and the states of being alive and being dead. Circumventing the philosophic and moral issues related to the question of when life begins—at the time of conception or some later stage of embryonic development—we will only in passing note the complexities and challenges involved in deciding when life ends and declaring whether a nonresponsive person is still alive. In this chapter, we will discuss various approaches toward assessing the health status of a person at any given time, and assessing the burden of death and disease in a population. Assessment of the burden of death and disease in a population is important for healthcare policy formulation and planning of health services. In discussing the health status of a person, we make a distinction between self-reported subjective declaration of personal health status and an objective assessment of an individual's health status by a healthcare professional—whether at the time of a routine annual physical examination or during an encounter with a healthcare provider necessitated by the emergence of a medical problem.

▶ 3.2 Definition of Disease, Disability, and Death

A *disease* (or the old medical term *dyscrasia*) is usually viewed as an objectively identifiable and clinically diagnosable condition distinct from *illness*, which is a subjective and often nondescript feeling of not being well. Taber's Cyclopedic Medical Dictionary[1] defines disease as "A condition marked by subjective complaints, a specific history, clinical signs and symptoms, and laboratory or radiographic findings . . . disease is usually objective and tangible or measurable." Whereas a disease is a specific, tangible, or objectively measurable condition, the concept of illness is intangible, highly personal, and tied, more or less, with the notion of suffering or distress. A disease such as hypertension (frequently referred to as the "silent killer"), though easily measurable, can exist without pain, distress, or feelings of illness. On the other hand, a feeling of not being well, or "feeling ill," may or may not arise from an underlying disease or pathology. Even when a "disease" is not clinically detected by a healthcare provider despite the use of all existing scientific tools and tests, neither can the possibility of the existence of a disease, whether known to medical science or hitherto unknown, be ruled out, nor can a person's feeling of being "ill" be dismissed as invalid. The complex interaction of body and mind frequently blurs the boundaries between "disease" and "illness." For example, scientists have been puzzled by the phenomenon of *phantom limb/phantom pain* since it was first reported in 1552 by a French surgeon named Ambroise Paré. In this medical mystery, patients who have lost a limb to trauma and/or surgical amputation continue to feel the existence of and pain in the lost limb for months or years. To date, neither a definitive explanation nor an effective treatment has been discovered for this condition.

A **disability** can be defined as a partial or complete physical or mental inability to perform normal tasks and activities of life and work. Both physical and mental disability can result from a disease or illness. For example, musculoskeletal disorders, with or without pain, can severely affect a person's ability to move, turn, or lift anything, whereas emotional or psychological disorders can affect the ability to focus, think, and act rationally or responsibly. In both cases, the effect is an inability to function normally. In the United States, the Americans with Disabilities Act (ADA), when it was passed in 1990, defined a disability as "physical or mental impairment that substantially limits one or more of the major life activities."[2]

Since 2011, pursuant to Section 4302 of the Affordable Care Act and the guidelines provided by the Department of Health and Human Services, research and data collection on disabilities must incorporate specifically functional types of disability such as visual, auditory, musculoskeletal, cognitive, and communicational impairment. According to one study,[3] in 2013, 22.2% of adult Americans (~53.32 million) reported having some disability. Impaired mobility (13.0%) was the most commonly reported disability, followed by cognitive disability (10.6%), inability to live independently (6.5%), impaired vision (4.6%), and difficulty in self-care (3.6%). Generally, women more frequently reported having some disability (24.4%) than did men (19.8%). Not surprisingly, prevalence of disabilities of various kinds, with the exception of cognitive problems, was highest among those age 65 years or older. **FIGURES 3.1** and **3.2** provide comparative U.S. data for the years 2005 and 2010 in terms of the number and percentage of people who reported having some disability, having a severe disability, or needing assistance because of a disability. **FIGURE 3.3** shows the age breakdown of people with disabilities in the United States in 2014. As reported by Courtney-Long et al.,[3] the vast majority of individuals with a disability are middle aged (45–64 years) or older (≥65 years). **TABLE 3.1** also shows data on the prevalence of self-reported disabilities of different kinds, as reported in the national Behavioral Risk Factor Surveillance System survey in the United States in 2013 by demographic characteristics. Notably, women, older individuals, blacks, Hispanics, those with an annual income less than $15,000, those who are unemployed, those who are unable to work, and individuals with less than a high school education more frequently reported having one disability or another.

At a glance, the definition of *death* (and conversely, of *life*) can seem deceptively simple. However, as underscored by several high-profile lawsuits in the United States in preceding years, the determination of whether a person is dead or still alive is fraught with ethical, moral, legal, and even economic complexities. The prospect of indefinite continuation of life support for patients in a prolonged vegetative state pits family members, healthcare providers, social activists, faith groups, the justice system, and even policy makers and economists on opposing sides of a highly emotional and complex debate. Aside from ethical, moral, and religious arguments, the legal ramifications of certifying the time of death can also be complex.

Given the complex nature of this issue, it is tremendously important to have a precise scientific definition of death. Taber's Cyclopedic Medical

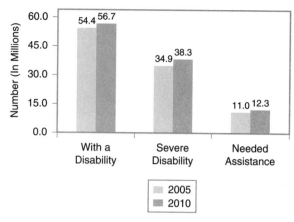

FIGURE 3.1 Number of people in the United States in 2005 and 2010 with a disability, in millions.

Reproduced from: Brault MW. Americans with disabilities: 2010. United States Census Bureau. Household Economic Studies. 2012;70–131. Available at: https://www.census.gov/newsroom/cspan/disability/20120726_cspan_disability_slides.pdf

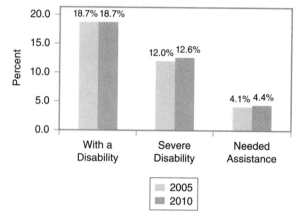

FIGURE 3.2 Percentage of people in the United States in 2005 and 2010 with a disability.

Reproduced from: Brault MW. Americans with disabilities: 2010. United States Census Bureau. Household Economic Studies. 2012;70–131. Available at: https://www.census.gov/newsroom/cspan/disability/20120726_cspan_disability_slides.pdf

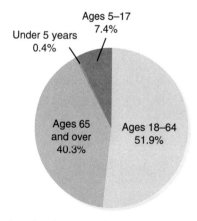

FIGURE 3.3 Age distribution in the U.S. population of civilians with disabilities, American Community Survey, 2014.

Reprinted with permission from: Kraus L. Disability statistics annual report. University of New Hampshire, Durham, NH. 2015.

Dictionary[4] offers a long definition that in part reads, "Permanent cessation of all vital functions including those of the heart, lungs, and brain."

TABLE 3.1 Prevalence of Any Disability and Disability Type† by Selected Demographic Characteristics Among Adults Aged ≥18 Years—Behavioral Risk Factor Surveillance System, United States, 2013

| Characteristic | Respondents§ (No.) | Type of Disability¶ | | | | | | | | | | | Any | |
| | | Vision | | Cognition | | Mobility | | Self-Care | | Independent Living | | | | |
		(%)	(95% CI)	(%)	(95% CI)	(%)	(95% CI)	(%)	(95% CI)	(%)	(95% CI)	(%)	(95% CI)
Sex													
Male	190,711	(4.2)	(4.0–4.4)	(9.3)	(9.1–9.6)	(11.3)	(11.0–11.5)	(3.5)	(3.3–3.7)**	(5.0)	(4.8–5.2)	(19.8)	(19.4–20.1)
Female	274,342	(5.0)	(4.9–5.2)	(11.9)	(11.6–12.2)	(14.6)	(14.3–14.9)	(3.7)	(3.5–3.8)	(7.9)	(7.7–8.1)	(24.4)	(24.1–24.8)
Age Group (yrs)††													
18–44	129,528	(2.9)	(2.7–3.1)	(10.1)	(9.8–10.4)	(5.5)	(5.2–5.7)	(1.9)	(1.8–2.0)	(4.4)	(4.2–4.6)	(15.7)	(15.3–16.0)
45–64	181,941	(6.5)	(6.2–6.7)	(12.0)	(11.7–12.3)	(18.2)	(17.8–18.5)	(5.6)	(5.4–5.8)	(8.4)	(8.1–8.7)	(26.2)	(25.8–26.6)
≥65	153,584	(6.6)	(6.3–6.9)	(9.9)	(9.5–10.2)	(27.4)	(27.0–27.9)	(5.3)	(5.1–5.5)	(9.8)	(9.5–10.1)	(35.5)	(35.0–36.0)
Race/Ethnicity													
White/Non-Hispanic	363,854	(3.6)	(3.5–3.7)	(10.1)	(9.9–10.3)	(12.0)	(11.8–12.2)	(3.1)	(3.0–3.2)	(6.1)	(5.9–6.2)	(20.6)	(20.3–20.9)
Black/Non-Hispanic	37,105	(7.4)	(6.9–7.9)	(13.3)	(12.7–14.0)	(18.7)	(18.0–19.4)	(5.7)	(5.3–6.1)	(9.2)	(8.7–9.7)	(29.0)	(28.1–29.9)
Hispanic	29,371	(7.4)	(6.8–8.0)	(12.1)	(11.5–12.8)	(14.6)	(13.8–15.3)	(4.7)	(4.2–5.1)	(7.3)	(6.8–7.9)	(25.9)	(25.0–26.8)
Other/Non-Hispanic	27,632	(5.5)	(4.8–6.3)	(10.2)	(9.4–11.1)	(11.8)	(10.9–12.7)	(3.4)	(3.0–3.9)	(6.4)	(5.7–7.1)	(21.1)	(20.0–22.3)
Veteran Status													
Veteran	58,713	(3.9)	(3.5–4.2)	(10.8)	(10.2–11.5)**	(13.4)	(12.8–14.0)**	(3.8)	(3.4–4.2)**	(5.9)	(5.4–6.4)	(22.1)	(21.3–22.9)
Non-veteran	406,010	(4.7)	(4.6–4.9)	(10.6)	(10.4–10.8)	(13.1)	(12.9–13.3)	(3.6)	(3.5–3.7)	(6.7)	(6.5–6.8)	(22.3)	(22.0–22.5)

	No.	(%)	(95% CI)	(%)	(95% CI)	(%)	(95% CI)	(%)	(95% CI)	(%)	(95% CI)	(%)	(95% CI)
Annual Household Income													
<$15,000	47,828	(12.4)	(11.8–13.0)	(26.1)	(25.3–27.0)	(29.2)	(28.5–30.0)	(10.1)	(9.6–10.6)	(18.1)	(17.4–18.8)	(46.9)	(46.0–47.9)
$15,000–<$25,000	72,390	(7.3)	(6.9–7.8)	(16.0)	(15.5–16.6)	(20.1)	(19.5–20.6)	(5.7)	(5.4–6.0)	(9.9)	(9.5–10.4)	(33.0)	(32.3–33.7)
$25,000–<$35,000	46,740	(4.6)	(4.2–5.1)	(10.2)	(9.6–10.8)	(14.1)	(13.5–14.7)	(3.6)	(3.2–4.0)	(6.1)	(5.6–6.5)	(23.6)	(22.8–24.4)
$35,000–<$50,000	59,235	(3.2)	(2.9–3.6)	(7.4)	(7.0–8.0)	(10.1)	(9.7–10.6)	(2.3)	(2.1–2.5)	(4.2)	(3.9–4.6)	(17.7)	(17.0–18.3)
$50,000+	176,210	(1.7)	(1.6–1.9)	(4.3)	(4.1–4.5)	(5.9)	(5.7–6.1)	(1.2)	(1.1–1.3)	(2.2)	(2.0–2.3)	(10.8)	(10.5–11.1)
Employment Status													
Employed	230,472	(2.5)	(2.3–2.6)	(5.6)	(5.4–5.8)	(6.0)	(5.8–6.2)	(1.0)	(0.9–1.1)	(1.7)	(1.6–1.9)	(12.6)	(12.3–12.9)
Unemployed	24,661	(7.2)	(6.5–8.0)	(18.2)	(17.2–19.2)	(17.2)	(16.3–18.2)	(4.8)	(4.2–5.4)	(9.6)	(8.8–10.5)	(33.5)	(32.3–34.7)
Retired/student/homemaker	172,385	(4.0)	(3.7–4.4)	(9.4)	(9.0–9.9)	(11.8)	(11.5–12.2)	(2.4)	(2.3–2.6)	(5.4)	(5.1–5.7)	(21.2)	(20.6–21.8)
Unable to work	35,690	(19.1)	(18.0–20.3)	(48.3)	(46.8–49.7)	(60.8)	(59.4–62.2)	(26.9)	(25.6–28.2)	(45.4)	(44.0–46.8)	(82.6)	(81.3–83.8)
Education Level[§§]													
<High school	36,615	(10.8)	(10.1–11.4)	(19.9)	(19.1–20.7)	(25.8)	(24.9–26.6)	(8.0)	(7.5–8.5)	(13.5)	(12.9–14.2)	(39.8)	(38.8–40.8)
High school	125,901	(5.4)	(5.1–5.7)	(12.1)	(11.7–12.5)	(16.3)	(15.9–16.7)	(4.4)	(4.2–4.7)	(7.9)	(7.6–8.2)	(26.0)	(25.5–26.5)
Some college	118,275	(4.0)	(3.8–4.3)	(10.2)	(9.9–10.6)	(14.0)	(13.6–14.4)	(3.8)	(3.6–4.0)	(6.7)	(6.5–7.0)	(22.9)	(22.4–23.3)
College graduate	157,878	(2.0)	(1.9–2.1)	(4.3)	(4.1–4.5)	(7.1)	(6.9–7.3)	(1.6)	(1.5–1.8)	(3.0)	(2.9–3.2)	(11.8)	(11.5–12.1)

Abbreviation: CI = confidence interval.

* Weighted estimates, age-adjusted to the 2000 U.S. standard population.

[†] Respondents were asked, "Are you blind or do you have serious difficulty seeing, even when wearing glasses?" (vision disability); "Because of a physical, mental, or emotional condition, do you have serious difficulty concentrating, remembering, or making decisions?" (cognition disability); "Do you have serious difficulty walking or climbing stairs?" (mobility disability); "Do you have difficulty dressing or bathing?" (self-care disability); and "Because of a physical, mental, or emotional condition, do you have difficulty doing errands alone such as visiting a doctor's office or shopping?" (independent living disability). Respondents who refused to answer, reported "don't know," and other missing responses were excluded from the analyses.

[§] Respondents with missing information on disability are not included; all groups might not add to the same total number or the overall number in Table 1.

[¶] Each disability type might not be independent; one respondent might have two or more disability types.

** Groups not significantly different with p-value ≥0.05 determined by two-sided chi-square test. All other group comparisons were statistically significantly different with p-values <0.05.

[††] Estimates not age-adjusted.

[§§] Limited to respondents aged ≥25 years.

Reproduced from: Courtney-Long EA, Carroll DD, Zhang QC, Stevens AC, Griffin-Blake S, Armour BS, Campbell VA. Prevalence of disability and disability type among adults – United States, 2013. Morbidity and Mortality Weekly Report. 2013; 64(29):777–783. Available at: http://www.cdc.gov/mmwr/pdf/wk/mm6429.pdf

It defines *biological death* as "Irreversible cessation of detectable cardiorespiratory and neural functioning." A number of other definitions from a variety of sources are also available. These definitions focus on, among other detectable signs, permanent cessation of all vital functions, including brainstem and spinal reflexes, and recordable electrical activity in the cerebral cortex and cardiac muscles. The 1981 report titled "Defining Death: Medical, Legal and Ethical Issues in the Determination of Death," prepared by the President's Commission for the Study of Ethical Problems in Medicine and Biomedical and Behavioral Research,[5] provides a comprehensive review of complex issues involved in defining and establishing death. Prior to the Commission's report, in 1980, the National Conference of Commissioners on Uniform State Laws[6] wrote and recommended for enactment in all states the Uniform Determination of Death Act. The Act was endorsed by the American Medical Association in 1980 and by the American Bar Association in 1981. Currently, the Act is followed by all 50 states and the District of Columbia. The Act includes language related to "irreversible cessation of all functioning of the brain, including the brain stem," as well as "irreversible cessation of circulatory and respiratory functions." However, the Act does not propose an exclusive or end-all definition, but rather concentrates on determination of death by qualified medical personnel on the bases of prevalent and acceptable medical standards. Finally, despite the currently available definitions and guidelines that attempt to provide a conclusive or uniform way of defining death, the fact is, there is still much confusion, debate, and disagreement on this matter.[7] One aspect of the ongoing discussion and debate relates to the question of reversibility of the cessation of brain, respiratory, and cardiovascular function—that is, how and at what point in time it can be stated unequivocally that the loss of function is irreversible. This is especially the case when one of the systems such as the central nervous system (that is, the cerebral cortex) shows loss of function, but another system, such as the cardiovascular system, continues to function—whether with the help of life support or spontaneously. The prevailing practice guidelines from the American Academy of Neurology for the determination of death in adult patients rely on a complete neurologic clinical examination rather than tests such as a CAT scan or an MRI, and they focus on loss of cerebral function and brainstem reflexes combined with loss of spontaneous respiratory function to declare that the individual is dead. These guidelines, however, do not apply to children because of the "plastic" nature of a child's brain.

▶ 3.3 Assessment of Personal Health

Assessment of the health status of a person begins in fetal stages during the prospective mother's antenatal visits. The antenatal care process monitors the health of the prospective mother and her unborn child to avoid the possibility of future adverse events for both. The prospective mother's health is monitored through periodic measurement of weight, blood pressure, heart rate, and urine and blood analysis to detect early warning signs of poor nutrition, anemia, hypertension, diabetes, and preeclampsia that can threaten the life of both mother and child. Antenatal care also monitors the development of the fetus through tests such as Doppler heart rate monitoring, ultrasound, and analysis of amniotic fluid. These tests can give valuable early information regarding genetic and developmental problems, including Down syndrome, spina bifida, cleft palate, and clubfoot.

The health of the newborn is assessed by healthcare professionals immediately after birth. Subsequently, periodic assessments of health status can continue throughout the life course of a person depending on one's socioeconomic circumstances and access to health services. With adequate access to services, periodic professional assessment of health can occur during childhood through annual or semiannual "well-child" visits to a doctor's office and during adult life through routine annual physicals. In both childhood and adult life, health status assessment also occurs through unplanned visits to a healthcare establishment prompted by an adverse event and parental or personal concerns.

The debate about the utility and cost of routine "head-to-toe" annual physical examinations has continued for the last three decades or more. The weight of empirical evidence puts into question the value of this exercise. Professional bodies such as the American Medical Association no longer endorse this practice. Routine physical examinations, however, are not to be confused with periodic screenings, such as Pap smears every 3 years for cervical cancer screening in women between 21 and 65 years of age, and colonoscopy every 10 years after age 50 for colon cancer screening in both men and women. Despite some controversy regarding the timing and frequency of periodic mammograms for breast cancer screening, the U.S. Preventive Services Task Force recommends that women between the ages of 50 and 74 get a mammogram every 2 years. In a different chapter, we have discussed in detail the epidemiologic parameters to assess the suitability of a screening test.

▶ 3.4 Assessment of Physiologic Health

Objective assessment of health status is typically carried out by a healthcare provider and involves an assessment of physiologic functions commonly referred to as "vital signs," including heart rate, respiration rate, body temperature, and blood pressure. Depending on the circumstance necessitating a professional assessment of a person's health status, more sophisticated measures may be required, such as a detailed physical or psychiatric evaluation and a battery of laboratory and clinical tests. It is important to note that a "clean bill of health" given by a healthcare provider does not necessarily translate into absence of any pathology; it only means that a routine checkup, such as annual physical examination, did not reveal an abnormality or, in the event that a test was performed to look into a specific concern on the part of the provider or the patient, the test results were normal. As alluded to previously, many policy makers and healthcare providers consider routine annual physical examinations to be of little value given that slow-growing, insidious disorders can exist for a long time before causing noticeable clinical signs and symptoms.

An objective appraisal of the health status of a person at any age, among other measures, also involves measurement of body weight. Aside from its psychosocial impact, excess body weight has serious pathophysiologic consequences. Overweight and obesity have steadily increased all over the world in the last several decades. Currently, more than half of women in Libya, Qatar, Samoa, Tonga, Kiribati, and the Federated States of Micronesia are obese.[8] In 2005, globally, 23.2% of the population was overweight, and 9.8% was obese.[9] In the United States in 2011–2012, 16.9% of 2- to 19-year-olds and 34.9% of those older than age 20 were obese. Overall, more than two-thirds of adults in the United States were overweight or obese.[10] In the last 30 years, the greatest increase in obesity among women occurred in Egypt, Saudi Arabia, Oman, Honduras, and Bahrain, and among men in New Zealand, Bahrain, Kuwait, Saudi Arabia, and the United States.[8]

Despite the debate whether obesity, whether measured in terms of body mass index (BMI) or as percentage of body fat above a cutoff level, can itself be characterized as a disease, its antecedent role and association with diseases such as diabetes, hypertension, coronary heart disease, stroke, and various cancers is beyond dispute.[11] BMI (weight of a person measured in kilograms divided by the square of height measured in meters, i.e., kg/m^2) is not only used as a scientific and objective measure of overweight and obesity but also frequently regarded as a good predictor of health status. In interpreting BMI values, it is important to consider the age of the subject. A high BMI in a young person is more indicative of obesity than it is in an older individual with the same BMI. In adults, a BMI >30 kg/m^2 is interpreted as obesity, and a BMI >25 kg/m^2 indicates overweight.

▶ 3.5 Assessment of Mental Health and Psychosocial Development

The informal assessment of mental or intellectual development of a child happens at an early age at home and/or in a childcare setting by parents and others who notice delays in achieving developmental milestones, such as responses to audiovisual stimuli and speech development. Confirmation or exclusion of possible developmental problems then happens in clinical settings through age-appropriate tests. During adolescence and adult life, informal and formal assessment of psychosocial health is called for by specific situations, such as aberrant behavior and delinquency. Adolescent behavioral and psychosocial problems are often noticed in school settings, leading to a referral for professional evaluation and therapy. Evaluation for adult-life psychosocial problems is usually initiated by the individual or close family members who may notice odd or aberrant behavior. In many instances, the person in question is not aware or conscious of the problem and is often resistant to the suggestion that he or she may have a problem. Because aberrant behavior can frequently be attributed to individual idiosyncrasies, psychiatric health problems often go unrecognized until the issue becomes serious and too obvious to be ignored.

Self-recognition and help seeking for psychosocial problems in adult life often result from personal tragedies, such as the loss of a loved one, divorce, financial crisis, posttraumatic stress, or postpartum blues. Evaluation of physical and mental health is required in certain professions. For example, commercial airline pilots have to go through an evaluation at the time of recruitment and periodically thereafter. The deliberate crash of a Germanwings airplane by the copilot in the French Alps on March 24, 2015, put a spotlight on the tragic consequences of unresolved psychiatric problems. In the United States in recent years, a number of shootings of civilians in public places have continued to fuel the debate on ways to limit the access to firearms of mentally unstable individuals.

▶ 3.6 Assessment of Functioning and Disability

The assessment of a person's ability to function in a manner sufficient to take care of his or her daily needs adequately, as well as the ability to live independently, is important to determine the nature and extent of assistance required from family members and caregivers of the elderly and those with disabilities. Such an assessment is also a part of the process to determine eligibility for social services from various local, state, and federal agencies, and eligibility for nursing home care, whether financed by the state Medicaid program or through long-term care insurance. A number of instruments and scales are available to make these determinations. Two commonly used instruments are the Katz Activities of Daily Living (ADL) scale and the Lawton Instrumental Activities of Daily Living (IADL) scale. An assessment of the ability to take care of oneself in terms of ADLs through an instrument such as Katz scale usually involves assessment of the following five categories of tasks: (1) personal hygiene, including bathing, grooming, and oral hygiene; (2) feeding, but not necessarily the ability to prepare food; (3) dressing, including the ability to choose and put on clothes; (4) toileting, including the ability to maintain continence and the physical and mental ability to use the toilet properly; and (5) transferring from the bed and the ability to get up and move around. The ability to live independently at home or in a communal setting requires greater mental and physical abilities than are needed to carry out ADLs. The Lawton scale for instrumental activities of daily living (IADLs) assesses this ability by exploring the following eight dimensions of functionality: (1) communication by using the telephone and other devices; (2) shopping, including the ability to make appropriate decisions and choices; (3) food preparation, including meal planning and safe use of kitchen equipment; (4) housekeeping, including the ability to maintain safe and hygienic living conditions; (5) laundry; (6) transportation, including driving, taking a taxi, or using public transportation; (7) managing medication, including the ability to take the right medicine in the right dose at the right time and making refill requests; and (8) managing finances in terms of paying bills, writing checks, and budgeting resources. Periodic use of Lawton or Katz scales allows caregivers and healthcare professionals to monitor and detect potential deterioration in the condition of their loved ones and patients and make appropriate decisions.

The International Classification of Functioning, Disability and Health (ICF), developed by the World Health Organization (WHO), is a framework for measuring and describing health and dysfunction. ICF goes beyond purely medical assessment of physical health and takes into consideration the impact of environment and other factors. ICF recognizes that "disability is a universal human experience" that can happen at any stage of life, with varying degrees of severity, and can be temporary or permanent in nature.[12] Endorsed by 191 member countries of the WHO at the 54th World Health Assembly in May 2001, ICF is now implemented in clinical settings in a number of countries to assess the functional status of individuals, set treatment goals, and measure outcomes of treatment.

Because diagnosis alone is not a good predictor of a person's return to work, work performance, and social integration, ICF, especially when used as a complement to International Statistical Classification of Diseases and Related Health Problems (ICD), discussed later in this chapter, is a very important tool for planning and management. ICF enables administrators, organizations, and communities to collect data on functional status and disability in a consistent and comparable manner to measure the overall health status of a population in order to assess future healthcare needs and past performance or effectiveness of the healthcare system. A marked increase in disability benefit claims in many countries in recent years also calls for collecting reliable and valid community-level data on disability and functional status.

ICF views disability as an outcome of the interaction between disease or injury and "contextual factors," which include both environmental (physical and social environment) and personal (gender, age, education, profession, and so on) factors. It identifies the following three ways in which functionality may be affected: *impairments, activity limitations,* and *participation restrictions.* Each form of dysfunctionality is further measured on a multiple-point scale. For example, the 5-point scale for measuring impairment is as follows: (1) none, (2) mild, (3) moderate, (4) severe, and (5) complete. As illustrated in **TABLE 3.2**, one, two, or all three forms of functionality (impairments, activity limitations, and participation restrictions) can be simultaneously affected by a disease or injury in a person. Because a given form of disability can result from a variety of causes, ICF does not focus on the etiology of the disability, but rather concentrates on assessing the level of disability and measuring functional status in a standardized manner. This approach puts all diseases "on an equal footing" and allows them to be compared on the bases of resulting limitations on functionality.[13]

TABLE 3.2 Examples of How the Three Forms of Functionality Can Be Affected by a Given Condition

Disease	Impairment	Activity Limitation	Participation Restriction
Leprosy	Loss of sensation in extremities	Difficulty grasping objects	Stigma of leprosy leads to unemployment
Spinal injury	Paralysis	Inability to use public transportation	Lack of mobility prevents participation in athletics
Vitiligo	Facial disfigurement	None	Stigma and fear of "contagion" leads to social isolation

Reprinted from: Toward a common language for functioning, disability and health. Geneva, Switzerland. Copyright © World Health Organization (WHO). 2002.

TABLE 3.3 Dimensions of Functionality That Can Be Affected by a Disease or Condition

Level of Hierarchy	Example	Code
First Level/Chapter	Chapter 2, *Sensory Functions and Pain*	b2
Second level	Seeing function	b210
Third level	Quality of vision	b2102
Fourth level	Color vision	b21021

Reprinted from: Toward a common language for functioning, disability and health. Geneva, Switzerland. Copyright © World Health Organization (WHO). 2002.

To allow consistent and valid data collection across all settings on functional status and disability, the WHO has also developed a questionnaire called the Disability Assessment Schedule. To meet the different needs of those collecting information in terms of detail and specificity of domain, the questionnaire has long and short versions. The questionnaire can be used across all diseases in both clinical and general population settings. Rather than focusing on the disease, it focuses on six domains of functionality: cognition, mobility, self-care, getting along, life activities, and participation. The long (36-item) version of the questionnaire allows computation of an overall functionality score as well as domain-specific scores, whereas the short (12-item) version allows only calculation of an overall functionality score. Both versions of the questionnaire can be self-administered or may be administered by an interviewer. The coding scheme for each domain has a hierarchy of four levels as shown in **TABLE 3.3**. ICF has a number of chapters such as *Mental Functions* (chapter 1), *Sensory Functions and Pain* (chapter 2), and *Voice and Speech Functions* (chapter 3).

In the coding scheme, each chapter constitutes the first of the four levels of coding (see Table 3.3). Information generated by the use of ICF is not only useful for research, management, and policy making, but also valuable for insurance companies, labor departments, economists, and legislation. Detailed information on how ICF can be used by various entities is available in the ICF manual developed by the WHO.[13]

▶ 3.7 Self-Assessment of Health and Well-Being

Measurement of health is considered *subjective* when the assessment is done by the patient himself or herself in response to written or verbal questions. A number of approaches are adopted in designing questions and compiling self-reported information on personal health status. For example, in *scaling* methods, descriptive responses to a battery of questions are converted into numeric estimates of severity.

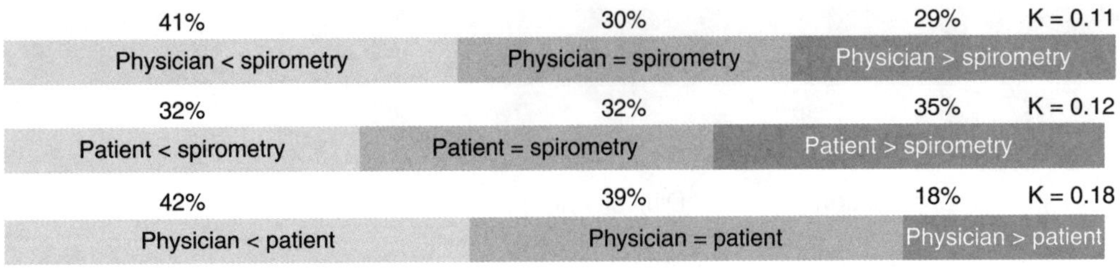

41%	30%	29%	K = 0.11
Physician < spirometry	Physician = spirometry	Physician > spirometry	

32%	32%	35%	K = 0.12
Patient < spirometry	Patient = spirometry	Patient > spirometry	

42%	39%	18%	K = 0.18
Physician < patient	Physician = patient	Physician > patient	

FIGURE 3.4 COPD severity estimate by physicians (pretest) versus spirometry. Patients* versus spirometry and physicians (pretest) versus patients.

*Total of 668 patients with spirometry results that could be rated for severity.

Reproduced from: Mapel DW, Dalal AA, Johnson P, Becker L, Hunter AG. A clinical study of COPD severity assessment by primary care physicians and their patients compared with spirometry. Am J Med. 2015;128(6):629–663. Copyright © 2015, with permission from Elsevier.

These numeric estimates are then pooled to obtain an aggregated score called the **health index**.[14] Typically, subjective or self-reported measurement of health focuses on determining the functional status of the individual. However, it is also common to ask subjects to rate their overall health as *excellent, good, fair,* or *poor*. Empirical evidence has shown a strong correlation between a person's self-reported health status and the assessment done by a healthcare provider using some objective criteria such as laboratory tests and a physical examination.[15-17] The assessment of functional status can be "global" in nature if it looks into all three aspects of health—physical, mental, and social functioning—or it can be an assessment of improvement in functional status after treatment for a specific disease. In the latter case, change in functional status is viewed to be the outcome of care and is taken as a measure of the success or failure of treatment.[14]

A number of instruments are available to assess self-reported or perceived health status. A good example of a tool for subjective or self-reported global (physical, mental, and social) assessment of health status is the Nottingham Health Profile (developed at Nottingham University in 1978)—a two-part questionnaire with 38 items in the first part and 7 in the second part. The Profile is used to assess patients' view of their own health in a number of areas.

Another important tool is the Short Form 36 (SF-36), a 36-item questionnaire developed by the RAND Corporation in 1988 for the health survey component of the well-known Medical Outcomes Study. SF-36 measures self-reported quality of life across the following eight domains: physical functioning, role limitations due to physical problems, bodily pain, general health perceptions, vitality, social functioning, role limitations due to emotional problems, and mental health. The questionnaire has been used in thousands of studies over the years and now has a commercial version, as well as the original version available free of charge in the public domain. Empirically validated shorter versions of the questionnaire as SF-12 and SF-8 are also available. Last, a commonly used instrument for healthcare outcomes assessment and program evaluation based on self-reported health status is the 68-item Sickness Impact Profile, which measures health status across six domains: somatic autonomy, mobility control, mobility range, social behavior, emotional stability, and psychological autonomy/communication.

FIGURE 3.4 provides an example of the degree of agreement or disagreement between physicians' clinical assessment and patients' personal assessment of the severity of a disease and their correlations with the findings of a confirmatory scientific test. Specifically, one of the objectives of this study was to assess how closely physicians' clinical assessment of their patients' chronic obstructive pulmonary disease (COPD) severity correlated with the airflow obstruction measured by a spirometry test. The researchers also examined how closely patients' own assessment of the severity of their condition matched the results of spirometry test. As shown in Figure 3.4, physicians' clinical assessment of the severity of disease agreed with the results of spirometry test in only 30% of the 668 cases. They underestimated the severity of disease in 41% of cases and overestimated it in 29% of cases. Likewise, 32% of patients underestimated the severity of their COPD, and 35% overestimated it. The concordance between physicians' and patients' assessment was also rather poor (39%). In 42% of cases, physicians' assessment was lower than that of patients, and in 18%, it was higher.

▶ 3.8 Assessment of Community Health

Under section 9007 of the Affordable Care Act of 2010, to maintain their tax-exempt status, nonprofit hospitals are required to conduct a community health needs assessment every 3 years and adopt strategies to meet those needs.[18] A community health assessment and improvement plan is also a prerequisite for voluntary public health accreditation standards that were implemented in 2011 by the Public Health Accreditation Board.[19] Assessment of community health status through systematic collection and analysis of data is a core public health function. Public health agencies have long carried out this function in conjunction with disease-monitoring and surveillance activities. Typically, community health assessment includes collection of information on behavioral socioeconomic and environmental determinants of health.

Hardcastle[20] has suggested that integration of public health and healthcare delivery systems is the best approach to deal with chronic diseases that have become the predominant cause of morbidity and mortality in the 21st century. Having a common set of metrics for community health assessment makes it easier to conduct comparisons across communities for research, policy formulation, and health services planning.[18] Currently, a unified definition of community health assessment (CHA) does not exist. The CDC uses the terms *community health assessment* and *community health needs assessment* (CHNA) interchangeably.[18] Historically, CHA activities by nonprofit community hospitals and other stakeholders have included various components of the broader concept of community health improvement, which encompasses both health outcomes indicators (for example, mortality and morbidity statistics) and identification of resources needed to address health-related problems and priorities.

Based on an extensive review of the literature, the CDC has proposed a common set of 42 metrics to assess the health status of a community.[18] **TABLE 3.4** shows the top 31 of the 42 metrics suggested by the CDC. Eleven of the 31 selected indicators constitute morbidity and mortality outcomes, whereas the remaining 20 represent demographic, behavioral, environmental, and healthcare-related determinants of health.

TABLE 3.4 Commonly Used Metrics for Community Health Assessment

Health Outcomes		Determinants of Health			
Mortality	Morbidity	Demographics and Social Environment	Health Behaviors	Physical Environment	Access and Quality of Health Care
Overall mortality and leading causes of death	Obesity	Age	Smoking	Housing	Health insurance coverage
Infant mortality	Cancer rates	Sex	Physical activity	Safe drinking water	Provider rates
Suicide	Hospital admission rates	Race/ethnicity	Immunizations and screenings	Air quality	Asthma-related hospitalizations
Homicide	Overall health status scores	Income	Alcohol use		
Motor vehicle and other injury-related mortality	Motor vehicle injury	Poverty level	Nutrition		
	STDs	Educational attainment	Unsafe sex		
		Employment status	Seat belt use		

Modified from: Centers for Disease Control and Prevention (CDC). Community health assessment for population health improvement: resource of most frequently recommended health outcomes and determinants. Atlanta, GA: Centers for Disease Control and Prevention; 2013.

Parrish[21] has suggested that "an ideal population health outcome metric should reflect a population's dynamic state of physical, mental, and social well-being." According to this approach, positive health outcomes at the individual level would include being alive, functioning well, and having a sense of total well-being. The negative outcomes would be the opposite of these three states. At the population level, health outcomes can be measured by aggregating the individual-level health outcomes and converting them into summary statistics, such as overall mortality rate or life expectancy, and measuring the functional status and well-being of the population. Assessment of population health and functional status can also be carried out through population surveys of self-reported health, such as the National Health Interview Survey or the Behavioral Risk Factor Surveillance System, and the National Health and Nutrition Examination Survey in the United States.[21]

▶ 3.9 Assessment of Burden of Disease and Summary Measures of Population Health

The term **burden of disease** relates to the estimation of the overall impact of a specific disease or a group of diseases in a population. It can be measured in terms of morbidity (the number of existing or new cases of a disease) or mortality, or used as a measure of economic loss, such as **years of potential life lost (YPLL)** or health-adjusted life years (HALYs) lost. The impact of premature deaths of individuals and/or their inability to function as fully active members of society can be estimated globally or at the level of a country, region, or province. When simply measured in terms of the number of deaths in a given period of time (crude mortality rate), the burden of disease can be estimated as either all-cause mortality or deaths resulting from a specific disease, such as HIV/AIDS.

One measure of the burden of diseases, YPLL, involves estimation of aggregated years of life lost in a population due to premature deaths. *Premature* in this instance is defined by average life expectancy in the population—that is, the number of years a person would have lived had he or she not died prematurely. The purpose of estimating YPLL is to estimate economic loss to a community or a region due to premature deaths caused by a particular disease. For example, average life expectancy

at birth for men in the United States is currently around 78 years, so the death of a young man at age 30 would result in 48 YPLL. A study of deaths from urological cancers in the United States[22] estimated that in 2004, urological cancers accounted for more than 244,000 YPLL. Each death from testicular cancer that typically affects younger men resulted in 37.9 YPLL. Considering that the average annual salary of American men aged 25–34 years in 2016 was approximately $40,000, a death from testicular cancer translates into more than $1.5 million (in 2016 currency) in lost productivity. The study[22] estimated that in 2004, the overall lifetime productivity loss due to urogenital cancer mortality in the United States was $10.4 billion.

Specific methods of calculating YPLL vary from author to author.[23] As an example, in the United States, the National Center for Injury Prevention and Control at the CDC estimated a total of 11,034,030 YPLL in 2013 due to deaths from all causes occurring before age 65 years, and 2,134,721 (19.3%) of these years were lost due to deaths from unintentional injuries. Likewise, 1,782,412 (16.2%) years of potential life were lost to deaths before age 65 years from all malignant neoplasms.[24]

Another method to assess the burden of disease in a population is to estimate the combined effects of both premature deaths (YPLL) as well as the disability resulting from a disease (or a group of diseases) during the time lived before death. Several such measures with varying uses and methodologies have been developed over the years to measure the combined impact of death and disability in a population. Health-adjusted life years (HALYs) is an umbrella term used for two such measures: **quality-adjusted life years (QALYs)** and **disability-adjusted life years (DALYs)**.[25] Both of these measures are useful for assessing the overall burden of disease in a population and for comparing the impact of two or more diseases in the same population. Both QALYs and DALYs incorporate into one measure the YPLL due to premature death as well as the years of healthy life lost due to the time lived before death in a state of less than full health (i.e., a state of disability). In both DALYs and QALYs, the level of disability or health-related quality of life (HRQOL) associated with a specific disease or condition is subjectively assessed on a scale from 0 to 1 and is multiplied with life expectancy in the population to get the overall measure of the burden of disease.[25] However, despite the conceptual similarities, there are important differences in the computational methods employed and the use of these two measures of the burden of disease. Because of these similarities and differences, more information is provided on QALYs and DALYs in the following sections.

3.9.1 Disability-Adjusted Life Years

As noted, the estimation of DALYs combines the impact of premature deaths as well as the "time lived in states of less than full health"—that is, the time before death in which the individual could not function as a fully productive member of society because of a physical or mental disorder.[25] The methods for assessing the value or worth of a year of life lived with a given level of disability by assigning weights to different levels of disability are complex and, in the past, varied from one study to another. In all such studies, however, a year of life lived with some level of disability was counted less than a year of life lived in good health.

The most known and currently used methodology for calculating DALYs was developed under the auspices of the World Bank and the WHO for the Global Burden of Disease (GBD) program, first launched in 1991 to assess the burden of diseases throughout the world. In this methodology, the value of time lived at different ages was computed such that it reflected the dependence of children and the elderly on working-age adults. Also, the time lived with a disability was "made comparable with the time lost due to premature mortality by defining six classes of disability severity" and by assigning a severity weight between 0 and 1 to each class of disability.[26] The most recent assessment

of GBD was based on data gathered from 187 countries for the years 1990 through 2010 on 291 different causes of disease and injury. In this study, the years of life lost due to premature deaths were calculated by multiplying the total number of deaths with the total number of remaining years based on life expectancy at the time of death in a reference population in which life expectancy at birth was 86.0 years. Based on the formula used to estimate years of life lost due to premature death, a death at age 25 years represented 61.4 years of life lost. The GBD 2010 study reported that 2.482 billion DALYs were lost worldwide due to premature deaths in 2010.[27]

DALYs also help in estimating the health effects of common risk factors such as low birth weight, unsafe sex, and tobacco use. For example, Ezzati et al.[28] have reported that globally, in 2000, 138 million DALYs were lost because of childhood and maternal underweight, 92 million DALYs because of unsafe sex, 64 million DALYs because of high blood pressure, and 59 million DALYs because of the use of tobacco. In a related study, Lopez et al.[29] calculated mortality, incidence, prevalence, and DALYs for 136 diseases and estimated that 56 million people had died in 2001 worldwide, of whom 10.6 million were children. More than half of the deaths in children resulted from acute respiratory infections, measles, diarrhea, malaria, and HIV/AIDS. **TABLE 3.5** from the study shows the comparative burden of disease in terms of DALYs in low- and middle-income countries (LMICs) and in high-income countries in 2001. As shown, ischemic

TABLE 3.5 Ten Leading Causes of Burden of Disease (DALYs) by Income Group, 2001

	Low- and Middle-Income Countries			High-Income Countries		
	Cause	DALYs*	% of Total DALYs	Cause	DALYs*	% of Total DALYs
1	Perinatal conditions	89.1	6.4%	Ischemic heart disease	12.4	8.3%
2	Lower respiratory infections	83.6	6.0%	Cerebrovascular disease	9.4	6.3%
3	Ischemic heart disease	71.9	5.2%	Unipolar depressive disorders	8.4	5.6%
4	HIV/AIDS	70.8	5.1%	Alzheimer's disease and other dementias	7.5	5.0%
5	Cerebrovascular disease	62.7	4.5%	Trachea, bronchus, lung cancer	5.4	3.6%

(continues)

TABLE 3.5 Ten Leading Causes of Burden of Disease (DALYs) by Income Group, 2001 *(continued)*

	Low- and Middle-Income Countries			High-Income Countries		
	Cause	DALYs*	% of Total DALYs	Cause	DALYs*	% of Total DALYs
6	Diarrheal diseases	58.7	4.2%	Hearing loss adult onset	5.4	3.6%
7	Unipolar depressive disorders	43.4	3.1%	Chronic obstructive pulmonary disease	5.3	3.5%
8	Malaria	40.0	2.9%	Diabetes mellitus	4.2	2.8%
9	Tuberculosis	35.9	2.6%	Alcohol use disorders	4.2	2.8%
10	Chronic obstructive pulmonary disease	33.5	2.4%	Osteoarthritis	3.8	2.5%

*Millions of years.

Reprinted from: Lopez D, Mathers CD, Ezatti M, Jamison DT, Murray CJL. Global and regional burden of disease and risk factors, 2001: systematic analysis of population health data. Lancet. 2006; 367:1747–1757. Copyright © 2006, with permission from Elsevier.

heart disease, with 12.4 million DALYs in high-income countries, and perinatal conditions, with 89.1 million DALYs in LMICs, were the leading causes of burden of disease.

3.9.2 Quality-Adjusted Life Years

QALYs, a measure of health improvement resulting from a healthcare intervention, were developed in the 1960s primarily to be used as the denominator in cost-effectiveness analysis (CEA), where they represent the unit of effect or health outcome resulting from a specific health-related intervention. The purpose of CEA is to derive the cost at which a standardized health outcome, such as QALYs, is achieved by one or another health-related intervention, such as a new medical technology.[25,30] Thus, QALY estimates are used in assessing the comparative merits of medical technologies and public health interventions and are linked with the idea that societal resources should be distributed to achieve the greatest good for the greatest number of people.[25]

QALYs are estimated by assigning weights to different HRQOL states that are not unique to a particular disease or condition. Instead, the weights assigned to different health states are based on values attached to different states of health either by patients who are or have been in those states, or by others who can make a judgment on behalf of those in such states of health. By convention, an interval scale of 0 to 1.0 is used for assigning quality to 1 year of life with a given health outcome. For example, the outcome of a health interven-

tion that results in perfect health would receive a score of 1.0. Conversely, a score of zero is assigned if the outcome of an intervention is death. Notably, on an interval scale, a change in health state or improvement in the quality of life from 0.2 to 0.4 numerically represents the same amount of improvement as a change in the quality of life from 0.5 to 0.7. In other words, a gain in quality of life from 0.2 to 0.4 is just as valuable[30] as a gain from 0.6 to 0.8. Because of the subjective method of assessing the value of a given health state or a health outcome, weights assigned to various health states can vary tremendously from one source to another—thus creating unwarranted variations in the calculation of QALYs.

▶ 3.10 Classification of Diseases and Procedures

3.10.1 International Classification of Diseases

The International Statistical Classification of Diseases and Related Problems, commonly known as the **International Classification of Diseases (ICD)**, is a standardized system of assigning diagnostic codes to diseases, injuries, abnormalities, and various signs and symptoms for the purpose of classification, reimbursement, and statistical analysis. Developed by the WHO in collaboration with 10 international centers and revised periodically, the ICD is intended to facilitate and promote comparison of morbidity and mortality data within and across countries to understand the shifting patterns of diseases and causes of death.

The history of attempts to develop a system of classifying diseases and causes of death can be traced back to John Graunt's (1620–1674 CE) "Bills of Mortality" and William Farr's (1807–1883) annual reports at the General Register Office in England. However, the most significant event in the development of a system of classifying diseases and causes of death was the commissioning of a list of causes of death by the International Statistical Institute in 1891 to a committee chaired by Jacques Bertillon (1851–1922), who was then the chief of Statistical Services of the City of Paris. The report of the committee with the proposed list of causes of death that later came to be known as Bertillon Classification of Causes of Death was submitted by Bertillon and adopted by the International Statistical Institute at its meeting in Chicago in 1893.[31]

Efforts to classify causes of death continued to evolve in the 20th century in Europe and North America. At its meeting in 1899, the International Statistical Institute recognized the need to revise the International List of Causes of Death every 10 years. About the same time, the need to classify causes of morbidity was also recognized. This recognition led to the task of revising the list of causes of death and developing a list of causes of morbidity being given to the Interim Commission of the World Health Organization at the International Health Conference held in New York in 1946. Since then, the WHO has taken the responsibility for revising and updating a uniform list of diseases and causes of death with a standardized system of coding.[31] A number of countries, including the United States, Australia, Germany, and France, make their own modifications to the WHO version of ICD and use it for a variety of purposes, including indexing of medical records, reimbursement to providers for services rendered, and development of automated decision support systems. Along the way, the WHO has also developed several other systems of classification that are included in the WHO Family of International Classifications.

Between 1893 and 1978, the classification of causes of death and diseases was revised and updated eight times. The ninth revision of the International Classification of Diseases (ICD-9) was adopted in 1979 by a number of countries. In the United States, the Department of Health and Human Services adopted its own modified version titled ICD-9-CM (Clinical Modification). The 10th revision (ICD-10), on which WHO had started work in 1983, was implemented by the WHO in 1994. Since then, it has been translated into 43 languages and is currently being used in its original, modified, or translated form by 117 different countries. As opposed to the numeric codes used in ICD-9, alpha-

numeric codes are used in ICD-10. The 11th revision of the ICD is scheduled by the WHO to be released in 2018 for implementation in or after 2018.[31-33]

In the United States, the National Center for Health Statistics (NCHS) is one of the 10 WHO collaborating centers and the federal agency responsible for implementing the use of ICD-10. As was done with ICD-9, the NCHS prepared a clinical modification of the classification of morbidities ICD-10-CM for implementation in the United States. ICD-10 has been used in the United States since 1999 for coding and classifying mortality data from death certificates. The clinical modification (CM) version of ICD-10 is used for coding, classifying, and compiling morbidity data from medical records in all inpatient and outpatient settings as well as for maintenance of electronic health records. The transition from ICD 9-CM to ICD-10-CM for all entities covered by Health Insurance Portability and Accountability Act (HIPAA) occurred on October 1, 2015. Another modification of ICD developed in the United States under the auspices of the Centers for Medicare and Medicaid Services (CMS) is the Procedure Coding System (PCS) that is used to code procedures done in inpatient settings. Developed over a period of 5 years, ICD-10-PCS, a multiaxial seven-character alphanumeric code, replaced Volume 3 (procedures) of ICD-9-CM and was implemented by the CMS on October 1, 2015, for coding and billing of inpatient procedures. ICD-10-PCS is used in conjunction with **Current Procedural Terminology (CPT)** that is used to code and bill for procedures carried out in outpatient or ambulatory care settings. In ICD-10, the diagnosis codes are much more detailed than ICD-9, and it requires more information. For example, in the case of an infection of the middle ear (otitis media), ICD-10 has different codes for left and right ear, and it distinguishes recurrent infection from a new infection. In contrast, ICD-9 did not require specification of right or left side of body for otitis media or for any other diagnosis.[32] As shown in **FIGURE 3.5**, an ICD-10 code always begins with a letter followed by a number. All categories have three characters before a decimal point, and characters 3–7 can be any combination of letters or numbers. For greater specification, subcategories can follow the decimal point with 4 or 5 characters. Hence, an ICD-10 code must always have 3 characters before the decimal point and altogether may have 3–7 characters. A category that does not need further specification will have altogether only three characters in the code.[32] Resources and tools to fully understand and appropriately use ICD-10 are available from the CMS at https://www.cms.gov/Medicare/Coding/ICD10/Downloads/ICD-10Overview.pdf.

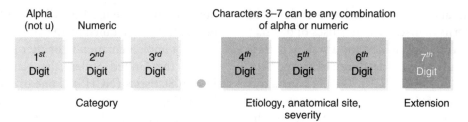

FIGURE 3.5 Format of an ICD-10 code.

3.10.2 Current Procedural Terminology (CPT) Codes

Developed, maintained, and regularly updated by the American Medical Association and first published in 1966, CPT is a system of 5-digit numeric codes that accurately, uniformly, and consistently describe services rendered by a healthcare provider in outpatient or ambulatory care settings. These codes are used nationwide by hospitals, physicians, and other healthcare providers to bill insurance companies and other payers, including the CMS, for all medical, surgical, anesthesiology, laboratory, radiology, and evaluation and management services provided on an outpatient basis. Updated by the CPT editorial panel, new editions of CPT are released every year.

Currently, the 5-digit numeric CPT codes range from 00100 to 99499. Two-digit modifiers, such as 23, 55, or 77, can be attached after the main code listed for a procedure (for example, 83408-23). There are specific guidelines in the published codebooks regarding the use of a given two-digit modifier. CPT codes are published in two different versions: (1) CPT: Physicians' Current Procedural Terminology and (2) CPT: Physicians' Current Procedural Terminology: Specially Annotated for Hospitals: Hospital Outpatient Services. There are three categories of CPT codes. Category I codes are the vehicle for billing all payers. The five-digit numeric code describes the service or procedure, including its descriptor nomenclature. Category II codes, on the other hand, are alphanumeric and usually optional or supplemental in nature and are intended to track the performance of a provider. These codes cannot be used for billing purposes or as a substitute for category I codes. Category III codes are temporary in nature and are used for new or emerging technologies, procedures, or services. They allow collection and analysis of data to assess new procedures and services. It is important to note that CPT differs from the ICD in that CPT codes represent services rendered by the provider, whereas ICD (or ICD-CM) codes represent a diagnosis. As mentioned in the section on ICD, the ICD-Procedure Coding System (ICD-PCS) is a set of codes for inpatient procedures, whereas CPT is a set of codes for procedures done in outpatient or ambulatory care settings, such as physicians' offices or hospital outpatient departments.

▶ 3.11 Reportable/Notifiable Diseases

Because of an interest in understanding and reporting the magnitude of a health problem and to prevent the spread of life-threatening infectious diseases, local, territorial, state, and federal agencies require mandatory or voluntary *reporting* or *notification* of such diseases by all healthcare providers. Based on whether a state or local agency or the CDC is the recipient of such information, a distinction is made between the terms *reporting* and *notification*. The CDC uses the term *notification* because information is voluntarily submitted to them by local, territorial, and state health departments, whereas state health departments use the term *reporting* because healthcare providers are legislatively or under regulations required to submit such information.

Each state in the United States has the legal authority to determine which diseases or conditions are of sufficient public health importance to be listed as State Reportable Conditions (SRCs). Suspected or confirmed cases of conditions on this list are reported to a designated entity in the state health department by all healthcare providers, including hospitals, doctors, laboratories, and city or county health departments. Reporting can occur based on clinical signs and symptoms, a confirmed laboratory test, or epidemiologic criteria known as the *reporting criteria*. Depending on the circumstances and risk to the public, the state health department, with or without the involvement of a federal agency such as the CDC, can launch an investigation to determine if a public health intervention, such as vaccination or quarantine of one or more individuals or removal of a food product from store shelves, is warranted. Because each state has the authority to determine which conditions are listed on the SRCs, lists of SRC can differ from one state to another.

The CDC is the federal agency that, in collaboration with the Council of State and Territorial

Epidemiologists, designates conditions and the criteria based on which designated conditions are listed on the National Notifiable Disease Surveillance System (NNDSS). To protect the health of people throughout the nation, in partnership with local, tribal, and state health authorities, the CDC also gets involved in the investigation and containment of a public health threat. The CDC requests that it be notified when a suspected or confirmed case of a condition listed in the NNDSS is identified by a state health department and it meets the CDC's case definition. This happens through a formal process of notification, in which deidentified case data are provided by the state health department to the CDC. Conditions listed on the NNDSS may or may not be listed as SRCs or vice versa.

Data from 57 state, tribal, and local reporting jurisdictions are reported to NNDSS and published in the Morbidity and Mortality Weekly Report issued by the CDC. Many sexually transmitted diseases and other infectious diseases, such as anthrax, plague, and tuberculosis, are listed on many of the SRC lists and the NNDSS. The occurrence of a listeria outbreak linked to Blue Bell ice cream products and the recall of all its ice cream products by the company in April 2015 is just one example of the public health importance of reportable conditions lists and the NNDSS. The time frame and mechanisms for reporting cases of reportable or notifiable conditions vary depending on the seriousness of the public health threat posed by the condition. Some diseases have to be reported electronically or via telephone immediately on suspicion or diagnosis, whereas others can be reported on paper over a period of days or even weeks. The time frame and procedure for reporting a given condition can also differ from one state to another.

▶ Exercise 3.1

In a community where normal life expectancy is 65 years, 100 people died in 2015. Look at **TABLES 3.6** and **3.7** and calculate YPLL and DALYs lost for the community in 2015.

TABLE 3.6 Table to Calculate Years of Potential Life Lost

	No. of Deaths	Age at Death	Calculate YPLL
A	20	65	
B	20	63	
C	20	61	
D	20	58	
E	20	53	
Total	100	—	

TABLE 3.7 Table to Calculate Disability-Adjusted Life Years Lost

Group	No. of Deaths	Age at Death	Calculate YPLL	Years Lived with Disability	Level of Disability*	Calculate DALYs Lost
A	20	65		2	0.8	
B	20	63		5	0.6	
C	20	61		7	0.9	
D	20	58		3	0.5	
E	20	53		2	0.7	
Total	100	—				

*Each year of disability in the corresponding group is equal to 0.8, 0.6, 0.9, 0.5, and 0.7 of a healthy year. These values are different because the nature and severity of disability in each group were different from another group.

🔍 CASE STUDY 3.1: Assessment of Burden of Disease

Modified from: Lortet-Tieulent J, Soerjomataram I, Lin CC, Coebergh JWW, Jemal A. U.S. burden of cancer by race and ethnicity according to disability-adjusted life years. Am J Prev Med. 2016; 51(5):673–681.

In a study published in the *American Journal of Preventive Medicine* in 2016, Lortet-Tieulent et al. estimated the burden of cancer in different racial and ethnic groups in the United States by estimating the total number of DALYs in 2011. The authors used 2013 data on the incidence of 24 most common malignant tumors and "all other cancers" from population-based cancer registries in the United States. To estimate the number of DALYs by sex and race, they first derived the two components of DALYs: (1) the years of life lost (YLL) to premature death and (2) years lived with disability (YLD). YLL was estimated by multiplying the number of deaths in each age group by the life expectancy at the midpoint of that age group. DALYs were calculated by adding estimates for YLL and YLD. Mortality data for 2011 were extracted from the NCHS files. To estimate YLD, data were obtained from the National American Association of Central Cancer Registries. Disability weights established by the 2013 GBD study for the level of disability resulting from various conditions, including cancer, were used to estimate differential YLDs for different cancers. The burden of cancer was also estimated through age-standardized DALY rates per 100,000 population using the U.S. standard population in 2000. To get the race/ethnicity-specific DALYs and age-standardized rates per 100,000 population, the authors employed the following race/ethnic categories in data analysis: non-Hispanic white, non-Hispanic black, Hispanic, and non-Hispanic Asian.

The results indicated that the burden of cancer combined for men and women in the United States in 2011 exceeded 9.8 million DALYs, with 4.9 million DALYs in each sex group. Lung cancer, with 24% of all DALYs, was the biggest contributor to cancer-related loss of health (**FIGURE 3.6**). Lung (24%), breast (10%), colorectal (9%), and pancreatic cancer (6%) collectively were responsible for nearly half of all DALYs. Approximately 91% of all DALYs resulted from the YLLs to premature deaths. The age-standardized DALY rate for men was 3,046 per 100,000 and 2,694 per 100,000 for women. The age-standardized DALY rates for breast, gallbladder, and thyroid cancer were higher in women than in men. All other cancer rates were higher in men.

FIGURES 3.6 and **3.7** show the proportion of DALYs from various cancers in the total population and in various racial/ethnic groups.

Questions

Question 1. What are the top three cancers for DALYs? Do they differ from one race/ethnic group to another?

Question 2. In which race/ethnic group are lung cancer DALYs the lowest?

Question 3. Which race/ethnic group has the highest DALYs from prostate and liver cancer?

Question 4. How much does stomach cancer contribute to DALYs in each race/ethnic group?

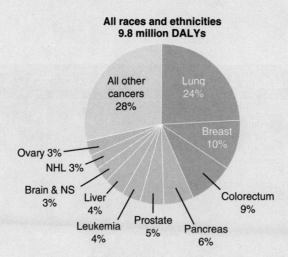

FIGURE 3.6 Proportion of DALYs from top 10 and all other cancers in all races/ethnicities in 2011.

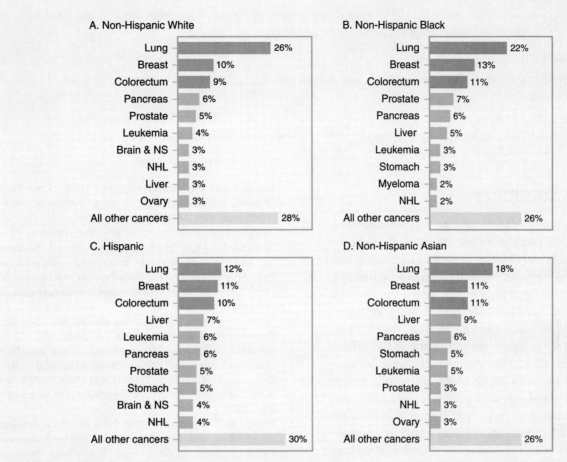

FIGURE 3.7 Proportion of DALYs from top 10 and all other cancers by race/ethnicity in 2011.

⌕ CASE STUDY 3.2: Influence of Gender and Age on Disability After Stroke

Modified / Adapted from: Kelly-Hayes M, Beiser A, Kase CS, Scaramucci A, D'Agostino RB, Wolf PA. The influence of gender and age on disability following ischemic stroke: the framingham study. Journal of Stroke and Cerebrovascular Disease. 2003;12(3):119–126.

The purpose of this 2003 study by Kelly-Hayes et al. was to assess whether there are gender-based differences in stroke -related disability in elderly patients. The study used the original Framingham Heart Study community-based cohort to identify the 108 cases included in the study of first-ever ischemic stroke between 1982 and 1999 at any age between 65 to 94 years and survival for at least 6 months after the stroke. The study compared these individuals with 102 age- and sex-matched controls who did not have a stroke. The demographic and clinical characteristics of both cases and controls compared by gender were statistically similar. About half of the 108 cases had moderate or severe neurologic deficit and 78.7% had hypertension, 29.6% had diabetes, 15.7% previously had myocardial infarction, and 12% had congestive heart failure. About 40% of the 108 cases had more than one comorbid condition. Women stroke patients as compared to their age- and sex-matched controls were significantly more likely to have had myocardial infarction (15.8% vs. 1.8%) and have congestive heart failure (14.0% vs. 3.5%). The study reported that, 6 months after stroke, women were more likely than men to be dependent in activities of daily living (ADLs; 33.9% vs. 15.6%), more likely to be unable to walk without assistance (40.3% vs. 17.8%), have bladder incontinence (28.6% vs. 13.3%), have social disability (36.8% vs. 23.1%), be institutionalized (34.9% vs. 13.3%), and have poorer subjective health (40.7% vs. 38.1%). However, based on odds ratio and their confidence intervals, the authors reported that all of these differences between

(continues)

women and men in the prevalence of disabilities were statistically not significant and older age at stroke onset was associated with greater disability than were gender or stroke subtype.

Questions

Question 1. How similar or dissimilar were men and women stroke patients from their respective age- and sex-matched controls?

Question 2. Based on the data reported in the study, was the prevalence of "bladder incontinence," "inability to walk unassisted," "social disability," and "poor subjective health" statistically similar or dissimilar in men and women?

▶ 3.12 Summary

Defining, counting, and measuring disease, disability, and death in a population are complex. Boundaries between health and disease, between functioning and disability, and between life and death can be blurred. To provide some guidelines in this regard, frameworks and standards have been developed by professional societies such as the American Medical Association, the American Bar Association, and the WHO. These guidelines and standards help in medicolegal decision making and in formulating social and public health policy. Such standards and guidelines not only provide a uniform and consistent framework for data collection and reporting, but also assist in comparing distribution and frequency of diseases in various populations, determining reimbursement rates, and setting priorities for public health policy. The ICD and CPT codes are examples of systems that serve these important functions. Understanding these and other classification and coding systems is essential for effective healthcare management.

Measuring and reporting disease-specific burden of disease and premature deaths in a population is also important for setting strategic goals and priorities. Estimation of YPLL to a disease or QALYs gained by the implementation of a technology or public health intervention is important for optimal allocation of limited societal and institutional resources. Developing a good understanding of concepts related to the assessment of health, measurement of disease and disability, and standardized procedures for estimating the burden of disease in different populations should be of great value to future and current healthcare managers.

References

1. Venes D, editor. Taber's cyclopedic medical dictionary [Internet]. 23rd ed. Philadelphia: FA Davis; 2017. Disease. [cited 2018 Jan 18]. Available from: http://online.statref.com/document.aspx?Offset=0&StartDoc=1&QueryID=-1&FxID=57&Lt=TOC&SessionID=281CBAFANNQENVWN#H&3&ChaptersTab&SGICMASe1GACwl3hpR8jbA%3d%3d&p37&57

2. United States Department of Justice (DOJ), Civil Rights Division. Information and Technical Assistance on the Americans with Disabilities Act. [cited 2017 Oct 23]. Available from: https://www.ada.gov/2010_regs.htm

3. Courtney-Long EA, Carroll DD, Zhang QC, et al. Prevalence of disability and disability type among adults—United States, 2013. MMWR Morb Mortal Wkly Rep. 2015;64(29):777–783. [cited 2017 Jul 24]. Available from: http://www.cdc.gov/mmwr/pdf/wk/mm6429.pdf

4. Venes D, editor. Taber's cyclopedic medical dictionary [Internet]. 23rd ed. Philadelphia: FA Davis; 2017. Death. [cited 2018 Jan 18]. Available from: http://online.statref.com/document.aspx?Offset=0&StartDoc=1&QueryID=-1&FxID=57&Lt=TOC&SessionID=281CBAFANNQENVWN#H&2&ChaptersTab&OkcFmw44Bg40BiG95XebXw%3d%3d&p37&57

5. President's Commission for the Study of Ethical Problems in Medicine and Biomedical and Behavioral Research. Defining death: medical, legal and ethical issues in the determination of death. 1981. [cited 2017 Jul 24]. Available from: http://euthanasia.procon.org/sourcefiles/PresCommDefiningDeath.pdf

6. National Conference of Commissioners on Uniform State Laws. Uniform Determination of Death Act. Chicago, IL. 1981. [cited 2017 Jul 24]. Available from: http://pntb.org/wordpress/wp-content/uploads/Uniform-Determination-of-Death-1980_5c.pdf

7. DeGrazia D. Biology, consciousness and the definition of death. Philos Public Policy Q. 1998;18(1–2):18–22. [cited 2017 Jul 24]. Available from: http://journals.gmu.edu/PPPQ/article/viewFile/288/216

8. Wise J. Obesity rates rise substantially worldwide. BMJ. 2014;348:g3582. http://dx.doi.org/10.1136/bmj.g3582

9. Kelly T, Yang W, Chen CS, Reynolds K, He J. Global burden of obesity in 2005 and projections to 2030. Int J Obes. 2008;32:1431–1437.

10. Ogden CL, Carroll MD, Kit BK, Flegal KM. Prevalence of childhood and adult obesity in the United States, 2011-2012. JAMA. 2014;311(8):806–814. [cited 2017 Jul 24]. Available from: http://jama.jamanetwork.com/article.aspx?articleid=1832542

11. Heshka S, Allison DB. Is obesity a disease? Int J Obes. 2001;25(10):1401–1404.

12. World Health Organization. Toward a common language for functioning, disability and health. Geneva: World Health Organization; 2002.

13. World Health Organization. How to use the ICF: a practical manual for using the International Classification of Functioning, Disability and Health (ICF). Exposure Draft for Comments. Geneva: World Health Organization; 2013.

14. Garcia P, McCarthy M. Measuring health: a step in the development of city health profiles. World Health Organization Regional Office for Europe. 1996 [cited 2017 Jul 24]. Available from: http://www.euro.who.int/__data /assets/pdf_file/0017/101645/WA95096GA.pdf

15. Maddox GL, Douglass EB. Self-assessment of health: a longitudinal study of elderly subjects. J Health Soc Behav. 1973;14(1):87–93.

16. Idler EL, Kasl SV, Lemke JH. Self-evaluated health and mortality among the elderly in New Haven, Connecticut, and Iowa and Washington Counties in Iowa, 1982–1986. Am J Epidemiol. 1990;131(1):91–103.

17. Shetterly SM, Baxter J, Mason LD, Hamman RF. Self-rated health among Hispanic vs. non-Hispanic white adults: the San Luis Valley Health and Aging Study. Am J Public Health. 1996;86(12):1798–1801.

18. Centers for Disease Control and Prevention. Community health assessment for population health improvement: resource of most frequently recommended health outcomes and determinants. Atlanta, GA: Centers for Disease Control and Prevention; 2013.

19. Public Health Accreditation Board. Standards and Measures (Version 1.5). 2013 [cited 2017 Jul 24]. Available from: http:// www.phaboard.org/wp-content/uploads/SM-Version-1.5 -Board-adopted-FINAL-01-24-2014.docx.pdf

20. Hardcastle LE, Record KL, Jacobson PD, Gosten LO. Improving the population's health: The Affordable Care Act and the importance of integration. J Law Med Ethics. 2011;39(3):317–327.

21. Parrish RG. Measuring population health outcomes. Prev Chronic Dis. 2010 7(4). [cited 2017 Jul 24]. Available from: http://www.cdc.gov/pcd/issues/2010/jul/10_0005.htm

22. Li C, Ekwueme DU, Rim SH, Tangka FK. Years of potential life lost and productivity losses from male urogenital cancer deaths–United States, 2004. Urology. 2010;76(3):528–535.

23. Gardner JW, Sanborn JS. Years of potential life lost (YPLL)– what does it measure? *Epidemiology*. 1990;1(4):322–329.

24. Centers for Disease Control and Prevention. Years of potential life lost (YPLL) 1999–2013. 2017 [cited 2017 Jul 24]. Available from: https://webappa.cdc.gov/sasweb/ncipc /ypll.html

25. Gold MR, Stevenson D, Fryback DG. HALYs and QALYs and DALYs, oh my: similarities and differences in summary measures of population health. Annu Rev Public Health. 2002;23:115–134.

26. Murray CJL. Quantifying the burden of disease: the technical basis for disability-adjusted life years. Bull World Health Organ. 1994;72(3):429–445.

27. Murray CJL, Lopez AD. Measuring the global burden of disease. N Engl J Med. 2013;369(5):448–457.

28. Ezzati M, Lopez AD, Rodgers A, Hoorn SV, Murray CJL. Selected major risk factors and global and regional burden of disease. Lancet. 2002;360:1347–1360.

29. Lopez D, Mathers CD, Ezatti M, Jamison DT, Murray CJL. Global and regional burden of disease and risk factors, 2001: systematic analysis of population health data. Lancet. 2006;367:1747–1757.

30. Weinstein MC, Torrance G, McGuire A. QALYs: the basics. Value Health. 2009;12(Supp. 1):S5–S9.

31. Moriyama IM, Loy RM, Robb-Smith AHT. History of the statistical classification of diseases and causes of death. In: Rosenberg HM, Hoyert DL, editors. Hyattsville, MD: National Center for Health Statistics; 2011 [cited 2017 Jul 24]. Available from: http://www.cdc.gov/nchs/data/misc /classification_diseases2011.pdf

32. Outland B, Newman MM, William MJ. Health policy basics: implementation of the International Classifications of Disease, 10th revision. Ann Intern Med. 2015;163(7): 554–556.

33. Manaker S. Time to get off the diagnosis dime onto the 10th revision of the International Classification of Diseases. Ann Intern Med. 2015;163(7):557–558.

© Monsitj/Getty Images

CHAPTER 4

Epidemiologic Measures of Population Health

LEARNING OBJECTIVES

Having mastered the materials in this chapter, the student will be able to:

1. Appropriately use and explain various measures of morbidity and mortality.
2. Use necessary data and calculate various measures of morbidity and mortality.
3. Use appropriate data and calculate age-, sex-, and race-adjusted morbidity and mortality rates.

CHAPTER OUTLINE

4.1 Introduction
4.2 Types of Summary Statistics Used in Population Health
    4.2.1 Ratio
    4.2.2 Proportion
    4.2.3 Rate
4.3 Measures of Disease Frequency in a Population
    4.3.1 Incidence Rate
    4.3.2 Incidence Density
    4.3.3 Cumulative Incidence
    4.3.4 Prevalence
    4.3.5 Relationship Between Incidence Rate and Prevalence
4.4 Measures of the Frequency of Death in a Population
    4.4.1 Crude Death (Mortality) Rate
    4.4.2 Age-Specific Death (Mortality) Rate
    4.4.3 Cause-Specific Death (Mortality) Rate
    4.4.4 Neonatal Mortality Rate
    4.4.5 Postneonatal Mortality Rate

    4.4.6 Infant Mortality Rate
    4.4.7 Fetal Mortality Rate and Ratio
    4.4.8 Maternal Mortality Rate and Ratio
    4.4.9 Case Fatality Rate
    4.4.10 Proportional Mortality
    4.4.11 Proportional Mortality Ratio
4.5 Other Commonly Reported Statistics
    4.5.1 Crude Birth Rate
    4.5.2 Life Expectancy at Birth
    4.5.3 Life Tables and Life Expectancy at Specific Age Intervals
    4.5.4 Observed and Relative Survival Rates
4.6 Adjustment or Standardization of Rates
    4.6.1 Direct Standardization
    4.6.2 Indirect Standardization
    4.6.3 Standardized Mortality Ratio
Case Study 4.1 – Example of Cumulative Incidence
Case Study 4.2 – Example of a Prevalence Study
Exercises 4.1
4.7 Summary

▶ 4.1 Introduction

This chapter provides a compendium of terms and concepts essential to understanding the health status of a population. For the healthcare manager, the significance of different measures of morbidity and mortality discussed in this chapter is that, in addition to the socioeconomic conditions in a population such as poverty, poor nutrition, lack of education, and poor environmental conditions, high morbidity and mortality rates in a population also reflect inadequate access to appropriate health services. For a host of reasons, including unsustainable cost of medical care and low returns on investment in episodic curative care, there is growing emphasis on population health and preventive services. Healthcare managers must develop a holistic perspective to address problems that result in preventable morbidity and mortality in their communities. Without fully understanding various measures of population health, healthcare managers neither have the information to influence healthcare policy at the local, regional, or national level, nor are they equipped to address these problems. Periodic review of available data on various measures of population health allows healthcare managers to remain cognizant of emerging and evolving health problems in their communities and formulate strategies to provide services that best meet the needs of the community in an efficient and timely manner.

The measures of morbidity and mortality discussed in this chapter give healthcare managers the tools to better understand issues related to healthcare access, planning, and quality. Because *ratio*, *proportion*, and *rate* are mathematical terms used to report measures of morbidity and mortality such as *incidence* and *prevalence*, the chapter begins by explaining these terms and by discussing why it is important to distinguish between them. After explaining these terms, the most commonly reported measures of population health are discussed with examples. The list of concepts discussed in this chapter is by no means exhaustive, but is sufficient to meet the needs of a competent healthcare manager.

▶ 4.2 Types of Statistics Reported in Population Health

4.2.1 Ratio

A **ratio**, usually expressed in a notational form as X:Y, is a comparison of the magnitude of two different numbers, or how many times one value is contained in another. Alternatively, a ratio is a statement of "the relationship in quantity, amount, or size between two or more things."[1] For example, we can compare the ratio of men to women in a population (men:women) or the number of schoolteachers and mine workers in a country (1,000,000 vs. 20,000, i.e., a ratio of 50:1). Mathematically, a ratio is obtained by dividing one of the numbers being compared by the other. Thus, a ratio of 10:20 is the same as a ratio of 7:14 or 4:8.

The usefulness of a ratio in epidemiology can be illustrated by observing that in 2013, the ratio of boys to girls among the newborns in the United States was approximately 1.05:1, whereas the ratio of boys to girls at birth in China and India was 1.12:1. On the other hand, at age 65 years or older, the ratio of men to women in the United States was about 0.75:1, whereas in China it was 0.93:1. These ratios mean that at birth in the United States, 1.05 boys are born as compared with 1 girl (or 105 boys and 100 girls), but in India and China, 1.12 boys are born for every girl (or 112 boys and 100 girls). In contrast, at age 65 or older in the United States, there are only 0.75 men per 1 woman, but in China, there are 0.93 men as compared with 1 woman. Various kinds of ratios, including *risk ratio*, *rate ratio*, and *incidence rate ratio*, are discussed in the chapter on observational studies in this book.

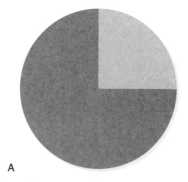 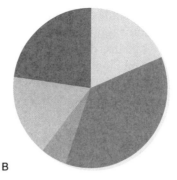

FIGURE 4.1 An illustration of how a proportion is represented by each slice of a pie chart.

4.2.2 Proportion

A **proportion** is a part of something considered in relation to the whole—that is, "the relation of one part to another or to the whole with respect to magnitude, quantity, or degree."[2] Mathematically, a proportion, also called a *fraction*, is a particular kind of ratio in which the numerator is a part or subset of the denominator. As an example, in pie chart A shown in **FIGURE 4.1**, the slice in light green is a proportion of the pie and represents 1/4, or 25%, of the whole, or the denominator. Similarly, in pie chart B, each slice is a part of the whole and represents a proportion. The relationship (i.e., ratio) between different slices is reflected by their relative magnitude, size, or quantity. When the quantity of one slice (i.e., one proportion) changes, the size of one or more of the other slices correspondingly changes to accommodate for the fact that the overall size of the pie, or quantity of the denominator, has remained constant.

The relationship between ratio and proportion can be understood by noting that a ratio can easily be used to derive a proportion, and proportions can easily be converted into a ratio. For example, the ratio of men to women at age 65 in the United States (0.75:1), as discussed in the previous section, can also be used to derive the proportion of men in the population in the following manner:

$$\text{Proportion of men in the population} = \frac{(\text{men})}{(\text{men} + \text{women})}$$

That is,

$$\text{Proportion of men in the population} = \frac{(0.75)}{(0.75 + 1)},$$

$$\text{or } \frac{(0.75)}{1.75} = \text{approximately } 0.43 \text{ or } 43\%$$

Conversely, the proportion of 43% men in the population can be used to derive the ratio between men and women as follows: Because 43% of the population

are men, women make 57% of the population (i.e., $100 - 43 = 57\%$). So, the ratio of men to women would be 0.43:0.57, or 0.43/0.57 = 0.75:1.

4.2.3 Rate

The simplest way to define a rate is to state that it is the frequency of the occurrence of an event in a specific population in a defined period. The dictionary[3] defines rate as: (1) "a quantity, amount, or degree of something measured per unit of something else," for example, death rate, heart rate, metabolic rate, pulse rate, or sedimentation rate; or (2) "the number of times something happens or is done during a particular period of time." Usually, a rate is expressed per unit of time, such as per minute, per hour, per month, or per year.

In epidemiology, **rate** is the measure of the frequency of death, disease, or other health-related events in a given population in a specified period. For example, the number of children born in the world in 2011 was estimated to be at the rate of approximately 4/second, 250/minute, 15,000/hour, or 360,000/day. Similarly, the death rate globally was approximately 2/second, 105/minute, 6,316/hour, or 151,600/day. In the preceding example, the numerator is the number of births or deaths, the denominator is the total population of the world and a unit of time is specified in which the event occurred. By convention, the denominator (in this case, the total world population) is simplified to a manageable and standardized form—usually per 1,000 or per 100,000. Thus, the global birth rate in 2011 can be expressed as approximately 19/1,000 population, while the death rate was estimated to be 8/1,000. It is important to note that this rate applied only to the year 2011, and a different rate may have been estimated for 2012.

From these examples, it becomes clear that, mathematically speaking, a rate is nothing but a number divided by another number, such that the denominator provides the context for the numerator. Often, the denominator is expressed in units of the size of a population, while the numerator represents the variable being measured, such as births, deaths, or episodes of a disease. In strict epidemiologic terms, time is an integral and explicit component of a rate, whether expressed in seconds, minutes, hours, days, or years. Therefore, the term *rate* should not be confused with the previously discussed terms *ratio* and *proportion*.

In calculating disease rates (morbidity rates) or death rates (mortality rates), the numerator represents the number of births, cases of a disease, or deaths, whereas the denominator represents the base population or the population that is at risk of getting the disease or dying in the specified time period. For example, the breast cancer rate in women between the ages of 25 and 75 years in Texas in 2015 might be estimated by the following expression:

$$\text{Breast cancer rate in women aged 25–75 in Texas in 2015} = \frac{\text{Total number of women aged 25–75 known to have breast cancer in Texas in 2015}}{\text{Total number of women aged 25–75 in Texas in 2015}} \times 1{,}000$$

Measurement of rates such as birth and death rates in a population in a specified period is central to the assessment of the health status of that population and for comparing the health status of one population with another in the same period. Comparison of rates in a population in different periods is also important for understanding the changes taking place in the health status of a given population—say, residents of Mississippi, Utah, or Rhode Island.

The frequency of the occurrence of an event such as disease or death in a population also serves as a measure of risk. The hypothetical example in **TABLE 4.1** illustrates how estimation of a rate can shed light on the level of risk of disease or death in different populations and why it is important to compare rates rather than compare the raw number of cases or deaths in two different populations.

In this example, although the total number of deaths of schoolteachers is 20 times greater than the total number of deaths of mine workers, the death rate in mine workers is 5 times greater than it is in teachers. In other words, mine workers experienced a 5-times-greater risk of death as compared with teachers. Observations regarding high or low rates of certain diseases in some populations or occupational groups in the past have provided valuable clues about the etiology or causal factors of those diseases. For example, high rates of lung cancer among smokers provided some clues about the relationship between smoking and lung cancer. Aside from the commonly reported measures of population health discussed in this chapter, some other epidemiologic rates, such as *attack rate* and *survival rate*, are discussed in other parts of this book.

▶ 4.3 Measures of Disease Frequency in a Population

Before discussing any of the specific measures of the frequency of disease and death, it is important to make two observations. First, at times, there is some confusion or a difference of opinion on whether a particular epidemiologic measure is a *rate*, a *proportion*, a *ratio*, or a *probability*. Case in point might be the use of the terms *case fatality ratio* or *case fatality rate*. Even the use of the terms *infant mortality rate* and *under-5 mortality rate* is questioned by some who argue that, strictly speaking, these measures of the frequency of death in children are not rates "but a probability of death derived from a life table."[4] Despite their practical implications, the complexity of such theoretical discussions is beyond the scope of this text, and for the sake of consistency with widely reported statistics, we will adhere to the conventional definition of these terms. In general, the accurate use of a term is both a function of the specific example under consideration and one's perspective on the use of the term in question.

Second, there is considerable variation in the use of an appropriate multiplier, such as *per 1,000 births* versus *per 100,000 births*. Again, the choice of a multiplier is a

TABLE 4.1 A Hypothetical Example of Relative Numbers and Death Rates in Schoolteachers and Mine Workers

	Schoolteachers	Mine Workers
Number of deaths in 2015	10,000	500
Total number in 2015	1,000,000	10,000
Death rate	10,000/1,000,000 = **0.01**	500/10,000 = **0.05**

matter of both preference and convention. As a general principle, it is better to say "4 deaths per 1,000 population" rather than "0.04 deaths per 100,000 population."

4.3.1 Incidence Rate

In common use, *incidence* means the frequency of occurrence of an event (e.g., low incidence of street crime). By definition, the frequency of occurrence of any event must specify the period in which the event of interest is being counted. In epidemiology, the term *incidence* is used to count the frequency of *new cases* of a disease, event, or condition in a specified population in a given time period. The length of time can be a day, a month, a year, or longer depending on the time it takes to develop the disease. Broadly speaking, **incidence rate** indicates the risk or probability that healthy individuals in a population will develop a particular disease during a specified period. The following formula indicates how incidence rate is generally estimated.

$$\text{Incidence rate} = \frac{\substack{\text{Number of new cases of a disease in a defined} \\ \text{population in a defined period of time}}}{\substack{\text{Total population at risk in the same} \\ \text{period of time}}} \times 1,000$$

The mathematical expression that was developed for breast cancer rate in section 4.2.3 can be changed for breast cancer incidence rate in women aged 25–75 in Texas in 2015 as follows:

$$\substack{\text{Breast cancer incidence rate} \\ \text{in women aged 25–75 in} \\ \text{Texas in 2015}} = \frac{\substack{\text{Total number of new cases of} \\ \text{breast cancer diagnosed} \\ \text{in women aged 25–75} \\ \text{in Texas in 2015}}}{\substack{\text{Total number of women aged} \\ \text{25–75 in Texas in 2015 who} \\ \text{previously did not have} \\ \text{breast cancer}}} \times 1,000$$

Three important points must be highlighted with regard to the previously noted definition. First, the counting of new cases can be tricky at times. Some disorders, such as malaria, asthma, or herpes, can be episodic in nature and can remain dormant for a period of time in the same individual. Reemergence of the disease in the same individual after a period of remission or the occurrence of another episode of the same disease in the same individual may not be counted as a new case. On the other hand, diseases that do not confer lasting immunity and can occur more than once in the same time period in the same individual because the person has been exposed to the same or a different strain of the same organism (such as the flu or the common cold) would count as new cases. Accurate knowledge of the time of onset of the disease

is also an important consideration in estimating incidence rate. In some diseases, such as gastroenteritis or stroke, the time of onset is easy to pinpoint. However, in conditions that develop slowly and remain dormant or asymptomatic for a long period of time, such as various kinds of cancers, the time of onset is nearly impossible to determine. In these circumstances, the date of definitive diagnosis is used as the date of onset.

Second, the specification of the population (the denominator) from which new cases (the numerator) emerge must also be carefully limited only to those individuals who are at risk of getting the disease. Those members of the population who either already have the disease or are not currently at risk because they previously have been vaccinated or exposed to the disease and have developed immunity against it would not be included in the "at-risk" population. Similarly, individuals who do not have the specific organ that is affected by the disease whose new cases are being counted cannot be considered at risk. This would be the case when counting the at-risk population for cancers of the gallbladder, uterus, ovary, or breast because in some individuals, these organs have been removed for other reasons. This would include preemptive removal of the breast in women with BRCA 1 and BRCA 2 gene mutations to avoid the future risk of breast cancer. Admittedly, the number of individuals in the population of interest (county, state, or country) who do not have these organs is likely to be small and may not substantially affect overall estimation of the incidence rate for a particular disorder.

Third, specification of the period in which the occurrence of new cases is being counted renders the estimation of incidence to be a rate rather than just a proportion. Usually, incidence rate is estimated and reported for a specific calendar year. For example, the *crude*, or overall, incidence rate of all cancers combined in the United States in 2011 was 513.5 per 100,000 population.[5] Note that the incidence rate in the overall population can be further categorized on the bases of sex, age, race, occupation, or some other subsets of the total population.

The size of the population in which new cases are being counted can vary widely. In clinical research studies, the number of at-risk individuals being followed can be quite small. On the other hand, in population studies that are based on population surveys, routine administrative data, or billing data, the at-risk population can be in the millions or tens of millions. In such cases, depending on the frequency or rarity of the disease, incidence rates may be expressed in terms of per 1,000 or per 100,000 population. For example, the incidence of prostate cancer in men in the United

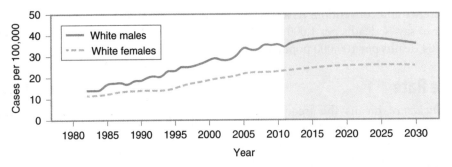

FIGURE 4.2 Observed and projected age-adjusted melanoma incidence rates by sex and race—United States, 1982–2030.

Reproduced from: Guy GP, Thomas CC, Thompson T, Watson M, Massetti GM, Richardson LC. Vital signs: melanoma incidence and mortality trends and projections — United States, 1982–2030. Morbidity and Mortality Weekly Report. 2015;64(21):591–596.
Available at: http://www.cdc.gov/MMWr/preview/mmwrhtml/mm6421a6.htm

TABLE 4.2 Hypothetical Example of Age-Stratified Estimates of Traumatic Brain Injury Incidence Rates Per Million Persons in the United States

Year	Age				
	≥15 to 24	≥25 to 44	≥45 to 64	≥65 to 74	≥75
1995	93	61	51	58	120
2005	69	53	58	70	132
2015	57	46	70	92	155

Modified from: Jain NB, Ayers GD, Peterson EN, Harris MB, Morse L, O'Connor KC, Garshick E. Traumatic spinal cord injury in the United States, 1993–2012. JAMA. 2015;313(22):2236–2243.

States in 2011 was 128.3/100,000, and that of breast cancer in women was 122.0/100,000.

FIGURE 4.2 provides an example of observed and future projection of the *age-adjusted incidence rate* of malignant melanoma per 100,000 white men and women in the United States. In contrast, **TABLE 4.2** is a hypothetical example of the incidence rate of traumatic brain injury *per million* persons stratified by age in three different periods in the United States.

4.3.2 Incidence Density

The estimation of incidence rate becomes more complicated in situations when (1) the at-risk population is dynamic rather than fixed, and (2) the period in which new cases are counted spans one or several years.

In any population in a given period, some people can die, others can move to a different area, while new people arrive and become part of the at-risk population. In such a situation, not all individuals in the population can be followed for the entire duration of the estimation period—especially if the population at risk needs to be followed for months or even years. This often happens in studies of uncommon or rare diseases in which no new cases may occur in a relatively short period. In

such circumstances, rather than incidence rate, a different measure of disease frequency called **incidence density** is estimated. As individuals in the at-risk population are followed for varying periods of time—say, some for 2 years, some for 3 years, and others for only half a year—the denominator in the incidence density calculation is the total number of *person years* rather than the total population at risk. The total number of person years is determined by the sum total of the duration for which each of the individuals in the study population was followed. We will revisit the estimation of incidence density in the context of cohort study design with illustrative examples in a later chapter.

4.3.3 Cumulative Incidence

Cumulative incidence is simply measured by dividing the number of new cases of a disease in a defined period in a given population by the total number of at-risk individuals over the same time period. Usually, estimation of cumulative incidence involves follow-up of a specific population over a period of time that can span years or even decades. Strictly speaking, cumulative incidence is not a rate, but rather a measure of the total burden of a disease in a population over a given period of time. The specification of a unit of time in this case is not integral to the estimation of cumulative incidence, and time is only mentioned to indicate the total period for which the population of interest was followed to count the total number of new cases. The word *cumulative* refers to the fact that the number of new cases from one month to the next or one year to the next are aggregated over time (e.g., 2, 4, or 7 years). A hypothetical example of cumulative incidence can be 20 new cases of liver disease in a population of 150 heavy drinkers of alcohol who were followed for a period of 5 years. Out of the 20 new cases, let us assume that 2 occurred in the second year, 8 occurred in the fourth year, and 10 occurred in the fifth year. Therefore, cumulative incidence in this example would be 20/150, or 0.13. Of course, this number can easily be converted into a percentage and expressed as such. So, in this example, cumulative incidence can also be stated as 13%.

In calculating cumulative incidence, no attempt is made to derive a yearly rate, and the proportion 20/150 is not converted into the estimated number of cases per 1,000 or 100,000 heavy drinkers of alcohol. Values of cumulative incidence, therefore, can only range between 0 and 1. It is important to note that the value of cumulative incidence is affected by the length of time for which the population of interest is followed. Clearly, longer periods of follow-up would result in higher values of cumulative incidence. Reporting of a *lifetime risk* of a disease—say, breast cancer in women with BRCA 1 and BRCA 2 gene mutations—is a common practice in epidemiology. Aside from assessing the average risk of a disease in a defined population over a given period of time (liver disease in the preceding

example), estimation of cumulative incidence can also provide clues about the etiology of a disease and can be used for planning services or developing health policy. Because of its fractional values, however, the interpretation of cumulative incidence can be a bit more difficult than interpreting incidence rate.

4.3.4 Prevalence

Prevalence is defined as the proportion of a population that has a particular disease, such as diabetes, or a group of diseases, such as cardiovascular diseases or cancers. Prevalence is the estimation of the total number of existing cases of a disease at any given point in time or during a specified period. If counting of cases of a disease is done at a point in time—say, on January 1, 2017—then the estimation is called *point prevalence*. However, if the number of cases is counted for a specified duration of time—say, from January 1 through December 31, 2017—the estimation is called *period prevalence*. In point prevalence, because the cases of a particular disease are counted at a point in time, strictly speaking, it should not be called a *rate*, but only a *count* of existing cases in the population—that is, a proportion. Period prevalence, on the other hand, is the sum total of the number of cases of a disease that already existed at the onset of the period (say, January 1, 2017) and the cases that newly occurred during the time period (say, January 1 through December 31, 2017). All cases of the disease are counted regardless of whether some of the new or old cases recovered, died, or were living on the last day of the period. **FIGURE 4.3** provides an example of trends

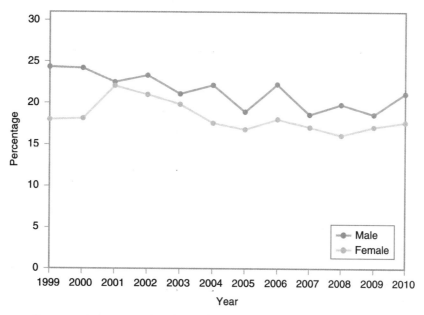

FIGURE 4.3 Prevalence of current cigarette smoking among adults in Kansas, 1999–2010.

Reproduced from: Neuberger JS, Lai SM. Cigarette consumption and cigarette smoking prevalence among adults in Kansas. Preventing Chronic Disease. 2015;12:150011. DOI: http://dx.doi.org/10.5888/pcd12.150011. Available at: http://www.cdc.gov/pcd/issues/2015/15_0011.htm/15_0011a.htm#1

in smoking prevalence in men and women from 1999 through 2010 in Kansas.

4.3.5 Relationship Between Incidence Rate and Prevalence

$$Prevalence = (Incidence\ rate) \times (Duration\ of\ the\ disease)$$

As shown in the preceding equation, prevalence is a function of both the incidence rate and the duration of the disease whose cases are being counted. Therefore, an increase in the prevalence of a disease over a period of time may reflect an increase in the number of new cases, an increase in the duration of the disease, or both. An increase in incidence rate from one period to the next can happen because of an increase in the number of people being exposed to the disease agent or risk factor. For example, an increased incidence rate of drug overdose may reflect an increase in the number of people using illicit drugs. Increased duration of the disease, on the other hand, can be due to earlier diagnosis of the disease than in the past, prolonged survival of cases of a disease resulting from better treatment and availability of new technologies to treat many fatal disorders such as cancers, or both. Improvement in the treatment for a variety of cancers in recent years has had a profound effect on the length of time people can expect to live with one type of cancer or another. Increased survival time for many cancers may have potentially increased prevalence for these conditions in recent years, as opposed to just a decade or two ago.

To understand the relationship between incidence rate and prevalence, imagine a room with some people in it and some people entering or exiting the room. Consider also the factors that can affect the total number of individuals in the room at any given time or during a specified period. Clearly, only the number of people entering or exiting the room during a minute, hour, or day can affect the total count of individuals in the room at any given time or during a specified period. Assume that at 9:00 a.m., 10 people were already in the room, and 5 people entered the room between 9:00 and 9:40 a.m. Thus, point prevalence at 9:00 a.m. was 10, the incidence rate of new arrivals for the hour between 9:00 and 10:00 a.m. would be 5, and prevalence for the hour would be 15. If 3 people left the room at 9:45 a.m., the period prevalence or prevalence for the hour would still be 15, but point prevalence at 9:50 a.m. would be 12, because 3 people left the total pool of people at 9:45 a.m. However, if 7 new people entered the room between 10:00 and 11:00 a.m. but

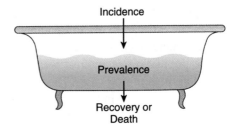

FIGURE 4.4 Prevalence pool.

no one left during that hour, the incidence rate for the hour between 10:00 and 11:00 a.m. would be 7, and prevalence would be 17. **FIGURE 4.4** also depicts the relationship between incidence rate and prevalence. The figure shows how changes in incidence rate and/or in mortality or recovery rates can affect prevalence of a given disease in a population.

It is important to note that if the value of two of the three variables in the equation

$$Prevalence = (Incidence\ rate) \times (Duration\ of\ the\ disease)$$

is known, it is quite simple to derive the value of the third variable. It is also easy to see that if patients neither quickly recover nor rapidly die and the incidence rate in each time interval remains constant, the prevalence of the disease would continue to increase over time as new cases are added to the existing pool of patients. In this situation, fewer people are exiting the pool of patients because of recovery or death than those being newly added. However, with more people being in the prevalence pool, the number of deaths in each time interval would also begin to increase until a balance between mortality rate and incidence rate is achieved. **FIGURE 4.5** graphically illustrates this point. In this example, the incidence rate is 100 per year, and the mortality rate is 20%. Note that in the earlier periods, prevalence increases rapidly but begins to slow down as time progresses and finally arrives at a steady state in which the incidence rate is equal to the mortality rate, and there is no increase or decrease in prevalence over time.

▶ 4.4 Measures of the Frequency of Death in a Population

4.4.1 Crude Death (Mortality) Rate

Crude death (mortality) rate (CDR) is a summary statistic based on the total number of deaths from all causes in a specified population in a given year.

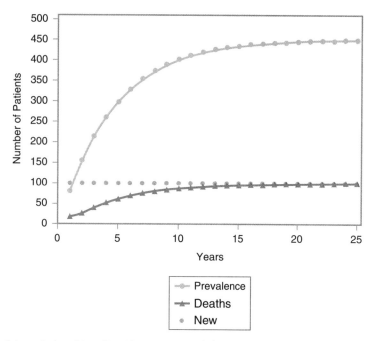

FIGURE 4.5 An illustration of the relationship of incidence rate and duration of disease with the prevalence of disease.
Courtesy of Advanced Renal Education Program–Fresenius Medical Care North America.

To allow easy comparisons of overall death rates in different populations in the same period or death rates in the same population in different periods, by convention, CDR is expressed as per 100,000 population. However, it is also common to report CDR and some other population health measures in terms of per 1,000 population. Because no attempt is made to adjust for differences in the number of individuals in different age, sex, or race subsets in the populations being compared, it is called a *crude* or *unadjusted* rate. For example, with approximately 2,512,873 deaths from all causes in the United States in 2011, CDR was 806.5 deaths per 100,000 population.[6] This rate does not take into account different death rates in various age, sex, or race subsets of the entire U.S. population in 2011. In consideration of the fact that, because of deaths, births, immigration, and emigration, every day there are changes taking place in the count of the total population, by convention, *average midyear population* is used as the denominator in calculating CDR as well as other population summary statistics. Despite the "crude" nature of its estimation, CDR is commonly used in public health and frequently reported by national and international agencies because of the simplicity of its calculation and easy availability of data on the total number of deaths in a specified population in a given year.

$$CDR = \frac{\text{Total number of deaths from all causes in a specified population in a given year}}{\text{Average midyear population in the same year}} \times 100,000$$

4.4.2 Age-Specific Death (Mortality) Rate

Age-specific death (mortality) rate (ASDR) is defined as the total number of deaths of individuals in a specific age group from all causes in a given year per 100,000 (or per 1,000) population in that age group. By convention, average midyear population in the specific age group is used as the denominator.

$$ASDR = \frac{\text{Total number of deaths of individuals in a specific age group in a given year}}{\text{Average midyear population in that age group in the same year}} \times 100,000$$

4.4.3 Cause-Specific Death (Mortality) Rate

The **cause-specific death (mortality) rate (CSDR)** is the total number of deaths in a population attributed or assigned to a specific causal agent, factor, or diagnosis in a given year. By convention, the CSDR also is reported per 100,000 population. However, depending on the size of the population, it may also be reported per 1,000 population. In 2011, 575,313 deaths were reported in the United States due to malignant neoplasms, with a CSDR of 184.6 per 100,000 population. Likewise, 73,282 deaths were reported for diabetes mellitus, with a CSDR of 23.5 per 100,000 population.[6]

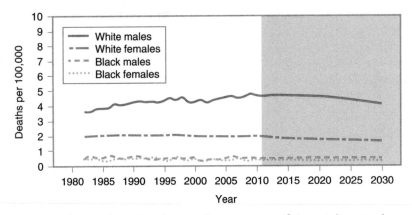

FIGURE 4.6 Observed and projected age-adjusted melanoma (i.e., cause-specific) mortality rates by sex and race: United States, 1982–2030.

Reproduced from: Guy GP, Thomas CC, Thompson T, Watson M, Massetti GM, Richardson LC. Vital signs: melanoma incidence and mortality trends and projections — United States, 1982–2030. Morbidity and Mortality Weekly Report. 2015;64(21):591–596. Available at: http://www.cdc.gov/MMWr/preview/mmwrhtml/mm6421a6.htm

$$CSDR = \frac{\text{Total number of deaths due to a specific disease or condition in a given years}}{\text{Average midyear population in the same year}} \times 100{,}000$$

FIGURE 4.6 provides an example of actual and future projections of age-adjusted CSDR by a malignant neoplasm known as melanoma for the entire U.S. population. Note that white men in the United States die from melanoma at a much higher rate than white women and black men and women.

4.4.4 Neonatal Mortality Rate

The **neonatal mortality rate (NMR)** is the number of deaths of children during the first 28 days after birth per 1,000 live births in a given year. Note that there are some variations of this definition available from various sources. The World Health Organization (WHO) defines *neonatal deaths* as the "number of deaths during *the first 28 completed days* of life per 1,000 live births in a given year or period. Neonatal deaths may be subdivided into early neonatal deaths, occurring during the first seven days of life, and late neonatal deaths, occurring after the seventh day but before the 28 completed days of life."[2]

Many other sources, including the American Pediatric Association, use <28 days or "before reaching 28 days of age" (i.e., 27 completed days) rather than 28 completed days to count neonatal deaths. **TABLE 4.3** shows the NMR and some other common epidemiologic measures for the United States and some other countries.

$$NMR = \frac{\text{Number of deaths of children during the first 28 days after birth in a given year}}{\text{Total number of live births in the same year}} \times 1{,}000$$

4.4.5 Postneonatal Mortality Rate

The **postneonatal mortality rate (PNMR)** is the number of deaths of children from the 29th day after birth to 1 year of age (i.e., <365 completed days) per 1,000 live births in a given year.

$$PNMR = \frac{\text{Number of deaths of children from the 29th day to 1 year after birth in a given year}}{\text{Total number of live births in the same year}} \times 1{,}000$$

4.4.6 Infant Mortality Rate

The **infant mortality rate (IMR)** includes both the neonatal mortality rate and the postneonatal mortality rate because both occur before the completion of the first year of life (i.e., <365 completed days); the IMR is therefore defined as the number of deaths of children under 1 year of age in a specified population per 1,000 live births in a given year.

$$IMR = \frac{\text{Number of deaths of children under 1 year of age in a given year}}{\text{Total number of live births in the same year}} \times 1{,}000$$

TABLE 4.3 Neonatal Mortality Rate and Some Other Common Epidemiologic Measures for Selected Countries, 2013

Country	Life Expectancy*	Neonatal Mortality**	Infant Mortality**	Under-5 Mortality**	Adult*** Mortality Male	Adult*** Mortality Female
United States	79	4	6	7	132	77
Switzerland	83	3	4	4	68	40
Norway	81	2	2	3	82	50
Singapore	82	1	2	3	73	41
Spain	82	3	4	4	83	39
France	82	2	4	4	109	52
Germany	81	2	3	4	96	52
Japan	83	1	2	3	77	40
India	66	29	41	53	236	156
China	75	8	11	13	102	75
Cuba	79	3	5	6	109	70
Botswana	47	25	36	47	699	731
Chad	51	40	89	148	391	362
Mozambique	50	30	62	87	489	475

* At birth.
** Per 1,000 live births.
*** 5-year adult mortality 2008–2013 per 1,000 adults (age ≥15 years).

Modified from: Table 2.21 Mortality. World Bank. 2015. World Development Indicators 2015. Washington, DC. © World Bank. Accessed May 12, 2015. http://wdi.worldbank.org/table/2.21#

4.4.7 Fetal Mortality Rate and Ratio

The **fetal mortality rate (FMR)** is defined as the number of fetal deaths in a specified population in a given year per 1,000 live births and fetal deaths. Note that the denominator in this case is the sum of all live births and fetal deaths in the same population in the same year. *Fetal mortality ratio* is defined as the number of fetal deaths divided by the total number of live births in a population in a given period.

Taber's Cyclopedic Medical Dictionary[7] defines *fetal death* as "spontaneous death of a fetus occurring after the 20th week of gestation." The Centers for Disease Control and Prevention (CDC) defines fetal death as follows:

> [D]eath prior to the complete expulsion or extraction from its mother of a product of human conception, irrespective of the duration of pregnancy and which is not an induced termination of pregnancy. The death is indicated by the fact that after such expulsion or extraction, the fetus does not breathe or show any other evidence of life, such as beating of the heart, pulsation of the umbilical cord, or definite movement of voluntary muscles.

Heartbeats are to be distinguished from transient cardiac contractions; respirations are to be distinguished from fleeting respiratory efforts or gasps.[8,9]

In the United States, approximately 1 million fetal deaths at any gestational age occur every year, with about 26,000 fetal deaths at 20 weeks of gestation or longer. State laws require the reporting of fetal deaths, and most states report fetal deaths of 20 weeks of gestation and/or 350 grams birthweight. Federal law also requires collection and publication of national fetal death data.[10]

$$FMR = \frac{\begin{array}{c}\text{Number of fetal deaths in a}\\\text{specified population}\\\text{in a given year}\end{array}}{\begin{array}{c}\text{Sum of all live births and fetal deaths}\\\text{in the same population}\\\text{in the same year}\end{array}} \times 1,000$$

4.4.8 Maternal Mortality Rate and Ratio

The **maternal mortality rate (MMR)** is the total number of deaths of women due to pregnancy-related (puerperal) causes per 100,000 live births in a specified population in a specified time period. Note that the WHO[11] uses the term *maternal mortality ratio*, whereas the CDC uses both terms.[12,13]

$$MMR = \frac{\begin{array}{c}\text{Number of deaths of}\\\text{women in a year from}\\\text{pregnancy-related causes}\end{array}}{\begin{array}{c}\text{Total number of live births}\\\text{in the same year}\end{array}} \times 100,000$$

Note that *maternal death* is defined by the WHO as follows:

[T]he death of a woman while pregnant or within 42 days of termination of pregnancy, irrespective of the duration and site of the pregnancy, from any cause related to or aggravated by the pregnancy or its management but not from accidental or incidental causes. To facilitate the identification of maternal deaths in circumstances in which cause of death attribution is inadequate, a new category has been introduced: Pregnancy-related death is defined as the death of a woman while pregnant or within 42 days of termination of pregnancy, irrespective of the cause of death.[2]

A *live birth* is defined by WHO[4] and by the CDC as follows:

[T]he complete expulsion or extraction from its mother of a product of conception, irrespective of the duration of the pregnancy, which, after such separation, breathes or shows any other evidence of life—e.g. beating of the heart, pulsation of the umbilical cord or definite movement of voluntary muscles—whether or not the umbilical cord has been cut or the placenta is attached. Each product of such a birth is considered live born.[8]

According to the CDC, in the United States, "the pregnancy-related mortality ratio" was 17.8 deaths per 100,000 live births in 2011, with 12.5 deaths per 100,000 live births for white women and 42.8 deaths per 100,000 live births for black women.[13] **FIGURE 4.7**

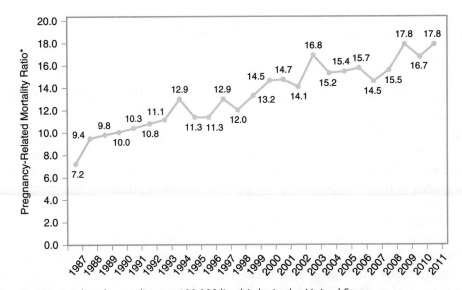

FIGURE 4.7 Trends in pregnancy-related mortality per 100,000 live births in the United States.

* Note: Number of pregnancy-related deaths per 100,000 live births per year.
Reproduced from: Centers for Disease Control and Prevention. (2017). Pregnancy mortality surveillance system. Retrieved from http://www.cdc.gov/reproductivehealth/maternalinfanthealth/pmss.html

shows trends in maternal mortality ratio in the United States from 1987 through 2011.

4.4.9 Case Fatality Rate

Usually discussed in the context of, but not strictly limited to, infectious diseases, **case fatality rate (CFR)** is the percentage or proportion of cases of a disease in a specified period of time that resulted in death. As is the case with several other definitions in this chapter, it can be argued whether this measure is a proportion, a ratio, or a rate because of the specification of time period. The CDC uses the term *case fatality ratio*. Regardless of the debate, it is important to understand that CFR is a measure of the fatality/lethality of a disease because it reports the frequency with which a particular disease proves to be fatal. For example, the CFR of rabies in unvaccinated humans is reported to be nearly 100%, and CFR of Ebola virus disease (EVD) is about 50%.

$$CFR = \frac{\begin{array}{c}\text{Number of deaths from disease X in a}\\\text{population in a given period}\end{array}}{\begin{array}{c}\text{Total number of cases of disease X in}\\\text{the same population in the same period}\end{array}} \times 100$$

4.4.10 Proportional Mortality

The **proportional mortality** is the percentage or proportion of all deaths in a population that occurred from a particular disease or condition during a specified period of time. For example, in 2011, there were 2,512,873 deaths in the United States, of which 122,777, or 4.9%, occurred from accidents (i.e., $[(122,777/2,512,873) \times 100]$).

$$\text{Proportional mortality} = \frac{\begin{array}{c}\text{Number of deaths in a}\\\text{population from a}\\\text{particular disease}\\\text{in a given period}\end{array}}{\begin{array}{c}\text{Total number of deaths}\\\text{from all causes in the}\\\text{same population in the}\\\text{same period}\end{array}} \times 100$$

4.4.11 Proportional Mortality Ratio

The **proportional mortality ratio (PMR)** is a ratio of the proportional mortality from a specific cause such as suicide or lung cancer in a subgroup of a population with the proportional mortality from the same cause in the general population.

$$PMR = \frac{\begin{array}{c}\text{Proportional mortality from disease}\\\text{A in an occupational group}\\\text{in a given period}\end{array}}{\begin{array}{c}\text{Proportional mortality from disease}\\\text{A in the entire population}\\\text{in the same period}\end{array}}$$

▶ 4.5 Other Commonly Reported Statistics

4.5.1 Crude Birth Rate

The **crude birth rate (CBR)**, sometimes also called the *live birth rate*, is the total number of live births per 1,000 population in a given year. As is the case with CDR, CBR is commonly reported because of the ease of estimation and the availability of reasonably accurate data on the number of births in a specified population in a given year.

The definition of a live birth used by the CDC[8] is provided earlier in the chapter, in the section on maternal mortality rate. In consideration of ongoing changes occurring in the size of any population throughout the year from deaths, births, and migration, by convention, midyear population is used as the denominator in calculating CBR.

$$CBR = \frac{\begin{array}{c}\text{Total number of live births}\\\text{in a given year}\end{array}}{\begin{array}{c}\text{Total average midyear population}\\\text{in the same year}\end{array}} \times 1,000$$

4.5.2 Life Expectancy at Birth

According to the World Bank, "Life expectancy at birth indicates the number of years a newborn infant would live if prevailing patterns of mortality at the time of its birth were to stay the same throughout its life."[14] Stated differently, **life expectancy at birth** in a given population represents the average number of years children born in a particular year are expected to live. In the United States, life expectancy at birth in 2013 was 79 years, whereas in Japan, Switzerland, and San Marino, it was 83 years. The United States in 2011 ranked 26th in life expectancy at birth among the 40 OECD + BRIICS (Organisation for Economic Cooperation and Development + Brazil, Russian Federation, India, Indonesia, China, and South Africa) countries.[15] Within the United States, there are also significant disparities in life expectancy at birth among the 50 states and between different racial groups, with white men and women, on average, enjoying several more years of life than black men and women. In 2010, life expectancy at birth for men in the United States was 76.3 years, and for women, it was 81.3 years. Asian American children born in the United States in 2010 with a life expectancy of 86.5 years on average could expect to live 7.6 years longer than white children born in the same year, and 11.9 years longer than black newborns. In the same year, Hawaii (81.3 years), Minnesota (81.1), Massachusetts (80.5 years), and New York (80.5) had the highest life expectancy at birth, whereas Mississippi (75 years), Alabama (75.4 years), West Virginia (75.4 years), and Louisiana (75.7 years) had the lowest.[16]

As shown in Table 4.3, life expectancy at birth in developing countries is considerably lower than that in developed countries. In most European developed countries, in 2013, average life expectancy was between 81 and 82 years. In Botswana, life expectancy at birth in 2013 was only 47 years, and in the Democratic Republic of Congo, Mozambique, Chad, and Angola, it was between 50 and 52 years. In 2013, "high-income" countries, on average, enjoyed a life expectancy at birth of 79 years, whereas the average for "low-income" countries was only 62 years.[14] In almost all countries, life expectancy at birth is greater for women than it is for men.

Among the 34 member countries of the OECD, the average life expectancy in excess of 80 years in 2011 represented an increase of 10 years since 1970. Women in OECD countries in 2011 could expect to live 5.5 years longer than men. **FIGURE 4.8** shows the relationship between life expectancy at birth and a country's healthcare spending per capita. The performance of the United States clearly falls short of most other OECD countries, all of which have much lower healthcare spending.[15]

4.5.3 Life Tables and Life Expectancy at Specific Age Intervals

There are several different types of life tables. A **cohort life table** starts at birth and follows the mortality experience of an actual group of individuals in consecutive calendar years until the last person in the cohort dies. For instance, a cohort life table might be developed for the birth cohort of 1900—that is, all individuals born in the year 1900. Usually starting with 100,000 individuals, this kind of life table would show life expectancy, mortality, and survivorship of individuals in each year of life. The table would also show the probability that a person of a given age will die before his or her next birthday. Development of a complete cohort life table is very difficult because it requires availability of accurate age-specific mortality data for the entire life span of that cohort. In many instances, development of such a table would require complex statistical projections into the future for a number of years because many of the individuals in the cohort might still be alive at the time of the development of such a table. For example, development of a cohort life table for the birth cohort of 1960 would mean that surviving members of the cohort in 2015 are only 55 years old, and many of them can be expected to live for another 30 or 40 years. Because

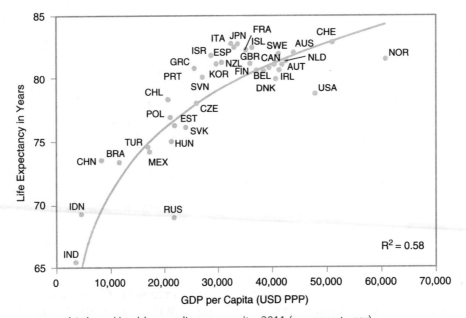

FIGURE 4.8 Life expectancy at birth and health spending per capita, 2011 (or nearest year).

complete data on the actual mortality experience of the entire cohort will not be available for the next 40 or 50 years, until the last person in the cohort dies, development of a cohort life table in 2015 for this cohort would necessitate projections of life expectancy based on statistical modeling for ages beyond 55 years.

Another kind of life table, called the *period life table*, is based on a hypothetical cohort of newborns to whom ASDRs of a known population in a given year are applied to derive the expected number of deaths and survivorship at each age interval. In other words, the period life table hypothetically follows a cohort of newborns into the future with the assumption that at each age, they will experience the ASDR of the known or reference population. To help countries that may not have up-to-date and accurate systems of vital statistics, the United Nations develops *model life tables*, which combine life tables and age-specific

mortality data from a number of countries where such records are routinely maintained.

TABLE 4.4 provides an example of a period life table based on 2010 ASDRs in the United States. It shows the probability of death for men and women at each age, the number of individuals surviving to the next age, and the remaining expected years of life at each age. This table is further discussed in the section on standardization of age-specific mortality and morbidity rates.

4.5.4 Observed and Relative Survival Rates

Observed survival rate, also known as **crude survival rate**, refers to the proportion or percentage of cases of a disease in which the person survives for a specified period of time (say, 5 or 10 years) regardless of the cause of death. In other words, it is the probability of living for the specified period (say, 5 years)

TABLE 4.4 2010 Period Life Table from the U.S. Social Security Administration

	Period Life Table, 2010					
	Male			Female		
Exact Age	Death Probability [a]	Number of Lives [b]	Period Life Expectancy	Death Probability [a]	Number of Lives [b]	Period Life Expectancy
0	0.006680	100,000	76.10	0.005562	100,000	80.94
1	0.000436	99,332	75.62	0.000396	99,444	80.39
2	0.000304	99,289	74.65	0.000214	99,404	79.43
–	–	–	–	–	–	–
10	0.000082	99,155	66.74	0.000090	99,304	71.50
11	0.000086	99,147	65.75	0.000096	99,295	70.51
12	0.000125	99,138	64.76	0.000111	99,285	69.52
61	0.011592	85,076	20.57	0.007046	90,994	23.49
62	0.012444	84,090	19.81	0.007686	90,352	22.65
–	–	–	–	–	–	–
71	0.026364	71,584	13.40	0.017882	81,397	15.59
72	0.028808	69,697	12.75	0.019693	79,941	14.87

(continues)

TABLE 4.4 2010 Period Life Table from the U.S. Social Security Administration						*(continued)*
Period Life Table, 2010						
	Male			**Female**		
Exact Age	**Death Probability** [a]	**No. of Lives** [b]	**Period Life Expectancy**	**Death Probability** [a]	**No. of Lives** [b]	**Period Life Expectancy**
81	0.067698	46,884	7.60	0.048808	60,580	9.03
82	0.074923	43,710	7.11	0.054434	57,624	8.47
91	0.186543	14,250	3.70	0.147181	24,938	4.45
92	0.205115	11,592	3.44	0.163161	21,268	4.13
101	0.374819	562	1.99	0.322673	1,888	2.31
102	0.393560	351	1.88	0.342033	1,279	2.17
111	0.610541	1	1.09	0.577858	7	1.17
112	0.641068	0	1.02	0.612530	3	1.08
117	0.818183	0	0.71	0.818183	0	0.71
118	0.859092	0	0.66	0.859092	0	0.66

[a] Probability of dying within 1 year.

[b] Number of survivors out of 100,000 born alive.

Note: The period life expectancy at a given age for 2010 represents the average number of years of life remaining if a group of persons at that age were to experience the mortality rates for 2010 over the course of their remaining life.

The *period life expectancy* at a given age is the average remaining number of years expected prior to death for a person at that exact age using the mortality rates for 2010 over the course of his or her remaining life.

Modified from: The U.S. Social Security Administration. Available from: http://www.ssa.gov/oact/STATS/table4c6.html

if a person has disease X, regardless of whether he or she dies in that period from disease X or some other disease. The time period of interest varies depending on the nature of disease. In some diseases, such as EVD, the survival rate is only about 50%, and victims either fully recover or die from the disease in a matter of days. Therefore, in this case, the period of interest cannot be 5 or 10 years. On the other hand, in diseases such as prostate cancer, short-term survival is nearly 100%, and patients can live for a number of years before dying from some other cause or finally succumbing to the disease. In such instances, survival rates are often expressed as a 1-year, 5-year, or 10-year survival rate. For example, 5-year survival rate of patient with stage II breast cancer in the United States in 2015 was 93%, and that of stage IV patients was 22%. In pancreatic cancer, stage IA patients have a 5-year survival rate of only 14%, and the prognosis for stage III patients is even worse, with a 5-year survival rate of 3%.[17] In these examples, the survival rates are not adjusted for the background or underlying risk of dying from some other cause in the same period. To get a more accurate estimation of surviving the disease of interest, another rate called *relative survival rate* is derived by adjusting for the risk of dying from some other cause in the same period and represents net survival "in the absence of other causes of death." As a rule of thumb, relative survival rate is always as high as or higher than the observed survival rate.

▶ 4.6 Adjustment or Standardization of Rates

Crude birth, death, or morbidity rates are useful summary statistics as snapshots of the health status of a given population during a specified time period. However, comparison of crude rates of two or more populations in the same time period (e.g., 2015) or of the same population in different time periods (e.g., Florida residents in 1975 vs. 2015) can be misleading for two reasons.

First, individuals are not equally distributed across various age groups in any population. That is, the number of children, adolescents, adults, and the elderly are neither equal in a given population nor the same in a specific age group in two different populations. For example, in some developing countries, such as Niger and Afghanistan, children younger than age 15 years may constitute as much as 40%–50% of the total population, and individuals older than age 65 years may constitute only 3%–4% of the population. In contrast, in some developed countries, such as Japan or Sweden, children younger than age 15 may constitute only 15%–18% of the population, and individuals older than age 65 may constitute 20%–25% of the total population. Demographic data for various countries are available from sources such as the World Bank, the WHO, and the NationMaster website.[18] The U.S. demographic structure in 2013 indicated that those between the ages of 0 and 14 years constituted 20% and those aged 65 years and older constituted 13.9% of the total

population.[18] In July 2016, 22.8% of U.S. population was younger than 18 years and 15.2% was 65 years or older.

Second, the risk of birth, death, or disease is strongly associated with age and is not equally distributed across all age groups in any population. This point is well illustrated in Table 4.4. For each age group, the table shows the probability of death within 1 year and the probability of remaining years of life for both males and females. Starting with a cohort of 100,000 hypothetical newborns of each gender, Table 4.4 successively shows the numbers that are projected to survive to the next year. Note that for both male and female children, the probability of death within 1 year is higher below age 1, after which it declines and is lowest at age 10. After age 10, the probability of death within the next year for both male and female individuals continues to increase with each passing year.

Although race and socioeconomic factors also affect the risk of health-related events such as death and disease, the most important element that affects the probability of these events is the age distribution of the population. For example, only women of childbearing age are exposed to the risk of disease and death associated with pregnancy and childbirth, and the elderly in a population are at a much greater risk of stroke or death from cancer. Generally, the risk of death and disease is much greater for those at the extremes of age—the very young and the very old. For the very young, the risk of death and disease diminishes with age. For the elderly, however, the risk of death and disease steadily increases with advancing age. **TABLE 4.5** shows

TABLE 4.5 Life Expectancy by Age in Men and Women						
Age in Years	**70**	**75**	**80**	**85**	**90**	**95**
Men	*Life Expectancy*					
Healthy	18.0	14.2	10.8	7.9	5.8	4.3
Average	12.4	9.3	6.7	4.7	3.2	2.3
Frail	6.7	4.9	3.3	2.2	1.5	1.0
Women	*Life Expectancy*					
Healthy	21.3	17.0	13.0	9.6	6.8	4.8
Average	15.7	11.9	8.6	5.9	3.9	2.7
Frail	9.5	6.8	4.6	2.9	1.8	1.7

life expectancy for men and women in three categories of health status from ages 70 to 95 years. Note that healthy men and women at age 70 have a life expectancy of 18.0 and 21.3 years, respectively. At age 95, however, life expectancy for men and women even in good health diminishes to only 4.3 and 4.8 years. In comparison, frail men and women at age 70, on average, can expect to live no more than 6.7 and 9.5 years, respectively.

Another example of differential distribution of risk associated with age and gender is related to homicidal deaths. As shown in **FIGURE 4.9**, the risk of death from homicide is much greater for men between the ages of 10 and 24 years than any other age group.[19] As such, populations that have high proportions of elderly or young children are likely to report higher morbidity and mortality rates in comparison with populations that comprise higher proportions of young adults and middle-aged individuals.

Because death and disease unequally affect different segments of all populations, for any comparisons to be valid, it is necessary to take into account the differences in the composition of the populations being compared. Simple comparisons between populations without adjusting for differences in age, gender, racial, or socioeconomic composition can lead to erroneous conclusions. For example, see **TABLE 4.6** comparing CDRs in hypothetical populations A and B. Note that although the two populations are exactly the same size (1 million each), the distribution of individuals in

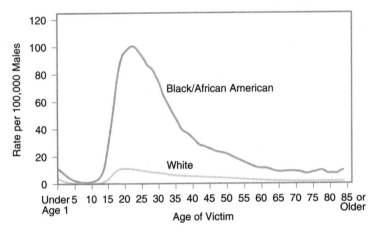

FIGURE 4.9 Male homicide rates by victim age and race, 2002–2011.

Reproduced from: Smith EL, Cooper A. Homicide in the U.S. known to law enforcement, 2011. Patterns & Trends U.S. Department of Justice, Office of Justice Programs, Bureau of Justice Statistics. 2013. Available at: http://www.bjs.gov/content/pub/pdf/hus11.pdf

TABLE 4.6 Calculation of Crude Death Rates in Two Hypothetical Populations, A and B

Age in Years	No. of Individuals	Age Composition of Population A	No. of Deaths	Death Rate*	No. of Individuals	Age Composition of Population B	No. of Deaths	Death Rate*
	Population A				**Population B**			
<15	400,000	40%	2,000	500	200,000	20%	600	300
15 to <45	300,000	30%	3,000	1,000	250,000	25%	1,500	600
45 to <65	250,000	25%	3,750	1,500	350,000	35%	4,200	1,200
≥65	50,000	5%	1,000	2,000	200,000	20%	5,000	2,500
Total	1,000,000	100%	9,750	975	1,000,000	100%	11,300	1,130
Crude death rate of population A				**975**	**Crude death rate of population B**			**1,130**

* per 100,000 population.

various age groups in the two populations is quite different. Population A largely consists of young people, which is the situation in some developing countries (e.g., Niger), whereas population B has a much older population that is reflective of demographic situation in some developed countries (e.g., Japan). In population B, age groups <15 years, 15 to <45 years, and 45 to <65 years experienced much lower ASDRs per 100,000 than those in the same age groups in population A. Those aged ≥65 in population B, however, experienced a much higher ASDR (i.e., 2,500 per 100,000 in B, as opposed to 2,000 per 100,000 in A). Also, note that CDRs for the two populations are different; the rate of 1,130 per 100,000 in B is considerably higher than the CDR of 975 per 100,000 in A. This is because in population B, the ASDR of 2,500 for those aged ≥65, as well as the proportion of those in this age group (20%), is much higher than population A, where only 5% of the total population is in this age bracket. Note that the CDR is nothing but the weighted average of ASDRs in a population. For population B, it would be $(.2 \times 300) + ([.25 \times 600)] + (.35 \times 1200) + (.2 \times 2500) = 1,130$. The greater proportion of those aged ≥65 (20% as opposed to 5%) and a much higher ASDR in this age group (2,500 as opposed to 2,000) greatly affected the CDR in population B and made it considerably greater than the CDR in population A (1,130 vs. 975).

To allow fair and valid comparisons of morbidity and mortality rates in different populations, two different methods have been developed to obtain *adjusted* or *standardized* rates that take into account differences in the composition of populations being compared. These methods are commonly known as *direct standardization* and *indirect standardization*.

4.6.1 Direct Standardization

In contrast to a crude rate, such as CDR, a standardized or age-adjusted rate is a summary statistic that allows a fair and appropriate comparison of overall mortality or morbidity rates of two or more populations (e.g., populations A and B) that may be quite different in their age composition. Through a statistical transformation process described next, **direct standardization** eliminates the effects of differences in the composition of the populations being compared. The transformation process involves arbitrary identification of a reference or "standard" population whose composition in terms of age groups or other characteristics such as gender and race is known. In common practice, U.S. total population is used as the standard or reference population to compare county, state, or regional mortality and morbidity rates. Typically, census data from the most recent census year are

used for this purpose. For international comparisons, total world population in a given year may be used as the reference population. Data for international comparisons are generally available from sources such as the World Bank and the WHO.

The statistical transformation process to obtain age-, sex-, or race-standardized mortality or morbidity rates requires knowledge of age, sex, or race-specific rates in the populations being compared as well as the age structure of the standard population. We will use age-specific mortality rates in two hypothetical populations, A and B, to demonstrate the statistical transformation procedures for direct standardization based on age distribution. The same procedures can be followed to carry out standardization based on race or sex distribution in two or more populations. Typically, direct age standardization or adjustment is carried out in the following sequential steps:

1. Age-specific mortality rates of the populations being compared (e.g., A and B) are applied to the corresponding age groups of the standard population (e.g., U.S. population) to obtain the expected number of deaths in each age group of the standard population.
2. The expected number of deaths in each age group of the standard population thus derived are aggregated to obtain the total number of expected deaths in the overall standard population.
3. The total number of expected deaths in the standard population is then converted into a rate (per 1,000 or per 100,000 population).

In essence, we first answer the question, *How many people in each age group in the standard population will die if they died at the same rate as those in the corresponding age group in population A or B?* Then, we aggregate the expected number of deaths for various age groups to derive the mortality rate for the entire standard population. In statistical terms, the overall mortality rate obtained for the entire standard population is the weighted average of all ASDRs. Based on hypothetical data, **TABLE 4.7** shows the age distribution of a standard population S and the original ASDRs of populations A and B. Table 4.7 also shows formulas to derive the expected number of deaths in each of the age groups in the standard population, and the standardized mortality rates for both populations. Note that, as compared with the CDRs of 975 and 1,130 derived in Table 4.6, the age-standardized rates for the standard population in Table 4.7 indicate that standardized mortality rates for population A are higher than those for population B (1,200 vs. 1,005). **FIGURE 4.10** shows a conceptual model of direct standardization.

TABLE 4.7 Example of Direct Age Standardization of Mortality Rates in Hypothetical Populations A and B Using the Age Structure of a Standard Population S

Age in Years	Standard Population (S)		Age-Specific Death rates* in Population A (X)	Expected No. of Deaths in the Standard Population S (X/100,000)	Age-Specific Death rates* in Population B (Y)	Expected No. of Deaths in the Standard Population S (Y/100,000)
<15	20%	200,000	500	1,000	300	600
15 to <45	35%	350,000	1,000	3,500	600	2,100
45 to <65	30%	300,000	1,500	4,500	1,200	3,600
≥65	15%	150,000	2,000	3,000	2,500	3,750
Total	100%	1,000,000		12,000		10,050

Directly age-standardized mortality rates*: population A = 1,200, population B = 1,005

* per 100,000 population.

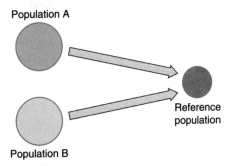

FIGURE 4.10 Conceptual model of direct standardization.
Direct standardization: Age-, race-, or sex-stratified rates of population A and population B are applied to the reference population.

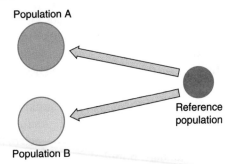

FIGURE 4.11 Conceptual model of indirect standardization.
Indirect standardization: Age-, race-, or sex-stratified rates of the reference population are applied to population A and population B.

4.6.2 Indirect Standardization

As shown in **FIGURE 4.11**, indirect standardization, or *indirect age adjustment*, is the opposite of direct standardization. Remember that in direct standardization, ASDRs of the populations A and B were applied to the standard or reference population to answer the question, *What would be the expected number of deaths in the standard population if individuals in various age groups in the standard population died at the rates observed in population A or population B?* In indirect standardization, the process is reversed. ASDRs of the standard population are applied to the corresponding age groups in the populations of interest to answer the question, *What would be the expected number of deaths in population A or in population B if individuals in various age groups in this population died at the rates observed in the standard population?* **TABLE 4.8** provides an example of indirect standardization using population S (say, the U.S. population) as the standard population. Note that in comparison with the CDRs of 975 and 1,130 obtained in Table 4.6, the indirectly age-standardized rates for populations A and B are now 835 and 1,175.

Remember also that the choice of standard population in both direct and indirect standardization is arbitrary. So far, in the hypothetical examples, we have used a third population (say, the 2010 U.S. population) as the

TABLE 4.8 Example of Indirect Age Standardization of Mortality Rates in Hypothetical Populations A and B Using the Age Structure of a Standard Population S

Age in Years	Death rates* in the Standard Population (S)	Age Composition of Population A (X)	Expected No. of Deaths in Population A X (S/100,000)	Age Composition of Population B (Y)	Expected No. of Deaths in Population B Y (S/100,000)
<15	400	400,000	1,600	200,000	800
15 to <45	800	300,000	2,400	250,000	2,000
45 to <65	1,300	250,000	3,250	350,000	4,550
≥65	2,200	50,000	1,100	200,000	4,400
Total		1,000,000	8,350	1,000,000	11,750

Indirectly age-standardized mortality rates*: population A = 835, population B = 1,175

*per 100,000 population.

TABLE 4.9 Example of Indirect Age Standardization of Mortality Rate in Hypothetical Population B Using Population A as the Standard Population

Age in Years	Age Composition of Population A	Actual No. of Deaths in Population A	Death rate* in Population A (D)	Age Composition of Population B (N)	Expected No. of Deaths in Population B N (D/100,000)	Actual No. of Deaths in Population B
<15	400,000	2,000	500	20,000	100	60
15 to <45	300,000	3,000	1,000	25,000	250	150
45 to <65	250,000	3,750	1,500	35,000	525	420
≥65	50,000	1,000	2,000	20,000	400	500
Total	1,000,000	9,750	975	100,000	1,275	1,130

Indirectly age-standardized mortality rate* in population B = 1,275

*per 100,000 population.

reference population. When comparisons are to be made between populations such that one population is much bigger than the other, it is quite reasonable to use the larger of the two populations as the standard population. For example, if mortality or morbidity rates of Vermont (population ~622,000) are to be compared with those of New York (population ~19.5 million), the population of New York can be used as the standard population. To illustrate this point, in **TABLE 4.9** we use population A as the standard population and apply its ASDRs to population B that we now assume to be only 100,000 rather than 1 million.

4.6.3 Standardized Mortality Ratio

Standardized mortality ratio (SMR) is a measure of whether people in the population of interest are dying at a higher or lower rate as compared with the standard or reference population. It is derived by dividing the actual death rate in the population of interest (population A or B in the previous examples) by the expected death rate in the same population derived through indirect standardization. For example, the actual (crude) death rates in populations A and B were, respectively, 975 and 1,130 (Table 4.6), whereas the indirectly standardized expected death rates were 835 and 1,175 (Table 4.8). Thus, the SMR for populations A and B would be as follows.

SMR for population A $= 975/835 =$ **1.17** (or 117%)

SMR for population B $= 1,130/1,175 =$ **0.96** (or 96%)

Therefore, based on the available data, the death rate in population A is 17% higher than the standard population, whereas that in population B is 4% less than the standard population. In other words, the actual number of deaths in population A is about 17% greater than the number of deaths that would have been expected based on the death rate in the standard population. Likewise, the actual number of deaths in population B is about 4% less than the expected number if people in this population had died at the same rate as the standard population. The SMR for population B based on indirect standardization carried out in Table 4.9 by using population A as the standard population would be as follows:

SMR for population B $= 1,130/1,275 =$ **0.89** (or 89%)

This means that the death rate in population B is about 11% less than if people in population B had died at the same rate as those in population A.

▶ Exercises 4.1

Exercise 1. Create a 25-year graph similar to Figure 4.5 showing point prevalence at the end of each year using an incidence rate of 100, a mortality rate of 25%, and a full recovery rate of 5% per year. Also, show lines for incidence rate and mortality rate.

Exercise 2. Create a 20-year graph similar to Figure 4.5 showing point prevalence at the end of each year using an incidence rate of 100, a mortality rate of 35%, and a full recovery rate of 5% per year. Also, show lines for incidence rate and mortality rate.

Exercise 3. Comment on the slope of the line showing point prevalence in the two graphs built in Exercises 1 and 2. Explain what happens to point prevalence given different incidence, mortality, and recovery rates in the population.

🔎 CASE STUDY 4.1: Example of Cumulative Incidence

Modified from: Lopes RD, Garacholou SM, Holmes DN, Thomas L, Wang TY, Roe MT, Peterson ED, Alexander KP. Cumulative incidence of death and rehospitalization among the elderly in the first year after NSTEMI. AM J Med. 2015;128(6):582–590. Copyright © 2015, with permission from Elsevier.

It is well known that age is often associated with health outcomes. In a study of 36,711 patients aged 65 and older who had previously had a myocardial infarction,* researchers examined the cumulative incidence of hospital readmission in the 1-year period after the initial or index episode of myocardial infarction. They also examined the cumulative incidence of death in each age group in the 1-year period after the initial myocardial infarction. **TABLE 4.10** shows the cumulative incidence rates of overall hospital readmissions as well as cause-specific hospital readmissions whether related or unrelated to cardiovascular disease.

* Non-ST-segment-elevation myocardial infarction.

Questions

Question 1. In this study, what effect, if any, did age have on the cumulative incidence of death?

Question 2. Did age have any effect on overall and cause-specific cumulative incidence of hospital readmissions?

Question 3. Was there a noteworthy difference or pattern in the cumulative incidence rates for CVD-related and non-CVD-related (cause-specific) hospital readmissions?

TABLE 4.10 Cumulative Incidence of Hospital Readmission and Death Within 1 Year After the Initial/Index Episode of Myocardial Infarction

	Age 65–79 (n = 21,586)	Age 80–84 (n = 7,324)	Age 85–89 (n = 5,007)	Age ≥90 (n = 2,794)
Overall readmissions	52.7%	59.6%	59.5%	56.5%
CVD*-unrelated readmissions	32.4%	38.4%	38.0%	34.5%
CVD*-related readmissions	38.4%	43.2%	43.2%	39.6%
MI/stroke† readmissions	8.6%	12.1%	13.6%	14.0%
Deaths	13.3%	23.6%	33.6%	45.5%

* CVD: cardiovascular disease.
† MI/stroke is a subset of readmissions related to CVD.
Reprinted from: Lopes RD, Garacholou SM, Holmes DN, Thomas L, Wang TY, Roe MT, Peterson ED, Alexander KP. Cumulative incidence of death and rehospitalization among the elderly in the first year after NSTEMI. AM J Med. 2015;128(6):582–590. Copyright © 2015, with permission from Elsevier.

🔎 *CASE STUDY 4.2: Example of a Prevalence Study*

Modified from: Mdodo R, Frazier EL, Dube SR, Mattson CL, Sutton MY, Brooks JT, Skarbinski J. Cigarette smoking prevalence among adults with HIV compared with the general adult population in the United States. Ann Intern Med. 2015;162(5):335–344. Copyright © 2016 American College of Physicians. All rights reserved. Reprinted with permission of American College of Physicians, Inc.

This study compared the prevalence of current cigarette smoking in adult HIV patients receiving medical care with the prevalence in the general U.S. adult population. The researchers used data from two nationally representative cross-sectional surveys: A sample of 4,271 adult HIV patients who participated in the Medical Monitoring Project, and a sample of 27,731 adults in the general population who participated in the National Health Interview Survey. The data on smoking were adjusted for the probability of being selected to participate in the survey, as well as for nonresponse. **TABLE 4.11** shows adjusted prevalence of current smokers stratified by age, sex, race, education, and income.

Questions

Question 1. How did age, race, sex, and education affect smoking prevalence in HIV- and non-HIV-positive adults in this study?

Question 2. What might explain higher smoking prevalence in HIV-positive adults in each demographic category of study participants?

TABLE 4.11 Adjusted Prevalence and Adjusted Prevalence Difference of Current Cigarette Smoking Among Adults with HIV Who Received Medical Care and the General Adult Population in the United States in 2009

Characteristic	Adjusted* Current Smoking Prevalence		Adjusted Prevalence Difference
	HIV Adults % (A)	General Adult Population % (B)	(A − B)
Total	37.6	20.6	17.0
Age			
18–29 years	35.7	23.6	12.1
30–39 years	39.2	24.9	14.3

TABLE 4.11 Adjusted Prevalence and Adjusted Prevalence Difference of Current Cigarette Smoking Among Adults with HIV Who Received Medical Care and the General Adult Population in the United States in 2009   *(continued)*

Age			
40–49 years	43.0	25.0	18.0
≥50 years	35.6	15.5	20.1
Sex			
Male	40.9	23.3	17.6
Female	34.6	18.0	16.6
Race			
White	40.3	23.7	16.6
Black	34.7	19.3	15.4
Hispanic	25.9	10.6	15.3
Education			
<High school	48.5	30.2	18.3
High school	43.0	27.9	15.1
>High school	32.3	14.9	17.4
Income			
≥Poverty level	35.4	19.6	15.8
<Poverty level	47.8	28.7	19.1

*Adjusted in multivariate logistic regression model for age, sex, race, educational level, and poverty level.
Modified from: Mdodo R, Frazier EL, Dube SR, Mattson CL, Sutton MY, Brooks JT, Skarbinski J. Cigarette smoking prevalence among adults with HIV compared with the general adult population in the United States. Ann Intern Med. 2015;162(5):335–344. Copyright © 2016 American College of Physicians. All rights reserved. Reprinted with permission of American College of Physicians, Inc.

▶ 4.7 Summary

In this chapter, we have described various epidemiologic measures of population health. With the help of these measures and available data from various sources, healthcare managers can develop a comprehensive morbidity and mortality profile of populations they serve. In the event that the population of interest is small, rates of a larger population, such as the state or a larger county, can be applied to the smaller population with techniques such as indirect standardization.

References

1. Merriam-Webster [Internet]. Ratio. 2017 [cited 2017 Jun 12]. Available from: https://www.merriam-webster.com/dictionary/ratio
2. Merriam-Webster [Internet]. Proportion. 2017 [cited 2017 Oct 24]. Available from: https://www.merriam-webster.com/dictionary/proportion
3. Merriam-Webster [Internet]. Rate. 2017 [cited 2017 Oct 24]. Available from: https://www.merriam-webster.com/dictionary/rate
4. World Health Organization. Indicator definitions and metadata. WHO Statistical Information System (WHOSIS); 2015 [cited 2017 Jun 12]. Available from: http://www.who.int/whosis/indicatordefinitions/en/
5. Centers for Disease Control and Prevention. United States Cancer Statistics: 1999–2011 Incidence. WONDER Online Database. United States Department of Health and Human Services, Centers for Disease Control and Prevention and National Cancer Institute; 2014 [cited 2015 May 13]. Available from: http://wonder.cdc.gov/cancer-v2011.html

6. Hoyert DL, Xu J. Deaths: preliminary data for 2011. National Vital Statistics Reports. 61(6). Hyattsville, MD: National Center for Health Statistics; 2012.

7. Venes D, editor. Fetal death. Taber's cyclopedic medical dictionary [Internet]. 23rd ed. Philadelphia: FA Davis; 2017. [cited 2018 Jan 19]. Available from: http://online.statref.com/document.aspx?FxId=57&DocID=1&SessionID=277A25DHLOXQVEWH#H&7&ChaptersTab&OkcFmw44Bg40BiG95XebXw%3d%3d&a8010&57

8. Kowaleski J. State definitions and reporting requirements for live births, fetal deaths, and induced terminations of pregnancy (1997 rev.). Hyattsville, MD: National Center for Health Statistics; 1997.

9. Barfield WD, Committee on Fetus and Newborn. Standard terminology for fetal, infant, and perinatal deaths. Pediatrics. 2011;128(1):177–181 [cited 2018 July 3]. Available from: http://pediatrics.aappublications.org/content/128/1/177.full.pdf+html

10. Centers for Disease Control and Prevention. National Vital Statistics System: fetal deaths. 2017 [cited 2017 Jun 13]. Available from: https://www.cdc.gov/nchs/nvss/fetal_death.htm

11. World Health Organization. Maternal mortality ratio. 2015 [cited 2017 Jun 13]. Available from: http://www.who.int/healthinfo/statistics/indmaternalmortality/en/

12. Hoyert DL. Maternal mortality and related concepts. National Center for Health Statistics. Vital Health Stat 3. 2007;33 [cited 2018 July 3]. Available from: http://www.cdc.gov/nchs/data/series/sr_03/sr03_033.pdf

13. Centers for Disease Control and Prevention. Pregnancy related deaths: 2015 [cited 2017 Jun 14]. Available from: http://www.cdc.gov/reproductivehealth/maternalinfanthealth/pmss.html

14. World Bank. 2015 [cited 2018 July 3]. Available at: http://databank.worldbank.org/data/Views/Metadata/MetadataWidget.aspx?Name=Life expectancy at birth, total (years)&Code=SP.DYN.LE00.IN&Type=S&ReqType=Metadata&ddlSelectedValue=&ReportID=37330&ReportType=Table

15. OECD. Health at a glance 2013: OECD indicators. OECD Publishing. 2013 [cited June 11, 2017]. Available from: https://www.oecd.org/els/health-systems/Health-at-a-Glance-2013.pdf

16. Kaiser Family Foundation. State health facts: life expectancy at birth in years. 2009 [cited 2017 Jul 24]. Available from: http://www.kff.org/other/state-indicator/life-expectancy/?currentTimeframe=0&sortModel=%7B%22colId%22:%22Location%22,%22sort%22:%22asc%22%7D

17. American Cancer Society. Breast cancer survival rate. 2017 [cited 2017 Jun 14]. Available from: http://www.cancer.org/cancer/breastcancer/detailedguide/breast-cancer-survival-by-stage

18. NationMaster. 2015 [cited 2017 Jun 14]. Available from: http://www.nationmaster.com/country-info/stats/People/Population

19. David-Ferdon C, Dahlberg LL, Kegler SR. Homicide rates among persons aged 10–24 years: United States, 1981–2010. MMWR Morb Mortal Wkly Rep. 2013;62(27):545–548.

CHAPTER 5

Descriptive Epidemiology

LEARNING OBJECTIVES

Having mastered the materials in this chapter, the student will be able to:

1. Analyze, evaluate, and report the demographic, geographic, and temporal distribution of health problems in communities and populations.
2. Interpret and use for health services planning data reported in descriptive epidemiological studies.
3. Explain the purpose of geographic information systems (GISs) and interpret the results of studies examining the interaction of multiple variables in the context of their spatial distribution.

CHAPTER OUTLINE

5.1 Introduction
5.2 Person
    5.2.1 Age
    5.2.2 Race
    5.2.3 Sex
    5.2.4 Occupation
    5.2.5 Socioeconomic Status
    5.2.6 Marital Status
5.3 Place
    5.3.1 Geographic Information Systems (GISs) and Descriptive Epidemiology

5.4 Time
5.5 Types of Epidemiologic Investigations
5.6 Descriptive Epidemiologic Studies
    5.6.1 Case Reports and Case Series
    5.6.2 Cross-Sectional Studies
Case Study 5.1 – Example of a Case Series Report
Case Study 5.2 – Example of a Cross-Sectional Study
Case Study 5.3 – Example of a Cross-Sectional Study
5.7 Summary

KEY TERMS

Case report
Cross-sectional study
Geographic information systems
Health geography

Marital status
Medical geography
Occupation
Person

Place
Race
Socioeconomic status

▶ 5.1 Introduction

To estimate the need for different kinds of services and to conduct market analysis, healthcare managers need to understand the nature of health problems and the characteristics of patient populations in their service area. For example, knowing the magnitude and distribution of problems such as Alzheimer's disease, hepatitis B, or substance abuse in their service area, managers can assess the need for screening, vaccination, detoxification, and rehabilitation services.

Descriptive epidemiology deals with the distributive component in the definition of epidemiology—that is, it allows us to understand the distribution of disease in one or more populations or localities. Because diseases are not randomly distributed, understanding the distribution of a disease in people (i.e., person), place, and time is important to develop hypotheses about its etiology, understand the magnitude of the problem, plan medical and nonmedical interventions, and estimate the need for health services. Descriptive epidemiology answers questions about *who*, *where*, and *when* in the distribution or occurrence of a disease. To answer these questions, decision makers, analysts, or policy makers can use existing data from various sources, or they may need to conduct targeted investigations to collect necessary information about the disease of interest. Either way, epidemiological studies that are done to describe the distribution of a disease or health problem are accordingly known as *descriptive studies*.

In this chapter, we will first discuss the importance of understanding the distribution of diseases in *person*, *place*, and *time*, and then describe how such information is gathered through descriptive studies such as *case reports* and *cross-sectional studies* so that it can be used by healthcare providers, administrators, and policy makers.

▶ 5.2 Person

Demographic characteristics of a **person** such as age, race, sex, occupation, and income allow us to group people into different categories. Apart from other societal interests in such groupings, these characteristics are important because people in one group may be more or less susceptible to one disease or another in comparison with some other group. The reasons for such susceptibilities or protections are varied and can result from differences in genetic makeup, the extent of exposure to risk factors, and levels of resistance or immunity against diseases. In the 18th and 19th centuries, recognition of an association between a par-

ticular vocation and some disease—despite a lack of understanding of the underlying pathophysiology—led people to coin names for diseases in relation to specific occupations. Names such as *wool sorter's disease* for anthrax, *chimney sweep's disease* for squamous cell carcinoma of the scrotum, *coal miner's disease* or *black lung disease* for pneumoconiosis, *nun's disease* for breast cancer, and *phossy jaw* for necrosis of the jaw bone (due to the deposition of white phosphorus in London match workers in the late 19th and early 20th century) are just a few examples.

5.2.1 Age

The age of a person has a strong positive or negative association with the risk of many diseases. Frequently, there are physiologic, genetic, or behavioral explanations for these age-related associations. Because of a lower physiologic reserve and potentially lower immunity, people at the two ends of life—the very young and the very old—are at risk of higher frequency and greater severity of some diseases, particularly infectious diseases. For behavioral and lifestyle reasons, health problems resulting from injuries and violence are more common during the teen years and young adulthood. Clearly, not everyone in an age group associated with a higher risk of some disease falls victim to that disease, and not everyone in another age group would be totally immune to the same disease; it just means that the statistical probability for that disease is higher or lower in one age group as compared with another.

Just like the graying of hair with age, some diseases, such as cataract of the eye lens, loss of hearing, incontinence, osteoporosis and resulting hip fractures, osteoarthritis in joints, or enlargement of the prostate gland in men, are linked with aging. The incidence of diseases such as Alzheimer's disease and congestive heart failure increases logarithmically with age.[1] Children or even most young adults are unlikely to develop these problems. On the other hand, children are more susceptible to certain infections because they have not been previously exposed and developed immunity against those organisms. Similarly, certain kinds of cancers are found more often in children, while others seem to strike later in life. We do not yet fully understand the reasons for such age-related associations. Nevertheless, knowing the age of a person gives us clues about the probability of a given disease and helps clinicians in making a differential diagnosis or rule out certain disorders.

In public health, morbidity and mortality data are routinely stratified by age groups in recognition of the fact that diseases differentially afflict people of different ages, and pooling of data for all age groups masks this important observation. Because populations differ in their age composition, age stratification is also important for comparing morbidity and mortality rates in different population groups. Pooling of data for all ages can give distorted information and lead to erroneous conclusions.

5.2.2 Race

The impact of genetic makeup and the role of **race** or ethnicity as one of the social determinants of health are discussed in more detail elsewhere in the book, in the context of individual and population health determinants. Here, it is important to note that although race or ethnicity independently affects the risk of some diseases, race or ethnicity is also intertwined with other social determinants of health, such as income and education. In the context of its independent impact on health—that is, separated from socioeconomic factors such as income and education—race can be viewed as a surrogate for the genetic makeup of individuals. This is true even though there is more genetic variation within racial groups (intragroup variation) than there is between racial groups (intergroup variation).

Because of distinct genetic traits or mutations passed down the generations within racial groups, the genetic makeup of a person determines the likelihood of inheriting genes or genetic mutations linked with various diseases. For example, Ashkenazi Jewish women, as compared with the rest of the female population, are at a higher risk of having hereditary BRCA1 and BRCA2 gene mutations, putting them at a higher risk of breast cancer. Ashkenazi Jewish ancestry is also linked with increased risk of a number of other diseases, such as Gaucher disease, glycogen storage disease 1A, and Tay-Sachs disease. Blacks or African Americans are known to have a much higher risk of diabetes, hypertension, and hereditary disorders such as sickle cell anemia, beta thalassemia, and glucose-6-phosphate dehydrogenase deficiency.

Because of the higher risk for various diseases, in combination with various social determinants of morbidity and mortality, disease and death rates in various groups can differ substantially in the same country, region, or county. For example, **FIGURE 5.1** shows age-adjusted death rates in blacks and whites in the United States from 1980 to 2013. Although the overall death rate declined substantially in both groups over this period, it has consistently remained higher in the black population.[2] The age-adjusted death rate for whites in 2013 was 731.0 deaths per 100,000, whereas for blacks, it was 860.8 per 100,000. For both diabetes and hypertensive renal disease, the mortality rate in blacks in 2013 was twice as high as in the white population, but for Parkinson's disease, it was only half the death rate in whites.[2]

Because of some confusion in people's minds about the extent to which race overlaps with ethnicity, culture, or place of origin, and the fact that in population surveys, many individuals identify themselves with more than one racial group, the temporal data on race can be inconsistent and unreliable. Following the guidelines from the Office of Management and Budget (OMB), the U.S. Census Bureau collects population data on race on the basis of self-identification and allows people to elect more than one race category. Because of an increasingly mixed ancestry in a diverse society, many people now choose to identify themselves with more than one racial group. The OMB requires the Census Bureau to use the following five *minimum* categories in

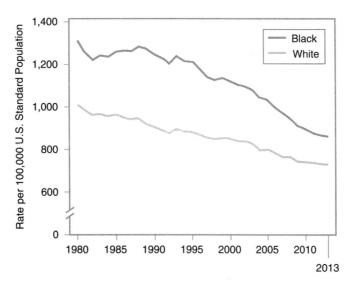

FIGURE 5.1 Age-adjusted death rates by race in the United States, 1980–2013.

data collection, compilation, and reporting: (1) White, (2) Black or African American, (3) American Indian or Alaska Native, (4) Asian, and (5) Native Hawaiian or Other Pacific Islander.[3]

The Census Bureau uses the following definitions for these racial categories.

White—A person having origins in any of the original peoples of Europe, the Middle East, or North Africa.

Black or African American—A person having origins in any of the Black racial groups of Africa.

American Indian or Alaska Native—A person having origins in any of the original peoples of North and South America (including Central America) and who maintains tribal affiliation or community attachment.

Asian—A person having origins in any of the original peoples of the Far East, Southeast Asia, or the Indian subcontinent, including, for example, Cambodia, China, India, Japan, Korea, Malaysia, Pakistan, the Philippine Islands, Thailand, and Vietnam.

Native Hawaiian or Other Pacific Islander—A person having origins in any of the original peoples of Hawaii, Guam, Samoa, or other Pacific Islands.

The Census Bureau notes that the concept of race is separate from the concept of Hispanic origin. Peo-ple who identify their origin as Hispanic, Latino, or Spanish may be of any race.

TABLE 5.1 shows the distribution of various groups in the 2016 estimated U.S. population. The racial mix of the population in the country is rapidly changing. **FIGURE 5.2** reflects this change, with the projection that Hispanic

TABLE 5.1 Estimated Population Distribution by Race/Ethnicity: United States, 2016

	No.	%
White	195,453,000	61%
Black	39,256,900	12%
Hispanic	57,670,000	18%
Asian	18,364,500	6%
America Indian/ Alaska Native	2,390,300	1%
Native Hawaiian/ Other Pacific Islander	1,043,200	<1%
Two or more races	6,194,100	2%
United States	320,372,000	100%

Modified from: Kaiser Family Foundation. Available at: http://kff.org/other/state-indicator/distribution-by-raceethnicity/. Reprinted with permission.

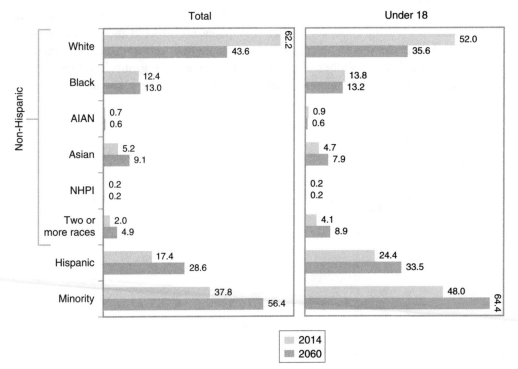

FIGURE 5.2 Distribution of the population by race and Hispanic origin for the total population and population under 18: 2014 and 2060.

population will grow from 17.4% in 2014 to 28.6% in 2060. Conversely, the proportion of the White population will decrease from 62.2% in 2014 to 43.6% in 2060.

5.2.3 Sex

The sex of a person at birth (not gender reassignment or gender transformation later in life) is a strong biologic and physiologic determinant of which diseases he or she may or may not be at risk for, or may be at a higher or lower risk for in a lifetime. Sex is also a strong determinant of the kind of sociopsychological stresses men and women differentially face in life. The gradient of sociopsychological stresses and social determinants of health for men and women differ from one country to another. Generally, women seem to have a biologic advantage in terms of lower risk of mortality and longer life expectancy at all ages (with the notable exception of greater risk of mortality for girls in preteen years in some countries). For example, the lifetime risk of being diagnosed with an invasive cancer for U.S. men has been estimated to be around 42%, whereas for women, it is about 38%. However, below age 50, women—presumably because of a much greater risk of breast cancer—are at a higher overall risk of cancer (5.4%) than are men (3.4%).[4] Like age,

adult height in both men and women has also been shown to be positively associated with the incidence and mortality from cancer.[5] About 33% of the difference between men and women in cancer incidence and mortality is accounted for by the difference in the average height of men and women.[6]

In the context of biologic determinants of risk, ovarian, uterine, and cervical cancers, for obvious anatomic reasons, occur only in women, whereas testicular and prostatic cancers occur only in men. For physiologic reasons, problems associated with hormonal changes occur only in women during the menopausal period. Breast cancer, although at times seen in men, predominantly affects women. In a small percentage of cases of breast cancer in women (about 10%), there is a hereditary genetic link (e.g., mutated or abnormal BRCA1 and BRCA2 genes). According to the American Cancer Society, in 2016, there were approximately 249,260 new cases of breast cancer in the United States, of which only 2,600 (1.0%) occurred in men, and 246,660 (99.0%) occurred in women. Similarly, out of a total of 40,890 breast cancer deaths in the country in the same year, only 440 (1.1%) were men, and 40,450 (98.9%) were women.[4]

TABLE 5.2 illustrates the differences between men and women in the estimated incidence and mortality

TABLE 5.2 Sex Distribution of Estimated Number of New Cases and Deaths from Selected Categories of Cancer: United States, 2016

	Estimated New Cases			Estimated Deaths		
	Male	**Female**	**Both Sexes**	**Male**	**Female**	**Both Sexes**
All sites	841,390 **(49.9%)**	843,820 **(50.1%)**	1,685,210 (100%)	314,290 **(52.8%)**	281,400 **(47.2%)**	595,690 (100%)
Esophagus	13,460 **(79.6%)**	3,450 **(20.4%)**	16,910 (100%)	12,720 **(81.1%)**	2,970 **(18.9%)**	15,690 (100%)
Colon	47,710 **(50.1%)**	47,560 **(49.9%)**	95,270 (100%)	26,020 **(52.9%)**	23,170 **(47.1%)**	49,190 (100%)
Liver	28,410 **(72.4%)**	10,820 **(27.6%)**	39,230 (100%)	18,280 **(67.3%)**	8,890 **(32.7%)**	27,170 (100%)
Lung & bronchus	117,920 **(52.5%)**	106,470 **(47.5%)**	224,390 (100%)	85,920 **(54.4%)**	72,160 **(45.6%)**	158,080 (100%)
Breast	2,600 **(1.0%)**	246,660 **(99.0%)**	249,260 (100%)	440 **(1.1%)**	40,450 **(98.9%)**	40,890 (100%)
Urinary bladder	58,950 **(76.6%)**	18,010 **(23.4%)**	76,960 (100%)	11,820 **(72.1%)**	4,570 **(27.9%)**	16,390 (100%)
Thyroid	14,950 **(23.3%)**	49,350 **(76.7%)**	64,300 (100%)	910 **(46.0%)**	1,070 **(54.0%)**	1,980 (100%)

Reprinted with permission from: Siegel RL, Miller KD, Jemal A. Cancer statistics, 2016. CA Cancer J Clin. 2016;66:7–30. doi:10.3322/caac.21332. Copyright © 2016 Wiley.

from seven selected categories of cancer in the United States. It has been estimated[4] that in 2016, most new cases of cancer in men were of prostate cancer, and in women, breast cancer. Cancer of lung and bronchus and that of colon and rectum were the second and third most common types of new cancer cases in both men and women.

The leading cause of cancer deaths in both men and women was estimated to be cancer of lung and bronchus, while the second most common cause in men was prostate cancer, and in women, breast cancer.

5.2.4 Occupation

Over the years, numerous studies have documented a bidirectional relationship between work and health.[7,8] The nature of work (i.e., **occupation**) as well as the physical and social environment at the workplace both have been shown to affect the physical and mental health of individuals. However, a division between the deleterious physical effects and mental effects of the work environment is rather artificial because the states of body and mind affect each other and are intertwined.[9] Workers in different industries can be exposed in varying degrees of intensity and duration to a variety of hazardous factors. The physical hazards at the workplace can range from mechanical and electrical to ergonomic and visual. There is a long list of diseases that have been linked with specific occupations, and the list continues to grow as new professions and occupations emerge with new technologies. The International Labor Organization (ILO) lists more than

100 disorders or groups of disorders related to occupational environments.[10] The most important point to remember in the context of occupational disorders is that they result from people's exposure to various biologic, chemical, physical, or psychological factors in the work environment, and all of these conditions can be prevented with appropriate protections and safeguards. The entire fields of occupational epidemiology and occupational medicine have emerged based on the recognition that work environment can pose special threats to health. A 2014 report sponsored by the ILO[11] estimated that every year, approximately 2.3 million people die worldwide for reasons attributed to work, and 15% of these deaths result directly from work-related injuries. According to this report, the most common causes of work-related death, in 2011, were circulatory disorders (35%), malignant neoplasms (29%), and accidents and violence (15%). Another estimate[12] indicated that, in 1998, there were 264 million nonfatal occupational accidents and 2 million work-related deaths globally. Approximately 346,000 of the 2 million work-related deaths resulted from traumatic injuries. The death rate from injuries in some developed countries was as low as <1 per 100,000 workers, whereas in some developing countries, it was as high as 30 per 100,000 workers.[12] **FIGURE 5.3** shows the total number of fatal work-related injuries in the United States every year from 1992 to 2014. Note the steady decline in the total number of deaths resulting from work-related injuries over the 22-year period. **FIGURE 5.4** shows the breakdown of 4,821 work-related deaths in 2014 by the nature of the work. Note that 41% of these deaths were related

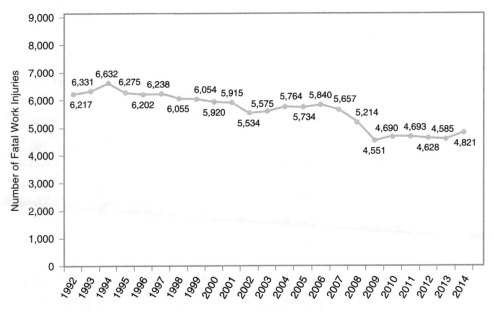

FIGURE 5.3 Number of fatal work injuries in the United States, 1992–2014.

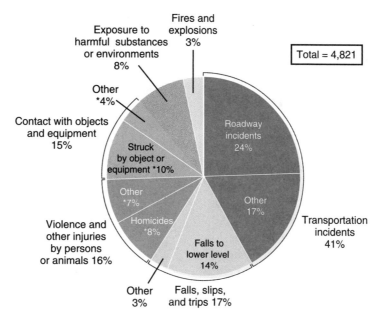

FIGURE 5.4 Percentage of work-related traumatic fatal injuries by source or cause of injury in the United States, 2014.

*Percentages do not add up to 100% because of rounding.

Reproduced from: U.S. Bureau of Labor Statistics. Census of fatal occupational injuries charts, 1992–2014 (revised data). 2016. Available at: http://stats.bls.gov/iif/oshwc/cfoi/cfch0013.pdf

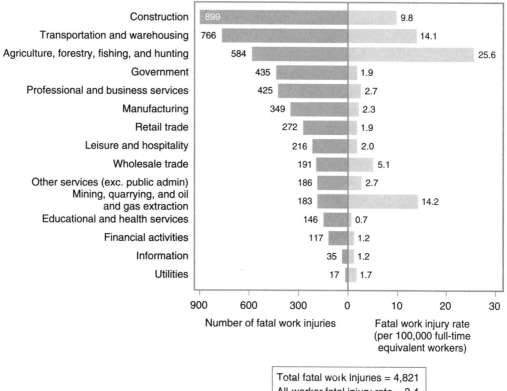

FIGURE 5.5 Number and rate of fatal occupational injuries by industry sector, 2014.

Reproduced from: U.S. Bureau of Labor Statistics. Census of fatal occupational injuries charts, 1992–2014 (revised data). 2016. Available at: http://stats.bls.gov/iif/oshwc/cfoi/cfch0013.pdf

to transportation incidents, and 17% were due to falls, slips, and trips. While the total number of deaths was highest in the construction industry (899), the rate of deaths per 100,000 full-time workers was the highest (25.6) in agriculture, forestry, fishing, and hunting (**FIGURE 5.5**).

The example of a cross-sectional study discussed later in this chapter about the investigation of cases of peripheral neuropathy resulting from exposure to hexane in solvents used in auto repair shops provides a good example of a disease associated with work environment.

5.2.5 Socioeconomic Status

Socioeconomic variables—including income, education, housing, and even religious affiliation—have long been shown to be associated with the health status of communities and population groups. A positive relationship between education and health, as well as between income and health, consistently has been shown across countries, across men and women, and across ethnic or racial groups. The positive incremental effect of education and income on health has also been shown to hold with increasing years of education and increasing amounts of family income—that is, those in the middle-income bracket have better health indicators than those in the low-income bracket, whereas those in the upper-income bracket fare better than those in the middle-income bracket.[13-15]

A recent study[16] that used deidentified tax records and involved more than 1.4 billion person-years of observation between 1999 and 2014 provided valuable information regarding the effects of **socioeconomic status** on health. Based on mortality data for 7 million individuals, the study showed a strong positive relationship between higher income and longer life, and a gap in life expectancy of 15 years for men and 10 years for women between those in the richest and the poorest fifth percentiles of the population.

5.2.6 Marital Status

Marital status, as an indicator of social support, is one of a number of socioeconomic and demographic characteristics that affect health status. Many research studies have shown that married people have better quality of life, better health status, and greater life expectancy than do unmarried people when faced with health problems such as lung, bladder, cervical, breast, and prostate cancer.[17-19] The specific clinical or physiologic pathways through which marital status and other social support variables impact health outcomes are not understood, but may include greater access to health care and earlier use of therapeutic and preventive health services such screening and vaccination.[19] The literature on the benefits of social support indicates that living together with a spouse or someone else reduces the need for formal and informal health care and improves both mental well-being and physical health.[20] Research has shown that married people are also more likely to have a primary care provider, are more likely to seek health care earlier, are more likely to receive influenza and pneumococcal vaccines, and have better pretreatment health indicators. Married people also seem to use better quality hospitals and have shorter lengths of hospital stay.[21] Publications based on the U.S. National Longitudinal Mortality Study (NLMS) have also shown that, overall, married people are at a lower risk of mortality,[22] lower risk of suicide,[23] and lower risk of homicide.[24] A study based on a recent release of the NLMS data found that divorced and separated individuals were 4.3 times more likely than married persons to die of HIV/AIDS, and single or never-married persons were 13 times more likely than married persons to die of HIV/AIDS. However, these differences were almost entirely applicable to men only and not to women.[25] In other studies, widowhood and bereavement have been shown to increase the risk of mortality in older couples.[26]

▶ 5.3 Place

Medical geography examines the spatial distribution of diseases. There is a long history of observed associations of **place** or geographic areas with different diseases. Long before the identification of the malarial parasite (*Plasmodium* of different types) and our understanding of the role that mosquitos play in the transmission of malaria, human beings had associated the signs and symptoms of malaria with swamps (mal-air or bad air). Because of the distribution of vector and host organisms and geoclimatic conditions that supported the populations of vector organisms, many infectious diseases in premodern times were associated with specific geographic areas. Many of these associations continue to exist even today. The names of diseases such as Congo hemorrhagic fever, Lassa fever, Lyme disease, Rocky Mountain spotted fever, and river blindness reflect such associations. Exclusive occurrence of a disease in an area (for example, Kuru disease in the past in Papua New Guinea) or a higher incidence of some diseases in certain areas may reflect the influence of culture, diet, housing, or exposure to natural elements. Such examples might include high incidence of stomach cancer in Japan or tuberculosis among the Inuit people of northern Canada.

A recent study by Chetty et al.,[16] in addition to the relationship between income and health, also revealed a relationship between geography and health status within the same income bracket. The study showed that life expectancy for those in the lowest 5% of income is 6 years longer in New York City as compared with those in Detroit. On the other hand, for those in the richest 5% of the population, life expectancy in various cities was nearly the same. This suggests that geography plays a much more significant role in affecting the health status of those in the lower socioeconomic gradient than those in the highest

FIGURE 5.6 Reported cases of Lyme disease in the United States, 2016.

Reproduced from: Centers for Disease Control and Prevention. Lyme disease maps. Updated November 1, 2017. https://www.cdc.gov/lyme/stats/maps.html

socioeconomic strata. The reported cases of Lyme disease in the United States in the last two decades show a clear pattern in the geographic distribution of this disease, with the highest number of cases reported in the northeastern states. This distribution can easily be linked to the population of deer ticks in various states. **FIGURE 5.6** from the U.S. Centers for Disease Control and Prevention (CDC) shows the distribution of reported cases of Lyme disease in 2016.

5.3.1 Geographic Information Systems (GISs) and Descriptive Epidemiology

Medical geography, also known as **health geography**, examines the impact of geography and climate on individual and population health. As the name suggests, it can be characterized as the field of research that combines medicine and geography to investigate the spatial distribution and determinants of health, disease, and healthcare delivery. Since Hippocrates's (ca 460- ca 377 BCE) observations in *On Airs, Waters, and Places,* and John Snow's (1854) street mapping of cholera cases in London, health geography has made tremendous advances in promoting our understanding of the role that geographic and environmental factors play in the etiology and spread of diseases in populations. *Disease geography,* described by some as a component of medical geography,[27] is descriptive in nature and, usually through frequency data, relates spatial distribution of a disease to geographic and environmental characteristics. The second component of medical geography focuses on the geography of healthcare delivery and utilization. In recent years, this component has made extensive use of **geographic information systems** (GISs), which are computer systems designed to integrate and analyze spatially or geographically referenced data—that is, in relation to the surface of Earth. Two-dimensional or three-dimensional (2D or 3D) GISs maps can show different kinds of variables layered or superimposed on top of each other to demonstrate patterns and reveal how different variables relate to one another.

Because of their versatility and countless potential applications, GISs are ubiquitous. In the United States, the range of GISs developers and users spans from telecommunication and telemarketing to telemedicine, and from 911 emergency locator systems to public health and homeland security. In public health, GISs are used extensively for disease surveillance and monitoring to identify high-risk populations. In health services research, they have most commonly been used to assess geographic and socioeconomic access to preventive and therapeutic services.[27,28] GISs are also developed and used by insurance companies and healthcare providers to understand the spatial distribution and clustering of patients. In combination with remote sensing data obtained through satellite sensors and aerial photography, GISs are now being used by

U.S. government agencies, such as the Environmental Protection Agency and the Department of Health and Human Services, to identify risks and incidents of infectious or chemically induced diseases that can be spread through air or water contamination.[27] In the past, a number of government agencies in the United States have used GISs to prepare atlases that show spatial distribution of cases of various diseases and resulting deaths. For example, the CDC has used human case data to develop the National Lyme Disease Risk Map. The CDC and the National Cancer Institute have also developed atlases of mortality statistics from various causes and racial disparities in health.[29-32]

As tools of *descriptive epidemiology*, GISs are used primarily for the purpose of understanding the interactive distribution and clustering of diseases and their determinants in *person, place,* and *time.* Epidemiologists can use multilayered maps and spatial statistical techniques to understand changes in the distribution of diseases or vectors and agents of infectious diseases in different time periods. For example, the mapping cluster functionality in ArcGIS Pro is designed to "identify statistically significant hot spots, cold spots, and spatial outliers."[33] GISs have also been used to investigate the effects of traffic patterns on asthma in children,[34] to examine power line magnetic fields as potential contributors to leukemia in children,[35] and to identify homes where children had high levels of exposure to lead.[36]

The CDC's Web-Based Injury Statistics Query and Reporting System (WISQARS; www.cdc.gov/injury /wisqars/) allows users to build state- or county-level maps for fatal injury rates stratified by race, sex, and age categories. Likewise, the National Cancer Institute's website (http://ratecalc.cancer.gov/) also allows users to create state- or county-level cancer mortality maps stratified by type of cancer and by race, sex, and age. **FIGURE 5.7** provides an example of a color-coded spatial display of geographic incidence data. The map shows categorical representation of the number of cases of Zika virus disease reported to the CDC by all U.S. states and territories from January 2015 to June 2016. For example, no cases of Zika virus disease were reported by North Dakota, South Dakota, Wyoming, and Idaho, whereas seven or more cases were reported by a number of states, including Texas, California, and Florida.

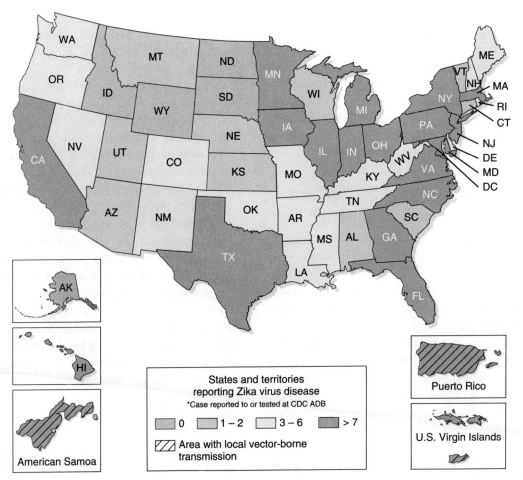

FIGURE 5.7 Geographic distribution of reported cases of Zika virus disease in the United States, January 2015–June 2016.

Reproduced from: Centers for Disease Control and Prevention. Zika virus disease in the United States, 2015–2016. Available at: http://www.cdc.gov/zika/geo/united-states.html

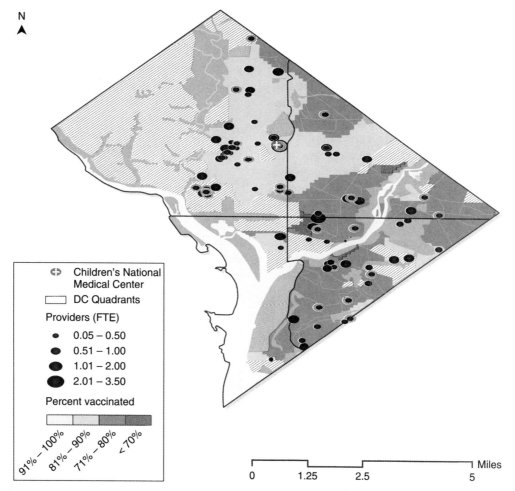

FIGURE 5.8 Relationship of pediatric primary vaccine completion to vaccine provider availability in the Washington, DC, metropolitan region.

Reproduced from: Jacobs B. Geospatial mapping and analysis of health care conditions in children. Washington, DC: Children's National Medical Center; 2012. Available at: http://s3.amazonaws.com/rdcms-himss/files/production/public/HIMSSorg/Content/HIMSS12PhysPosters/BrianJacobs.pdf

FIGURE 5.8 provides an example of the use of GISs to show the relationship between geographic accessibility of services and levels of health services utilization. The researchers examined the spatial accessibility of pediatric immunization services and vaccine compliance in a low-income urban population of 4,195 children between 19 and 35 months of age.[37] The study discovered that children who had greater spatial accessibility to pediatric vaccination services were 36% more likely to be up to date on vaccinations.

▶ 5.4 Time

Information related to the timing of a disease in a person or in a population is the third component in the person-place-time (who, where, and when) triad of descriptive epidemiology.

The study of the distribution of a disease over short or long periods of time can reveal interesting patterns of incidence and prevalence. Many infectious diseases, including viral respiratory disorders or vector-borne parasitic diseases such as malaria, typically display seasonal and cyclical epidemic patterns. These patterns are associated with environmental or climatic conditions, such as temperature and rainfall, as well as patterns of human behavior related to these natural phenomena. For example, incidence and prevalence of malaria, dengue, and West Nile fever is linked with hot and humid climates and rainy seasons that favor breeding of mosquito vectors and easy access of mosquitos to exposed human skin during summer months. Likewise, incidence of Lyme disease also shows a seasonal pattern of transmission during the summer months because of higher levels of human exposure to deer ticks carrying the *Borrelia burgdorferi* spirochete organism. Epidemics of upper respiratory viral infections, on the other hand, occur mostly during the winter season due to people spending more time indoors in close proximity to one another and longer survival time of viruses on surfaces in relatively dry, colder temperatures.

Plotting of an *epidemic curve* for relatively short-lived foodborne bacterial or viral outbreaks can also be instructive regarding the source of infection and the nature of the organism responsible for the outbreak. An epidemic curve is a bar chart displaying the frequency of cases on y-axis, and duration of time in days, weeks, or months along the x-axis. Thus, an epidemic curve is nothing but a visual expression of the distribution of the number of cases of a disease over time. Epidemic curves can manifest different patterns depending on whether the outbreak resulted from a single or point source; continuing exposure of susceptible individuals over time to a single source, such as a contaminated water supply system; or sequential person-to-person spread of disease over time. **FIGURE 5.9** provides an example of a point-source short-lived (single incubation period) outbreak.

Graphs of changing patterns of incidence, prevalence, or mortality from chronic diseases such as cancers, diabetes, or cardiovascular disease in a population over longer periods of time can also provide valuable information about the success or failure of health policies and effects of new diagnostic technologies, new treatments, screening programs, or educational interventions. Similarly, temporal changes in the frequency of health-related behaviors such as smoking, use of illicit drugs, unsafe sex, or rates such as teen pregnancy and obesity also provide useful information for healthcare policy and planning. Understanding trends in the prevalence of a risk factor and the incidence and prevalence of a disease can give important clues about a potential association between the two. For example, trends in the sale or consumption of alcohol and/or illicit drugs in a community and trends in the frequency of DUI (driving under the influence) charges, automobile crashes, rate of violent crimes, or homicide rates can point toward an association between the risk factor and the health outcome.

▶ 5.5 Types of Epidemiologic Investigations

The chart shown in **FIGURE 5.10** provides a schematic diagram of various kinds of epidemiologic investigations. The grouping of various kinds of studies under different titles or categories is intended only to provide a conceptual framework with a keen awareness of the fact that some studies can straddle more than one category. For example, many ecological studies can be cross-sectional in design and may just as appropriately be characterized as descriptive studies. In principle, such studies do not involve a temporal or longitudinal observation of some phenomenon, process, or health indicator in a population. Also, the label *descriptive*, as opposed to *analytic*, does not imply a total avoidance of statistical or quantitative analysis in descriptive studies—it only suggests that the nature of analysis and the methods employed are descriptive rather than inferential.

To maintain the distinction between descriptive and analytic study designs, descriptive epidemiologic studies, including case reports and cross-sectional studies, are discussed in this chapter, whereas observational and experimental analytic studies are discussed separately in other chapters.

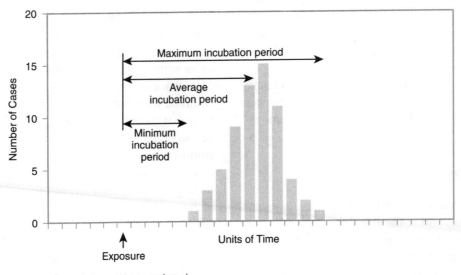

FIGURE 5.9 Epidemic curve for a point-source outbreak.

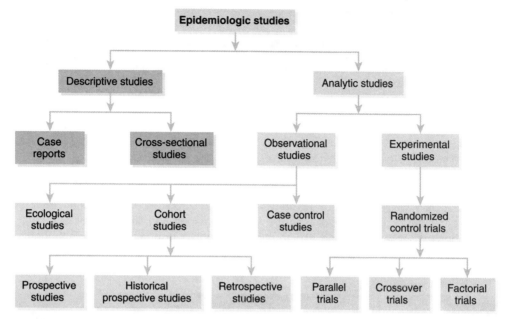

FIGURE 5.10 A schematic diagram of different types of epidemiologic studies.

Data from Friis, 2010; Swallen KC, University of Wisconsin-Madison.

To keep the reader reminded of this conceptual framework, the chart shown in Figure 5.10 is also displayed in the chapters on observational and experimental studies.

▶ 5.6 Descriptive Epidemiologic Studies

5.6.1 Case Reports and Case Series

Case reports are descriptive accounts of clinical presentation and demographic characteristics of individual patients of a previously unknown disease or an unusual presentation of a known disease, including details of circumstances in which the disease may have been acquired by the individual. Case reports have clinical and epidemiologic importance because they constitute the earliest events that draw attention of researchers, clinicians, and public health professionals toward a newly emerging disease or a condition that may have previously existed at low levels but could potentially become a significant public health problem in the future. Most times, case reports originate in clinical settings, such as doctor's offices or research establishments, and are either reported to public health agencies or appear in scientific literature as short reports.

At times, reports of isolated cases may not get sufficient attention from public health agencies until reports of similar cases begin to appear in scientific journals or news media. Often, case reports represent the proverbial tip of the iceberg and point toward a problem that might have gone unnoticed for a long time for a variety of reasons. For example, HIV/AIDS first came to the attention of healthcare professionals in the United States through a report on June 5, 1981, of five cases of *Pneumocystis carinii* pneumonia, an uncommon opportunistic infection, in young gay men in Los Angeles; two of the five patients had died.[38] Subsequent reports of cases of Kaposi's sarcoma, another uncommon disease, and reports of additional cases of *P. carinii* from New York and other areas led to the discovery of HIV/AIDS. However, now it is known that the transmission of HIV had started in Africa in the period 1920–1930 in the country now called the Democratic Republic of Congo. Similarly, the first case of Alzheimer's disease was described by Dr. Alois Alzheimer in Germany in 1906.[39] However, it was not until 1976 that Alzheimer's disease began to be recognized as a common form of dementia and a major public health problem associated with aging.

These examples underscore the importance of descriptive case reports as harbingers of potentially larger problems that merit the attention of clinicians, researchers, and policy makers. These days, many clinical journals routinely publish case reports. Likewise, local, state, and national public health agencies in the United States require timely reporting of a number of infectious diseases and compile time-series data on a variety of conditions from various sources, including clinical case reports. **CASE STUDY 5.1** described on the next page provides an example of a *case series report*.

🔍 *CASE STUDY 5.1: Example of a Case Series Report*

Source: Sircar AD, Abanyie F, Blumberg D, et al. Raccoon roundworm infection associated with central nervous system disease and ocular disease — six states, 2013–2015. Morbid Mortal Wkly Rep. 2016;65:930–933. doi:10.15585/mmwr.mm6535a2

Baylisascaris procyonis is a roundworm found in raccoons all over North America. Infected raccoons are typically asymptomatic and pass worm eggs in feces. Human infection occurs through ingestion of materials contaminated with egg-containing raccoon feces. Larvae from ingested *Baylisascaris* eggs migrate through the brain, eyes, and other organs. Unless treated promptly, infection in humans can cause fatal disease or severe neurologic outcomes. Because Baylisascariasis is not a nationally notifiable disease in the United States, little is known about its prevalence and clinical characteristics. Between 1973 and 2010, only 22 confirmed cases were reported in the United States. Because no serologic test is commercially available in the United States, clinical and laboratory diagnosis of the disease is difficult. This case series report includes circumstances of exposure and demographic and clinical characteristics of seven cases of Baylisascariasis diagnosed between 2013 and 2015 through immunoblot testing at the CDC. Although all seven individuals survived, nearly half were left with persistent neurologic problems. **TABLE 5.3**, from the report, provides specific information about each of the seven cases.

TABLE 5.3 Seven Cases of *Baylisascaris Procyonis* Infection, United States, 2013–2015

Year	State	Age	Sex	Test	Clinical Findings	Suspected Exposure	Outcome
2013	Oklahoma, Arkansas	31 years	Female	Positive serum & CSF*	Eosinophilic meningitis	Pet raccoon	Survived; neurologic deficit
2014	Ohio	15 months	Male	Positive serum	Eosinophilic meningitis	Raccoon pelts	Survived; full recovery
2014	Massachusetts	32 years	Female	Positive serum	Eosinophilic meningitis	Hiking in raccoon-prevalent area	Survived; full recovery
2015	California	63 years	Male	Positive serum & CSF	Eosinophilic meningitis	Working in raccoon-prevalent area	Survived; neurologic deficit
2015	California	3 years	Male	Positive serum & CSF	Eosinophilic meningitis	Living in raccoon prevalent area	Survived; neurologic deficit
2015	Virginia	10 months	Female	Positive serum & CSF	Eosinophilic meningitis	Geophagia in raccoon-prevalent area	Survived; neurologic deficit
2015	Minnesota	7 years	Male	Positive serum	Ocular larva migrans	Living in raccoon-prevalent area	Survived; full recovery

*CSF: cerebrospinal fluid.
Reproduced from: Sircar AD, Abanyie F, Blumberg D, et al. Raccoon roundworm infection associated with central nervous system disease and ocular disease — six states, 2013–2015. Morbid Mortal Wkly Rep. 2016;65:930–933. doi:10.15585/mmwr.mm6535a2

5.6.2 Cross-Sectional Studies

Cross-sectional studies are usually conducted in the form of surveys and are the most common form of epidemiologic research in public health. In contrast, prospective cohort studies or randomized controlled trials (RCTs) are the most common epidemiologic investigations in medicine and clinical research. (Prospective cohort studies and RCTs are described in the chapters on observational and experimental studies.)

In a cross-sectional study, the selection of the population to be investigated is based on some geographic, demographic, or socioeconomic characteristics. The interest of the investigator lies in describing the characteristics of a population or in discovering the frequency of one or more diseases and risk factors in a population. The researcher may also describe the difference in the characteristics of those who have a disease, as opposed to those who do not have the disease. These studies can be done in the form of one-on-one personal interviews, questionnaires distributed to groups of individuals in face-to-face settings, questionnaires mailed out through postal services to randomly or nonrandomly selected individuals, telephone surveys through random or nonrandom dialing, or online computerized surveys using commercially available software platforms or websites. Some surveys may involve taking measurements such as height, weight, or blood pressure or collection of samples such as blood, urine, and sputum. Naturally, such measurements and collection of samples can limit the size of the survey because of high costs and logistic difficulties.

Whatever the mechanism for soliciting desired information from voluntarily participating individuals, the common element in all survey research is the fact that the information is obtained during a narrowly defined window of time—whether a few days or a few weeks—and represents a snapshot of the situation existing in the population of interest at that specific point in time. In cross-sectional studies, researchers gather and report information about the concurrence or coexistence of diseases, risk factors, or health-related behaviors in a representative sample of the population of interest at a given point in time. Consequently, cross-sectional studies are commonly used to report the prevalence of diseases and various risk factors, but they cannot be used to draw causal inferences. The purpose of these studies frequently is to develop a hypothesis for further research or to use the information for public health planning and policy formulation. Because measurement of disease and exposure to a risk factor is done at the same time, it cannot be determined whether the disease occurred before or after exposure. This is especially true for chronic diseases that progress slowly over a long period of time before their signs and symptoms become overt. In such situations, it is extremely difficult to pinpoint the time of onset of disease.

Statistically speaking, these studies can only establish associations or correlations and can report the relative prevalence of a disease or risk factor in one population as compared with another. For obvious reasons, these studies can suffer from bias introduced by potential self-selection of respondents and issues related to poor recall or intentional under- or overreporting by participants. Another potential source of bias is the difference between healthy and sick individuals' likelihood of participating in the study. On one hand, sick individuals may not be available or might be too sick to participate in the study; on the other hand, sick individuals or those with greater severity of disease may be more motivated to participate in a study. Both scenarios are problematic because of the potential for under- or overrepresentation of such individuals in the study. Another problem with cross-sectional studies is that individuals with a longer duration or chronic form of a disease are likely to be overrepresented because those with short or nonchronic disease recover and enter the pool of healthy individuals. Discovery of simultaneous presence of diseases and risk factors allows researchers to generate hypotheses about causal relationships, but not the ability to test hypotheses. A lack of temporal data makes it impossible to establish whether the occurrence of a disease succeeded or preceded exposure to a potential risk factor. To make a case for a causal relationship between a risk factor and a disease, it is necessary to demonstrate that exposure to the risk factor occurred before the development of the disease and not concurrently or subsequently.

The advantage of cross-sectional studies is that they are easier to design, faster to implement, and simpler to analyze. In many instances, data are readily and publicly available from previously conducted national, regional, or local surveys by government or nongovernment agencies. At times, data from repeated surveys, such as those conducted annually (e.g., the U.S. National Health Interview Survey), are available to understand trends in exposure and disease occurrence. **CASE STUDIES 5.2** and **5.3** described on the following pages provide examples of cross-sectional study design.

🔍 CASE STUDY 5.2: Example of a Cross-Sectional Study

Source: Beckman S, Eisen EA, Bates MN, Liu S, Haegerstrom-Portnoy G, Hammond SK. Acquired color vision defects and hexane exposure: a study of San Francisco Bay Area automotive mechanics. Am J Epidemiol. 2016 May. doi:10.1093/aje/kwv328

In May 2016, Beckman et al. reported in the *American Journal of Epidemiology* the results of the Bay Area Solvent Study (BASS)—a cross-sectional study of 835 automotive repair workers in the San Francisco Bay Area of California.

Previously, a case series report and a small follow-up study had suggested a potential link between occupational exposure to hexane in aerosol solvents used in auto repair shops and peripheral neuropathy and blue-yellow color vision defects. Color vision defects in humans can be hereditary or acquired after birth: Hereditary color vision defects result from missing or abnormal photoreceptors, while acquired color vision defects result from damage to the retina or the optic nerve. Blue-green hereditary color vision defects are somewhat more common (10% of men and 0.5% of women) than blue-yellow hereditary defects, which are quite rare (1 in 1 million people) and are associated with age, alcoholism, eye diseases like glaucoma and cataract, and exposure to solvents such as hexane.

The study participants were 835 males younger than 60 years of age still living in the San Francisco Bay Area who had worked as auto repair mechanics at any time during the period from 1989 to 2000, when hexane was being used in solvent automobile cleaners. The 835 participants in the study were recruited from 1,765 men found to be eligible after contacting via telephone or postal service all the individuals in a pool of 2,848 potentially eligible workers identified through union records. Between 2008 and 2011, the participants visited a clinic through individual appointments, where they responded to a questionnaire and were tested for color vision. The questionnaire obtained demographic, clinical, and work history information, including the frequency and duration of work that involved the use of specific solvent products. To aid their memory, study participants were shown pictures of solvent products that had been available during the last 20 years. Based on self-reported work history, the study estimated cumulative exposure to hexane. Color vision in the study participants was tested through a laboratory test (Lanthony desaturated D-15 panel test).

Out of the 835 participants, 81 were excluded from final analysis because of missing hexane exposure data (n = 18), having congenital color vision defects (n = 53), or inadequate color vision assessment (n = 10). For the analysis of blue-yellow color vision defect, 65 participants who had nonspecific or red-green color vision defect were also excluded. Thus, cross-sectional data from 689 individuals were analyzed to explore a possible association between cumulative exposure to solvents and blue-yellow color vision defects in automotive mechanics.

The results of the Lanthony desaturated D-15 panel test for blue-yellow color vision defects were treated as binary (yes, no) variables. Different levels of cumulative exposure to solvents such as hexane and acetone were estimated based on reported frequency and duration of tasks, types and brands of solvents used, and quantity of solvents use in various tasks. Because age was found to be strongly associated with color vision defects as well as the level of cumulative exposure, it was treated as a confounding variable in all statistical analytic models. Because color vision deteriorates after age 50, age-stratified analyses were carried out to reduce bias resulting from color vision defects occurring because of age. The investigators used log-binomial regression models to estimate prevalence ratios for the risk of color vision defects by different levels of exposure to nonhexane, hexane, and hexane-acetone combination solvents. Statistical models were adjusted for potentially confounding variables such as race, smoking, alcohol consumption, and previous history of concussion and head trauma. **TABLE 5.4** shows partial results of statistical analysis.

Questions

Question 1. In statistical analysis, what was the issue related to age? How did the researchers address that issue?

Question 2. Why was statistical analysis adjusted for smoking, alcohol consumption, and previous history of concussion and head trauma?

Question 3. In Table 5.4, what do the prevalence ratios for nonhexane solvent exposure in All Participants and Participants age ≤50 years indicate? Do these ratios provide conclusive evidence of an association between blue-yellow color vision defect and exposure to nonhexane solvents?

Question 4. In Table 5.4, what is the difference between the prevalence ratios for exposure to nonhexane and hexane solvents? What does that difference suggest?

TABLE 5.4 Categorical Exposure Response Relationship Between Blue-Yellow Vision Defects and Cumulative Exposure to Nonhexane and Hexane Solvents Among Participants Completing the Lanthony Desaturated D-15 Panel Test

Model and Exposure Category	All Participants			Participants Age ≤50 Years		
	No. of Cases	PR*	95% CI**	No. of Cases	PR*	95% CI**
Nonhexane Solvents						
Exposure, mg/m³-year						
0–670.9	155	1.00	Reference	60	1.00	Reference
>670.9–1,364.3	29	1.25	0.81–1.92	12	1.75	0.89–3.46
>1,364.3–2,470.7	39	1.16	0.75–1.78	18	1.98	0.98–4.02
>2,470.7	40	1.31	0.86–2.00	17	2.17	1.03–4.56
Age	47	1.04	1.02–1.07	13	1.02	0.96–1.08
Hexane Solvents						
Exposure, mg/m³-year						
Unexposed to hexane	155	1.00	Reference	60	1.00	Reference
>0–33.7	81	0.73	0.51–1.04	25	0.77	0.41–1.42
>33.7	33	0.94	0.68–1.29	13	1.26	0.76–2.11
Age	41	1.05	1.02–1.07	22	1.04	0.99–1.10

*Prevalence ratio.
**95% confidence interval.
Modified with permission from: Oxford University Press: Beckman S, Eisen EA, Bates MN, Liu S, Haegerstrom-Portnoy G, Hammond SK. Acquired color vision defects and hexane exposure: a study of San Francisco Bay Area automotive mechanics. Am J Epidemiol. 2016 May. doi:10.1093/aje/kwv328

🔎 *CASE STUDY 5.3: Example of a Cross-Sectional Study*

Data from: Sahakyan KR, Somers VK, Rodriguez-Escudero JP, et al. Normal-weight central obesity: implications for total and cardiovascular mortality. Ann Intern Med. 2015;163(11):2827–2835.

Obesity, regardless of whether it is measured in terms of body mass index (BMI) or through indicators of central obesity such as Waist-to-Hip Ratio (WHR), is known to be associated with total mortality and cardiovascular mortality. However, measures of central obesity have been shown to be more strongly associated with total and cardiovascular mortality than BMI. In this cross-sectional study, Sahakyan et al. investigated the risk of total and cardiovascular mortality associated with central obesity and normal BMI. They hypothesized that persons with normal BMI and central obesity would have greater risk of mortality than those who have any other combination of BMI and central obesity.

(continues)

The authors used 1988–1994 cohort data from the Third National Health and Nutrition Examination Survey (NHANES III)—a cross-sectional survey of the U.S. population with stratified multi-stage probability sampling. NHANES III used a total sample of 39,695, of which 33,994 were interviewed and 30,818 were examined at mobile examination centers. The examination involved anthropometric, physiologic, and laboratory testing, as well as hip and waist measurements. WHR data were available for 16,124 adults 18 years or older. The researchers restricted analysis to 15,184 individuals with BMI >18.5 kg/m^2 (7,249 men and 7,935 women) and used survival modeling to estimate the relative risk of mortality adjusting for variables such as age, sex, education, and smoking, which are independently associated with both obesity and the risk of mortality. A BMI between 18.5 and 24.9 kg/m^2 was considered the normal range, between 25 and 29.9 kg/m^2 defined overweight, and ≥30.0 kg/m^2 indicated obesity.

The results showed that 6,062 (39.9%) individuals had a normal BMI, 5,249 (34.6%) were overweight, and 3,873 (25.1%) were obese. Using the World Health Organization's criteria of WHR ≥0.85 in women and ≥0.90 in men for central obesity, 10,655 individuals (70.2%) were characterized as centrally obese. Of those with normal BMI, 322 men (11.0%) and 105 women (3.3%) had a WHR ≥1.0. Of those who were characterized as overweight, 1,064 men (37.0%) and 289 women (12.0%) had a WHR ≥1.0. Lastly, of obese individuals, 928 men (63.0%) and 336 women (14.0%) had a WHR ≥1.0. During the mean follow-up period of 14.3 years, there were 3,222 deaths (1,413 in women), of which 1,404 were due to cardiovascular disease.

For men, the effect of central obesity on 5-year and 10-year survival across all age groups was quite remarkable. The expected survival overall and within each age group consistently favored both men and women with less central obesity. It also showed that men with normal BMI but central obesity had much greater risk of mortality than those with any other combination of BMI and WHR. In comparison to men with normal weight but central obesity, those who were overweight but did not have central obesity had a much lower risk of mortality. A similar risk of mortality associated with central obesity was observed for women overall and in various age groups. The authors concluded that central obesity with normal weight is associated with higher risk of mortality than when BMI-based obesity is not accompanied by central obesity.

▶ 5.7 Summary

The primary function of epidemiology—the one that is foundational to the definition and origins of the field—is to develop an understanding of the distribution of disease, disability, and injury in populations in relation to geography and time. Because diseases and injuries are not randomly distributed, understanding their distribution in the context of person, place, and time provides important clues about the sources, origins, and causes of diseases and allows researchers to develop testable hypotheses. The simplest methods to understand the distribution of diseases in person, place, and time are descriptive studies that include case reports and cross-sectional surveys conducted to gather necessary information from a sample of the population. For appropriate planning and proportionate allocation of resources, healthcare managers must understand not only the nature and magnitude of problems in the communities they serve but also the characteristics of those who suffer from these problems and the methods used to generate this information. The data, figures, tables, and case studies reported in this chapter will go a long way in helping future healthcare managers develop the skills to carry out health services planning effectively and assess the adequacy of currently available services in the community.

References

1. Brody JA, Grant MD. Age-associated diseases and conditions: implications for decreasing late life morbidity. Aging. 2001;13(2):64–67.
2. Xu J, Murphy SL, Kochanek KD, Bastian BA. Deaths: final data for 2013. Natl Vital Stat Rep. 2016;64(2).
3. The United States Census Bureau. Race. 2016 [cited 2018 May 2]. Available from: https://www.census.gov/topics /population/race/about.html
4. Siegel RL, Miller KD, Jemal A. Cancer statistics, 2016. CA Cancer J Clin. 2016;66:7–30.
5. Wiren S, Haggstrom C, Ulmer H, et al. Pooled cohort study on height and risk of cancer and cancer deaths. Cancer Causes Control. 2014;25(2):151–159.
6. Walter RB, Brasky TM, Buckley SA, Potter JD, White E. Height as an explanatory factor for sex differences in human cancer. J Natl Cancer Inst. 2013;105(12):860–868.
7. Takala J, Hämäläinen P, Saarela LK, et al. Global burden of injury and illness at work in 2012. J Occup Environ Hyg. 2014;11(5):326–337.
8. Burton J. WHO healthy workplace framework and model: background document and supporting literature and practices. Geneva: WHO; 2010.

9. Robert Wood Johnson Foundation Commission to Build a Healthier America. Issue Brief 4: Work and Health: Work Matters. 2008 [cited 2018 May 2]. Available from: http://www.commissiononhealth.org/PDF/0e8ca13d-6fb8-451d-bac8-7d15343aacff/Issue%20Brief%204%20Dec%2008%20-%20Work%20and%20Health.pdf

10. International Labour Organization. ILO list of occupational diseases. Geneva: International Labour Organization; 2010 [cited 2018 May 2]. Available from: http://www.ilo.org/wcmsp5/groups/public/@ed_protect/@protrav/@safework/documents/publication/wcms_125137.pdf

11. Nenonen N, Saarela KL, Takala J, et al. Global estimates of occupational accidents and work-related illnesses 2014. Tempere, Finland: Tempere University of Technology; 2014 [cited 2018 May 2]. Available from: https://www.wsh-institute.sg/files/wshi/upload/cms/file/Global%20Estimates%20of%20Occupational%20Accidents%20and%20Work-related%20Illness%202014.pdf

12. Hämäläinen P, Takala J, Saarela KL. Global estimates of occupational accidents. Saf Sci. 2006;44:137–156.

13. Crimmins EM, Preston SH, Cohen B, editors. Explaining divergent levels of longevity in high-income countries. National Research Council. Washington, DC: National Academies Press; 2011.

14. Cutler D, Lleras-Muney A. Education and health: evaluating theories and evidence. Working Paper 12352. Cambridge, MA: National Bureau of Economic Research; 2006 [cited 2018 May 2]. Available from: http://www.nber.org/papers/w12352.pdf

15. Marmot M. Social determinants of health inequalities. Lancet. 2005;365:1099–1104.

16. Chetty R, Stepner M, Abraham S, et al. The association between income and life expectancy in the United States, 2001–2014. JAMA. 2016;315(14):1715–1766.

17. Robards M, Evandrou M, Falkingham JF, Vlachantoni A. Marital status, health, and mortality. Maturitas. 2012;73(4):295–299.

18. Pruthi RS, Lentz AC, Sand M, Kouba E, Wallen EM. Impact of marital status in patients undergoing radical cystectomy for bladder cancer. World J Urol. 2009;27:573–576.

19. Gore JL, Kwan L, Saigal CS, Litwin MS. Marriage and mortality in bladder carcinoma. Cancer. 2005;104(6):1188–1194.

20. Cafferata GL. Marital status, living arrangements, and the use of health services by elderly persons. J Gerontol. 1987;42(6):613–618.

21. Iwashyna TJ, Christakis NA. Marriage, widowhood, and health-care use. Soc Sci Med. 2003;57:2137–2147.

22. Johnson NJ, Backlund E, Sorlie PD, Loveless CA. Marital status and mortality: the National Longitudinal Mortality Study. Ann Epidemiol. 2000;10(4): 224–238.

23. Kposowa AJ. Marital status and suicide in the National Longitudinal Mortality Study. J Epidemiol Community Health. 2000;54(4):254–261.

24. Kposowa AJ, Singh GK, Breault KD. The effects of marital status and social isolation on adult male homicides in the United States: evidence from the National Longitudinal Mortality Study. J Quant Criminol. 1994;10(3):277–289.

25. Kposowa AJ. Marital status and HIV/AIDS mortality: evidence from the U.S. National Longitudinal Mortality Study. Int J Infect Dis. 2013;17(10):e868–e874.

26. Shah SM, Carey IM, Harris T, DeWilde S, Victor CR, Cook DG. The effect of unexpected bereavement on mortality in older couples. Am J Public Health. 2013;103(6):1140–1145.

27. Cromley EK. GIS and disease. Annu Rev Public Health. 2003;24:7–24.

28. Higgs G. A literature review of the use of GIS-based measures of access to health care services. Health Serv Outcomes Res Methodol. 2004;5:119–139.

29. Centers for Disease Control and Prevention. Atlas of United States mortality: motor vehicle deaths for black male. 2015 [cited 2018 May 2]. Available from: http://www.cdc.gov/nchs/products/other/atlas/mvibm.htm

30. Centers for Disease Control and Prevention. Atlas of United States mortality: lung cancer for white male. 2015 [cited 2018 May 2]. Available from: http://www.cdc.gov/nchs/products/other/atlas/lcwm.htm

31. Devesa SS, Grauman DJ, Blot WJ, Pennello GA, Hoover RN, Fraumeni JF. Atlas of cancer mortality in the United States 1950–94. National Institutes of Health. NIH Publication No. 99-4564. 1999 [cited 2018 May 2]. Available from: http://eot.us.archive.org/eot/20130214054413/http://ratecalc.cancer.gov/archivedatlas/

32. National Cancer Institute. State cancer profiles; 2018 [cited 2018 May 2]. Available from: https://statecancerprofiles.cancer.gov/index.html

33. Esri. ArcGIS Pro [cited 2018 July 3]. Available from: http://www.esri.com/en/software/arcgis-pro

34. English P, Neutra R, Scalf R, Sullivan M, Waller L, Zhu L. Examining associations between childhood asthma and traffic flow using a geographic information system. Environ Health Perspect. 1999;107:761–767.

35. Kheifets L, Crespi CM, Hooper C, et al. Epidemiologic study of residential proximity to transmission lines and childhood cancer in California: description of design, epidemiologic methods and study population. J Expo Sci Environ Epidemiol. 2015;25:45–52.

36. Reissman DB, Staley F, Curtis GB, Kaufmann RB. Use of geographic information system technology to aid health department decision making about childhood lead poisoning prevention activities. Environ Health Perspect. 2001;109(1):89–94.

37. Jacobs B. Geospatial mapping and analysis of health care conditions in children. Washington, DC: Children's National Medical Center; 2012 [cited 2018 May 2]. Available from: http://s3.amazonaws.com/rdcms-himss/files/production/public/HIMSSorg/Content/HIMSS12PhysPosters/BrianJacobs.pdf

38. Centers for Disease Control and Prevention. Pneumocystis pneumonia: Los Angeles. MMWR Morb Mortal Wkly Rep. 1981;30:250–252.

39. Graeber MB, Mehraein P. Reanalysis of the first case of Alzheimer's disease. Eur Arch Psychiatry Clin Neurosci. 1999;249:Suppl. 3:III/10–III/13.

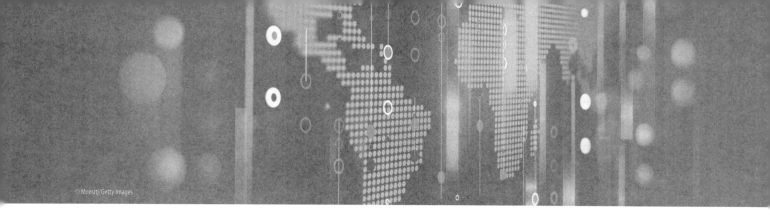

© Monsitj/Getty Images

CHAPTER 6
Behavioral Epidemiology

LEARNING OBJECTIVES

Having mastered the materials in this chapter, the student will be able to:

1. Explain the magnitude, demographic distribution, and socioeconomic impact of the following: (1) physical inactivity, (2) combustible and e-cigarette smoking, (3) obesity and poor nutrition, (4) alcohol and substance abuse, (5) cardiovascular disease, and (6) diabetes.
2. Explain the nature and effectiveness of monetary and nonmonetary incentives for patients to engage in a healthy lifestyle and behavior.
3. Explain the nature and effectiveness of incentives for healthcare providers to promote delivery of preventive care and adoption of a healthy lifestyle in patients.

CHAPTER OUTLINE

6.1   Introduction
6.2   Behavioral Epidemiology
6.3   Epidemiology of Physical Activity
6.4   Epidemiology of Smoking
    6.4.1 E-Cigarettes
6.5   Epidemiology of Obesity and Poor Nutrition
6.6   Epidemiology of Alcohol and Substance Abuse
6.7   Epidemiology of Cardiovascular Disease
    6.7.1 LIFE's Simple 7 to Improve Cardiovascular Health

6.8   Epidemiology of Diabetes
6.9   Patient Incentives to Promote Healthy Behavior
6.10   Incentives for Providers
Case Study 6.1 – Behavioral Factors and Risk of Gestational Diabetes
Case Study 6.2 – Body Mass Index, Waist Circumference, and Risk of Mortality
6.11   Summary

KEY TERMS

Behavioral epidemiology
Body mass index
E-cigarette

Gestational diabetes mellitus
Life's Simple 7
Metabolic equivalent

My Life Check
Waist circumference

▶ 6.1 Introduction

The use of digital behavior change interventions (DBCIs), including smartphone apps (i.e., applications), smartwatches, wearable sensors, and Internet websites, to promote healthy lifestyles and to monitor and reduce high-risk activities is an emerging area of research in behavioral epidemiology.[1] In the last few years, there has been an explosion in startup technology companies developing self-management, skills training, therapist-supported illness management, symptom tracking, and biofeedback apps and devices.[2] The use of mobile health technologies generally known as *mHealth* to monitor and improve health outcomes is becoming increasingly common. Between 2013 and 2015, the number of mHealth apps available on the Apple operating system known as iOS more than doubled, from about 43,700 to more than 90,000. By some estimates, more than 165,000 mHealth apps are currently available.[3] Most of these apps are geared toward wellness promotion and disease management.[4] Numerous smartphone apps are currently available to reduce excessive consumption of alcohol, increase physical activity, improve women's health, promote weight loss, and enhance treatment compliance for chronic conditions. However, the real impact of this new approach to influence health-related behaviors and lifestyle choices is not fully known. Some of the negative effects of electronic entertainment technologies such as video games, interactive social media such as Facebook, and mobile technologies such as smartphones on the physical and psychosocial health of individuals have been reported in recent literature[5-7] and are now an active area of research. Studies on health-related behaviors have also found that physicians, residents, and medical students get insufficient sleep, exercise insufficiently, and have depression, substance abuse, and alcohol dependence problems at higher rates than the rest of the population.[8,9]

For healthcare mangers, these technological developments are highly relevant because of the high prevalence of lifestyle- and behavior-related health problems and their ramifications for the healthcare system in terms of cost, healthcare utilization, workforce training, and additional services to be provided. On one hand, healthcare managers have to tackle issues arising from the diverse needs of patients with lifestyle-related health problems. On the other hand, they face administrative challenges posed by the existence of the same problems in their employees. The challenges of making special arrangements to meet patient needs range from having armless chairs and sofas, larger stretchers, and motorized wheelchairs to providing bariatric beds and operating tables with greater weight capacity to accommodate large patients. Staff need to be trained to "choose your words wisely" and use nonstigmatizing terminology but also to protect themselves and avoid injury while transporting, repositioning, and providing other care to large or overweight patients.

Existence of lifestyle-related health problems in the healthcare work force means greater absenteeism, lower productivity, more worker's compensation claims, more injuries, higher insurance costs, greater risk of liability, and theft of prescription drugs. Incentive programs are an important tool for healthcare managers to motivate patients and employees to take better care of themselves and to encourage healthcare providers to be more diligent about providing preventive care and patient counseling. This chapter is designed to give healthcare managers a better understanding of behavioral health issues and their impact on the healthcare system as well as the design and use of incentive programs for both patients and healthcare providers.

▶ 6.2 Behavioral Epidemiology

Behavioral epidemiology is defined as the investigation of the distribution and etiology of health-related behaviors in populations. This includes identification and description of demographic correlates of such behaviors—that is, how a behavior varies by age, sex, ethnicity, socioeconomic status, and other variables.[10] Behavioral epidemiology seeks to prevent disease and promote health by focusing on issues related to personal choice and behavior, including substance abuse, alcohol use, sexual behavior, obesity, and smoking. It explores the link between health-related behaviors and health outcomes such as cardiovascular disease, diabetes, and depression, and the distribution of these outcomes in various populations. Additionally, it relates to the study of outcomes such as hypertension, osteoporosis, and physical injury that also are affected by lifestyles and choices.[11]

Although epidemiologic investigations do not shed light on how to change behaviors that are implicated in the occurrence of various diseases, they can be used to evaluate behavioral change interventions. For example, randomized trials can be used to assess the efficacy of interventions designed to promote healthful behaviors or to modify unhealthful behaviors.[10] Once a behavioral intervention is shown to be effective, it can be implemented in schools, worksites, places of worship, healthcare facilities, and broader community settings to attain desired health outcomes at the population level.

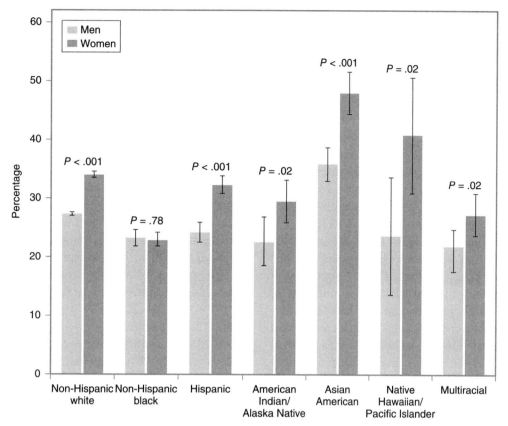

FIGURE 6.1 Age-adjusted prevalence of engaging in four or five health-related behaviors* among adults aged 21 years or older, Behavioral Risk Factor Surveillance System, 2013. Error bars indicate 95% confidence intervals.

* Never smoking, getting regular physical activity, consuming no alcohol or only moderate amounts, maintaining a normal body weight, and getting sufficient daily sleep.

Reproduced from: Liu Y, Croft JB, Wheaton AG, et al. Clustering of five health-related behaviors for chronic disease prevention among adults, United States, 2013. Prev Chronic Dis. 2016;13:160054. doi:10.5888/pcd13.160054

Key health-related behaviors to prevent chronic disease include never smoking, regular physical activity, alcohol abstinence or only moderate consumption, maintaining normal body weight, and sleeping at least 7 hours per 24-hour period. In 2013, only 6.3% of Americans reported engaging in all five behaviors, and 24.3% reported engaging in four of the five behaviors.[12] With the exception of Asian men, Asian women, and Native Hawaiian/Pacific Islander women, fewer than 30% of men and fewer than 40% of women in all racial groups in the United States in 2013 engaged in four or five key chronic disease prevention behaviors (**FIGURE 6.1**).

▶ 6.3 Epidemiology of Physical Activity

Metabolic equivalent is a measure of functional capacity in terms of the amount of oxygen consumed per minute. Sedentary behavior is defined as sitting or lying posture that involves ≤1.5 metabolic equivalents per minute.[13] The distribution of time spent in sleep, sedentary behavior, and light-intensity physical activity is strongly associated with greater body mass index (BMI), **waist circumference** (WC), triglycerides, plasma glucose, plasma insulin, and high systolic and diastolic blood pressure in adults and children. The proportion of time spent in moderate to vigorous physical activity, on the other hand, is reported to have a strikingly favorable effect on all of these health markers.[14,15]

In modern societies, people spend 50%–70% of their waking hours engaged in sedentary behavior, 25%–45% in low-intensity physical activity, and less than 5% in medium- to high-intensity physical activity.[16] Prolonged sedentary behavior is an independent risk factor for cardiometabolic disorders and all-cause mortality. Periodic breaking up of prolonged sitting, however, is shown to improve the cardiometabolic profile.[17] Breaking up prolonged sitting with periodic 5-minute bouts of light-intensity standing or walking has been shown to reduce blood sugar and insulin levels in postmenopausal overweight or obese women.[18]

In 2008, the U.S. Department of Health and Human Services (HHS) released its Physical Activity Guidelines for Americans of all ages. The guidelines for children 6 years or older are 60 minutes of daily aerobic, muscle-strengthening, and bone-strengthening physical activity. For adults, the HHS recommends 150 minutes each week of moderate-intensity (e.g., brisk walking or tennis) or 75 minutes of vigorous-intensity (e.g., jogging or swimming laps) aerobic physical activity or an equivalent combination of moderate- and vigorous-intensity aerobic physical activity. The guidelines also recommend that adults and older individuals engage in muscle-strengthening activities of moderate or high intensity and involving all major muscle groups (e.g., lifting weights or using resistance bands) two or more days a week.

Currently, only about 21% of adult Americans meet the guidelines for both weekly aerobic physical activity and muscle strength activity. About 23% of non-Hispanic whites, 16% of Hispanics, and 18% of non-Hispanic blacks meet the guidelines for both aerobic and muscle strength activity. A little over half of the men (54%) and fewer than half of women (46%) in the country meet the aerobic physical activity guidelines.[19,20] For both men and women, as age increased, the percentage of those who met the guidelines decreased.[19] Fewer women in each age group met the guidelines than did men. In 2015, the percentage of individuals 18 years or older who met both the muscle strength and aerobic guidelines rose to 21.6% from 14.3% in 1998. However, only 27.1% of high school students in the United States met the recommendation of 60 minutes or more of physical activity on all seven days of the week—14.3% of high school students reported no physical activity at all during the preceding 7 days.[21] Among adult Americans, those with more education, family income above the federal poverty level, and younger age are more likely to meet the HHS 2008 physical activity guidelines than their older, poorer, and less-educated counterparts.[22] Those living in the South are less likely to engage in physical activity as compared to those living in other regions of the country.[20]

▶ 6.4 Epidemiology of Smoking

Smoking has been causally linked to the diseases of almost all organs in human body and is known to harm the fetus in pregnant women. Secondhand smoke also seriously affects the health of exposed infants, children, and adults. Secondhand smoke has specifically been linked to cardiovascular and respiratory diseases and various cancers.[23,24] With 480,000 smoking-related deaths every year (20% of all deaths) and more than 16 million individuals living with a smoking-related disease, tobacco use is still the leading cause of

preventable death and disease in the United States.[24,25] Since 1964, more than 20 million deaths in the country have been attributed to cigarette smoking.

In 2015, about 52 million (20%) individuals age 12 years or older in the United States were estimated to be current cigarette smokers.[26] In the same year, with 36.5 million smokers 18 years of age or older (16.7% of men and 13.6% of women), smoking prevalence in the adult U.S. population was estimated to be 15.1%—a significant decline from 20.9% in 2005. Large disparities in tobacco use continue to exist across racial, educational, and socioeconomic divides. A higher tobacco use rate is associated with low socioeconomic status; being disabled; having mental illness; being Native American; and lesbian, gay, or transgender status. Among adult Americans, smoking prevalence is highest in Native Americans and Alaska Natives (20.9%) and lowest among Asian Americans (7.0%). In 2015, West Virginia had the highest overall tobacco use (26.7%), Kentucky had the highest adult smoking prevalence (25.9%), and Utah had the lowest overall tobacco use and adult smoking prevalence (9.7% and 9.1%, respectively).[21,27,28] In the same year, 26.1% of adult Americans living below the federal poverty level were current smokers. Cigarette smoking in U.S. non-college peers of the same age is much higher (23.4% in 2015) than full-time college students (11.3% in 2015). **FIGURE 6.2** shows the trends in the prevalence of cigarette smoking among adolescents and adults by sex and age.

Hookahs (also known as hubble-bubble and by a variety of other names), used in India, Pakistan, and Iran for hundreds of years, have rapidly become popular in the United States, Europe, Russia, and the Middle East in the last couple of decades. Hookah use by youth and high school or college students is also on the rise. According to Monitoring the Future, an annual survey of 8th-, 10th-, and 12th-grade U.S. students sponsored by the U.S. National Institute on Drug Abuse (NIDA), in 2010, 17% of boys and 15% of girls among U.S. high school seniors reported having used a hookah in the past year. There seems to be a downward trend in hookah smoking among American college students, of whom 23.4% in 2015 and 27.9% in 2011 reported smoking a hookah.[29]

The negative economic impact of smoking is staggering. Every year, smoking-related illness is estimated to cost the United States in excess of $300 billion. Of this amount, about $170 billion (8.7% of total healthcare spending) is spent on medical care of adults and $156 million is attributed to lost productivity.[24,25] On the other side, in 2014, cigarette and smokeless tobacco companies spent more than $9 billion (almost $25 million per day) on advertising in the United

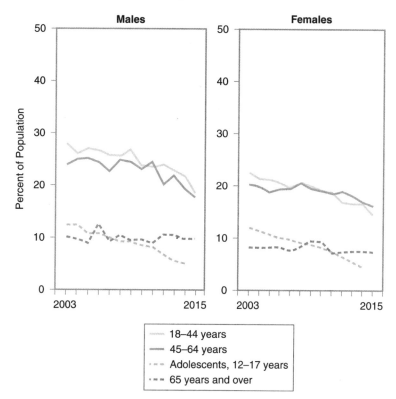

FIGURE 6.2 Trends in the prevalence of cigarette smoking among adolescents (past month) and adults (current) by sex and age (NHIS, 2003–2015; NSDUH, 2003–2014)*.

* NSDUH stands for National Survey on Drug Use and Health; NHIS stands for National Health Interview Survey.

Reproduced from: Benjamin EJ, Blaha MJ, Chiuve SE, et al. Heart disease and stroke statistics—2017 update: a report from the American Heart Association. Circulation. 2017;135. doi:10.1161/CIR.0000000000000485 e1

States alone. Of this amount, $6.8 billion was paid to wholesalers and retailers to reduce the price of cigarettes to consumers.[30] A considerable part of tobacco companies' advertising and promotional efforts is targeted at adolescents and youth. At the end of 2014, the average retail price of a pack of 20 cigarettes, including state and federal taxes, ranged from $5.06 in Missouri to $10.56 in New York.[31] Price increase is the single most effective way to reduce consumption, especially in youth and young adults, who are known to be two to three times more sensitive to price increase. A 10% price increase is estimated to reduce consumption by 3%–5%.[30]

6.4.1 E-Cigarettes

Various forms of electronic cigarettes (**e-cigarettes**), pipes, and hookahs are collectively known as electronic nicotine delivery systems (ENDSs). These are battery-operated devices that heat and deliver flavored or nonflavored aerosolized vapors of e-liquid nicotine and other chemicals for inhalation. As has long been known, nicotine is an addictive substance hazardous to human health. Secondhand exposure to e-cigarette emissions containing carcinogenic chemicals such as formaldehyde, benzene, and nitrosamines

is also hazardous to nonsmoker bystanders.[32] Varying amounts of nicotine are delivered by e-cigarettes of different brands and strengths, with little consistency within the same brand and labeled strength. Currently more than 500 brands and 7,700 flavors of e-cigarettes are available in the marketplace.[32] Despite various claims by manufacturers regarding the role of e-cigarettes in helping people to quit combustible cigarette smoking, as of May 2017, the U.S. Food and Drug Administration had not approved any e-cigarettes as a risk-free and effective method to help smokers of conventional cigarettes quit. Evidence indicates that many smokers of conventional cigarettes continue to smoke while concurrently using e-cigarettes. The U.S. Centers for Disease Control and Prevention (CDC) reported that in 2015, nearly 60% of those who had recently used e-cigarettes were current smokers of conventional cigarettes.[33]

In 2015, 3 million U.S. high school and middle school students—16% of high school and 5.3% of middle school students—were current e-cigarette users. This represented a marked increase from 1.5% and 0.6%, respectively, in 2011.[34] Other reports suggest that nearly 40% of high school students in the United States in 2015 smoked e-cigarettes, and twice as many boys as girls used e-cigarettes.[35] In the same year, 12.9% of noncollege peers of the same age and 8.8% of U.S. college students reported having used e-cigarettes in the past month.[36] The 2016 report of the U.S. Surgeon General on e-cigarette use among youth and young adults concluded that e-cigarette smoking is strongly linked with the use of other tobacco products in these groups. The report also found that from 2011 through 2015, there was an increase of 900% in e-cigarette use among high school students. Flavoring of e-cigarettes was the primary reason for their use by youth and young adults.[37] In another study, 81% of youth e-cigarette users reported flavoring of e-cigarettes to be the primary reason for use.[38] Although teens more often use e-cigarettes than conventional cigarettes, about 31% of teen e-cigarette smokers start smoking combustible conventional cigarettes within 6 months.[35,39]

Considering e-cigarettes to be a significant public health concern, in August 2016, the U.S. Food and Drug Administration began to enforce provisions of the Family Smoking Prevention and Tobacco Control Act that relate to the manufacturing, marketing, and sale of e-cigarettes.[21,37]

▶ 6.5 Epidemiology of Obesity and Poor Nutrition

Body mass index (BMI) is a measure of body fat in adult men and women age ≥20 years. It is derived by dividing body weight in kilograms by the height of the person in meters squared (i.e., kg/m^2). When weight and height are measured in pounds and inches, BMI is calculated by multiplying the weight in pounds with 703 and dividing the product by height in inches squared (i.e., weight in lbs. $\times 703/inches^2$). The U.S. National Heart, Lung, and Blood Institute; the American Heart Association; and many other organizations use the following categories of BMI: Underweight = BMI <18.5 kg/m^2; Normal weight = BMI 18.5–24.9 kg/m^2; Overweight = BMI 25–29.9 kg/m^2; Obese = BMI ≥ 30 kg/m^2. For adults, obesity is further categorized as Class I = BMI 30 to 34.9 kg/m^2; Class II = BMI 35 to 39.9 kg/m^2; and Class III = BMI ≥40 kg/m^2. For children (aged 2–19 years), instead of the BMI measurement itself, BMI percentiles, which are based on the CDC's age and sex-specific growth charts, are used as an indicator of body fat. In children, overweight is defined as 85th to <95th percentile, and obese is defined as ≥95th percentile.[40,41] The American Heart Association has recommended that severe obesity in children ≥2 years should be defined as BMI ≥120% of the 95th percentile for a given age and sex group, or

an absolute BMI ≥35 kg/m^2—whichever of the two is lower.[42] The American Heart Association notes that U.S. BMI and WC guidelines underestimate the obesity rate and the risk of cardiovascular disease in Asian and South Asian populations.[21]

A variety of BMI charts based on different height and weight ranges for men, women, and children are available online from multiple sources. Different charts also show the BMI ranges for underweight, normal weight, overweight, and obese somewhat differently. **FIGURE 6.3** is an example of a chart used by the Allegheny County Medical Society in Pittsburgh, Pennsylvania, and posted on the Society's website. A BMI calculator for adults and a BMI percentile calculator for child and teen percentiles are available from the CDC at its website:

Adult BMI Calculator:
www.cdc.gov/healthyweight/assessing/bmi
/adult_bmi/english_bmi_calculator/bmi
_calculator.html

Child and Teen BMI Percentile Calculator:
https://nccd.cdc.gov/dnpabmi/Calculator.aspx

Obesity affects health outcomes throughout the life course of an individual.[43] The physical, social, and psychological effects of obesity are multifaceted. Among youth, overweight and obesity are associated with poor academic performance, smoking, alcohol use, and premature sexual activity. In comparison with normal-weight adolescents, overweight or obese adolescents are 16 times more likely to have severe obesity (BMI ≥40) in adulthood, with accompanying risks of cardiovascular disease, hypertension, venous thromboembolism, sleep apnea, diabetes, stroke, depression, and overall lower quality of life. Variations in obesity-related health outcomes are influenced by both genetic and socioeconomic factors.

In the United States, the prevalence of obesity among adults increased significantly from 1999 through 2000 and in children from 1999 through 2014. However, the rate of increase in obesity prevalence began to level off in all age groups from 2003–2004 onward, and the increase in obesity prevalence through 2011–2012 in adults and through 2013–2014 in children was statistically not significant. According to the National Health and Nutritional Examination Survey (NHANES), in the period 2009–2012, overall, 69% of American adults (73% of men and 65% of women) were overweight or obese. Nearly 80% of Hispanic men, 73% of white men, and 69% of black men were overweight or obese, and 82% of black women, 76% of Hispanic women, and 61% of white women were overweight or obese.[40] In 2011–2014,

To determine your BMI*, find the column closest to your weight in pounds.
Follow the column down until it crosses the row that closely approximates your height in feet and inches.

Weight (lbs)	100	110	120	130	140	150	160	170	180	190	200	210	220	230	240	250	260	270	280	290	300	310	320	330
5'0"	20	21	23	25	27	29	31	33	35	37	39	41	43	45	47	49	51	53	55	57	59	61	63	65
5'1"	19	21	23	25	27	28	30	32	34	36	38	40	42	44	45	47	49	51	53	55	57	59	61	62
5'2"	18	20	22	24	26	27	29	31	33	35	37	38	40	42	44	46	48	49	51	53	55	57	59	60
5'3"	18	19	21	23	25	27	28	30	32	34	36	37	39	41	43	44	46	48	50	51	53	55	57	59
5'4"	17	19	21	22	24	26	28	29	31	33	34	36	38	40	41	43	45	46	48	50	52	53	55	57
5'5"	17	18	20	22	23	25	27	28	30	32	33	35	37	38	40	42	43	45	47	48	50	52	53	55
5'6"	16	18	19	21	23	24	26	27	29	31	32	34	36	37	39	40	42	44	45	47	49	50	52	53
5'7"	16	17	19	20	22	24	25	27	28	30	31	33	35	36	38	39	41	42	44	46	47	49	50	52
5'8"	15	17	18	20	21	23	24	26	27	29	30	32	34	35	37	38	40	41	43	44	46	47	49	50
5'9"	15	16	18	19	21	22	24	25	27	28	30	31	33	34	36	37	38	40	41	43	44	46	47	49
5'10"	14	16	17	19	20	22	23	24	26	27	29	30	32	33	35	36	37	39	40	42	43	45	46	47
5'11"	14	15	17	18	20	21	22	24	25	27	28	29	31	32	34	35	36	38	39	41	42	43	45	46
6'0"	14	15	16	18	19	20	22	23	24	26	27	29	30	31	33	34	35	37	38	39	41	42	43	45
6'1"	13	15	16	17	19	20	21	22	24	25	26	28	29	30	32	33	34	36	37	38	40	41	42	44
6'2"	13	14	15	17	18	19	21	22	23	24	26	27	28	30	31	32	33	35	36	37	39	40	41	42
6'3"	13	14	15	16	18	19	20	21	23	24	25	26	28	29	30	31	32	34	35	36	38	39	40	41
6'4"	12	13	15	16	17	18	20	21	22	23	24	26	27	28	29	30	32	33	34	35	37	38	39	40

Height (feet / inches)

Underweight (BMI less than 18) | Healthy weight (BMI 18–24.9) | Overweight (BMI 25–29.9) | Obese (BMI 30–39.9) | Severely obese (BMI>40)

*Chart for adults 20-years and older

FIGURE 6.3 Body mass index (BMI) chart.
Allegheny County Medical Society, 713 Ridge Avenue, Pittsburgh, PA 15212. Accessed on June 2, 2017. https://www.acms.org/wp-content/uploads/2015/10/2015BMIChart.pdf

36.5% of U.S. adults (38.3% of women and 34.3% of men) and 17% of youth were obese. The prevalence of obesity was much higher among those 40–59 years old (40.2%) and those 60 or older (37%) than younger adults (32.3%). With 11.7% obesity prevalence, Asian men were less likely to be obese than all other ethnic or racial groups (whites 34.5%, Hispanics 42.5%, and blacks 48.1%). A similar pattern of obesity was observed among women of different racial groups, with 11.9% of Asian women and 56.9% of black women being obese. In the 2011–2014 survey period, 17% of U.S. youth were obese, with 8.9% of preschool children (2–5 years old) and 20% of adolescents (12–19 years old) being obese. Similar patterns of obesity existed in both boys and girls. With 8.6% of Asian and 21.9% of Hispanic youth being obese, differences in obesity prevalence in children from different racial groups mimicked those in adults.[44] In 2015, Louisiana had the highest overall obesity prevalence of 36.2%, and Colorado had the lowest at 20.2%. In the same year, obesity prevalence exceeded 35% in four states (Alabama, Louisiana, Mississippi, West Virginia) and 30% in another 21 states.[45] **FIGURE 6.4** shows the prevalence of obesity in U.S. children and adolescents from 2011 to 2014.

Globally, poor nutrition is related to more disability and death than any other preventable health problem.[43,46] In the United States, inadequate diet is associated with nearly 1,000 diabetes and cardiovascular

disease–related deaths every day. Most of the diet-related cardiometabolic deaths are attributed to a diet that is high in sodium, low in nuts and seeds, high in processed meat, low in seafood omega-3 fats, low in vegetables and fruits, and high in sugar-sweetened beverages.[40,47] According to the 2015–2020 Dietary Guidelines for Americans issued by the U.S. Dietary Guidelines Advisory Committee, a healthy diet is high in vegetables, fruits, and whole grains; low in red and processed meat; low in sugar-sweetened content; and high in nuts, legumes, seafood, and low-fat or nonfat dairy products.[48] Between 1999 and 2012, the American Heart Association's Healthy Diet scores for Americans improved across all socioeconomic, ethnic, and educational strata. However, gains were more modest in lower income, lower education, and minority groups in comparison with the gains in scores of those in higher socioeconomic and educational strata. Consequently, disparities between groups widened in the same period.[21]

The financial burden of diet-related chronic diseases in the United States is estimated to be about $1 trillion per year. The economic cost of morbidity, mortality, and loss of productivity related to overweight and obesity in the United States and Canada was estimated in 2011 to be around $300 billion, of which $270 billion was attributed to the United States. Medical costs resulting from overweight and obesity accounted for $127 billion, and loss of productivity resulting from

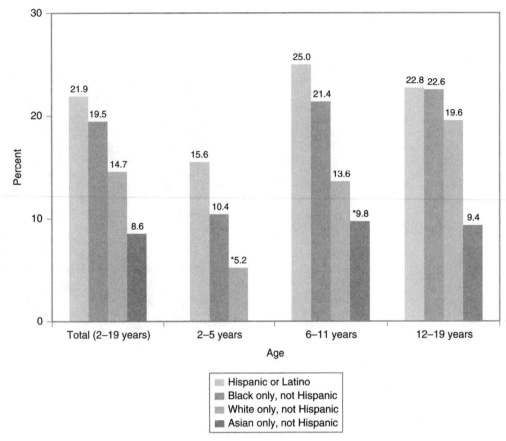

FIGURE 6.4 U.S. children and adolescents with obesity by race/ethnicity, 2011 to 2014*.

*Obesity defined as body mass index (BMI) at or above the sex-and-age-specific 95th percentile. BMI cutoff points are from the 2000 Centers for Disease Control and Prevention (CDC) growth charts.

Reproduced from Benjamin EJ, Blaha MJ, Chiuve SE, et al. Heart disease and stroke statistics—2017 update: a report from the American Heart Association. Circulation. 2017;135. doi:10.1161/CIR.0000000000000485 e1

excess mortality related to overweight and obesity equaled $49 billion.[49] Finkelstein et al.[50] estimated that the direct medical cost of obesity in the United States in 2008 had risen to $147 billion. Obese individuals pay about $1,429 (42%) higher per person in health-care costs as compared with those of normal weight. In 2008, obese beneficiaries cost Medicare $1,723, Medicaid $1,021, and commercial insurers $1,140 more than normal-weight beneficiaries. Likewise, they had 27% more frequent outpatient visits and 46% higher inpatient costs, and they spent 80% more on prescription medication than normal-weight individuals.[50]

▶ 6.6 Epidemiology of Alcohol and Substance Abuse

Alcohol consumption is associated with about 3.3 million deaths worldwide and is a component cause of more than 200 diseases. Excessive use of alcohol and its negative impact is differentially distributed in men and women worldwide, with much higher use and negative effects in men.[51] In 2015,

about 138.3 million Americans aged 12 years or older reported current use of alcohol. Of those, 66.7 million (24.9%) reported binge drinking (i.e., 5 or more drinks at the same time or within 2 hours), and 17.3 million (6.5%) reported heavy alcohol use (i.e., binge drinking on 5 or more days in the past 30 days).[26] The National Survey on Drug Use and Health (NSDUH) data from 2011 through 2014 indicated that close to 5.4 million (60.1%) full-time U.S. college students age 18–22 years old reported drinking alcohol in the past month. About 3.5 million (39%) of them had engaged in binge drinking, and 1.2 million (13.2%) in heavy alcohol use. In 2015, 31.9% of full-time U.S. college students reported having engaged in binge drinking in the past 2 weeks, and 38.4% reported having been drunk at least once in the past month. The statistics for the same behavior among noncollege individuals of the same age were 23.7% and 24.9%, respectively.[36] The 2016 Monitoring the Future survey of U.S. high school students found that 33.2% of 12th-grade students, 19.9% of 10th-grade students, and 7.3% of 8th-grade students reported having consumed alcohol in the past month.[29]

As of May 2017, recreational marijuana use was legal in eight U.S. states (Alaska, California, Colorado, Maine, Massachusetts Nevada, Oregon, and Washington) and the District of Columbia, and 28 states had passed laws allowing medical use of marijuana. A recent study reported that adult illicit marijuana use and marijuana use disorders are more common in states that have medical marijuana laws.[52] In 2015, approximately 27.1 million individuals (10.1%) aged 12 years or older in the United States reported using an illicit drug in the past 30 days, with 22.2 million using marijuana, and 3.8 million using prescription pain medication.[26] In the same year, about 4.6% of college students reported using marijuana on a daily basis—an increase from 3.7% in 1995.[36] However, the use of synthetic marijuana among U.S. college students declined by 80% between 2011 and 2015 and the use of salvia (a hallucinogenic herb in the mint family) declined by 90% between 2009 and 2015.[36] The Monitoring the Future survey reported that in 2016, nearly 69% of high school seniors did not consider regular marijuana smoking to be harmful, and 22.5% of 12th-grade students, 14.0% of 10th-grade students, and 5.4% of 8th-grade students reported having used marijuana in the past month.[29]

Among full-time and part-time college students in the United States, substance abuse is an ongoing serious problem.[53] In fact, attending college appears to be an independent risk factor for marijuana use. A recent study[54] based on longitudinal panel data gathered through annual surveys of 19- to 22-year-old individuals who had never used marijuana by 12th grade reported a consistently increasing probability of marijuana use in college in the past year. The increased probability of marijuana use after going to college was 31% in 2013 and 51% in 2015. The NSDUH 2011–2014 survey data showed that about 2 million (22.2%) of the 9 million full-time students reported using an illicit drug in the past month.[53] In any given year, of the approximately 11 million full-time or part-time college students, about 1 million start drinking alcohol for the first time—that is, 2,632 new college student drinkers every day. Of the 2 million part-time students, 1.1 million (56.4%) reported drinking alcohol in the past month. About 707,000 (35.5%) of them reported binge drinking, and 207,000 (10.4%) had engaged in heavy alcohol use. About 448,000 (22.5%) of the 2 million part-time students had used an illicit drug in the past month.[53]

Among Americans who are 65 years or older, substance use is an emerging public health problem.[55] Of the more than 1 million individuals 65 or older with a substance use disorder in 2014, 978,000 had an alcohol use problem, and 161,000 used illicit drugs.[56] By 2020, the number of older individuals with a substance abuse problem is expected to grow to approximately 5.7 million, more than doubling from 2.8 million in 2006.[57] Data from the NSDUH, conducted every year from 2007 through 2014, indicated that about 16.2 million Americans 65 years or older had reported consuming alcohol in the past month.[55] Among the 16.2 million were 3.4 million who reported binge drinking (5 or more drinks at the same time or within 2 hours) and 772,000 who reported heavy alcohol use (binge drinking on 5 or more days in the past 30 days). About 469,000 of individuals 65 or older reported using illicit drugs in the past 30 days. On any given day in the past month, 6 million older Americans had consumed alcohol, 132,000 used marijuana, and 4,300 had used cocaine. Data from the Drug Abuse Warning Network (DAWN) indicated that in 2011, older Americans made more than 750,000 drug-related visits (2,056 per day) to emergency departments. Nearly 106,000 of these visits were related to illicit drug and/or alcohol use, and about 645,000 involved adverse reactions to or accidental ingestion of prescription drugs.[55]

The ongoing epidemic of drug overdose in the United States resulted in more than 47,000 drug overdose deaths (14.7 deaths per 100,000) in 2014—more than double the rate of 6.2 deaths per 100,000 in 2000. The death rate from overdose in 2014 represented an increase of 6.5% from 13.8 overdose deaths per 100,000 in 2013. As a subgroup of overall drug overdose deaths, the rate of opioid overdose deaths increased from 7.9 in 2013 to 9.0 per 100,000 in 2014. The significant increase in all drug overdose deaths and opioid overdose deaths has affected both men and women; those between 25 and 44 years of age and those 55 years or older; non-Hispanic whites and non-Hispanic blacks; and the northeastern, midwestern, and southern regions of the country. Among opioid overdose deaths, the greatest increase (80%) from 2013 to 2014 was due to nonmethadone synthetic opioids such as fentanyl.[58]

In 2014, approximately 1,741 Americans between the ages of 18 and 25, nearly 5 per day, died of prescription drug overdose—more than four times of those (418) in 1999.[59] In 2016, there were close to 32,500 deaths (about 89 per day) involving prescription opioids, including nearly 17,100 deaths (about 47 per day) from synthetic opioid use. **FIGURE 6.5** shows trends in overdose deaths from different forms of opioids in the United States from 2000 to 2016.

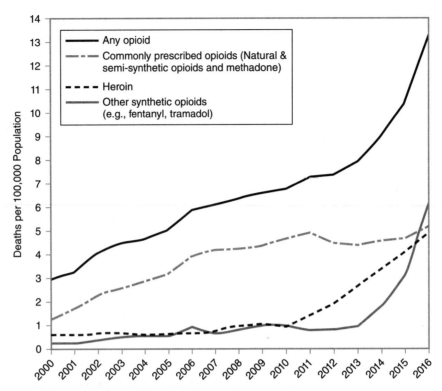

FIGURE 6.5 Overdose deaths involving opioids, United States, 2000–2016.

CDC/NCHA, National Vital Statistics System, Mortality. CDC WONDER. Atlanta, GA: US Department of Health and Human Services, CDC, 2017. https://wonder.cdc.gov/

▶ 6.7 Epidemiology of Cardiovascular Disease

With more than 810,000 deaths every year (approximately 2,200 every day)—about 31% of all deaths in the country—cardiovascular disease is the leading cause of death in the United States. Coronary heart disease is responsible for more than >45% of these deaths—about 370,000 annually. Approximately 790,000 individuals in the United States have a heart attack every year, and 114,000 die from it.[60] When considered separately from other cardiovascular diseases, stroke is the fifth leading cause of death in the United States. Historical data have shown that 40.6% of cardiovascular disease mortality in the United States is attributable to high blood pressure, 13.7% to smoking, 13.2% to poor diet, 7.8% to insufficient physical activity, and 7.5% to high blood glucose.[61] Currently, about 92.1 million adult Americans are living with one or more forms of cardiovascular disease. This includes 85.7 million who have high blood pressure (systolic blood pressure ≥140 mmHg and/or diastolic blood pressure ≥90 mmHg) and 16.5 million with coronary heart disease (some have both hypertension and coronary heart disease). About 27.6 million individuals in the country (11.5% of population) have one or the other type of heart disease, such as congestive heart failure, angina pectoris, or myocardial infarction.[62] The overall societal cost of cardiovascular disease in the United States in 2012–

2013 was estimated to be in excess of $316 billion.[21] From 2004 to 2014, the annual age-standardized death rate from coronary heart disease declined by about 35.5% and stroke-related death rate by 28.7%. Overall, annual age standardized death rate from cardiovascular diseases dropped from 295.7 per 100,000 in 2004 to 220.8 per 100,000 in 2014—a drop of 25%.[21,60]

Social risk factors for cardiovascular disease include low income, minority status, low education, and single-living status. These factors are also linked with lower probability of attaining good cardiovascular health.[63] Close to half of all African American men and women suffer from some form of cardiovascular disease and have twice the risk of first-ever stroke than whites. African Americans also have a much higher stroke death rate. While the prevalence of coronary heart disease is similar in whites, blacks, and Hispanics, the prevalence of hypertension is higher in blacks. Overall, mortality data from 2001 through 2010 showed that the avoidable mortality rate in blacks was nearly twice of that in whites.[21]

6.7.1 LIFE's Simple 7 to Improve Cardiovascular Health

Successful health improvement strategies focus on the individual and target lifestyle changes. These strategies encourage, facilitate, and reward the efforts of providers and patients to achieve better health through lifestyle changes. In a study of almost 45,000 Americans

20 years or older, between 2005 and 2010, only 1.2% were adhering to all seven criteria considered essential for optimal heart health by the American Heart Association.[64] These individuals had a 76% lower risk of dying from a heart-related problem and, overall, had a 51% lower risk of death as compared with those who were adhering to only one or none of the seven criteria. Achieving a high score on cardiovascular health metrics is associated with lower risk of cardiovascular disease, stroke, and cardiovascular mortality.[21]

The American Heart Association has declared a 20% improvement in the cardiovascular health of all Americans and a 20% reduction in deaths from cardiovascular diseases and stroke as its 2020 Impact Goal.[21] The Association hopes to achieve this goal by promoting the following seven changes in personal health that contribute to cardiovascular health: (1) no smoking, (2) maintaining a healthy weight, (3) engaging in regular physical activity, (4) eating a healthy diet, (5) maintaining normal blood pressure, (6) maintaining normal blood cholesterol, and (7) maintaining a normal blood sugar level. The Association calls this strategy **Life's Simple 7.** "Ideal cardiovascular health," according to the Association, is characterized by the absence of "clinically manifest cardiovascular disease with the simultaneous presence of optimal levels of all 7 metrics."[21] To help individuals achieve these targets and monitor progress, the Association has developed an online self-assessment tool called **My Life Check** (http://mylifecheck.heart.org). This tool allows individuals to enter their demographic information and data on the seven components of Life's Simple 7 and instantly receive a cardiovascular health status report. By periodically carrying out this self-assessment, individuals can keep track of changes in their Life's Simple 7 components and improvement in their cardiovascular health score on a scale of 0 to 10.

▶ 6.8 Epidemiology of Diabetes

The prevalence of type 2 diabetes in the United States almost doubled from 5.5% in 1994 to 9.3% in 2012. Although the number of newly diagnosed cases of diabetes has begun to decline, currently about 23.4 million adult Americans have diagnosed diabetes mellitus, and 7.6 million are living with undiagnosed diabetes. The CDC estimated that in 2016, 86 million U.S. adults—more than one-third of the total population—had prediabetes, and 90% of them were unaware of their condition.[21,65] About 95% of diagnosed cases of diabetes are type 2, and 5% are type 1 (commonly known as juvenile-onset diabetes). With more than 76,000 deaths attributed to diabetes-related complications in 2014, diabetes was the seventh most common cause of death in the United States. It is also the most common cause of kidney failure, lower limb amputation, and adult blindness. Additionally, it is a major risk factor for cardiovascular disease, stroke, and peripheral artery disease. Gestational diabetes, which is diagnosed during pregnancy, is often a precursor of type 2 diabetes later in life. It is also a strong risk factor for pregnancy-related hypertension (preeclampsia) in women and birth defects in newborns.[21,65]

In 2009, out of 3.4 million children under the age of 20 years, 6,666 (1.93 per thousand) were diagnosed with type 1 diabetes, with the highest prevalence (2.55 per 1,000) in white children and the lowest (0.55 per 1,000) in Native American children. In the same year, 819 children out of 1.8 million (0.46 per 1,000) were diagnosed with type 2 diabetes, with the highest prevalence (1.06 per 1,000) in black children and the lowest (0.17 per 1,000) in white children. Type 2 diabetes, typically found in those age ≥40, has been on the rise in American youth in recent years. Children with type 2 diabetes are usually overweight or obese and have a family history of diabetes. Among black diabetic youth, nearly 58% had type 2 diabetes, whereas in white diabetic youth, the prevalence of type 2 diabetes was only about 15%; the rest had type 1 diabetes.[66] Overall, type 2 diabetes in American youth increased by 30.5% between 2001 and 2009.[67] Currently, about 186,000 youth.

▶ 6.9 Patient Incentives to Promote Healthy Behavior

Financial incentives to promote healthy behavior have been used in the United States and other countries, including the United Kingdom, Germany, Canada, and South Africa, for a number of years with mixed results.[71,72] Large employers in the private sector have been particularly active in adopting incentive programs to promote healthy behavior among employees. In 2011, 80% of surveyed large U.S. employers planned to use financial incentives in the next year.[73] In 2013, 90% of U.S. employers reportedly offered wellness incentives or financial rewards averaging $521 per employee to get healthier.[74] Through federal funding, Medicaid programs in a few states provide incentives in the form of credits that can be exchanged for goods; premium assistance for preventive services such as wellness visits; and vouchers to attend healthy lifestyle programs, including those for weight loss and smoking cessation. In 2015, 15 states provided healthy lifestyle incentives to various segments of the state Medicaid population. Some of the programs encourage use of health services, such as attending primary care appointments, getting prenatal care, attending a postpartum visit, and filling prescriptions for chronic conditions, whereas others focus on smoking cessation, decreasing systolic blood pressure, maintaining healthy diet, and increasing physical activity.[75]

Drivers of incentive programs include concerns about rising healthcare costs and poor health outcomes in patients with chronic conditions. Despite a growing body of literature showing that, in varying degrees, financial incentives are effective in promoting healthy behavior, gaps persist in our understanding regarding the most responsive health-related behaviors and patient characteristics, size of financial incentives, and optimal design of incentive programs.[76] One clear finding, however, is that incentive programs are more successful in changing behaviors related to one-time preventive services, such as vaccination for flu or pneumonia, and less effective for problems such as obesity, hypertension, or smoking, which require ongoing engagement of patients.[71] Past research has shown that cash incentives are much preferred over noncash incentives such as vouchers and gifts.[77] Studies have also shown that there is a clear relationship between the magnitude of an incentive and its effectiveness, and that people generally respond more to immediate rewards than delayed rewards, such as reduction in insurance premiums next year.[78] According to some estimates, in 2011 financial incentives of $100 or more were needed to get about 75% of employees to participate in wellness, healthy diet, and fitness programs.[74,79] Inadequate communication with the target population, heavy reliance on provider participation, and administrative complexities also reduce the chances of an incentive program being successful.[71] Both immediate and delayed modest cash or prize awards to elementary school children in Utah for eating at least one serving of fruits and vegetables during school lunch have been shown to significantly enhance school children's consumption of fruits and vegetables. This impact was even more pronounced in schools with larger proportions of low-income children.[80] A 2011 pilot program in Hampden County, Massachusetts, with 7,500 participating households also showed that a modest amount of additional cash to buy fruits and vegetables resulted in a notable increase in daily consumption of fruits and vegetables.[81,82] The subjects of this study were recipients of the federal Supplemental Nutrition Assistance Program (SNAP, formerly known as "food stamps").

According to a 2013 *Wall Street Journal* report,[74] Caterpillar Inc. reduced premiums by $75 per month for employees who participated in a health-risk assessment program. About 90% of Caterpillar's eligible employees participated in the program. JetBlue Airways offered employees from $25 to $400 for engaging in a range of healthy lifestyle activities, from teeth cleaning to completing an Ironman triathlon. To avoid a payroll surcharge of $25 per month, the city of Houston required employees to complete a health-risk assessment; have a biometric screening; and participate in a health coaching, weight management, or breast-screening program. Nearly 90% of employees had completed three or more of these activities. The Florida Blue insurance company offered employees up to $500 for reducing multiple risk factors such as high cholesterol, hypertension, and overweight. Employees of Johnson & Johnson received a discount of up to $500 on annual health insurance premiums for submitting a personal health profile, and an additional incentive of $100–$250 for participating in health improvement activities.

In summary, the following lessons have been gleaned from the literature on the design and implementation of financial or nonfinancial incentives:[83]

1. The goals of behavioral change should be simple and clearly delineated, such as weight management, exercise, and smoking cessation.
2. Incentives involving office visits for screening, vaccination, or wellness are more effective because they require direct action of the participant and feedback from the provider.
3. Financial or cash incentives should be available immediately rather than being delayed.
4. Potential participants should be given direct and clear information about the availability of incentives.
5. Incentive programs that use physicians as gatekeepers are not very effective.
6. Programs that involve default enrollment rather than active engagement and action on the part of the participant are not very effective.
7. Programs that use vouchers (e.g., for a gym) but do not address other barriers such as transportation or child care are not very effective.

▶ 6.10 Incentives for Providers

Financial incentives, generally known as *pay-for-performance* (P4P), are commonly provided to healthcare providers to improve the quality of care and health outcomes. Essentially, P4P is a payment model that gives financial rewards to providers for achieving health and wellness targets or imposes penalties for failing to achieve those targets. Incentives in this model take the form of both reward and punishment—that is, carrot and stick—for attaining or failing to attain specified goals. These programs mostly target preventive care modalities such as vaccinations; screenings; counseling; and attainment of intermediate health outcomes such as blood pressure, cholesterol, and blood sugar control. Typically, P4P programs give bonuses to providers in addition to their base salary or fee schedule. Sometimes they take the form in which part of the base salary is withheld and released at the end of the year if targets for wellness, preventive care, or intermediate health outcomes, such as attainment of normal blood pressure in hypertensive patients, are achieved by the provider.

Research literature indicates that processes of care and the use of preventive services are relatively easier to improve. Sustained improvement in health outcomes is more difficult to achieve.[84] For example, in the United Kingdom, the nationwide P4P program known as Quality Outcomes Framework (QOF), which was imple-mented in 2004 by the U.K. National Health Service (NHS), has shown improvements in the overall quality of diabetes care provided by primary care physicians. In the United States, increased numbers of HbA1c tests and diabetic eye examinations have been reported in association with P4P programs implemented by various entities such as insurance companies and federally qualified community health centers.[84] Brief interventions in the form of advice from primary care physicians provided opportunistically and regularly on smoking cessation and alcohol consumption are known to have a positive impact on patient behavior. However, advice to reduce alcohol consumption is given much less often than advice for smoking cessation.[85] At this time, it is not clear how much impact P4P programs actually have on long-term health outcomes in patients.

🔍 CASE STUDY 6.1: Behavioral Factors and Risk of Gestational Diabetes

Modified from: Badon SE, Enquobahrie DA, Wartko PD, et al. Healthy lifestyle during early pregnancy and risk of gestational diabetes mellitus. Am J Epidemiol. 2017 May 6. doi:10.1093/aje/kwx095. Accessed May 22, 2017.

Gestational diabetes mellitus (GDM) poses a serious threat to the health of both mother and child. In this prospective cohort study conducted by Badon et al. in 2017, the researchers examined the independent and overall combined effect of diet, physical activity, nonsmoking, and low stress during early pregnancy on the risk of GDM. In total, 4,602 pregnant English-speaking women 18 years or older who had received prenatal care at clinics associated with the Swedish Medical Center and Tacoma General Hospital in Washington State from 1996 through 2008 were recruited for the study. The participants completed an in-person structured interview around the 15th week of pregnancy and provided demographic, socioeconomic, medical, reproductive, and lifestyle information. Participants were followed until delivery. Information related to the course of pregnancy, including GDM and other complications, was abstracted from medical records. Pre-pregnancy body mass index (BMI) was calculated on the bases of reported pre-pregnancy height and weight.

Based on questions related to leisure-time physical activity, diet during the preceding 12 weeks, current smoking status and history, and various forms of stress during the preceding 12 weeks, each of these lifestyle behaviors was treated as a dichotomous (yes/no or 1/0) variable and categorized as healthy or unhealthy (healthy = 1, unhealthy = 0). The number of healthy lifestyle behaviors were added for each participant to obtain an aggregated lifestyle score. As such, the combined score for the four lifestyle factors for each participant ranged from zero to four (0–4). All participants were tested for GDM between 24 and 28 weeks of pregnancy using a 50 g glucose challenge test and a follow-up 100 g 3-hour oral glucose tolerance test if they failed the 50 g glucose challenge test. Altogether, 140 participants were diagnosed with GDM.

After excluding those with preexisting type 1 or type 2 diabetes, missing data, or implausible values of variables, data on 3,005 participants were used for statistical analysis. Of the 3,005 participants, 20% had a healthy diet, 66% were physically active, 95% were nonsmokers, and 55% had low stress. Descriptive statistical analysis showed that those with higher healthy lifestyle scores were more likely to be white, nulliparous, married, have at least a high school education, have normal body weight before pregnancy (18.5–24.9 kg/m²), and have no family history of diabetes than those with low healthy lifestyle scores. In addition to descriptive statistical analysis, adjusting for various extraneous factors, separate regression models were developed to assess the relative risk (RR) of GDM associated with each of the lifestyle components individually (**TABLE 6.1**) and for each 1-point-change in the overall lifestyle score. Regression analysis in Model I adjusted for age, race, and nulliparity; analysis in Model II adjusted for age, race, nulliparity, and pre-pregnancy BMI; and analysis in Model III adjusted for age, race, nulliparity, pre-pregnancy BMI, pre-pregnancy physical activity, and pre-pregnancy smoking status. Overall, the results showed that after adjusting for age, race, and absence of previous children (nulliparous), a 1-point increase in lifestyle score was associated with a 21% lower risk of developing GDM (RR = 0.79; 95% CI = 0.65–0.96). Women with a healthy lifestyle score of 0 had 4.43 times the risk of GDM when compared with women who had a lifestyle score of 4. Those with a lifestyle score of 4 were at a 35% lower risk of GDM than women who had a score of 3 or less, although this finding was statistically not significant.

(continues)

Table 6.1 shows some of the results of this study.

Questions

Question 1. Based on the data shown in Table 6.1, were any of the lifestyle components truly associated with lower relative risk (RR) of GDM? Explain which ones and why.

Question 2. Which lifestyle factor seems to reduce the risk of GDM the most? Explain with the help of data from Table 6.1.

Question 3. Which lifestyle factor seems to have the least effect in lowering the risk of GDM? Explain with the help of data from Table 6.1.

TABLE 6.1 Association of Each Healthy Lifestyle Component During Early Pregnancy With Reduced Risk of Gestational Diabetes

Lifestyle Component	No. With Healthy Score	No. With GDM*	Relative Risk of GDM* Unadjusted	Relative Risk of GDM* Model 1	Relative Risk of GDM* Model II	Relative Risk of GDM* Model III
Healthy diet	611	25 (4%)	0.86 (0.57–1.32)[†]	0.85 (0.56–1.30)[†]	0.90 (0.59–1.37)[†]	0.92 (0.61–1.41)[†]
Physically active	1,990	85 (4%)	0.82 (0.59–1.14)[†]	0.88 (0.63–1.22)[†]	0.89 (0.64–1.24)[†]	0.97 (0.69–1.36)[†]
Nonsmoker	2,854	129 (5%)	0.68 (0.37–1.23)[†]	0.55 (0.30–0.99)[†]	0.58 (0.33–1.03)[†]	0.47 (0.24–0.92)[†]
Low stress	1,666	65 (4%)	0.72 (0.52–0.99)[†]	0.75 (0.55–1.04)[†]	0.78 (0.56–1.07)[†]	0.80 (0.58–1.09)[†]

*Gestational diabetes mellitus.
[†]95% confidence interval.
Modified with permission from: Oxford University Press: Badon SE, Enquobahrie DA, Wartko PD, et al. Healthy lifestyle during early pregnancy and risk of gestational diabetes mellitus. Am J Epidemiol. 2017 May 6. doi:10.1093/aje/kwx095. Accessed May 22, 2017.

🔎 CASE STUDY 6.2: Body Mass Index, Waist Circumference, and Risk of Mortality

Chen Z, Klimentidis YC, Bea JW, Ernst KC, Hu C, Jackson R, Thomson CA. Body mass index, waist circumference, and mortality in a large multiethnic postmenopausal cohort – results from the women's health initiative. J Am Geriatr Soc. 2017 Feb 23. doi:10.1111/jgs.14790. Accessed on June 1, 2017.

Obesity, whether measured through body mass index (BMI) or through waist circumference (WC), is a known underlying cause of death in men and women. The purpose of this prospective cohort study by Chen et al., published in the *Journal of American Geriatric Society* in 2017, was to examine whether the relationship between obesity and mortality varies by age and racial or ethnic background in postmenopausal American women. Overall, 161,808 postmenopausal women aged 50–79 years were recruited between 1993 and 1998 in a larger study known as the Women's Health Initiative. Their height, weight, and WC were measured and BMI (kg/m²) calculated at the onset of the study, and they were followed for a mean of 11.4 ± 3.2 years. Demographic, health, and lifestyle information was obtained at the onset of the study. During the follow-up period that continued until May 2011, 18,320 women died from various causes—mostly cancer and cardiovascular disease. Verification of death and information on the circumstances of death were obtained from multiple sources, including the National Death Index, hospital records, autopsy records, and death certificates.

For statistical analyses, patients were grouped by different categories of BMI and WC (see **TABLE 6.2**). All-cause mortality was used as the outcome of interest. The researchers carried out *t*-tests and chi square statistical tests to compare demographic and lifestyle characteristics of subjects in various BMI groups. Cox regression models were used to examine the relationship of different categories of BMI and WC with all-cause mortality in various age and race groups with or without adjusting for differences in demographic and lifestyle characteristics. Three different Cox regression models were developed. The first model was unadjusted for any variables; the second was adjusted for age; and the third was adjusted for variables such as age, annual income, alcohol intake, physical activity, and several other characteristics (see Table 6.2). Hazard ratios were derived by dividing the annual risk of mortality (hazard rate) in each category of BMI and WC by the annual risk of mortality (hazard rate) in the reference category. Normal BMI (18.5–24.9 kg/m²) and normal WC (80–89 cm) were used as reference groups in respective sets of analyses.

Table 6.2 shows partial results of this study.

Questions

Question 1. From Table 6.2, among those with BMI <18.5, which racial group has the highest risk of mortality?

Question 2. From Table 6.2, what observations can you make about the risk of mortality in obesity levels II (BMI 35.0–39.9) and III (BMI >40) and WC categories 105–114 and ≥115?

TABLE 6.2 Body Mass Index and Waist Circumference Cox Model for All-Cause Mortality Stratified According to Ethnicity

	Model 1			Model 2			Model 3		
Factor	African American	Hispanic	Non-Hispanic White	African American	Hispanic	Non-Hispanic White	African American	Hispanic	Non-Hispanic White
BMI, kg/m² (reference 18.5–24.9)									
BMI	**Hazard Ratio* (95% Confidence Interval)**								
<18.5	1.98 (1.13–3.45)	3.10 (1.14–8.46)	2.09 (1.83–2.38)	1.89 (1.08–3.30)	3.15 (1.16–8.57)	1.94 (1.70–2.21)	1.68 (0.96–2.95)	3.52 (1.28–9.65)	1.67 (1.45–1.92)
25.0–29.9	0.98 (0.83–1.13)	0.97 (0.74–1.26)	1.01 (0.98–1.05)	1.00 (0.86–1.16)	0.99 (0.75–1.29)	0.98 (0.94–1.02)	1.02 (0.87–1.20)	0.97 (0.72–1.31)	0.94 (0.90–0.98)
30.0–34.9	1.02 (0.87–1.19)	1.42 (1.08–1.88)	1.13 (1.08–1.18)	1.10 (0.94–1.38)	1.55 (1.17–2.04)	1.14 (1.08–1.19)	1.10 (0.93–1.31)	1.42 (1.04–1.95)	1.02 (0.97–1.07)
35.0–39.9	1.31 (1.11–1.55)	1.69 (1.20–2.39)	1.30 (1.23–1.39)	1.50 (1.26–1.78)	2.00 (1.42–2.83)	1.42 (1.33–1.51)	1.37 (1.14–1.66)	1.99 (1.36–2.91)	1.21 (1.13–1.29)
≥40	1.22 (1.01 1.48)	2.50 (1.70–3.69)	1.50 (1.39–1.63)	1.54 (1.27–1.86)	2.89 (1.96–4.26)	1.83 (1.69–1.99)	1.36 (1.10–1.68)	2.41 (1.57–3.70)	1.44 (1.32–1.57)
WC, cm (reference 80–89)									
WC	**Hazard Ratio* (95% Confidence Interval)**								
≤79	0.87 (0.74–1.02)	0.87 (0.66–1.14)	0.87 (0.84–0.91)	0.87 (0.74–1.02)	0.86 (0.66–1.13)	0.94 (0.90–0.98)	0.88 (0.74–1.05)	0.96 (0.71–1.30)	0.98 (0.93–1.02)
90–104	1.28 (1.13–1.45)	1.40 (1.10–1.79)	1.21 (1.16–1.26)	1.31 (1.16–1.48)	1.41 (1.10–1.81)	1.21 (1.16–1.26)	1.18 (1.03–1.35)	1.40 (1.06–1.85)	1.11 (1.06–1.16)

(continues)

TABLE 6.2 Body Mass Index and Waist Circumference Cox Model for All-Cause Mortality Stratified According to Ethnicity *(continued)*

Factor	Model 1			Model 2			Model 3		
	African American	Hispanic	Non-Hispanic White	African American	Hispanic	Non-Hispanic White	African American	Hispanic	Non-Hispanic White
105–114	1.51 (1.28–1.77)	2.49 (1.80–3.44)	1.45 (1.37–1.54)	1.67 (1.42–1.96)	2.74 (1.98–3.78)	1.57 (1.48–1.67)	1.36 (1.14–1.62)	2.66 (1.86–3.80)	1.36 (1.27–1.45)
≥115	1.77 (1.47–2.13)	3.09 (2.05–4.68)	1.89 (1.75–2.03)	2.16 (1.80–2.61)	3.15 (2.08–4.76)	2.24 (2.08–2.41)	1.72 (1.41–2.10)	2.30 (1.43–3.69)	1.74 (1.61–1.88)

Model 1: Unadjusted.
Model 2: Adjusted for age.
BMI Model 3: Adjusted for age, annual income, alcohol intake, physical activity, smoking status, diabetes mellitus, study arm (interventions).
WC Model 3: Adjusted for age, height, annual income, alcohol intake, physical activity, smoking status, diabetes mellitus, study arm (interventions).
*Hazard ratio compares the risk of death in a BMI or WC category with the risk of death in the reference category. For example, in WC Model 3, a ratio of 1.72 indicates that, after adjusting for a number of other risk factors, postmenopausal African American women whose waist circumference was ≥115 centimeters were at 72% greater risk of death as compared with those postmenopausal African American women whose waist circumference was between 80 and 89 centimeters.

▶ 6.11 **Summary**

This chapter provides an overview of the most common health-related behaviors and their impact on the healthcare system and the society. Diabetes and cardiovascular disease are the leading causes of morbidity, mortality, and disability in the United States and all over the world. The socioeconomic costs of these diseases in terms of healthcare utilization and loss of productivity are staggering. These diseases are causally linked with a lack of physical activity, smoking, poor nutrition, obesity, and alcohol and substance abuse, which are themselves connected to each other. In turn, all these factors are linked with low education, low income, and minority status, creating a cycle of social disadvantage and deprivation. Ironically, these factors are also amenable to low-cost, low-technology educational and behavioral interventions that can be implemented at a fraction of the cost of resources employed to deal with the consequences of these lifestyle choices. In a multidimensional approach, a variety of monetary and nonmonetary incentives for patients and providers, as well as social programs and legislative actions, can be used to address these behavioral epidemiologic issues. It is imperative for effective healthcare managers to understand the dimensions of behavioral epidemiology and the scope of various interventions. The materials presented in this chapter can be of value in developing such an understanding.

References

1. Crane D, Garnett C, Brown J, West R, Michie S. Factors influencing usability of a smartphone app to reduce excessive alcohol consumption: think aloud and interview studies. Front Public Health. 2017;5 [cited 2017 May 2]. Available from: http://journal.frontiersin.org/article/10.3389/fpubh.2017.00039/full

2. Doneva R. Digital intervention for mental health. Medium. 2016 [cited 2017 May 2]. Available from: https://medium.com/experience-design-for-ptsd/digital-interventions-for-mental-health-e99e16c6a718

3. Institute for Healthcare Informatics. Patient adoption of mHealth: use, evidence and remaining barriers to mainstream acceptance. 2015 [cited 2017 May 23]. Available from: http://www.imshealth.com/files/web/IMSH%20Institute/Reports/Patient%20Adoption%20of%20mHealth/IIHI_Patient_Adoption_of_mHealth.pdf

4. Kao C, Liebovitz DM. Consumer mobile health apps: current state, barriers, and future directions. J Phys Med Rehabil. 2017;9:S106–115.

5. Cookingham LM, Ryan GL. The impact of social media on the sexual and social wellness of adolescents. J Pediatr Adolesc Gynecol. 2015;28(1):2–5.

6. Moreno MA, Kolb J. Social networking sites and adolescent health. Pediatr Clin North Am. 2012;59(3):601–612.

7. Strasburger VC, Jordan AB, Donnerstein E. Health effects of media on children and adolescents. Pediatrics. 2010;125(4):756–767.

8. Hull SK, DiLalla LF, Dorsey JK. Prevalence of health-related behaviors among physicians and medical trainees. Acad Psychiatry. 2008;32(1):31–38.

9. Garg A, Chavan BS, Singh GP, Bansal E. Patterns of alcohol consumption in medical students. J Indian Med Assoc. 2009;107(3):151–152.

10. Sallis JF, Owen N, Fotheringham MJ. Behavioral epidemiology: a systematic framework to classify phases of research on health promotion and disease prevention. Ann Behav Med. 2000;22(4):294–298.

11. Raymond JS. Behavioral epidemiology: the science of health promotion. Health Promot Int. 1989;4(4):281–286.

12. Liu Y, Croft JB, Wheaton AG, et al. Clustering of five health-related behaviors for chronic disease prevention among adults, United States, 2013. Prev Chronic Dis. 2016;13:160054. doi:http://dx.doi.org/10.5888/pcd13.160054

13. Chevance G, Foucaut AM, Bernard P. State of knowledge on sedentary behaviors. Presse Med. 2016;45(3):313–318.

14. Chastin SF, Palarea-Albaladejo J, Dontje ML, Skelton DA. Combined effects of time spent in physical activity, sedentary behaviors and sleep on obesity and cardio-metabolic health markers: a novel compositional data analysis approach. PLoS ONE. 2015;13(10). doi:10.1371/journal.pone.0139984.

15. Vaisto J, Eloranta AM, Viitasalo A, et al. Physical activity and sedentary behavior in relation to cardiometabolic risk in children: cross-sectional findings from the Physical Activity and Nutrition in Children (PANIC) study. Int J of Behav Nutr Phys Act. 2014 Apr 26;11:55.

16. Rotman D, Constantini N. A paradigm shift in the perception of health maintenance from increasing physical activity to decreasing physical inactivity. Harefuah. 2016;155(6):374–377.

17. Benatti FB, Ried-Larsen M. The effects of breaking up prolonged sitting time: A review of experimental studies. Med Sci Sports Exerc. 2015;47(10):2053–2061.

18. Henson J, Davies MJ, Bodicoat DH, et al. Breaking up prolonged sitting with standing or walking attenuates the postprandial metabolic response in postmenopausal women. A randomized acute study. Diabetes Care. 2016;39(1):130–138.

19. Ward BW, Clarke TC, Nugent CN, Schiller JS. Early release of selected estimates based on data from the 2015 National Health Survey. U.S. Department of Health and Human Services, Centers for Disease Control and Prevention. 2016 May [cited 2017 Jun 5]. Available from: https://www.cdc.gov/nchs/data/nhis/earlyrelease/earlyrelease201605.pdf

20. Centers for Disease Control and Prevention. Facts about physical activity. 2014 [cited 2017 May 24]. Available from: https://www.cdc.gov/physicalactivity/data/facts.htm

21. Benjamin EJ, Blaha MJ, Chiuve SE, et al. Heart disease and stroke statistics—2017 update: a report from the American Heart Association. Circulation. 2017 Mar 7;135. doi:10.1161/CIR.0000000000000485 e1

22. Centers for Disease Control and Prevention. Facts about physical activity. 2016 [cited 2017 Apr 14]. Available from: https://www.cdc.gov/physicalactivity/data/facts.htm

23. Centers for Disease Control and Prevention. Current cigarette smoking among adults in the United States. 2015 [cited 2017 Jun 5]. Available from: https://www.cdc.gov/tobacco/data_statistics/fact_sheets/adult_data/cig_smoking/

24. U.S. Department of Health and Human Services. The health consequences of smoking—50 years of progress: a report of the Surgeon General. Atlanta, GA: Centers for Disease Control and Prevention, Office on Smoking and Health; 2014.

25. Xu X, Bishop EE, Kennedy SM, Simpson SA, Pechacek TF. Annual healthcare spending attributable to cigarette smoking: an update. Am J Prev Med. 2015;48(3):326–333.

26. Bose J, Hedden SL, Lipari RN, Park-Lee E, Porter JD, Pemberton MR. Key substance use and mental health indicators in the United States: results from the 2015 National Survey on Drug Use. 2016 [cited 2017 May 17]. https://www.samhsa.gov/data/sites/default/files/NSDUH-FFR1-2015/NSDUH-FFR1-2015/NSDUH-FFR1-2015.pdf

27. Jamal A, King BA, Neff LJ, Whitmill J, Babb SD, Graffunder CM. Current cigarette smoking among adults—United States, 2005–2015. MMWR Morb Mortal Wkly Rep. 2016;65(44):1205–1211 [cited 2017 May 4]. Available from: https://www.cdc.gov/mmwr/volumes/65/wr/mm6544a2.htm?s_cid=mm6544a2_w

28. Centers for Disease Control and Prevention. State Tobacco Activities Tracking & Evaluation (STATE) system. Map of current cigarette use among adults (Behavioral Risk Factor Surveillance System). 2015 [cited 2017 May 4]. Available from: https://www.cdc.gov/statesystem/cigaretteuseadult.html

29. National Institute on Drug Abuse. Monitoring the future: 2016 survey results [cited 2017 May 10]. Available from: https://www.drugabuse.gov/related-topics/trends-statistics/infographics/monitoring-future-2016-survey-results

30. Centers for Disease Control and Prevention. Fact sheet: economic trends in tobacco [cited 2017 May 4]. Available from: https://www.cdc.gov/tobacco/data_statistics/fact_sheets/economics/econ_facts/index.htm

31. Orzechowski and Walker. The tax burden on tobacco. Arlington, VA: Orzechowski and Walker; 2014 [cited 2017 May 3]. Available from: http://old.taxadmin.org/fta/tobacco/papers/tax_burden_2014.pdf

32. American Lung Association. E-cigarettes and lung health. 2016 [cited 2017 May 4]. Available from: http://www.lung.org/stop-smoking/smoking-facts/e-cigarettes-and-lung-health.html

33. Centers for Disease Control and Prevention. Quick stats: percent distribution of cigarette smoking status among adult current e-cigarette users, by age group, National Health Interview Survey, United States, 2015. MMWR Morb Mortal Wkly Rep. 2016;65(42):1177.

34. Centers for Disease Control and Prevention. Tobacco use among middle and high school students—United States, 2011–2015. MMWR Morb Mortal Wkly Rep. 2016;65(14):381–385.

35. Johnston LD, O'Malley PM, Miech RA, Bachman JG, Schulenberg JE. Monitoring the future—national survey results on drug use: 2015 overview; key findings on adolescent drug use. 2015 [cited 2017 May 10]. Available from: http://monitoringthefuture.org/pubs/monographs/mtf-overview2015.pdf

36. National Institute on Drug Abuse, National Institutes of Health, U.S. Department of Health and Human Services. Drug and alcohol use in college-age adults in 2015. 2015 [cited 2017 May 10]. https://www.drugabuse.gov/related-topics/trends-statistics/infographics/drug-alcohol-use-in-college-age-adults-in-2015

37. U.S. Department of Health and Human Services. E-Cigarette use among youth and young adults: a report

of the Surgeon General. Atlanta, GA: Centers for Disease Control and Prevention, National Center for Chronic Disease Prevention and Health Promotion, Office on Smoking and Health; 2016.

38. Villanti AC, Johnson AL, Ambrose BK, et al. Flavored tobacco product use in youth and adults: findings from the first wave of the PATH study (2013–2014). Am J Prev Med. 2017;10. doi:10.1016/j.amepre.2017.01.026

39. Leventhal AM, Strong DR, Kirkpatrick MG, et al. Association of electronic cigarette use with initiation of combustible tobacco product smoking in early adolescence. JAMA. 2015;314(7):700–707.

40. Mozaffarian D, Benjamin EJ, Go AS, et al. Heart disease and stroke statistics—2016 update: a report from the American Heart Association. Circulation. 2016;133(4):e38–e360.

41. National Heart, Lung, and Blood Institute, National Institutes of Health. Aim for healthy weight: calculate your body mass index. 2017 [cited 2017 May 11]. Available from: https://www .nhlbi.nih.gov/health/educational/lose_wt/BMI/bmicalc .htm

42. Kelly AS, Barlow SE, Rao G, et al. Severe obesity in children and adolescents: identification, associated health risks, and treatment approaches: a scientific statement from the American Heart Association. Circulation. 2013;128(15):1689–1712. doi:10.1161/CIR.0b013e3182a5cfb3.

43. World Health Organization. Report of the Commission on Ending Childhood Obesity. 2016 [cited 2017 May 3]. Available from: http://apps.who.int/iris/bitstream/10665 /204176/1/9789241510066_eng.pdf

44. Ogden CL, Carroll MD, Fryar CD, Flegal KM. Prevalence of obesity among adults and youth: United States, 2011–2014. NCHS data brief, no. 219. Hyattsville, MD: National Center for Health Statistics. 2015 Nov [cited 2017 May 11]. Available from: https://www.cdc.gov/nchs/data/databriefs /db219.pdf

45. Robert Wood Johnson Foundation. The state of obesity: better policies for a healthier America. 2016 [cited 2017 Jun 5]. Available from: http://www.rwjf.org/en/library/articles -and-news/2016/09/report-finds-obesity-rates-decreased -in-four-states.html

46. Mozaffarian D. Conflict of interest and the role of the food industry in nutrition research. JAMA. 2017;317(17):1755–1756.

47. Micha R, Penalvo JL, Cudhea F, Imamura F, Rehm CD, Mozaffarian D. Association between dietary factors and mortality from heart disease, stroke, and type 2 diabetes in the United States. JAMA. 2017;317(9):912–924.

48. USDA. U.S. Department of Agriculture Dietary Guidelines Advisory Committee. Dietary guidelines for Americans 2015–2020. 8th ed. 2015 [cited 2018 July 3]. Available from: https://health.gov/dietaryguidelines/2015/guidelines/

49. Society of Actuaries. The economic cost of obesity. Insur J. 2011 [cited 2017 Apr 27]. Available from: http://www .insurancejournal.com/news/national/2011/01/11/180022 .htm?print

50. Finkelstein EA, Trogdon JG, Cohen JW, Dietz W. Annual medical spending attributable to obesity: payer and service specific estimates. Health Aff. 2009;28(5):w822–w831.

51. World Health Organization. Global status report on alcohol and health 2014. 2014 [cited 2017 May 2]. Available from: http:// apps.who.int/iris/bitstream/10665/112736/1/9789240692763 _eng.pdf

52. Hasin DS, Sarvet AL, Cerda M, et al. U.S. adult illicit cannabis use, cannabis use disorder, and medical marijuana laws: 1991–1992 to 2012–2013. JAMA Psychiatry. 2017 [cited 2017 May 10]. doi:101.1001/jamapsychiatry.2017.0724. Available from: http://jamanetwork.com/journals/jamapsychiatry /fullarticle/2619522

53. Lipari RN, Jean-Francois BA. A day in the life of college students aged 18 to 22: substance use facts. The CBHSQ Report: May 26, 2016. Rockville, MD: Center for Behavioral Health Statistics and Quality, Substance Abuse and Mental Health Services Administration; 2016 [cited 2018 July 3]. Available from: https://www.samhsa.gov/data/sites/default/files/report_2361 /ShortReport-2361.html

54. Miech RA, Patrick ME, O'Malley PM, Johnston LD. The influence of college attendance on risk for marijuana initiation in the United States: 1977 to 2015. Am J Public Health. 2017 Apr 20;e1–e7.

55. Mattson M, Lipari RN, Hays C, Van Horn SL. A day in the life of older adults: substance use facts. The CBHSQ Report, Substance Abuse and Mental Health Services Administration. 2017 [cited 2017 May 16]. Available from: https://www.samhsa.gov/data/sites/default/files/report_2792 /ShortReport-2792.pdf

56. Hedden SL, Kennet J, Lipari R, Medley G, Tice P. Results from the 2014 National Survey on Drug Use and Health: detailed tables. Rockville, MD: Substance Abuse and Mental Health Services Administration; 2015 [cited 2017 May 16]. Available from: https://www.samhsa.gov/data/sites/default /files/NSDUH-FRR1-2014/NSDUH-FRR1-2014.pdf

57. Wu LT, Blazer EG. Illicit and nonmedical drug use among older adults: a review. J Aging Health. 2011;23(3):481–504.

58. Rudd RA, Aleshire N, Zibbel JE, Gladden RM. Increase in drug and opioid overdose deaths—United States, 2000–2014. MMWR Morb Mortal Wkly Rep. 2016;64(50):1378–1382.

59. National Institute on Drug Abuse, National Institutes of Health, U.S. Department of Health and Human Services [cited 2017 Jun 1]. Available from: https://www.drugabuse .gov/related-topics/trends-statistics/infographics/abuse -prescription-rx-drugs-affects-young-adults-most

60. American Heart Association. Heart disease and stroke statistics 2017 at-a-glance [cited 2018 July 3]. Available from: https://www.heart.org/idc/groups/ahamah-public/@wcm /@sop/@smd/documents/downloadable/ucm_491265.pdf

61. Younus A, Aneni EC, Spatz ES, et al. A systematic review of the prevalence and outcomes of ideal cardiovascular health in U.S. and Non-U.S. populations. Mayo Clin Proc. 2016;91(5):649–670.

62. Farvid MS, Ding M, Pan A, et al. Dietary linoleic acid and risk of coronary heart disease: a systematic review and meta-analysis of prospective cohort studies. Circulation. 2014; 130(18):1568–1578.

63. Caleyachetty R, Echouffo-Tcheugui JB, Muennig P, Zhu W, Muntner P, Shimbo D. Association between cumulative social risk and ideal cardiovascular health in U.S. adults: NHANES 1999-2006. Int J Cardiol. 2015;191:296–300.

64. Yang Q, Cogswell ME, Flanders WD, et al. Trends in cardiovascular health metrics and associations with all-cause and CVD mortality among U.S. adults. JAMA. 2012;307(12):1273–1283.

65. Centers for Disease Control and Prevention, the U.S. Department of Health and Human Services. Diabetes: data

and statistics [cited 2017 May 12]. Available from: https://www.cdc.gov/diabetes/data/

66. Dabelea D, Bell RA, D'Agostino RB Jr, et al. Incidence of diabetes in youth in the United States. JAMA. 2007;297(24):2716–2724. [Errata appeared in JAMA, 2007;298(6):627.]

67. Dabelea D, Mayer-Davis EJ, Saydah S, et al. Prevalence of type 1 and type 2 diabetes among children and adolescents from 2001 to 2009. JAMA. 2014;311(17):1778–1789.

68. Vehik K, Hamman RF, Lezotte D, et al. Increasing incidence of type 1 diabetes in 0 to 17 Year Old Colorado Youth. Diabetes Care. 2007;30:503–509.

69. Hummel K, McFann KK, Realsen J, Messer LH, Klingensmith GJ, Chase HP. The increasing onset of type 1 diabetes in children. J Pediatr. 2012;161:652–657.

70. Robert Wood Johnson Foundation. The state of obesity: better policies for a healthier America. 2015 [cited 2017 Jun 5]. Available from: http://www.rwjf.org/en/library/articles-and-news/2015/09/State-of-Obesity-Report-2015.html

71. Blumenthal KJ, Saulsgiver KA, Norton L, et al. Medicaid incentive programs to encourage healthy behavior show mixed results to date and should be studied and improved. Health Aff. 2013;32(3):497–507.

72. Ries NM. Financial incentives for weight loss and health behaviours. Healthc Policy. 2012;7(3):23–27.

73. Towers Watson/NBGH. Shaping health care strategy in a post-reform environment: 16th annual Towers Watson/National Business Group on Health employer survey on purchasing value in health care. Arlington, VA: Towers Watson/NBGH. 2011 [cited 2017 Jun 5]. Available from: https://www.towerswatson.com/Insights/IC-Types/Survey-Research-Results/2011/03/16th-Annual-Towers-WatsonNational-Business-Group-on-Health-Employer-Survey-on-Purchasing-Value-in

74. Wieczner J. Your company wants to make you healthy: a look at the pros and cons of the most popular wellness programs used by companies. Wall Street Journal. 2013 Apr 8 [cited 2017 Apr 27]. Available from: https://www.wsj.com/articles/SB10001424127887323393304578360252284151378

75. Medicaid and CHIP Payment and Access Commission. The use of healthy behavior incentives in Medicaid. Issue Brief. 2016 [cited 2017 May 2]. Available from: https://www.macpac.gov/wp-content/uploads/2016/08/The-Use-of-Healthy-Behavior-Incentives-in-Medicaid.pdf

76. Lee TH. Financial versus non-financial incentives for improving patient experience. J Patient Exp. 2015;2(1):4–6.

77. Kane RL, Johnson PE, Town RJ, Butler M. A structured review of the effect of economic incentives on consumers' preventive behavior. Am J Prev Med. 2004;27(4):327–352.

78. Volpp KG, Asch DA, Galvin R, Loewenstein G. Redesigning employee health incentives—lessons from behavioral economics. New Engl J Med. 2011;365(5):388–390.

79. Lowenstein G, Volpp KG, Asch DA. Incentives in health: different prescriptions for physicians and patients. JAMA. 2012;307(13):1375–1376.

80. Just D, Price J. Using incentives to encourage healthy eating in children. J Hum Resour. 2013;48(4):855–872.

81. Wilde P, Klerman JA, Olsho LEW, Bartlett S. Explaining the impact of USDA's Healthy Incentives Pilot on different spending outcomes. Appl Econ Perspect Policy. 2016;38(4):655–672.

82. Klerman JA, Bartlett S, Wilde P, Olsho L. The short-run impact of the Healthy Incentives Pilot program on fruit and vegetable intake. Am J Agric Econ. 2014;96(5):1372–1382.

83. Greene, J. Medicaid efforts to incentivize healthy behaviors: Resource paper. Center for Health Care Strategies, Inc. 2007 Jul [cited 2018 May 4]. Available from: http://www.chcs.org/media/Medicaid_Efforts_to_Incentivize_Healthy_Behaviors.pdf

84. Lorincz IS, Lawson BCT, Long JA. Provider and patient directed financial incentives to improve care and outcomes for patients with diabetes. Curr Diab Rep. 2013;13(2):188–195.

85. Brown J, West R, Angus C, et al. Comparison of brief interventions in primary care on smoking and excessive alcohol consumption: a population survey in England. Br J Gen Pract. 2016. doi:10.3399/bjgp16X683149.

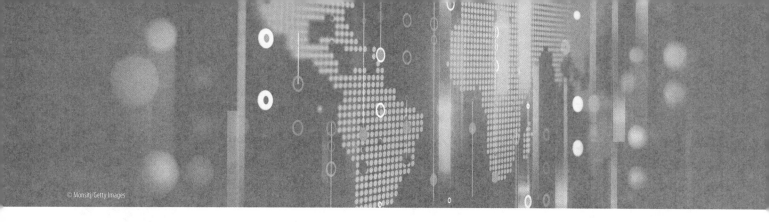

© Monsitj/Getty Images

CHAPTER 7

Infectious Disease Epidemiology

LEARNING OBJECTIVES

Having mastered the materials in this chapter, the student will be able to:

1. Recognize the global, national, and local socioeconomic impact of infectious diseases.
2. Assess the burden of illness and need for specialized health services resulting from infectious diseases in a population.
3. Accurately use epidemiologic concepts and terminology related to the transmission of infectious diseases.
4. Evaluate the healthcare challenges presented by newly emerging infectious diseases as well as the resurgence of those previously known.
5. Evaluate the importance and results of outbreak investigations reported in literature.

CHAPTER OUTLINE

7.1 Introduction
7.2 Infectious Diseases in the United States
7.3 Global Burden of Infectious Diseases
7.4 Emergence of New and Resurgence of Previously Known Infectious Diseases
7.5 The Infectious Disease Triad
7.6 Important Definitions Related to Infectious Diseases
   7.6.1 Agent
   7.6.2 Acute Diseases or Conditions
   7.6.3 Attack Rate
   7.6.4 Case Fatality Rate (Case Fatality Ratio)
   7.6.5 Carrier
   7.6.6 Chronic Diseases or Conditions
   7.6.7 Convalescent Period
   7.6.8 Endemic

7.6.9 Environment
7.6.10 Epidemic
7.6.11 Host
7.6.12 Incubation Period
7.6.13 Infection
7.6.14 Infectious
7.6.15 Infectivity/Invasiveness
7.6.16 Infestation
7.6.17 Microorganism, Microbe, or Microbial Organism
7.6.18 Outbreak
7.6.19 Pathogen
7.6.20 Pathogenesis
7.6.21 Pathogenicity
7.6.22 Prodromal Stage
7.6.23 Transmission

7.6.24 Vector
7.6.25 Virulence
7.7 Infectious Disease Outbreaks or Epidemics
7.8 Outbreak Investigation
7.9 Example of an Outbreak Investigation

7.10 Zika Virus Outbreak 2015
7.11 Ebolavirus Outbreak: West Africa 2014
Case Study 7.1 – California Measles Outbreak 2014
Case Study 7.2 – Ohio Botulism Outbreak 2015
7.12 Summary

KEY TERMS

Acute
Agent
Attack rate
Carrier
Case fatality rate
Chronic
Common source outbreak
Convalescent period
Ebola virus disease
Endemic
Environment

Epidemic
Fecal transplant
Host
Incubation period
Infection
Infectious
Infectivity
Infestation
Microbe
Microbiome
Microorganism

Outbreak
Pathogen
Pathogenesis
Pathogenicity
Point source
Prodromal stage
Propagated outbreak
Transmission
Vector
Virulence
Zika virus

▶ 7.1 Introduction

Healthcare-associated infections (HAIs) are a source of concern for healthcare managers. They reflect poorly on the quality of care, and avoidance of HAIs is an important part of a healthcare organization's risk management strategy. Every year, hundreds of millions of patients all over the world fall victim to HAIs.[1,2] It has been estimated that 7 out of every 100 hospitalized patients in developed countries and 10 of 100 in developing countries acquire at least one HAI. Approximately 30% of patients in intensive care units (ICUs) in high-income countries develop at least one HAI.[2] The frequency of HAIs in ICU patients in low-income countries is estimated to be 2–3 times greater than in developed countries.[3,4] The European Center for Disease Control and Prevention estimates that in Europe, every year, about 4.1 million patients are affected by 4.54 million episodes of HAIs that are directly responsible for 37,000 deaths.[5] In 2013, the total annual cost of five major HAIs in the United States—central line-associated bloodstream infections, ventilator-associated pneumonias, surgical site infections, *Clostridium difficile* infections, and catheter-associated urinary tract infections—was estimated to be about $9.8 billion, with surgical site infections accounting for 33.7% of the total cost.[6]

Humans and other animals have had a complex and intimate relationship with microbial organisms for thousands of years. Mostly this relationship has been of coevolution, synergism, and mutual benefit. Over millennia, host animals, including humans, have provided a suitable growth environment and nourishment to the microbial organisms in various parts of our bodies—mostly the intestinal tract. The microbes have returned the favor by producing enzymes, vitamins, and other materials that are vital to our physiologic processes and defense mechanisms. Our bodies act as a "complex ecosystem, in which a variety of microbial organisms flourish and evolve throughout the life cycle of a person."[7] The mix of these organisms, of which there are at least as many as the total number of cells in our own bodies[8,9] or possibly several times as many—more than 100 trillion microbes per person[10,11]—is unique to each individual. The study of the combined genetic material of the microorganisms in a particular environment, commonly referred to as the **microbiome**, is a new and exciting field of research.[12]

Recognizing the vital role that nonpathogenic skin and intestinal tract microbes or *normal intestinal flora* play in maintaining our overall health, and more so of our digestive system, a new treatment called **fecal transplant** or *fecal flora reconstitution* is emerging.[13] It involves rectal administration of diluted liquefied feces from a healthy donor, usually a close relative, into the proximal part of the colon of the patient. The purpose of this treatment is to restore populations of normal intestinal microorganisms in patients whose normal intestinal flora may have been destroyed by broad-spectrum antibiotics administered to treat an infectious disease. For example, fecal transplantation has successfully been used to treat patients suffering from life-threatening diarrhea caused by an opportunistic pathogenic organism known as *C. difficile*.[13]

On the other hand, infectious diseases have taken the heaviest toll on human beings over thousands of years. The scourges of cholera, plague, leprosy, tuberculosis (TB), and malaria have killed millions upon millions of people over centuries throughout the world. Since the discovery of the human immunodeficiency virus (HIV) in 1983, almost 78 million people have been infected by the virus, and nearly 39 million have died from HIV/AIDS worldwide. In recent years, not only have some of the previously known diseases resurfaced in the form of multidrug-resistant TB and drug-resistant malaria, but a number of new viral infections, such as H1N1 (swine flu), H1N5 (avian flu), and Middle East respiratory syndrome coronavirus, have also emerged. The spread of the Zika virus and its effects, especially on the brain of the developing fetus in pregnant women, are a source of concern throughout the Americas and the Caribbean. The Ebola virus epidemic that started in December 2013 in Guinea, West Africa, quickly spread to Liberia and Sierra Leone, affecting nearly 29,000 individuals and claiming more than 11,000 lives in the three countries.[14,15]

▶ 7.2 Infectious Diseases in the United States

In the United States in 2012, the number of new cases of sexually transmitted diseases included about 14 million cases of human papillomavirus, more than 1.4 million cases of chlamydia, over 330,000 cases of gonorrhea, about 50,000 cases of HIV, and more than 15,600 cases of syphilis. In the same year, about 48,000 new cases of whooping cough and approximately 10,000 new cases of TB were reported. It was also estimated that in 2012, between 700,000 and 1.4 million people in the country had chronic hepatitis B infection, and between 2.5 million and 3.9 million people had chronic hepatitis C infection.[16]

Infectious disease mortality declined from 797 deaths per 100,000 persons in 1900 to 283 in 1937, at a rate of 2.8% decline per year, and then to 75 deaths per 100,000 individuals in 1952, at an accelerated decline of 8.2% per year (though a sharp spike in infectious disease and all-cause mortality occurred around 1918 because of the influenza pandemic of that year).[17] From 1952 to 1980, the decline continued at a slower rate of 2.3% per year, reaching a death rate of 36 per 100,000 persons. After 1980, infectious disease mortality in the United States increased—largely due to the HIV/AIDS epidemic—at a rate of 4.8% per year, with the mortality rate reaching 63 deaths per 100,000 in 1995. The decline in infectious disease mortality mirrored the decline in all-cause mortality in the 20th century. The crude mortality rate from noninfectious diseases remained relatively unchanged throughout the 20th century.[17]

The steady decline in infectious disease mortality from 1900 to 1980 in the United States occurred in all age groups at about the same rate.[17] Similar decline occurred in mortality from nine infectious diseases and in the proportion of all deaths attributed to those nine diseases in age groups 0–4 years and 5–24 years. The nine diseases were as follows: (1) pneumonia and influenza, (2) TB, (3) diphtheria, (4) pertussis, (5) measles, (6) typhoid, (7) dysentery, (8) syphilis, and (9) AIDS. Notably, the increase in the infectious disease death rate in the United States after 1980 was primarily due to deaths from HIV/AIDS and largely affected those in the 25–44 and 45–65 years age groups.[17] **TABLE 7.1** shows the numbers of new cases of 10 selected infectious diseases in the United States in selected years. As shown, the numbers of new cases of most of these diseases have steadily declined in the United States from 1950 through 2012.[18]

▶ 7.3 Global Burden of Infectious Diseases

In developing countries, most people still die of infectious diseases. Tropical diseases such as trypanosomiasis, onchocerciasis, schistosomiasis, dengue, and leishmaniasis are endemic in 199 low- and middle-income countries (LMICs).[1] The five biggest killers—acute respiratory infections, HIV/AIDS, diarrheal diseases, malaria, and TB—collectively account for nearly one-third of all deaths in developing countries. Out of the total global death toll of 12 million claimed by communicable disease every year, approximately 80% occur in low-income countries.[19] In 2012, 70% of 2.3 million new HIV infections in the world occurred in sub-Saharan Africa.[1] In the same year, about 1.6 million people died of HIV/AIDS—a vast majority of them in low-income countries. Diarrhea is among the top 10 causes of death, with 1.5 million deaths in 2012, and TB, with 900,000 deaths in the same year, is among the top 15 killers. In 2012, about 6.6 million children younger than 5 years died worldwide; 99% of these deaths occurred in developing countries largely due to prematurity, pneumonia, and diarrheal diseases. About 15% of under-5 deaths

TABLE 7.1 New Cases of Selected Notifiable Diseases in the United States in Selected Years

Disease	1950	1970	1990	2010	2012
Hepatitis A	-	56,797	31,441	1,670	1,562
Hepatitis B	-	8,310	21,102	3,374	2,895
Whooping cough	120,718	4,249	4,570	27,550	48,277
Measles	319,124	47,351	27,786	63	55
Salmonella*	-	22,096	48,603	54,424	53,800
Shigellosis	23,367	13,845	27,077	14,786	15,283
Tuberculosis	-	37,137	25,701	11,182	9,945
Syphilis	217,558	91,382	135,590	45,844	49,903
Chlamydia	-	-	323,663	1,307,893	1,422,976
Gonorrhea	286,746	600,072	690,042	309,341	334,826

* Excluding typhoid fever.
Data from: National Center for Health Statistics. Health, United States, 2014: with special feature on adults aged 55–64. Hyattsville, MD: National Center for Health Statistics; 2015.

in sub-Saharan Africa were due to malaria.[20] In 2012, 80% of the 207 million cases of malaria and 90% of the 627,000 malaria deaths occurred in Africa.[1]

Globally, in 2012, more than 35 million people were living with HIV, and 2.3 million people were newly infected.[1] Of the 2.3 million new infections in 2012, 70% were in sub-Saharan Africa. In the same year, 1.6 million people died from HIV/AIDS—a reduction of 700,000 from the peak of 2.3 million deaths in 2005. The global infection rate in 2012 represented a 33% decline from 3.4 million new HIV infections in 2001. From 2003 onward, millions of lives have been saved all over the world, especially in sub-Saharan Africa, with the effective use of antiretroviral HIV/AIDS treatment. **FIGURE 7.1** shows the positive global impact of antiretroviral treatment (ART) on HIV/AIDS-related deaths. In 2012, ART saved more than 1 million lives globally.

An estimated 8.6 million people developed TB worldwide, and 1.3 million died from the disease. This figure includes 320,000 TB-related deaths among HIV-positive individuals.

In 2000, 103 countries were identified as having active malaria transmission. Worldwide, approximately 207 million cases and 627,000 deaths occurred from malaria in 2012, of which 80% of cases and 90% of deaths occurred in Africa, with children under

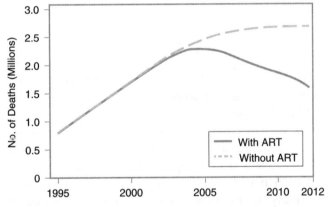

FIGURE 7.1 The impact of antiretroviral treatment use on the estimated number of deaths due to HIV/AIDS (millions) that would otherwise have occurred in low- and middle-income countries, 1995–2012.

Reprinted from: World Health Organization (WHO). World Health Statistics. Geneva, Switzerland: World Health Organization; 2014. Copyright © 2014 World Health Organization (WHO).

5 years of age bearing 77% of the total burden of malaria deaths (**FIGURE 7.2**). Between 2000 and 2012, the incidence of malaria worldwide fell by 25%, and malaria mortality fell by 42%. A host of other infectious diseases, including leprosy, Chagas disease, rabies, and schistosomiasis, are termed by the World Health Organization as *neglected tropical diseases*. These diseases affected more than 1 billion people in

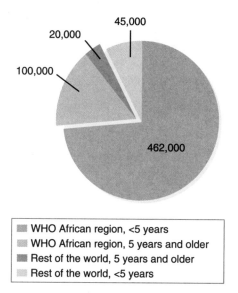

FIGURE 7.2 Estimated number of global deaths due to malaria in 2012.

Reprinted from: World Health Organization (WHO). World Health Statistics. Geneva, Switzerland: World Health Organization; 2014. Copyright © 2014 World Health Organization (WHO).

143 countries where they were still endemic in 2012. In the 2014 World Health Statistics report, dengue was noted as the world's fastest growing viral infection, with 2.5 billion people at risk. **FIGURE 7.3** shows the crude death rate by three broad causal groups from 2000 to 2012 by WHO region. In 2000 and in 2012, communicable diseases were the most common cause of death in Africa.

The situation, however, is getting better in all low-income countries that experience the highest burden of communicable diseases. In the last 10 years, the number of cases of HIV/AIDS, TB, and malaria have steadily declined all over the world. For example, the estimated 2.3 million new cases of HIV/AIDS in 2012 represented a decline of 33% as compared with the 3.4 million new cases reported in 2001.[1] Likewise, the 1.6 million HIV/AIDS deaths in the same year were about 700,000 fewer than the high-water mark of 2.3 million deaths in 2005. Since 1990, the number of TB-related deaths has also dropped by 45%. Between 2000 and 2012, the annual incidence of malaria dropped by 25% globally and by 31% in Africa. During the same period, malaria mortality also declined by almost half in Africa and by 42% all over the world.

▶ 7.4 Emergence of New and Resurgence of Previously Known Infectious Diseases

In the last three or four decades, a number of new infectious diseases have been identified, and several of the previously known diseases have drawn renewed attention because of their increased incidence. The increased incidence is largely attributable to the causative organisms having become resistant to existing antimicrobial drugs. Infectious diseases such as Lyme disease and babesiosis, transmitted by the hard-bodied (ixodid) deer tick known as the blacklegged tick, were identified in the 1980s. The latest addition to the list in 2011 was *Borrelia miyamotoi* disease caused by an organism previously thought to be nonpathogenic;[21] cases of this disease have been identified in Russia,

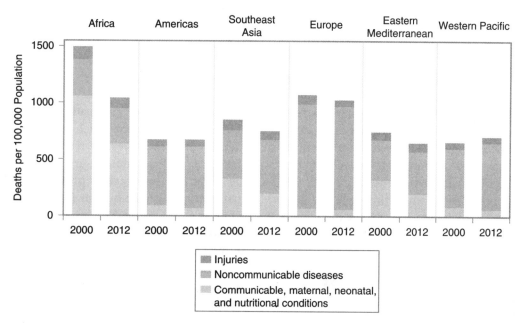

FIGURE 7.3 Crude death rate by broad cause groups, 2000 and 2012.

Reprinted from: World Health Organization (WHO). Causes of death by WHO region: situation and trends. Geneva, Switzerland: World Health Organization; 2015. Accessed July 3, 2017. http://www.who.int/gho/mortality_burden_disease/causes_death/region/en/. Copyright © 2015 World Health Organization (WHO).

TABLE 7.2 Emerging Infectious Diseases and Their Global Impact

Emerging Disease	Year Identified	Estimated Global Impact	
		Cases	Deaths
Ebola virus disease	1976	28,616	11,310
HIV/AIDS	1981	78 million	35 million[†]
Variant Creutzfeldt-Jakob disease (mad cow disease)	1996	229	229
H5N1 (bird flu)	1997	850*	449
Severe acute respiratory syndrome (SARS)	2003	8,096	774
H1N1 (swine flu)	2009	Unknown	>284,500
Middle East respiratory syndrome (MERS)	2012	2,090	730
H7N9 (bird flu)	2013	1,589	616

Note: Cases and deaths reflect the cumulative number of cases and deaths (as of March 14, 2018). Different sources report somewhat different estimates.

[†] Reported by UNAIDS as of June 2017.

*Cumulative cases and deaths from 2003 to the present.

Henry J. Kaiser Family Foundation. The U.S. government & global emerging infectious disease preparedness and response. 2014 Dec 8. Available at: http://kff.org/global-health-policy /fact-sheet/the-u-s-government-global-emerging-infectious-disease-preparedness-and-response/#endnote_link_92191-6. Reprinted with permission.

Japan, The Netherlands, and the United States. The term *emerging infectious diseases* (EIDs) is sometimes used to include HIV, SARS, H1N1, Ebola, and several other infectious diseases that have attained recognition or prominence in recent years. Since 1980, one to three new human infectious diseases have been identified every year. In one report, the Institute of Medicine listed 87 novel pathogens identified since 1980.[22]

An EID can be defined as "an infectious disease that is newly recognized as occurring in humans; one that has been recognized before but is newly appearing in a different population or geographic area than previously affected; one that is newly affecting many more individuals; and/or one that has developed new attributes (e.g., resistance or virulence)."[23]

TABLE 7.2 provides summary information about the occurrence and global impact of some of the more notable EIDs.

▶ 7.5 The Infectious Disease Triad

Infectious diseases occur as a result of a complex interaction among the causative organism, or *agent*; the victim, or *host* organism (humans and other animals); and the physical *environment* in which both exist. In a philosophic sense, both agent and host are engaged in a struggle for their own survival and propagation. From an evolutionary perspective, in the struggle and adaptation for survival, the relationship between humans and microbes in some instances has been of mutual support and benefit, in others of just harmless coexistence, and in still others of antagonism and survival at the cost of the other. The physical, biochemical, transformative, and pathogenic characteristics of the microbial agent—such as multiplication rate, transferability, heat or cold resistance, pathogenicity, virulence, and mutability—are all designed to help the organism survive and propagate. Likewise, the characteristics of the human (or animal) host determine its ability to fend for itself and survive. Over a period of millennia, humans have developed not only an internal biologic response mechanism in the form of an immune system, but also scientific tools, such as antimicrobial drugs and vaccines, to deal with the problem of microbial attacks.

Suitable environmental conditions are necessary for both agent and host to survive, grow, and multiply. Both microbes and humans have adapted to the characteristics of the surrounding physical environment, such as temperature, humidity, and sunlight. For humans, healthy living conditions include appropriate temperature, humidity, ventilation, and nutrition. Crowded living and working quarters promote interpersonal transfer of infectious agents, while damp, dark, and poorly ventilated areas allow microbes to live longer and remain potent. Many of the microbes not only use more than one host to complete their life cycle and to go through morphologic changes at different stages of their life cycle, but also use these hosts as *vectors*, or vehicles for transmission and transfer from one susceptible host to another. Insects such as ticks and mosquitoes are the most common examples of vectors for a number of parasitic, bacterial, and viral disorders, including Lyme disease, malaria, leishmaniasis, dengue, and Zika virus disease.

▶ 7.6 Important Definitions Related to Infectious Diseases

Note: Some of the following definitions have been adapted from Porta's dictionary of epidemiology.[24]

7.6.1 Agent

In epidemiology, the term **agent** is broadly used in reference to a physical, chemical, or biologic entity that can cause disease in an animal or a person. In the context of infectious diseases, it specifically refers to a living microscopic or macroscopic organism.

7.6.2 Acute Diseases or Conditions

Typically, an **acute** disease or disorder has at least two of the following three characteristics, if not all three: (1) rapid onset, (2) severe symptoms, and (3) short duration. It is important to bear in mind that *rapid*, *severe*, and *short* are relative terms that lack precision and specificity. Therefore, boundaries between *acute*, *subacute*, and *chronic* are somewhat blurred and arbitrary.

7.6.3 Attack Rate

Attack rate is defined as the proportion of individuals or subjects who became sick after being exposed to an infectious agent or pathogen. It represents the magnitude of a potential problem or volume of patients who can be expected in a population. However, attack rate in a population depends on the proportion of individuals who are susceptible to the disease or are *at risk* at the time of exposure. If most people in the population were immune to the disease at the time of exposure, the attack rate would be relatively low. On the other hand, if a vast majority of individuals in the population were susceptible to the infectious disease in question, the attack rate would be expected to be quite high. In addition to the pathogenicity of the organism and the proportion of immune individuals in the population, attack rate can also be affected by other factors, such as the extent and duration of exposure. If calculated for the entire population, without stratification for age, race, sex, or other demographic characteristics, it is called *crude attack rate*. If attack rates are calculated for specific subgroups in the population on the bases of age, race, or sex, they are called *stratified attack rates*. For obvious reasons, the term *attack rate* is restricted to infectious diseases and is not used for disorders such as cancers, kidney stones, or infertility.

7.6.4 Case Fatality Rate (Case Fatality Ratio)

Case fatality rate is an indicator of the severity of a disease and is defined as the proportion of cases of a disease that resulted in death. The numerator in obtaining this rate is the number of deaths from the disease (e.g., meningitis), and the denominator is all clinically diagnosed or known symptomatic cases of meningitis. Usually, it is expressed as a percentage of cases of a disease—for example, a case fatality rate of 10%–15%. Technically, it should not be referred to as a rate because no time period is specified. More accurately, it should be called a proportion. It can also be expressed as a ratio; for example, the case fatality ratio for meningitis is about 1:10.

7.6.5 Carrier

A **carrier** is an animal or a person who does not show the signs and symptoms of a disease but harbors the infectious agent and acts as a vehicle of transmission to other hosts. A carrier can be a *healthy carrier* if no apparent or discernable disease exists, an *incubatory carrier* in the stages before clinically overt disease appears, or a *convalescent carrier* during the recovery stages of the disease.

7.6.6 Chronic Diseases or Conditions

Chronic conditions are the opposite of acute disorders and, therefore, are slow in onset and progression, have relatively less severe but sustained symptoms, and are usually long-lasting. By convention, a condition that lasts 3 months or longer is considered chronic.

7.6.7 Convalescent Period

The **convalescent period** is the period of recovery from a disease; there is no specification or limit to the duration. Depending on the nature and severity of the disease, it can be days or months.

7.6.8 Endemic

When a disease, particularly an infectious disease, is constantly and continuously present in a specified geographic area, it is known as a disease **endemic** to that area. For example, malaria is endemic almost all over Africa and Asia, and Zika virus (ZKV) is endemic in a number of Southeast Asian countries such as Vietnam, Laos, and Cambodia.

7.6.9 Environment

The term **environment** refers to the physical environment, including air, temperature, light, humidity, water, and other conditions that facilitate or promote the survival and growth of the infectious agent and the interaction of the vector with the host. The environment also plays a critical role in the survival and multiplication of the vector and the vulnerability and exposure of the host to the vector and the infectious agent.

7.6.10 Epidemic

An **epidemic** is the occurrence of new cases of a disease in a population during a specified time period clearly in excess of its usual occurrence. The number of cases required to make such a pronouncement is a function of the nature of the disease in question and past experience of the population with the disease over an extended period. The occurrence of a few cases of polio or measles in a matter of days in a population from which the disease had been completely eradicated would constitute an epidemic. On the other hand, the occurrence of a few hundred cases of malaria in Lagos, Nigeria, in a 6-month period may be considered normal.

7.6.11 Host

A **host** is a person or animal in which an infectious agent harbors, grows, and multiplies. The host may or may not manifest the symptoms and signs of the disease caused by the infectious agent.

7.6.12 Incubation Period

The term **incubation period** is often used interchangeably with the term *latent period* and is defined as the time elapsed from the moment of exposure to a pathogenic organism to the first appearance of the signs and/or symptoms of a disease. Though also used in the context of exposure to chemicals and radiation, the term is predominantly used in the context of infectious diseases. Different organisms have different incubation periods. While the incubation period for some organisms can be as short as a day, in other cases, it can be months or even years. The incubation period for the same organism can also vary from one exposed individual to another depending on a variety of factors, including the degree or dose of exposure and the characteristics of the host, such as immunity or resistance. The incubation periods for some common infectious diseases are shown in **TABLE 7.3**.

7.6.13 Infection

Infection is defined by Taber's Cyclopedic Medical Dictionary[25] as "a disease caused by microorganisms, esp. those that release toxins or invade body tissues. . . . Infection differs from colonization of the body by microorganisms in that during colonization, microbes reside harmlessly in the body or perform useful functions for it, e.g., bacteria in the gut that produce vitamin K. By contrast, infectious illnesses typically cause bodily harm."

7.6.14 Infectious

A microorganism is **infectious** if it is capable of being transmitted or passed from one host to another and can produce *infection* or disease. Frequently, the term *infectious diseases* is broadly used to include diseases caused by both microscopic unicellular and macroscopic multicellular organisms.

7.6.15 Infectivity/Invasiveness

Infectivity or invasiveness refers to an organism's ability to invade and multiply or replicate in the body of the host—regardless of whether the organism is pathogenic or nonpathogenic. Thus, a nonpathogenic organism can be highly infective because of its quick replication or high rate of multiplication, whereas a pathogenic organism may be less infective because of its slow rate of multiplication.

7.6.16 Infestation

Usually the term **infestation** refers to the lodgment, development, and reproduction of parasites—especially the macroscopic forms such as worms or arthropods—on the skin of an animal or person.

Parasites can harbor on the skin or surface of the body (ectoparasites) or can be inside the body, such as in the digestive tract, the bloodstream, and various organs (endoparasites).

TABLE 7.3 Incubation Periods for Some Well-Known Infectious Diseases

Disease	Incubation Period (Days)*
Bronchiolitis	3 – 6
Chicken pox	10 – 21
Common cold	2 – 5
Diphtheria	2 – 5
Hand, foot, and mouth disease	3 – 5
Hepatitis A	14 – 50
Hepatitis B	50 – 180
Herpes simplex	5 – 8
Infectious mononucleosis	30 – 50
Influenza	1 – 2
Measles	8 – 12
Meningitis (Bacterial)	2 – 10
Meningitis (Viral)	3 – 6
Mumps	12 – 25
Rota virus diarrhea	1 – 3
Rubella	14 – 21
Scarlet fever	3 – 6
Strep throat	2 – 5
Warts	30 – 180
Whooping cough	7 – 10

* The time it takes for first appearance of symptoms after exposure to the infectious agent. In literature, different sources report somewhat different estimates.

7.6.17 Microorganism, Microbe, or Microbial Organism

A **microorganism** or **microbe** is defined as a "microscopic biological entity (living) that is typically too small to be seen with the naked eye."[26] Usually the term is reserved for microscopic unicellular or multicellular organisms such as bacteria and fungi, or noncellular proteinaceous particulate organisms such as viruses and prions. These organisms can enter, reside, and multiply within the cells in various parts of the body of a host animal or person and can only be seen with the help of a high-resolution microscope or an electron microscope.

7.6.18 Outbreak

Although commonly used interchangeably with any *epidemic*, the term **outbreak** usually refers to a relatively short-lived but rapidly accelerating infectious disease epidemic in a localized area or a small and well-defined population—for example, a foodborne salmonella outbreak in a village or a waterborne cholera outbreak in a community. However, relatively large and somewhat extended epidemics, such as Ebola virus disease (EVD) in three West African countries in 2014, were titled in various reports as an outbreak.

7.6.19 Pathogen

The term **pathogen** refers to any organism, but usually a microorganism, that can cause disease in humans or other animals.

7.6.20 Pathogenesis

The term **pathogenesis** refers to the biological mechanisms of development of disease or the chain of biological processes and changes in the body of the host through which a pathogen causes disease.

7.6.21 Pathogenicity

The qualitative term **pathogenicity** refers to the inherent ability of an organism to cause damage or disease in the host. In simple terms, pathogenicity refers to whether or not an organism is able to cause disease or whether it is harmful or harmless.

7.6.22 Prodromal Stage

The term **prodromal stage** refers to the early stages of a disease in which nonspecific symptoms, such as malaise, aches, and fatigue, appear as harbingers of approaching disease shortly before full-blown specific symptoms, such as rash, fever, diarrhea, vomiting, or cough, and signs such as enlargement of lymph nodes, appear. The length of the prodromal stage can vary from one disease to another but is usually in hours or a day or two.

7.6.23 Transmission

The term **transmission** refers to mechanisms through which an infectious agent is passed from a carrier or a host—whether a sick animal or person—to another host. The transmission of infectious agents from one host to another can take place in a number of ways, including the following:

1. Coughing, sneezing, or spitting by a carrier or a sick host and inhalation by a susceptible host of the suspended infectious agent on minute droplets or dust particles in the air.

2. Direct mechanical transfer through skin contact of the carrier or sick host with a susceptible host, such as through handshaking. Infectious agents, such as bacteria and viruses or eggs of parasites such as pinworms, can then pass from the hand of the susceptible host to his or her mucosal surfaces, such as the eyes, nose, or mouth. Parasites such as lice or fungi such as ringworm (tinea versicolor, tinea corporis, tinea capitis, and so on) can pass from one host to another through direct contact and mechanical transfer.

3. Fomites such as doorknobs, combs, hats, knives, and utensils are also common objects of direct mechanical transfer of microbial organisms from one person to another.

4. Sexual contact and intimate physical interaction, including kissing, can result in the transmission of infectious agents from one person to another through skin, saliva, and bodily fluids.

5. Some infectious agents can be passed from mother to child through placenta or breastmilk.

6. One of the most common modes of transmission of infectious agents is the fecal–oral route. Food and water contaminated with the feces of an infected individual or a carrier can contain live infectious agents or eggs of various kinds of parasites. Healthy, susceptible hosts are infected by ingesting contaminated food or water. Contamination of food and water can occur because of unsanitary and unhygienic practices, such as inadequate handwashing by carriers or infected individuals. The use of untreated sewage for agriculture and untreated or nonchlorinated drinking water supply are also common causes of fecal–oral transmission and spread of infectious diseases in many developing countries. In developed countries, most foodborne outbreaks result from unhygienic practices of food handlers.

7.6.24 Vector

The **vector** is an organism, usually an insect such as a mosquito or a flea, that passes the infectious organism or agent from one host to another—usually through the process of biting and feeding on the host. The agent frequently spends part of its life cycle and changes, grows, and multiplies in the body of the vector.

7.6.25 Virulence

Virulence is also a trait of the pathogenic organism, but, as opposed to pathogenicity, it refers to the extent, severity, or intensity of disease caused by a pathogen. It can be characterized as a measure of potential damage to the host that can be caused by a pathogen. In other words, the higher the virulence of a pathogen, the greater the risk of serious damage, disability, or death for the host.

▶ 7.7 Infectious Disease Outbreaks or Epidemics

Every year, thousands of infectious disease outbreaks occur all over the world. Most of these outbreaks are relatively short-lived and are caused by food or waterborne microorganisms that spread through a common source. The well-known outbreaks of cholera in London that killed thousands of people in the mid-1850s resulted from common sources of the water supply. Likewise, the cholera epidemic in Haiti that started in October 2010, months after a devastating eartquake, killed thousands of Haitians and most likely spread through the contaminated water of a river (Arbonite River) that served as a source of drinking water for many Haitians. In the United States in recent years, a number of foodborne outbreaks have been linked to regional distribution of food, such as as eggs, scallops, meat, ice cream, cantaloupes, and even pistachios, by commercial suppliers. The U.S. Centers of Disease Control and Prevention (CDC) listed 13 foodborne outbreaks that it had investigated in 2016 alone.[27]

Outbreaks are usually characterized as either a **common source outbreak** or a **propagated outbreak**. If a group of susceptible individuals contract a disease by simultaneously or at different times being exposed to the same source of infection, the outbreak is called a common source outbreak. Exposure to a common source can occur, for example, in the form of drinking water from the same river or consuming the same batch or pot of contaminated food (e.g., eggs, milk, salad, or strawberries) at the same church cookout, or bought at different times at different grocery stores in different states. If a group of individuals is exposed to a common source at a specific point in time, the resulting outbreak is referred to as a **point source** outbreak. It should be noted that a common source outbreak can also be a propagated outbreak if members of a community continue to be exposed to the same common source over an extended period of time (e.g., contaminated water from a river), as happened in Haiti in the cholera outbreak of 2010.

As the name suggests, a propagated outbreak can occur as a result of propagated or sequential exposure of healthy susceptible individuals to sick (or apparently healthy) germ-carrying individuals. Such exposure can occur through some form of direct physical contact (e.g., sexual contact); contact with germ-carrying fomites, syringes, or bodily fluids (saliva, vomit, urine, or stools); or through inhalation of germ-carrying airborne droplets emitted by the sick individual through coughing or sneezing. Propagated exposure can also occur through vectors, such as mosquitos or ticks, carrying a virus or parasite from one person to another. In a propagated outbreak, the disease is sequentially passed from disease-carrying persons to healthy individuals. Therefore, the propagation of the outbreak depends not only on the nature and intensity of exposure and the number of people being exposed to a sick person, but also on whether the exposed individuals are susceptible to the disease in question—that is, the level of herd immunity in the population.

If most of the individuals being exposed to a diseased individual are immune to the disease—whether by virtue of previous experience with the disease or through vaccination (i.e., high levels of herd immunity)—the disease would not continue to spread. The term *herd immunity* refers to the requisite proportion of a population being resistant to a disease so as to prevent its continued propagation. Of course, the proportion of the population or the level of herd immunity necessary to prevent propagation of a disease or continuation of an outbreak varies from one disease to another and depends on a number of factors, including the density of the population and how long a diseased person remains contagious. Mathematical models have been developed for various diseases to estimate the level of herd immunity necessary to interrupt the continuation of an outbreak. Clearly, herd immunity can occur as a result of a proportion of the population falling victim to the disease and recovering from it, through vaccination, or a through combination of both of these senarios. Obviously, most vaccination programs aspire to achieve near 100% coverage of the target population.

▶ 7.8 Outbreak Investigation

The purpose of any outbreak investigation is twofold: first, to identify the cause of the epidemic and take necessary actions to stop it, and second, to devise measures and take necessary actions to prevent future outbreaks.

The investigation of an outbreak, often characterized as "shoeleather epidemiology," begins with the development of the definition of a *case*. The definition of a case is important because it sets the criteria to determine whether a person has the disease in question and to understand the characteristics of such individuals. In situations in which the nature or specific diagnosis of the disease is not clear at the onset of the outbreak, the signs and symptoms of the index case allow investigators to develop some preliminary ideas about the nature of the disease and, if necessary, quickly take some actions, such as isolation of the index case and his or her contacts. The definition of a case may be based on the results of one or more laboratory tests; the signs and symptoms of the disease; participation in a specific event, such as visit to an area or travel to another country; or some combination of these factors.

The first case of the disease in a community or population is usually known as the *index case*. In a propagated outbreak, the index case can be the source that triggered the outbreak. More important, in both common source and propagated outbreaks, the identification of the index case allows investigators to determine the point in time when the outbreak started and develop the timeline of events, including identification and tracking of people who were in the same proximity or came into direct contact with the index case. In foodborne or other common source outbreaks, identification of the index case allows investigators to estimate the incubation period since the time of exposure (e.g., to potentially contaminated food) and develop some ideas about the source and cause of the outbreak.

Along with the identification and tracking of cases of the disease, a critical step in outbreak investigation is the development of an *epidemic curve*, which requires plotting a barchart graph of the number of cases over time. The investigators should also develop a spot map to understand the geographic distribution of cases in a populaion and stratify data by age, sex, race, occupation, and other demographic characteristcs of affected individuals. Such analysis can help investigators to develop some hypotheses about the cause of the outbreak. For example, if all the cases in a localized outbreak are small children, the outbreak may have resulted from a common source exposure at a place such as a childcare center where all the children may have received care during a specified period of time.[28] Further investigation and analysis of data should allow investigators to confirm or reject a hypothesis. Once a hypothesis is cofirmed and evidence about the source of an outbreak is established, investigators can take necessary action to stop the continuation of the outbreak and prevent future occurrences.

FIGURES 7.4 through **7.7** provide examples of epidemic curves for outbreaks of different kinds. For example, Figure 7.4 shows the epidemic curve for a point source outbreak in which all the cases resulted from exposure to the same source without further spread of disease through person-to-person exposure. In contrast, Figure 7.5 shows the situation in which the outbreak started as a result of multiple individuals being exposed to the same common source or index case, but the outbreak lasted a little longer because of some person-to-person spread. Figure 7.6 provides an example of an epidemic curve for a propagated outbreak, such as the outbreak of hand, foot, and mouth disease in Shandong province in China, and the outbreak of Chikungunya virus disease in two villages in northern Italy discussed later in this chapter. In these situations, individuals who became sick after exposure to the index case themselves became the source of infection and propagation of the outbreak by infecting other people. Finally, Figure 7.7 shows epidemic curves for intermittent outbreaks of the same disease in a geographic district or regions. The EBV outbreak in western Africa that started in early 2014 and continued until 2016 provides an example of intermittent outbreaks involving relatively few individuals after the first large outbreak that affected thousands of people had been contained through international collaborative efforts and active surveillance.

▶ **7.9 Example of an Outbreak Investigation**

Modified from: Zhang Y, Tan X, Wang H, et al. An outbreak of hand, foot, and mouth disease associated with subgenotype c4 of human enterovirus 71 in Shandong, China. J Clin Virol. 2009;44:262–267.

An outbreak of hand, foot, and mouth disease (HFMD) occurred in the Shandong province of China from March 13 through May 22, 2007, affecting a total of 1,149 children. HFMD is an enterovirus (Coxsackievirus) infection that usually affects children younger than 5 years of age. The clinical signs and symptoms include fever; sore throat; malaise;

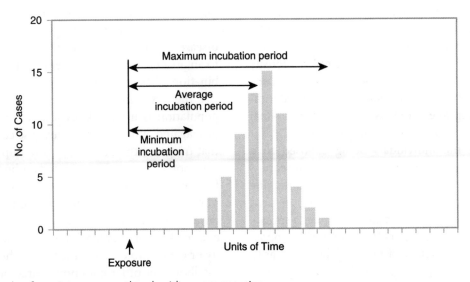

FIGURE 7.4 Example of a point source outbreak with no propagation.

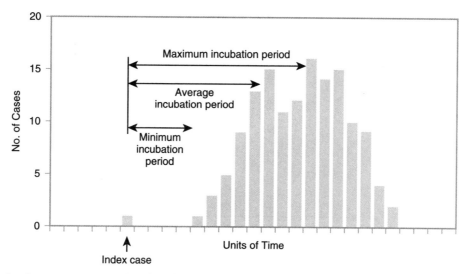

FIGURE 7.5 Example of a point source outbreak with index case and limited spread.

Reproduced from: University of Ottawa. University of Ottawa medical curriculum: society, the individual, and medicine (SIM). Available at: https://www.med.uottawa.ca/sim/data/Public_Health_Epidemic_Curves_e.htm

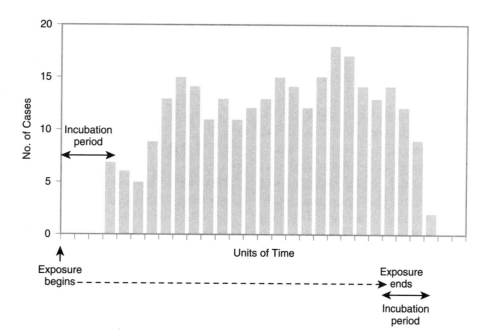

FIGURE 7.6 Example of a continuing source or propagated outbreak.

Reproduced from: University of Ottawa. University of Ottawa medical curriculum: society, the individual, and medicine (SIM). Available at: https://www.med.uottawa.ca/sim/data/Public_Health_Epidemic_Curves_e.htm

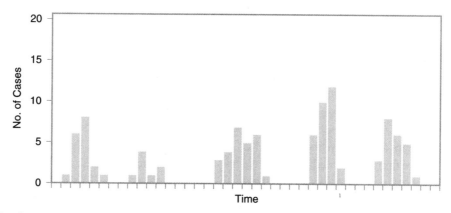

FIGURE 7.7 Example of an intermittent outbreak.

Reproduced from: University of Ottawa. University of Ottawa medical curriculum: society, the individual, and medicine (SIM). Available at: https://www.med.uottawa.ca/sim/data/Public_Health_Epidemic_Curves_e.htm

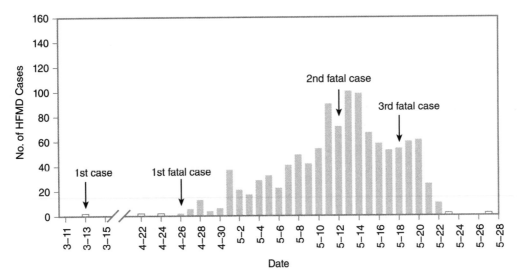

FIGURE 7.8 Distribution of hand, foot, and mouth disease (HFMD) patients in Linyi City, Shandong Province, by date. On March 13, 2007, the first HFMD case appeared. The number of similar cases had increased dramatically by April 27. By May 22, the outbreak had affected 1,149 children. The arrows indicate the dates of onset of the three fatal cases.

Reprinted from: Zhang Y, Tan X, Wang H, et al. An outbreak of hand, foot, and mouth disease associated with subgenotype C4 of Human Enterovirus 71 in Shandong, China. J Clin Virol. 2009;44: 262–267. Copyright © 2009, with permission from Elsevier.

and a blistery (vesicular) skin rash (exanthema) on the palms of hands, the soles of the feet, inside and around the mouth, and sometimes on the buttocks. The disease spreads through direct contact with the nasal secretions, saliva, fluids from blisters, and stools of the sick person or through inhalation of the virus droplets in the air from the sick person's coughing and sneezing. The infection usually resolves spontaneously after a few days, but serious complications, including death, can occur in a small number of cases.

In this outbreak, the first case was a child who was clinically diagnosed with HFMD on March 13, 2007. The number of cases began to increase quickly, with cases in all 12 counties or various districts of Linyi City; most cases were concentrated in three counties. The investigators defined a case as a patient with a fever and maculopapular, or vesicular rash, on the hands, feet, and mouth, with or without a rash on the buttocks. By May 22, 2007, the Chinese notifiable disease reporting system had identified a total of 1,149 patients who met this definition. Of the total number of cases, 970 (84.4%) were children younger than 5 years of age. The peak period of the outbreak was week 10, in which 540 cases were reported. Eleven of the 1,149 cases were severe, with complications including encephalitis and meningitis. The outbreak resulted in the deaths of three children, all younger than age of 3 years. **FIGURE 7.8** shows the epidemic curve for this outbreak. Virological tests of 233 specimens obtained from 105 hospitalized

children indicated that the outbreak was mainly caused by human enterovirus 71 (HEV71).

▶ 7.10 Zika Virus Outbreak 2015

Zika virus is an arbovirus of the genus *Flavivirus*, which was first islolated from a rhesus monkey in the Zika forest of Uganda in 1947.[29,30] The virus is transmitted from one person to another by the bite of an infected *Aedes aegypti* mosquito and other *Aedes* mosquito species. Infection with Zika virus in humans in most instances is either asymptomatic or associated with mild flulike symptoms. However, in pregnant women, it can affect fetal brain development and lead to microcephaly in the newborn. In a small number of cases among adults, it has been associated with Guillain-Barré syndrome, a relatively uncommon but serious neurological disorder that can ultimately result in total paralysis. The long-term effects of Zika virus infection in asymptomatic or mildly symptomatic cases are not known. Zika virus disease and Zika virus congenital infection are nationally notifiable conditions in the United States.

An outbreak of Zika virus, which was still ongoing in November 2016, started in northeastern Brazil in May 2015 and quickly spread all over the Americas and the Caribbean region. Previously, an outbreak of Zika virus had been reported in 2007 on the island of Yap in Micronesia, and in 2013 in French Polynesia.[31] By the end of 2016, the 2015 outbreak had affected millions of individuals in more than 40 countries, and the incidence of Guillain-Barré syndrome in some parts of Latin America had increased twentyfold. Cases of Zika infection, microcephaly in newborns, and Guillain-Barré syndrome were reported all over Central and South America, the Caribbean, Mexico, the United States and its territories, and the Pacific Islands. In Africa, its transmission was reported in Cape Verde. In the United States, most cases were travel related, although locally acquired cases, whether through mosquito transmission or sexual transmission, were also reported.

As of November 16, 2016, a total of 4,255 cases of Zika virus had been reported in the United States. Of these cases, 4,115 were travel associated, one was laboratory acquired, and 139 were acquired locally through mosquito-borne transmission.[32] These num-

bers included 1,087 pregnant women with laboratory evidence of possible Zika virus infection. On the same date, the CDC reported that 32,068 cases of Zika virus had been reported in U.S. territories, including Puerto Rico, the U.S. Virgin Islands, and American Samoa; 50 of these individuals developed Guillain-Barré syndrome. As of November 10, 2016, 2,451 cases of Zika virus infection in pregnant women had been reported in U.S. territories. **FIGURE 7.9** shows the distribution and density of reported Zika virus disease cases in the United States and its territories. By the end of 2016, the transmission of Zika virus remained ongoing, and prospects for preventing it through mosquito control measures seemed to be limited, as has been the case in the past with other mosquito-borne diseases such as malaria. In the United States, efforts have focused on mosquito control through pesticide spraying in known

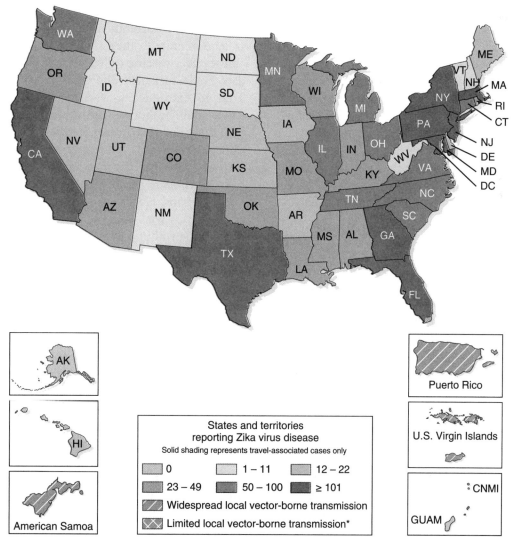

FIGURE 7.9 Laboratory-confirmed Zika virus disease cases reported to ArboNET by state or territory (as of November 16, 2016).

*Case counts include all symptomatic Zika virus disease cases including cases in travelers returning from affected areas, cases acquired through presumed local mosquito-borne transmission, and cases acquired through other routes. Cross hatching signifies areas with reported sustained local mosquito-borne transmission.

Reproduced from: Centers for Disease Control and Prevention. Zika cases reported in the United States: laboratory-confirmed Zika virus disease cases reported to ArboNET by state or territory (as of November 16, 2016). Available at: https://www.cdc.gov/zika/intheus/maps-zika-us.html

areas of transmission (mostly in Miami, Florida) and travel advisories issued by the CDC. Internationally, efforts are actively under way to develop a vaccine against Zika virus. Considering that Zika virus is now endemic in about 75 different countries, development of an effective vaccine seems to be the most promising way to deal with this problem. Currently, a number of Phase I clinical trials are underway to develop a safe and effective vaccine against Zika virus disease. In January 2018, the U.S. Food and Drug Administration granted a fast track designation to Takeda Pharmaceutical company's Zika vaccine candidate TAK-429. On July 5, 2018, the FDA also approved the Procleix Zika Virus Assay developed by Grifols Diagnostic Solutions Inc. to detect Zika virus RNA in plasma.

▶ 7.11 Ebola Virus Outbreak: West Africa 2014

Ebola virus disease, formerly knowns as Ebola hemorrhagic fever, a relatively rare but frequently fatal disease in humans and other primates, is caused in humans by four of the five strains of the *Ebolavirus* genus of the family Filoviridae. These strains are found in several African countries. The virus was first identified in 1976 near the Ebola River in the Democratic Republic of the Congo.[33] The natural reservoir of the virus is not definitively known, but it is believed to have an animal host, most likely bats. How the virus transfers from the animal host to humans is not understood, but the disease spreads among humans through direct contact (skin, eye, or oronasal mucuous membranes) with the blood or bodily fluids (saliva, sweat, semen, breast milk, vomit, urine, or feces) of a person with EVD, objects such as needles and syringes contaminated with the bodily fluids of an EVD patient, or contact with bats and nonhuman primates (monkeys and apes). Sexual contact with a person with the virus is also a mode of transmission of EVD. Transmission during outbreaks commonly occurs through contact with family members, caregivers, and funeral preparations and ceremonies. The clinical presentation of the diseases includes fever, vomiting, severe headache, fatigue, malaise, abdominal pain, diarrhea, and unexplained bleeding. Patients who survive EVD develop antibodies that last for 10 or more years.[33]

In the last two decades, there have been several outbreaks of EVD in various African countries, including Uganda, Gabon, Sudan, and Congo.[14,15,33]

The largest and most recent outbreak started in Guinea in early 2014 and quickly spread to Liberia and Sierra Leone. It took a concerted international effort under the United Nations Mission for Ebola Emergency Response to bring this outbreak under control by the spring of 2015, although sporadic cases continued to be reported from Liberia, Sierra Leone, and Guinea until September 2015.[14,15] It was only on January 14, 2016, that the World Health Organization declared all three of these countries to be free of Ebola transmission. Altogether, this outbreak resulted in 28,616 cases of Ebola in these three West African countries, with 15,227 laboratory-confirmed cases and 11,310 deaths. Additionally, 36 travel-related Ebola cases were reported in seven other countries (Italy, Mali, Nigeria, Senegal, Spain, the United Kingdom, and the United States), with 34 laboratory-confirmed diagnoses and 15 deaths.[14,15]

A combined phase II and phase III unblinded vaccine trial is currently under way in Sierra Leone in collaboration with the CDC to assess the safety and efficacy of a vaccine called the rVSV-ZEBOV candidate Ebola vaccine.[34] The trial, named Sierra Leone Trial to Introduce a Vaccine (STRIVE), involves 8,650 adult healthcare and other frontline workers, including doctors, nurses, ambulance teams, laboratory technicians, pharmacy workers, and burial workers. The participants were randomly divided into *vaccination* (immediate) and *defferred vaccination* groups. No placebo was given to any participants in this trial. The vaccination group was given the vaccine within 1 week of enrollment, whereas the defferred vaccination group was given the vaccine 6 months later. The follow-up period was 6 months. The first 400 participants were enrolled in a substudy involving more frequent follow-up to detect adverse events such as fever, rash, and headache. The participants were asked to keep a diary of events and were followed through scheduled monthly phone calls. An immunogenicity substudy with 500 participants is also being conducted to assess the immune response to the vaccine. The vaccine being used in STRIVE is a recombinant vesicular stomatitis virus, *Zaire ebolavirus vaccine*, which was developed in Canada. It contains a weakened vesicular stomatitis virus in which a single gene of the virus is replaced with a single ebolavirus gene. Because the whole ebolavirus is not used, the vaccine cannot cause EVD. Other studies with the same vaccine have been conducted and are continuing in Gabon, Kenya, Germany, Canada, and the United States. Similar phase II and phase III trials are being conducted in Liberia and and Guinea.

⌕ CASE STUDY 7.1: California Measles Outbreak 2014

Modified from: Zipprich J, Winter K, Hacker J, Xia D, Watt J, Harriman K. Measles outbreak – California, December 2014–February 2015. Morbid Mortal Wkly Rep. 2015;64(6):153–154. Accessed July 3, 2017. https://www.cdc.gov/mmwr/pdf/wk/mm6406.pdf

A suspected case of measles—an 11-year-old unvaccinated hospitalized child with a rash that started on December 28, 2014—was reported to the California Department of Public Health (CDPH) on January 5, 2015. The only notable part of the history was a visit to one of the two adjacent Disney theme parks in Orange County, California. On the same date, CDPH was notified of six other suspected cases of measles; four were California residents and two were Utah residents. All six had visited one or both Disney theme parks during the period December 17–20, 2014. By January 7, 2015, there were seven confirmed cases in California. By February 11, a total of 125 confirmed U.S. resident cases (110 California residents and 15 in seven other states) linked to this outbreak with rash onset between December 28, 2014 and February 8, 2015 had been reported. Additionally, 11 linked cases were reported from Mexico (1) and Canada (10). Out of the 110 California resident cases, 39 (35%) had visited one or both of the theme parks during December 17–20, 2014. Of the remaining 71 California cases, 34 were secondary cases (mostly household or close contacts), while source of exposure for 37 was unknown. Among the 110 California cases, 49 (45%) were unvaccinated, 47 (43%) had unknown vaccination status, and 14 were partially (12) or completely (1) vaccinated or had immunoglobuline G seropositivity (1). Among the 49 unvaccinated cases, 12 were too young to be vaccinated and 28 were intentionally unvaccinated because of personal beliefs. The age range for cases was 6 weeks to 70 years. The two Disney theme parks in California have approximately 24 million visits every year, with many international visitors from measles-endemic countries.

FIGURE 7.10 shows the epidemic curve for this outbreak.

Questions

Question 1. What was the approximate length of the incubation period? Explain your answer with the help of data from the outbreak and Figure 7.10.

Question 2. Was this a point source, common source, or mixed propagated outbreak? Explain your answer with the help of data from the outbreak.

Question 3. When did the peak of the outbreak occur? Explain your answer with the help of data from the outbreak and Figure 7.10.

Question 4. Did the outbreak end spontaneously, or did it end because of control measures implemented by the local health authorities? Explain your answer with the help of data from the outbreak.

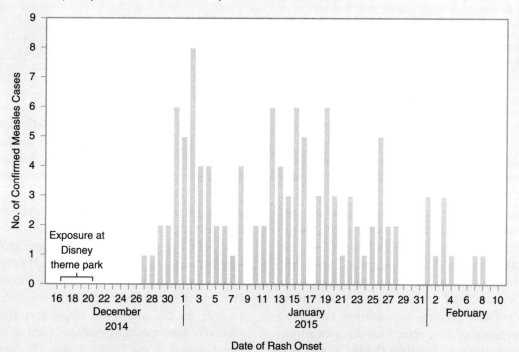

FIGURE 7.10 Number of confirmed measles cases (N = 110)* by date of rash onset, California, December 2014–February 2015.

*Reported to California Department of Health as of February 11, 2015.

Reproduced from: Zipprich J, Winter K, Hacker J, Xia D, Watt J, Harriman K. Measles outbreak – California, December 2014–February 2015. Morbid Mortal Wkly Rep. 2015;64(6):153–154. Accessed July 3, 2017. https://www.cdc.gov/mmwr/pdf/wk/mm6406.pdf

$\mathcal{P}$ *CASE STUDY 7.2: Ohio Botulism Outbreak 2015*

Modified from: McCarty CL, Angelo K, Beer KD, Cibulskas-White K, Quinn K, de Fijter S, Bokanyi R, et al. Large outbreak of botulism associated with a church potluck meal – Ohio, 2015. Morbid Mortal Wkly Rep. 2015;64929:802–803. Accessed July 3, 2017. https://www.cdc.gov/mmwr/pdf/wk/mm6429.pdf

On April 21, 2015, the Ohio Department of Health (ODH) was notified of a suspected case of botulism in Fairfield County, Ohio. Because botulism is a potentially fatal neuroparalytic disease and a single case can point toward a possible outbreak, the report of a single case is taken as a public health emergency. Within 2 hours of the notification of the first case, four more cases with similar clinical features had been identified at the local hospital, of which one died the same afternoon. All these individuals had eaten at a widely attended church potluck meal on April 19, 2015. For the investigation of this outbreak, ODH and the CDC defined a case as a clinically compatible illness in a person who had eaten food at the potluck meal and had either (1) laboratory-confirmed botulism or two or more signs of botulism, or (2) one sign and two or more symptoms of botulism. Symptoms of botulism include blurred vision, double vision, dizziness, slurred speech, thick-feeling tongue, hoarseness, dry mouth, and difficulty swallowing. Signs of botulism include paralysis of eye muscles, drooping of the eyelids, sluggishly reactive pupils, facial paralysis, palatal weakness, impaired gag reflex, musculoskeletal paralysis or weakness, and evidence of declining respiratory function. Out of the 77 individuals who ate food at the potluck meal, 29 (38%) met the case definition. The age range for patients was 9 to 87 years, and 17 (59%) were female. In 26 patients, median time for the onset of symptoms and signs was 2 days. In 19 cases, serum and stool specimens were positive for botulinum neurotoxin, or *Clostridium botulinum* microbe. Of the 77 individuals who had eaten any of the 52 food items at the potluck meal, 75 were interviewed. By cross-matching the items consumed by these individuals, consumption of potato salad was found to have the highest association with botulism case status (risk ratio = 13.9). Of the 12 specimens of food collected from the church dumpster, six were positive for botulinum neurotoxin; five of the specimens contained potato salad, and one contained macaroni and cheese. The specimen of macaroni and cheese was deemed to have been contaminated with botulinum neurotoxin from the potato salad after having been discarded in the dumpster. Further investigation revealed that the potato salad had been inadequately/unsafely canned and served.

Questions

Question 1. What was the cause or source of the outbreak?

Question 2. What was the approximate length of the incubation period? Explain your answer with the help of the information provided in the case study.

Question 3. Was this a point source, common source, or mixed propagated outbreak? Explain your answer with the help of the information provided in the case study.

Question 4. Did the outbreak end spontaneously, or did it end because of any measures implemented by the public health authorities?

▶ 7.12 Summary

Infectious diseases relentlessly continue to take a heavy toll in morbidity and mortality all over the world. Millions of people die every year from HIV, malaria, TB, and other viral, bacterial, and parasitic diseases. Previously known communicable diseases are resurging for a variety of reasons, including resistance to antimicorbial drugs by infectious agents and to pesticides by insect vectors, mutations and other adaptations by viruses, and greater exposure of humans through population growth, urbanization, and global travel. Emergence of new infectious diseases almost every year continues to lengthen the list of agents to which hundreds of millions of humans are exposed globally. The rising global temperature and climate change may very well favor the growth of vectors and transmission of microbial agents in the future. Limited resources to combat infectious diseases and vast numbers of people traveling nationally and internationally further complicate the situation. All of this simply means a huge burden of infectious diseases and demand for health services globally. The socioeconomic impact of infectious diseases globally every year runs into hundreds of billions, if not trillions, of dollars. In high-income countries, millions of people every year suffer from common infectious diseases such as the flu and upper respiratory infections, or relatively less common diseases such as hepatitis or Lyme disease in the United States. However, those in low-income developing countries bear the brunt of infectious diseases.

References

1. World Health Organization. World Health Statistics 2014. Geneva, Switzerland: World Health Organization; 2014 [cited 2018 July 24]. Available from: http://apps.who.int/iris/bitstream/10665/112738/1/9789240692671_eng.pdf

2. World Health Organization. Health care-associated infections: Fact Sheet. 2016 [cited 2018 July 24]. Available from: http://www.who.int/gpsc/country_work/gpsc_ccisc_fact_sheet_en.pdf

3. Rosenthal VD, Maki DG, Mehta Y, et al. International Nosocomial Infection Control Consortium (INICC) report, data summary of 43 countries for 2007–2012: Device-associated module. Am J Infect Control. 2014;42(9):942–956.

4. Rosenthal VD. Epidemiology of HAIs: findings of the International Nosocomial Infection Control Consortium (INICC). 20th International Intensive Care Symposium; 2015 May 8; Istanbul, Turkey.

5. European Centre for Disease Prevention and Control. Annual Epidemiological Report on Communicable Diseases in Europe 2008. Stockholm: European Centre for Disease Prevention and Control; 2008 [cited 2018 July 24]. Available from: https://ecdc.europa.eu/sites/portal/files/media/en/publications/Publications/0812_SUR_Annual_Epidemiological_Report_2008.pdf

6. Zimlichman E, Henderson D, Tamir O, et al. Health care-associated infections: a meta-analysis of costs and financial impact on the U.S. health care system. JAMA Intern Med. 2013;173(22):2039–2046.

7. Janoff EN, Gustafson C, Frank D. The world within: living with our microbial guests and guides. Transl Res. 2012;160(4):239–245.

8. Sender R, Fuchs S, Milo R. Are we really vastly outnumbered? Revisiting the ratio of bacterial to host cells in humans. Cell. 2016;164(3):337–340.

9. Rosner JL. Ten times more microbial cells than body cells in humans? Microbe. 2014;9(2):47.

10. Backhed F, Ley RE, Sonnenburg JL, Pererson DA, Gordon JI. Host-bacterial mutualism in the human intestine. Science. 2005;307(5717):1915–1920.

11. Gill SR, Pop M, Deboy RT, et al. Metagenomic analysis of the human distal gut microbiome. Science. 2006;312(5778):1355–1359.

12. Jandhyala SM, Talukdar R, Subramanyam C, Vuyyuru H, Sasikala M, Reddy DN. Role of the normal gut microbiota. World J Gastroenterol. 2015;21(29):8787–8803.

13. Brandt LJ. Fecal transplantation for the treatment of *Clostridium difficile* infection. Gastroenterol Hepatol. 2012;8(3):191–194.

14. Centers for Disease Control and Prevention. Outbreak chronology: Ebola virus disease. 2016 [cited 2018 July 24]. Available from: http://www.cdc.gov/vhf/ebola/outbreaks/history/chronology.html

15. Centers for Disease Control and Prevention. 2014 Ebola outbreak in West Africa—case counts. Atlanta, GA: Centers for Disease Control and Prevention. 2014 [cited 2018 July 24]. Available from: http://www.cdc.gov/vhf/ebola/outbreaks/2014-west-africa/case-counts.html

16. Centers for Disease Control and Prevention. Health, United States, 2012 [cited 2017 Jul 26]. Available from: https://www.cdc.gov/nchs/data/hus/hus12.pdf

17. Armstrong GL, Conn AA, Pinner RW. Trends in infectious diseases mortality in the United States during the 20th century. JAMA. 1999;281(1):61–66.

18. National Center for Health Statistics. Health, United States, 2014: with special feature on adults aged 55–64. Hyattsville, MD: National Center for Health Statistics; 2015.

19. Boutayeb A. The burden of communicable and non-communicable disease in developing countries. In: Preedy VR, Watson RR, editors. Handbook of disease burden and quality of life measures. New York: Springer; 2010. 531–546 p. [cited 2018 July 24]. Available from: http://link.springer.com/referenceworkentry/10.1007%2F978-0-387-78665-0_32

20. World Health Organization. Fact sheet: world malaria report 2015 [2018 July 24]. Available from: http://www.who.int/malaria/media/world-malaria-report-2015/en/

21. Molloy PJ, Telford SR, Chowdri HR, et al. Borrelia miyamotoi disease in the northeastern United States: a case series. Ann Intern Med. 2015;163:9198.

22. Institute of Medicine. Microbial evolution and co-adaptation: a tribute to the life and scientific legacies of Joshua Lederberg: workshop summary. Forum on Microbial Threats. Washington, DC: National Academies Press; 2009.

23. Henry J. Kaiser Family Foundation. The U.S. Government & Global Emerging Infectious Disease Preparedness and Response. 2014 Dec 8 [cited 2018 July 24]. Available at: http://kff.org/global-health-policy/fact-sheet/the-u-s-government-global-emerging-infectious-disease-preparedness-and-response/#endnote_link_92191-6

24. Porta M. Agent. A dictionary of epidemiology [Internet]. 6th ed. New York: Oxford University Press; 2014 [cited 2018 Mar 14]. Available from: http://www.irea.ir/files/site1/pages/dictionary.pdf

25. Venes D, editor. Infection. Taber's cyclopedic medical dictionary [Internet]. 23rd ed. Philadelphia: FA Davis; 2017 [cited 2018 Mar 14]. Available from: http://online.statref.com/document.aspx?Offset=0&StartDoc=1&QueryID=-1&FxID=57&Lt=TOC&SessionID=28A9406VQJPDJETN#H&1&ChaptersTab&JhoCcUe-vTNq8LwxN1HjEQ%3d%3d&p37&57

26. Porta M. Microorganism (syn Microbe). A dictionary of epidemiology [Internet]. 6th ed. New York: Oxford University Press; 2014. [cited 2018 Mar 14]. Available from: http://irea.ir/files/site1/pages/dictionary.pdf

27. Centers for Disease Control and Prevention. List of selected multistate foodborne outbreak investigations. 2016 [cited 2018 July 24]. Available from: http://www.cdc.gov/foodsafety/outbreaks/multistate-outbreaks/outbreaks-list.html

28. Mausner JS, Kramer S. Epidemiology: an introductory text. Philadelphia: WB Saunders Company; 1985.

29. Musso D, Gubler DJ. Zika virus. Clin Microbiol Rev. 2016;29(3):487–524.

30. Dick GWA, Kitchen SF, Haddow AJ. Zika virus (I). Isolations and serological specificity. Trans R Soc Trop Med Hyg. 1952;46(5):509–520.

31. Anderson KB, Thomas SJ, Endy TP. The emergence of Zika virus: a narrative review. Ann Intern Med. 2016;165:175–183.

32. Centers for Disease Control and Prevention. Zika virus update: 2016 case count in the U.S. 2017 [cited 2017 Jul 26]. Available from: https://www.cdc.gov/zika/reporting/2016-case-counts.html

33. Dallatomasina S, Crestani R, Squire JS, et al. Ebola outbreak in rural West Africa: epidemiology, clinical features and outcomes. Trop Med Int Health. 2015;20(4):448–454.

34. Centers for Disease Control and Prevention. Sierra Leone Trial to introduce a vaccine against Ebola (STRIVE). 2016 [cited 2018 July 24]. Available from: https://www.cdc.gov/vhf/ebola/strive/

© Monsitj/Getty Images

CHAPTER 8

Injury Epidemiology

CHAPTER OUTLINE

8.1   Introduction
8.2   Nature, Distribution, and Impact of Injuries in the United States
8.3   Epidemiology of Intentional Injuries in the United States
8.4   Epidemiology of Road Traffic Injuries and Death in the United States
8.5   Epidemiology of Traumatic Brain Injury in the United States
8.6   Epidemiology of Burns in the United States
8.7   Economic Impact of Injuries in the United States
8.8   The U.S. National Violent Death Reporting System

8.9   The U.S. National Electronic Injury Surveillance System
8.10 Global Injury Epidemiology
    8.10.1 Global Epidemiology of Injury
    8.10.2 Global Epidemiology of Burns
    8.10.3 Global Epidemiology of Drowning
    8.10.4 Global Epidemiology of Road Traffic Injuries
8.11 Example of a Study of Injury Epidemiology
Case Study 8.1 – Hospital-Based Injury Surveillance
Case Study 8.2 – Unintentional Firearm Deaths
8.12 Summary

KEY TERMS

Brain injury
Burn
Firearm
Fatality

Homicide
National Electronic Injury Surveillance System (NEISS)

National Violent Death Reporting System (NVDRS)
Trauma

8.1 Introduction

Injuries of various kinds place considerable demand on a healthcare system for specialized services, including orthopedic, burn, neurosurgical, and rehabilitation services. The nature and frequency of injuries in a community are largely determined by its demographic characteristics. Populations with a high proportion of the elderly are more likely to encounter injuries resulting from falls, whereas those with a high proportion of young adults are likely to experience higher numbers of violence- or sports-related injuries. Emergency departments (EDs) of hospitals experience significant demand for injury-related services. Tertiary care hospitals provide more complex injury-related services than do secondary care hospitals and frequently develop specialized departments such as a *burn unit* or a *trauma unit*. To be designated a level I **trauma** center, a tertiary care medical center in the United States must meet specific criteria established by the local or state government. These criteria are based on demonstrated commitment, readiness, volume of patients, and resources to provide optimal care for trauma patients and define the standards for trauma care. Verification of the availability of *resources for optimal care of the injured patient* is independently carried out by the American College of Surgeons. For various levels of trauma care (i.e., levels I, II, III, IV, or V), hospitals are separately designated for adult and pediatric trauma care. These standards can vary from one state to another and are developed by a legislative or regulatory process. Having a good understanding of the nature of, scope of, and demand for injury-related services is necessary for healthcare managers in both rural and urban settings. This chapter provides an overview of the epidemiology of injuries in the United States and globally, including the nature, distribution, and overall burden of various kinds of injuries.

8.2 Nature, Distribution, and Impact of Injuries in the United States

In 2010, with an average medical cost in excess of $11,600 per death, the total cost of nearly 181,000 injury-related deaths in the United States was estimated to be about $2.1 billion.[1] In 2013, the rate of fatal injuries in the United States was 61 per 100,000 population, and unintentional injuries ranked as the fourth most common cause of death. The combined medical and work-loss costs of fatal injuries were more than $214 billion and represented about one-third of the $671 billion in medical and work-loss costs associated with all injuries in 2013.[2] **TABLE 8.1** shows the total number of deaths resulting from injuries and the

TABLE 8.1 Injury-Related Mortality Data for 2013 and 2014

Cause	No. of Deaths in 2013	No. of Deaths in 2014	Rate per 100,000 in 2013	Rate per 100,000 in 2014
Total number of deaths due to injuries	192,945	199,756	61.0	62.7
Unintentional injuries	130,557	136,053	41.3	42.7
Unintentional falls	30,208	31,959	9.6	10.0
All poisoning deaths (includes drugs)	48,545	51,966	15.4	16.3
Unintentional poisoning (includes drugs)	38,851	42,032	12.3	13.2
Motor vehicle traffic deaths	33,804	33,736	10.7	10.6
All firearms deaths	33,636	33,599	10.6	10.5
All suicides	41,149	42,773	13.0	13.4

Firearm suicides	21,175	21,334	6.7	6.7
All homicides	16,121	15,809	5.1	5.0
Firearm homicides	11,208	10,945	3.5	3.4

Data from: Centers for Disease Control and Prevention. FastStats – injuries. Available at http://www.cdc.gov/nchs/fastats/default.htm. Data from: Centers for Disease Control and Prevention. Fatal injury reports, National and Regional, 1999 – 2014. Available at: http://webappa.cdc.gov/sasweb/ncipc/mortrate10_us.html. Data from: Florence C, Simon T, Haegerich T, Luo F, Zhou C. Estimated lifetime medical and work-loss costs of fatal injuries – United States, 2013. Morbid Mortal Wkly Rep. 2015;64(38): 1074–1077.

breakdown of deaths from various sources of injuries in 2013 and 2014.

Males accounted for 67% of injury deaths and about 78% of medical and work-loss costs of fatal injuries. About 66% of injury deaths were unintentional and represented $129.7 billion (61%) of fatal injury costs. About 20% of injury-related deaths were suicides, which accounted for $50.8 billion (24%) of medical and work-loss costs related to fatal injuries. About 8% of injury-related deaths were homicides and accounted for $26.4 billion (12%) of total injury-related costs. Males accounted for 82% of the cost of suicides ($41.7 billion) and 86% of the costs of homicides ($22.5 billion). Table 8.1 also shows that **homicide** rates were higher among young people, whereas suicide rates were higher among the middle-aged. The lowest proportion of costs of fatal injuries was among those 65 years or older. The mean medical cost and work-loss cost of any injury-related death in 2013 was more than $1.1 million. The cost of a homicide was estimated to be about $1.6 million, and that for a suicide was $1.2 million.[2]

In 2013, there were a total of 33,636 firearm-related deaths in the United States, of which 21,175 (63%) were suicides, 11,208 (33%) were homicides, 505 were due to unintentional discharges, 467 were on account of legal intervention or were war related, and 281 had undetermined etiology or explanation. Altogether, there were 16,121 homicides in the country, with a rate of 5.1 homicides per 100,000 population and 3.5 firearm-related homicides per 100,000 population.[3]

According to the Centers for Disease Control and Prevention (CDC),[4] in 2011, there were 31.0 million visits to EDs for unintentional injuries and 2.1 million visits that were due to assaults. Self-inflicted injuries resulted in 836,000 visits to EDs. The number of medically attended injury and poisoning episodes in 2013 was 37.4 million, at a rate of 121.2 per 1,000 population. The number of hospital discharges for fractures was 1.1 million. **TABLE 8.2** shows the top 10 causes of death in each age group in the United States in 2014.

Different colored cells in the table represent different sources of injury. Cells in light green represent deaths from suicide, those in the darker green represent deaths from unintentional injuries, and those in the darkest green represent homicidal deaths. As can be noted, in each age group, one, two, or all three of these sources of injury were among the top 10 causes of death for that age group. **FIGURE 8.1** shows the percentage distribution of the top 10 causes of death by sex in the United States in 2012.

▶ 8.3 Epidemiology of Intentional Injuries in the United States

From 2000 through 2008, about 340,000 children between the ages of 0 to 17 were treated in EDs in the United States for intentional injuries. This constitutes about 1.2% of all pediatric visits to EDs in the country.[5] Between 2010 and 2012, every year, on average, more than 32,500 individuals died in the country from a **firearm**-related injury, constituting an age-adjusted rate of 10.2 deaths per 100,000 population.[6] Of these deaths, 60% (20,012) were suicides, 35% (11,256) were homicides, and 2% (582) were unintentional. In the same period, every year, about 67,200 individuals received medical treatment in an ED for a firearm-related injury at an age-adjusted annual rate of 21.6 persons per 100,000 population. More than half of these individuals (53.9%) had to be admitted to a hospital for their injuries. The case **fatality** rate for suicidal attempts with a firearm was 85%. Fowler et al.[6] have reported that between 2010 and 2012, 86% of all firearm-related deaths and 90% of those treated for nonfatal firearm injuries were men. The rate of firearm-related deaths was 6.5 times higher among men than women (18.1 vs. 2.8 per 100,000). Those between the ages of 25 and 34 had the highest rate of firearm-related death. However, those aged 65 years or older had the highest rate of firearm suicides (10.9 per

TABLE 8.2 10 Leading Causes of Death, United States, 2014, All Races, Both Sexes

Rank	<1	1–4	5–9	10–14	15–24	25–34	35–44	45–54	55–64	65+	All Ages
					Age Groups (Years)						
1	Congenital Anomalies 4,746	Unintentional Injury 1,216	Unintentional Injury 730	Unintentional Injury 750	Unintentional Injury 11,836	Unintentional Injury 17,357	Unintentional Injury 16,048	Malignant Neoplasms 44,834	Malignant Neoplasms 115,282	Heart Disease 489,722	Heart Disease 614,348
2	Short Gestation 4,173	Congenital Anomalies 399	Malignant Neoplasms 436	Suicide 425	Suicide 5,079	Suicide 6,569	Malignant Neoplasms 11,267	Heart Disease 34,791	Heart Disease 74,473	Malignant Neoplasms 413,885	Malignant Neoplasms 591,699
3	Maternal Pregnancy Complications 1,574	Homicide 364	Congenital Anomalies 192	Malignant Neoplasms 416	Homicide 4,144	Homicide 4,159	Heart Disease 10,368	Unintentional Injury 20,610	Unintentional Injury 18,030	Chronic Lower Respiratory Disease 124,693	Chronic Lower Respiratory Disease 147,101
4	SIDS 1,545	Malignant Neoplasms 321	Homicide 123	Congenital Anomalies 156	Malignant Neoplasms 1,569	Malignant Neoplasms 3,624	Suicide 6,706	Suicide 8,767	Chronic Low. Respiratory Disease 16,492	Cerebro-vascular 113,308	Cerebro-vascular 133,103
5	Unintentional Injury 1,161	Heart Disease 149	Heart Disease 69	Homicide 156	Heart Disease 953	Heart Disease 3,341	Homicide 2,588	Liver Disease 8,627	Diabetes Mellitus 13,342	Alzheimer's Disease 92,604	Alzheimer's Disease 93,541
6	Placenta Cord Membranes 965	Influenza & Pneumonia 109	Chronic Lower Respiratory Disease 68	Heart Disease 122	Congenital Anomalies 377	Liver Disease 725	Liver Disease 2,582	Diabetes Mellitus 6,062	Liver Disease 12,792	Diabetes Mellitus 54,161	Diabetes Mellitus 76,488
7	Bacterial Sepsis 544	Chronic Lower Respiratory Disease 53	Cerebro-vascular 45	Chronic Lower Respiratory Disease 71	Influenza & Pneumonia 199	Diabetes Mellitus 709	Diabetes Mellitus 1,999	Cerebro-vascular 5,349	Cerebro-vascular 11,727	Influenza & Pneumonia 44,836	Influenza & Pneumonia 55,227
8	Respiratory Distress 460	Septicemia 53	Influenza & Pneumonia 57	Cerebro-vascular 43	Diabetes Mellitus 181	HIV 583	Cerebro-vascular 1,745	Chronic Lower Respiratory Disease 4,402	Suicide 7,527	Unintentional Injury 48,295	Nephritis 48,146
9	Circulatory System Disease 444	Benign Neoplasms 38	Benign Neoplasms 36	Influenza & Pneumonia 41	Chronic Lower Respiratory Disease 178	Cerebro-vascular 579	HIV 1,174	Influenza & Pneumonia 2,731	Septicemia 5,709	Nephritis 39,957	Suicide 42,773
10	Neonatal Hemorrhage 441	Perinatal Period 38	Septicemia 33	Benign Neoplasms 38	Cerebro-vascular 177	Influenza & Pneumonia 549	Influenza & Pneumonia 1,125	Septicemia 2,514	Influenza & Pneumonia 5,390	Septicemia 29,124	

Legend: ■ Unintentional Injuries; ■ Homicidal Deaths; ■ suicide

WISQARS™ produced by: National Center for Injury Prevention and Control, Centers for Disease Control and Prevention Data. Source: National Center for Health Statistics (NCHS), National Vital Statistics System. Available at: http://webappa.cdc.gov/sasweb/ncipc/leadcaus10_us.html

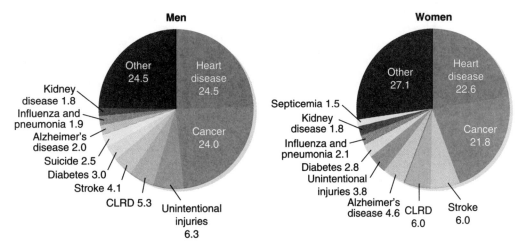

FIGURE 8.1 Percentage distribution of the 10 leading causes of death by sex, United States, 2012.

Reproduced from: Heron M. Deaths: leading causes for 2012. Centers for Disease Control and Prevention, National Center for Health Statistics: Vital Statistics System. National Vital Statistics Reports. 2015;64(10).

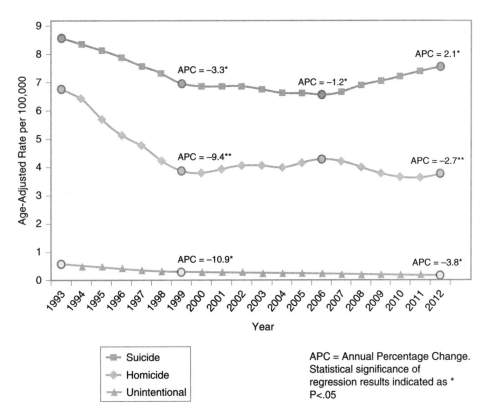

FIGURE 8.2 Age-adjusted fatal firearm injury rates by intent and year, United States, 1993–2012.

Reprinted from: Fowler KA, Dahlberg LL, Haileyesus T, Annest JL. Firearm injuries in the United States. Prev Med. 2015;79:5–14. Copyright © 2015 with permission from Elsevier.

100,000), whereas the firearm homicide rate (8.9 per 100,000) was the highest among those 15–24 years of age. **FIGURE 8.2** shows age-adjusted fatal firearm injury rates by intent and year in the United States from 1993 through 2012. Although there has been considerable decline in the rate of firearm-related deaths (particularly in the rate of homicides), firearm-related injuries take a heavy toll not only in human lives and suffering but also in tens of billions of dollars in healthcare costs and lost productivity every year (**FIGURE 8.3**).

Wintemute[7] examined the relationship between alcohol misuse and firearm ownership as well as the risk of perpetrating interpersonal and self-directed violence and reported that in an average month, 8.9 to 11.7 million owners of firearms binge drink (≥5 drinks on one occasion for males and ≥4 for females). Further, 16.9% of respondents in the 2012 U.S. Behavioral Risk Factor Surveillance System (BRFSS) survey reported binge drinking, and 6.1% reported heavy drinking (>2 drinks per day

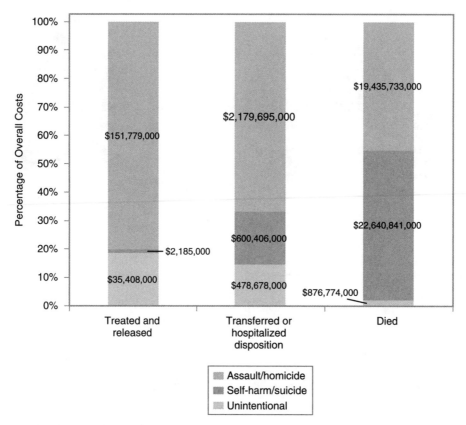

FIGURE 8.3 Percentage distribution of total lifetime costs by intent of firearm injury and disposition, United States, 2010–2012.

for males and >1 for females) in the last 30 days. Alcohol-Related Disease Impact (ARDI)—an online application from the CDC—estimated that alcohol-attributable death rates for violence exceed those for automobile traffic crashes.[8] A study by Branas et al.[9] showed an odds ratio of 5.5 (95% confidence interval 2.9–12.1) for firearm suicide associated with "nonexcessive" acute alcohol consumption and 85.8 (95% confidence interval 10.0–732.3) for "excessive consumption." In 2000, the total cost of deaths and nonfatal injuries resulting from interpersonal and self-directed violence was more than $70 billion, out of which $64.4 billion (92%) represented the cost of lost productivity and $5.6 billion on the medical care of 2.5 million injured individuals.[10] In 2006, the total societal cost of excessive drinking was estimated to be $223.5 billion, and the cost of alcohol-related crimes was about $73.3 billion.[11] In 2012, the total societal cost of firearm deaths and injuries was estimated to be about $229 billion.[12]

According to the National Trauma Institute (NTI), every year, nearly one-third of older adults experience at least one fall. In 2009, more than 8 million individuals were treated in EDs for nonfatal injuries resulting from falls, and more than 581,000 of them had to be hospitalized. Of the 8 million treated in EDs, about 2.2 million were aged 65 or older.[13]

▶ 8.4 Epidemiology of Road Traffic Injuries and Death in the United States

The National Highway Traffic Safety Administration has reported a steady decline in road traffic crash fatalities over the last decade, from 43,510 deaths in 2005 to 32,675 in 2014—a decrease of 25%. Of the more than 21,000 passenger vehicle occupants who were killed in crashes in 2014, 49% were not restrained.[14,15] Also, in 2014, a total of 2.3 million individuals were injured in 6.1 million police-reported road traffic crashes. The number of injured people also represents a decline of 13% from the number of injured people in 2005. This improvement is even more important in view of the increased total population and increased number of drivers on roads, as well as more miles driven as compared with preceding years. The number of pedestrians and cyclists killed in road traffic crashes in 2014 was 4,884 and 726, respectively.

Of the 32,675 fatalities in 2014, 31% (9,967) involved alcohol-impaired driving (drunk driving). Out of the 9,967 crash fatalities that involved alcohol-impaired driving, 64% were drivers with blood alcohol levels ≥0.08 g/dL, 15% were passengers riding with the alcohol-impaired driver, 12% were occupants of other vehicles, and 8% were nonoccupants such as pedestrians, cyclists, or others. In 2014, 1,070 children age ≤14 were killed in road traffic crashes. 19% of these deaths involved drunk drivers. Most of these children (56%) were occupants in vehicles with an alcohol-impaired driver. Alcohol-impaired driving fatalities have declined by 27% in the last 10 years, from 13,582 in 2005 to 9,967 in 2014. The rate of fatalities per 100 million vehicle miles traveled (VMT) has also declined by 27%, from 0.45 fatalities in 2005 to 0.33 in 2014. The economic cost of all road traffic crashes in the United States in 2010, the most recent year for which economic cost data are available, was estimated to be $242 billion, with a cost of $44 billion attributed to alcohol-impaired driving crashes.[16]

Preliminary data reported by the U.S. Federal Highway Administration indicated that in the first 9 months of 2015, the number of VMT increased by 80.2 billion miles—a 3.5% increase from the number of VMT in the same period in 2014. The fatality rate per 100 million VMT also decreased steadily, from 1.32 in 2005 to 0.99 in 2014.[16] Importantly, in the states that did not have universal helmet laws, 10 times more unhelmeted motorcyclists died in 2014 than in states where such universal laws existed—1,565 deaths

vs. 151 deaths.[15] A total of 10% of crash fatalities (3,179) in the same year involved distracted driving related to cell phone use and other devices. Massachusetts, North Dakota, and Texas had the highest percent of drunk-driving fatalities, at 41% each, while Vermont with 20% and Utah with 22% had the lowest percentage of such fatalities in 2014.

The steady decline in the number of road traffic fatalities can be attributed to a number of factors, including safer vehicles and roads and more vigorous implementation of road traffic safety laws, such as those related to speed limits, drunk driving, seatbelt use, and child restraints. The seatbelt use rate has steadily improved from 70.7% in 2000 to 88.5% in 2015. There has been a corresponding decrease in unrestrained passenger fatality rates, from 51.6% to 40.3%, over the same years (**FIGURE 8.4**). Seatbelt use has continued to be high in those states in which vehicle occupants can be pulled over for not wearing a seatbelt ("primary law states") as compared with states that have weaker laws or do not have a seatbelt law.

▶ 8.5 Epidemiology of Traumatic Brain Injury in the United States

Traumatic **brain injury** (TBI) is defined as "an injury that disrupts the normal function of the brain."[17,18] The CDC has estimated that in 2010, TBIs, whether

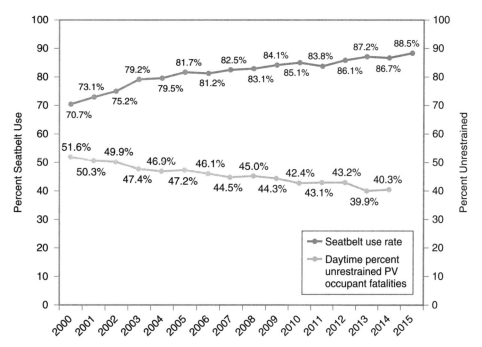

FIGURE 8.4 National seatbelt use rate and daytime percentage of unrestrained passenger vehicle occupant fatalities.

reported as isolated injuries or in combination with other injuries, resulted in about 2.5 million ED visits, hospitalizations, and deaths in the United States. About 87% (>2.2 million) of these individuals were treated in and released from EDs, 11% (>283,000) were hospitalized and later discharged, and about 2% (>52,800) died.[19] Between 2002 and 2006, on average, 1.7 million TBIs occurred every year and resulted in 52,000 deaths, 275,000 hospitalizations, and 1.37 million ED visits (**FIGURE 8.5** and **TABLE 8.3**). However, these numbers do not represent the full magnitude of TBIs because they do not include individuals who sought care at Veterans Affairs hospitals, those who received care at an outpatient facility or doctor's office,

military personnel or their family members who received care at military hospitals, and those who did not receive any medical care at all.[20]

Based on their neurological presentation, TBIs are classified as mild, moderate, or severe. Depending on the severity of the injury, the nature, duration, and severity of neurological presentations can vary from one individual to another. In some cases, the signs and symptoms can resolve completely, whereas in others, there is a life-long impact with permanent disability.[19] TBIs have a wide range of short- and long-term health effects, including impaired cognition, emotional and behavioral disturbances, physical disability, and secondary neurological disorders such as mood disorders

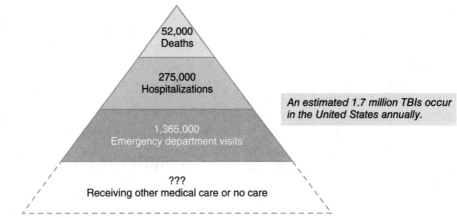

Of the 1.7 million TBIs occurring each year in the United States, 80.7% were emergency department visits, 16.3% were hospitalizations, and 3.0% were deaths.

FIGURE 8.5 Estimated average number of traumatic brain injury-related deaths, hospitalizations, and emergency department visits per year, United States, 2002–2006.

Reproduced from: Faul M, Xu L, Wald MM, Coronado V. Traumatic brain injury in the United States: emergency department visits, hospitalizations and deaths, 2002–2006. Atlanta, GA: Centers for Disease Control and Prevention, National Center for Injury Prevention;2010.

TABLE 8.3 Traumatic Brain Injury-Related Emergency Department Visits, Hospitalizations, and Deaths as a Percentage of All Injuries and as a Percentage of All Causes of Emergency Department Visits, Hospitalizations, and Deaths, United States, 2002–2006

Category	All Causes	All Injuries		Traumatic Brain Injuries		
	No.	No.	% of All Visits	No.	% of All Injuries	% of All Visits
ED visits	96,839,411	28,697,028	29.6	1,364,797	4.8	1.4
Hospitalizations	36,693,646	1,826,548	5.0	275,146	15.1	0.7
Deaths	2,432,714	169,055	6.9	51,538	30.5	2.1
Total	135,965,771	30,692,631	22.6	1,691,481	5.5	1.2

Reproduced from: Faul M, Xu L, Wald MM, Coronado V. Traumatic brain injury in the United States: emergency department visits, hospitalizations and deaths, 2002–2006. Atlanta, GA: Centers for Disease Control and Prevention, National Center for Injury Prevention;2010.

and posttraumatic epilepsy. According to various estimates, at any given time, between 3.2 million to 5.3 million individuals in the United States are living with disabilities resulting from a TBI.[21-23] Victims of moderate or severe TBIs discharged from rehabilitation facilities after recovery have been found to be twice as likely to die within 3.5 years as compared with the general public.[24,25] TBIs also have considerable negative impact on family and caregivers in terms of stress, depression, and dysfunctional relationships.[19] Because of the invisible nature of its long-term effects and complications such as cognitive impairment, memory loss, and behavioral or mood disorders, TBIs are often referred to as the "silent epidemic."[20]

In the United States, those aged 75 or older have the highest rate of hospitalization and death due to a TBI. The most common causes of nonfatal TBIs include falls (35%), motor vehicle crashes (17%), and trauma to the head from direct blows and strikes, including sports activities (17%).[20] As shown in **FIGURE 8.6**, the rate of TBI-related ED visits per 100,000 population increased from 457.5 to 715.7 between 2007 and 2010. During the same period, the rates of hospitalization and deaths from TBIs, however, remained relatively stable. In fact, the TBI-related death rate decreased from 18.2 to 17.1 per 100,000 population.[19]

▶ 8.6 Epidemiology of Burns in the United States

The American Burn Association (ABA) estimated that in 2015, approximately 486,000 **burn** injury patients received medical treatment in U.S. hospitals and EDs.[26] Because this estimate did not include those who received care at hospital outpatient clinics, community health centers, and private medical offices, it is probably an underestimation of the overall frequency of burn injuries in the United States. The ABA also estimated that in 2015, about 3,240 deaths resulted from burn injuries, including >2,800 deaths from residential fires, 300 from motor vehicle crash fires, and 85 from other sources. According to the same estimate, about 40,000 hospitalizations resulted from burn injury, including 30,000 admissions to hospital burn centers. Altogether, 60% of these admissions occurred at 128 burn centers in the country.

The National Burn Repository Annual Report has been compiled by the ABA every year since 2005. This report is an important source of longitudinal data on burn injury in the United States and is based on voluntary participation of hospitals that provide specialized services at burn centers. Despite some limitations,[27]

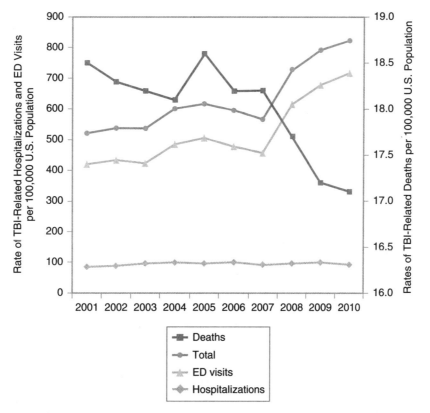

FIGURE 8.6 Rates of traumatic brain injury-related emergency department visits, hospitalizations, and deaths, United States, 2001–2010.

the report is a valuable source of information on the epidemiology of burn injury in the United States.

The 2015 report included data for acute burn admissions to U.S. hospitals from 2005 through 2014 and comprised >203,000 records from 99 hospitals in 36 states and the District of Columbia. The data showed that more than 68% of patients were men, and the mean age of all cases was 32 years. Children younger than age 5 years accounted for 19% of cases, and those 60 years or older accounted for 13%. Most of the burn cases (75%) involved less than 10% of total body surface area (TBSA), and the overall mortality rate for burns was only 3.2%. The two most common causes of burns, fire/flame and scalding, accounted for nearly 80% of cases. Children younger than 5 years mostly had scald injuries, while fire/flame was the most common cause in all other age groups. **TABLE 8.4** provides information on the etiology and circumstances of burn cases reported in 2015 by the participating hospitals. Notably, 72% of burn injuries were reported as non-work-related accidents. Only 3.3% of cases were listed as nonaccidental, and 12.7% were listed as work related. In 81% of cases, the burn injury involved less than 20% of TBSA. The report also indicated that 73% of burn injuries occurred in homes. The average length of stay in the hospital in 2014 was about 8.6 days, and 87% of admitted patients were sent home at the end of the hospital stay. The average total cost per person for those who survived was approximately $91,000, with an average daily cost of about $7,700. The average total cost per person for those who died from the burn injury or its complications was >$302,000, with an average daily cost of almost $24,000. The most common clinical complication— pneumonia—occurred in 5% of fire/flame burn cases. Pneumonia most commonly occurred in cases that involved 4 or more days of mechanical ventilation and was more frequent in older age groups, reaching a rate of almost 20% among those ages 80 or older.

Scald injury is the most common source or cause of burn in children younger than 5 years of age and overall represented 34% of all burn injuries in the 2015 National Burn Repository data, and fire/flame is the most common cause of burn injury after age 5 and overall accounted for 43% of burn cases in the repository. Generally, the average length of stay for

TABLE 8.4 Etiology and Circumstances of Burn Injuries in the United States, 2015

Etiology	Cases	% of Valid	Circumstance of Injury	Cases	% of Valid
Fire/Flame	79,303	42.6%	Accident, Non-Work Related	135,118	71.7%
Scald	63,247	34.0%	Accident, Work Related	25,892	13.7%
Contact with Hot Object	16,588	8.9%	Accident, Recreation	8,009	4.2%
Electrical	6,689	3.6%	Accident, Unspecified	7,934	4.2%
Chemical	6,301	3.4%	Other	4,747	2.5%
Burn, Unspecified	5,079	2.7%	Suspected Assault/Abuse	2,481	1.3%
Other, Non-Burn	4,689	2.5%	Suspected Child Abuse	2,011	1.1%
Inhalation Only	3,231	1.7%	Suspected Self-Inflicted	1,993	1.1%
Radiation	478	0.3%	Suspected Arson	290	0.2%
Skin Disease	415	0.2%			
Unknown	17,402		Unknown	14,947	
Total	**203,422**		**Total**	**203,422**	

American Burn Association. National burn repository, version 11.0. 2015. Available at: http://www.ameriburn.org/2015NBRAnnualReport.pdf

TABLE 8.5 Total Number of Years of Potential Life Lost Because of Deaths from Various Causes Before Age 65 in the United States in 2014: All Races, Both Sexes, and All Deaths

Cause of Death	YPLL*	Percentage
All Causes	11,134,297	100.0%
Unintentional Injury	**2,202,441**	**19.8%**
Malignant neoplasms	1,769,480	15.9%
Heart disease	1,339,215	12.0%
Suicide	**831,205**	**7.5%**
Perinatal period	771,707	6.9%
Homicide	**492,262**	**4.4%**
Congenital anomalies	413,136	3.7%
Liver disease	287,017	2.6%
Diabetes mellitus	239,256	2.1%
Cerebrovascular	221,132	2.0%
All others	2,567,446	23.1%

*Years of potential life lost. Bolded entries indicate years of potential life lost due to common causes of injuries.

Centers for Disease Control and Prevention (CDC). Available at: http://webappa.cdc.gov/sasweb/ncipc/ypll10.html

scald injury is shorter than that for fire/flame burn injury. It has been estimated that in 2013 in the United States, more than 50,000 years of potential life were lost (YPLL) because of burn fatalities.[28]

▶ 8.7 Economic Impact of Injuries in the United States

Every year, injuries account for approximately 41 million ED visits and more than 2.3 million hospital admissions in the United States.[1] The CDC estimates that, on average, the economic burden of trauma, including healthcare costs and loss of productivity, in the United States is about $585 billion per year. For example, in 2010, the combined medical and work-loss costs for injury-related deaths, hospitalizations, and ED visits were estimated by the CDC to be more than $586 billion.[28] In 2014, trauma accounted for 30% of all YPLL in the country. In comparison, all cancers combined account for only about 16% and heart disease accounts for only 12% of life years lost (**TABLE 8.5**). Because trauma affects people of all ages, its impact on life years lost is equal to cancer, heart disease, and HIV combined.[1]

The CDC's web-based Injury Statistics Query and Reporting System (WISQAR)—an interactive online database—contains comprehensive data from various sources on fatal and nonfatal injuries, injury-related hospitalizations, ED visits, cost of medical care, and cost to society through loss of productivity. WISQAR allows researchers, public health professionals, and other interested users to generate tables that are stratified on a number of variables. **TABLE 8.6** shows the number of deaths, hospitalizations, ED visits, and costs in 2010 by source or cause of injury. **TABLE 8.7** shows the total number of injury-related deaths, death rates per 100,000 population, and estimated lifetime medical and work-loss costs by sex, age group, and intent in the United States in 2013.

▶ 8.8 The U.S. National Violent Death Reporting System (NVDRS)

With funding received from the federal government in 2002, the CDC created an active surveillance system called the **National Violent Death Reporting System (NVDRS)** in 2003 with the initial participation of seven states. By 2015, 32 states were participating in this state-based system that collects data on all violence-related deaths, including the following: (1) homicides, (2) suicides, (3) unintentional firearms deaths, (4) legal deaths (those resulting from the use of deadly force by law enforcement authorities but excluding executions), and (5) deaths from undetermined intent.[17,28,29] The CDC provides funding and support to states for their participation and data collection efforts.

The NVDRS uses multiple complementary sources of data, including death certificates, coroners' or medical examiners' reports, law enforcement reports, and crime laboratories. Other sources of data used by some states include hospital data, crime laboratory data, and Bureau of Alcohol, Tobacco, Firearms and Explosives

TABLE 8.6 Cost of Fatal and Nonfatal Injuries in the United States in 2010 by Source or Cause of Injury

	Intent					
	Unintentional	Suicide	Homicide	Undetermined	Legal Intervention	Total
No. of Deaths	120,859	38,364	16,259	4,908	412	**180,802**
Medical cost*	$1,721,946	$154,032	$177,932	$40,580	$3,207	**$2,097,697**
Work-loss* cost	$111,571,569	$44,520,795	$24,893,055	$5,808,041	$640,187	**$187,433,647**
No. of Hospitalizations	2,067,006	5,247	135,563	316,572	4,779	**2,529,167**
Medical cost*	$72,480,028	$104,932	$3,958,544	$3,519,174	$121,753	**$80,184,431**
Work-loss cost*	$126,753,295	$347,842	$16,278,572	$6,300,746	$542,956	**$150,223,411**
No. of ED Visits	26,737,581	62,645	1,531,219	134,202	84,776	**28,550,423**
Medical cost*	$61,858,894	$210,795	$4,051,155	$464,155	$211,211	**$66,796,210**
Work-loss cost*	$93,423,379	$307,292	$5,915,331	$145,992	$315,691	**$100,107,685**
Total Cost*	**$467,809,111**	**$45,645,688**	**$55,274,589**	**$16,278,688**	**$1,835,005**	**$586,843,081**

*In thousands.

Modified from Centers for Disease Control and Prevention (CDC). National Center for Injury Prevention and Control. Data & Statistics (WISQARS™): Cost of Injury Reports. Available at https://wisqars.cdc.gov:8443/costT/.

TABLE 8.7 Injury Deaths, Rates per 100,000 Population, and Estimated Lifetime Medical and Work-Loss Costs by Sex, Age Group, and Intent, United States, 2013

		Sex		Age Group (Years)				
Intent	Total	Male	Female	0–14	15–24	25–44	45–64	≥65
All Intents								
No. of deaths	192,945	129,912	63,033	5,501	21,320	53,205	58,350	54,524
Rate*	61.03	83.46	39.28	9.00	48.50	63.87	70.23	121.97
Costs**	214,394	166,717	47,355	7,786	41,527	95,540	55,250	9,164
Unintentional								
No. of deaths	130,557	81,916	48,641	3,993	11,619	31,563	37,414	45,942
Rate*	41.30	52.63	30.31	6.54	26.43	37.89	45.03	102.77
Costs**	129,726	97,091	32,585	5,628	22,371	56,079	35,122	7,439
Homicide								
No. of deaths	16,121	12,726	3,395	896	4,329	6,817	3,164	905
Rate*	5.10	8.18	2.12	1.47	9.85	8.18	3.81	2.02
Costs**	26,350	22,572	3,817	1,235	8,622	12,858	3,159	202

Suicide								
No. of deaths	41,149	32,055	9,094	395	4,878	12,899	15,756	7,215
Rate*	13.02	20.59	5.67	0.65	11.10	15.49	18.96	16.14
Costs**	50,795	41,747	8,913	664	9,578	23,242	15,038	1,443

*Deaths per 100,000 population.
**In millions of U.S. dollars.

Reproduced from: Florence C, Simon T, Haegerich T, Luo F, Zhou C. Estimated lifetime medical and work-loss costs of fatal injuries – United States, 2013. Morbid Mortal Wkly Rep. 2015;64(38): 1074–1077.

reports. Updated and historical data are made available by the CDC to the general public and interested stakeholders through WISQARS. According to the CDC, "Linking information about the 'who, when, where, and how' from data on violent deaths provides insights about 'why' they occurred."[17,29] The data reported by the NVDRS can be used by various agencies to develop, implement, and evaluate national, state, and local programs and policies to prevent and reduce violent deaths. By linking data from multiple sources, the NVDRS provides detailed information on the circumstances that result in violent deaths. This information allows researchers and policy makers to understand the circumstances and context of each death and link multiple deaths that are related to one another.

▶ 8.9 The U.S. National Electronic Injury Surveillance System

The **National Electronic Injury Surveillance System (NEISS)** was developed and implemented by the U.S. Consumer Products Safety Commission (CPSC). The NEISS collects survey data from a sample of hospitals in the United States and its territories every year through a probability sample of hospitals. Patient information from surveyed hospitals is collected for every emergency visit resulting from an injury associated with the use of a consumer product. From sample data, the total number of product-related injuries treated in the EDs of hospitals nationwide is estimated for a given year. The CPSC allows free public access to their web-based query system to retrieve estimates based on a number of variables such as age, sex, product, locale, and period. The products can be chosen using NEISS product codes; note, however, that product codes change over time, and queries for specific periods must use product codes relevant for that

specific period. Injury estimates for 2014 reported by the CPSC are grouped under 14 main categories, such as Toys, Child Nursery Equipment, Sports and Recreational Equipment, and Yard and Garden Equipment. Each of these groups has further categories. For example, Sports and Recreational Equipment allows queries related to specific sports such as baseball and softball, basketball, boxing, football, and a number of other categories. Altogether, queries can be generated from the NEISS for injuries related to 87 different kinds of subcategories in a given period, including the mentioned subcategories. Based on a sample of 96 surveyed hospitals in 2014, **TABLE 8.8** shows the estimated number of injuries and rates per 100,000 population for a few common sources of injuries in children and adults.

▶ 8.10 Global Injury Epidemiology

8.10.1 Global Epidemiology of Injury

Injuries are an important global public health problem. Every year, more than 5 million people worldwide die from various kinds of injuries. In 2000, the estimated number of injury deaths worldwide was 5,026,000.[30] According to the World Health Organization's (WHO) Global Health Estimates, in 2012, about 5,144,000 individuals—9.2% of all deaths globally—died of various kinds of injuries, including road traffic crashes, homicide, suicide, falls, burns, drowning, and poisoning.[31] The number of deaths resulting from injuries globally is more than 1.7 times the total number of deaths caused by HIV/AIDS, tuberculosis, and malaria combined. Unintentional injuries were responsible for 3.7 million (72.2%) of these deaths, and intentional injuries accounted for the remaining 1.4 million (27.8%) deaths. Deaths caused by intentional injuries included 804,000 (15.6%) suicides ("self-harm") and 505,000 (9.8%) homicides ("interpersonal violence").

TABLE 8.8 Estimated Numbers and Rates of Injury per 100,000 Population in Select Categories by Age and Sex in 2014

Product Groupings	Estimated Total No. of Injuries (Rate per 100,000)	Age (Years)					Sex	
		0–4	5–14	15–24	25–64	≥65	Male	Female
All nursery equipment	97,541 (30.6)*	71,776 (361.1)	3,244 (7.9)	4,129 (9.4)	16,330 (9.7)	2,062 (4.5)	45,276 (28.9)	52,264 (32.3)
All toys	240,658 (75.5)	83,728 (421.2)	95,680 (232.3)	18,922 (43.0)	36,848 (22.0)	5,479 (11.8)	141,897 (90.4)	98,761 (61.0)
Baseball, softball	225,712 (70.8)	3,888 (19.6)	94,443 (229.3)	69,876 (158.9)	54,934 (32.8)	2,571 (5.6)	141,856 (90.4)	83,856 (51.8)
Basketball	522,817 (164.0)	1,973 (9.9)	179,306 (435.3)	245,817 (558.9)	94,673 (56.5)	1,048 (2.3)	419,675 (267.4)	103,142 (63.7)
Bicycle & accessories	510,905 (160.2)	22,822 (114.8)	170,038 (412.8)	87,807 (199.7)	198,890 (118.7)	31,317 (67.7)	372,903 (237.6)	138,002 (85.2)
Exercise equipment	466,162 (146.2)	8,354 (42.0)	51,775 (125.7)	103,450 (235.2)	254,572 (151.9)	48,011 (103.8)	255,767 (163.0)	210,395 (129.9)
Football	396,457 (124.3)	1,435 (7.2)	200,687 (487.2)	158,408 (360.2)	35,427 (21.1)	499 (1.1)	373,384 (237.9)	23,073 (14.2)
Soccer	239,943 (75.3)	2,538 (12.8)	104,838 (254.5)	93,151 (211.8)	39,314 (23.5)	103 (0.2)	157,001 (100.0)	8,2941 (51.2)

*Estimated rate per 100,000 population.

Modified from: Consumer Products Safety Commission's National Electronic Injury Surveillance System (NEISS) Data Highlights – 2014.

The remaining 119,000 (2.3%) were accounted for by "collective violence and legal intervention," including executions, armed conflicts, terrorism, and intended or unintended killings by law enforcement agencies.[30,31] **FIGURE 8.7** shows the breakdown of global injury deaths by cause of death in 2012. Road traffic injuries were the ninth most common cause of death globally in 2012; by 2030, they are expected to become the seventh most common cause of death worldwide.[32] **FIGURE 8.8** shows the rising trend of road traffic fatalities in Cambodia and India from 2001 through 2012. Unfortunately, low-income countries are the worst affected by injuries and violence (see **FIGURE 8.9**).

8.10.2 Global Epidemiology of Burns

A burn injury can result from a variety of sources, including fire/flame, electricity, radiation, or chemicals

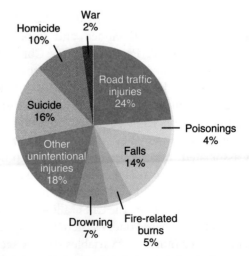

FIGURE 8.7 Breakdown of global injury deaths by cause of death in 2012.

Reprinted from: World Health Organization(WHO). Injuries and violence: 2014 – global health estimates 2014. Available at: http://apps.who.int/iris/bitstream/10665/149798/1/9789241508018_eng.pdf?ua=1&ua=1&ua=1 Source for injury related data: http://www.who.int/mediacentre/factsheets/fs344/en/. Copyright © 2014 WHO.

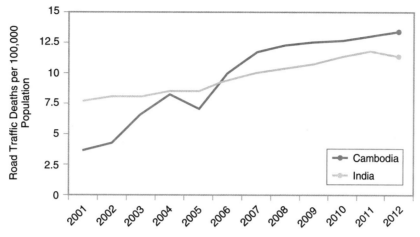

FIGURE 8.8 Trend of increasing road traffic fatalities in Cambodia and India from 2001 through 2012.

Reprinted from: World Health Organization (WHO). Global health estimates 2014. Available at: http://apps.who.int/iris/bitstream/10665/149798/1/9789241508018_eng.pdf?ua=1&ua=1&ua=1. Copyright © 2014 WHO.

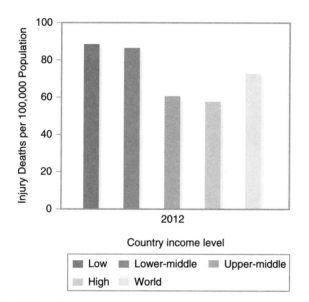

FIGURE 8.9 Injury death rates by country income level, 2012.

Reprinted from: World Health Organization (WHO). Global health estimates 2014. Available at: http://apps.who.int/iris/bitstream/10665/149798/1/9789241508018_eng.pdf?ua=1&ua=1&ua=1. Copyright © 2014 WHO.

and, depending on the intensity and duration of exposure, can affect skin, muscles, and other tissues of the body in varying degrees. Damage to lungs results directly from the inhalation of smoke and toxic gases or fumes linked with fires.

Globally, burn injury is the fourth most common cause of injury, after traffic accidents, falls, and interpersonal violence. About 90% of burns occur in low- and middle-income countries (LMICs).[33] The WHO has estimated that 265,000 people die every year from fires alone. Deaths from other forms of burns, such as scalds and electrocution, would substantially increase this estimate.[34,35] More than 96% of fire-related burn deaths also occur in LMICs and are largely preventable. For example, the WHO has reported that boys younger than age 5 years in LMICs of the Eastern

Mediterranean region are 6 times more likely to die from burns than are boys of the same age in Europe.[35] Further, nonfatal burn injuries are one of the leading causes of morbidity, disability, and disfigurement in developing countries. In 2014, about 11 million individuals received medical care for burns worldwide, and the incidence of burn injury was estimated to be about 1.1 per 100,000 population. In LMICs, the incidence was approximately 1.3, as opposed to only 0.14 per 100,000 population in high-income countries.[35] However, a recent study based on outpatient and inpatient cohort data of 1 million individuals in Taiwan reported a much higher incidence of 671 burn injuries per 100,000 men and 853 burn injuries per 100,000 women in 2010.[36] At a country level, the WHO reported that in Bangladesh, more than 1 million people get moderately or severely burned every year—approximately 173,000 of them are children. Likewise, burns account for 5% of all disabilities in Nepal and are the second most common form of injury in rural areas.[32-35] **TABLES 8.9** and **8.10** show estimated incidence and the number of burn-related deaths globally and in different WHO regions in 2004.

Most burn injuries occur in household settings and are associated with food preparation activities.[37,38] This is particularly true for burns in children, of which 84% occur at home and 80% occur when children are unsupervised. Among adult women, most burns occur at home, whereas adult men experience burn injury mostly at work or in outdoor settings.[38,39] A 2012 survey of 1,843 households with 3,645 individuals reported that 3.98% of the individuals reportedly had at least one burn injury in the preceding 12 months, with the highest rate of burns (5.4%) occurring in children younger than 5 years of age.[40] Burn injury data from developing countries do not fully reflect the magnitude of the problem because of a variety of

TABLE 8.9 Estimated Annual Incidence of Fire-Related Burn Injuries* in 2004, by World Health Organization Region

	Africa	The Americas	EMR	Europe	SEAR	WPR	World
Population†	689,632	874,380	519,688	883,311	1,671,904	1,738,457	6,436,826
Burns†	982	163	970	523	4,069	388	7,105
Incidence rate per 1,000	1.33	0.19	1.87	0.59	0.24	0.22	1.1

*Includes only burns covering 20% or more of TBSA.
†In thousands.
Abbreviations: EMR = Eastern Mediterranean region; SEAR = Southeast Asia region; WPR = Western Pacific region.

Reprinted from: Peck MD. UpToDate®. Epidemiology of burn injuries globally. Available at: http://www.uptodate.com/contents/epidemiology-of-burn-injuries-globally?source=see
_link&sectionName=Incidence&anchor=H4#H4 Data from: World Health Organization. Disease and injury estimates for 2004. Morbidity and Mortality. Prevalence for selected causes, in WHO regions, estimates for 2004. www.who.int/healthinfo/global_burden_disease/estimates_regional/en/index.html. Copyright © 2004 WHO.

TABLE 8.10 Estimated Deaths from Fire-Related Burn Injuries* in 2004, by World Health Organization Region

	Africa	The Americas	EMR	Europe	SEAR	WPR	World
Population†	737,536	874,380	519,688	883,311	1,671,904	1,738,457	6,436,826
Burn deaths†	48	8	29	23	186	16	310
Percentage of deaths§	6.51	0.91	5.58	2.6	1.11	0.92	0.53

*Includes only burns covering 20% or more of TBSA.
†In thousands.
§Percentage of all deaths attributed to burn injuries.
Abbreviations: EMR = Eastern Mediterranean region; SEAR = Southeast Asia region; WPR = Western Pacific region.

Reprinted from: Peck MD. UpToDate®. Epidemiology of burn injuries globally. Available at: from: World Health Organization. Disease and injury estimates for 2004. Morbidity and Mortality. Prevalence for selected causes, in WHO regions, estimates for 2004. www.who.int/healthinfo/global_burden_disease/estimates_regional/en/index.html. Copyright © 2004 WHO.

problems, including underreporting of assaults and potential overreporting of allegedly self-inflicted or accidental burn injuries in women.[41]

According to various estimates,[26,33,42,43] most burn injuries are unintentional or accidental. In fact, less than 5% of all burn injuries are considered to be intentional—whether resulting from self-burning or abuse. However, there are important regional exceptions in this regard. The greatest number of intentional self-burning (self-immolation) cases are reported in India, but the highest incidence per 1,000 population of intentional self-burning has been reported in Sri Lanka.[44] Self-immolation or self-burning is relatively rare in higher-income countries, accounting for only about 1% of suicide attempts. In developed countries, deliberate self-burning is most commonly associated

with mental illness or history of substance abuse, and most victims are men. For example, it has been reported that among those who had 20% or more of TBSA affected by a burn injury, 36.9% had a psychiatric disorder or substance abuse problem. In developing countries, on the other hand, most cases of deliberate self-burning occur in women, and self-immolation is more frequently associated with socioeconomic and marital issues.[41] According to one report,[45] almost 30% of burn-related hospital admissions in Nepal resulted from intentional burn injury, and 90% of them were reportedly self-immolations—only 10% of these cases were attributed to assault or abuse. Most cases of intentional burn injury in this report were married women between the ages of 25 and 30 years. Another recent report from Nepal indicated that most cases of unintentional or accidental burn injury admitted to a tertiary care hospital were caused by kerosene or biomass flames and occurred in women at home during cooking.[46] In other studies as well, most accidental burns in home settings in developing countries have been associated with the use of kerosene oil stoves for cooking and heating.[34]

The economic impact of burns at a global level is quite staggering. For example, in South Africa, approximately US $26 million is spent every year on providing medical care to individuals burned in kerosene stove cooking fire incidents. In Norway, the hospital care cost for burns exceeded €10.5 million (US $12.4 million) in 2007.[31]

8.10.3 Global Epidemiology of Drowning

The WHO estimates that about 372,000 people drown every year worldwide. In other words, globally, more than 42 individuals die from drowning every hour of every day. More than 90% of these deaths occur in LMICs where drowning rates per 100,000 population are more than 3 times higher than in high-income countries.[47,48] For individuals younger than 24 years, drowning is one of the 10 leading causes of death—drowning deaths in this age group account for more than half of all drowning deaths globally. In Bangladesh, drowning accounts for 43% of deaths of children 1–4 years of age.[47,48] In terms of gender distribution, drowning deaths are twice as frequent in males as they are in females. Among all unintentional injury deaths, drowning ranks number 3 and is responsible for 7% of total injury deaths in the world every year. The WHO notes that reported or estimated drowning deaths do not include suicidal or homicidal drownings, and, because of many challenges in the collection and reporting of data from various sources, such estimates may underestimate the magnitude of this public

health problem by as much as 50%.[47,48] In many countries, alcohol use, especially among adolescent and adult males, is an important risk factor. In the Western Pacific Region of the WHO, drowning is the leading cause of death of children 5–9 years of age. In high-income countries, it is the second most common cause of death of children 5–9 years. National-level estimates of the direct and indirect economic impact of drownings in Canada, Australia, and the United States range from US $85 million to $4.1 billion per year.[47,48]

Since 2014, refugee and migrant drownings in the Mediterranean Sea have become the most notable and visible global public health crisis. According to the International Organization for Migration estimates, in 2015, close to 3,800 refugees and migrants, largely from African countries, drowned in the Mediterranean Sea, and almost 4,700 in 2016.[49]

Risk factors for drowning include a lack of physical barriers between people and water; lack of or inadequate supervision of children near water; uncovered or unprotected water supplies and lack of safe water crossings; risky behavior, including swimming alone; water travel in poorly maintained and overcrowded vessels; and natural water-related events such as floods, tsunamis, and hurricanes.[48] **FIGURES 8.10** and **8.11** show age-standardized drowning rates in low- and middle-income countries within various WHO regions of the world and the distribution of places in which children in Bangladesh have reportedly drowned, respectively.

8.10.4 Global Epidemiology of Road Traffic Injuries

In March 2010, the United Nations General Assembly proclaimed 2011–2020 to be the Decade of Action for Road Safety, with the official goal of "stabilizing and then reducing" global road traffic fatalities by 2020. The Decade was officially launched in more than 100

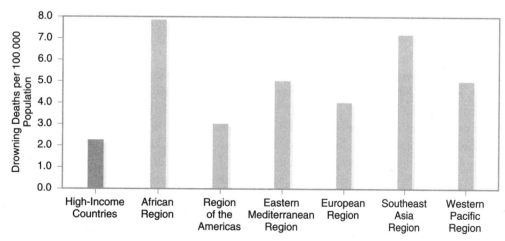

FIGURE 8.10 Age-standardized drowning deaths per 100,000 population by region and income level.

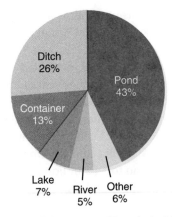

FIGURE 8.11 Place of drowning of Bangladeshi children younger than 5 years.

Reprinted from: Global report on drowning: preventing a leading killer. 2014. Available at: http://apps.who.int/iris /bitstream/10665/143893/1/9789241564786_eng.pdf?ua=1&ua=1. Copyright © 2014 WHO.

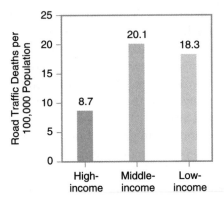

FIGURE 8.12 Road traffic death rates per 100,000 population by country income status.

Reprinted from: Global status report on road safety 2013: Supporting a decade of action. Copyright © 2013 World Health Organization (WHO). Available at: http://www.who.int/violence_injury_prevention/road_safety_status/2013/en/

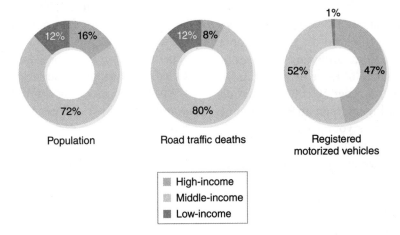

* Registered vehicle data provided only for countries participating in the survey.

FIGURE 8.13 Population, road traffic deaths, and registered motorized vehicles* by country income status.

Reprinted from: World Health Organization (WHO). Global status report on road safety 2013: supporting a decade of action. Available at: http://www.who.int/violence_injury_prevention/road_safety_status/2013/en/. Copyright © 2013 WHO.

countries on May 11, 2011, through many national and local events. At the launching of the Decade, a number of countries, including Australia, China, France, and New Zealand, either revised existing road safety laws or adopted new laws. To raise monies from private sector donors worldwide to support nongovernmental initiatives and to help implement national plans of WHO member countries, the Road Safety Fund was established, which is jointly managed by the WHO and the FIA Foundation, an independent charity organization based in the United Kingdom that is also a member of the United Nations Road Safety Collaboration. The Collaboration has developed a Global Plan as the framework to guide activities and initiatives to achieve the goals of the Action for Road Safety decade.[50]

Road traffic fatalities and injuries are an important public health issue in high-income countries and one of the leading causes of death and trauma in LMICs.

According to the WHO's 2013 Global Status Report on Road Safety,[50] which was developed to provide baseline data regarding the state of global road safety at the beginning of the Decade of Action and to help monitor progress toward its goals, 1.24 million individuals were killed in road traffic crashes in 2010.[50,51] This number is expected to rise to 1.9 million by 2020. More than 90% of road traffic deaths occur in developing countries. **FIGURE 8.12** shows the rate of road traffic fatalities in high-, middle-, and low-income countries in 2010. Notably, middle-income countries, especially those in Africa, are becoming more motorized and are the most affected.[50,51] These countries had 72% of the world's population, 52% of all registered motorized vehicles, and 80% of all road traffic deaths (**FIGURE 8.13**). In contrast, high-income countries had 16% of the global population, 47% of globally registered motorized vehicles, and only 8% of all road traffic deaths.

About 27% of global road traffic casualties in 2010 occurred in pedestrians and cyclists, but in some developing countries, pedestrians and cyclists account for 75% of road traffic fatalities. Every year, approximately 50 million people are injured worldwide in road traffic crashes; many of these individuals remain disabled for the rest of their lives. Globally, road traffic injuries are the leading cause of death of young people between the ages of 15 and 29, with young men accounting for more than 73% of deaths. The annual economic burden of road traffic injuries in the world is estimated to be $100 billion. The global burden on hospitals and healthcare systems from road traffic crashes is just as staggering. However, the report also shows that, despite a 15% increase in the number of registered vehicles worldwide, the number of global road traffic deaths plateaued between 2007 and 2010, and in 88 countries where almost 1.6 billion (~20%) of the world's total population lives, the number of road traffic deaths actually declined in the same period.[50] The main risk factors for road traffic injuries are high speed, drunk driving, riding a motorcycle without a helmet, and not using seatbelts and child restraints. Between 2008 and 2011, 35 countries passed laws to address one or more of these risk factors, but the number of countries that already had comprehensive laws to address all five of these risk factors remained unchanged at 28 since last reported in 2009.[50] Although more than one-third of road traffic deaths in developing countries are accounted for by pedestrians and cyclists, less than one-third of these countries have policies and laws to protect them from motorized and high-speed traffic. Likewise, 88% of high-income countries have child-restraint laws, but only 30% of low-income and 43% of middle-income countries have such laws.[50]

▶ 8.11 Example of a Study of Injury Epidemiology

Source: Crifasi CK, Pollack KM, Webster DW. Assault against U.S. law enforcement officers in the line-of-duty: situational context and predictors of lethality. Inj Epidemiol. 2016;3(29).

As compared with the overall rate of 3.3 fatal occupational injuries per 100,000 workers in the United States, the rate of fatal occupational injuries among law enforcement officers (LEOs) is about 14.2/100,000. Assaults on LEOs are primarily situational and frequently occur during a suspect's attempt to escape after having committed a crime. The nature of the weapon used in an assault most often makes the difference between a fatal or nonfatal attack. Firearms account for about 75%–90% of weapons used during a fatal assault on a LEO. In the United States, states with higher gun ownership rates also experience higher numbers of fatal assaults on LEOs.

The purpose of this study was to provide descriptive epidemiology of assaults on LEOs and compare situational characteristics of fatal and nonfatal assaults. The study also looked at officer and encounter characteristics through inferential statistical methods to identify factors that increase the odds or risk of an assault being fatal. The data used for this study were extracted from a database maintained by the U.S. Federal Bureau of Investigation (FBI) and named Law Enforcement Officers Killed and Assaulted. The database includes a number of variables related to the context and situation of the encounter as well as the characteristics of the officers involved. For this study, the researchers used longitudinal data from 1998 through 2013.

TABLES 8.11 and **8.12** show the descriptive characteristics of fatal and nonfatal attacks and estimated

TABLE 8.11 Descriptive Statistics of Fatal and Nonfatal LEO Assaults, 1998–2013		
Characteristics	**Fatal %** **(N = 791)**	**Nonfatal %** **(N = 2,022)**
Mean age (years)*	37.7	35.6
Average experience (months)*	127.3	118.3
Male	94	95
White	85	86

(continues)

TABLE 8.11 Descriptive Statistics of Fatal and Nonfatal LEO Assaults, 1998–2013   *(continued)*

Characteristic	Fatal % (N = 791)	Nonfatal % (N = 2,022)
Firearm*	92	66
Handgun*	65	48
Rifle*	19	10
Shotgun	7	8
LEO wearing body armor*	67	83
LEO disarmed*	13	4
LEO fired weapon*	22	37
Primary Wound Location		
Head/neck/throat*	61	25
Upper torso/back*	30	18
Lower torso/back*	6	9
Below waist*	2	19
Arms/hands*	0	29
Assignment		
One-officer vehicle	59	60
Two-officer vehicle*	9	13
Detective	6	5
Off-duty*	9	4
Special assignment	7	8
Undercover	3	3
Other	7	7
Encounter		
Investigative activities*	14	18
Disturbance call*	7	11
Domestic call*	7	11
Attempting other arrest	11	11

Ambush*	8	2
Unprovoked attack*	12	5
Burglary in progress	2	2
Robbery in progress	6	6
Tactical situations*	7	10
Traffic pursuits and stops*	18	11
Drug-related	4	4
Handling mentally deranged persons*	2	6
Handling/transporting/custody of prisoners	3	3

*$p < 0.05$

Reproduced from: Crifasi CK, Pollack KM, Webster DW. Assault against U.S. law enforcement officers in the line-of-duty: situational context and predictors of lethality. Inj Epidemiol. 2016;3(29).

TABLE 8.12 Multiple Logistic Regression Estimates of Odds Ratios for Lethal Outcomes

Independent Variable	OR[a]	95% CI[b]	p-value
Age of LEO	1.02**	1.00 to 1.03	<0.001
Suspect used firearm	4.37**	3.10 to 6.10	<0.001
LEO wearing body armor	0.43**	0.32 to 0.58	<0.001
LEO disarmed	2.24**	1.48 to 3.38	<0.001
LEO fired weapon	0.34**	0.27 to 0.44	<0.001
Primary Wound (Reference category = head/neck/throat)			
Upper torso/back	0.68**	0.54 to 0.87	0.002
Lower torso/back	0.24**	0.17 to 0.36	<0.001
Below waist	0.03**	0.02 to 0.06	<0.001
Assignment (Reference category = two-officer vehicle)			
One-officer vehicle	1.45*	1.02 to 2.07	0.041
Detective	1.40	0.80 to 2.50	0.242
Off-duty	2.68**	1.50 to 4.81	0.001
Special assignment	1.44	0.86 to 2.42	0.165
Undercover	1.18	0.59 to 2.39	0.641

(continues)

TABLE 8.12 Multiple Logistic Regression Estimates of Odds Ratios for Lethal Outcomes (continued)

Independent Variable	OR[a]	95% CI[b]	p-value
Encounter (Reference category = investigative activities)			
Disturbance call	0.99	0.63 to 1.55	0.948
Domestic call	1.10	0.70 to 1.74	0.688
Attempting other arrest	1.46	0.96 to 2.21	0.076
Ambush	3.27**	1.83 to 5.85	<0.001
Unprovoked attack	2.24**	1.44 to 3.47	<0.001
Burglary in progress	1.06	0.48 to 2.36	0.887
Robbery in progress	1.45	0.89 to 3.38	0.139
Tactical situations	1.12	0.70 to 1.79	0.647
Traffic pursuits and stops	2.38**	1.64 to 3.46	<0.001
Drug-related	1.75	0.90 to 3.40	0.097
Handling mentally deranged persons	0.56	0.27 to 01.16	0.121
Handling/transporting/custody of prisoners	0.95	0.45 to 2.00	0.887

[a]Odds ratio.
[b]Confidence interval.
*$p < 0.05$. **$p < 0.001$.

Reproduced from: Crifasi CK, Pollack KM, Webster DW. Assault against U.S. law enforcement officers in the line-of-duty: situational context and predictors of lethality. Inj Epidemiol. 2016;3(29).

odds or risk of a fatal outcome associated with various factors. Some observations from these tables are noted next to assist the student in interpreting the data reported in these tables. The student is strongly encouraged to carefully make note of other observations reported in these tables to better understand the epidemiology of LEO injuries and the findings of this study.

1. Between 1998 and 2013, there were 791 fatal and 2,022 nonfatal assaults on law enforcement officers in the United States.
2. Assaults that involved the use of a firearm as compared with other weapons increased the risk of a fatal outcome by more than fourfold (odds ratio = 4.37).
3. Use of body armor by the officer at the time of assault reduced the risk of a fatal outcome by 57% (odds ratio = 0.43).
4. The risk of an officer being killed in the assault increased by more than twofold (odds ratio = 2.24) if the officer was disarmed during the assault.
5. The risk of the officer being killed was reduced by 66% (odds ratio = 0.34) if the officer discharged his or her weapon during the assault, as compared with when he or she did not fire his or her gun.
6. The officer was 45% more likely to be killed (odds ratio = 1.45) in an assault if the officer was assigned to a one-officer vehicle, as compared with being assigned to a two-officer vehicle.

🔍 CASE STUDY 8.1: Hospital-Based Injury Surveillance

Modified from: Lakshmi PVM, Tripathy JP, Tripathy N, Singh S, Bhatia D, Jagnoor J, Kumar R. A pilot study of a hospital-based injury surveillance system in a secondary level district hospital in India: lessons learn and way ahead. Inj Epidemiol. 2016;3(24).

Every year, 5.8 million deaths, about 10% of total global mortality, result from injuries. About 90% of these deaths occur in low- and middle-income countries. The traffic-related mortality rate in India is among the highest in the world. Based on data collected from January through December 2012 in the ED of a district hospital (secondary care-level facility) serving a population of approximately 600,000, Lakshmi et al. shed some light on the epidemiology of injury in Punjab state in northern India. Using a paper-based questionnaire developed by the research team, the data were collected by emergency medical officers (EMOs) for all patients arriving in the ED of the district hospital in Fatehgarh Sahib District in Punjab, India. The information was obtained directly from patients and/or their family members, with supplemental data included based on the professional observation and assessment of the attending EMO. An electronic database was created on Epi Info and subsequently analyzed with the help of SPSS 16 statistical software package. Of the 1,548 patients who arrived in the ED during the study period, 649 (42%) were reported as injury cases. **TABLE 8.13** provides some descriptive data on the characteristics of injured patients and the nature, context, and circumstances of injury by sex and age groups.

Questions

Question 1. Does this hospital-based study accurately reflect the magnitude or burden of injuries in this population? Explain your answer.

Question 2. Only 0.9% of injury outcomes are reported as death. Does this number accurately reflect the number of injuries that resulted in death? Explain your answer.

Question 3. No firearm-related injuries are reported in this study. Does that accurately reflect the situation in this population? Explain your answer.

Question 4. Do the data on self-harm in Table 8.13 accurately reflect the frequency of self-harm injuries? Explain your answer.

Question 5. What is the extent of missing data in this study, and what problems do missing data present?

TABLE 8.13 Sex Distribution of the Intent, Nature, Circumstance, and Mechanism of Injury Among Emergency Department Patients at Fatehgarh Sahib District Hospital, Punjab, India, 2012

Characteristics of Injury	Male	Female	Total
Intent of Injury			
Unintentional	403 (82%)	89 (18%)	493 (100%)
Intentional	89 (73%)	33 (27%)	122 (100%)
Self-harm	11 (92%)	1 (8%)	12 (100%)
Nature of Injury			
Fracture	51 (81%)	12 (19%)	63 (100%)
Cut wound	259 (84%)	51 (16%)	310 (100%)
Concussion	14 (67%)	7 (33%)	21 (100%)
Others	135 (74%)	47 (26%)	182 (100%)

(continues)

TABLE 8.13 Sex Distribution of the Intent, Nature, Circumstance, and Mechanism of Injury Among Emergency Department Patients at Fatehgarh Sahib District Hospital, Punjab, India, 2012 _(continued)_

Characteristics of Injury	Male	Female	Total
Activity During Injury			
Work	111 (74%)	39 (26%)	150 (100%)
Traveling	266 (81%)	64 (19%)	330 (100%)
Sports	17 (94%)	1 (6%)	18 (100%)
Others	33 (81%)	8 (19%)	41 (100%)
Mechanism of Injury			
Road traffic crash	274 (81%)	64 (19%)	338 (100%)
Fall	62 (78%)	18 (22%)	80 (100%)
Quarrel	79 (72%)	31 (28%)	110 (100%)
Others	94 (86%)	16 (14%)	110 (100%)

Modified from: Lakshmi PVM, Tripathy JP, Tripathy N, Singh S, Bhatia D, Jagnoor J, Kumar R. A pilot study of a hospital-based injury surveillance system in a secondary level district hospital in India: lessons learn and way ahead. Inj Epidemiol. 2016;3(24).

⌕ CASE STUDY 8.2: Unintentional Firearm Deaths

Modified from: Hemenway D, Solnick SJ. Children and unintentional firearm deaths. Inj Epidemiol. 2015;2:26. Accessed on July 3, 2017. https://injepijournal.springeropen.com/track/pdf/10.1186/s40621-015-0057-0?site=injepijournal.springeropen.com

The rate of unintentional firearm fatalities of children between the ages of 0 and 14 years is about 10 times higher in the United States as compared with other high-income countries. The authors of this study used data available from 16 states in the U.S. National Violent Death Reporting System (NVDRS) for the years 2005–2012. The NVDRS is a state-based surveillance system that incorporates data from multiple sources. The purpose of the study was to estimate the number of unintentional firearm deaths in the 0–14 age group annually and to describe the circumstances of events and characteristics of those involved.

The authors examined all the suicide (n = 574), homicide (n = 2,143), and undetermined intent (n = 268) fatality data of children 0–14 years old in the 8-year study period. The authors estimated that from 2005 through 2012, a total of 229 unintentional firearm-related deaths of children 0–14 years had occurred in the 16 states. **TABLE 8.14** shows some of the descriptive data reported by the authors. Based on the data shown in the table, answer the following questions.

Questions

Question 1. Was the risk of unintentional firearm-related death equally distributed between boys and girls? Explain your answer with the help of data from Table 8.14.

Question 2. In which age group or groups were children more at risk of self-inflicted unintentional firearm-related death? Explain your answer with the help of data from Table 8.14.

Question 3. In which age group or groups were boys more at risk of unintentional firearm-related death? Explain your answer with the help of data from Table 8.14.

TABLE 8.14 Unintentional Firearm Fatalities of Children Between the Ages of 0–14 Years in 16 States, United States, 2005–2012

Age	No. of Cases	Male	Female	Self-Inflicted	Other-Inflicted	Inflicted by Unknown
0–1	7	2 (29%)	5 (71%)	1 (14%)	6 (86%)	0 (0%)
2–4	42	37 (88%)	5 (12%)	27 (64%)	11 (26%)	4 (10%)
5–10	69	52 (75%)	17 (25%)	18 (26%)	46 (67%)	5 (7%)
11–12	51	40 (78%)	11 (22%)	13 (25%)	35 (69%)	3 (6%)
13–14	60	54 (90%)	6 (10%)	12 (20%)	43 (72%)	5 (8%)
Total	229	185 (81%)	44 (19%)	71 (31%)	141 (62%)	17 (7%)

Modified from: Hemenway D, Solnick SJ. Children and unintentional firearm deaths. Inj Epidemiol. 2015;2:26. Accessed on July 3, 2017. https://injepijournal.springeropen.com/track/pdf/10.1186/s40621-015-0057-0?site=injepijournal.springeropen.com

▶ 8.12 Summary

Injuries result in high levels of morbidity and mortality all over the world and cost hundreds of billions of dollars annually in medical care and lost productivity—more than the morbidity, mortality, and cost of several of the leading communicable diseases, such as HIV/AIDS, malaria, and tuberculosis, combined. EDs of secondary and tertiary care hospitals in every big city of every country in the world every year attend to the needs of thousands of patients of all ages with severe injuries—both intentional and unintentional. Hundreds of research studies investigating various dimensions of the epidemiology of injuries of one kind or another are published every year in research journals globally. For example, an Internet search on Google Scholar using the words "suicide in veterans" resulted in 123,000 links to research articles and books on this subject. The case study in this chapter on unintentional firearm-related deaths of children 0–14 years of age in the United States and the case study on the characteristics of injury cases arriving in the ED of a secondary care hospital in India provide examples of studies on the epidemiology of specific issues of public health importance. Hundreds of legislative or public health initiatives all over the world, whether related to the safe use of automobiles and road traffic, safe work environment, or safe recreational and sporting conditions, all are designed to prevent injuries. With a number of tables and figures showing national and international data, this chapter provides a comprehensive overview of the epidemiology of various kinds of injuries. Understanding the epidemiology of injuries is important for healthcare providers, managers, and policy makers because virtually all injuries are preventable.

References

1. Centers for Disease Control and Prevention. Data and Statistics (WISQARS) Cost of Injury Reports. 2016 [cited 2018 May 11]. Available from: https://www.cdc.gov/injury/wisqars/overview/cost_of_injury.html
2. Florence C, Simon T, Haegerich T, Luo F, Zhou C. Estimated lifetime medical and work-loss costs of fatal injuries—United States, 2013. MMWR Morb Mortal Wkly Rep. 2015;64(38):1074–1077.
3. Heron M. Deaths: leading causes for 2013. Natl Vital Stat Rep. 2016;65(2). [cited 2018 May 11] Available from: https://www.cdc.gov/nchs/data/nvsr/nvsr65/nvsr65_02.pdf
4. Centers for Disease Control and Prevention. FastStats—Injuries. [cited 2018 May 11]. Available from: http://www.cdc.gov/nchs/fastats/default.htm
5. Monuteaux MC, Lee L, Fleegler E. Children injured by violence in the United States: emergency department utilization, 2000–2008. Acad Emerg Med. 2012;19:535–540.
6. Fowler KA, Dahlberg LL, Haileyesus T, Annest JL. Firearm injuries in the United States. Prev Med. 2015;79:5–14.
7. Wintemute GJ. Alcohol misuse, firearm violence perpetration, and public policy in the United States. Prev Med. 2015;79:15–21.
8. Gonzales K, Roeber J, Kanny D, et al. Alcohol-attributable deaths and years of potential life lost—11 states, 2006–2010. MMWR Morb Mortal Wkly Rep. 2014;63(10):213–216.

9. Branas CC. Alcohol & firearms: research, gaps in knowledge, and possible interventions. Paper Presented at the Institute of Medicine's Forum on Global Violence Prevention, Washington, DC. December 2014.

10. Corso PS, Mercy JA, Simon TR, Finkelstein EA, Miller TR. Medical costs and productivity losses due to interpersonal and self-directed violence in the United States. Am J Prev Med. 2007;32(6):474–482.

11. Bouchery EE, Harwood HJ, Sacks JJ, Simon CJ, Brewer RD. Economic costs of excessive alcohol consumption in the U.S., 2006. Am J Prev Med. 2011;41(5):516–524.

12. Follman M, Lurie J, Lee J, West J, Miller T. The true cost of gun violence: what does gun violence really cost? Mother Jones. 2015 May/Jun [cited 2018 May 11]. Available from: http://www.motherjones.com/politics/2015/04/true-cost-of-gun-violence-in-america

13. National Trauma Institute. Trauma statistics. 2014 [cited 2018 May 11]. Available from: http://www.nationaltraumainstitute.org/home/trauma_statistics.html

14. National Highway Traffic Safety Administration. Traffic safety facts: 2014 crash data key findings. DOT HS 812219. 2015 [cited 2018 May 11]. Available from: https://crashstats.nhtsa.dot.gov/Api/Public/ViewPublication/812219

15. National Highway Traffic Safety Administration. Early estimates of motor vehicle traffic fatalities for the first nine months (Jan-Sep) of 2015. DOT HS 812 240. 2016 [cited 2018 May 11]. Available from: https://crashstats.nhtsa.dot.gov/Api/Public/ViewPublication/812240

16. National Highway Traffic Safety Administration. Traffic safety facts—2014 data: alcohol-impaired driving. 2015 [cited 2018 May 11]. Available from: https://crashstats.nhtsa.dot.gov/Api/Public/ViewPublication/812231

17. Centers for Disease Control and Prevention. The National Violent Death Reporting System (NVDRS): A powerful tool for prevention. 2015 [cited 2018 May 11]. Available from: http://www.cdc.gov/violenceprevention/pdf/nvdrs_overview-a.pdf; http://www.cdc.gov/violenceprevention/pdf/nvdrs_factsheet-a.pdf; and http://www.cdc.gov/violenceprevention/nvdrs/

18. Marr AL, Coronado VG, editors. Central nervous system injury surveillance data submission standards—2002. Atlanta, GA: Centers for Disease Control and Prevention, National Center for Injury Prevention and Control; 2004.

19. Centers for Disease Control and Prevention. Traumatic brain injury in the United States: epidemiology and rehabilitation. 2015 [cited 2018 May 11]. Available from: http://www.cdc.gov/traumaticbraininjury/pdf/TBI_Report_to_Congress_Epi_and_Rehab-a.pdf

20. Faul M, Xu L, Wald MM, Coronado V. Traumatic brain injury in the United States: emergency department visits, hospitalizations and deaths, 2002–2006. Atlanta: Centers for Disease Control and Prevention, National Center for Injury Prevention; 2010.

21. Selassie AW, Zaloshnja E, Langlois JA, Miller T, Jones P, Steiner C. Incidence of long-term disability following traumatic brain injury hospitalization, United States. J Head Trauma Rehabil. 2003;23(2):123–131.

22. Thurman DJ, Alverson C, Dunn KA, Guerrero J, Sniezek JE. Traumatic brain injury in the United States: a public health perspective. J Head Trauma Rehabil. 1999;14(6):602–615.

23. Zaloshnja E, Miller T, Langlois JA, Selassie AW. Prevalence of long-term disability from traumatic brain injury in the civilian population of the United States, 2005. J Head Trauma Rehabil. 2008;23(6):394–400.

24. Harrison-Felix C, Kolakowsky-Hayner SA, Hammond FM, et al. Mortality after surviving traumatic brain injury: risks based on age groups. J Head Trauma Rehabil. 2012;27(6):E45–E56.

25. Harrison-Felix CL, Whiteneck GG, Jha A, DeVivo MJ, Hammond FM, Hart DM. Mortality over four decades after traumatic brain injury rehabilitation: a retrospective cohort study. Arch Phys Med Rehabil. 2009;90:1506–1513.

26. American Burn Association. Burn incidence fact sheet: burn incidence and treatment in the United States: 2015 [cited 2018 May]. Available from: http://ameriburn.org/resources_factsheet.php

27. Taylor SL, Lee D, Nagler T, Lawless M, Curri T, Palmieri TL. A validity review of the NBR. J Burn Care Res. 2013;34(2):274–280.

28. Centers for Disease Control and Prevention. Injury Reporting System: WISQARS™. 2016 [cited 2018 July 25]. Available from: https://www.cdc.gov/injury/wisqars/index.html

29. Karch DL, Dahlberg LL, Patel N, et al. Surveillance for violent deaths—National Violent Death Reporting System, 16 states, 2006. MMWR Morb Mortal Wkly Rep. 2009;58(SS01):1–44.

30. World Health Organization. Global burden of disease—global health estimates 2014: Causes of death 2000–2012. 2014 [cited 2018 May 11]. Available from: http://www.who.int/healthinfo/global_burden_disease/estimates/en/index1.html

31. World Health Organization. Injuries and violence: the facts 2014 [cited 2018 May 11]. Available from: http://www.who.int/violence_injury_prevention/media/news/2015/Injury_violence_facts_2014/en/

32. World Health Organization: Injuries and violence: 2014—Global health estimates. 2014 [cited 2018 July 25]. Available from: http://www.who.int/healthinfo/global_burden_disease/en/

33. Peck MD. Epidemiology of burns throughout the world. Part II: intentional burns in adults. Burns. 2012;38(5):630–637.

34. Peck MD. UpToDate. Epidemiology of burn injuries globally. [cited 2018 May 11]. Available from: http://www.uptodate.com/contents/epidemiology-of-burn-injuries-globally?source=see_link&sectionName=Incidence&anchor=H4#H4

35. World Health Organization. Burns—fact sheet. Updated 2014 Apr [cited 2018 May 11]. Available from: http://www.who.int/mediacentre/factsheets/fs365/en/

36. Chen SH, Chen YC, Chen TJ, Ma H. Epidemiology of burns in Taiwan: a nationwide report including inpatients and outpatients. Burns. 2014;40(7):1397–1405.

37. Centers for Disease Control and Prevention. Fire deaths and injuries: fact sheet. 2013 [cited 2018 May 11]. Available from: http://gardencityguardian.blogspot.com/2013/08/fire-deaths-and-injuries-fact-sheet.html

38. Hameda M, Maher A, Mabrouk A. Epidemiology of burns admitted at Ain Shams University Burns Unit, Cairo, Egypt. Burns. 2003;29(4):353–358.

39. Davies JW. The problem of burns in India. Burns. 1990;Suppl. 1:S1–S24.

40. Wong EG, Groen RS, Kamara TB, et al. Burns in Sierra Leone: A population-based assessment. Burns. 2014;40(8):1748–1753.

41. Poeschla B, Combs H, Livingstone S, Romm S, Klein MB. Self-immolation: socioeconomic, cultural and psychiatric patterns. Burns. 2011;37(6):1409–1457.

42. American Burn Association. National Burn Repository, Version 13.0. 2017 [cited 2016 April 11]. Available from: http://ameriburn.org/wp-content/uploads/2018/04/2017_aba_nbr_annual_report_summary.pdf.

43. Tung KY, Chen ML, Wang HJ, et al. A seven-year epidemiology study of 12,381 admitted burn patients in Taiwan—using the Internet registration system of the Childhood Burn Foundation. Burns. 2005;31:Suppl 1:S12–S7.

44. Laloe V. Patterns of deliberate self-burning in various parts of the world. A review. Burns. 2004;30(3):207–215.

45. Lama BB, Duke JM, Sharma NP, et al. Intentional burns in Nepal: a comparative study. Burns. 2015;41(6):1306–1314.

46. Sharma NP, Duke JM, Lama BB, et al. Descriptive epidemiology of unintentional burn injuries admitted to a tertiary-level government hospital in Nepal: gender-specific patterns. Asia Pac J Public Health. 2015;27(5):551–560.

47. World Health Organization. Drowning: fact sheet. 2014 [cited 2018 May 11]. Available from: http://www.who.int/mediacentre/factsheets/fs347/en/

48. World Health Organization. Global report on drowning: preventing a leading killer. 2014 [cited 2018 May 11]. Available from: http://apps.who.int/iris/bitstream/10665/143893/1/9789241564786_eng.pdf?ua=1&ua=1

49. International Organization for Migration. Mediterranean migration arrivals reach 112,018 in 2017; 2,361 deaths. [cited 2018 May 11]. Available from: https://www.iom.int/news/mediterranean-migrant-arrivals-reach-112018-2017-2361-deaths

50. World Health Organization. Global status report on road safety 2013: supporting a decade of action. 2013 [cited 2017 Jul 27]. Available from: http://www.who.int/violence_injury_prevention/road_safety_status/2013/en/

51. World Health Organization. Global status report on road safety. 2015 [cited 2017 Jul 27]. Retrieved from: http://www.who.int/violence_injury_prevention/road_safety_status/2015/en/

© Monsitj/Getty Images

CHAPTER 9

Epidemiology and Measurement of Quality

LEARNING OBJECTIVES

Having mastered the materials in this chapter, the student will be able to:

1. Explain the relationship of structure, process, and outcome to one another and their relevance to quality of health care.
2. Monitor and assess healthcare quality in an organization.
3. Explain the significance of case mix and severity adjustment in healthcare quality assessment.
4. Explain the purpose and mechanisms for physician and hospital online quality reporting.
5. Explain various indicators of inpatient and outpatient healthcare quality.

CHAPTER OUTLINE

9.1 Introduction
9.2 Definition and Goals of Healthcare Quality
9.3 Determinants of Healthcare Quality
9.4 Distribution of Healthcare Quality (Person, Place, Time)
    9.4.1 Healthcare-Associated Infections/ Nosocomial Infections
    9.4.2 Medical Errors or Preventable Adverse Events
    9.4.3 Potentially Preventable Hospitalizations
    9.4.4 Hospital Readmissions
    9.4.5 Patient Safety and Sentinel Events
9.5 Severity of Disease and Assessment of Quality

9.6 Use of Checklists in Quality Improvement
9.7 Physician Quality Reporting System
9.8 Hospital Quality Reporting System— Hospital Compare
9.9 Hospital Readmission Reduction Program
9.10 Institute for Healthcare Improvement— Triple Aim
9.11 Example of a Quality Assessment Study
Case Study 9.1 – Reasons for Postsurgical Hospital Readmissions
Case Study 9.2 – Impact of a Rapid Response System on Inpatient Mortality and Length of Stay
9.12 Summary

KEY TERMS

Active errors	Healthcare-associated infection	Potentially preventable
Adverse event	Hospital readmission	hospitalizations
Case mix	Latent errors	Process
Case mix index	Length of stay	Risk management
Comorbidities	Medical error	Run charts
Comorbidity measures	National Healthcare Safety Network	Sentinel event
Control charts	Never event	Severity of disease
Excess readmission ratio	Outcome	Structure

▶ 9.1 Introduction

The assessment, monitoring, and reporting of healthcare quality constitute a critical component of every healthcare organization and an important part of managerial functions. Although specific individuals and departments in larger organizations are responsible for collecting and reporting quality-related data and for recommending specific actions to address quality-related issues, the attainment of highest standards of healthcare quality is a shared responsibility of all employees. The quality of care in a healthcare organization is related to all three components in Donabedian's[1] well-known triad of *structure, process, and outcome.* Identification of metrics and standards for all three of these drivers of quality is necessary to assess, report, and improve quality of care.

In hospitals, quality improvement and risk management functions are usually separated and are considered the domain of two separate departments. The main purpose of the department of quality improvement, whether an independent department or one housed within a larger administrative unit, is to protect the health and well-being of patients, whereas the main objective of the department of **risk management** is to protect the organization from potential risk of litigation and liability.[2] Because potential threats to the health and well-being of patients are closely linked to the risk of litigation and liability for the organization, there is a good deal of overlap in the interests and activities of these two departments in a hospital.

Poor quality of care leads to avoidable pain, inconvenience, dissatisfaction, disability, and even death for the patient. It also results in a waste of resources through avoidable hospitalizations, unplanned readmissions, prolonged hospital and intensive care unit (ICU) stays, duplication of tests and procedures, and cost of litigation and legal settlements for the healthcare provider.

▶ 9.2 Definition and Goals of Healthcare Quality

The Oxford English Dictionary[3] defines *quality* as "The standard of something as measured against other things of a similar kind; the degree of excellence of something." As indicated by the definition, quality is an attribute that is comparative in nature and involves meeting expectations or standards. Griffin[2] has defined quality of healthcare as "The degree to which patient care services increase the probability of desired patient outcomes." This definition borrows directly from the definition of quality of care proposed by the U.S. Institute of Medicine: "The degree to which health services for individuals and populations increase the likelihood of desired health outcomes and are consistent with current professional knowledge."[4,5] The U.S. Agency for Healthcare Research and Quality (AHRQ) defines quality health care as "doing the right thing, at the right time, in the right way, for the right person—and having the best possible results."[6]

Meeting expectations and standards in the practice of medicine to increase the likelihood of desired health outcomes translates into the pursuit of evidence-based standards and best practices in therapeutic and preventive services to achieve excellence in both technologic and interpersonal aspects of care. For healthcare managers, "meeting expectations" means meeting industry standards of performance in terms of hospital and ICU **length of stay** (LOS), **hospital readmission** rates, rates of postsurgical complications, rates of **healthcare-associated infections** (HAIs), frequency of medical errors, waiting times for services, and overall patient satisfaction levels.

In statistical terms, "meeting standards" translates into minimizing variance from the standards of clinical care and industry norms for outcomes such as unplanned hospital readmission rates and inpatient mortality. Unacceptable or "too much" variance

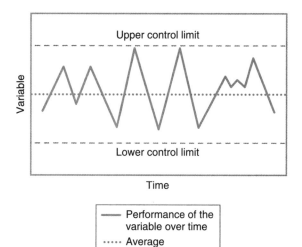

FIGURE 9.1 Example of a typical control chart.

Reproduced from: Varkey P, Reller MK, Resar RK. Basics of quality improvement in health care. Mayo Clinic Proceedings. 2007; 82(6):735–739.

from the industry standard (i.e., statistical mean or median) translates into poor quality of care. In simple terms, the goal of providers and managers alike is to achieve maximum adherence to best practices and minimal variance from statistical standards of performance. Ongoing monitoring and assessment of performance through statistical quality control can be carried out with the help of *control charts* or **run charts. Control charts** involve plotting of data points for a performance measure (e.g., waiting times or the frequency of unplanned hospital readmissions) over regular time intervals. The temporal distribution of data can reveal trends in performance and variance from industry standards that are shown in the form of a central horizontal line representing the average performance of comparable organizations. The upper and lower statistical bounds of performance in a control chart are based on random variations in performance and acceptable levels of variance from the average or typical performance of other comparable organizations. **FIGURE 9.1** provides example of a typical control chart.

For healthcare systems to improve quality of care, the Institute of Medicine[5] and the World Health Organization (WHO)[7] recommend the following six dimensions of quality to focus on:

1. **Effectiveness**: evidence-based care that results in better health outcomes for individuals and communities.
2. **Efficiency**: delivery of care that maximizes the use of resources and minimizes waste.
3. **Accessibility**: timely and geographically reasonable care that utilizes skills and resources in proportion to medical need.

4. **Acceptability** (also known as **patient-centered care**): care that takes into consideration the preferences and values of individuals and cultural norms of communities.
5. **Equitability**: care whose standards are consistent and unrelated to the gender, race, ethnicity, or socioeconomic status of the patient.
6. **Safety**: care that minimizes risk of harm to patients.

▶ 9.3 Determinants of Healthcare Quality

In nonhealthcare settings, quality of a product is considered a function of the following four "Ms": *man, method, machine,* and *material.* In health care, these four Ms can translate into the *structure* and *process* of care. In other industries, thinkers such as Walter Shewhart (1891–1967), Edward Deming (1900–1993), and Joseph Juran (1904–2008) led the quality improvement movement by pioneering ideas related to statistical quality control, routine monitoring, appropriate skills, continuous training, and—most of all—teamwork. In the healthcare industry, these ideas have found their implementation only in the last couple of decades. The pioneer of healthcare quality improvement, Avedis Donabedian (1919–2000), recognized structure, process, and outcome to be intricately interconnected. **Structure**, the equivalent of *man, machine,* and *material* in the industrial model of quality, includes all the physical, technologic, human, and financial resources involved in the delivery of care—that is, the total organizational environment in which health care is delivered. This includes the availability and use of appropriate technologies and qualified personnel. **Process** of care is what emanates from the structural elements of care and includes evidence-based practice of medicine, adherence to appropriate protocols, use of best practices and technologies, coordinated care, meeting standards of care, and engagement of the patient through appropriate communication and decision making. Clearly, in the absence of all essential structural elements, it is virtually impossible for high-quality processes to take place. However, the existence of necessary structural elements in and of itself does not translate into the right execution of the right processes.

Deficiencies in the structural elements of the settings of care and/or in the processes of care have a direct bearing on the quality of care and its potential outcomes. Although appropriate structure and processes do not guarantee desired health outcomes, they are essential to the attainment of desired outcomes. In other words, appropriate structure and process are necessary but not sufficient conditions to achieve desired health outcomes in terms of improved health status, functionality, avoidance of disability, and alleviation of pain and suffering. Although failure to achieve desired or anticipated health outcomes at times can be attributed to deficiencies in the structural or procedural aspects of care (i.e., the quality of care), frequently they result from factors outside the control of the healthcare provider. Factors that have a direct bearing on health outcomes but are outside the control of the healthcare provider include patient characteristics, disease characteristics, and characteristics of the environments in which patients live.

Outcome in Donabedian's model of healthcare quality is a multidimensional construct. It includes not only the attainment of positive results in terms of prevention of disease, attainment and maintenance of full functional status, and satisfaction with the structure and process of care, but also, first and foremost, avoidance of adverse outcomes in terms of complications, disability, pain, and death.

▶ 9.4 Distribution of Healthcare Quality (Person, Place, Time)

Numerous studies from various countries have furnished abundant historical evidence that healthcare quality is unevenly or differentially distributed across rural versus urban, rich versus poor, white versus black, and more educated versus less-educated divides. In the United States, those who are poor, live in rural areas, are less educated, and are from a racial or ethnic minority are worse off in the quality of care they receive and in the outcomes of care than their richer, urban, more educated, and white counterparts.[8–11] Typically, health disparities across geographic areas and population groups, nationally and internationally, are linked with the distribution of and access to healthcare resources. However, not all the reasons for these disparities are fully understood. In the United States, parallel and corresponding degrees of improvement in healthcare quality and outcomes have occurred across all geographic and socioeconomic divides in the last two to three decades. Consequently, despite the improvements in the conditions of each group in comparison with its own baseline, the same degrees of disparity continue to exist across groups.

9.4.1 Healthcare-Associated Infections/ Nosocomial Infections

The U.S. Centers for Disease Control and Prevention (CDC) estimated that in 2011, about 721,800 cases of HAIs occurred in U.S. acute care hospitals, and on any given day, 1 out of every 25 patients in U.S. acute care hospitals has a HAI[12,13] (**TABLE 9.1**). The most common HAIs were pneumonias and surgical site infections. A 2013 meta-analysis of the financial impact of HAIs estimated that the five most common HAIs cost the U.S. healthcare system nearly $10 billion.[14] At an approximate cost of $45,814 per case, central line-associated bloodstream infections (CLABSIs) were estimated to be the costliest, followed by ventilator-associated pneumonias, with an estimated cost of $40,144 per case. However, surgical site infections were found to contribute the most to the overall cost of HAIs (33.7%). Urinary tract infections (UTIs) are among the most common HAIs reported to the CDC's **National Healthcare Safety Network** (NHSN), the most widely used HAI tracking system in the United States.[12] About 75% of UTIs are related to the use of urinary catheters. Approximately 15%–25% of hospitalized patients at some point during their hospital stay are estimated to require a urinary catheter. Recent studies have also estimated that implementation of current prevention methods can

TABLE 9.1 The Frequency of Various Types of Healthcare-Associated Infections in U.S. Acute Care Hospitals, 2011

Major Site of Infection	Estimated No.
Pneumonia	157,500
Gastrointestinal illness	123,100
Urinary tract infections	93,300
Primary bloodstream infections	71,900
Surgical site infections from any inpatient surgery	157,500
Other types of infections	118,500
Estimated total number of infections in hospitals	**721,800**

Reproduced from: Centers for Disease Control and Prevention. HAI data and statistics: HAIs at a glance. 2014. Available at: https://www.cdc.gov/hai/surveillance/index.html

result in a 70% reduction in some of the HAIs in U.S. hospitals[15] and approximately $25 billion to $31.5 billion in medical cost savings.[16] However, a 2012 study[17] reported that Medicare's "no pay for errors" policy had not had any appreciable improvement in the rates of catheter-associated bloodstream or urinary tract infections in U.S. hospitals.

The U.S. Department of Health and Human Services, through its Centers for Medicare and Medicaid Services (CMS), and the CDC is actively engaged in addressing the issue of HAIs. Growing concerns regarding the spread of multidrug-resistant organisms and limited availability of effective antimicrobial agents have given impetus to these efforts. Inappropriate or unwarranted use of antibiotics is linked with the emergence of drug-resistant microbial strains. As is well known, most of the use of antibiotics in ambulatory care settings occurs in primary care office settings. The research study by Jones et al.[18] discussed later in this chapter shows some data related to the unnecessary use of antibiotics to treat acute respiratory infections (ARIs). The Healthcare Infection Control Practices Advisory Committee, a 14-member committee of external experts, provides counsel and guidance to the CDC and the U.S. Department of Health and Human Services regarding surveillance, prevention, and control of HAIs in healthcare facilities nationwide. In addition to the 14 regular voting members, the committee includes six ex-officio members from other federal agencies as well as 21 nonvoting liaison representatives from various interest groups, such as professional societies, public health agencies, and consumer groups.

According to the CDC's 2014 *National and State Healthcare-Associated Infections Progress Report*, CLABSIs were reduced by 50% in U.S. hospitals between 2008 and 2013. Surgical site infections (SSIs) from 10 selected procedures were also reduced by 17% in the same period. The national goal by the Department of Health and Human Services was to achieve a 50% reduction in CLABSIs and a 25% reduction in SSIs by the end of 2013. SSI rates for various procedures still vary widely, and significant improvements have been seen in SSIs for cardiac and rectal surgery in U.S. hospitals. The CDC also reported an 8% reduction nationally in hospital-acquired *Clostridium difficile* infection rates and a 13% reduction in MRSA (methicillin-resistant *Staphylococcus aureus*) bloodstream infections since 2011. Catheter-associated urinary tract infections (CAUTIs) remained unchanged from 2009 through 2013. Since 2014, nationwide improvement in CAUTIs has been reported in non-ICU settings by the CDC.

9.4.2 Medical Errors or Preventable Adverse Events

The Oxford English Dictionary[19] defines an *error* as "The state or condition of being wrong in conduct or judgement." A **medical error** can be defined in terms of failing to execute a plan in the manner in which it was intended for a given situation, not using any plan at all, or using the wrong plan.[20-22] As such, medical errors can be characterized as errors of execution or nonexecution, or acts of omission or commission.[23,24] The term **adverse event** refers to a negative development or outcome that occurred during or after the process of health care and that may have resulted from the process of medical care rather than the underlying problem for which care was being given.[21] In other words, an adverse event is an unplanned and unintended negative health effect or injury that can be attributed to the actions or inactions of healthcare providers.

Adverse events can be classified in several ways. For example, they can be classified on the bases of the setting in which they occur (i.e., inpatient care or outpatient care adverse events). Alternatively, they can be grouped according to the nature of service or activity (i.e., surgical or postsurgical adverse events, as opposed to medication-related or diagnostic-services-related adverse events). Another way to classify adverse events or medical errors is in terms of the immediacy or latency of their effects. That is, they are characterized as **active errors** or **latent errors** depending on the duration of time elapsed before their effects are manifested.[25,26] The effects of active errors typically appear rather quickly, whereas those of latent errors can remain dormant for a long time. For example, the effects of inadequate management of diabetes or Lyme disease may not be noted for months or even years. Usually, active errors are believed to be associated with the characteristics and decisions of individuals (i.e., human error), whereas latent errors are believed to be a function of organizational or system-related factors. Leape[24] has grouped preventable adverse events or medical errors (**BOX 9.1**) into the following four categories: (1) diagnostic, (2) treatment, (3) prevention, and (4) other.

Adverse events are frequently classified as either *preventable adverse events* or *nonpreventable adverse events*. At times, it is difficult to establish with absolute certainty whether an event can be characterized as totally preventable or unpreventable. However, an event such as wrong-site surgery or a foreign object left in the body of a patient after a surgical procedure are considered by entities such as the U.S. National

Box 9.1 Classification of Medical Errors

Types of Errors

Diagnostic

Error or delay in diagnosis
Failure to employ indicated tests
Use of outmoded tests or therapy
Failure to act on results of monitoring or testing

Treatment

Error in the performance of an operation, procedure, or test
Error in administering the treatment
Error in the dose or method of using a drug
Avoidable delay in treatment or in responding to an abnormal test
Inappropriate (not indicated) care

Preventive

Failure to provide prophylactic treatment
Inadequate monitoring or follow-up treatment

Other

Failure of communication
Equipment failure
Other system failure

Reprinted with permission from: Kohn LT, Corrigan JM, Molla SD. (eds). To err is human: building a safer health system. Washington, DC: National Academy Press. 1999. Accessed on July 11, 2017. Available at: http://www.nationalacademies.org/hmd/~/media/Files/Report%20Files/1999/To-Err-is-Human/To%20Err%20is%20Human%201999%20%20report%20brief.pdf. Copyright © 2011 National Academy of Sciences.

Quality Forum (NQF) as a **never event**. Irrespective of the question of whether some events can or cannot be legitimately characterized as preventable or a never event, the term *medical error* is commonly used interchangeably with the term *preventable adverse event*.

The current "never event" list of the NQF that was revised in 2011 includes 29 conditions grouped under the following seven categories: (1) surgical, (2) product or device, (3) care management, (4) patient protection, (5) radiologic, (6) environmental, and (7) criminal events. The 2015–2016 official "never event" list of the United Kingdom National Health Service contains 14 events. Some of the events on the list include the following: (1) misplaced nasogastric tubes, (2) neck or chest entrapment in bed rails, (3) falls from poorly restricted windows, (4) transfusion or transplantation of ABO-incompatible blood or organs, (5) wrong implant or prosthesis, (6) wrong route administration of medication, and (7) insulin

overdose due to abbreviations or use of a wrong device. The Joint Commission[27] in the United States (for accreditation of healthcare organizations), however, uses the term **sentinel event** for adverse events associated with the delivery of health care and defines a sentinel event as "an unexpected occurrence involving death or serious physical or psychological injury, or the risk thereof. Serious injury specifically includes loss of limb or function." This definition includes all the events defined as never events by the NQF.

The Joint Commission routinely reviews and reports sentinel event statistics voluntarily reported to it by all accredited organizations. Because of the voluntary reporting of data, these statistics do not accurately represent the magnitude of various sentinel events and quite likely only represent the tip of the iceberg. In reporting these data, The Joint Commission includes the following cautionary note about drawing any epidemiologic conclusions from these data: "Data Limitations: The reporting of most sentinel events to The Joint Commission is voluntary and represents only a small proportion of actual events. Therefore, these data are not an epidemiologic data set and no conclusions should be drawn about the actual relative frequency of events or trends in events over time."[28]

In its 1999 report titled *To Err is Human: Building a Safer Health System*,[23] the U.S. Institute of Medicine reported that preventable inpatient medical errors, complications, or adverse events killed at least 44,000 individuals and possibly as many as 98,000 every year and cost society between $17 billion and $29 billion every year. A 2008 literature review of eight studies based on 74,485 patient records from the United States, Canada, Australia, New Zealand, and the United Kingdom indicated that 9.2% of patients experienced at least one adverse event during their hospital stay, and about 43.5% of these events were preventable. Reportedly, more than half of the adverse events did not cause any serious harm to the patient. Almost 40% of the events were related to surgery, and 15% were medication related.[29] Studies from The Netherlands[30,31] and Sweden[32] have shown the frequency of inpatient adverse events to be in the range of 5.7% to 12.3%. In The Netherlands, more than 50% of adverse events were related to surgery, and 12.8% resulted in permanent disability or contributed to death. In Sweden, 70% of adverse events were deemed preventable, but only 9% of the events led to permanent disability, and 3% resulted in death. Based on national health expenditures from 2000 to 2016 and data reported by the WHO, the economic cost of preventable adverse events to 30 European Union countries has been estimated to be about €17 billion (~$19.9 billion USD) to €38 billion (~$44.5 billion USD).[33] It has been estimated that in 2008, potentially preventable infections in American hospitals added to in-hospital deaths by 3.1% and to hospital readmissions by 7.7%, with each episode of preventable infection resulting in $19,480 additional payment to the hospital.[34,35] Likewise, preventable metabolic problems added to in-hospital deaths by 3% and to hospital readmissions by 6.3% with an average additional payment of $11,797 to the hospital for each incident.

The ultimate economic impact of these events translates into higher insurance premiums for everyone in the insurance pool. The analysis of 11,883 records of patients admitted to 21 randomly selected hospitals in The Netherlands in 2004 and 20 hospitals in 2008 showed that the rate of adverse events actually increased from 4.1% in 2004 to 6.2% in 2008, although the rate of preventable adverse events remained stable, at 1.8% of admissions.[30]

9.4.3 Preventable Hospitalizations

Potentially preventable hospitalizations (PPHs) are those admissions to hospitals for acute or chronic conditions that, if adequately managed in ambulatory care settings, including primary care, should not result in a hospital admission. In short, the rate of PPHs in a country or region reflects the quality of ambulatory care—the higher the rate of PPHs, the poorer the quality of ambulatory care. The AHRQ[36] has identified the following 16 *prevention quality indicators* (commonly known as *ambulatory care sensitive conditions*) for which hospital admission would indicate unacceptable quality of outpatient care: (1) bacterial pneumonia; (2) hypertension; (3) dehydration; (4) adult asthma; (5) pediatric gastroenteritis; (6) pediatric asthma; (7) urinary tract infection; (8) chronic obstructive pulmonary disease; (9) perforated appendix; (10) diabetes short-term complication; (11) low birth weight; (12) diabetes long-term complication; (13) angina without procedure; (14) uncontrolled diabetes; (15) congestive heart failure; and (16) lower-extremity amputation among patients with diabetes.

FIGURE 9.2 shows the rates of PPHs in the United States for acute conditions from 2005 through 2011 by locations where hospitalized patients lived. As shown, despite a significant reduction in PPHs over the 7-year period in all locations of patients' residence, the rates of PPHs were still quite high in 2011. Because of a well-known association of preventable hospitalizations with socioeconomic conditions and with various measures of access to health care, not surprisingly, the rates were the highest for patients who lived in remote rural areas.

9.4.4 Hospital Readmissions

Preventable readmissions to hospitals within a short time after discharge (e.g., 30 days) are usually viewed

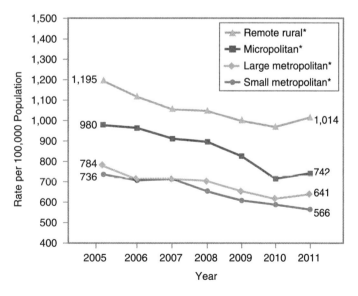

* The difference in rates between 2005 and 2011 is statistically significant at $p < 0.05$. Rates are per 100,000 population.

FIGURE 9.2 Rates of potentially preventable hospitalizations for acute conditions by location of patient residence, 2005–2011.

Reproduced from: Torio CM, Andrews RM. Geographic variation in potentially preventable hospitalizations for acute and chronic conditions, 2005–2011. Agency for Healthcare Research and Quality (AHRQ), Center for Delivery, Organization, and Markets, Healthcare Cost and Utilization Project (HCUP). 2014.

as an indication of poor quality of care. Preventable admissions usually occur because of the recurrence of a medical problem, inadequate postdischarge coordination and communication, complications resulting from previous treatment, or unaddressed problems clinically related to the primary condition. Studies have shown socioeconomic factors and severity of illness to be linked with preventable readmissions for conditions such as heart failure, pneumonia, and acute myocardial infarction.[37–41] Readmissions not only expose patients to greater risk of morbidity and mortality but also result in avoidable costs to the healthcare system. About 20% of Medicare patients have been found to be readmitted within 30 days after discharge, and unplanned readmissions were estimated to cost Medicare $17.4 billion in 2004.[37] PricewaterhouseCoopers' Health Research Institute[42] estimated that preventable hospital readmissions costs the U.S. healthcare system $25 billion every year. **TABLE 9.2** shows the frequency of potentially preventable readmissions (PPRs) of Texas Medicaid and Children's Health Insurance Program (CHIP) enrollees and costs of these readmissions during fiscal year (FY) 2013. Overall, potentially preventable admissions for Medicaid and CHIP enrollees cost the state of Texas more than $135 million in FY 2013 alone.[43]

9.4.5 Patient Safety and Sentinel Events

Ensuring patient safety is the primary responsibility of the healthcare provider and a cornerstone of a tacit agreement between the healer and the patient. Inclusion of the Latin phrase *primum non nocere* (first, do no harm) in the Hippocratic Oath for nearly 2,500 years and in biomedical ethics since the early 19th century is a testament to that responsibility. In modern times, adherence to this principle and monitoring of conditions necessary to ensure patient safety in all healthcare settings by accrediting and regulatory

TABLE 9.2 Potentially Preventable Readmission by Clinical Relationship to the Initial Admission

PPR Clinical Relationship Reasons[a]	No. of PPR Admissions	% of Total PPR Events	Expenditures for PPR Admissions[b]	% of Total PPR Expenditure
Recurrence	3,687	23.64%	$36,327,123.04	26.90%
Unrelated ambulatory care sensitive condition	500	3.21%	$3,567,770.24	2.64%
Unrelated chronic problem	1,171	7.51%	$12,325,269.11	9.13%
Acute medical condition related to care for the condition of the initial admission	4,816	30.88%	$45,359,366.68	33.59%
Surgical recurrence	239	1.53%	$6,068,303.43	4.49%
Surgical complication	290	1.86%	$5,779,610.89	4.28%
Mental health readmission following a non-MH/SA[c] admission	515	3.30%	$2,412,434.10	1.79%
Substance abuse readmission following a non-MH/SA[c] admission	87	0.56%	$507,068.15	0.38%
MH/SA[c] readmission following a MH/SA[c] admission	4,290	27.51%	$22,706,541.13	16.81%

[a] The 3M category for the clinical relationship between the initial admission and the PPR admission.
[b] Expenditure data include the detail paid amount from fee for service claims, which is an estimated cost.
[c] Mental health or substance abuse.

Texas External Quality Review Organization. Potentially preventable readmissions in Texas medicaid and CHIP programs, FY 2013. 2014. Available at: https://hhs.texas.gov/sites/hhs/files/ppr-statewide-report-fy2013.pdf

bodies has required that there be some agreed-upon standards of patient safety. The WHO has identified patient safety as one of the six necessary elements of healthcare quality to be focused on by all healthcare providers.

Many international and national organizations have been involved in setting standards of patient safety that healthcare providers can pursue and regulatory organizations can use for monitoring patient safety. The Patient Safety Advisory Group of the The Joint Commission has identified the following seven National Patient Safety Goals (NPSGs) for 2016 for all U.S. hospitals.[44] The group comprises professionals from various health-related fields, including nurses, physicians, pharmacists, risk managers, and clinical engineers.

1. **Identify patients correctly**: Use at least two ways to identify patients. For example, use the patient's name and date of birth. This is done to make sure that each patient receives the correct medicine and treatment.
2. **Improve staff communication**: Get important test results to the right staff person on time.
3. **Use medicines safely**: Before a procedure, label medicines that are not labeled—for example, medicines in syringes, cups, and basins.
4. **Use alarms safely**: Make improvements to ensure that alarms on medical equipment are heard and responded to on time.
5. **Prevent infection**: Use the hand-cleaning guidelines from the CDC or the WHO. Set goals for improving hand cleaning.
6. **Identify patient safety risks**: Find out which patients are most likely to attempt suicide.
7. **Prevent mistakes in surgery**: Make sure that the correct surgery is done on the correct patient and at the correct site on the patient's body.

From the preceding list, Goals 1, 3, 5, and 7 (identify patients correctly, use medicines safely, prevent infection, prevent mistakes in surgery) are also designated by The Joint Commission as 2016 Ambulatory Care National Patient Safety Goals.[45]

Based on voluntarily reported data by U.S. hospitals between 2004 and the second quarter of 2016, the summary statistics of sentinel events reviewed by The Joint Commission showed that 9,922 patients experienced sentinel events that resulted in the deaths of 5,394 (54.4%) patients, loss of function for 823 (8.3%) patients,

TABLE 9.3 The 10 Most Common Sentinel Events Reported to The Joint Commission, 2014

Most Frequently Reported Sentinel Events January 1–December 31, 2014 (764 total)	
Unintended retention of a foreign object	112
Falls	91
Suicide	82
Delay in treatment	73
Other unanticipated events*	73
Wrong patient, wrong site, or wrong procedure	67
Operative/postoperative complication	52
Criminal event (assault/rape/homicide)	47
Perinatal death/injury	32
Medication error	18

* Includes asphyxiation, burns, choking, drowning, and being found unresponsive.

Copyright © The Joint Commission, 2017. Reprinted with permission. Available at: http://www.jointcommission.org/assets/1/23/jconline_April_29_15.pdf

and unexpected additional care for 2,624 (26.4%) patients.[28] **TABLE 9.3** shows the 10 most commonly reported sentinel events in 2014. The Commission noted that voluntarily reported data on sentinel events do not accurately reflect the actual frequency of these events and "represent only a small proportion of actual events."[28]

The NQF, a nonprofit organization that works to improve healthcare quality by developing and endorsing evidence-based measures and standards of care, has developed a list of preventable clinical events called *serious reportable events* (SREs; also known as never events) to assess and report the performance of healthcare organizations in providing safe care to their patients. Public- and private-sector healthcare organizations or other interested parties can use these measures to assess and report the quality of health services. The NQF is supported by the U.S. federal government and is regarded by the Office of Management and Budget (OMB) as a "consensus-based organization" that promotes evidence-based approaches to improve healthcare quality. **BOX 9.2** shows the NQF's most current list of SREs grouped by five healthcare-related domains.

Box 9.2 National Quality Forum's List of Serious Reportable Events

1. **SURGICAL OR INVASIVE PROCEDURE EVENTS**
   1A. Surgery or other invasive procedure performed on the wrong site
   1B. Surgery or other invasive procedure performed on the wrong patient
   1C. Wrong surgical or other invasive procedure performed on a patient (updated)
   1D. Unintended retention of a foreign object in a patient after surgery or other invasive procedure
   1E. Intraoperative or immediately postoperative/postprocedure death in an ASA Class 1 patient*

2. **PRODUCT OR DEVICE EVENTS**
   2A. Patient death or serious injury associated with the use of contaminated drugs, devices, or biologics provided by the healthcare setting
   2B. Patient death or serious injury associated with the use or function of a device in patient care, in which the device is used or functions other than as intended
   2C. Patient death or serious injury associated with intravascular air embolism that occurs while being cared for in a healthcare setting

3. **PATIENT PROTECTION EVENTS**
   3A. Discharge or release of a patient/resident of any age, who is unable to make decisions, to other than an authorized person
   3B. Patient death or serious injury associated with patient elopement (disappearance)
   3C. Patient suicide, attempted suicide, or self-harm that results in serious injury, while being cared for in a healthcare setting

4. **CARE MANAGEMENT EVENTS**
   4A. Patient death or serious injury associated with a medication error (e.g., errors involving the wrong drug, wrong dose, wrong patient, wrong time, wrong rate, wrong preparation, or wrong route of administration)
   4B. Patient death or serious injury associated with unsafe administration of blood products
   4C. Maternal death or serious injury associated with labor or delivery in a low-risk pregnancy while being cared for in a healthcare setting
   4D. Death or serious injury of a neonate associated with labor or delivery in a low-risk pregnancy
   4E. Patient death or serious injury associated with a fall while being cared for in a healthcare setting
   4F. Any Stage 3, Stage 4, and unstageable pressure ulcers acquired after admission/presentation to a healthcare setting
   4G. Artificial insemination with the wrong donor sperm or wrong egg
   4H. Patient death or serious injury resulting from the irretrievable loss of an irreplaceable biological specimen
   4I. Patient death or serious injury resulting from failure to follow up or communicate laboratory, pathology, or radiology test results

5. **ENVIRONMENTAL EVENTS**
   5A. Patient or staff death or serious injury associated with an electric shock in the course of a patient care process in a healthcare setting
   5B. Any incident in which systems designated for oxygen or other gas to be delivered to a patient contain no gas, the wrong gas, or are contaminated by toxic substances
   5C. Patient or staff death or serious injury associated with a burn incurred from any source in the course of a patient care process in a healthcare setting
   5D. Patient death or serious injury associated with the use of physical restraints or bedrails while being cared for in a healthcare setting

6. **RADIOLOGIC EVENTS**
   6A. Death or serious injury of a patient or staff associated with the introduction of a metallic object into the MRI area

7. **POTENTIAL CRIMINAL EVENTS**
   7A. Any instance of care ordered by or provided by someone impersonating a physician, nurse, pharmacist, or other licensed healthcare provider
   7B. Abduction of a patient/resident of any age
   7C. Sexual abuse/assault on a patient or staff member within or on the grounds of a healthcare setting
   7D. Death or serious injury of a patient or staff member resulting from a physical assault (i.e., battery) that occurs within or on the grounds of a healthcare setting

* American Society of Anesthesiology (ASA) Physical Status Classification System: Class 1 is a normal, healthy patient.

▶ 9.5 Severity of Disease and Assessment of Quality

As alluded to earlier in this chapter, the relationship of the structure and process of care with health outcomes is tenuous because health outcomes are affected by many factors other than the quality of health care. One such factor is the nature and severity of disease. **Severity of disease** can be defined and assessed in various ways. One definition of severity of disease is that it is the "likelihood of death or organ failure resulting from disease progression and independent of the treatment process."[46] However, severity of disease is related not only to the likelihood of death or organ failure but also to the level of pain or suffering, disability, and risk of complications.

Irrespective of the quality of care, in many instances, the nature of the disease and/or the advanced stage of disease make attainment of outcomes such as avoidance of death more or less unrealistic. In such circumstances, the goal of health care may not be avoidance of death but rather attainment of dignity, comfort, and palliation. Assessment of quality, particularly in comparison with other providers, must therefore account for differences in the severity of disease among patients in one setting as compared with another. Unadjusted comparisons of mortality statistics or complication rates among hospitals can unfairly make tertiary care hospitals or academic medical centers look worse than other hospitals. By definition, such comparisons cannot be considered valid because the populations from which such data are drawn are statistically different and not comparable.

To allow fair and valid comparisons of the quality of care provided by different providers, scores of severity assessment methods, scales, and indices (**case mix index**) have been developed over the years. These scales and indices are used to adjust for differences in the **case mix** of different hospitals, nursing homes, and home health agencies and represent different approaches toward *severity adjustment, case mix adjustment,* or *risk adjustment.* In the United States, some of the most well-known severity adjustment methods are related to the disease classification system called the *diagnosis-related groups* (DRGs) used since the 1980s by CMS—previously known as the Healthcare Financing Administration—to pay hospitals that participate in its Inpatient Prospective Payment System (IPPS). Since the 1980s, the DRG-related severity adjustment methodologies have been revised many times. These revisions have been driven, at least in part, by concerns regarding the unfairness of unadjusted comparisons of mortality rates at different hospitals.

The DRG-based severity adjustment methods developed by various entities include, for example, *all payer severity-adjusted DRGs* (APS-DRGs developed by HSS) and *all patient refined DRGs* (APR-DRGs developed by 3M). The DRGs-related risk adjustment methods use hospital administrative or claims data, whereas other methods such as *disease staging* developed by MEDSTAT and AHRQ's **comorbidity measures** (AHRQ-CM) and *Elixhauser Comorbidity* software use clinical data. Disease staging uses four stages of increasing complexity to measure progression of disease and includes scales not only for assessing the risk of mortality, but also for predicting hospital LOS and amount of charges.[47] AHRQ-CM allows adjustment for coexisting medical conditions that are unrelated to the primary diagnosis or the reason for admission to a hospital. Adjusting for **comorbidities** before comparing hospital quality of care and health outcomes is important because comorbid conditions can prolong hospital stay, lead to poor outcomes, and increase the cost of care.

Severity adjustment and risk standardization methods have also been developed for healthcare settings such as nursing homes, ICUs, and emergency departments. For severity adjustment in ICUs, many hospitals use the Acute Physiology and Chronic Health Evaluation (APACHE) computer algorithms developed by Cerner Corporation in the United States. APACHE uses regression models to assign an Acute Physiologic Score (APS) to each patient to predict his or her risk of mortality and length of ICU stay. Severity-adjusted mortality rates and average LOS can be used to compare health outcomes of ICUs at different hospitals. An examination of the association between APAHCE's APSs and ICU mortality rates reveal a direct positive correlation between the severity of disease (or patients' APSs) and the risk of mortality. Typically, the risk of mortality increases almost in a linear fashion as the severity of disease increases.

Other severity or acuity scoring systems developed for ICU patients include the *simplified acute physiology score* (SAPS), the *mortality prediction model* (MPM), the *sepsis-related organ failure assessment* (SOFA), and the *multiple organ dysfunction score* (MODS).[48] For the purpose of triage in the emergency department, severity assessment scales or indices have been developed in the United Kingdom, Canada, Australia, and the United States. These scales help in deciding which patients need to be seen first by a healthcare provider and how long a patient can safely wait in the emergency department. The Emergency

Severity Index (ESI), a five-level emergency triage algorithm originally sponsored by the AHRQ, allows assessment of resources needed to discharge or admit patients or transfer them to other facilities, in addition to assessment of the level of acuity.[49]

▶ 9.6 Use of Checklists in Quality Improvement

A book titled *The Checklist Manifesto: How to Get Things Right*, written in 2010 by the well-known medical writer Atul Gawande[50] of Harvard University, brought the simple idea of using checklists in operating rooms and other healthcare settings to the forefront of healthcare quality discussions. The role of checklists in the proper execution of tasks that involve a series of activities, often carried out by different actors or teams, has been understood for a long time. In other industries, such as construction and aviation, checklists have been routinely used for many years to minimize the risk of human error in carrying out complex tasks. In the healthcare industry, rather than being a standard practice, the use of checklists so far has been sporadic at best.

A number of studies have shown the difference a checklist can make in improving healthcare quality, saving lives, and reducing costs. Some of the earlier studies on patient safety and the impact of checklists on central line-associated infections in ICUs were conducted by Peter Pronovost and his colleagues.[51] In a multihospital international study, the implementation of a 19-point checklist in operating rooms at eight different hospitals in several countries over a 6-month period led to a 36% drop in postsurgical complications and a 47% reduction in deaths.[52] In 2010, de Vries et al.[53] reported substantial reduction in complication and mortality rates in The Netherlands after the implementation of a comprehensive multidisciplinary surgical safety list. Studies by van Klei et al.[54] and Salzwedel et al.[55] have also demonstrated the positive effects of implementing surgical safety and postanesthesia handover checklists. In the last few years, numerous studies from various countries have demonstrated dramatic reductions in the incidence of HAIs after implementing central venous line and surgical safety checklists. According to the WHO, since 2009, surgical safety checklists have been implemented in 1,790 hospitals all over the world.[56] However, the success of checklists depends on the implementation process and the commitment of those involved. Empirical evidence shows that checklist implementations have not been equally and consistently effective across hospitals and services.[57] Clearly, checklists are not a solution for all quality-related challenges in the healthcare industry. However, they serve to demonstrate that, as previously shown by Pronovost et al.,[51] there are low-technology solutions for many of the quality-related issues in health care and that adherence to protocols, such as routine handwashing before and after patient contact, can go a long way in improving quality and addressing problems such as HAIs.

▶ 9.7 Physician Quality Reporting System

The U.S. Physician Quality Reporting System (PQRS) for individual healthcare professionals or group practices was first implemented by CMS in 2006. It became a permanent program in 2008.[58] The purpose of the program is to encourage healthcare providers to assess and improve the quality of care they provide to Medicare patients through online reporting of compliance with CMS's standards of care for various services.

By participating and reporting relevant data in PQRS, healthcare providers can assess how frequently they meet any of CMS's quality metrics for specific services. The standards of care used in PQRS are developed by provider associations and quality groups as well as by CMS, and they assign a numeric score to the quality of care for each of the included services by every participating healthcare provider. These measures change from one year to the next. Generally, these measures of healthcare quality focus on patient safety and engagement of the patient in the processes of care, coordination of care among providers, effectiveness of clinical care, and effective delivery of preventive care.

The program requires eligible healthcare professionals to voluntarily report information related to a host of services provided to Medicare patients that are covered under the Medicare Physician Fee Schedule. The list of services covered by PQRS ranges from preventive to therapeutic services and from acute to chronic care services, as well as a number of procedures and rehabilitative services. Several different options or mechanisms, including codes on claims data and qualified registries, are available to healthcare professionals and group practices to report compliance with standards of care. Assessment of compliance with CMS's codes is based on the proportion of cases (numerator) in a given class or category of patients seen by a provider (denominator) who met the relevant compliance code. The performance of healthcare providers is reported every year by CMS through a list published online of providers who successfully reported compliance with PQRS standards. For the purpose of transparency and comparison with other providers, some performance scores are available to the general public, patients, and other interested parties at CMS-sponsored Physician Compare web pages.

Although participation on the part of eligible providers is voluntary, since its inception, the program has employed financial incentives to encourage provider participation. For the first few years, the program provided incentive payments on top of regular reimbursement rates to eligible participants for reporting compliance with CMS-specified standards of care in the previous year(s). These payments were reduced through periodic decrements over several years and eventually turned into financial penalties through negatively adjusted reimbursement rates for future services. The program began to use these "negative payment adjustments" in 2015. The negative payment adjustments that were slated to take effect in 2017 and 2018 on the bases of lack of reporting to PQRS in 2015 and 2016 have been temporarily deferred because of issues related to the implementation of ICD 10 (International Classification of Diseases version 10).

▶ 9.8 Hospital Quality Reporting System—Hospital Compare

Hospital Compare, a web-based consumer platform, was created by CMS with input from multiple stakeholder organizations, including providers, employers, and patient advocacy groups. The purpose of this platform is to allow consumers the opportunity to make informed choices about where they might seek inpatient care after comparing information from different hospitals. A secondary objective of the platform is to promote transparency and motivate hospitals to improve their quality of care. Hospital Compare contains information on more than 100 measures of quality in seven different categories: (1) mortality, (2) safety of care, (3) unplanned readmissions, (4) effectiveness of care, (5) timeliness of care, (6) efficient use of medical imaging, and (7) patient experience. More than 4,000 CMS-certified hospitals in the country voluntarily submit this information to CMS every year through its Hospital Inpatient Quality Reporting (IQR) program. Aside from general information about a hospital, consumers can find an overall hospital rating score of 1–5 stars that is based on 57 different measures of quality. To determine the final

rating score every year, CMS uses sophisticated statistical techniques to assign weights to different variables. Other information includes recently discharged patients' evaluation of their experience at the hospital and the quality of care received. Consumers can find information related to the timeliness and effectiveness of care in terms of adherence to recommended treatment for conditions such as heart attack, stroke, and pulmonary embolism; avoidance of postsurgical complications; unplanned 30-day readmission rates; and inpatient mortality rates in comparison with national averages. Quality of care data for U.S. Veterans Health Administration hospitals are also available at the Hospital Compare website (https://www.medicare.gov/hospitalcompare/search.html).

▶ 9.9 Hospital Readmission Reduction Program

Under Section 3025 of the Affordable Care Act of 2010, CMS implemented the Hospital Readmission Reduction Program (HRRP) in October 2012 (federal FY 2013) for hospitals participating in Medicare's IPPS. This "pay for performance" program is designed to improve quality of care by levying a financial penalty to hospitals for poor performance. The measure of quality employed in this case is the rate of readmissions related to the primary diagnosis within 30 days after discharge. The list of applicable medical conditions included in the program has been incrementally expanded since 2013. The program currently applies to readmissions for high-cost conditions such as acute myocardial infarction, heart failure, pneumonia, chronic obstructive pulmonary disease, elective total hip arthroplasty, and coronary artery bypass graft surgery.[59]

The HRRP reduces payments to hospitals that have more than expected (*excess*) readmissions per 100 discharges as compared with the national average for peer hospitals—that is, hospitals with similar case mix. The judgment regarding excessive readmission rates is based on Medicare's predictive statistical models. For each applicable condition such as heart failure, CMS applies 3 years' discharge data and a minimum of 25 cases to estimate the **excess readmission ratio** (ERR). The ratio of a hospital's *predicted readmission rate* or *adjusted actual readmissions* (the numerator) with its *expected readmission rate* (the denominator) in a given period can be greater than 1.0000 if the hospital's performance is poorer than that of its peers and can be less than 1.0000 if its performance is better than the average performance of other comparable hospitals.

The penalty that applies to the base DRG for a given hospital discharge started in 2013 at the rate of 1% and reached the maximum penalty of 3% in 2015. To avoid unfair penalties to hospitals with sicker and more complex cases, in addition to using the relevant national average of readmission rates at peer institutions for a given condition (the denominator), the methodology to calculate ERR also uses a risk-adjustment procedure that accounts for patient characteristics such as age, gender, frailty, and comorbidities. However, the risk standardization methodology does not account for socioeconomic factors such as poverty and lack of timely access to appropriate postdischarge services. CMS believes doing so would "mask disparities in quality of care" rendered by hospitals. Such factors can affect readmission rates and may be outside the control of the hospital.[37–39,60] In August 2016, CMS indicated that it was going to reduce payments to 2,597 hospitals under HRRP in FY 2017,[61] a slight decline from 2,665 hospitals in FY 2016. The FY 2017 reductions were estimated to be about $528 million—an increase of $108 million over FY 2016.[62] In a recent study, Joynt and Jha[40] examined the risk of HRRP-related financial penalties for hospitals that provide care to more complex and socioeconomically deprived patients; most large, teaching, and safety net hospitals fall into this category. The researchers found that large, teaching, and safety net hospitals were at greater risk of being subjected to financial penalties by CMS than small, nonteaching, and non-safety-net hospitals.

▶ 9.10 Institute for Healthcare Improvement—Triple Aim

Launched in 2007 by the U.S. Institute for Healthcare Improvement (IHI), *Triple Aim* is a framework that simultaneously focuses on enhancing patient experience in terms of quality, access, and satisfaction; improving the health status of a defined population; and reducing per capita healthcare cost. This framework has been pilot-tested at more than 100 organizations around the world and successfully implemented by a number of organizations in the United States. Triple Aim involves identification of the target population, specification of the objectives of the healthcare system, developing a portfolio of projects sufficient in number and scope to yield system-level results, and rapid testing techniques that can be adapted to meet local needs and conditions. The framework also involves community

participation, a broader role for community-based services such as primary care, and adoption of innovative financing mechanisms. The broader scope of primary care may involve extended hours and nighttime availability, coordination of care, and adoption of a patient-centered medical home model. At the inpatient level, it may involve sanctions for avoidable events such as hospital readmissions and HAIs. Successful implementation of the Triple Aim framework requires system integration and linking organizations across the continuum of care. To integrate services at the local or regional level, the framework necessitates the existence of an organization that is willing to implement the Triple Aim framework and that can serve as a micro- or macro-integrator. The organization must accept the responsibility to simultaneously attain the three-dimensional objectives of Triple Aim in a defined population. The role of the micro- or macro-integrator organization extends to developing partnerships with individuals, families, and other organizations; redesigning and broadening the scope of primary care; and managing the costs at a sustainable and acceptable level. The fundamental principle of Triple Aim is equitable treatment of all members of the target population in terms of access, quality, and cost of care.[63] In addition to estimating total cost per member of the population per month and monitoring hospital and emergency department utilization rates, the IHI recommends the following population level measures of healthcare improvement:

1. Health or functional status assessment through survey instrument such as Health Related Quality of Life-4 (HRQOL-4), Short Form-12 (SF-12), or EuroQol.
2. Risk status assessment and estimation of a composite Health Risk Appraisal (HRA) score.
3. Burden of disease estimation based on the incidence and prevalence of major chronic conditions and assignment of an overall summary score.
4. Estimation of standardized mortality rates and years of potential life lost (YPLL).

▶ 9.11 Example of a Quality Assessment Study

Source: Jones BE, Sauer B, Jones MM, et al. Variation in outpatient antibiotic prescribing for acute respiratory infections in the veteran population: a cross-sectional study. Ann Intern Med. 2015;163(2):73–80.

Unwarranted use of antibiotics is largely responsible for the development of resistance to antibiotics in bacteria. Much of the use of antibiotics occurs in primary care settings. Antibiotics are commonly prescribed to treat ARIs, most of which are viral in nature.

This 2015 study by Jones et al. was designed to examine trends in prescribing antibiotics to treat ARIs at outpatient facilities in the Veterans Affairs (VA) health system from January 2005 through December 2012. The researchers wanted to understand patient-, provider-, and setting-related factors associated with the use of antibiotics. The study further aimed to investigate variations among providers, clinics, and medical centers in prescribing antibiotics to treat ARIs.

The VA system serves about 6.5 million veterans at more than 1,700 clinics and 152 hospitals, with about 13 million primary care visits every year. Visits to primary and urgent care centers and to emergency departments for acute naso-pharyngitis, pharyngitis, sinusitis, acute bronchitis, laryngitis, tonsillitis, and other acute upper respiratory infections were included in the study. Data on patient, provider, and setting characteristics and on prescriptions written were extracted from the VA's systemwide electronic health records and health information system.

Out of 2,481,520 visits for ARIs to VA facilities during the 8-year study period, 1,044,523 were included in the analysis. These patients were seen by 45,619 providers at 990 clinics or emergency departments in 130 VA medical centers. The results of the study showed that antibiotics were prescribed in 86% of diagnoses of sinusitis, in 85% of diagnoses of bronchitis, 78% of cases with high fever, and 75% of ARI visits to urgent care centers. The highest 10% of providers prescribed antibiotics during 95% or more of their ARI visits, while the lowest 10% prescribed them during 40% or fewer of visits. The highest 10% of clinics prescribed antibiotics during 89% or more of their ARI visits, while the lowest 10% of clinics prescribed them during 41% or fewer visits. Overall, providers accounted for 59% of variation in antibiotic prescribing, clinics for 28%, and medical centers for 13% of variation in antibiotic prescribing for ARIs.

TABLE 9.4 shows the characteristics of patients, providers, and settings for veterans' ARI visits.

The authors concluded that providers were the greatest source of variation in antibiotic prescribing during veterans' visits to VA facilities for ARIs.

TABLE 9.4 Patient, Provider, and Setting Characteristics in ARI Visits for the Veteran Population*

Characteristic	All Visits N = 1,044,523	Antibiotics Prescribed N = 714,552	No Antibiotics Prescribed N = 329,971
Sex			
Male	85.8%	85.5%	86.6%
Female	14.1%	14.5%	13.4%
Median age, years	61	60	61
Diagnosis			
Upper respiratory infection	51.5%	42.5%	70.9%
Bronchitis	23.9%	29.7%	11.5%
Sinusitis	18.5%	23.4%	8.0%
Pharyngitis	10.7%	10.55	11.3%

(continues)

TABLE 9.4 Patient, Provider, and Setting Characteristics in ARI Visits for the Veteran Population* *(continued)*

Characteristic	All Visits N = 1,044,523	Antibiotics Prescribed N = 714,552	No Antibiotics Prescribed N = 329,971
Comorbid Conditions			
>10 conditions	50.9%	51.1%	48.9%
Cardiovascular disease	51.9%	51.1%	48.9%
Psychiatric disease	42.4%	42.6%	42.1%
Pulmonary disease	24.1%	24.6%	22.9%
Infectious disease	19.3%	20.0%	17.8%
Renal disease	3.7%	3.6%	3.7%
Clinical Features			
No fever (temp. <100.4°F)	98.0%	97.7%	98.5%
Fever (temp. 100.4–101.9°F)	1.6%	1.8%	1.2%
High fever (temp. ≥102.0°F)	0.4%	0.4%	0.3%
Provider Type			
Physician	62.4%	62.3%	62.7%
Midlevel provider	24.5%	25.1%	23.3%
Nurse	11.1%	10.4%	12.9%
Other	1.9%	2.3%	1.1%
Median age, years	50	50	49
Setting			
Primary care clinic	72.4%	70.6%	76.3%
Emergency department	22.9%	24.2%	20.0%
Urgent care clinic	7.2%	7.9%	5.7%
Community-based outpatient clinic	30.1%	27.9%	34.8%
VAMC	69.9%	72.1%	65.2%

ARI: acute zrespiratory infection; ED: emergency department; VAMC: Veterans Affairs medical center.

* Percentages may not sum to 100 because of rounding.

Modified from: Jones BE, Sauer B, Jones MM, et al. Variation in outpatient antibiotic prescribing for acute respiratory infections in the veteran population: a cross-sectional study. Ann Intern Med. 2015;163(2):73–80. Copyright © 2015 American College of Physicians. All Rights Reserved. Reprinted with the permission of American College of Physicians, Inc.

🔍 *CASE STUDY 9.1: Reasons for Postsurgical Hospital Readmissions*

Source: Merkow RP, Ju MH, Chung JW, et al. Underlying reasons associated with hospital readmission following surgery in the United States. JAMA. 2015;31q3(5):483–495.

The purpose of this study by Merkow et al. was to understand the reasons, timing, and factors associated with unplanned 30-day postsurgery readmissions. The authors used abstracted data from clinical records for the period January 1, 2012, through December 31, 2012, from 346 U.S. hospitals continuously enrolled in the National Surgical Quality Improvement Program of the American College of Surgeons. Readmission rates and reasons for readmission were assessed for all surgical procedures and for the following six operations: (1) bariatric surgery, (2) colectomy and proctectomy, (3) hysterectomy, (4) total hip and knee arthroplasty, (5) ventral hernia repair, and (6) lower extremity vascular bypass surgery.

The overall unplanned readmission rate for the 498,875 operations included in the analysis was 5.7%. Surgical site infection was the most common reason for hospital readmission. The median time after surgery for an unplanned readmission was 8 days (interquartile range 3–14 days). The rate of unplanned readmissions was 14.9% (944/6,341) after lower extremity vascular bypass surgery, 10.9% (3,830/35,112) after colectomy or proctectomy, 5.2% (950/18,143) after bariatric surgery, 4.6% (1,549/33,895) after ventral hernia repair, 4.3% (1,676/38,671) after total hip or knee arthroplasty, and 3.8% (945/25,119) after a hysterectomy. The median length of a hospital stay for an unplanned readmission varied from 6 days (interquartile range 4–8 days) after colectomy or proctectomy to 0 days (interquartile range 0–2 days) for ventral hernia repair.

🔍 *CASE STUDY 9.2: Impact of a Rapid Response System on Inpatient Mortality and Length of Stay*

Modified from: Kollef MH, Heard K, Chen Y, Lu C, Martin N, Bailey T. Mortality and length of stay trends following implementation of a rapid response system and real-time automated clinical deterioration alerts. Am J Med Qual. 2017:32(1):12–18.

Deterioration of a patient's clinical condition in general medical units happens from time to time. Rapid response systems (RRSs) implemented to identify and treat deteriorating patients can make a big difference in health outcomes. This study examined the potential impact of an RRS that used an automated real-time clinical deterioration alert (RTCDA) in eight general medicine units at the Barnes-Jewish hospital, a 1,250-bed academic medical center in St. Louis, Missouri. The RRS was implemented in 2006. The RTCDA was implemented in a staged manner in 2009.

The rapid response team comprises a registered nurse, a medical resident physician, and a respiratory therapist. The nurse on the rapid response team carries a hospital-issued mobile phone to which the automated system sends RTCDAs directly. The nurse must respond to an alert within 20 minutes to do triage and take necessary follow-up action. The RTCDA uses 398 clinical variables from the real-time central data repository and operates around-the-clock, 7 days a week to generate automated alerts regarding "at-risk" patients. To avoid "alert fatigue" resulting from a system that generates too many false positive alerts and to have a manageable number of alerts per hospital unit per day, the RTCDA is set to achieve 40% sensitivity of detection—that is, 40% of those patients who are truly at risk of clinical deterioration are correctly identified by the RTCDA.

The outcomes of interest in this study were year-to-year decrease in mortality rate, cardiopulmonary arrests, and median LOS. Based on data from the eight general medicine units, retrospective statistical analysis used linear regression models to assess the strength of association between the intervention and each of the health outcomes while adjusting for extraneous factors such as comorbidities and patients' age and sex. To evaluate the impact of RRS and RTCDAs, the yearly hospital mortality, incidence of cardiopulmonary arrests, and median LOS data were compared from 2003 to 2014.

FIGURE 9.3 and **FIGURE 9.4** show some of the findings of this study.

(continues)

Questions

Question 1. Looking at Figure 9.3, what impact, if any, did the RRS and RTCDA system have on hospital mortality?

Question 2. Looking at Figure 9.4, what impact, if any, did the RRS and RTCDA system have on median hospital length of stay?

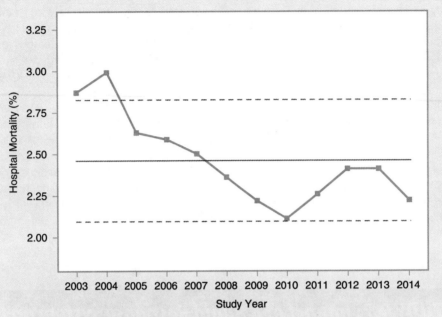

Solid line represents the mean value with the dotted lines depicting the upper and lower limits of the 95% confidence intervals.
P = .002 for the year-to-year decrease in hospital mortality for patients admitted to the general medicine units.

FIGURE 9.3 Hospital mortality for January 1, 2003, through December 31, 2014, for the 8 general medicine units.

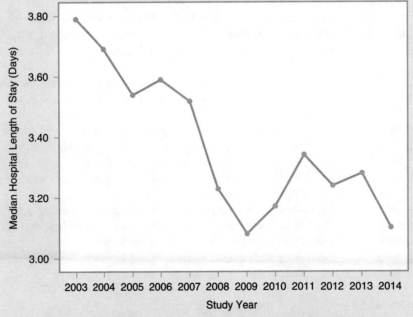

Hospital length of stay showed a statistically significant decrease over this time period for patients admitted to the general medicine units (P = .001).

FIGURE 9.4 Hospital length of stay between January 1, 2003, and December 31, 2014, for the 8 general medicine units.

9.12 Summary

Assessment, reporting, and improvement of quality in healthcare organizations are important subjects for healthcare mangers. Data on quality indicators, including health disparities, patient satisfaction, medical errors, avoidable hospitalizations, and HAIs provide clear evidence of systemic problems that need to be addressed. Effective and practical solutions such as implementation of checklists and staff training protocols are available to address many of the existing problems. Accreditation standards, financial incentives, and regulatory mechanisms are increasingly being used to promote the application of appropriate tools and technologies to improve the quality of care.

Variations in healthcare quality across geographic areas and population groups are linked to human actions or inactions. Organizational characteristics and other factors have much less to do with quality than staff characteristics and human behavior. Therefore, the focus of quality improvement efforts, more than anything else, ought to be staff training, retraining, and tools to facilitate change in personal behavior supported by the use of appropriate technologies and evidence-based protocols. Financial incentives, commonly known by the acronym P4P (pay for performance) are an effective and proven way of influencing human behavior.

References

1. Donabedian A. The definition of quality and approaches to its assessment: exploration in quality assessment and monitoring. Volume 1. Ann Arbor, MI: Health Administration Press; 1980.
2. Griffin DJ. Hospitals: what they are and how they work. 4th ed. Griffin DJ, editor. Sudbury, MA: Jones and Bartlett Learning; 2012.
3. Oxford English Dictionary. Oxford University Press. 2017 [cited 2017 July 7]. Available from: https://en.oxforddictionaries.com/definition/quality
4. Lohr K, Committee to Design a Strategy for Quality Review and Assurance in Medicare, editors. Medicare: a strategy for quality assurance. Vol. 1. Washington, DC: IOM, National Academy Press; 1990.
5. Institute of Medicine. Crossing the quality chasm: a new health system for the 21st century. Washington, DC: National Academy Press; 2001.
6. Agency for Healthcare Research and Quality. Your guide to choosing quality health care. Rockville, MD: Agency for Healthcare Research and Quality; 2001 [cited 2018 May 14]. Available at: http://archive.ahrq.gov/consumer/qnt/
7. World Health Organization. Quality of care: a process for making strategic choices in health systems. Geneva, Switzerland: WHO; 2006 [cited 2018 June 14]. Available from: http://www.who.int/management/quality/assurance/QualityCare_B.Def.pdf
8. Agency for Healthcare Research and Quality. 2016 National Healthcare Quality and Disparities Report [cited 2018 June 14]. Available from: https://www.ahrq.gov/sites/default/files/wysiwyg/research/findings/nhqrdr/nhqdr16/2016qdr.pdf
9. Agency for Healthcare Research and Quality. National healthcare quality and disparities report 2015 [cited 2018 June 14]. Available from: http://www.ahrq.gov/research/findings/nhqrdr/nhqrdr15/index.html
10. Agency for Healthcare Research and Quality. National healthcare quality and disparities report 2014 [cited 2018 June 14]. Available from: http://www.ahrq.gov/research/findings/nhqrdr/nhqrdr14/index.html
11. Centers for Disease Control and Prevention. Health disparities and inequalities report. MMWR supplements. 2013;62 Suppl.(3):1–187 [cited 2018 June 14]. Available from: https://www.cdc.gov/mmwr/preview/ind2013_su.html#HealthDisparities2013
12. Centers for Disease Control and Prevention. HAI data and statistics: HAIs at a glance. 2014 [cited 2018 June 14]. Available from: https://www.cdc.gov/hai/surveillance/index.html
13. Centers for Disease Control and Prevention. *National and state healthcare—associated infections progress report.* 2016 [cited 2018 June 14]. Available from: https://www.cdc.gov/hai/surveillance/progress-report/index.html
14. Zimlichman E, Henderson D, Tamir O, et al. Health care-associated infections: a meta-analysis of costs and financial impact on the U.S. Health Care System. JAMA Intern Med. 2013;173(22):2039–2046 [cited 2018 June 14]. Available from: http://archinte.jamanetwork.com/article.aspx?articleid=1733452
15. Magill SS, Edwards JR, Bamberg W, et al. Multistate point-prevalence survey of health care-associated infections. N Engl J Med. 2014;370:1198–1208.
16. Scott RD. The direct medical costs of healthcare-associated infections in U.S. hospitals and the benefits of prevention. Atlanta, GA: Centers for Disease Control and Prevention; 2009 [cited 2018 June 14]. Available from: https://www.cdc.gov/HAI/pdfs/hai/Scott_CostPaper.pdf
17. Lee GM, Kleinman K, Soumerai SB, et al. Effect of nonpayment for preventable infections in U.S. hospitals. N Engl J Med. 2012;367:1428–1437.
18. Jones BE, Sauer B, Jones MM, et al. Variation in outpatient antibiotic prescribing for acute respiratory infections in the veteran population: a cross-sectional study. Ann Intern Med. 2015;163(2):73–80.
19. Oxford English Dictionary. Oxford University Press. 2017 [cited 2017 Nov 4]. Available from: https://en.oxforddictionaries.com/definition/error
20. La Pietra L, Calligaris L, Molendini L, Quattrin R, Brusaferro S. Medical errors and clinical risk management: state of the art. Acta Otorhinolaryngol Ital. 2005;25(6):339–346.
21. Kalra J. Medical errors: an introduction to concepts. Clin Biochem. 2004;37:1043–1051.
22. Hofer TP, Kerr EA, Hayward RA. What is an error? Eff Clin Pract. 2000;6:261–269.
23. Kohn LT, Corrigan JM, Molla SD. To err is human: building a safer health system. Washington, DC: National Academy Press;1999.
24. Leape LL. Error in medicine. JAMA. 1994;272(23):1851–1857.
25. Vincent C. Understanding and responding to adverse events. N Engl J Med. 2003;348:1051–1056.

26. Agency for Health Care Quality and Research. Patient safety primer: systems approach. 2015 Mar [cited 2018 June 14]. Available from: https://psnet.ahrq.gov/primers/primer/21/systems-approach

27. The Joint Commission. Comprehensive accreditation manual for hospitals 2013: sentinel events. 2013 [cited 2017 Nov 14]. Available from: https://www.jointcommission.org/assets/1/6/CAMH_2012_Update2_24_SE.pdf

28. The Joint Commission. Summary data of sentinel events reviewed by the Joint Commission. 2016 [cited 2017 Nov 14]. Available from: https://www.jointcommission.org/assets/1/18/Summary_2Q_2016.pdf

29. de Vries EN, Prins HA, Crolla R, et al. Effects of comprehensive surgical safety systems on patient outcomes. N Engl J Med. 2010;363:1928–1937.

30. Baines RJ, Langelaan M, de Bruijne MC, et al. Changes in adverse event rate in hospitals over time: a longitudinal retrospective patient record review study. BMJ Qual Saf Health Care. 2013;22:290–298.

31. Zegers M, de Bruinje MC, Wagner C, et al. Adverse events and potentially preventable deaths in Dutch hospitals: results of a retrospective patient record review. BMJ Qual Saf Health Care. 2009;18:297–302.

32. Soop M, Fryksmark U, Koster M, Haglund B. The incidence of adverse events in Swedish hospitals: a retrospective medical record review study. Int J Qual Health Care. 2009;21(4):285–291.

33. Agbabiaka TB, Lietz M, Mira JJ, Warner B. A literature-based economic evaluation of healthcare preventable adverse events in Europe. Int J Qual Health Care. 2017;29(1):9–18.

34. Encinos WE, Hellinger FJ. 2008. The impact of medical errors on ninety-day costs and outcomes: an examination of surgical patients. Health Serv Res. 43(6):2067–2085.

35. Milstein A. 2009. Ending extra payment for "Never Events" – stronger incentives for patients' safety. New Eng J Med. 360(3): 2388–2389.

36. Agency for Healthcare Research and Quality. Guide to prevention quality indicators: hospital admission for ambulatory care sensitive conditions. AHRQ Pub. No. 02-R0203. Rockville, MD: Agency for Healthcare Research and Quality; 2001.

37. Jencks SF, Williams MV, Coleman EA. Rehospitalizations among patients in the Medicare fee-for-service program. N Engl J Med. 2009;360(14):1418–1428.

38. Allaudeen N, Vidyarthi A, Maselli J, Auerbach A. Redefining readmission risk factors for general medicine patients. J Hosp Med. 2011;6(2):54–60.

39. Joynt KE, Orav EJ, Jha AK. Thirty-day readmission rates for Medicare beneficiaries by race and site of care. JAMA. 2011;305(7):675–681.

40. Joynt KE, Jha AK. Characteristics of hospitals receiving penalties under the Hospital Readmission Reduction Program. JAMA. 2013;309(4):342–343.

41. Rathore SS, Foody JM, Wang Y, et al. Race, quality of care, and outcomes of elderly patients hospitalized with heart failure. JAMA. 2003;289(19):2517–2524.

42. Price Waterhouse Coopers' Health Research Institute. The price of excess: identifying waste in healthcare spending. 2008 [cited 2018 June 14]. Available from: http://www.oss.net/dynamaster/file_archive/080509/59f26a38c114f2295757bb6be522128a/The%20Price%20of%20Excess%20-%20Identifying%20Waste%20in%20Healthcare%20Spending%20-%20PWC.pdf

43. Texas External Quality Review Organization. Potentially preventable readmissions in Texas Medicaid and CHIP programs, FY 2013, 2014 [cited 2017 Nov 15]. https://hhs.texas.gov/sites/default/files/documents/about-hhs/process-improvement/medicaid-chip-qei/PPR-FY2013.pdf

44. The Joint Commission. Hospital national patient safety goals. 2016 [cited 2018 June 14]. Available from: https://www.jointcommission.org/assets/1/6/2016_NPSG_HAP_ER.pdf

45. The Joint Commission. Ambulatory care national patient safety goals. 2016 [cited 2018 June 14]. Available from: https://www.jointcommission.org/assets/1/6/2016_NPSG_AHC_ER.pdf

46. Medstat. Disease staging software user guide. Ann Arbor, MI: Medstat Group, Inc; 2001.

47. Agency for Healthcare Research and Quality. Overview of disease severity measures disseminated with the Nationwide Inpatient Sample (NIS) and Kid's Inpatient Database (KID). 2005 [cited 2018 June 14]. Available from: http://www.hcup-us.ahrq.gov/db/nation/nis/OverviewofSeveritySystems.pdf

48. Bouch DC, Thompson JP. Severity scoring systems in the critically ill. Contin Educ Anaesth Crit Care Pain. 2008;8(5):181–185.

49. Gilboy N, Tanabe T, Travers D, Rosenau AM. Emergency Severity Index (ESI): a triage tool for emergency department care, version 4. Implementation handbook 2012 edition. AHRQ Publication No. 12–0014. Rockville, MD: Agency for Healthcare Research and Quality; 2011.

50. Gawande AA. The checklist manifesto: how to get things right. New York, NY: Metropolitan Books–Henry Holt and Co; 2010.

51. Pronovost P, Needham D, Berenholtz S, et al. An intervention to decrease catheter-related bloodstream infections in the ICU. N Engl J Med. 2006;355:2725–2732.

52. Haynes AB, Weiser TG, Berry WR., et al. A surgical safety checklist to reduce morbidity and mortality in a global population. N Engl J Med. 2009;360:491–499.

53. de Vries EN, Ramrattan MA, Smorenburg SM, Gouma DJ, Boermeester MS. The incident and nature of the in-hospital adverse events: a systematic review. Qual Saf Health Care. 2008;17:216:223.

54. Van Klei WA, Hoff RG, van Aarnhem EE, et al. Effects of the introduction of the WHO "Surgical Safety Checklist" on in-hospital mortality: a cohort study. Ann Surg. 2012;55(1):44–49.

55. Salzwedel C, Bartz HJ, Kühnelt I, et al. The effect of a checklist on the quality of post-anaesthesia patient handover: a randomized controlled trial. Int J Qual Health Care. 2013;25(2):176–181.

56. World Health Organization. Patient safety: surgical safety web map. 2014 [cited 2018 June 14]. Available from: http://maps.cga.harvard.edu/surgical_safety/index.html

57. Conley DM, Singer SJ, Edmondson L, Berry WR, Gawande AA. Effective surgical safety checklist implementation. J Am Coll Surg. 2011;212:873–879 [cited 2018 June 14]. Available from: http://scoap.org/wp-content/uploads/2011/12/Implementation_JACS.pdf

58. Anumula N, Sanelli PC. Physician quality reporting system. Am J Neuroradiol. 2012;32:2000–2001.

59. Centers for Medicare and Medicaid Services. Readmission Reduction Program. 2016 [cited 2018 June 14]. Available from: https://www.cms.gov/medicare/medicare-fee-for

-service-payment/acuteinpatientpps/readmissions-reduction -program.html

60. Akin D, Ward M. Rethinking the hospital readmission reduction program. TrendWatch. American Hospital Association. 2015 [cited 2018 June 14]. Available from: http://www.aha.org/research/reports/tw/15mar-tw -readmissions.pdf

61. Centers for Medicare and Medicaid Services. Details for title: FY 2017 final rule and correction notice data files. 2016 [cited 2018 June 14]. Available from: https://www.cms.gov/Medicare /Medicare-Fee-for-Service-Payment/AcuteInpatientPPS /FY2017-IPPS-Final-Rule-Home-Page-Items/FY2017-IPPS -Final-Rule-Tables.html

62. Rau J. Medicare's readmission penalties hit new high. Kaiser Health News. 2016 [cited 2018 June 14]. Available from: http://khn.org/news/more-than-half-of-hospitals-to-be -penalized-for-excess-readmissions/

63. Berwick DM, Nolan TW, Whittington J. The triple aim: care, health, and cost. Health Aff. 2008;27(3):759–769.

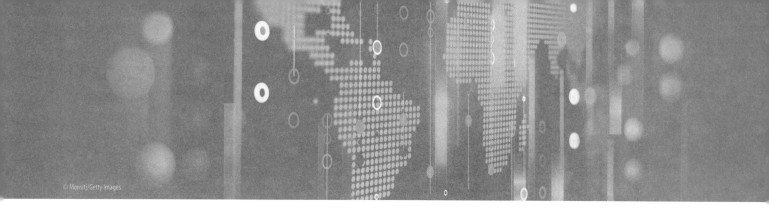

© Monsitj/Getty Images

CHAPTER 10

Community Health Needs Assessment

CHAPTER OUTLINE

10.1 Introduction
10.2 Determinants of Healthcare Needs
    10.2.1 Size and Demographic Characteristics of the Population
    10.2.2 Health Status of the Population
10.3 Need Versus Demand
10.4 Definition and Scope of a Community Health Needs Assessment
10.5 Requirements of the U.S. Affordable Care Act
10.6 Methods and Process of Needs Assessment
10.7 Planning for a Community Health Needs Assessment
10.8 Nature and Type of Data for a Community Health Needs Assessment

10.9 Sources of Data for a Community Health Needs Assessment
10.10 Priority Setting for Healthcare Needs
10.11 Community Health Needs Assessment After a Disaster
10.12 Assessment of Unmet Healthcare Needs— Market Analysis
10.13 Estimation of Future Healthcare Needs
10.14 Forecasting Methods
Case Study 10. 1 – Healthcare Needs of the Homeless
Case Study 10. 2 – Impact of Unmet Healthcare Needs
10.15 Summary

▶ 10.1 Introduction

For managers, assessing and striving to meet the healthcare needs of the communities they serve have a business, moral, and professional imperative. The business imperative stems from the fact that unmet healthcare needs represent a business opportunity, whereas offering services for which there is no need reflects wasted resources. The moral imperative is based on the argument that neglecting the needs of a community, whether for economic, social, or political reasons, is morally questionable and amounts to a dereliction of duty. The professional imperative derives from the position that failing to meet the needs of a community because of a lack of awareness or understanding is nothing short of incompetence and poor management.

The objective of this chapter is to provide a conceptual framework for assessing the needs of a community and to demonstrate how existing epidemiologic data can be used for this purpose. In the same way that doctors assess the healthcare needs of individual patients, managers and policy makers can assess the healthcare needs of communities or populations. However, needs should not be confused with wishes, demands, or aspirations, and needs assessment should not be confused with opinion polls and market surveys. Needs can be assessed by using existing quantitative data that reflect the nature and magnitude of health problems in a community. These data can also help in identifying gaps in services and shortage of resources. Reliance on quantitative data alone, however, can be problematic because they can fail to reveal the concerns or priorities of a population. Therefore, a carefully designed assessment should include collection of both quantitative and qualitative data that provide the evidence on which priorities can be based and resources can be allocated. A carefully conducted assessment can lead to changes in existing programs and development of new services. Such an undertaking can be narrowly focused to determine the need for a specific service, or it can be broad and comprehensive in scope to understand the full range of the needs of a population.

▶ 10.2 Determinants of Healthcare Needs

In broad terms, the following factors can influence the current and future healthcare needs of a population:

1. The demographic characteristics of the population, including its size, socioeconomic characteristics, and risk profile
2. The health status of the population, including various measures of morbidity, disability, and mortality

FIGURE 10.1 shows the relationship of these factors with the healthcare needs of a population. Healthcare needs can be defined in terms of physical, human, and technological resources required to deliver the necessary type, quantity, and quality of services. Depending on the demographic characteristics and health status of a given population, the spectrum of required services can be broad or relatively narrow, and the quantity of required services can be large or small. In the following section, we further discuss the role of demographic characteristics and health status as drivers of population healthcare needs.

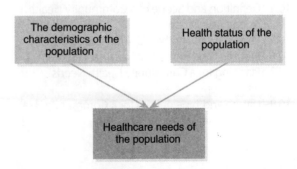

FIGURE 10.1 A conceptual model of the determinants of healthcare needs of a population.

10.2.1 Size and Demographic Characteristics of the Population

There is a direct statistical relationship between the size of a population and the need for healthcare resources. Generally, a relatively small population—say, a town of 10,000 people—will be expected to have fewer health-related events such as deliveries, heart attacks, or injuries in a given period of time as compared with a much larger population, such as a town of 100,000 people. For example, if the birth rate in both populations is 5 per 1,000, the smaller population will have only 50 babies born in one year, whereas the larger population will have 500 babies born in the same period. Under ordinary circumstances, the need for healthcare resources increases in direct proportion to the size of the population. Naturally, the health status of the population also has an important bearing on the need for healthcare resources.

Personal characteristics such as age, sex, race, education, income, and personal behavior have a tremendous effect on the health status and healthcare needs of individuals and populations. The composition of a population in terms of age, sex, and racial distribution, as well as average education; average family income; proportion of the population with health insurance coverage; urban or rural location; and environmental conditions, including availability of clean drinking water, sanitation, and air quality; are powerful determinants of healthcare needs.[1]

Populations with high fertility rates and a high proportion of women of reproductive age will have a greater need for obstetric and pediatric services than populations that have relatively lower fertility rates and a small proportion of women of childbearing age. Similarly, populations with a high percentage of retirees and elderly people will have a greater need for geriatric and long-term care services. For example, the amount and nature of healthcare resources needed in Finland or Denmark, where approximately 20% of the population is age ≥65 years, are likely to be different from those needed in Iran, where median age in 2014 was only 28.3 years and approximately 60% of the population was younger than age 35 years. In the United States, the amount and type of health services needed in Scottsdale, Arizona, and Clearwater, Florida, are likely to be different from those needed in East Lansing, Michigan, and Flagstaff, Arizona. In Scottsdale and Clearwater, the median age in 2013 was about 45.1 and 44.8 years, respectively, whereas the median age in Lansing and Flagstaff in the same year was only 21.6 and 26.3 years, respectively.

10.2.2 Health Status of the Population

The current health status of a population in terms of its morbidity, mortality, and disability rates broken down by various age, race, and sex categories is the most direct determinant of its healthcare needs. Records of vital statistics from state or county health departments and healthcare utilization records and billing data available from various healthcare providers can allow planners and researchers to prepare a detailed health profile of a **community**. The availability of these records over multiple years can allow analysts and policy makers to understand trends and changes in the health status of a population over time and make predictions regarding its healthcare needs. Comparisons of these data across subgroups within a population and across different populations render useful information regarding intrapopulation and interpopulation health disparities. Empirical data from many studies have clearly established a link between the health status of individuals and their use of healthcare resources.[2] Generally, young and healthy individuals use fewer resources and less-complicated services such as screening and preventive services, whereas those who are sicker and older use more healthcare resources and need more technologically advanced services.

Research conducted in the United States and other countries over many years has also provided clear evidence of healthcare disparities across different socioeconomic groups within a population.[3] Individuals such as those with chronic mental conditions often do not seek health care even though they are in dire need of such help.[4] Numerous instances of violent crimes in the United States in recent years have provided tragic examples of individuals with chronic mental disorders who did not seek or receive timely help. Mass shootings at Marjory Stoneman Douglas High School in Parkland, Florida in February 2018; a country music festival in Las Vegas in October 2017 and at First Baptist Church in Texas in November 2017; the Pulse nightclub in Orlando, Florida, in June 2016; at Sandy Hook elementary school in Newtown, Connecticut, in December 2012; and at Virginia Tech in Centerville, Virginia, in 2007 could possibly have been prevented by timely interventions to help the mentally affected or deranged individuals who carried out these acts.

Descriptive epidemiologic measures such as data on the incidence and prevalence of various diseases do not, per se, equate with healthcare need, but are a good starting point in needs assessment because they provide a good estimation of the burden of disease.

In this regard, crude; standardized; and age-, sex-, and race-specific incidence and prevalence data are important in developing an estimation of the burden of disease and the need for healthcare resources in a population. Even if current epidemiologic data for the population of interest are not available, data from similar populations allowing generalizability are still useful in estimating the burden of disease.[5] **TABLE 10.1** and **TABLE 10.2** show the rates of the 10 most common reasons for hospitalizations and the 10 most common procedures done for patients living in the poorest communities in the United States in 2006 as compared with the rates in other communities. Clearly, hospitalization rates for pneumonia; congestive heart failure; coronary atherosclerosis; skin infections; and procedures such as cardiac catheterization, respiratory intubation, and gastrointestinal endoscopy were much higher for patients residing in the poorest communities.

These differences suggest a poorer health status of individuals living in the poorest communities as compared with those residing in other communities.

Illustrating the relationship between income and health status, **FIGURE 10.2** shows hospitalization rates for ambulatory care sensitive conditions (i.e., conditions for which individuals can be adequately managed in primary care settings and should not need to get into a hospital) in the poorest communities in the United States in 2006 as compared with other communities. As shown, the poorest communities experienced much higher admission rates for all ambulatory care sensitive conditions as compared with other communities in the United States. Previously it has been shown that those in low- and middle-income countries died both in 1990 and in 2000 at much higher rates for all conditions than did their counter parts in high-income countries.[6] These data are useful in understanding the

TABLE 10.1 Top 10 Most Common Reasons for Admission to the Hospital for Patients Residing in the Poorest Communities in the United States in 2006

Rank (Poorest Areas)	Principal Diagnosis	Rate* in the Poorest Communities	Rate* in all Other Communities	Percent Difference	Rank (Other Areas)
1	Newborn infants	155.6	136.1	14%	1
2	Pneumonia	51.4	36.1	42%	3
3	Congestive heart failure	48.2	32.0	51%	4
4	Coronary atherosclerosis	42.2	38.3	10%	2
5	Nonspecific chest pain	34.1	25.8	32%	6
6	Chronic obstructive pulmonary disease	28.3	16.7	69%	16
7	Skin infections	25.8	17.3	49%	15
8	Trauma to perineum	25.5	27.2	–6%	5
9	Cardiac dysrhythmias	25.1	24.4	3%	8
10	Diabetes with complications	25.0	14.1	77%	25

Note: "Poorest communities" had a median household income in the patient's ZIP code of less than $38,000. "All other communities" had a median household income in the patient's ZIP code of greater than or equal to $38,000.

*Per 10,000 population.

Modified from: Wier LM, Merrill CT, Elixhauser A. Hospital stays among people living in the poorest communities, 2006. Healthcare Cost and Utilization Project: Statistical Brief # 73. National Health Disparities Report. Rockville, MD: Agency for Healthcare Research and Quality; 2008. Source: AHRQ, Center for Delivery, Organization, and Markets, Healthcare Cost and Utilization Project, Nationwide Inpatient Sample, 2006.

TABLE 10.2 Top 10 Most Common Inpatient Procedures for Patients Residing in the Poorest Communities in the United States in 2006

Rank (Poorest Areas)	Procedure	Rate* in the Poorest Communities	Rate* in all Other Communities	Percent Difference	Rank (Other Areas)
1	Blood transfusion	89.6	74.4	20%	1
2	Cardiac catheterization	55.6	54.5	2%	2
3	Respiratory intubation	51.7	39.1	32%	6
4	Cesarean section	48.3	42.9	13%	4
5	Gastrointestinal endoscopy	46.9	37.5	25%	7
6	Repair of obstetric laceration	43.1	45.8	−6%	3
7	Vaccinations	40.3	27.4	47%	11
8	Circumcision	39.0	40.9	−5%	5
9	Hemodialysis	37.7	20.9	80%	13
10	Fetal monitoring	37.3	28.9	29%	10

Notes: "Poorest communities" had a median household income in the patient's ZIP code of less than $38,000. "All other communities" had a median household income in the patient's ZIP code of greater than or equal to $38,000.

*Per 10,000 population.

Modified from: Wier LM, Merrill CT, Elixhauser A. Hospital stays among people living in the poorest communities, 2006. Healthcare Cost and Utilization Project: Statistical Brief # 73. National Health Disparities Report. Rockville, MD: Agency for Healthcare Research and Quality; 2008. Source: AHRQ, Center for Delivery, Organization, and Markets, Healthcare Cost and Utilization Project, Nationwide Inpatient Sample, 2006.

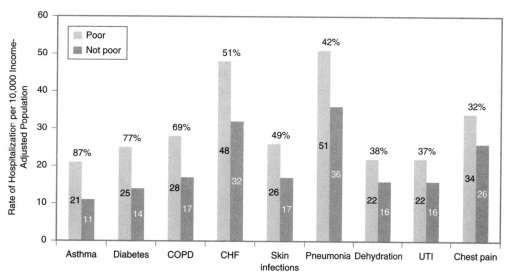

FIGURE 10.2 Rates of hospital admissions for ambulatory care sensitive conditions in the poorest communities as compared with other communities, United States, 2006.

Reproduced from: Wier LM, Merrill CT, Elixhauser A. Hospital stays among people living in the poorest communities, 2006. Healthcare Cost and Utilization Project: Statistical Brief # 73. National Health Disparities Report. Rockville, MD: Agency for Healthcare Research and Quality; 2008. Source: AHRQ, Center for Delivery, Organization, and Markets, Healthcare Cost and Utilization Project, Nationwide Inpatient Sample, 2006.

evolving burden of disease and healthcare needs in various countries and regions. Clearly, developing countries of sub-Saharan Africa and South Asia have the greatest burden of disease and healthcare needs. Much of the burden of disease and mortality for these countries results from preventable and treatable infectious diseases rather than cancer and cardiovascular disease, which pose the biggest problems for the developed countries of Europe and North America.

▶ 10.3 Need Versus Demand

Before discussing the objectives and methods of needs assessment, it is appropriate to clarify the difference between *need* and *demand*. Oxford Dictionary defines *need*[7] as "require (something) because it is essential or very important rather than just desirable," and *demand*[8] as "an insistent and peremptory request, made as of right" or "the desire of consumers, clients, employers, etc. for a particular commodity, service, or other item." Thus, **need** refers to a perception or assessment by the individual or someone else about what ought to happen, while **demand**, on the other hand, is the articulation and communication by one or more people (whether verbally, in writing, or in some other fashion) regarding what ought to happen.[4] Another definition of *need* is "the capacity to benefit."[4,9] This definition implies that the determination of the capacity to benefit is best made by experts based on some previously established criteria.

At times, valid needs remain unarticulated or unexpressed because of sociopolitical factors and a lack of clout on the part of the affected population. For example, the healthcare needs of homeless or undocumented individuals in a community frequently are neither expressed nor met. In any large city such as New York, Los Angeles, Toronto, London, or Bombay there are large numbers of homeless individuals on any given day. According to the U.S. Department of Housing and Urban Development,[10] on any given night in January 2015, there were more than 5.64 million homeless people in the United States. There is no easy way to understand the healthcare needs of these individuals.

Conversely, some demands are not based on a valid need. Complying with demands that do not represent valid needs can result in waste of resources and potential harm to the individual. Of course, the validity or legitimacy of a need or demand can be disputed by the parties involved. For example, in the current age of "direct to consumer marketing" by the pharmaceutical industry, patients suffering from viral infections frequently demand to be treated with antibiotics while, in the assessment of primary care doctors, there may not be a need for antibiotics in these circumstances. Clearly, the nature, degree, and urgency of need for healthcare services depend upon several factors and can vary a great deal from one population to another. **FIGURE 10.3** clarifies the relationship among "need," "demand," and supply of resources. As shown, some valid healthcare needs remain unmet despite being articulated while some invalid needs—both expressed and unexpressed—are met on account of sociopolitical factors.

To illustrate the relationship among need, demand, and supply, Wright et al.[4] have developed a model of three overlapping circles with one circle representing need, one representing demand, and the third representing supply of resources. The critical area in the model is where all three circles overlap (i.e., valid needs are effectively communicated and met with adequate supply of resources). Legitimate need for a service such as treatment for drug dependence may not be met because of ineffective communication or lack of resources. For services such as counseling and treatment for child abusers, there might be a need, but no demand or supply; for services to terminate a pregnancy, there might be a need and demand, but no supply. On the other hand, there might be a need and availability for some screening and counseling services, but no real demand in the population.[4]

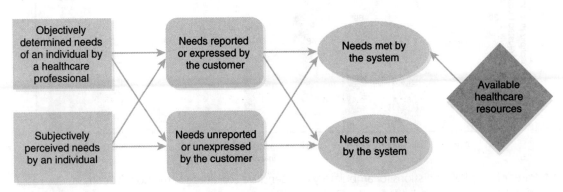

FIGURE 10.3 Perceived and expressed healthcare needs in relation to available healthcare resources.

Modified from: Wright J, Williams R, Wilkinson JR. Development and importance of health needs assessment. BMJ. 1998;316:1310–1313.

▶ 10.4 Definition and Scope of a Community Health Needs Assessment

Witkin and Altschuld[11] have defined a **needs assessment** as "procedures undertaken for the purpose of setting priorities and making decisions." Generally, the term *community health needs assessment* (CHNA) refers to the collection, analysis, and interpretation of data on the **determinants of health** and health outcomes in a population and identification of resources needed to address high-priority healthcare needs.[11] A number of different definitions of community health assessment and CHNA are available in the literature. Often these terms are used interchangeably.[12-15] Despite some differences in the finer details of various definitions, such as the question of whether community engagement and intervention planning is a part of CHNA, all definitions have two elements in common: (1) identification and prioritization of the healthcare needs of a population through data collection and analysis, and (2) some level of input from the community. Both in concept and in practice, a CHNA also includes identification of health disparities between population subgroups in a geographic area.

As mentioned in the introduction to this chapter, it is important to make a distinction between the healthcare needs of individuals and those of communities or populations. A careful assessment of the needs of individual patients is essential to the delivery of appropriate clinical care. Such an assessment, ideally conducted by a team of healthcare professionals, can optimize the quality of care and achieve best health outcomes for the individual patient. Likewise, the assessment of healthcare needs of a population, systematically conducted by a team of analysts, public health professionals, and healthcare planners, is essential for the optimal allocation of healthcare resources to achieve the highest levels of population health. To conduct a scientifically sound and administratively useful needs assessment, it is necessary to develop and implement an explicit framework.[12,15,16]

CHNA involves the use of epidemiologic methods to assess health problems in a population, identify disparities in health status and **access** to health services of different groups, and set priorities for the allocation of resources. As such, the purpose of needs assessment is to ensure that healthcare resources are used most efficiently to improve the health status of the population.[17] Steven and Gillam[9] suggest that efficient and equitable allocation of resources can be done by identifying the following:

1. Those who can benefit from services but are not receiving them (*unmet need*)
2. Those who are receiving ineffective care (*and releasing those resources for unmet need*)
3. Those who are receiving inefficient care (*and releasing those resources for unmet need*)
4. Those who are receiving inappropriate care (*and giving them appropriate care to improve health outcomes*)

One of the objectives of needs assessment is to achieve adequate *spatial* or geographic allocation of resources.[18] This involves assessment of the health status of the population through surrogate measures, such as standardized mortality ratios, and by estimating the level of resource *deprivation* in the geographic district of interest. For this purpose, scientists have developed *deprivation indices* that allow comparison of the level of deprivation in two or more geographic districts.

Assessment of healthcare needs of a population should be central to the design and delivery of health services in a geographic area. Wright et al.[4] have argued that public health professionals, hospital administrators, and clinical practitioners all should aim to develop services to "match the needs of their local populations." Population health needs can be assessed at all administrative levels: national, regional, provincial, and local. Issues related to social determinants of health, such as poverty and education, can be assessed at national or regional levels, whereas programmatic needs for behavioral determinants of health, such as smoking cessation and teen pregnancy prevention, can be assessed at a local level. A focused assessment can target specific specialties, such as the need for mental health services, specific diseases such as HIV/AIDS, or population subgroups such as the elderly and single mothers.[19]

The 1988 report of the U.S. Institute of Medicine[20] entitled *The Future of Public Health* identified CHNA to be a core public health function and made a recommendation for all public health agencies to conduct such an assessment routinely. The primary responsibility in this regard was placed with local health departments. A number of developments in recent years have drawn greater attention in the United States toward the role of various stakeholders in conducting a CHNA. For example, the 2011 standards for voluntary accreditation of state, local, tribal, and territorial public health departments launched by the Public Health Accreditation Board (PHAB) require documentation of a comprehensive community health assessment and community improvement plan. Similarly, the Community Transformation Grants (CTGs) program (2011–2014), which was designed under the Patient Protection and Affordable Care Act to reduce the burden of chronic diseases such as cancer, stroke, and heart disease, also required grantees to conduct a CHNA and develop plans for improvement.[12,13]

▶ 10.5 Requirements of the U.S. Affordable Care Act

Under the provisions of the **Patient Protection and Affordable Care Act** of 2010 (commonly known as Obamacare and currently standing the risk of being repealed by the new administration), to retain their tax-exempt status, all nonprofit hospitals—501(c)(3) hospitals—in the country are required to conduct a CHNA at least once every 3 years. They are also required to report progress toward the achievement of identified needs to the Internal Revenue Service (IRS) through Schedule H (Form 990). In conducting a CHNA, nonprofit hospitals are required to consult and seek input from at least one state, local, tribal, or regional government health department.[12,13] The provisions of the Act and guidelines from the IRS also require nonprofit hospitals to provide a categorized listing of community benefit services and activities undertaken by the hospital. Nonprofit hospitals are also required to indicate in clear and specific terms how they identify and define their community. In defining the community, IRS rules mandate that the definition not exclude vulnerable population groups, such as minorities or low-income individuals and families in the same geographic area. In fact, the planning process for needs assessment must seek input from such vulnerable groups.[13] In defining the community, hospitals and other service organizations should explicitly identify their primary and secondary service areas and various patient/client subgroups. If needs assessment is being conducted jointly by several organizations, then all members of the coalition have to agree on a common definition of their collective community.

▶ 10.6 Methods and Process of Needs Assessment

There are many different models and approaches to conduct a CHNA. Depending on whether the assessment is based on expert opinion or is *participatory* (i.e., involves those whose needs are being determined), these approaches can be divided into two groups. Steven and Gillam[9] have suggested that for a given situation, a practical way to assess the usefulness of one or the other model is by answering the following questions:

1. Does the proposed methodology focus on populations or individuals in a population?
2. Are there clear rules and criteria for setting priorities among competing needs?
3. Is the needs assessment formative or summative in nature? (That is, it is being done to make decisions regarding the allocation of resources, or only to shed light on the nature and magnitude of problems, not follow up with necessary action?)
4. Does it rely on expert opinion or on participatory methods to identify the most important needs?

Steven and Gillam have argued that if needs assessment does not result in specific decisions, follow-up actions, and changes in the allocation of resources, then it may just be an exercise in futility. Moreover, needs assessment should not be seen as a "one-shot" effort, but rather an iterative process that should lead to a consensus among policy makers, managers, and healthcare providers regarding priorities for health services development.[11]

In common practice, a needs assessment may include the following steps or stages: (1) planning the study, (2) implementation and data collection, (3) data analysis, (4) compilation of findings and results, and (5) implementation of recommendations.[11,21] In this sequence, stage 1 is designed to understand and report the existing conditions in the community, including the demographic profile and health status of the target population. Stages 2 and 3 help identify the gap between existing or prevailing conditions and the desired or expected conditions. As a rule, a CHNA should not just focus on current needs, but also must make projections of future needs. Naturally, projections of future needs would necessitate making assumptions about future changes in the demographic, technologic, and socioeconomic conditions of the target population. Because programs and services have to address the root causes of problems, the current and future needs of a population have to be understood in the context of factors that cause those problems in the first place. Needs assessment must also be considered in the context of the healthcare delivery system. The characteristics of healthcare organizations and providers also contribute to the emergence and continuation of health needs.[11,21]

Comprehensive needs assessment can take place in phases over time. However, the time frame for the completion of a phased needs assessment must not be too long, otherwise changes taking place in the socioeconomic, political, and technologic environment can make the findings irrelevant. Further, it is not sufficient to identify the breadth and depth of needs; it is also necessary to identify the steps that must be taken to meet those needs. Therefore, the breadth and depth of an assessment are closely tied to the context of the study. Unless the scope of the study is carefully defined and agreed on by all stakeholders, a lot of time and resources can be wasted on a needs assessment that does not meet the expectation of all stakeholders and fails to produce desired results. Every needs assessment must weigh and compare various alternatives and formulate a plan of action for decision makers.

The Association for Community Health Improvement has developed a six-step process[14] depicted in **FIGURE 10.4**. In this model, the first step is to develop the necessary infrastructure that involves identification of resources and creation of a plan of action to conduct the CHNA. This step includes identification of partners and clarification of their roles in carrying out the assessment. In step 2, the purpose, scope, target population, and/or geographic area to be covered in the needs assessment are defined. In this stage, researchers clarify what they want to learn about the community and the indicators of health for which they want to collect data. Step 3 involves collection

and analysis of data specified in the previous step. To avoid potential waste of time and other resources, it is best to first identify sources from which existing demographic, behavioral, epidemiologic, and healthcare utilization data might be obtained. Assessment regarding the need for additional data can be made with the help of other stakeholders and community participants. In step 4, the process of setting priorities begins. During this stage, it is critically important to seek input from community representatives to ensure that focus remains on issues that are of greatest importance and relevance to the community. Priorities must also be set in proportion to available resources. Setting ambitious goals and priorities without sufficient resources can only result in frustration and disillusionment on the part of all stakeholders, including community representatives. It can also undermine the prospects for undertaking another CHNA in the future. Step 5 involves documentation of study findings and identified priorities in a comprehensive report with supporting data, maps, and charts. Finally, in step 6, a plan of action with appropriate allocation of resources must be developed to address community health needs in the rank order of priorities.[14]

The Catholic Health Association of the United States (CHA) also uses a similar six-step approach for conducting a CHNA. However, the model developed by CHA is much more detailed in terms of describing how a CHNA should be conducted and how strategies for implementation ought to be developed.[13] In the CHA model, the needs assessment process comprises the following six steps:

1. Planning and preparation for the needs assessment
2. Determination of the purpose and scope of the assessment
3. Identification of data that describe the health status and needs of the community
4. Understanding and interpreting the data
5. Defining and validating community health priorities
6. Documentation and communication of results to all stakeholders

Notably, the CHA model explicitly emphasizes the following: (1) collaboration with other interested parties, (2) careful definition and specification of the community that is the focus of the needs assessment, (3) building on previously conducted assessments and existing healthcare utilization and public health data, and (4) periodically updating assessment and implementation strategies. According to the CHA model, the planning stage of a CHNA must include the determination of team members, the proposed process of

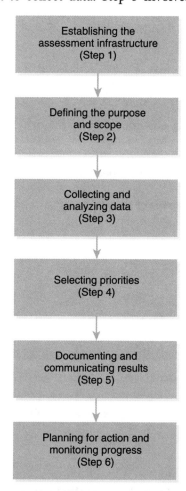

FIGURE 10.4 Steps for community health needs assessment.

Modified from: Bilton M. Executive Briefing 3: Community Health Needs Assessment. Trustee. 21–24. October 2011. Available at: http://www.trusteemag.com/subscribers/PDFs/executivebriefings/2011/TRU1011pExBrief_new.pdf; Bilton M. Association for Community Health Improvement. Available at: https://www.ihaconnect.org/Leadership/Documents/2012GovernanceIssues.pdf

assessment, and identification and procurement of necessary resources to conduct the assessment. At the time when the scope of the assessment is being determined, availability of necessary resources must be carefully weighed in proportion to the scope of the study. **BOX 10.1** shows various elements of data that should be included in a CHNA. Notably, the elements listed in Box 10.1 are similar to those used in 2011 by the Primary Care Office of the Maryland Department of Health and Mental Hygiene to conduct a CHNA in 23 counties in Maryland.

Because of considerable variation in the methods, processes, goals, and reporting of the findings of

CHNAs, Myers and Stoto[15] have developed 21 criteria to assess the usefulness of a CHNA. These criteria include essential elements that should be part of the content and format of a CHNA report. For example, the content of the CHNA report should clearly state its goals and objectives, include the most important community health issues, allow a comparison of data from other communities, allow temporal analysis of data from the same community, and allow analysis of subgroup data in the community. The CHNA report should also provide information regarding the process and methods used to conduct the assessment.[15] Likewise, the format of the report should allow the reader to easily find

---

BOX 10.1 Suggested Information to Be Included in a Community Health Needs Assessment

A. **Demographic and Socioeconomic Status**
   A1. Community overview: age, sex, race, socioeconomic status, academic attainment
   A2. Poverty by age and race/ethnic subgroups
   A3. Unemployment rate

B. **Access to Health Care**
   B1. Healthcare staffing shortages by Health Professional Shortage Area (HPSA), Dental HPSA
   B2. Primary care physicians per 10,000 population
   B3. Number of hospital beds per 10,000 population
   B4. Percent of adults (age ≥18) and children (age <18) who are uninsured
   B5. Percent of population with Medicare coverage
   B6. Percent of population with Medicaid coverage

C. **Health Status of Overall Population and by Subgroups (Uninsured, Low-Income, and Minority)**
   C1. Leading causes of death (age adjusted if available)
   C2. Admission rates: top 10 causes
   C3. Rates of preventable hospitalizations (asthma, diabetes, pneumonia, congestive heart failure, chronic obstructive pulmonary disease [COPD])

D. **Behavioral Risk Factors and Conditions Associated with Top 10 Causes of Death**
   D1. Tobacco use, obesity rate, and related behaviors
   D2. Screening utilization rates

E. **Child Health**
   E1. Infant mortality rate
   E2. Low birth weight rates
   E3. Proportion of women who receive late or no prenatal care
   E4. Teen pregnancy rate

F. **Infectious Diseases**
   F1. Sexually transmitted infection incidence rate (chlamydia, gonorrhea, syphilis)
   F2. HIV incidence rate
   F3. Tuberculosis incidence rate

G. **Natural Environment**
   G1. Air quality annual rating

H. **Social Environment**
   H1. Violent crime rate
   H2. Child abuse rate
   H3. Housing affordability rate

I. **Resources Available to Address Community Health Needs (Federally Qualified Health Centers, School Clinics)**

desired information presented in a consistent format in various sections of the report in both text and graphic form. The proposed solutions for a community's unmet healthcare needs should at least meet the following criteria: feasibility, acceptability, and impact. The evaluator, policy maker, or healthcare planner should then consider alternative solutions and compare their merits based on these three criteria. A CHNA should also answer the question, "Why have critical needs not been met or remained unaddressed?"[15]

Witkin and Altschuld[11] have identified the following factors that affect whether a particular need of a population is addressed:

1. The size of the gap existing between the current and desired health status of a community
2. Factors that led to the emergence of a need in the first place and the degree of difficulty in addressing such factors
3. The seriousness of the consequences for various stakeholders if the need is not addressed
4. The economic, social, and political cost of implementing the proposed solutions

▶ 10.7 Planning for a Community Health Needs Assessment

Planning for a CHNA involves setting the objectives and goals of the study and specifying the scope of the study. Additionally, during the planning phase of a study, indicators of a specific need, whether a service or a resource, have to be explicitly identified. A CHNA can be a one-time stand-alone activity, or it can be a part of an ongoing cyclical planning process. Even when it is a one-time activity, it does not occur in a vacuum, but has some context and background in the organization's mission and the community's concerns. Therefore, planning and implementation of a needs assessment should include the involvement and participation of the community whose needs are being assessed. The leadership or executives who commission the study must commit themselves to using the findings and implementing the recommendations of the study. Unless there is an explicit and enduring commitment to using the finding of the study, a CHNA can be an exercise in futility.[22]

Key questions that should be asked at the onset of the study include the following:

1. What do we already know about the issue?
2. What more would we like to know?
3. What data are currently available?
4. Are those data sufficient and of good quality?
5. What additional data are needed?
6. How best can those additional data be generated?

▶ 10.8 Nature and Type of Data for a Community Health Needs Assessment

Two forms of data are collected in a CHNA: (1) quantitative historical data that are based on facts, and (2) qualitative data that reflect opinions or perceptions of those surveyed or interviewed.[11] Qualitative data can be collected through community surveys, focus group discussions, *key informant* interviews, and *nominal group* process. The kinds of data necessary for needs assessment and planning include the following:

1. Epidemiologic indicators of population health status, such as morbidity and mortality statistics (i.e., incidence and prevalence of disease data)
2. Health services utilization data, including hospital admissions and discharges and outpatient clinic visits per year
3. Socioeconomic data, including median income and the proportion of the population and the number of persons in the community who are below federal poverty level
4. Existing healthcare resources, including the number of hospitals and hospital beds and healthcare personnel of various cadres, such as doctors, nurses, dentists, and technicians
5. Data related to environment and living conditions, such as access to clean water, sanitation, and levels of air pollution

Descriptive data from specific geographic areas are used to identify the nature, frequency, and severity of health problems and the extent to which needs are met or remain unmet. Sociodemographic data also help in estimating need for specific services and resources. General social conditions such as housing, educational opportunities, employment, health insurance, environment, and measures of social stability and well-being are also helpful in making such estimates. All these factors combined provide an excellent picture of the socioeconomic conditions of the community.[21]

Analytic tools such as tables, charts, and graphs of trends in longitudinal data are helpful in getting a detailed profile of social and health-related indictors of a community and for making national, regional, and local comparisons.[21] Data to develop a community profile and to carry out comparative analyses are usually available from public sources, such as the Census Bureau, Centers for Disease Control and Prevention (CDC), and state and local health departments. However, one must be careful about the accuracy of various sources of data. More important, one must be careful about direct application of national or regional data to a small jurisdiction, such as a municipality or ZIP code. Demographic characteristics and morbidity and mortality rates or the incidence of a disease in a small community can be quite different from what is observed at a national or regional level. A review of literature to identify available survey instruments and other tools for health needs assessment found 31 instruments that had been used in 52 studies related to cancer, mental health, palliative care, cardiovascular disease, and multiple sclerosis.[23]

These instruments covered a range of approaches, from interviews to self-administered questionnaires.

The variables on which data are collected can also differ from one assessment to another and from one organization to the next. One example of CHNA and metrics used for the collection of relevant data comes from the Maryland Department of Health and Mental Hygiene. In 2011, the Primary Care Office of the Maryland Department of Health and Mental Hygiene looked at 29 different variables grouped under *health status indicators* and *healthcare access indicators* (**TABLE 10.3**) to assess the need for primary care services in the 23 counties and Baltimore jurisdiction of Maryland. The CDC has identified 42 metrics (**TABLE 10.4**) as the most commonly available indicators of population

TABLE 10.3 Health Status and Healthcare Access Indicators Used by the Primary Care Office of the Maryland Department of Health and Mental Hygiene

No.	Health Status Indicators	No.	Healthcare Access Indicators
1	Life expectancy	1	Population living in poverty
2	Self-reported health status	2	Affordability of doctor visits
3	Prevalence of obesity	3	Mammogram screenings level
4	Prevalence of hypertension	4	Pap smear screenings level
5	Prevalence of high cholesterol	5	Colonoscopy screening level
6	Prevalence of smoking	6	Flu shot prevalence
7	Prevalence of diabetes	7	Prenatal care in first trimester
8	Prevalence of asthma	8	Low-birth-weight infants
9	Anxiety disorder diagnosis	9	Dental visit in the past year
10	Depressive disorders diagnosis	10	Permanent tooth removal
11	HIV/AIDS rate	11	Insurance status
12	Total mortality rate	12	Medicaid enrollment
13	Infant mortality rate	13	Medicare enrollment
14	Heart disease mortality rate		
15	Stroke mortality rate		
16	Cancer mortality rate		

Modified from: Primary Care Office, Maryland Department of Health and Mental Hygiene. 2010 primary care needs assessment. October 2011. Accessed on July 10, 2017. http://phpa.dhmh .maryland.gov/IDEHASharedDocuments/PCO_Needs_Assessment_11_16_11.pdf

TABLE 10.4 Metrics for Community Health Needs Assessment

Health Outcome Metrics		Health Determinant and Correlate Metrics			
Mortality	**Morbidity**	**Health Care (Access & Quality)**	**Health Behaviors**	**Demographics & Social Environment**	**Physical Environment**
Mortality—leading causes of death	Obesity	Health insurance coverage	Tobacco use/smoking	Age	Air quality
Infant mortality	Low birth weight	Provider rates (PCPs, dentists)	Physical activity	Sex	Water quality
Injury-related mortality	Hospital utilization	Asthma-related hospitalization	Nutrition	Race/ethnicity	Housing
Motor vehicle mortality	Cancer rates		Unsafe sex	Income	
Suicide	Motor vehicle injury		Alcohol use	Poverty level	
Homicide	Overall health status		Seatbelt use	Educational attainment	
	STDs (chlamydia, gonorrhea, syphilis)		Immunizations and screenings	Employment status	
	AIDS			Foreign born	
	Tuberculosis			Homelessness	
				Language spoken at home	
				Marital status	
				Domestic violence and child abuse	
				Violence and crime	
				Social capital/social support	

Modified from: Centers for Disease Control and Prevention (CDC). Community health assessment for population health improvement: resource of most frequently recommended health outcomes and determinants, Atlanta, GA: Centers for Disease Control and Prevention; 2013. Available at: http://wwwn.cdc.gov/CommunityHealth/PDF/Final_CHAforPHI_508.pdf

health that can be used for CHNA at the level of a metropolitan statistical area, county, or census tract. Different measures of mortality and morbidity are listed under *health outcome metrics*, whereas *determinants of health metrics* are grouped under (1) *health care*, (2) *health behaviors*, (3) *demographic and social environment*, and (4) *physical environment*. Comparison of data on these metrics across different communities allows the development of a common understanding of factors that affect population health and promotes collaboration between different organizations.[12]

It is important to note that in the United States and some of the other developed countries, health status indicators such as incidence, longevity, disability, and especially mortality rates have become somewhat insensitive to increased availability of services and improvements in healthcare delivery. This is partly because of a relatively weak link between morbidity and healthcare delivery or between morbidity and mortality, and partly because of diminishing marginal impact of the healthcare system on further lowering mortality rates beyond a certain level. For example, reducing the infant mortality rate from 100 per 1,000 live births to 50 per 1,000 live births is considerably easier than reducing it from 8 per 1,000 live births to 4 per 1,000 live births. For that reason, behavioral health indicators such as obesity, smoking, alcohol and substance abuse, and environmental indicators, including air pollution levels, are now being viewed as more relevant to the assessment of population needs and more cost-effective strategies for improving population health.

▶ 10.9 Sources of Data for a CHNA

Schedule H of IRS is designed for hospitals and their suborganizations to provide information regarding activities, policies, and community benefits rendered during a given year. For this purpose, CHSI 2015 (Community Health Status Indicators 2015), an online interactive web application developed by the CDC, can be an extremely valuable tool.[24] This freely available web application can generate a comparative public health profile of any of the 3,143 counties in the United States with descriptive charts and graphs. Each county's profile can include information on morbidity, mortality, healthcare access and quality, health behaviors of the population, social factors such as economic condition and poverty, and the physical environment of the county in comparison with its peers. CHSI 2015 also shows peer counties on a nationwide

map with their comparative ranking on the indicator being examined. It also shows a summary page with a tabulated list of variables on which a given county may be performing better than, on a similar level to, or worse than its peer counties. For example, in 2016, Oklahoma County in Oklahoma, with an Alzheimer's disease mortality rate of 25.2 per 100,000 population, performed moderately and ranked 23rd in comparison with its peer counties; Richmond County in New York, with an Alzheimer's disease mortality rate of only 3.1 per 100,000, ranked number 1. Similarly, Cleveland County in Oklahoma, with a teen birth rate of 23.4 per 1,000 females aged 15–19, performed best and ranked number 1 as compared with its peer counties in the nation. In contrast, Pinal County in Arizona, with a teen birth rate of 55.9 per 100,000, performed the worst and ranked 28th in the same peer group.

Another extremely valuable source of community-level data on health-, economy-, education-, and environment-related variables is the *Community Commons* (www.chna.org) website where researchers, educators, planners, and others can freely generate customized data reports for CHNA or other purposes. Community Commons partners with the CDC, the Robert Wood Johnson Foundation, Kaiser Permanente, the American Heart Association, and the University of Missouri to provide a platform for readily accessible extensive data on health outcomes and various determinants of health. The website also allows comparison of current health status indicators of a community, state, or county with the U.S. Healthy People 2020 targets for a given health status indicator to assess how far along the state, county, or community is in achieving those targets. Through Community Commons, researchers can also access the Kaiser Permanente Community Health Needs Assessment (KP CHNA) hub, which also generates, at the click of a button, customized community health status reports. The Kaiser Permanente hub is specifically designed to help hospitals report community benefits to the IRS under the requirements of the Patient Protection and Affordable Care Act. This hub can also help planners, policy makers, and community organizations understand the drivers of health and prioritize healthcare needs.

Other sources of information, such as census data, hospital and physicians' office records, and data at public health agencies, and different methods of assessment, including data analysis, community surveys, and focus group discussions, provide complementary information for a comprehensive or targeted CHNA. Health information systems play a critical role in conducting needs assessment and health services planning by providing the necessary data.

Population health data are developed, collected, analyzed, and reported by the health information system. The scope and sophistication of the system depend on the resources of the organization that owns and operates the health information system. To avoid being drowned in a mountain of data, healthcare analysts and managers need to be selective in deciding what data they would want to collect and analyze with the help of available health information technology.

▶ 10.10 Priority Setting for Healthcare Needs

Priority setting for healthcare needs can occur in two stages. In the first stage, priorities are set in terms of broad needs—for example, the need for preventive services or the needs of those aged 65 years or older. In the second stage, priorities are subselected within the broad categories previously identified—say, preventive services (for example, preventive services can be educational activities or clinical services such as vaccinations). Wilkinson[19] has suggested that, among other things, the priority-setting process must consider the following points:

1. The resources, expertise, and likelihood of achieving a change
2. The cost-effectiveness of strategies to achieve specific objectives—that is, the proportionality of resources consumed to achieve a specific outcome
3. What are the perspectives of various stakeholders on the importance of different health-related issues and problems in the target population?
4. Which problems or issues are outside the sphere of influence or control of the organization conducting the needs assessment?

▶ 10.11 Community Health Needs Assessment After a Disaster

To mount an effective and timely response to a natural or manmade disaster in a small or large community, it is critical to gather accurate and reliable public health information in a quick, efficient, and inexpensive manner. To assist public health officials in gathering such information, the CDC has developed a toolkit called **Community Assessment for Public Health**

Emergency Response (CASPER).[25] Using this toolkit, public health officials can rapidly assess the health status and basic needs of the affected community and set priorities to allocate critical resources. Based on the rapid needs assessment (RNA) methods first developed by the World Health Organization in the 1970s, CASPER was developed by the CDC in 2009 and widely distributed to the public health community in the United States. The CASPER toolkit can also be used in nonemergency situations to assess the healthcare needs of a community, understand public health perceptions, and a conduct health impact assessment.

CASPER uses a two-stage cluster sampling method to obtain a representative sample for collecting household-level survey data with the help of an electronic or on-paper data collection instrument (questionnaire). The template for a two-page prototype questionnaire and sample questionnaires for a 10- to 15-minute interview are available from the CDC. In Stage I, using census data, 30 clusters or blocks are randomly identified and geo-mapped. In Stage II, seven housing units are identified through *simple random sampling* or *systematic random sampling* in each cluster for interviewing. Overall, 210 interviews are conducted to obtain necessary information from one adult per household who speaks for all members of the household.[25] **FIGURE 10.5** shows the steps involved in conducting a CASPER.

▶ 10.12 Assessment of Unmet Healthcare Needs—Market Analysis

Unmet need refers to a perceived (or scientifically demonstrated) healthcare need for which care is not provided.[26] A need can remain unmet if the service provided is insufficient in quantity or inappropriate in nature. The level of unmet need is frequently estimated through population surveys to learn how frequently individuals in a community forgo health care or experience hardship in accessing services. Long waiting times to receive care in one setting or another; inability to get primary, secondary, or tertiary levels of care; or inability to afford prescription medication are common examples of unmet healthcare needs. In most instances, individuals in the lower socioeconomic strata of a population report greater degree and frequency of unmet healthcare need.[17] For example, uninsured and poor individuals experience greater barriers to preventive services and treatment for chronic conditions than acute care, for

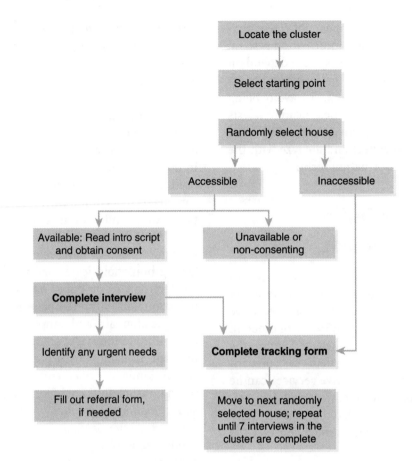

FIGURE 10.5 Steps involved in conducting a Community Assessment for Public Health Emergency Response (CASPER).

Reproduced from: Centers for Disease Control and Prevention (CDC). Community Assessment for Public Health Emergency Response (CASPER) toolkit. (2nd ed.). Atlanta, GA: Centers for Disease Control and Prevention; 2012.

which many turn to the emergency department of a nearby hospital.[2,26] Studies have also shown that uninsured individuals receive fewer screenings for cancer and cardiovascular risk factors, experience avoidable hospitalization, and are at a greater risk of death while hospitalized.[2] It is important to note that unmet healthcare need, especially in developed countries, is primarily a function of the socioeconomic characteristics of individuals rather than a reflection of the availability or supply of services. In the United States, for example, unmet healthcare needs of uninsured individuals have persisted for decades despite an adequate supply of healthcare resources, such as physicians and hospitals in the same geographic districts. In developing countries, on the other hand, unmet need is frequently the result of both the individuals' inability to pay for services and the society's inability to provide adequate services.[2,17]

In the United States, since 1984, one good source of data that has allowed researchers and policy makers insights into individuals' access to health services, self-reported risk factors and health status, and socioeconomic conditions is the Behavioral Risk Factor Surveillance System—a nationally representative survey conducted annually in all 50 states and the District of Columbia. Information on unmet healthcare needs in Canada is derived from the periodically conducted National Population Health Survey. In Europe, the Survey of Income and Living Conditions and the Survey of Health, Aging, and Retirement in Europe have been used in some studies to estimate the level of unmet healthcare need.

▶ 10.13 Estimation of Future Healthcare Needs

Estimation of future healthcare needs of a population must carefully focus on the need for preventive, therapeutic, and rehabilitative services and would involve the use of appropriate forecasting methods and historical data on past healthcare needs, utilization of services, and levels of unmet needs.[21]

Examples of preventive services include immunizations for infectious diseases; surveillance, early detection, and reporting systems; and screenings for chronic or latent infectious and noninfectious disorders that can benefit from early detection and intervention. Tuberculosis is an example of a chronic infectious disease for which screening can be done and may be warranted in some communities or populations. Colorectal cancer is an example of a latent condition for which colonoscopy screening every 10 years is recommended in men and women after age 50. Similarly, screening every 3 years for cancer of the cervix through a Pap smear in women between the ages of 21 and 65 years is recommended by the U.S. Preventive Services Task Force.[27]

For individual patients, these services are routinely provided in predominantly ambulatory care settings on a case-by-case basis. Healthcare administrators and policy makers in general do not have a good understanding of the need for, demand for, and utilization of these services. Healthcare managers would be hard pressed to know the degree to which the need for these services in various segments or subgroups of the community is being met in a given year and by whom. Based on previous years' utilization or billing data, healthcare managers may have an idea of the overall volume or market for a given service in a geographic area and their own market share. However, it is important to understand that utilization or billing data from a previous year do not accurately reflect the need for a particular service; it only reflects demand for that service in that geographic area.

Despite an estimation of the burden of various diseases in a community through available data on incidence and prevalence, an estimation of the burden of disability resulting from those disorders and the need for rehabilitative services is difficult to assess. Specific efforts have to be made to estimate the prevalence and degree of disability among the cases with varying levels of severity of a disease. Because of the underrecognition and underreporting of mental and behavioral disorders, the estimation of the need for psychiatric and behavioral services is even more challenging.

Examples of rehabilitative services include speech therapy and physical therapy in patients after a stroke or orthopedic surgery. Therapeutic services include the full range of ambulatory and inpatient services required to treat patients with acute, subacute, or chronic disorders that equally affect men and women of all ages or that selectively affect men, women, children, or the elderly.

Utilization data for various services can be gleaned from billing and medical claims data available from both public and private sources. In the United States, these sources can include third-party payers such as state Medicaid programs, Medicare, hospital discharge data sets available from state health departments, or publicly reported data available on platforms such as Medicare's Hospital Compare platform and Healthcare Cost and Utilization Project of the Agency for Healthcare Research and Quality. Some of these sources are discussed in the Healthcare Planning and Marketing chapter, see in the Sources of Epidemiologic Data section.

▶ 10.14 Forecasting Methods

Estimation of future healthcare needs in a population must rely on quantitative forecasting methods that employ historical or *time series* data from the same population or other populations that are similar in size, demographic characteristics, and morbidity and mortality profile to the population of interest. Techniques such as weighted moving averages, exponential smoothing, and regression models of healthcare utilization with trend analysis can be used for this purpose. Projections regarding the future healthcare needs of a population must also take into consideration prospects for changes in healthcare technology as well as in the social, political, financial, and legislative environment of the population.[21] A healthcare manager may or may not be called on to forecast independently the future healthcare needs of a population without the help of quantitatively trained analysts. However, a manager may certainly be called on to interpret the results, findings, and recommendations of analysts or consultants. Therefore, having some degree of familiarity with forecasting techniques is advisable for the healthcare manager. It should be noted that forecasting involves projections of both the quantity and the spectrum of services needed in the future—that is, what type of services would be needed in the next 2, 3, or 5 years, and in what quantity? By definition, forecasts are probabilistic in nature and have at least some margin of error. The quality of a forecast can only be determined after the fact, or *a posteriori*, and is not characterized in a binary fashion as accurate or inaccurate, but rather by the degree of error between the actual need (or demand) and the forecast.

A comprehensive CHNA can be a complex, slow, and time-consuming process that requires excellent analytic, communication, negotiating, and leadership skills on the part of those involved. Aside from the evidence and rationale provided by epidemiologic investigations and quantitative data, the priority setting process must take into consideration the competing interests, agendas, and expectations of various stakeholders. **BOX 10.2** provides a hypothetical example of a comprehensive community health needs assessment in an imaginary community.

BOX 10.2 Example of a Community Health Needs Assessment

Acknowledgment: The following hypothetical example of a model healthcare needs assessment is used with permission from the Catholic Health Association of the United States of America with some abridgement and reformatting.

NOTE: This example is abridged from Appendix G of the book titled Assessing & addressing community health needs.

Harris County Healthcare Needs Assessment–2012

Jointly conducted by St. Agnes Catholic Hospital, Ryan Community Hospital, and Harris County Health Department.

I. Executive Summary

During 2012, a community health needs assessment (CHNA) was jointly conducted by St. Agnes Catholic Hospital, Ryan Community Hospital, and the Harris County Health Department for the 100,000 residents of Harris County, Kansas. Harris County includes the county seat, Best City, a city of 50,000 residents located in the midst of rolling farmland in central Kansas. The two hospitals, St. Agnes Catholic Hospital and Ryan Community Hospital, serve this city and the surrounding rural area in Harris County.

II. Description of Community Served by the Hospitals

Harris County includes both urban and rural areas. The local economy is heavily agricultural. About 10 years ago, a chicken processing plant opened on the east side of Best City bringing new workers to the community and increasing its cultural diversity. The average annual family income for the city is currently $58,000. Those below the median income have been disproportionately impacted by the recession. The proportion of the population living below poverty has increased from 13% to 17% over the past decade. A map and demographic data including income levels, age, race/ethnicity, and educational attainment for the city and surrounding counties with a comparison with the state and national data are included in Attachment A.

III. Who Was Involved in Assessment

The healthcare needs assessment process was initiated and co-chaired by the two hospitals in collaboration with the County Health Department. The three entities provided roughly equal financial and in-kind support. The municipal departments, school district, and all agencies providing health or related services within the city were also invited to participate. To ensure input from persons with broad knowledge of the community, notices of all meetings were announced, as a public service, on the local radio station and posted in the local paper with a link to previous meeting minutes. Invitations were sent to organizations representing ethnic and patient-type groups, including the Spanish Club and the county mental health association. Staff from the public health department and faculty from Harris University collated and analyzed the public health data.

   Those who committed to participating in the assessment process and attending semi-monthly meetings became the 18 members of Harris County Health Assessment Team (CHAT), which continues to meet semi-monthly to assess progress and modify plans as needed. Attachment B to this assessment lists the CHAT members and all those who attended planning meetings during 2012.

IV. Description of the Assessment Process

The Harris County CHNA began with a review of the 2009 public health assessment conducted by the Harris County Health Department. Information in the previous assessment was updated with recent statistics from city, county, state, and national sources. New data sources were identified and incorporated, including the newly published County Health Rankings and additional data from both hospitals (discharge information and interviews with medical, social service, and ED staff). Recent health indicator data for comparisons were also collected from both Healthy People 2020 and the Kansas State Department of Health. These data were collated and presented with the assistance of faculty members from the Economics and the Social Services Departments at Harris University.

   The CHAT's initial review included analysis of trends and comparisons within the community and with other like-sized communities. Data were also compared with indicators established by Healthy People 2020 and by the Kansas State Department of Health. Based on this analysis, the CHAT, with assistance from Harris University, developed discussion topics for a variety of community engagements, including town hall meetings, interviews with key informants, and focus groups. A variety of community settings were selected with a special emphasis on those persons and areas most impacted by health disparities. Information from these forums was collated and presented to the CHAT. With the assistance of Harris University, a list of 20 community needs was developed (Attachment F). CHAT members agreed on a set of criteria to use to evaluate the list of 20 health needs identified through the fact-finding process. The criteria included:

1. The numbers of persons affected,
2. The seriousness of the issue,
3. Whether the health need particularly affected persons living in poverty or reflected health disparities, and
4. Availability of community resources to address the need.

Each team member used the criteria to rank the health needs. These individual results were then shared with the CHAT for discussion. Team members were then given an opportunity to revise their rankings. These individual rankings were then summed to produce a composite ranking. Information was widely disseminated in the local news with invitations for electronic responses. Several town hall meetings were held to discuss and affirm the selections. The prioritization process identified four priority issues for the community:

1. High school graduation rates
2. Access to health care for the uninsured and underinsured
3. Obesity rates
4. Teenage smoking

It should be noted that the assessment process identified some gaps in information. There was not, for example, good information about air quality for the city or the county. The CHAT also determined a need to have more information on the social determinants of some of the key health issues to address one of the overarching goals of Healthy People 2020 better.

V. Healthcare Needs Identified

The city and county have always prided themselves on the health status of the residents. Historical data collected from various sources by the Health Department have shown that on the average, the county has regularly met or exceeded most national benchmarks published by Healthy People and even met or exceeded the national objectives for a number of Healthy People indicators.

While morbidity and mortality data still demonstrate that the city and surrounding county are near the national benchmarks for most of the Healthy People 2020 indicators, a trend analysis detected a concerning decline in the high school graduation rate, an important determinant of future health status. Reanalysis of the data showed that there was a disparity in graduation rates. The East Side High School reported that 67% of 18 year olds in their district had graduated, while the West Side High School reported a graduation rate of 85%. Interviews with school representatives uncovered high absenteeism related to improperly controlled asthma that many considered a factor in the lower graduation rates. Analysis of public health data also found high rates of diabetes in the city and county, mirroring the high rates of disease at the national level and the increase in obesity rates in the county.

Although focus groups and interviews were new processes, it was noted that both picked up air quality complaints, especially near the chicken processing plant. There was also a concerning increase in two health risk factors as reported by the school district. While overall tobacco use in the community continues to decline, there appears to be a slight increase in smoking among teenagers. Further, childhood obesity rates are steadily increasing.

Both hospitals reported an increase in visits to their emergency departments and an increase in preventable hospitalizations. In the last three years alone, the costs of uncompensated care for uninsured and Medicaid patients increased by 33%. The hospitals estimated that about one third of the ED visits could be avoided if patients had adequate access to care.

VI. Community Resources Identified

The assessment identified a number of strong community assets (Attachment C), including the two hospitals and their community benefit programs, a community clinic, an adequate supply of primary care physicians and dentists, a public school system with active home and school associations, and numerous religious congregations.

VII. Assessments and Priorities

Assessment data are summarized in Attachment D. Attachment F lists all needs identified and describes the priority setting approach. CHAT members committed to focus on the affirmed priorities. In summary, priority needs identified were:

1. High school graduation rates
2. Access to health care for the uninsured and underinsured
3. Obesity rates
4. Teenage smoking

VIII. Next Steps

CHAT established separate teams to develop implementation strategies for each priority (Attachment F); leaders for each of the four teams also committed to continued service on CHAT. Each leader is responsible for:

1. Finding out what other community organizations are doing regarding the priority.
2. Organizing a team that includes both field professionals and representative community members.
3. Guiding the work of the team, including development of a work plan.
4. Establishing metrics including measurable outcomes indicators.
5. Assuring work is coordinated with other CHAT implementation teams.
6. Communicating appropriately with the community at large.

(continues)

BOX 10.2 Example of a Community Health Needs Assessment (continued)

CHAT is developing a community report card including metrics for both the city and the surrounding county to be published on an annual basis. CHAT is committed to conducting another comprehensive needs assessment in 3 years. CHAT will also be charged with attempting to fill the information gaps and with developing a better understanding of the social determinants of some of the health issues identified to address one of the overarching goals of Healthy People 2020 better. This assessment summary is available on the websites of the Harris County Health Department and St. Agnes and Ryan Community Hospitals. A copy can also be obtained by contacting the administrative offices of any of the three organizations.

- **Appendices**:

Attachment A.   Demographic data and maps
Attachment B.   List of participants with their affiliations
Attachment C.   Harris County resources/asset analysis
Attachment D.   Comparative health indicator data for Harris County and neighboring counties with trend projections
Attachment E.   Community input including dates and locations of meetings, interviews and list of community participants and Key Informants
Attachment F.   List of prioritized healthcare needs with description of prioritization process.

🔍 CASE STUDY 10.1: Healthcare Needs of the Homeless

Modified from: Baggett TP, O'Connell JJ, Singer DE, Rigotti NA. The unmet health care needs of homeless adults. Am J Public Health. 2010;100(7):1326–1333.

Every year, about 2.3 to 3.5 million people experience homelessness in the United States. A vast majority of homeless people have one or more health problems. The authors of this study used the Health Care for the Homeless (HCH) User Survey data for 2003 to understand the unmet needs of homeless adults in the United States. The federal HCH program funds about 205 grantees throughout the country and in Puerto Rico who serve more than 700,000 homeless people every year. The HCH User Survey carried out by the Research Triangle Institute staff used a three-stage sampling methodology to conduct in-person interviews of service recipients at 79 clinic sites. The authors analyzed interview data on utilization of health services in the preceding year by 966 respondents representing more than 436,000 homeless adult clinic users nationwide. They used a conceptual framework in which *realized access* to health services is considered to be a function of the following three factors: (1) predisposing factors, (2) enabling factors, and (3) need factors. Predisposing factors are defined as those characteristics of the individual that affect his or her "propensity for seeking healthcare services." Enabling factors are the ones that "facilitate or impede" healthcare utilization. Need factors are the medical conditions for which health care may be required.[28] The outcome of interest (i.e., unmet need) was defined in terms of unrealized access or lack of utilization of (1) medical or surgical care, (2) prescription medication, (3) mental health care or counseling, (4) eye care, and (5) dental care. The authors conducted statistical analysis of data from 966 interviews (logistic regression models) to identify factors independently associated with unmet need (i.e., nonutilization) for each of the five services. **TABLE 10.5** shows factors associated with unmet need for each of the five services in the preceding 1 year.

Questions

Question 1. How much higher was the unmet need for prescription medication among older homeless individuals as compared with those aged 18–29 years? Answer with the help of data shown in Table 10.5.

Question 2. What was the level of unmet need for medical or surgical care among homeless veterans as compared with all other homeless individuals? Answer with the help of data shown in Table 10.5.

Question 3. Did homeless individuals who had history of out-of-home placement as a minor have greater or lesser unmet need for the five services as compared with other homeless individuals in the study? Answer with the help of data shown in Table 10.5.

Question 4. How did being uninsured affect the level of unmet need for each of the five services? Answer with the help of data shown in Table 10.5.

Question 5. How did food insufficiency affect the level of unmet need for each of the five services? Answer with the help of data shown in Table 10.5.

TABLE 10.5 Factors Associated With Past-Year Unmet Need for Medical or Surgical Care, Prescription Medications, Mental Health Care, Eyeglasses, and Dental Care Among Homeless U.S. Adults: Health Care for the Homeless User Survey, 2003

	Unmet Need for Medical or Surgical Care, AOR (95% CI)[a]	Unmet Need for Prescription Medications, AOR (95% CI)[a]	Unmet Need for Mental Health Care, AOR (95% CI)[a]	Unmet Need for Eyeglasses, AOR (95% CI)[a]	Unmet Need for Dental Care, AOR (95% CI)[a]
Predisposing Factors					
Age in years					
18–29 (Ref)	1.00	1.00	1.00	1.00	1.00
30–44	1.04 (0.42 – 2.57)	2.71* (1.20 – 6.13)	1.61 (0.47 – 5.53)	0.94 (0.51 – 1.73)	1.21 (0.38 – 3.87)
≥45	1.20 (0.58 – 2.52)	2.80* (1.47 – 5.34)	1.11 (0.38 – 3.21)	1.66 (0.97 – 2.84)	0.96 (0.34 – 2.70)
Male	0.91 (0.34 – 2.42)	0.86 (0.36 – 2.03)	0.57 (0.32 – 1.02)	0.60 (0.35 – 1.03)	0.72 (0.47 – 1.09)
Race/ethnicity					
White, non-Hispanic (Reference)	1.00	1.00	1.00	1.00	1.00
Black, non-Hispanic	0.90 (0.60 – 1.35)	0.52 (0.25 – 1.09)	1.28 (0.75 – 2.20)	0.80 (0.45 – 1.44)	1.38 (0.81 – 2.34)
Hispanic/other	1.00 (0.47 – 2.13)	0.61 (0.29 – 1.30)	2.03* (1.17 – 3.51)	0.63 (0.29 – 1.36)	1.63 (0.77 – 3.45)
Veteran	1.76* (1.14 – 2.70)	0.74 (0.29 – 1.85)	0.71 (0.22 – 2.33)	2.00 (0.90 – 4.44)	1.42 (0.85 – 2.38)
Married/partnered	0.83 (0.43 – 1.60)	0.78 (0.41 – 1.48)	0.08* (0.02 – 0.28)	1.13 (0.51 – 2.47)	0.98 (0.49 – 1.97)
High school diploma or higher	1.07 (0.52 – 2.18)	1.06 (0.47 – 2.40)	1.25 (0.59 – 2.65)	0.58* (0.35 – 0.95)	1.05 (0.62 – 1.76)

(continues)

TABLE 10.5 Factors Associated With Past-Year Unmet Need for Medical or Surgical Care, Prescription Medications, Mental Health Care, Eyeglasses, and Dental Care Among Homeless U.S. Adults: Health Care for the Homeless User Survey, 2003 *(continued)*

	Unmet Need for Medical or Surgical Care, AOR (95% CI)[a]	Unmet Need for Prescription Medications, AOR (95% CI)[a]	Unmet Need for Mental Health Care, AOR (95% CI)[a]	Unmet Need for Eyeglasses, AOR (95% CI)[a]	Unmet Need for Dental Care, AOR (95% CI)[a]
Predisposing Factors					
Out-of-home placement as a minor[b]	2.52* (1.80 – 3.52)	1.71* (1.08 – 2.73)	1.44 (0.77 – 2.68)	1.10 (0.63 – 1.91)	0.90 (0.54 – 1.50)
Two or more homeless episodes at least 30 days in duration	0.92 (0.65 – 1.29)	0.85 (0.49 – 1.47)	0.95 (0.49 – 1.83)	1.17 (0.70 – 1.95)	1.26 (0.72 – 2.20)
Physical/sexual assault in past year	0.91 (0.49 – 1.67)	2.26* (1.44 – 3.55)	1.97* (1.13 – 3.42)	1.22 (0.78 – 1.93)	0.77 (0.38 – 1.54)
Substance abuse in past year	0.96 (0.40 – 2.31)	1.06 (0.56 – 2.01)	1.10 (0.68 – 1.77)	1.26 (0.82 – 1.96)	1.36 (0.76 – 2.43)
Mental illness history	1.18 (0.51 – 2.76)	1.79 (0.91 – 3.51)	2.58* (1.27 – 5.23)	1.83* (1.14 – 2.93)	1.04 (0.53 – 2.04)
Enabling Factors					
No usual source of care	1.72 (0.98 – 3.04)	2.16 (0.79 – 5.88)	3.36* (1.92 – 5.89)	0.89 (0.38 – 2.07)	1.17 (0.47 – 2.92)
Uninsured	1.75* (1.14 – 2.69)	1.94* (1.26 – 3.00)	2.03* (1.08 – 3.82)	1.72* (1.10 – 2.67)	1.08 (0.58 – 1.99)
Employment in past year	1.70* (1.22 – 2.37)	1.60* (1.09 – 2.35)	0.84 (0.45 – 1.57)	1.48 (0.87 – 2.52)	1.22 (0.75 – 2.00)
Food insufficiency[c]	2.06* (1.19 – 3.57)	1.61* (1.04 – 2.50)	1.55* (1.02 – 2.38)	1.11 (0.58 – 2.13)	1.06 (0.65 – 1.72)
Vision impairment	1.11 (0.59 – 2.09)	1.48 (0.86 – 2.56)	2.17* (1.17 – 4.01)	1.88* (1.16 – 3.04)	1.81* (1.25 – 2.63)
Need Factors					
No. of medical comorbidities[d]					
0 (Reference)	1.00	1.00	1.00	1.00	1.00

1	2.22* (1.08 – 4.52)	1.46 (0.88 – 2.44)	1.57 (0.70 – 3.56)	1.47 (0.93 – 2.32)	1.07 (0.63 – 1.83)
≥2	3.44* (1.61 – 7.36)	2.82* (1.39 – 5.73)	1.85 (0.61 – 5.57)	1.63 (0.89 – 2.97)	1.20 (0.57 – 2.54)
Dental problem in past year	—	—	—	—	2.97* (1.89 – 4.67)

AOR: adjusted odds ratio; CI: confidence interval. Ellipses indicate that the factor was not applicable for that need.
[a]Adjusted for all of the variables presented, via multivariable logistic regression.
[b]Defined as placement into foster care, a group home, or an institution before the age of 18 years.
[c]Defined as "sometimes" or "often" not getting enough food to eat.
[d]Medical comorbidities included hypertension, diabetes, cardiovascular disease (coronary artery disease or stroke), obstructive lung disease (asthma or chronic obstructive pulmonary disease), HIV infection, cancer, kidney disease, liver disease, and arthritis or past-year chronic joint problems.
*$P < .05$.

Reprinted with permission from: Baggett TP, O'Connell JJ, Singer DE, Rigotti NA. The unmet health care needs of homeless adults. Am J Public Health, 100(7):1326–1333. Copyright © 2010.

○ CASE STUDY 10.2: *Impact of Unmet Healthcare Needs*

Modified from: Hargreaves DS, Bliott MN, Viner RM, Richmond T, Schuster MA. Unmet health care need in U.S. adolescents and adult health outcomes. Pediatrics. 2015;136(3). Accessed July 10, 2017. http://pediatrics.aappublications.org/content/pediatrics/136/3/513.full.pdf

In this study, Hargreaves et al. used survey data collected in 1994/1995 and 2008 in phases I and IV of the National Longitudinal Study of Adolescent to Adult Health to examine the effect of unmet healthcare needs in adolescence on self-reported health outcomes in adult life. Data for 14,800 subjects who participated in the study as adolescents (mean age 15.9 years) in 1994/1995 and as adults in 2008 were analyzed through logistic regression models. The following five self-reported measures of health were used as dichotomous (Yes/No) health outcomes or dependent variables in logistic regression analyses: (1) fair or poor general health, (2) functional impairment, (3) time off from work or school, (4) depressive symptoms, and (5) suicidal ideation. The statistical analyses were adjusted for the potential effects of baseline health status in 1994/1995, health insurance status, age, race, gender, parents' education, and family income in 1994/1995. The researchers hypothesized that after adjusting for these factors, the odds (risk) of adverse health outcomes such as functional impairment or depressive symptoms would be higher among those who had reported unmet healthcare needs in adolescence as compared with those who did not have any unmet healthcare needs. The presence or absence of unmet healthcare needs was determined in the 1994/1995 adolescent survey by asking the participants, "Has there been any time over the past year when you thought you should get medical care, but you did not?" Subjects, who responded Yes to this question were asked to indicate the number one reason for not getting medical care. In the analysis, these reasons were divided into the following four categories: (1) cost; (2) nonfinancial access-related factors; (3) perceived negative consequences of accessing health care; and (4) perceived low importance of the health problem. First, the prevalence of unmet needs and health outcomes was calculated. Next, logistic regression models were developed to examine the association of unmet needs with each of the health outcomes. **TABLES 10.6** and **10.7** show some of the study results.

Questions

Question 1. In Table 10.6, was the prevalence of unmet healthcare need among different racial/ethnic groups substantially different? Can we make such an assessment with confidence?

Question 2. In Table 10.6, what effect did insurance status have on the prevalence of unmet healthcare need?

Question 3. In Table 10.6, did household income and the level of parental education have any effect on the prevalence of unmet healthcare need?

Question 4. Were the overall health outcomes of those with unmet healthcare need better or worse than those with no unmet healthcare needs? Explain your answer with the help of data shown in Table 10.7.

Question 5. Were those with unmet healthcare need more or less likely to have depressive symptoms and suicide ideation as compared with those with no unmet healthcare need? Explain your answer with the help of data shown in Table 10.7.

(continues)

TABLE 10.6 Sample Description and Prevalence of Unmet Healthcare Need, 1994/1995

Characteristic	N	%	Prevalence of Unmet Healthcare Need (%)
Total number of participants	14,800	100.0	19.2
Gender			
Male	6,932	46.8	18.3
Female	7,866	53.2	20.1
Total	14,798	100.0	
Year of Birth			
1974–1977	3,694	25.0	24.6
1978–1979	5,753	38.9	21.2
1980–1984	5,343	36.1	14.3
Total	14,790	100.0	
Race/Ethnicity			
Hispanic	2,343	15.9	20.7
Non-Hispanic white	7,877	53.3	17.6
Non-Hispanic black	2,978	20.2	23.1
Other/mixed	1,575	10.7	22.5
Total	14,773	100.0	
Insurance Status in 1994/1995			
Medicaid/Medicare	1,183	9.6	17.2
Individual/group (e.g., Blue Cross, Cigna)	6,293	50.8	17.0
Prepaid (e.g., HMO/CHAMPUS*)	2,883	23.3	18.3
Other	505	4.1	21.3
None	1,528	12.3	24.1
Total	12,392	100.0	

Household Income, $			
Low (<20,000 per year)	2,285	20.4	21.5
Medium (20,000–49,000 per year)	4,712	42.0	17.9
High (≥50 000 per year)	4,218	37.6	16.9
Total	11,215	100.0	
Parental Education			
Did not graduate high school	2,148	16.9	20.4
High school diploma or equivalent	3,739	29.5	19.4
Some college/university	3,749	29.6	16.9
Graduated college/university	3,053	24.1	17.0
Total	12,689	100.0	

*CHAMPUS: Civilian Health and Medical Program of the Uniformed Services; HMO: health maintenance organization
N: number of observations in each category.
Reproduced with permission from: Hargreaves DS, Bliott MN, Viner RM, Richmond T, Schuster MA. Unmet health care need in U.S. adolescents and adult health outcomes. Pediatrics. 2015; 136(3). Accessed July 10, 2017. Copyright © 2015 by the AAP.

TABLE 10.7 Prevalence of Adverse Health Outcomes in 2008 According to Unmet Healthcare Need in 1994/1995

Health Outcome	No Unmet Need	Any Unmet Need	P
Fair/poor general health	8.7%	11.9%	<.001
Functional impairment	8.5%	12.0%	<.001
Missed school/work	17.4%	21.3%	<.001
Depressive symptoms	19.3%	28.1%	<.001
Suicidal ideation	6.6%	9.7%	<.001

Reprinted with permission from: Hargreaves DS, Bliott MN, Viner RM, Richmond T, Schuster MA. Unmet health care need in U.S. adolescents and adult health outcomes. Pediatrics. 2015; 136(3). Accessed July 10, 2017. Copyright © 2015 by the AAP.

▶ 10.15 Summary

Community health needs assessment is an important strategic activity for healthcare organizations. A number of theoretical models with common principles and methodological elements are available to guide those who aspire to conduct a CHNA. This chapter describes the steps that should be taken in a logical fashion to conduct a scientifically rigorous needs assessment to produce results that are valid and recommendations that are appropriate to meet those needs. The needs of all communities are continuously evolving and changing. Therefore, needs assessment is an iterative process to be undertaken periodically rather than done as a one-time activity. Successful CHNA is a team effort rather than a solo endeavor. Organizations that want to be fully immersed in their communities can do so by periodically engaging in a participatory community-based needs assessment.

To that end, it is important to develop and support a team that has adequate community representation. Community participation in this activity not only brings to attention important community priorities and concerns but also lends a degree of legitimacy to this effort and an opportunity to tap into valuable communal resources. Many organizations invest resources in developing programs and services that are symbolically appealing but that are not steeped in reality and fail to meet the needs of a community. It is obligatory on the part of organizational leaders to put together a team of skilled professionals capable of conducting a first-rate CHNA. The skills to conduct a methodologically sound CHNA can be developed over time and improved with practice. For a successful healthcare manager, it is well worth the time and effort to develop those skills. This chapter provides the healthcare manager with necessary tools to get on the path of developing those skills.

References

1. Wier LM, Merrill CT, Elixhauser A. Hospital stays among people living in the poorest communities, 2006. Healthcare Cost and Utilization Project: Statistical Brief No. 73. National Health Disparities Report. Rockville, MD: Agency for Healthcare Research and Quality; 2008.

2. Ayanian JZ, Weissman JS, Schneider EC, Ginsburg JA, Zaslavsky AM. Unmet health needs of uninsured adults in the United States. JAMA. 2000;284(16):2061–2069.

3. Robert Wood Johnson Foundation. Health policy brief: achieving equity in health. Health Aff. 2011 Oct 6 [cited 2018 May 16]. Available from: http://healthaffairs.org/healthpolicybriefs/brief_pdfs/healthpolicybrief_53.pdf

4. Wright J, Williams R, Wilkinson JR. Development and importance of health needs Assessment. BMJ. 1998;316: 1310–1313.

5. Williams R, Wright J. Epidemiologic issues in health needs assessment. BMJ. 1998;316:1379–1382.

6. Lopez A.D., Mathers C.D., Ezzati M., Jamison D.T., Murray C.J.L. Global and regional burden of disease and risk factors, 2001: systematic analysis of population health data. Lancet, 367(9524): 1747-1757. 2006.

7. Oxford Online Dictionary. Need. Oxford University Press [cited 2018 May 16]. Available at: https://en.oxforddictionaries.com/definition/need

8. Oxford Online Dictionary. Demand. Oxford University Press [cited 2018 May 16]. Available from: https://en.oxforddictionaries.com/definition/demand

9. Stevens A, Gillam S. Needs assessment: from theory to practice. BMJ. 1998;316:1448–1452.

10. Meghan H, Shivji A, De Sousa T, Cohen R. The 2015 Annual Homeless Assessment Report (AHAR) to Congress. The U.S. Department of Housing and Urban Development. 2015 [cited 2018 May 16]. Available from: https://www.hudexchange.info/resources/documents/2015-AHAR-Part-1.pdf

11. Witkin BR, Altschuld JW. Planning and conducting needs assessment: a practical guide. Thousand Oaks, CA: SAGE; 1995.

12. Centers for Disease Control and Prevention. Community health assessment for population health improvement: resource of most frequently recommended health outcomes and determinants. Atlanta: Centers for Disease Control and Prevention; 2013 [cited 2018 May 16]. Available from: http://c.ymcdn.com/sites/www.cste.org/resource/resmgr/CrossCuttingI/FinalCHAforPHI508.pdf

13. Catholic Health Association. Assessing and addressing community health needs. 2013 [cited 2018 May 16]. Available from: https://www.chausa.org/docs/default-source/general-files/cb_assessingaddressing-pdf.pdf?sfvrsn=4

14. Bilton M. Executive briefing 3: community health needs assessment. Trustee. October 2011 [cited 2018 Mar 15]. Available at: http://www.hospitalalliancetn.com/hpdf/CHNA%20Executive%20Briefing.pdf

15. Myers S, Stoto MA. Criteria for assessing the usefulness of community health assessments: a literature review. Technical report. Santa Monica, CA: RAND Corporation; 2006 [cited 2018 May 16]. Available from: http://www.rand.org/content/dam/rand/pubs/technical_reports/2006/RAND_TR314.pdf

16. Wilkins K, Nsubuga P, Mendlein J, Mercer D, Pappaioanou M. The Data for Decision Making project: assessment of surveillance systems in developing countries to improve access to public health information. J R Inst Public Health. 2008;122:914–922.

17. Allin S, Grignon M, Le Grand J. Subjective unmet need and utilization of health care services in Canada: What are the equity implications? Soc Sci Med. 2010; 70:465–472.

18. Wang F, Luo W. Assessing spatial and nonspatial factors for healthcare access: toward an integrated approach to defining health professional shortage areas. Health Place. 2005;11:131–146.

19. Wilkinson JR. Assessment in primary care: practical issues and possible approaches. BMJ. 1998;316(7143):1524–1528.

20. Institute of Medicine. The future of public health. Washington DC: National Academy Press; 1988.

21. Hymen HH. Health planning: a systematic approach. 2nd ed. Rockville, MD: Aspen Systems Corporation; 1982.

22. Jordan J, Dowswell T, Harrison S, Lilford RJ, Mort M. Whose priorities? Listening to users and the public. BMJ. 1998;316:1668–1670.

23. Asadi-Lari M, Gray D. Health needs assessment tools: progress and potential. Int J Technol Assess Health Care. 2005;21(3):288–297.

24. Centers for Disease Control and Prevention. Community health status indicators: CHSI 2015 [cited 2018 May 16]. Available from: https://www.cdc.gov/ophss/csels/dphid/CHSI .html

25. Centers for Disease Control and Prevention. Community Assessment for Public Health Emergency Response (CASPER) toolkit. 2nd ed. Atlanta: Centers for Disease Control and Prevention; 2012.

26. Bryant T, Leaver C, Dunn J. Unmet healthcare need, gender, and health inequalities in Canada. Health Policy. 2009;91:24–32.

27. United States Preventive Services Taskforce. Cervical cancer screening. 2012 [cited 2017 Jul 27]. Available from: https:// www.uspreventiveservicestaskforce.org/Page/Document /UpdateSummaryFinal/cervical-cancer-screening

28. Baggett TP, O'Connell JJ, Singer DE, Rigotti NA. The unmet health care needs of homeless adults. Am J Public Health. 2010;100(7):1326–1333.

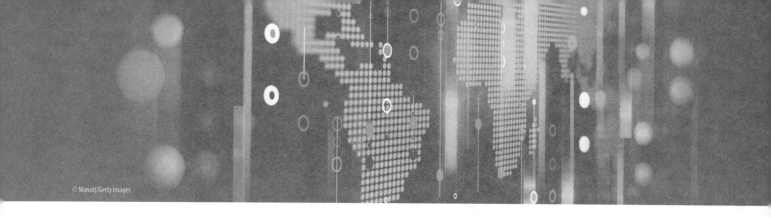

CHAPTER 11

Healthcare Planning and Marketing

LEARNING OBJECTIVES

Having mastered the materials in this chapter, the student will be able to:

1. Set the boundaries or parameters of a geographic market.
2. Compare and contrast various methods of setting the boundaries of a geographic market.
3. Estimate the service area or geographic market of a hospital or a group of hospitals.
4. Estimate the market share of a healthcare provider and identify its competitors.
5. Measure the degree of market concentration and competition in a geographic market.
6. Explain how the Health Resources and Services Administration designates populations or geographic areas as Medically Underserved or Health Professional Shortage Areas.

CHAPTER OUTLINE

11.1 Introduction
11.2 Definition and Purpose of Planning
11.3 Determinants of Geographic Markets and Service Areas
11.4 Estimation of Geographic Markets and Service Areas
11.5 Estimation of Service Area and Market Share: Hospital Administrator Perspective
    11.5.1 Expanding Radius Method
    11.5.2 Contiguous Zip Codes Method
    11.5.3 Estimation of Market Share
11.6 Estimation of a Geographic Market: Policy Maker Perspective
    11.6.1 Geopolitical Boundaries Approach
    11.6.2 Distance Between Hospitals: Radius and Hospital Cluster Approach

11.6.3 Elzinga–Hogarty Test Approach
11.6.4 Hospital Clustering Based on Patient Origin Data
11.7 Measuring the Level of Competition in a Geographic Market
11.8 Priority Setting and the Role of Healthy People
11.9 Small Area Health Planning
11.10 Facility Location Planning
11.11 Certificate of Need Programs
11.12 Designation of Health Professional Shortage Areas
11.13 Determinants of Access to Health Services
11.14 Sources of Epidemiologic Data
    11.14.1 State Inpatient Databases
    11.14.2 State Emergency Department Databases

11.14.3 State Ambulatory Surgery and Services Databases
11.14.4 National Inpatient Sample
11.14.5 Kids' Inpatient Database
11.14.6 National Emergency Department Sample
11.15 Healthcare Marketing
11.15.1 Definition, Scope, and Purpose of Marketing

11.15.2 Digital Marketing and Use of Social Media
11.15.3 Use of Big Data in Healthcare Marketing
Exercise 11.1
Exercise 11.2
Case Study 11.1 – Example of Regional Market Analysis
Case Study 11.2 – Planning for Mental Health Services
11.16 Summary

KEY TERMS

Commitment index
Elzinga–Hogarty test
Geographic market
Health Professional Shortage Areas

Herfindahl–Hirschman index
Little In From Outside (LIFO)
Little Out from Inside (LOFI)
Market share
Medically Underserved Areas

Medically Underserved Populations
Planning
Relevance index
Service area

▶ 11.1 Introduction

Experienced healthcare managers routinely engage in estimating the geographic boundaries of their primary and secondary service areas, the degree of competition in the marketplace and market share held by different providers, utilization patterns and growth potential for various services, availability of services, and patient preference. Increasingly, healthcare managers are being called on to assess the healthcare needs of communities they serve, show the extent to which they are meeting those needs, and demonstrate how they plan to address the unmet need for various services. The dynamic nature of the healthcare marketplace also requires managers to periodically assess the situation and develop new plans. To carry out these activities effectively, healthcare managers need the necessary tools and skills.

An important objective of the application of epidemiologic data in healthcare planning is to establish a cohesive and coordinated system of care in which different tiers represent a hierarchy of technologies and complexity of skills. The establishment of such a system is essential to reduce inefficiency, duplication, and confusion. A system of care in which stand-alone independent facilities or integrated multifacility systems compete for market share does not lend itself to the highest levels of efficiency and effectiveness that can be attained through coordination and cooperation rather than competition. However, in both competitive and collaborative environments, there is a great need to use epidemiologic data to guide and support administrative decisions such as planning of new services, merger or divestiture of existing services, and strategic

responses to evolving market conditions. Epidemiologic data related to the prevalence and incidence of morbidity, mortality, and disability allow estimation of future demand for various services. Projections regarding anticipated volume of patients allow healthcare managers to estimate their own market share for existing services and have a better understanding of the segments of the market held by other providers.

Section V of the American College of Healthcare Executives (ACHE) Code of Ethics, titled The Healthcare Executive's Responsibilities to Community and Society, states the following:[1]

"The healthcare executive shall:

1. Work to identify and meet the healthcare needs of the community;
2. Work to support access to healthcare services for all people;
3. Encourage and participate in public dialogue on healthcare policy issues, and advocate solutions that will improve health status and promote quality health care;
4. Apply short- and long-term assessments to management decisions affecting both community and society; and
5. Provide prospective patients and others with adequate and accurate information, enabling them to make enlightened decisions regarding services."

These clauses in the ACHE Code of Ethics indicate that the work of a healthcare manager involves collaboration with the community and policy makers to assess the healthcare needs of the community and participate in the planning process to meet those needs. This chapter is designed to help current and future healthcare managers in developing necessary skills for community health planning, assessing population health needs, and understanding the boundaries and characteristics of geographic markets.

▶ 11.2 Definition and Purpose of Planning

Some define **planning** as "rational future oriented actions."[2] Another definition declares planning to be "an organized intelligent effort to develop flexible patterns of action to meet the uncertainties of the future."[3] Davidoff and Reiner[4] have defined planning as "a process for determining appropriate future action through a sequence of choices." In other words, planning is the process by which a course of action is selected to achieve specific outcomes. Some planners make a distinction between problem-oriented planning and goal-oriented planning, whereas others debate whether the planning process should put more emphasis on means or on outcomes and goals. Regardless of such theoretical debates, it is generally understood that planning for any future action must have the following two essential elements: (1) rationality of choices and (2) specification of expected outcomes.

By definition, the word *decision* implies availability and examination of two or more alternatives and selection of the most desirable course of action. The selection of a course of action, however, cannot be made willy-nilly or arbitrarily; rather, it must be based on some explicit criteria that would establish the suitability or "goodness" of the decision. Clearly, every decision is subject to prevailing conditions in the internal and external environment of an organization and the assumptions made by the decision maker regarding future changes in the environment. If predictions regarding future conditions in the social, political, demographic, or economic conditions in the external environment or operative conditions within the organization prove to be erroneous, the outcomes of the chosen course of action may not turn out to be favorable for the organization and its stakeholders. Although the purpose of planning is to mitigate risk and prepare for the future, it is not an exact science. Therefore, even most carefully developed plans cannot be guaranteed to achieve specified targets or intended outcomes—hence the age-old adages, "the best laid plans of mice and men. . ." and "man proposes, God disposes."

Notably, health services planning is different from health policy analysis. Policy analysis deals with the political aspects of decision making through quantitative analytic tools and attempts to understand the ramifications of ideological positions taken by decision makers. Health services planning converts health policies into concrete programs that can be implemented to achieve the desired result of a policy. In operational terms, healthcare planning involves identification of the problem, understanding the root causes of the problem, collecting and analyzing data related to those causes, formulating goals, identifying alternative strategies, defining a time frame, implementing programs, and concluding with the measurement and evaluation of outcomes.[2]

▶ 11.3 Determinants of Geographic Markets and Service Areas

The delineation of a geographic market for health services planning is different from the delineation of the **geographic market** or **service area** of a healthcare provider. The former deals with a specific geographic district and examines the question of which providers most individuals in this area seek healthcare from, and which healthcare providers operate in this geographic district. The latter looks at a healthcare provider, such as a hospital or a multispecialty group practice, and examines which areas most of the patients of this provider come from and who its competitors are.

The geographic market or service area of a healthcare provider depends on a number of factors, including the urban or rural location, the size of the facility in terms of the number of beds, the specialized nature and spectrum of services, the quality and price of services, and the number of other similar facilities in the area. The geographic market of a healthcare provider can be arbitrarily divided into *primary* and *secondary* service areas depending on the intensity and frequency of use by residents of different communities or geographic districts. The overall service area of a healthcare provider can be relatively small, such as a single county or a cluster of ZIP codes, or it can encompass multiple counties and dozens, if not hundreds, of ZIP codes. In most instances, there is a direct relationship between the size or resources of a healthcare provider and the size of its service area. In contrast, there is usually an inverse relationship between the size of a geographic area and the market share of a particular provider. Often, providers of general services draw most patients locally, whereas providers of specialty services draw patients from relatively larger areas and longer distances. The estimation of geographic market or service area of a healthcare provider can be based on the total number of patients, patient visits, number of admissions or discharges, bed days, or total revenues. In the case of hospitals, estimation of service area is mostly based on the number of admissions or discharges originating from a given ZIP code or a cluster of ZIP codes.

Delineating the geographic markets or service areas of healthcare providers has become more complex since the advent of the managed care system in the United States. The service area of a provider is not only determined by the preferences of patients based on travel time, perceived quality of care, or history of association with a provider, but also by the nature of insurance coverage and financial incentives provided by an insurance carrier or a third-party payer. Because of negotiated price arrangements with healthcare providers, managed care plans such as health maintenance organizations (HMOs) and preferred provider organizations (PPOs) use financial incentives to steer their members in the direction of network providers.[5]

Consequently, patient origination data from hospital admissions and discharge records do not accurately reflect patients' choice of providers or the ability of a provider to capture a geographic market. When faced with financial incentives, insured patients demonstrate greater willingness to travel longer distances or seek care from network providers with whom they previously may not have had a relationship. In the absence of financial penalties imposed by insurance carriers to discourage the use of *out-of-network* providers, some patients may opt for providers geographically close to their residence, whereas others may choose to travel longer distances to go to a preferred place of care. Because of the ever-changing nature of health insurance markets and evolving demographic characteristics of populations, geographic markets and service areas change over time and are subject to fluctuating social, political, and economic conditions. Likewise, patient flow patterns to healthcare facilities during a given period are not determined by geopolitical boundaries but result from the interaction of economic forces and socioeconomic conditions.

In research literature,[6,7] the proportion of patients from an area who use a particular hospital is called the **relevance index**. Essentially, this index indicates the degree to which a healthcare provider (hospital X) is "relevant" to the needs of community Y.[8] For example, if only 10% of patients from community Y are admitted at hospital X, then the hospital is minimally relevant to community Y's needs. However, if 50% of patients from this ZIP code or county are admitted at hospital X, then it is highly relevant to the needs of the community. On the other hand, the proportion of

all patients admitted to or discharged from hospital X who originated from a specific area, such as county Y, is called the **commitment index**. Simply put, this index reflects the degree to which hospital X is "committed" to community Y.

▶ 11.4 Estimation of Geographic Markets and Service Areas

Market areas for health services, especially those for hospitals, can be examined from two different perspectives: (1) the perspective of a hospital administrator and (2) the perspective of a planner or a policy maker. Hospital administrators are interested in answering the following questions:

1. What is the primary service area or geographic market of my hospital (i.e., where are most of the patients admitted at my hospital coming from)?
2. How much market share does my hospital have (i.e., of all the patients in my hospital's primary service area, what proportion are being admitted at my hospital)?
3. Which hospitals are my competitors, and how much market share does each of them have from this geographic market?

It is necessary for hospital administrators to have answers to these three questions before developing strategies to maintain and enhance the market share for a specific service. Healthcare planners and policy makers, on the other hand, are concerned about the adequate supply of health services to meet demand. Their concerns are based on the need to ensure that there is neither a shortage nor oversupply of services. Both of these scenarios are problematic because of either inadequate access, or waste of resources and out-of-control healthcare costs. Policy makers are also interested in understanding the comparative characteristics of different geographic markets, such as healthcare costs in one area as compared with another. Thus, policy makers need answers to the following questions:

1. What are the boundaries or the size of a particular healthcare market?
2. Which hospitals compete in this geographic market and how much market share does each of them have?

Because of the difference in health administrators' and policy makers' perspectives and differences in the nature of questions they want answered, different methods have been developed to define healthcare markets. We discuss these approaches in the following sections. It is important to note that, depending on the setting in which a given health administrator or a policy maker might be operating, data required to determine the size of a geographic market and the market share of each healthcare provider may or may not be available. In the United States, such data are almost universally available to administrators and policy makers from various sources.

▸ 11.5 Estimation of Service Area and Market Share: Hospital Administrator Perspective

To answer the question, "What is the primary service area of my hospital?", hospital administrators can use the two methods described next.

11.5.1 Expanding Radius Method

In this method of identifying the geographic market (or service area) of a hospital (e.g., hospital X), the process begins by selecting a radius (e.g., 15 miles) around the hospital and identifying all the ZIP codes (or postal codes) in that radius. The number of admissions to hospital X originating from each of the ZIP codes during a specified period (e.g., in the last 1 year) is counted and aggregated to obtain the total number of admissions from all the ZIP codes within the radius. This number (e.g., A) is then divided by the total number of admissions at hospital X (e.g., B) during the same period to obtain the proportion of admissions (A/B) that originated from all the ZIP codes within the radius (note that this proportion, as discussed in the Determinants of Geographic Markets and Service Areas section, is known as the commitment index). This proportion is then compared with an arbitrarily selected expected proportion (e.g., 80%), which is used as a cutoff to define the hospital's primary market or primary service area. If admissions from the ZIP codes in the radius account for a smaller proportion (e.g., 50%) of all admissions at the hospital, the radius is incrementally increased to enlarge the service area. With each new radius, the process of calculating the proportion of admissions at the hospital is repeated until the ZIP codes in the radius meet or exceed the expected cutoff (e.g., 80%) of all admissions at the hospital in the preceding year. These ZIP codes are

then accepted as the geographic market or primary service area of the hospital.[9]

11.5.2 Contiguous ZIP Codes Method

This method of determining the geographic market or primary service area of a hospital is similar to the *expanding radius method.* The process begins by identifying all contiguous ZIP codes surrounding the facility (e.g., hospital X) and sequentially adding them to the service area one at a time based on the number of admissions to hospital X (or percentage of all admissions) contributed by the ZIP codes (or postal codes) during a specified period (e.g., the last calendar year). The first ZIP code to be selected is the one that contributed the most admissions (or the highest proportion) to hospital X. The process of adding ZIP codes to the service area on the bases of successively diminishing contributions to the total pool of admissions is continued until a predefined arbitrary cutoff, such as 80% of admissions to the hospital during the last 1 year, is reached. Beyond this point, no other ZIP codes are added to the primary service area even if some small proportion of admissions to the hospital originated from there.[8]

11.5.3 Estimation of Market Share

Once the primary service area of a hospital has been identified, the hospital administrator can attempt to answer the question, "How much **market share** does my hospital have in the primary service area?"

The answer to this question can be found by first determining the total number of admissions to or discharges from any hospital anywhere that originated from each of the ZIP codes in the primary service area of a given hospital (e.g., hospital X) during a specified period of time (say, the last 1 year). These numbers are then aggregated to obtain the total number of admissions (e.g., K) at all the hospitals from the primary service area of hospital X. In the next step, the total number of admissions at hospital X from its primary service area (e.g., L) during the specified period is divided by the aggregated number of admissions from the primary service area to all the hospitals combined during the same period to obtain the proportion (L/K) that represents hospital X's market share. Note that, as discussed in the Determinants of Geographic Markets and Service Areas section, the market share of a hospital from a specified geographic area is also known as the relevance index. Other hospitals that have significant proportions of market share in the primary service area of a given hospital (e.g., hospital X) would be considered competitors by the administrators of hospital X.

▶ 11.6 Estimation of a Geographic Market: Policy Maker Perspective

Policy makers can use various analytic approaches to answer the following two questions:

1. What are the boundaries or the size of a particular healthcare market?
2. Which hospitals compete in this geographic market, and how much market share does each have?

Three methodologic approaches to delineate a geographic market and to identify competing providers in that healthcare market are briefly described next from the perspective of a healthcare planner or policy maker. Each of these methods has its advantages and disadvantages. Over the years, researchers have modified and refined these methods in many different ways. A full discussion of the complexities of these approaches is beyond the scope of this text.

11.6.1 Geopolitical Boundaries Approach

This straightforward approach uses administratively defined geographic areas such as counties and standard metropolitan statistical areas (SMSAs) as distinct healthcare markets.[6] This approach has the advantage of simplicity, convenience, and availability of data. However, there are some obvious problems with this approach. For example, it ignores concentration of healthcare providers in urban areas and scant distribution of providers in rural areas.[10] Because patient flows and utilization patterns do not follow geopolitical boundaries, this approach does not reflect the realities of utilization patterns, preference for specific providers, dictates of insurance policies, travel time considerations, and competition across geopolitical boundaries. For example, some counties or SMSAs such as Los Angeles and New York are so large that not all healthcare facilities within them can be legitimately considered as competitors. On the other hand, hospitals located near county lines routinely receive patients from neighboring counties and make legitimate competitors for hospitals in those other counties. In this approach, however, they are disregarded as competitors. The geopolitical boundary approach also does not take into account the fact that sizes of geographic markets for different services vary tremendously. For example, the market for obstetric care is usually local, whereas that for transplant or neurosurgery service can be large and can attract patients from long distances.

11.6.2 Distance Between Hospitals: Radius and Hospital Cluster Approach

In this method of determining the boundaries of a geographic market in an area such as a county or city, one hospital in the area of interest is arbitrarily identified as the index hospital, and all hospitals within a given radius (e.g., 15 miles) around this hospital are listed as the initial or first cluster. In the next step, for all the hospitals in the initial cluster, the process is then repeated by applying the same radius and adding new hospitals to the list that fall within the radius of each of these hospitals but were not a part of the initial cluster. The process of adding new hospitals to the cluster is continued in the same fashion until no additional hospitals can be added. Consequently, each hospital in the cluster is within the specified radius (e.g., 15 miles) of another hospital in the cluster, but more than the distance of the radius from a hospital not included in the cluster. A cluster of hospitals identified in this manner is considered a distinct geographic market. Other markets are identified in the same manner. This method ensures that hospitals in one geographic market are separated from hospitals in another geographic market by a distance greater than the length of the radius.[6,9]

Aside from the fact that the radius used to define a cluster is entirely arbitrary, there are other problems with this approach. It does not take into account the fact that geographic markets for different services vary, and a radius that might be adequate for one service may be too small or too large for another service. Moreover, to capture the same level of competition in different geographic markets appropriately, a smaller radius would be required in densely populated urban areas, and a much larger radius would be required in rural areas. Because travel time is an important determinant of health service utilization, it is important to point out that straight-line distances (i.e., "crow's flight" distances) used in this method do not accurately reflect travel time.

11.6.3 Elzinga–Hogarty Test Approach

In sectors of the economy that involve trade and shipment of products into and out of an area, the definition of a geographic market is based on a test called the **Elzinga–Hogarty test** (EHT).[5,11] The test specifies that in order to be considered a defined geographic market, an area should meet the criteria of **Little In From Outside (LIFO)** and **Little Out From Inside (LOFI)**. These criteria simply mean that few shipments or sales of a given product are coming in from outside the geographic area, and few are going out of the geographic area. The measure of "little" in this definition is quite subjective. Generally, little is arbitrarily set at 25% for a weakly competitive market and 10% for a strongly competitive market—that is, in a weakly competitive market, 75% of transactions are expected to take place within the demarcated geographic area, and 90% in a strongly competitive market.[10]

Because of patients' preference to minimize travel time to a healthcare facility, health care is largely considered a local activity. Thus, healthcare markets can be defined by utilization patterns and the application of the EHT.

The underlying principle of EHT is that most of the healthcare needs of residents are met by healthcare facilities within the geographic area (LOFI), and most of the clientele or business for the facilities located in the market area also originate from within the geographic area (LIFO). The use of the Elzinga–Hogarty criterion involves two parallel sets of analyses. First, a cluster of ZIP codes or a geographic district such as a county is identified, and the healthcare utilization of its residents is examined to see what proportion of patients from the area were admitted at facilities within the area and what proportion were admitted at facilities outside the area during a specified period (e.g., the last 1 year). If a relatively small proportion of patients (e.g., 50%) from the initially identified geographic area were admitted at local facilities during the last year, then the geographic area is enlarged by adding more ZIP codes or counties so that more facilities fall into the cluster of "local" facilities. The utilization pattern of residents of the now expanded geographic market is examined again, and the process of expansion of the market is continued until a desired level of LOFI (e.g., 10%) is reached.[10] This means that 90% of patients from within the specified geographic area who needed to be hospitalized were admitted at one of the hospitals within the market area.

At each stage of demarcating a geographic market on the basis of the LOFI criterion, the flip side of the analysis is also carried out to see what proportion of admissions at all the facilities within the geographic market comprised patients from within the market area and what proportion came from outside. Every time the market is expanded by including additional ZIP codes or counties, this analysis is repeated until the predetermined level of LIFO (e.g., 5%) is achieved. This would mean that 95% of admissions that occurred at all the facilities within the demarcated geographic area originated from within the area, and only 5% of admissions were patients who came from outside the area. When both LIFO and LOFI criteria are met, the geographic market can be considered self-contained because few patients from within the area went to facilities outside the area, and few patients from other geographic areas made use of facilities located in this particular geographic market.

11.6.4 Hospital Clustering Based on Patient Origin Data

In this approach to define the boundaries of a geographic hospital market, an index hospital is arbitrarily selected and its geographic market is estimated based on its patient origin data—admissions or discharges. ZIP codes (or postal codes) from where "most" of the index hospital's admissions originated during a specified period of time, such as the last year, are listed in descending order, and a cumulative frequency table is developed. The criterion for most admissions, whether 60%, 70%, or 80%, is arbitrary and subject to the preferences of the analyst. Based on trial and error, this criterion can be changed in multiple cycles of analysis to see which cutoff makes more sense. Once the ZIP codes from where most patients are drawn are listed in rank order, the ZIP codes that collectively contributed the specified percentage of patients (e.g., 60%) are selected as the geographic market for the index hospital (e.g., hospital X). For example, if ZIP codes A, B, C, D, and E respectively contributed 25%, 22%, 18%, 10%, and 6% of admissions at the hospital in the preceding year, ZIP codes A, B, and C would be used as the geographic market of the hospital because they collectively contributed 65% of admissions at the hospital (25% + 22% + 18% = 65%). The remaining two ZIP codes, D and E, would be excluded from the estimation of hospital X's geographic market.

In the next step, the proportions of all hospital admissions that originated from each of these three ZIP codes (A, B, and C) in the last year for any other hospital are estimated. For example, let us assume that out of the total number of admissions from ZIP code A, 21%, 19%, 15%, 10%, 6%, and 4%, respectively, went to hospitals L, M, N, O, P, and Q. If a 10% cutoff is arbitrarily used as the definition of a *competitor*, then hospitals L, M, N, and O would be included in the list of competitors for the index hospital X, but hospitals P and Q would not be considered its competitors. Similarly, competitor hospitals in ZIP codes B and C are identified using the same parameter to define a competitor—that is, 10% or more of the admissions from each of the ZIP codes B and C must go to a hospital for it to be considered a competitor for hospital X.

In the last step, the same process is repeated to delineate geographic markets for hospitals L, M, N, and O and to identify their respective competitors. To that end, the parameters used for hospital X (collectively 60% of admissions from the top-ranking

ZIP codes and 10% cutoff of admissions for a hospital to be considered a competitor in a given ZIP code) would also be applied to hospitals L, M, N, and O. The process is repeated until no additional hospitals are brought in by new ZIP codes. The cluster of ZIP codes identified through this process is considered one geographic market, and the hospitals identified through this process are considered competitors. Clearly, not every hospital in the cluster competes at the same level with every other hospital in the same geographic market. To define the boundaries of a different geographic market, a hospital not included in another cluster is found, and the entire process is repeated.

▶ 11.7 Measuring the Level of Competition in a Geographic Market

Geographic mapping (or *geo-mapping*) techniques have shown that healthcare facilities, especially hospitals, are often clustered in a relatively close *geographic proximity* to one another in urban or suburban areas. The definition of geographic proximity in terms of a radius, whether 10 miles or 15 miles, is subjective and is only in comparison with the distribution of healthcare facilities in the rest of a state or province. In many instances, a radius of 15 miles might be considered a reasonably close geographic proximity. Clustering of healthcare providers such as hospitals in a relatively small area can raise the specter of market control and price fixing by a few big players.

To assess the degree of market concentration, a measure known as the **Herfindahl–Hirschman index** (HHI) has been developed. In contrast to the EHT, which identifies the boundaries of a geographic market, HHI measures the degree of concentration of healthcare resources, such as hospital beds, in a geographic market. The index is derived by aggregating the squared market share of each of the hospitals in a geographic area, such as a county or a SMSA.[8,9,11] Market share can be defined both in terms of the proportion of patients from a geographic market admitted (or discharged) to a hospital or the proportion of all hospital beds in an area that are housed in a given hospital. The possibility of market control and price fixing becomes a real concern when two or more hospitals in the same geographic market decide to merge. HHI is calculated to assess the potential for a violation of antitrust laws and price fixing.

The index can have a low value, at times approaching zero, if there are a large number of competitors in the same geographic market with each holding nearly equal market share. For example, if there are 34 hospitals in the same geographic market, with each competitor having about 3% of the market share, the total score for the index will only be 306 ($34 \times [3]^2 = 306$). The maximum possible value of HHI is 10,000 and can occur only when a single hospital serves the entire geographic market (i.e., a monopoly situation with one hospital controlling 100% of the market).[8] Remember that HHI is derived by getting the square of the market share of a provider, which in a monopoly situation would be 100 (i.e., $100 \times 100 = 10,000$). If a hospital owns 20% of all beds in a given market, its HHI would be only 400 (i.e., $20^2 = 400$). Because of the way this index is calculated, the values of the index increase at an increasingly sharper rate with higher values of market share. For example, if a hospital controls 50% of the market share, the index value would be only 2,500. However, if the market share of the same hospital increases to 75%, the corresponding HHI value more than doubles, to 5,625. By convention, a HHI value of 1,800 in a geographic market raises concerns about too much market power in the hands of just a few hospitals, or possibly even a single hospital. This situation can arise if a single hospital controls 42.4% of market share, or with two hospitals that each control 30% of the market. If a proposed merger between two hospitals causes HHI to increase by more than 50 points above the base value of 1,800, the U.S. Department of Justice may closely review the proposal for potential antitrust problems.[11]

Depending on how a geographic market is defined or demarcated, the HHI can be the same for all hospitals in a market (based on the combined market share of all hospitals in the geographic area), or it can be specific for each hospital and thus different from one hospital to another. If a market is defined in terms of geopolitical boundaries such as SMSA or is based on Elzinga–Hogarty criteria (i.e., LIFO and LOFI), then a single HHI is calculated by combining the market share of all hospitals in the geographic area and is the same for any of the hospitals included in the area. On the other hand, if the market is defined by patient flows to various hospitals or is defined by a variable radius around each hospital, then HHI is calculated separately for each hospital based on its market share and is specific to that particular hospital.[10]

▶ 11.8 Priority Setting and the Role of "Healthy People" Reports

During the last three decades, a number of countries, including the United States, Britain, Canada, Australia, and South Africa, have periodically articulated in various policy papers national health priorities and specific targets to improve population health. The overall purpose of these efforts is to establish a system of monitoring change in population health status and to assess the impact of health improvement programs.

Efforts to set national health priorities in the United States date back to 1979, when the U.S. Surgeon General issued the first "Healthy People" (HP) report. The report focused on five stages of life, from infancy to old age, and included 15 public health priorities. Since then, the U.S. Department of Health and Human Services (HHS) has released an updated report every 10 years with greater numbers of priority areas and objectives. Healthy People 2000 was released in 1990, Healthy People 2010 in 1998, and Healthy People 2020 in 2010. The "overarching goals" of Healthy People 2020 include the following:

- Attain high-quality, longer lives free of preventable disease, disability, injury, and premature death.
- Achieve health equity, eliminate disparities, and improve the health of all groups. Create social and physical environments that promote good health for all.
- Promote quality of life, healthy development, and healthy behaviors across all life stages.

Critics have asserted that Healthy People reports include too many objectives and suffer from inconsistencies across priority areas, and many of the objectives are not measurable. The case in point might be that Healthy People 2020 includes 1,200 separate objectives that span 42 different public health topics. Others have charged that federal politics has tainted the process of setting priorities and reasonable objectives.

The 2014 update of HP 2020 (**FIGURE 11.1**) reports that four (15.4%) of the 26 Leading Health Indicators—a selected subset of high-priority health issues—were met by March 2014, and another 10 (38.5%) were showing improvement. Of the remaining 12 indicators, 8 (30.8%) showed no improvement, and 3 (11.5%; suicide, adolescents with major depression, and visits to dentists) actually got worse (**TABLE 11.1**).

▶ 11.9 Small Area Health Planning

In countries that have some form of a national health service or where government is actively engaged in facilitating access and delivery of health care, planning and delivery of health care is also a function of the government. In those circumstances, the ministries of health and other federal or provincial bodies strive for

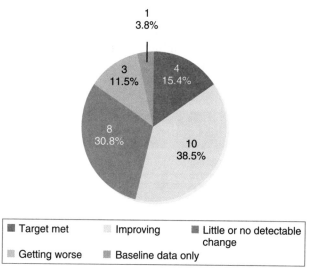

FIGURE 11.1 Status of the 26 Healthy People 2020 Leading Health Indicators, March 2014.

geographically equitable distribution of resources.[12] While decision makers are concerned about efficiency and effectiveness at the central level of healthcare planning, at the peripheral or local level, decision makers are most concerned about responsiveness to the local population and meeting the needs of individuals and families.

Because of the competing demands of different stakeholders, the process of setting priorities and allocating resources is inherently political and fraught with compromises at all levels of bureaucracy. Nonetheless, planners and policy makers need to be as rational and objective in setting priorities as they can be. Although priorities are usually articulated in broad terms, such as improving the health status of the population, they must be carefully translated into specific objectives and measurable outcomes, such as 20% reduction in infant mortality or 50% reduction in the incidence of HIV/AIDS cases.

When healthcare planning is carried out at the level of a community or in the context of an organization, the goals and objectives have to be tailored accordingly. Because of the small size of the target population and the modest scale of activities, it is unrealistic to measure the impact of services in terms of statistically meaningful health outcomes such as reduction in incidence, prevalence, or mortality rate. In these situations, planning and needs assessment can appropriately focus on processes of care and units of services delivered, such as number or proportion of pregnant women who will receive prenatal care, expected number of babies to be delivered at the facility, or the number of women who will receive Pap smear screening for cervical cancer.

For the purpose of community-based healthcare planning, it is necessary to group healthcare facilities into clusters and geographic areas into regions of similar healthcare utilization.[13] Based on healthcare utilization patterns by the population, various forms of cluster analysis methods are used to group healthcare facilities and communities into health service areas. In some of these approaches, healthcare facilities are

TABLE 11.1 Healthy People 2020 Leading Health Indicators: Progress Update

✓ Target met[1]	+ Improving[2]	O Little or no detectable change[3]	— Getting worse[4]

Progress Toward Target[5,6]	Leading Health Topic and Indicator	Baseline (Year)	Most Recent (Year)	Target
	Access to Health Services			
O	**AHS-1.1** Persons with medical insurance (percent, <65 years)	83.2% (2008)	83.1% (2012)	100.0%
O	**AHS-3** Persons with a usual primary care provider (percent)	76.3% (2007)	77.3% (2011)	83.9%
	Clinical Preventive Services			
+	**C-16** Adults receiving colorectal cancer screening based on most recent guidelines (age adjusted, percent, 50–75 years)	52.1% (2008)	59.2% (2010)	70.5%
+	**HDS-12** Adults with hypertension whose blood pressure is under control (age adjusted, percent, 18+ years)	43.7% (2005–08)	48.9% (2009–12)	61.2%
O	**D-5.1** Persons with diagnosed diabetes whose A1c value is >9 percent (age adjusted, percent, 18+ years)	17.9% (2005–08)	21.0% (2009–12)	16.1%
+	**IID-8** Children receiving the recommended doses of DTaP, polio, MMR, Hib, hepatitis B, varicella, and PCV vaccines (percent, aged 19–35 months)	44.3% (2009)	68.5% (2011)	80.0%
	Environmental Quality			
✓	**EH-1** Air Quality Index (AQI) exceeding 100 (number of billion person days, weighted by population and Air Quality Index value)	2.237% (2006–08)	1.252% (2009–11)	1.980%
✓	**TU-11.1** Children exposed to secondhand smoke (percent; nonsmokers, 3–11 years)	52.2% (2005–08)	41.3% (2009–12)	47.0%
	Injury and Violence			
+	**IVP-1.1** Injury deaths (age adjusted, per 100,000 population)	59.7% (2007)	57.1% (2010)	53.7%
✓	**IVP-29** Homicides (age adjusted, per 100,000 population)	6.1% (2007)	5.3% (2010)	5.5%
	Maternal, Infant, and Child Health			
+	**MICH-1.3** Infant deaths (per 1,000 live births, <1 year)	6.7% (2006)	6.1% (2010)	6.0%
+	**MICH-9.1** Total preterm live births (percent, <37 weeks gestation)	12.7% (2007)	11.5% (2012)	11.4%
	Mental Health			
—	**MHMD-1** Suicide (age adjusted, per 100,000 population)	11.3% (2007)	12.1% (2010)	10.2%
—	**MHMD-4.1** Adolescents with major depressive episodes (percent, 12–17 years)	8.3% (2008)	9.1% (2012)	7.5%
	Nutrition, Physical Activity, and Obesity			
✓	**PA-2.4** Adults meeting aerobic physical activity and muscle-strengthening Federal guidelines (age adjusted, percent, 18+ years)	18.2% (2008)	20.6% (2012)	20.1%
O	**NWS-9** Obesity among adults (age adjusted, percent, 20+ years)	33.9% (2005–08)	35.3% (2009–12)	30.5%
O	**NWS-10.4** Obesity among children and adolescents (percent, 2–19 years)	16.1% (2005–08)	16.9% (2009–12)	14.5%
O	**NWS-15.1** Mean daily intake of total vegetables (age adjusted, cup equivalents per 1,000 calories, 2+ years)	0.8% (2001–04)	0.8% (2007–10)	1.1%

Progress Toward Target[5,6]	Leading Health Topic and Indicator	Baseline (Year)	Most Recent (Year)	Target
	Oral Health			
−	**OH-7** Persons who visited the dentist in the past year (age adjusted, percent, 2+ years)	44.5% (2007)	41.8% (2011)	49.0%
	Reproductive and Sexual Health			
Baseline data only[7]	**FP-7.1** Sexually experienced females receiving reproductive health services in the past 12 months (percent, 15–44 years)	78.6% (2006–10)	Not available	86.5%
+	**HIV-13** Knowledge of serostatus among HIV-positive persons (percent, 13+ years)	80.9% (2006)	84.2% (2010)	90.0%
	Social Determinants			
+	**AH-5.1** Students awarded a high school diploma 4 years after starting 9th grade (percent)	74.9% (2007–08)	78.2% (2009–10)	82.4%
	Substance Abuse			
+	**SA-13.1** Adolescents using alcohol or illicit drugs in past 30 days (percent, 12–17 years)	18.4% (2008)	17.4% (2012)	16.6%
O	**SA-14.3** Binge drinking in past 30 days—Adults (percent, 18+ years)	27.1% (2008)	27.1% (2012)	24.4%
	Tobacco			
+	**TU-1.1** Adult cigarette smoking (age adjusted, percent, 18+ years)	20.6% (2008)	18.2% (2012)	12.0%
O	**TU-2.2** Adolescent cigarette smoking in past 30 days (percent, grades 9–12)	19.5% (2009)	18.1% (2011)	16.0%

Top legend: ✓ Target met[1]   + Improving[2]   O Little or no detectable change[3]   − Getting worse[4]

clustered by evaluating the proportion of patient visits or admissions originating in the *home area unit* of a facility or hospital. The definition of a home area can vary from one program or study to another. The importance or *relevance* of a healthcare provider for a specific geographic area is determined by the proportion of total utilization of health services (visits, admissions, discharges, or bed days) in the geographic district made at that particular facility. In these approaches, the importance of a healthcare provider for the community is directly related to the size of the facility and its proximity to the community. In general, the travel time to and from a healthcare provider is an important determinant of its utilization by the local population.

▸ 11.10 Facility Location Planning

Facility location planning, or location allocation, is a multiobjective complex activity that is subject to many strategic constraints. Two of the most important considerations in facility location planning are cost

efficiency and patient retention. Cost efficiency is a function of a number of factors, including the level of services provided in terms of severity or acuity and the capacity of the facility. Services involving high levels of severity or advanced technologies cost more and require larger volumes of patients to attain optimal efficiency. Patient retention refers to the proportion of patients retained as the distance between a facility and potential patient location varies. Patient retention is a measure of access under the assumption that patients choose a nearby facility, as opposed to a more distant one, as long as the quality of care at the two facilities is comparable. Optimal location allocation involves development of sophisticated mathematical and simulation models that use integer or goal programming techniques. These models can be deterministic or probabilistic in design and can involve large numbers of variables, assumptions, and constraints. Facility location models have been extensively developed for health services planning, and a large body of research literature on rural hospitals, trauma care, blood banks, transplant services, and U.S. Veterans Administration facility location planning exists. However, empirical evidence of the effective use of these models and resulting efficiencies seems to be scant.

▶ 11.11 Certificate of Need Programs

In the United States, healthcare planning has been attempted at different times, with the aim of ensuring enough supply to meet the needs of the population and containing cost by limiting the supply of services at levels that do not exceed the population's needs.[13,14] Certificate of Need (CON) programs have been used in the past to achieve these objectives and continue to be used in a number of states to regulate the supply of health services. CON programs were started in some U.S. states in the mid-1960s as regulatory mechanisms to reduce healthcare costs by avoiding duplication of services. Improvement in the quality of care through increased volume of patients at existing facilities was also a desired indirect benefit of the CON program.

In 1975, the U.S. Congress passed the National Health Planning and Resource Development Act of 1974, with the primary objective of containing healthcare costs. The Act enabled the federal government to provide powerful financial incentives and guidelines to state and local planning and regulatory agencies to implement CON programs. Although the Act was repealed by the U.S. Congress in 1986, a number of states have maintained their CON programs in various forms.[14,15] As of August 2015, 36 states still had some form of a CON program, with 28 of the states using such programs to evaluate the current and future supply of hospital beds in relation to their estimated need at the regional level.

CON or similar programs require proposals for new services or facilities to demonstrate an unmet need. Approval of such services or facilities must be obtained before their development.[16] This condition applies to all for-profit or nonprofit entities that want to build new facilities, expand existing facilities, or purchase costly equipment. The scope and extent of the regulatory authority of a planning agency varies from one state to another and may include or exclude regulation of acute care hospitals, hospices, skilled nursing, and intermediate care facilities, and purchase of major medical equipment.

Over the last 50 years, CON programs have been the subject of intense debate, and their merits have been frequently contested. The underlying argument to support the implementation of the CON program has been that excess capacity of healthcare resources (facilities, beds, equipment) lead to an increase in healthcare costs through price inflation. Purportedly, price inflation occurs because facilities with excess capacity have higher fixed costs than those without excess capacity, and organizations attempt to recoup excess fixed costs by increasing the price of services. Although many studies have been conducted to examine the success or failure of these programs in containing costs and avoiding duplication of resources, their findings have been inconclusive, and no consensus has emerged. The proponents and opponents of these programs have a philosophical disagreement on the fundamental issue of regulation versus open market. In principle, CON for a particular service should be granted only when there is evidence of community need. However, the opponents of these programs charge, with some justification, that other factors, including political power and organizational influence, frequently determine the outcome of an application for a CON.[14,15] It has been reported that, because of the increasing number of physician-owned freestanding ambulatory and long-term care facilities, in recent years, CON programs have concentrated more on these facilities rather than acute care general hospitals.

▶ 11.12 Designation of Health Professional Shortage Areas

Uneven geographic distribution of both healthcare providers and consumers results in uneven spatial access to health services.[17] Access to health services is also affected by *nonspatial* socioeconomic and demographic factors, including age, sex, and ethnicity. Spatial disparity in access to health services is determined by measuring travel time and distance between providers and consumers. Historically, policy makers have attempted to address spatial disparities in access by designating geographic areas or population groups as **Health Professional Shortage Areas** (HPSAs), **Medically Underserved Areas** (MUAs), and **Medically Underserved Populations** (MUPs). Eligibility for some federal grants is determined based on these designations. The Health Resources and Services Administration (HRSA) of the HHS makes the official determination whether a geographic area, population group, or healthcare facility has inadequate access to healthcare providers. HRSA employs established criteria to decide whether there is a shortage of primary care physicians, dentists, and mental health professionals and designates those areas or populations with a shortage as HPSAs, MUAs, or MUPs.[18]

Geographic areas, such as a whole county, a group of contiguous counties, minor civil divisions (MCDs), or a group of metropolitan census tracts, can be designated a MUA or a primary care HPSA. For example, in 2014, out of 77 counties in Oklahoma, 65 were designated by HRSA as partially or wholly MUAs or MUPs, and part of one county was listed as Exceptional Medically Underserved Population or Oklahoma Governor Service Area. Notably, 30 of the 77 counties in Oklahoma have remained designated MUAs since 1978.[19]

If a population group—such as low-income individuals, migrants, American Indians/Alaska Natives, or the homeless—within a geographic district can be shown by a state to meet HRSA's established criteria for barriers to access and shortage of primary medical care professionals, it can be designated as a MUP or primary care population group HPSA. However, the geographic area within which such a group resides must also be defined in terms of counties, civil divisions, or census tracts, as is required for designating a geographic area as a MUA. If a geographic area or a population group does not meet HRSA's criteria for MUA or MUP designation, a state governor or other interested party can request it to be designated as a Certified Shortage Area for Rural Health Clinics or Exceptional Medically Underserved Population (EMUP). However, the state must make the case that unusual local conditions exist that create a barrier to access or availability of *personal health services* for that population.[20]

The designation of MUA is based on the Index of Medical Underservice (IMU) score that is derived from health-related data of a geographic area. The variables used to calculate IMU are as follows: (1) the ratio of primary care physicians per 1,000 population, (2) infant mortality rate, (3) percentage of population age 65 years or older, and (4) percentage of the population with income below the federal poverty limit. Weights applied to the value of each of these variables for a given area are summed to get an aggregated score, the IMU. **TABLE 11.2** shows the weights assigned to different values of each of the four variables used

TABLE 11.2 Weights for Different Values of the Four Variables Used to Calculate the Index of Medical Underservice

Infant Mortality Rate	Weighted Value	% Age ≥65 Years	Weighted Value	Primary Care Physician Ratio	Weighted Value	% Below Poverty	Weighted Value
0–8	26.0	0–7.0	20.2	0–.050	0	0	25.1
8.1–9.0	25.6	7.1–8.0	20.1	.051–.100	0.5	0.1–20.0	24.6
9.1–10.0	24.8	8.1–9.0	19.9	.101–.150	1.5	2.1–4.0	23.7
10.1–11.0	24.0	9.1–10.0	19.8	.151–.200	2.8	4.1–6.0	22.8
11.1–12.0	23.2	10.1–11.0	19.6	.201–.250	4.1	6.1–8.0	21.9
12.1–13.0	22.4	11.1–12.0	19.4	.251–.300	5.7	8.1–10.0	21.0
13.1–14.0	21.5	12.1–13.0	19.1	.301–.350	7.3	10.1–12.0	20.0
14.1–15.0	20.5	13.1–14.0	18.9	.351–.400	9.0	12.1–14.0	18.7
15.1–16.0	19.5	14.1–15.0	18.7	.401–.450	10.7	14.1–16.0	17.4
16.1–17.0	18.5	15.1–16.0	17.8	.451–.500	12.6	16.1–18.0	16.2
17.1–18.0	17.5	16.1–17.0	16.1	.501–.550	14.8	18.1–20.0	14.9
18.1–19.0	16.4	17.1–18.0	14.4	.551–.600	16.9	20.1–22.0	13.6
19.1–20.0	15.3	18.1–19.0	12.8	.601–.650	19.1	22.1–24.0	12.2

(continues)

TABLE 11.2 Weights for Different Values of the Four Variables Used to Calculate the Index of Medical Underservice *(continued)*

Infant Mortality Rate	Weighted Value	% Age ≥65 Years	Weighted Value	Primary Care Physician Ratio	Weighted Value	% Below Poverty	Weighted Value
20.1–21.0	14.2	19.1–20.0	11.1	.651–.700	20.7	24.1–26.0	10.9
21.1–22.0	13.1	20.1–21.0	9.8	.701–.750	21.9	26.1–28.0	9.3
22.1–23.0	11.9	21.1–22.0	8.9	.751–.800	23.1	28.1–30.0	7.8
23.1–24.0	10.8	22.1–23.0	8.0	.801–.850	24.3	30.1–32.0	6.6
24.1–25.0	9.6	23.1–24.0	7.0	.851–.900	25.3	32.1–34.0	5.6
25.1–26.0	8.5	24.1–25.0	6.1	.901–.950	25.9	34.1–36.0	4.7
26.1–27.0	7.3	25.1–26.0	5.1	.951–1.000	26.6	36.1–38.0	3.4
27.1–28.0	6.1	26.1–27.0	4.0	1.001–1.050	27.2	38.1–40.0	2.1
28.1–29.0	5.4	27.1–28.0	2.8	1.051–1.100	27.7	40.1–42.0	1.3
29.1–30.0	5.0	28.1–29.0	1.7	1.101–1.150	28.0	42.1–44.0	1.0
30.1–31.0	4.7	29.1–30.0	0.6	1.151–1.200	28.3	44.1–46.0	0.7
31.1–32.0	4.3	30+	0	1.201–1.250	28.6	46.1–48.0	0.4
32.1–33.0	4.0			Over 1.250	28.7	48.1–50.0	0.1
33.1–34.0	3.6					50+	0
34.1–35.0	3.3						
35.1–36.0	3.0						
36.1–37.0	2.6						
37.1–39.0	2.0						
39.1–41.0	1.4						
41.1–43.0	0.8						
43.1–45.0	0.2						
45.1+	0						

Modified from: Health Resources and Services Administration (HRSA), U.S. Department of Health and Human Services. Shortage designation: Health professional shortage areas & medically underserved areas/populations. Accessed on July 12, 2017. https://datawarehouse.hrsa.gov/topics/shortageareas.aspx

in determining whether a geographic area qualifies for the designation of MUA. For example, if 0% of the population is below poverty level, a weight of 25.1 is assigned to this variable; if 24.1% to 26.0% of the population is below poverty level, the assigned weight is 10.9; and if 50% or more of the population is below poverty level, the weight given to this variable is zero. The total IMU score of an area resulting from the sum of the weights for all four variables, therefore, can range from 0 to 100, where 0 represents a completely underserved area, and a score of 100 means the area is well served. A score of 62.0 or less qualifies an area to be designated as a MUA. The designation of a MUP in an area of residence also requires collection of data from the population of interest on the same four variables and calculation of IMU.

Facilities that receive Community Health Center (CHC) grants are required by law to serve populations or geographic areas that are designated by HRSA as medically underserved. Healthcare facilities that meet the definition of a CHC under section 330 of the U.S. Public Health Service Act, but are not receiving any funds under that law, can be eligible for certification as a Federally Qualified Health Center (FQHC). Certified FQHCs can charge a cost-based fee to Medicaid programs for services rendered to Medicaid patients as long as such facilities serve in a designated MUA or serve a MUP.

HRSA can also designate healthcare facilities, such as those within federal and state correctional institutions, or public and private nonprofit medical facilities, such as migrant health centers, as having a shortage of primary care medical professionals if these facilities meet the criteria for such designation. Likewise, physicians' offices or medical practices can be designated as a Rural Health Clinic (RHC) or a Governor-Certified RHC. In most instances, such clinics are located in HPSAs or MUAs. To qualify as a Governor-Certified RHC, the applicant clinic or facility must meet the following conditions: (1) it must be located in a designated Governor's Certified Shortage Area; (2) it must accept patients who have Medicare, Medicaid, or State Children's Health Insurance coverage; (3) it must have a sliding-scale fee structure for individuals under 200% of the federal poverty limit; and (4) it must have a service area with a primary care physician-to-population ratio of at least 1:2,400.[20] In 2016, 12 states had active governor-certified shortage areas.

The list of HPSAs is updated annually by HRSA. After receiving comments and updated information from State Primary Care Offices, Primary Care Associations, and other stakeholders, HRSA makes the final determination regarding areas that can maintain their designated MUA or MUP status and areas that would lose their status if they no longer meet the criteria. The list of approved HPSAs can be found online at HRSA's website or the National Health Service Corps website. As of June 2014, approximately 6,100 approved Primary Care HPSAs, 4,900 Dental HPSAs, and 4,000 Mental Health HPSAs existed in the country.

The designation of Primary Care HPSA is based on the longstanding physician-to-population ratio of 1:3,500 (as well as other HRSA-established criteria). Based on this ratio, in 2014, HRSA estimated that 8,200 additional primary care physicians were required to eliminate Primary Care HPSA designations in the country. This estimate, however, did not take into consideration the availability of nonphysician primary care providers such as nurse practitioners and physician assistants. Many other public policy organizations, however, use a physician-to-population ratio of 1:2,000 to estimate the need for primary care physicians. Based on this ratio, HRSA estimated that 16,000 additional primary care physicians were needed in 2014 to eliminate all HPSAs.[20]

To replace HRSA's current methods of identifying access and areas of physician shortage, which are based on population-to-physician ratio (usually 1:3,500), Wang and Luo[17] have proposed integration of spatial/geographic and nonspatial measures (e.g., poverty, education, ethnicity) of access into a single index of access that can be used to designate HPSAs and MUPs. The proposed integration of spatial and nonspatial measures of access has two parts. First, a two-step *floating catchment area* method is used to measure spatial access based on travel time between healthcare providers and consumers. The second part involves the use of a statistical analytic technique called factor analysis to integrate various nonspatial factors, such as socioeconomic and demographic determinants of access, into a single composite variable. The measures of spatial and nonspatial access are then combined to generate a single quantitative index or score that can be used to designate areas and populations as HPSAs and MUPs.

▶ 11.13 Determinants of Access to Health Services

Primarily, access to healthcare is a function of the availability or existence of services in a geographic market, district, or region. If services of one or the other kind do not exist, people have to do without them. For example, if transplant services do not exist in a town, state, or province, people do not have access to them.

However, existence or availability of a service or technology in a geographic area does not translate into access for all residents of that area. There is an extensive body of research literature related to disparities in the health status of different population groups in the United States, Canada, United Kingdom, Australia, and other countries.[21–27] In the United States, stark disparities in health status, quality of care, and health outcomes continue to exist between groups. Evidence shows that these disparities are directly linked to inequities in socioeconomic, geographic, and cultural access to health services. Minority status, poverty, lack of education, rural settings, and cultural factors have a direct bearing on people's access to health services. Combinations of racial, economic, geographic, and cultural barriers to access explain most of the disparities in health outcomes. For more information on the subject of healthcare disparities in the United States, the reader is encouraged to see the October 2011 issue of the journal *Health Affairs*, which was entirely devoted to exploring various aspects of disparities in health care: http://www.healthaffairs.org /toc/hlthaff/30/10

▶ 11.14 Sources of Epidemiologic Data

Nonmedical and medical sources of data such as census data; disease registries for cancer or HIV/AIDS; and hospital records on discharges, length of stay, and bed occupancy, and ambulatory records are all useful sources of information for healthcare planning as long as planners and policy makers are mindful of the limitations of these sources. An excellent source of longitudinal epidemiologic and healthcare utilization data is the Healthcare Cost and Utilization Project (H-CUP), a family of data sets and related software programs sponsored by the U.S. Agency for Healthcare Research and Quality. Available online, these data sets provide nationwide encounter-level data on adult and pediatric hospital discharges and emergency department visits from 1988 onward. The H-CUP family of databases includes the following national- or state-level databases.

11.14.1 State Inpatient Databases

The State Inpatient Databases (SID) is a set of databases containing inpatient discharge data from community hospitals in the participating states. Starting with the participation of only eight states in the first year, 44 states were making these data publicly available in 2011. By 2015, 48 states were participating in SID.

Translated into a uniform format, the SID now cover about 97% of discharges from community hospitals in the country. Collectively, the multiyear databases provide a longitudinal view of inpatient care in a given state or geographic market. Covering more than 100 clinical and nonclinical variables, the data files contain information on demographic characteristics, principal and secondary diagnoses, procedures performed during the hospital stay, length of stay, hospital characteristics, total charges, expected source of payment, and admission and discharge status of the patient. In 2015, data files from 1990 through 2012 were available for a fee through HCUP Central Distributor.

11.14.2 State Emergency Department Databases

The State Emergency Department Databases (SEDD) are available from 1999 onward (through 2011 in 2015) and include information on those visits to hospital-affiliated emergency departments that do not result in hospitalization. Information regarding patients who are initially seen in the emergency department and then admitted to the same hospital is included in the SID. Presented in a uniform format, SEDD include a core set of more than 100 variables encompassing demographic, diagnostic, and financial data typically available in a hospital discharge abstract. Although not all elements included in the core set are available from all states, additional variables that are not part of the core set are included in the data from some of the states. The SEDD are annual state-specific files that can also be linked to hospital data from other sources such as the American Hospital Association (AHA).

11.14.3 State Ambulatory Surgery and Services Databases

The State Ambulatory Surgery and Services Databases (SASD) include state-specific encounter-level data on ambulatory surgery and other outpatient services such as lithotripsy, imaging, radiation and chemotherapy, and labor and delivery services provided at hospital-owned facilities in participating states. Available from 1997 onward, data from some of the states also include services provided at facilities that are not owned by hospitals. Similar to the SEDD, the SASD do not mask state and hospital identifier information. As such, they can be easily linked with other sources of hospital-level information such as that available from the AHA. The core set of elements in these databases includes clinical and nonclinical variables typically available in other data sets.

11.14.4 National Inpatient Sample

The National Inpatient Sample (NIS), called the Nationwide Inpatient Sample until 2012, is a set of publicly available longitudinal hospital inpatient databases drawn from SID. Containing data on about 7 million hospital stays every year, NIS represents a 20% stratified sample of discharges from all community hospitals included in SID. Until 2012, the sampling was done at the hospital level, and all data on all discharges from hospitals included in the sample were retained. Starting from 2012, all community hospitals in SID are now included in the NIS database with a 20% stratified sample of discharges taken from each hospital. Although available in previous years, state and hospital identifiers are no longer available in the currently de-identified database. Annual NIS data sets are available from 1988 onward and contain information on all the variables included in SID.

11.14.5 Kids' Inpatient Database

The national Kids' Inpatient Database (KID) contains information on inpatient hospital stays of patients younger than 21 years of age. Released every 3 years, KID spans the period from 1997 through 2012. In the 2015 release, it contained data from approximately 3 million hospital discharges at more than 4,100 community hospitals in 44 states and included more than 100 clinical and nonclinical variables. The data are deidentified to mask the identity of each state, hospital, and patient. Thus, longitudinal or cross-sectional analysis of morbidity, mortality, utilization, charges, quality, and outcomes is possible at the national level but not the state, regional, or hospital level.

11.14.6 National Emergency Department Sample

Obtained from both SID and SEDD, the Nationwide Emergency Department Sample (NEDS) contains information on approximately 30 million discharges from hospital-affiliated emergency departments in the country every year. The data set includes information on patients first seen in the emergency department and then admitted to the same hospital, as well as visits to the emergency department that did not result in an admission. The databases span from 2006 through 2015. The 2015 NEDS database contains discharge data for emergency department visits from 953 hospitals located in 34 states and the District of Columbia — approximating a 20% stratified sample of U.S. hospital-based emergency departments. The database includes demographic information such as hospital and patient characteristics, geographic area, and reasons for emergency department visits. It also includes charge information for 85 percent of patients, including those covered by Medicare, Medicaid, or private insurance, as well as those who are uninsured.

▶ 11.15 Healthcare Marketing

Effective marketing of products and services is critically important for healthcare organizations – especially those operating in highly competitive environments. In the age of Google and Facebook, the methods and scope of marketing have dramatically shifted away from conventional approaches. In the last couple of decades, much of the focus of marketing had already transitioned from print media to television commercials. Various parts of the healthcare system in the United States—particularly, the pharmaceutical industry—have made effective use of direct-to-consumer marketing through television ads. Now, the pervasive use of computers, smart phones, and social media for communication and news is likely to even reduce the scope and impact of television commercials. Rapid growth in the availability and use of big data is also changing the landscape of healthcare marketing. The following sections discuss some of these changes in healthcare marketing.

11.15.1 Definition, Scope, and Purpose of Marketing

The American Marketing Association defines marketing as "the activity, set of institutions, and processes for creating, communicating, delivering, and exchanging offerings that have value for customers, clients, partners, and society at large."[28]

The purpose of marketing is to inform and influence the population of future customers by giving the right information to the right population at the right time. Effective marketing requires a multidimensional approach that includes business intelligence, market analysis, digital marketing, and efficient use of marketing resources. It also requires carefully considered choice of technologies that are best suited to meet the goals and objectives of an organization.[29] The process begins with the development of a marketing plan that specifies the technologies to be used for communicating with the target population and evaluative mechanisms to assess the effectiveness of the campaign. A marketing plan includes market analysis, identification of target customers, gauging the level of competition, and an assessment of one's strengths and weaknesses. It also involves development of goals and objectives, strategies for implementation, a timeframe to achieve goals and objectives, and a proposed budget for all marketing activities.

Identification of target customers involves delineation of the size and demographic characteristics of the market for a specific service or a product. It also involves analysis of customer behavior in terms of the use of services, loyalty to one's brand, sources of information used by customers, and customer attitude toward a specific product or service. Healthcare consumers are becoming more informed and more assertive. They read reviews, compare prices, and are getting more involved in the decision-making process. Different population cohorts—whether Millennials or baby boomers—not only have different healthcare needs, but also have different attitudes towards health and health care. An effective marketing plan for a healthcare product or service must understand the needs and attitudes of the customer and quantify tangible and intangible benefits of the service or product being marketed. These benefits can translate into improvement in the quality of life, relief from pain, avoidance of disability, enhancement of productivity, and improvement in one's appearance.

Zeithaml et al.,[30] the developers of SERVQUAL, a widely used survey instrument to understand consumers' expectations and perceptions regarding service quality, have identified the following five dimensions of service environment that customers use to evaluate the quality of a service: (1) The appearance of physical facilities, staff, and equipment (Tangible); (2) the ability to deliver the service in a dependable and consistent manner (Reliability); (3) the willingness to meet the needs of the customer in a timely and efficient manner (Responsiveness); (4) the ability of employees to generate confidence and trust through high level of competence (Assurance); and (5) the ability and desire to provide individualized care and attention (Empathy). This model of assessing service quality is commonly known as the *gaps model* and has been used across a range of industries and settings. A number of criticisms have been leveled against the consumer expectations construct employed in the instrument, as well as the validity, reliability, and length of the questionnaire. One criticism is that the survey instrument captures consumer satisfaction rather than actual service quality. Research[31] has shown considerable variation in the rank order of consumer expectations. For example,[32] information science (library) customers seem to value reliability (32%) and responsiveness (22%) more than the other three dimensions; the physical appearance of facilities, staff, or equipment seems to rank last in the order of importance for customers (11%). Needless to say, an effective marketing strategy must focus on all of these dimensions.

11.15.2 Digital Marketing and Use of Social Media

Traditional marketing platforms such as television, newspapers, billboards, yellow pages, and mailed brochures are one-way communication channels. In contrast, Internet-based social media are two-way communication channels that allow customer input and feedback in near real-time. Through digital media, consumers have access to any information at any time in any place. In addition to being a source of entertainment, news, and social interaction, digital media are an ever-increasing source of information to an ever-increasing number of people. Therefore, it is necessary for marketers to communicate with their customers across all communication channels and in a form to which consumers are most likely to be receptive. In health care, social media can be used to do surveys, inform patients about new services, fill vacant appointment slots, and generate customer interest in new services and technologies.

Driven by the overwhelming use of digital media to get news, information, and entertainment, there has been an industrywide shift of healthcare marketing dollars from traditional media to digital marketing. Healthcare marketers understand that the vast majority of patient encounters with healthcare providers now take place after a digital query or keyword search on the Internet. The use of digital networks such as Facebook in conjunction with in-house customer relations and retention software programs allow healthcare marketers to target specific consumer groups with great precision and send text messages and advertisements to those in need of a checkup or test.

Northwell Health, a New York City–based company, reportedly increased the share of its digital advertising budget from 1% before 2016 to about 20% in 2017.[33] Most of this advertising occurred on Public Broadcasting Service Digital and *New York Times* Digital to reach a population of more than 8 million consumers. Ascension, the largest not-for-profit hospital conglomerate in the United States, spent about 10% of its marketing budget on digital media in 2016. In 2017, the company was expected to increase that share to 25%, with about 70% of the allocated dollars going to Facebook and Google.[33] With increased spending on digital media, Ascension ensures that its advertisements appear on the first webpage that opens after a keyword search on Google.

It is important to note that despite its unparalleled reach, digital marketing has its limitations and does not entirely replace other forms of marketing. The sheer volume of available data and growing intensity of competition for consumer attention across common digital platforms such as Facebook and Google pose a challenge for marketers. Marketing research and public surveys indicate that because of the complexity of health-related information, a majority of consumers, particularly those 35 years or older, still prefer receiving healthcare marketing messages via print media and television.

11.15.3 Use of Big Data in Healthcare Marketing

The term "big data" refers to data sets that are too big for a single computer to handle. The assessment of how big is big enough to be characterized as big data depends entirely on the capabilities of users and the power of their equipment. These data sets are constantly increasing in size because they contain information that is continuously being generated through minute-by-minute business transactions and countless millions of people interacting on social media. According to some estimates, 2.5 exabytes of data (i.e., 2.5×10^{18}, or 1 billion, gigabytes) are being generated through business transactions across the globe every day. In health care, the use of mHealth (mobile health applications), eHealth, and wearable technologies are also producing large volumes of data.

Because data come from a variety of sources, big data are complex and difficult to use. Part of the difficulty of organizing and using big data stems from the fact that not only is it continuously growing, but it also requires linkages across multiple sources and systems. The volume, velocity, and variety of data necessitate the use of multiple software programs simultaneously running parallel to one another on hundreds or thousands of servers all over the country, or even across the world. Because conventional analytic and statistical software programs are designed for installation on individual computers and are designed to work with specific operating systems, they are unable to handle big data. A number of consumer-driven software programs are now available from many nonprofit entities and are commonly used to analyze big data. One example of an open access data storage and processing platform suitable for the use of big data is Hadoop, which was released in 2005 by Apache Software Foundation (http://hadoop.apache.org/). Because of its flexible nature and ease of use, Hadoop is one of the most commonly used systems for big data analysis. More than half of the Fortune 500 companies are believed to use Hadoop in some adjusted, modified, or expanded form.

Despite the messiness and the challenges posed by the sheer volume, velocity, and variety of big data,

it provides valuable information regarding trends in customer behavior. In addition to understanding customer behavior, big data is useful in developing new products and services, innovative marketing strategies, and evidence-based decision making. Big data gives companies the opportunity to analyze data in near-real time to reduce costs, increase revenue, gain competitive advantage, and understand sources of risk and causes of failure. In health care, the use of big data lies in improving the quality of care through personalized prescription analytics, risk management and forecasting, standardization and reduction of care variability, and automated data reporting.

▶ Exercise 11.1

In a mythical town named Qasba, there is a total of 750,000 people and three acute care general hospitals, A, B, and C. Every year, 3% of the population of Qasba is admitted to these hospitals. Hospital A gets one-half of those admissions, B gets one-third of them, and C gets the remainder. In 2016, hospital A admitted 18,750 patients, out of which 11,250 were residents of Qasba; hospital B admitted a total of 25,000 patients, of which 7,500 were residents of Qasba; and hospital C admitted a total of 5,000 patients, of which 3,800 were residents of Qasba. The remainder of admissions at each of these hospitals came from neighboring towns.

Question 1. Based on the information provided, calculate the relevance index and commitment index for each of the hospitals and indicate which hospitals are the most and least relevant to the population of Qasba.

Question 2. To which hospitals is the population of Qasba most and least committed?

▶ Exercise 11.2

The combined Herfindahl–Hirschman index for a geographic area with four hospitals (A, B, C, and D) is 2,010. Hospitals A, B, and C, respectively, control 30%, 25%, and 17% of market share.

Question 1. Should the regulatory authorities be concerned about the situation in this market? Explain why or why not.

Question 2. Calculate the market share and HHI of hospital D.

Question 3. Hospitals A and C have proposed a merger. Should the regulatory authorities be concerned about the postmerger market power of hospitals A and C combined? Explain why or why not.

🔍 *CASE STUDY 11.1: Example of Regional Market Analysis*

Modified from: Hamadi H, Apatu E, Spaulding A. Does hospital ownership influence hospital referral region health rankings in the United States. Int J Health Policy Manag. 2018;33(1):e168–e180. Accessed June 20, 2018. https://doi.org/10.1002/hpm.2442.

Example of Regional Market Analysis

The Dartmouth Atlas of Health Care has aggregated 3,436 hospital service areas (HSAs) in the United States into 306 regional healthcare markets called hospital referral regions (HRRs). The boundaries of these regional markets are based on referral patterns of patients for major cardiovascular surgical procedures and neurosurgery. Consequently, each HRR includes a major city and at least one tertiary care hospital. Based on the overall performance of the healthcare system in each of these regional markets (HRRs) and its performance on four distinct categories of healthcare quality, the Commonwealth Fund ranks all 306 HRRs in the country every year. The four categories of healthcare quality used for ranking the HRRs are as follows: *access and affordability, prevention and treatment, avoidable hospital use and cost,* and *healthy lives.* As such, the Commonwealth Fund gives each HRR five different rank scores every year (i.e., an aggregated overall performance score and a score on each of the four above named categories of healthcare quality).

This 2017 study by Hamadi et al. examined the association of HRR rank scores with a number of characteristics of the referral region. The purpose of the study was to investigate which characteristics or variables, if any, significantly affect HRR's rankings. The characteristics of interest included the ownership of hospitals, the aggregated Hospital Value-Based Purchasing Scorecard (HVBP) performance score, the percentages of Medicare and Medicaid patients, the size of the population, per capita income, and the Herfindahl-Hirschman Index (HHI) for the referral region. The researchers were particularly interested in exploring whether the number of for-profit or not-for-profit hospitals in the HRR is associated with indicators of health system performance such as access and affordability or prevention and treatment.

The authors combined data from the 2016 Commonwealth Fund Scorecard on Local Health System Performance, the 2016 American Hospital Association data set, and the 2016 HVBP data set from the Centers for Medicare and Medicaid Services (CMS). The HVBP data set includes participating hospitals' scores on clinical processes of care, health outcomes, patient experience, efficiency, and overall performance.

Multivariate linear regression models were developed to explore the association of HRR ranking scores (dependent variable) with independent variables such as hospital ownership, HVBP scores, average length of stay, the number of staffed beds, and several other hospital- and market-level variables (see **TABLE 11.3**). The unit of analysis in all regression models was the HRR. All independent variables, such as the number of for-profit hospitals or HVBP scores,

TABLE 11.3 Multivariate Association of Hospital Referral Region Characteristics With Local Health System's Ranking on a Performance Indicator ($n = 301$)

	Local Health System's Performance Indicators							
	Access and Affordability		**Prevention and Treatment**		**Avoidable Hospital Use and Cost**		**Healthy Lives**	
Hospital ownership	Coefficient (SE)	Sig.	Coefficient (SE)	Sig.	Coefficient (SE)	Sig.	Coefficient (SE)	Sig.
Investor owned	4.87 (1.18)	***	2.39 (0.63)	***	2.32 (1.18)	*	0.78 (1.09)	
Not-for-profit	−4.45 (0.76)	***	−1.95 (0.4)	***	0.26 (0.76)		0.17 (0.7)	
Local and government owned	6.05 (2.09)	***	3.59 (1.11)	***	3.5 (2.1)	*	6.98 (1.93)	***
Herfindahl–Hirschman index	1.65 (15.32)		−14.32 (8.13)	*	−8.95 (15.36)		−10.9 (14.15)	

Population per million	4.89 (2.84)	*	3.39 (1.51)	**	−5.68 (2.85)	**	−12.36 (2.63)	***
Per capita income (1,000s)	−2.56 (0.34)	***	−0.93 (0.18)	***	−0.93 (0.35)	***	−3.26 (0.32)	***
Total performance score	−0.32 (0.51)		−1.19 (0.27)	***	−0.61 (0.52)		−0.62 (0.48)	
Hospital Medicare percentage	19.39 (66.26)		97.79 (35.17)	***	−75.67 (66.47)		−44.07 (61.22)	
Hospital Medicaid percentage	−189.51 (52.68)	***	−41.33 (27.96)		234.76 (52.84)	***	117.75 (48.67)	**
Average length of stay	−8.42 (2.04)	***	−4.1 (1.08)	***	4.72 (2.05)	**	2.48 (1.89)	
Staffed beds	0.03 (0.04)		0.07 (0.02)	***	0.22 (0.04)	***	0.12 (0.04)	***
***Significant at $P < .01$	R^2	0.3908	R^2	0.3864	R^2	0.2446	R^2	0.4338
**Significant at $P < .05$	Adj. R^2	0.3676	Adj. R^2	0.363	Adj. R^2	0.2158	Adj. R^2	0.4122
*Significant at $P < .1$	Prob. > F	0.000	Prob. > F	0.000	Prob. > F	0.000	Prob. > F	0.000

Modified from: Hamadi H, Apatu E, Spaulding A. Does hospital ownership influence hospital referral region health rankings in the United States. Int J Health Policy Manag. 2018;33(1):e168–e180. Accessed June 20, 2018. https://doi.org/10.1002/hpm.2442. Reprinted with permission from John Wiley & Sons.

were aggregated at the HRR level. Therefore, all independent and dependent variables (i.e., HRR ranking scores) in the regression models were continuous variables.

A high score on the Commonwealth Fund overall rank or rank on a quality indicator such as access and affordability signifies poorer performance of a referral region than referral regions with lower scores. Therefore, a positive value of the coefficient in the regression models (see Table 11.3) indicates increasingly poor performance of the HRR in association with increasing values of an independent variable. For example, increasing numbers of for-profit hospitals in the referral region may be associated with lower ranking of the referral region by the Commonwealth Fund. Conversely, negative values of the coefficient in a regression model indicate increasingly better performance of the referral region in association with higher values of the independent variable (e.g., the number of not-for-profit hospitals in the HRR).

Table 11.3 presents some of the results of the study.

Based on the results shown in Table 11.3, the authors concluded that a greater number of not-for-profit hospitals in the referral region was associated with better access and affordability (coefficient = −4.45) and prevention and treatment (coefficient = −1.95). On the other hand, referral regions with greater numbers of for-profit hospitals were associated with worse outcomes on all measures of quality other than healthy lives. Likewise, a greater number of local- and government-owned hospitals in a referral region was associated with worse outcomes on all four measures of the health system's performance. The corresponding coefficient values on these measures for local- and government-owned hospitals in Table 11.3 are 6.05, 3.59, 3.5, and 6.98. The results also showed that, in all four regression models, a higher per capita income in the HRR was associated with better outcomes on all four measures of quality (coefficients, −2.5, −0.93, −0.93, and −3.26). In addition, a large population size in the referral region was associated with better performance on avoidable hospital use and cost and with healthy lives (corresponding coefficients, −5.68 and −12.36).

🔍 *CASE STUDY 11.2: Planning for Mental Health Services*

Modified from: Harris MG, Buckingham WJ, Pirkis J, Groves A, Whiteford H. Planning estimates for the provision of core mental health services in Queensland 2007–2017. Aust N Z J Psychiatry 2012;46(10):982–994.

According to the guidelines developed by the World Health Organization, mental health service planning involves specification of strategies, time frames, indicators, and resources to achieve the objectives articulated in the health policy of a country or region. The following case study describes the methods adopted by a team of Australian researchers to develop resource target recommendations to guide the development of Queensland Plan for Mental Health Services 2007–2017. The purpose of the plan is to deliver the following core public mental health services: (1) inpatient services, (2) adult residential rehabilitation services, (3) supported accommodation, (4) ambulatory care mental health services, and (5) community support services. The methods adopted by the researchers were based on a combination of empirical evidence and planning models reported in the literature on health services planning. The work to develop recommendations for Queensland Plan for Mental Health Services 2007–2017 was done in the five steps described next.

In step 1, the researchers assessed the need for mental health services in the population by estimating the prevalence of mental disorders in Queensland by age group and severity. This was done by using a model that employs data from the Australian National Survey of Mental Health and Well Being, supplemented by data from other local and international surveys. National-level prevalence estimates of mental disorders thus derived were then applied to the population of Queensland to get the number of mental health patients in each age and severity group. Employing health services utilization data from various sources, the researchers then estimated the proportion of people with a specific mental disorder and level of severity who would have received treatment in various parts of the healthcare system. In step 2, the mix and level of specialized mental health services availability in Queensland were compared with reference standards against which the performance of Queensland could be assessed. The indicators used for benchmarking included the number of designated psychiatric beds, full-time equivalent direct-care staff in ambulatory care settings, and community accommodation (housing) support services.

In step 3, the impact of standards set in 1996 under Queensland Ten-Year Mental Health Strategy was assessed by examining 5-year trends in the utilization of inpatient and ambulatory care public mental health services. In step 4, benchmark information on resource targets from government-endorsed mental health plans and other sources was reviewed to develop age-specific standardized mental health resource targets per 100,000 population for the five core mental health service components in Queensland. In the fifth and final step, information obtained in steps 1–4 was combined to set resource targets for the five core service components in Queensland.

The researchers estimated that, overall, 16.6% of the population suffered from mental disorders, with 2.5% having severe and 4.5% having moderate-intensity mental health problems. Among children and adolescents (0 to 17 years), 15.6% suffered from mental disorders, with 2.1% having severe and 5.5% having moderate-intensity mental disorders. Among individuals 65 years or older, the prevalence of mental disorders was 12.9%.

TABLES 11.4 and **11.5** show some of the results of this study, including the number of people at each level of severity treated by health services in 2004 and resource implications of the recommended targets for service delivery in Queensland. Based on the data shown in Tables 11.4 and 11.5, answer the following questions.

TABLE 11.4 Estimated Number of People with Mental Disorders in Queensland, at Each Level of Severity, Treated by Health Services in 2004–2005[a,b,c,d]

Treated by Health Services							
Severity Level	State and territory public mental health services[e]	Private sector mental health services[f]	General practitioner only[g]	Other health services[h]	Total	Percent coverage	Not treated by health services
Mild	n.a.	17,000	25,000	15,000	57,000	15%	317,000
Moderate	n.a.	14,000	28,000	7,000	49,000	28%	127,000
Severe	52,000	14,000	23,000	6,000	95,000	96%	4,000

Total	52,000	45,000	76,000	28,000	201,000	31%	448,000
% total seen	26%	23%	38%	14%	–	–	–

aEstimates are based on non-duplicated person counts, with persons seen assigned to only one category in the following order of priority: state and territory public mental health, private sector mental health services, general practitioner only, and other health services.

b'Treated by health services' does not imply treatment is provided at adequate or optimal levels.

cEstimates are rounded to the nearest thousand.

dPopulation data are estimated resident population of Queensland, as at June 2004 (Australian Bureau of Statistics, 2005).

eBased on ambulatory service utilization data 2004–2005 provided by Queensland Health, adjusted for over-counting due to the lack of a state-wide unique person identifier and to allow for individuals who use only inpatient services (as recommended by Queensland Health). All individuals seen by the public sector are assumed to have severe disorders, however this may not be the case across all areas, particularly where there is a shortage of primary care services to deal with mild and moderate conditions.

fDerived from the National Mental Health Report 2007 (Department of Health and Ageing, 2007), with splits by severity based on a profile of private psychiatrist activity (Harris and Boyce, 1996; Solomon et al., 1993).

gFor the 18+ year population, based on analyses of 1997 National Survey of Mental Health & Wellbeing (NSMHWB) (Andrews et al., 2001b), with adjustments as per the MH-CCP model (New South Wales Department of Health, 2001); for the 0–17 year population, based on the child and adolescent component of the NSMHWB (Sawyer et al., 2000).

hDerived from analyses of the 1997 NSMHWB (Andrews et al., 2001a). Other health services include private psychologist, accident and emergency departments, community health services, and non-psychiatric units in general hospitals.

Reproduced from: Harris MG, Buckingham WJ, Pirkis J, Groves A, Whiteford H. Planning estimates for the provision of core mental health services in Queensland 2007–2017. Aust N Z J Psychiatry 2012;46(10):982–994. Reprinted by permission from: SAGE Publications, Ltd.

TABLE 11.5 Resource Implications of the Recommended Targets for Queensland Service Provision

	Targets per 100,000 Population		Comparison of Current and Recommended Resources If Targets Implemented		
	Current Resources (2005)	Recommended	Current (2005)	Targets Applied to 2005	Targets Applied to 2017
Inpatient Services					
Acute beds	17.4	20	691	793	883
Non-acute beds	16.5	10	653	397	442
Total	**33.9**	**30**	**1,344**	**1,190**	**1,325**
Adult Residential Rehabilitation Services					
24-hour clinical	2.0	10	80	397	442
Non-clinical	–	15	–	714	794
Total	**2.0**	**25**	**80**	**1,111**	**1,236**
Supported Accommodation					
Supervised hostel places	n.a.	35	n.a.	1,388	1,546
Supported public housing places	–	35	–	1,388	1,546
Total	**n.a.**	**70**	**n.a.**	**2,776**	**3,092**

(continues)

	Targets per 100,000 Population		Comparison of Current and Recommended Resources If Targets Implemented		
	Current Resources (2005)	Recommended	Current (2005)	Targets Applied to 2005	Targets Applied to 2017
Ambulatory Care Clinical Staffing					
Staffing	33.1	70	1,306	2,776	3,092
NGO-Managed Community Support Services (% total funding)					
% total funding	6.4%	15%	$24m	$58m	*

n.a., Information not available

– nil service provision

* Allocation is dependent upon 2017 mental health funding allocations that cannot be estimated at this time.

Reproduced from: Harris MG, Buckingham WJ, Pirkis J, Groves A, Whiteford H. Planning estimates for the provision of core mental health services in Queensland 2007–2017. Aust N Z J Psychiatry. 2012;46(10):982–994. Reprinted by permission from: SAGE Publications, Ltd.

Question 1. What proportion of treated patients with severe mental disorders was treated by general practitioners only?

Question 2. What proportion of patients with severe mental disorders was not treated by health services?

Question 3. Based on the data presented in Table 11.5, what are the resource implications of recommended targets in Queensland for inpatient acute and non-acute beds, ambulatory care clinical staffing, and financial implications of NGO-managed community support services in 2005 and 2017?

▶ 11.16 Summary

Planning and marketing of health services to ensure adequate supply, distribution, and utilization entail a variety of activities, from the delineation of a geographic market to the specification of the population to be served, from setting priorities to assessing whether a geographic area or population is adequately served. A number of different methods are available to determine the size and boundaries of a geographic area, whether from the perspective of a public policy maker or that of a hospital administrator. Different techniques have also been developed to assess market share of healthcare providers, identify competitors, and determine the degree of competition in the marketplace. From a regulatory point of view, low market concentration and greater competition serve the interests of communities, payers, patients, and policy makers better by promoting lower prices and better quality of service. Consumers utilize services with disregard for administrative geographic boundaries, such as county lines and SMSAs, and they demonstrate their assessment of quality

through preference for one provider or the other and willingness to travel a greater distance to seek care from a provider of choice.

Depending on the configuration of the healthcare system and the role of government, regulatory authorities can engage in healthcare planning either directly or indirectly. Direct methods of healthcare planning involve establishment of planning agencies, awards of grant monies to establish new healthcare facilities, and stringent licensing and certification requirements. Indirect methods of healthcare planning involve differential reimbursement policies and variable compensation rates for different localities, providers, and services. Designation of geographic units and populations within certain geographic districts as medically underserved is used to promote availability of services to socially and economically marginalized populations and localities.

This chapter provides students with the necessary tools to understand issues related to healthcare planning from different perspectives and methods to engage in data-driven, evidence-based health services planning.

References

1. American College of Healthcare Executives. ACHE Code of Ethics. 2016 [cited 2017 Jul 28]. Available from: https://www.ache.org/abt_ache/code.cfm

2. Hymen HH. Health planning: a systematic approach. Rockville, MD: Aspen Systems Corporation; 1982.

3. Forester J. Planning in the face of power. Berkeley: University of California Press; 1989.

4. Davidoff P, Reiner TA. A choice theory of planning. J Am Inst Plann. 1962;28(2):103–115.

5. Frech III HE, Langenfeld J, McCluer FF. Elzinga-Hogarty tests and alternative approaches for market share calculations in hospital markets. Antitrust Law J. 2004;71(3):921–947.

6. Garnick DW, Luft HS, Robinson JC, Tetreault J. Appropriate measures of hospital market areas. Health Serv Res. 1987;22(1):69–89.

7. Griffith JR. Quantitative techniques for hospital planning and control. Lexington, MA: Lexington Books; 1972.

8. Zwanziger J, Melnick GA, Mann JM. Measures of hospital market structure: a review of the alternatives and a proposed approach. Socioecon Plann Sci. 1990;24(2):81–95.

9. Phibbs CS, Robinson JC. A variable-radius measure of local hospital market structure. Health Serv Res. 1993;28(3):313–324.

10. Lindrooth RC. Research on the hospital market: recent advances and continuing data needs. Inquiry. 2008;45(Spring):19–29.

11. Morrisey MA, Sloan FA, Valvona J. Defining geographic markets for hospital care. Law Contemp Probl. 1988;51(2):165–195.

12. Knox EG. Epidemiology in health care planning: a guide to the uses of a scientific method. Oxford: Oxford University Press; 1979.

13. Delmater PL, Shortridge AM, Messina JP. Regional health care planning: a methodology to cluster facilities using community utilization patterns. BMC Health Serv Res. 2013;13:333.

14. U.S. Federal Trade Commission and US Department of Justice. Improving health care: a dose of competition. Technical Report. Washington, DC: U.S. Government Printing Office; 2004 [cited 2018 May 17]. Available from: https://www.ftc.gov/sites/default/files/documents/reports/improving-health-care-dose-competition-report-federal-trade-commission-and-department-justice/040723healthcarerpt.pdf

15. National Conference of State Legislatures. Certificate of Need: state health laws and programs [cited 2018 May 17]. Available from: http://www.ncsl.org/research/health/con-certificate-of-need-state-laws.aspx

16. Ferrier GD, Leleu H, Valdmanis VG. The impact of CON regulation on hospital efficiency. Health Care Manag Sci. 2010;13:84–100.

17. Wang F, Luo W. Assessing spatial and nonspatial factors for healthcare access: towards an integrated approach to defining health professional shortage areas. Health Place. 2005;11:131–146.

18. Luo W, Wang F. Measures of spatial accessibility to health care in a GIS environment: synthesis and a case study in the Chicago region. Environ Plann B Plann Des. 2003;30:865–884.

19. Oklahoma State Department of Health, Center for Health Innovation & Effectiveness. 2014 [cited 2018 May 17]. Available from: https://www.ok.gov/health2/documents/Medically%20Underserved%20Areas.pdf

20. HRSA, U.S. Department of Health and Human Services. Shortage Designation: Health Professional Shortage Areas & Medically Underserved Areas/Populations. 2016 [cited 2017 Nov 20]. Available from: https://bhw.hrsa.gov/shortage-designation/hpsas

21. Elgar FJ, Pfortner T, Moor I, Clercq BD, Stevens GWJM, Currie C. Socioeconomic inequalities in adolescent health 2002–2010: a time-series analysis of 34 countries participating in the Health Behaviour in School-Aged Children study. Lancet. 2015;385(9982):2088–2095.

22. Bahls C. Achieving equality in health: racial and ethnic minorities face worse health and health care disparities—but some interventions have made a difference. Health Policy Brief. Health Aff. Hasnian-Wynia R, Agres T, Dentzer S, editors. 2011 Oct 6 [cited 2018 May 17]. Available from: http://www.rwjf.org/content/dam/farm/reports/issue_briefs/2011/rwjf71161

23. Mead H, Cartwright-Smith L, Jones K, Ramos C, Siegel B, Woods K. Racial and ethnic disparities in U.S. health care: a chartbook. The Commonwealth Fund. 2008 [cited 2017 Nov 20]. Available from: http://www.commonwealthfund.org/~/media/files/publications/chartbook/2008/mar/racial-and-ethnic-disparities-in-u-s--health-care--a-chartbook/mead_racialethnicdisparities_chartbook_1111-pdf.pdf

24. Laird LD, Amer MM, Barnett ED, Barnes LL. Muslim patients and health disparities in the U.K. and the U.S. Arch Dis Child. 2007;92(10):922–926.

25. Dyer O. Disparities in health widen between rich and poor in England. BMJ. 2005;331:419.

26. Donato R, Segal L. Does Australia have the appropriate health reform agenda to close the gap in indigenous health? Aust Health Rev. 2012;37(2):232–238.

27. Durey A, Thompson SC. Reducing the health disparities of indigenous Australians: time to change focus. BMC Health Serv Res. 2012;12:151.

28. American Marketing Association. About AMA [cited 2017 Nov 15]. Available from: https://www.ama.org/AboutAMA/Pages/Definition-of-Marketing.aspx

29. Bierbaum B4 Steps to implementing Market Technology Effectively. Spectrum. 2015 Nov/Dec.

30. Zeithaml VA, Parasuraman A, Berry LL. Delivering Quality Service: Balancing Customer Perceptions and Expectations. New York, NY. The Free Press; 1990:15–34.

31. Sachdev SB, Verma HV. Relative importance fo service quality dimensions: a multisectoral study. J Serv Res; 2004;4(1):93–116.

32. Landrum H, Prybutok V, Zhang X, Peak D. Measuring IS system service quality with SERVQUAL: Users' perceptions of relative importance of the five SERVPERF dimensions. Informing Sci: Int J Emerging Transdis. 2009;12:17–35 [cited 2018 July 27]. Available from: http://inform.nu/Articles/Vol12/ISJv12p017-035Landrum232.pdf

33. Barkholz D. Hospitals work to harness the power of digital marketing. Modern Healthcare. 2017 [cited 2017 Nov 22]. Available from: http://www.modernhealthcare.com/article/20170605/NEWS/170609951

34. New South Wales Department of Health. Mental health clinical care and preventive model: A population health model MH-CCP version 1.11. Sydney, Australia: New South Wales Department of Health. 2001 [cited 2017 Nov 20]. Available from: http://www.health.nsw.gov.au/mentalhealth/Documents/mh-ccp-v-1-11.pdf

35. Australian Bureau of Statistics. Population by age and sex, Australian States and Territories (ABS Cat. 3210.0). Canberra: Australian Bureau of Statistics; 2005.

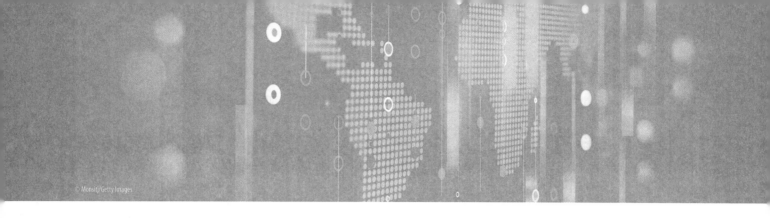

CHAPTER 12

Prevention, Detection, and Monitoring of Disease

LEARNING OBJECTIVES

Having mastered the materials in this chapter, the student will be able to:

1. Use various modalities of disease prevention in planning and evaluation of services.
2. Plan and organize community-based primary prevention programs.
3. Plan and organize community-based screening programs.
4. Plan and organize community- and facility-based active surveillance programs.

CHAPTER OUTLINE

12.1 Introduction
12.2 The Nature, Scope, and Levels of Prevention
    12.2.1 Primary Prevention
    12.2.2 Secondary Prevention
    12.2.3 Tertiary Prevention
12.3 Screening
    12.3.1 Definition of Screening
    12.3.2 Purpose of Screening
    12.3.3 Criteria for Effective Screening
    12.3.4 Characteristics of a Good Candidate Disease for Screening
        12.3.4.1 Seriousness of the Disease
        12.3.4.2 Treatability of the Disease
        12.3.4.3 Benefits of Treatment in Presymptomatic Stage
        12.3.4.4 Low Side Effects of Treatment
        12.3.4.5 Availability of a Definitive Diagnostic Test
        12.3.4.6 Prevalence of the Disease

12.3.5 Various Aspects of Screening Tests
    12.3.5.1 High Accuracy for Detectable Preclinical Phase
        12.3.5.1.1 Validity
        12.3.5.1.2 Sensitivity
        12.3.5.1.3 Specificity
        12.3.5.1.4 Reliability
    12.3.5.2 Relationship Between Sensitivity and Specificity
    12.3.5.3 Detection of Disease Before Reaching Critical Point
    12.3.5.4 Little Morbidity, Invasiveness, and Inconvenience
    12.3.5.5 High Availability and Affordability
    12.3.5.6 Predictive Values of Positive and Negative Screening Test Results
    12.3.5.7 Lead-Time Bias
    12.3.5.8 Length Bias

12.4 Surveillance
  12.4.1 Definition and Distinction from Screening
  12.4.2 Passive Surveillance
  12.4.3 Active Surveillance
  12.4.4 Sentinel or Categorical Surveillance
  12.4.5 Syndromic Surveillance
  12.4.6 U.S. National Electronic Disease
       Surveillance System

12.4.7 Triple-S: The European Syndromic
     Surveillance Project
Exercise 12.1
Exercise 12.2
Case Study 12.1 – Nosocomial Infection Surveillance
Case Study 12.2 – Screening for Colorectal Cancer
12.5 Summary

KEY TERMS

Active surveillance	Predictive value negative	Sensitivity
Critical point	Prevalence	Sentinel surveillance
Lead-time bias	Primary prevention	Specificity
Length bias	Reliability	Syndromic surveillance
Passive surveillance	Secondary prevention	Tertiary prevention
Predictive value positive	Screening	Validity

▶ 12.1 Introduction

Prevention and early detection of diseases that are responsible for significant morbidity, disability, and premature death are essential components of an effective healthcare system. Monitoring and surveillance activities to identify new cases and to keep track of previously existing cases of diseases that pose serious public health threats are also important for effective healthcare planning and delivery. Numerous studies on the cost-effectiveness of preventive services such as immunization programs have shown a tremendous payoff for societal investment in these programs.[1,2] Studies on the cost-effectiveness of newborn screening programs to identify serious congenital disorders such as cystic fibrosis, hypothyroidism, and phenylketonuria, or periodic screening in women for cervical and breast cancer have also shown significant overall cost savings for healthcare systems. Aside from societal cost savings, disease prevention, screening, and surveillance programs have considerable positive impact on the health and well-being of countless individuals all over the world. Healthcare managers need to be fully cognizant of the role of these activities in protecting, improving, and maintaining the health of communities they serve. Engaging in disease prevention and health promotion activities allows healthcare managers to demonstrate community benefits to payers, policy makers, and regulatory agencies. Low-cost programs for disease prevention and early detection, such as vaccinations and screenings at community events, are not only good for community relations, but also offer a high return on investment through reduced burden on healthcare facilities. In this chapter, we discuss the nature, scope, and epidemiologic dimensions of disease prevention, screening, and surveillance programs.

▶ 12.2 The Nature, Scope, and Levels of Prevention

At the onset, it is important to note that prevention of the occurrence, progression, and complications of diseases is a collaborative effort with a holistic approach and community-based perspective. All stakeholders, including policy makers, community leaders, educators, local health departments, and healthcare providers, have to work as partners toward the common goal of promoting health and preventing disease from birth to the end of life. Historically, the focus of payers, providers, and patients alike had remained on disease management through episodic reactive care rather than a consistent proactive focus on health promotion and disease prevention. The locus of decision making resided primarily with healthcare providers, while patients passively accepted the modalities of care offered to them. Contact with the healthcare system was mostly initiated by the patient and was triggered by the appearance of signs and symptoms of some disease. Only in recent decades did scheduled well-baby or well-child visits and annual physical

TABLE 12.1 Definitions of Various Grades of Recommendations for Preventive Services Issued by the United States Preventive Services Task Force, July 2012

Grade	Definition	Suggestions for Practice
A	The USPSTF recommends the service. There is high certainty that the net benefit is substantial.	Offer or provide this service.
B	The USPSTF recommends the service. There is high certainty that the net benefit is moderate or there is moderate certainty that the net benefit is moderate to substantial.	Offer or provide this service.
C	The USPSTF recommends selectively offering or providing this service to individual patients based on professional judgment and patient preferences. There is at least moderate certainty that the net benefit is small.	Offer or provide this service for selected patients depending on individual circumstances.
D	The USPSTF recommends against the service. There is moderate or high certainty that the service has no net benefit or that the harms outweigh the benefits.	Discourage the use of this service.
I Statement	The USPSTF concludes that the current evidence is insufficient to assess the balance of benefits and harms of the service. Evidence is lacking, of poor quality, or conflicting, and the balance of benefits and harms cannot be determined.	Read the clinical considerations section of USPSTF Recommendation Statement. If the service is offered, patients should understand the uncertainty about the balance of benefits and harms.

Reproduced from: U.S. Preventive Services Task Force. Grade definitions. June 2016. Accessed June 21, 2018. https://www.uspreventiveservicestaskforce.org/Page/Name/grade-definitions#grade-definitions-after-july-2012

examinations become a part of the healthcare lexicon. Almost universal availability of vaccines for a number of infectious disorders, tests for early detection of a host of diseases, and widespread recognition of the role of lifestyle as the most important determinant of health have brought prevention of diseases to the forefront of the healthcare system. In the last two or three decades, policy makers, public health agencies, and payers, including insurance companies and employers, have increasingly focused on disease prevention and shifted the burden of responsibility for staying healthy toward individuals and families. Employers and insurance companies have developed financial incentives to facilitate and reward adoption of healthy lifestyles on the part of the consumer, and delivery of preventive services, such as counseling, on the part of the provider.

The nature of activities undertaken by individuals, healthcare providers, communities, and public health professionals is a function of whether the objective is to prevent the occurrence, progression, or complication of a disease. Based on their objectives, preventive services are categorized as (1) *primary prevention*, (2) *secondary prevention,* and (3) *tertiary prevention.*

The United States Preventive Services Task Force (USPSTF) makes recommendations to practitioners and other interested parties regarding various preventive services. The Task Force grades these recommendations on a scale from A to I. **TABLE 12.1** shows the definition of each of these grades, and **TABLE 12.2** shows the list of preventive services that are currently listed as "A" grade—that is, the Task Force recommends these preventive services because there is a high level of certainty that the net benefit of each of these services is substantial.

12.2.1 Primary Prevention

Primary prevention activities are designed to prevent the occurrence of a disease in the first place. Successful primary preventions activities, such as high levels of vaccination coverage in a population, can have a direct positive effect on the incidence of infectious diseases—for example, high pneumonia vaccination rates among the elderly can reduce the incidence of pneumonia in that group. Educational programs targeting youth and young adults can reduce the incidence of sexually transmitted diseases. Regulatory and educational activities focused on tobacco smoking can have both short- and long-term impact on the incidence of respiratory diseases and lung cancer. At the individual level, primary prevention occurs through pursuing a lifestyle free of behaviors that are known to increase the risk of one or the other disease. Notably, because of the multifactorial etiology of diseases such as cardiovascular diseases, diabetes, and cancer, a

TABLE 12.2 List of A Grade Preventive Services Recommendations by the U.S. Preventive Services Task Force: September 2016

1	Screening pregnant women for asymptomatic bacteriuria
2	Screening adults aged 18 years or older for high blood pressure
3	Screening women ages 21 to 65 years for cervical cancer every 3 years
4	Screening men age 35 years and older for lipid disorders
5	Screening women age 45 years and older for lipid disorders if they are at increased risk
6	Screening men and women for colorectal cancer starting at age 50 years
7	Daily folic acid supplement for all women planning or capable of pregnancy
8	Ocular topical medication of all newborns to prevent gonococcal eye infection
9	Screening newborns for sickle cell disease
10	Screening pregnant women for hepatitis B infection
11	Screening nonpregnant adolescents and adults ages 15 to 65 years for HIV
12	Screening all pregnant women for HIV
13	Screening newborns for congenital hypothyroidism
14	Testing all pregnant women for Rh blood (D) typing and antibodies
15	Tobacco use counseling and offering behavioral intervention to all adults by clinicians
16	Tobacco use counseling and offering behavioral intervention to all pregnant women
17	Screening for syphilis infection all persons who are at increased risk
18	Screening all pregnant women for syphilis infection

nonrisky lifestyle does not guarantee complete avoidance of disease. For example, lung cancer does occur among nonsmokers; however, the risk of lung cancer increases by an order of magnitude among smokers, whereas nonsmokers can expect to have a much lower risk of developing lung cancer. Regular exercise; a nutritious, balanced diet; safer sex; nonuse of illicit drugs; and wearing a seatbelt are all common examples of individual-level primary prevention. Availability of clean drinking water, sanitary toilet facilities, clean air, proper housing, safe work environments, community parks, sidewalks, and bike trails are examples of primary prevention at the community and public policy level. Availability of age- and risk-appropriate counseling services at public health agencies and healthcare facilities, including primary care physicians' offices, represents system-level primary prevention. Programs that provide condoms and disposable syringes at no cost to population groups such as gay men and intravenous drug users are examples of primary prevention programs designed to reduce the occurrence of diseases such as HIV/AIDS.

12.2.2 Secondary Prevention

As opposed to primary prevention, which is designed to prevent the onset of disease in the first place, **secondary prevention** aims to arrest or alter the course of the pathologic process and natural progression of disease through early detection and intervention. It targets a disease in its presymptomatic stage with the aim of reducing severity and preventing adverse effects, including long-term disability. An excellent example of secondary prevention is the screening of newborn children for a number of congenital disorders by testing a heel stick dried blood spot. Screening of children shortly after birth allows for arresting the progression of life-threatening diseases through appropriate early intervention. In the United States, all states have a newborn screening program to identify serious congenital disorders shortly after birth. BOX 12.1 shows 58 conditions for which newborns are routinely screened in the state of California. According to the California Department of Public Health,[3] approximately 15–18 newborns with phenylketonuria (PKU), 70 with cystic fibrosis, 26 with congenital adrenal hyperplasia, 100–125 with sickle cell disease, and 275 with primary congenital

---

BOX 12.1 Congenital Conditions for Which Newborns Are Screened in California

A. Amino Acid Disorders

1. Argininemia (ARG)
2. Argininosuccinic aciduria (ASA)
3. Benign hyperphenylalaninemia (H-PHE)
4. Biopterin defect in cofactor biosynthesis (BIOPT-BS)
5. Biopterin defect in cofactor regeneration (BIOPT-REG)
6. Citrullinemia, Type I (CIT)
7. Citrullinemia, Type II (CIT II)
8. Classic phenylketonuria (PKU)
9. Homocystinuria (HCY)
10. Hypermethioninemia (MET)
11. Hyperornithine with gyrate deficiency (Hyper ORN)
12. Maple syrup urine disease (MSUD)
13. Ornithine transcarbamylase deficiency (OTC)
14. Prolinemia (PRO)
15. Tyrosinemia, Type I (TYR I)
16. Tyrosinemia, Type II (TYR II)
17. Tyrosinemia, Type III (TYR III)

B. Endocrine Disorders

1. Congenital adrenal hyperplasia (CAH)
2. Primary congenital hypothyroidism (CH)

C. Fatty Acid Oxidation Disorders

1. Carnitine acylcarnitine translocase deficiency (CACT)
2. Carnitine palmitoyltransferase I deficiency (CPT-IA)
3. Carnitine palmitoyltransferase II deficiency (CPT-II)
4. Carnitine uptake defect (CUD)
5. Glutaric acidemia, Type II (GA-2)
6. Long-chain L-3 hydroxyacyl-CoA dehydrogenase deficiency (LCHAD)
7. Medium-chain acyl-CoA dehydrogenase deficiency (MCAD)
8. Medium/short-chain L-3 hydroxyacyl-CoA dehydrogenase deficiency (M/SCHAD)
9. Short-chain acyl-CoA dehydrogenase deficiency (SCAD)
10. Trifunctional protein deficiency (TFP)
11. Very long-chain acyl-CoA dehydrogenase deficiency (VLCAD)

D. Hemoglobin Disorders

1. Hemoglobinopathies (Var Hb)
2. S, beta-thalassemia (Hb S/ßTh)
3. S, C disease (Hb S/C)
4. Sickle cell anemia (Hb SS)

(continues)

BOX 12.1 Congenital Conditions for Which Newborns Are Screened in California *(continued)*

E. Organic Acid Conditions

1. 2-methyl-3-hydroxybutyric acidemia (2M3HBA)
2. 2-methylbutyrylglycinuria (2MBG)
3. 3-hydroxy-3-methylglutaric aciduria (HMG)
4. 3-methylcrotonyl-CoA carboxylase deficiency (3-MCC)
5. 3-methylglutaconic aciduria (3MGA)
6. Beta-ketothiolase deficiency (BKT)
7. Ethylmalonic encephalopathy (EME)
8. Glutaric acidemia, Type I (GA-1)
9. Holocarboxylase synthetase deficiency (MCD)
10. Isobutyrylglycinuria (IBG)
11. Isovaleric acidemia (IVA)
12. Malonic acidemia (MAL)
13. Methylmalonic acidemia (cobalamin disorders) (Cbl A,B)
14. Methylmalonic acidemia (methylmalonyl-CoA mutase deficiency) (MUT)
15. Methylmalonic acidemia with homocystinuria (Cbl C, D, F)
16. Propionic acidemia (PROP)

F. Other Disorders

1. Adrenoleukodystrophy (ALD)
2. Biotinidase deficiency (BIOT)
3. Classic galactosemia (GALT)
4. Cystic fibrosis (CF)
5. Formiminoglutamic acidemia (FIGLU)
6. Hearing loss (HEAR)
7. Hyperornithinemia-hyperammonemia-homocitrullinuria syndrome (HHH)
8. Severe combined immunodeficiency (SCID)

Reproduced with permission from: Baby's first test: California Department of Public Health. California Newborn Screening Program;2016. Accessed July 14, 2017. http://www.babysfirsttest.org/newborn-screening/states/california#second-section

hypothyroidism are identified through the newborn screening program in California every year. Periodic screening of women for cervical and breast cancer and of both men and women after age 50 for colorectal cancer allows healthcare providers to start treatment at an early stage of the disease, thereby reducing the burden of disease and increasing the likelihood of survival. Clearly, early detection by itself without early intervention does not constitute secondary prevention. As discussed later in this chapter, the criteria to screen for a disease include treatability of the disease and availability of effective therapeutic modalities.

In epidemiologic terms, secondary prevention (i.e., treatment in the preclinical stage of a disease) can reduce the prevalence of a disease by delaying or altogether avoiding the appearance of signs and symptoms and by reducing the duration of a disease if it is curable. On the other hand, if the disease is not curable, but secondary prevention allows longer survival of sick individuals (provided incidence remains unchanged), it can have the effect of increased prevalence in a population. In the event the disease in

question cannot be cured altogether, secondary prevention can still be extremely valuable if it can reduce the severity of disease, enhance the quality of life, and increase the productive life span of an individual. For example, early detection and treatment of breast cancer in women can potentially eliminate the likelihood of metastasis and recurrence and, at the very least, can increase healthy and productive life span by several years. Timely treatment of sexually transmitted diseases can interrupt the spread of disease to other individuals and, while it serves as a secondary prevention strategy for the cases of the disease, it works as primary prevention for future sexual partners of diseased individuals.[4]

12.2.3 Tertiary Prevention

Whereas secondary prevention attempts to reduce the severity and duration of disease and prevent the occurrence of resultant complications or disability, **tertiary prevention** focuses on restoration of function and avoidance of permanent disability. For example, rehabilitation and restoration of function after major trauma, stroke, and heart attack falls under tertiary prevention. As such, tertiary prevention attempts to improve the quality of life through appropriate and timely management of resulting disability and dysfunction. The main purpose of tertiary prevention is to avoid further loss of function, mobility, or intellect and restore residual stock of physical and mental function. Tertiary care during and after a debilitating illness can include psychosocial evaluation, counseling, and vocational rehabilitation. It is important to note that, at times, boundaries between secondary and tertiary prevention can be blurred, and these definitions are intended only to provide a degree of conceptual clarity. As an example, while appropriate treatment of diabetes and avoidance of its complications may be considered secondary prevention, the management of its complications, such as reduced kidney function and poor healing of wounds, may be considered tertiary prevention.

▶ 12.3 Screening

12.3.1 Definition of Screening

Several closely related definitions of **screening** are available in epidemiologic and medical literature. The most commonly used definition, which also appears in *A Dictionary of Epidemiology*,[5] was developed in 1951 by the United States Commission on Chronic Illness. It states that screening is

> The presumptive identification of unrecognized disease or defect by the application of tests, examinations, or other procedures which can be applied rapidly. Screening tests sort out apparently well persons who probably have a disease from those who probably do not. A screening test is not intended to be diagnostic. Persons with positive or suspicious findings must be referred to their physicians for diagnosis and necessary treatment.

The Dictionary of Epidemiology[5] adds the following information to the definition

> The initiative for screening usually comes from an agency or organization rather than from a patient with a complaint. Screening is usually concerned with chronic illness and aims to detect disease not yet under medical care. Screening may identify risk factors, genetic predisposition, and precursors, or early evidence of disease. There are different types of medical screening, each with its own aim:

1. Mass screening usually means the screening of a whole population.
2. Multiple or multiphasic screening involves the use of a variety of screening tests on the same occasion or sequentially.
3. Prescriptive screening has as its aim the early detection in presumptively healthy individuals of specific diseases that can be controlled better if detected early in their natural history.

An example is the use of mammography to detect breast cancer. The characteristics of a screening test must include accuracy, estimates of yield, precision, reproducibility, sensitivity, specificity, and validity.

In 1994, Wald[6] defined screening as "The systematic application of a test or enquiry to identify individuals at sufficient risk of a specific disorder to warrant further investigation or direct preventive action, amongst persons who have not sought medical attention on account of symptoms of that disorder." Another commonly used definition states that screening is the "Identification of disease in asymptomatic individuals by application of rapid tests to separate persons who probably have the disease from those who probably do not have the disease."[7] As indicated in the section on secondary prevention in this chapter, because it does not prevent the occurrence of disease, but rather helps in mitigating the severity and outcome of disease by early identification and intervention, screening is a form of secondary prevention.

12.3.2 Purpose of Screening

As a tool for secondary prevention, the main use of screening has been to identify early stage disease in asymptomatic individuals to improve their prognosis in terms of severity of disease and health outcomes by early intervention. However, at times, screening programs have been used to understand the frequency of disease in a population or to protect the public from the spread of an infectious disease by early detection of cases.[4,8] The underlying assumption, of course, is that if the disease is identified in its early stages, then adequate therapeutic intervention will result in better health outcomes in terms of a shorter and/or less severe course of disease and potential avoidance of mortality. The economic case for screening is made on the basis of it being a cost-effective strategy that not only helps individual patients through early detection and treatment, but also results in overall cost savings for the society or insurance companies by obviating the need for late-stage expensive treatment.

Medical literature is replete with discussions about the suitability of one or the other candidate medical condition—whether abdominal aneurysm[9] or hepatocellular carcinoma[10]—for screening as a cost-effective way of identifying large numbers of individuals who could benefit from early detection of their condition. For example, clinical scientists have debated whether adult men, especially those older than 40 years, should be screened for low testosterone levels or hypogonadism. Proponents of screening for low testosterone levels cite studies showing 5.6% to 38.8% of men in different age groups having hypogonadism. By some estimates, about 14 million men 45 years or older in the United States are at risk for problems related to low testosterone levels.[11] The opponents in this debate argue that age-related decrease in serum testosterone levels is a part of normal aging process, and there are significant deleterious effects associated with testosterone replacement therapy. They also argue that the demand for testosterone replacement therapy is largely generated by the marketing strategies of the pharmaceutical industry.[12]

12.3.3 Criteria for Effective Screening

Obuchowski et al.[13] have developed a useful set of criteria to systematically examine diseases and tests to decide what kind of diseases are good candidates for screening and what conditions must be met by a screening test to be worthy of implementation. In a modified form, these criteria are shown in **TABLE 12.3** and briefly discussed in the paragraphs that follow.

12.3.4 Characteristics of a Good Candidate Disease for Screening

Factors that must be taken into account while considering candidate diseases for implementing a screening program include the following.

12.3.4.1 Seriousness of the Disease

The candidate disease for screening should pose a serious risk of death and/or long-term complications if it is not identified and treated in early stages. In consideration of limited societal and institutional resources for which there are many competing demands, screening for minor ailments or conditions that do not pose a serious threat of mortality, morbidity, or disability may not be justifiable.

12.3.4.2 Treatability of the Disease

Whether the disease under consideration is treatable is an important consideration for a screening

TABLE 12.3 Characteristics of a Good Candidate Disease for Screening and a Good Screening Test

Characteristics of:	Specific Criteria
Disease and its treatment	1. Seriousness of the disease 2. Treatability of the disease 3. Benefits of treatment in presymptomatic stage 4. Low side effects of treatment 5. Availability of a diagnostic test 6. High prevalence of detectable preclinical phase
Screening test	1. High accuracy for detectable preclinical phase 2. Detection of disease before reaching critical point 3. Little morbidity, invasiveness, and inconvenience 4. High availability and affordability

Modified from: Obuchowski NA, Graham RJ, Baker ME, Powell KA. Ten criteria for effective screening: their application to multislice CT screening for pulmonary and colorectal cancers. Am J Radiol. 2001;176:1357–1362.

program. The existence of an effective treatment is essential to justify screening for any disease. In the absence of a treatment to improve health outcomes, screening can only be an academic exercise from which neither the patient nor society benefits in a meaningful way. Even if the disease poses a serious threat to the life and well-being of the affected individual, if there is no remedy or available treatment, there would be no point in screening and making early diagnoses because nothing will be done about it. However, if the life of the affected person cannot be saved by early diagnosis but survival time after diagnosis is longer and/or the quality of life before death is improved by early diagnosis, a case may be made to implement a screening program. For a number of diseases, such as Alzheimer's disease, multiple sclerosis, and Parkinson's disease, no effective treatment is currently available, and early detection does not offer better health outcomes.

12.3.4.3 Benefits of Treatment in Presymptomatic Stage

For screening to be cost-effective, the treatment for the disease should have better outcomes and lesser side effects if it is begun during the presymptomatic stage than when the treatment starts after the appearance of symptoms. If earlier start of treatment does not hold additional benefits than its later implementation, the extra effort and costs incurred by the early detection of a disease through a screening test cannot be justified. This can happen in diseases that progress slowly and respond quickly to treatment. In such situations, the lead-time gained through early detection becomes relatively immaterial. As a rule, it is difficult to demonstrate the additional benefits of early detection as compared with effective treatment after the appearance of symptoms.[13]

12.3.4.4 Low Side Effects of Treatment

For a disease to be a good candidate for screening, the side effects of treatment ought not be serious—that is, the side effects of a treatment should not outweigh its benefits. The issue of side effects of treatment becomes critically important if the screening test has a relatively high proportion of false-positive results and test-positive individuals are likely to be given treatment. Because the findings of a screening test ordinarily would be followed by one or more confirmatory tests, the scenario of false-positive individuals being treated can exist only if there is no diagnostic test available or it is imperfect.

12.3.4.5 Availability of a Definitive Diagnostic Test

For a disease to be a good candidate for screening, a definitive diagnostic test must be available to confirm or refute the findings of the screening test. If the level of suspicion is falsely raised by a screening test but there is no way to unequivocally rule out the existence of a disease, the patient would be unnecessarily subjected to a high level of anxiety and fear, or worse, be subjected to unnecessary treatment. Alternatively, if the screening test is accurate in raising the level of suspicion but the results cannot be confirmed by a definitive test, both the patient and the healthcare provider may disregard the findings of the screening test and disease may progress unchecked to a clinically overt stage with tragic consequences.

12.3.4.6 Prevalence of the Disease

To justify the allocation of scarce resources and to make a screening program reasonably cost-effective, the disease in question must be quite prevalent. If a disease was relatively uncommon, a large number of individuals would have to be screened to find just a few cases of the disease. In such a situation, the cost of finding one case of the disease would be prohibitively high and would raise questions about the cost-effectiveness of the program. Priorities for optimal allocation of resources ought to be based on the comparative cost-effectiveness of various interventions. Another problem related to the frequency of disease is that if the disease is uncommon, even with a good screening test, a high proportion of individuals identified as diseased would actually not have the disease—that is, there would be a high level of false-positive test results.

As shown in **TABLE 12.4** (Scenario 1), if the **prevalence** of a disease is only 1% in a population of 10,000 people, a screening test that accurately identifies 95% of the cases and justly rules out 99% of those without the disease would result in 194 individuals being labeled as diseased. However, only 95 (49%) of the 194 test-positive individuals would actually have the disease. This situation would result in 99 (51%) individuals being wrongly labeled as diseased (i.e., 51% false positivity).

On the other hand, if the prevalence of the disease was 10% rather than 1% (Scenario 2 of Table 12.4), then the same test would yield 1,040 positive results, of which 950 (91.3%) would actually have the disease and 90 (8.7%) would be falsely identified as disease-positive. That is a false-positive rate of only 8.7%. In this scenario, the fact that prevalence of disease increased to 10% as compared with 1% in the first scenario had a profound effect on false-positive test results, which were reduced from 51% to 8.7%. It is noteworthy that there is only a small change (0.05% to 0.56%) in the proportion of false-negative test results from one scenario to the other. This is because, in both scenarios, a vast majority of individuals in the population (9,900 and 9,000, respectively) did not have the disease, and the test is able to rule out accurately 99% of those who do not have the disease. Later in this chapter, we will explore issues related to the predictive values of positive and negative screening test results.

12.3.5 Various Aspects of Screening Tests

Screening tests can be deemed good or bad depending upon a number of characteristics. In broad terms, a good screening test must be accurate, simple, quick, inexpensive, nonintrusive, convenient, and free of pain and morbidity. These and other issues related to screening tests are discussed in the next section in more detail.

TABLE 12.4 Example of the Impact of Disease Prevalence on the Predictive Value of a Screening Test

	Those Who Have Disease	Those Who Do Not Have Disease	Total
Scenario 1 Disease Is Relatively Uncommon (i.e., prevalence is = 1%)			
Test positive	95*	99**	194
Test negative	5***	9801†	9,806
Total	100	9,900	10,000
Scenario 2 Disease Is More Common (i.e., prevalence is = 10%)			
Test positive	950*	90**	1,040
Test negative	50***	8,910†	8,960
Total	1,000	9,000	10,000

*True positive **False positive *** False negative †True negative.

Note: The screening test correctly identifies 95% of cases and correctly rules out 99% of those without the disease.

12.3.5.1 High Accuracy for Detectable Preclinical Phase

The level of accuracy refers to how close the results of a test are to the truth or reality. The accuracy of a test designed to identify a disease is determined by how frequently it does so without error. The Dictionary of Epidemiology[5] provides the following definition of accuracy.

1. The degree to which a measurement or an estimate based on measurements represents the true value of the attribute that is being measured. Relative lack of error. In statistics, accuracy is sometimes measured as the mean squared error.
2. The ability of a diagnostic test to correctly classify the presence or absence of the target disorder. The diagnostic accuracy of a test is usually expressed by its sensitivity and specificity.

The term *validity* is used interchangeably with *accuracy*. It refers to the question whether a test actually does what it purports to do. In the context of identifying a disease accurately, there are two parts to accuracy or validity: (1) sensitivity of the test and (2) specificity of the test.

12.3.5.1.1 Validity. In research literature, **validity** refers to the question whether a survey instrument or questionnaire discovers "truth." In the context of screening tests, validity refers to accuracy—that is, does a screening test do what it is intended to do or what it purports to do?[14] Because the terms *sensitivity* and *specificity* of a screening test refer to the ability of a test to accurately identify cases of the disease in question and accurately exclude noncases, respectively, the term *validity* encompasses both of these terms. The Dictionary of Epidemiology[15] makes a distinction between testing a specimen, such as a blood or sputum sample, and testing a person for the presence or absence of a disease. For testing a specimen, it uses the term *analytical validity*, and for testing individuals, it uses the term *clinical validity*. For analytical validity, it provides the following definition: "The ability of a test to correctly identify a property or characteristic in a specimen. This term encompasses both analytical sensitivity and analytical specificity."[15] The definition for *clinical validity* is "the ability of a test to correctly identify a person who does or does not have the disease of interest. This term encompasses both *clinical sensitivity* and *clinical specificity*.[15]

To be highly valid (i.e., to be highly accurate), a screening test must have both a high level of sensitivity (say 95%) and a high level of specificity (say 99%). It can be argued that, by definition, a test with a high degree of validity will also be highly reliable—that is, it will produce the same results repeatedly. The converse, however, is not true: A test that produces the same results repeatedly may be testing something altogether different from what it is supposed to measure.

It is worth noting that validity is not purely a function of the quality of a screening test, but is also influenced by extraneous factors, such as the condition of the subject's immune system or the presence of another disease at the time of testing. For example, a screening test can be falsely negative if administered in the early stage of a disease; if the subject is immunocompromised because of the presence of another disease, such as HIV/AIDS; or if the subject is receiving immunosuppressive medication for the treatment of another disease, such as cancer.[4] Likewise, a screening test can also give false-positive results due to cross-reactivity with a medication being given to the subject for another disease or with the antibodies produced in response to another disease.

When using survey instruments for health services research, the measurement of validity becomes more complex and subjective. Kimberlin and Winterstein[16] have argued that validity is not a characteristic of a test or survey instrument, but is related to the intended use of the test or instrument. Thus, assessment of validity is based on the interpretation of the results or findings of a test or survey (i.e., are the results and their interpretation representative of the construct being operationalized?). They suggest that constructs such as *severity of disease, drug efficacy, burden of disease,* and *quality of life* cannot be directly measured and have to be translated into a measurable operational definition. Therefore, a conceptual definition of a construct such as drug efficacy must first be turned into an operational definition, which is then measured as a representation or proxy measure of the construct in question. For example, the theoretical construct known as drug efficacy can be operationalized as "the amelioration of specific signs and symptoms such as swelling of lymph nodes, pain, and nausea." Consequently, an operationalized measure of the efficacy of a drug can be relief from pain, nausea, and swollen lymph nodes. The following definitions of different ways to assess validity are drawn from an article by Kimberlin and Winterstein.[16]

1. *Face validity* refers to the assessment of whether a survey instrument or a set of items, in the consensus opinion of experts, appears to measure what it purports to measure.
2. *Content validity* is conceptually very similar to face validity and involves assessment by experts in the field as to whether a set of items/questions in a survey instrument

intended to operationalize a construct such as drug efficacy, quality of life, or severity of disease truly represents the construct it purports to measure.
3. *Criterion validity* assesses the characteristics of a survey instrument in comparison with an accepted "gold standard." In other words, criterion validity determines how well the scores/responses on a set of questions in an instrument correlate with the scores/responses in a proven or established measure of a construct.
4. *Construct validity* assesses whether a survey instrument truly depicts a specific construct, idea, or hypothesis and can produce results that are in accordance with the theoretical expectations of the construct, such as burden of disease, patient satisfaction, or quality of communication. As can be noted from the preceding definitions of face validity, content validity, and criterion validity, all of these different ways of assessing validity are encompassed by and "contribute to the evidence of construct validity."[16]

12.3.5.1.2 Sensitivity. The term **sensitivity** refers to the ability of a screening test to correctly identify those with asymptomatic preclinical disease (i.e., the proportion of those with asymptomatic disease who are correctly labeled as such by the test). In other words, it is the probability that the screening test will be positive if asymptomatic preclinical disease is present. For example, if the screening test for carcinoma of the cervix correctly identifies 90% of women who actually have preclinical carcinoma of the cervix but declares 10% of such women as free of detectable cancer (i.e., it misses 10% of the cases), the test would be considered 90% sensitive. It should be noted that sensitivity of a screening test is based entirely on the test results of diseased individuals in the population and is unaffected by the test results of those who do not have the disease.[4] **TABLE 12.5** and **TABLE 12.6** illustrate how sensitivity of a test is calculated.

12.3.5.1.3 Specificity. The term **specificity** pertains to the ability of the screening test to rule out correctly those without a detectable disease for which screening is being done. In other words, it is the probability that the screening test will be negative if the disease is not present. For example, if the screening test for cancer of the cervix correctly clears 95% of women

TABLE 12.5 Calculation of Sensitivity and Specificity of a Screening Test—Notational Example

Test	Disease		Total
	Disease Positive (D$^+$)	Disease Negative (D$^-$)	
Test positive (T$^+$)	a	b	a + b
Test negative (T$^-$)	c	d	c + d
Total	a + c	b + d	a + b + c + d
Sensitivity of the screening test			a / a + c
Specificity of the screening test			d / b + d

TABLE 12.6 Calculation of Sensitivity and Specificity of a Screening Test—Numeric Example

Test	Disease		Total
	Disease Positive (D$^+$)	Disease Negative (D$^-$)	
Test positive (T$^+$)	True positive (TP) 39	False positive (FP) 313	352
Test negative (T$^-$)	False negative (FN) 11	True negative (TN) 637	648
Total	50	950	1,000
Prevalence of disease		50/1000 = **5%**	
Sensitivity of the screening test (SE)		SE = TP/(TP + FN) = 39/50 = **0.78**	
Specificity of the screening test (SP)		SP = TN/(TN + FP) = 637/950 = **0.67**	

who do not have carcinoma of the cervix but falsely labels 5% of the disease-free women as diseased (who, on confirmatory testing, are found to be free of cancer of the cervix), then the specificity of the test would be 95%. Notably, the specificity of a test is based only on the test results of those who, in the population being tested, are free of disease and is unaffected by the test result of those who have the disease.[4] Ideally, we would want a screening test to be 100% sensitive and 100% specific—that is, it should correctly identify all the diseased individuals and correctly rule out all the nondiseased individuals. Unfortunately, that goal is practically impossible to achieve, and there is an inverse relationship between the sensitivity and specificity of a screening test. This point will be illustrated with examples a bit later in this chapter.

Tables 12.5 and 12.6 illustrate how specificity of a test is calculated.

Typically, the sensitivity of a screening test is judged by implementing it to known cases of disease (i.e., clinically symptomatic patients), and specificity is assessed by testing a group of individuals known to be free of disease. However, this approach is likely to produce erroneously higher estimates of sensitivity because a test is more likely to identify correctly disease in its symptomatic stages than when the disease is in an asymptomatic preclinical stage. Ideally, the sensitivity and specificity of a test should be estimated by testing a sufficiently large cohort of asymptomatic individuals and then following them for a sufficiently long time to see which individuals developed clinical disease and which ones remained free of disease.

The determination of the size of the asymptomatic cohort and the length of follow-up time in such a study would depend on the incidence and natural history of the disease. If the incidence of the disease of interest is low and the disease progresses slowly to a symptomatic stage, the size of the cohort would have to be large and the follow-up period would need to be relatively long, and vice versa.

12.3.5.1.4 Reliability.
The measurement of any clinical, physiologic, or socioeconomic variable is subject to errors in measurement resulting from problems associated with instruments, techniques, and skills of those administering the test (in management science referred to as 4 Ms: man, method, machine, and material). **Reliability**, also known as *stability, repeatability,* or *reproducibility,* refers to the ability of a test or survey instrument to produce the same results when administered again to the same subject at another occasion. In other words, reliability represents the degree of association or correlation between two sets of observations carried out at two different occasions by the same individual or by two different individuals. The purpose of assessing the reliability of a test or instrument is to minimize, if not eliminate, the level of error in measurement. If the test or survey instrument produces the same or similar results repeatedly, it is deemed highly reliable. Conversely, if it produces different results upon readministration to the same subject, it is considered unreliable.

The question of how much time should be allowed to elapse between two consecutive applications of the test or survey instrument is subjective and depends on the nature of the variable being measured. If the test involves measurement of a physiologic indicator such as blood sugar or cholesterol level, then repeating the test on a fresh sample or the same sample of blood immediately or within a few minutes of the first test can be perfectly acceptable. On the other hand, if the reliability of data obtained through a survey or interview is being tested, then sufficient time must be allowed to pass to ensure that the subject does not remember the response provided to the same question at an earlier occasion. However, if the time interval between two consecutive tests or surveys is too long, the possibility of a real change taking place in the subject's blood chemistry, opinion, or health status can produce a truly variant response at a later testing and lead to erroneous conclusions about the reliability of the test or survey instrument. Ideally, the interval between two administrations of a test or survey should be such that the results obtained from the second administration are not affected by the results of the previous administration, whether through memory of

the previous results or change in the health status of the subject.[16]

The results of a test to assess the health status, quality of life, or severity of disease in a subject can be affected by difference in the skills and techniques of different observers and changes in the technique and skill of the same observer over time. Depending on how and when observations are made, assessment of reliability is categorized as *interrater reliability* (or *interobserver agreement*) and *intrarater reliability* (or *intrarater agreement*). As the names suggest, intrarater reliability examines consistency or degree of agreement in the results of a test performed on the same subject by the same person at two different occasions. Interrater reliability, on the other hand, assesses the degree of agreement between the results of a test or survey administered to the same subject at different times by two or more different technicians or interviewers. Naturally, for appropriate assessment of interrater reliability, there must be no communication between raters, and each must be unaware of or blinded to the results of testing by the other rater. Typically, interrater reliability is best when definitions and criteria for normal and abnormal or for categories such as poor, satisfactory, good, and excellent are clear and specific, and raters are well trained in the use of these criteria.

In the case of survey instruments, the purpose of reliability assessment is to examine the stability of results obtained and the equivalence or *internal consistency* of different sets of questions included in the questionnaire. The statistical measure or coefficient of internal consistency or strength of association between two sets of items or questions is Cronbach's alpha (α), which is a function of the average correlation between pairs of items and the number of items or questions in the questionnaire. The value of Cronbach's alpha can vary between 0 and 1. Generally, the internal consistency of a scale or set of items is good if $\alpha \geq 0.8$ and poor if $\alpha \geq 0.5$ but <0.8. Any value of $\alpha < 0.5$ is considered unacceptable. When, instead of measuring the value of a continuous variable, observers classify measurements into categories such as A, B, C, and D, or poor, satisfactory, good, and excellent, Cohen's kappa is used to estimate the coefficient of agreement between the ratings of different raters.[16–18]

12.3.5.2 Relationship Between Sensitivity and Specificity

Errors in the findings of screening tests can occur for a number of reasons, including faulty equipment, quality of materials, variations in technique, or inadequate skills of the person administering the test. However, the main and most important source of error is the subjective nature of the criteria on which the determination of the existence or absence of disease is based. The states of unequivocal health and unquestionable presence of disease exist at the two ends of a continuum. The gradual transition from health to disease that occurs imperceptibly over a period of time creates ambiguity and a situation in which there is an overlap between the physiologic or psychological states of healthy and sick individuals. Between the physiologic or psychological states of the clearly healthy and the clearly sick is a zone in which it is difficult to judge with absolute certainty whether the disease is present or a person is still healthy. This is especially true for diseases such as hypertension and diabetes, in which blood pressure and serum sugar levels are measured to assess the presence or absence of disease. Blood pressure and serum sugar level are continuous variables (rather than binary or present vs. absent) that, even under normal conditions, can have different values in different individuals and in the same individual at different times. The criteria regarding the presence or absence of disease in such conditions are based on empirical evidence and are quite subjective or arbitrary. Because of the subjective nature of such criteria, rather than a hard cutoff point between normal and abnormal, usually a range of normalcy is agreed on by professionals. For example, the range for a normal serum fasting sugar level may be considered 80–100 mg/dL. However, in many perfectly healthy individuals, the level may well be lower than 80 or greater than 100 mg/dL. The ambiguity or the element of subjectivity involved in defining normal and abnormal states becomes critically important in life-threatening disorders such as cervical, breast, and colorectal cancer, in which early detection in a preclinical state can make a difference between life and death.

Ambiguity and subjectivity in assessing the presence or absence of a disease becomes even more problematic when screening for a disease such as HIV/AIDS, in which identification of cases in preclinical asymptomatic stage is important not only to save the lives of patients, but also for protecting others, including sexual partners or children born to HIV/AIDS-positive women. In such situations, determining what criteria must be used to declare normalcy or sickness, though difficult, becomes critically important, and a tradeoff between high sensitivity and high specificity becomes unavoidable. Both scenarios—erring on the side of high sensitivity with consequent higher numbers of false positive test results or high specificity with higher numbers of false negative test results—pose serious ethical and operational

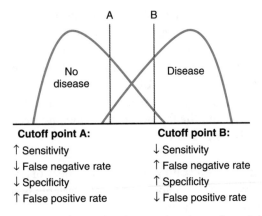

FIGURE 12.1 Overlap in the diagnostic values of a variable between diseased and nondiseased individuals and tradeoff between high sensitivity and high specificity of a screening test.

Reproduced with permission from: Kocher MS, Zurakowski D. Current concepts review – clinical epidemiology and biostatistics: a primer for orthopaedic surgeons. J Bone Joint Surg, 86-A(3):607–620. Copyright © 2004 Wolters Kluwer.

dilemmas. As shown in **FIGURE 12.1**, there is an intrinsic overlap between healthy and diseased individuals over a range of diagnostic values of the variable being measured (X axis)—for example, serum sugar level, intraocular pressure, or tissue dysplasia. A cutoff at any point in the overlapping distribution of values in the nondiseased and diseased population would unavoidably result in some false-positive and false-negative test results. In Figure 12.1, if the cutoff was at point A, a high level of sensitivity (test-positive results are to the right of the line) would be attained at the cost of low specificity and a high proportion of false-positive individuals. Conversely, if the cutoff point was at B, then a high level of specificity (test-negative results are to the left of the line) would be achieved at the cost of low sensitivity and a high proportion of false-negative individuals.

The problem that results from the tradeoff between high sensitivity and high specificity is either the high proportion of false-positive or of false-negative results that cause avoidable distress for individuals falsely labeled as sick, or unwarranted relief for those falsely declared as free of disease. False-positive individuals are then subjected either to the readministration of the screening test or to a potentially invasive and costly confirmatory test or procedure. False-negative individuals, on the other hand, face potentially delayed intervention and progression of disease to a symptomatic stage, with the prospect of poor health outcomes and greater morbidity, disability, and even mortality. As such, the tradeoff between high sensitivity and high specificity is made by weighing the consequences of higher numbers of false-positive test results, as opposed to higher numbers of false-negative test results.

12.3.5.3 Detection of Disease Before Reaching Critical Point

The **critical point** in the natural progression of a disease represents a point of no return and implies serious consequences, including disability or death, if treatment is not initiated before this point. It is important to clarify that critical point does not categorically mean that treatment has no effect or value after this point in the natural progression of disease; it only means that onset of treatment beyond this point will only yield less than maximum benefit and may not reverse the damage already done. The relevance of critical point to a screening test is that the screening test must be able to detect the disease not only in presymptomatic stages, but also sufficiently before the disease reaches its critical point. If the critical point occurs before the disease becomes detectable by a screening test, the screening test has much less value because, at that point, some irreversible damage may have already occurred. Even if the critical point occurs shortly after the disease has become detectable through a screening test, the screening test may have little impact on the course of disease. Finally, if the critical point occurs after the disease has become symptomatic, screening after the appearance of symptoms would offer no additional benefit because the disease is already clinically detectable. In this scenario, initiation of treatment after the appearance of symptoms would be the optimum course of action.

12.3.5.4 Little Morbidity, Invasiveness, and Inconvenience

A good screening test should have no or little pain, inconvenience, or risk of morbidity associated with it. A test that involves taking a mucosal cell sample through cheek swab, urinalysis, or stool sample for chemical testing is much more acceptable to the target population than a test such as colonoscopy that involves considerable preparation, embarrassment, and inconvenience. Even relatively low levels of pain, inconvenience, or risk of morbidity can have a considerable effect on the acceptance of a screening test by the target population. For example, a screening test that involves periodic radiation exposure and potential risk of cancer may not be as readily accepted as mucosal cheek swab or even a blood sample.

12.3.5.5 High Availability and Affordability

A desirable screening test should be widely available in all urban and rural areas and should be relatively inexpensive to be within the financial reach of the target population. Participation rates can drop precipitously if the test is just too expensive for the general population or involves long-distance travel and/or time-consuming appointments.

12.3.5.6 Predictive Values of Positive and Negative Screening Test Results

Predictive value positive, or the predictive value of a positive test, is the probability that a test-positive individual actually has the disease for which the person was tested. It represents the proportion of individuals who, among all those who tested positive, actually have the disease. From the notations shown in **TABLE 12.7**, this value would be represented by the formula a / a + b. Conversely, **predictive value negative** is the probability that a test-negative individual truly does not have the disease. This, from the notations in Table 12.7, would be calculated as d / c + d. The predictive value of a positive test is strongly influenced by the prevalence of the disease for which the population is being screened. As prevalence of a disease increases, the predictive value of a test of a given level of sensitivity and specificity also increases—that is, our ability to predict the presence of a disease with a given screening test in a test-positive individual is greater if the prevalence of the disease is high as compared with when the prevalence is low. **TABLE 12.8** and **TABLE 12.9** further illustrate this point. In Table 12.8, the sensitivity of the test is 0.78 (i.e., 39/50), specificity is 0.67 (i.e., 637/950), and the prevalence of the disease is only 5% (i.e., [50/1000] × 100). As shown, the predictive value of a positive test is only 0.11 and the predictive value of a negative test is 0.98. This means that the probability is only 0.11 that a test-positive individual actually has the disease. Alternatively, it can be said that almost 9 out of 10 test-positive individuals do not have the disease (i.e., a high number of false-positive individuals). Further, the probability that a test-negative individual truly does not have the disease is 0.98. That is, almost 10 out of 10 individuals who do not have the disease will be correctly ruled out by the test (i.e., a small number of false-negative individuals).

To illustrate the relationship between the prevalence of a disease and the positive and negative predictive values of a test, in Table 12.9, prevalence of the disease has been increased to 35% of the population (i.e., [350/1000] × 100), while sensitivity and specificity of the test remain unchanged at 0.78 (i.e., 273/350) and 0.67 (i.e., 436/650), respectively. Note that in this scenario, the predictive value of a positive test has increased to 0.56 (i.e., 273/487)—that is, the probability that a test-positive individual actually has

TABLE 12.7 Notational Representation of Predictive Values of Positive and Negative Test Results

Test	Disease		Total
	Disease Positive (D⁺)	Disease Negative (D⁻)	
Test positive (T⁺)	a	b	a + b
Test negative (T⁻)	c	d	c + d
Total	a + c	b + d	a + b + c + d
Predictive value of a positive test			**a / a + b**
Predictive value of a negative test			**d / c + d**

TABLE 12.8 Predictive Values of Positive and Negative Test Results When Prevalence of Disease Is Relatively Low

Test	Disease		Total
	Disease Positive (D⁺)	Disease Negative (D⁻)	
Test positive (T⁺)	True positive (TP) 39	False positive (FP) 313	352
Test negative (T⁻)	False negative (FN) 11	True negative (TN) 637	648
Total	50	950	1,000
Prevalence of disease			50/1000 = **5%**
Predictive value of a positive test (PV⁺)			PV⁺ = TP/(TP + FP) = 39/352 = **0.11**
Predictive value of a negative test (PV⁻)			PV⁻ = TN/(TN + FN) = 637/648 = **0.98**

TP = true positive; FP = false positive; FN = false negative; TN = true negative.

Modified with permission from: Dawson B, Trapp RG. Basic and clinical biostatistics. 4th ed. McGraw-Hill Companies;2004. Accessed July 17, 2017. http://accessmedicine.mhmedical.com/book .aspx?bookID=356

the disease is 0.56. In other words, nearly 6 out of 10 test-positive individuals actually have the disease. In contrast, with the prevalence of the disease increasing from 5% to 35%, the predictive value of a negative test (sensitivity and specificity still being 0.78 and 0.67) has dropped from 0.98 to 0.85 (i.e., 436/513), and the number of false-negative individuals has increased from 11 to 77. Conversely, with the increase in prevalence of the disease from 5% to 35%, the number of false-positive individuals has dropped from 313 to 214. It is important to note that, similar to an inverse relationship between the sensitivity and specificity of a test, there is an inverse relationship between predictive values of positive and negative test results.

12.3.5.7 Lead-Time Bias

The length of time elapsed between the detection of disease in its asymptomatic preclinical stage through a screening test and the first appearance of signs and symptoms is known as the *lead time*. **Lead-time bias** is the bias introduced in the estimation of survival time because of the overestimation of survival time in patients of a disease when the disease is detected earlier than usual with the help of a screening test, as compared to those in whom the disease is clinically diagnosed after the appearance of signs and symptoms. Lead time results from the ability of a screening test to identify disease during the *detectable preclinical phase* (DPCP). Depending on the point in time during

TABLE 12.9 Predictive Values of Positive and Negative Test Results When Prevalence of Disease Is Relatively High

Test	Disease		Total
	Disease Positive (D⁺)	**Disease Negative (D⁻)**	
Test positive (T⁺)	True positive (TP) 273	False positive (FP) 214	487
Test negative (T⁻)	False negative (FN) 77	True negative (TN) 436	513
Total	350	650	1,000
Prevalence of disease		200/1,000 = **35%**	
Predictive value of a positive test (PV⁺)		$PV^+ = TP/(TP + FP) = 273/487 =$ **0.56**	
Predictive value of a negative test (PV⁻)		$PV^- = TN/(TN + FN) = 436/513 =$ **0.85**	

TP: true positive; FP: false positive; FN: false negative; TN: true negative.

Modified with permission from: Dawson B, Trapp RG. Basic and clinical biostatistics. 4th ed. McGraw-Hill Companies;2004. Accessed July 17, 2017. http://accessmedicine.mhmedical.com/book.aspx?bookID=356

the DPCP when the disease is identified and the natural course and duration of disease, lead time can vary from one person to another. For those who are screened, estimation of *survival time* begins from the time of detection during DPCP and ends at the time of death. For those who are not screened, the computation of survival time begins at a later stage, when signs and symptoms appear and a diagnosis is made because of the clinical manifestation of the disease—with or without a laboratory test. The addition of lead time to the survival time of screened patients creates a semblance of longer survival time as compared with those who are not screened. An apparently longer survival time among those who are screened can lead to an overestimation of the benefits of screening.[19]

If early initiation of treatment in screened individuals truly has greater benefit than later onset of treatment, then screened individuals would definitely enjoy longer survival. On the other hand, if early treatment in screened individuals offers no additional benefit, then survival time of screened individuals would erroneously appear to be longer because of lead time being added to their total duration of survival. Separating the effect of lead time from the effect of earlier start of treatment is difficult when comparing the survival time of screened and unscreened individuals.

12.3.5.8 Length Bias

Even in the absence of treatment, the rate of progression of a disease can be quite different in different individuals because of the difference in their age, race, sex, and genetic makeup. Individuals in whom a disease progresses at a slower rate would have a longer duration of detectable asymptomatic disease or DPCP as compared with those in whom it progresses at a faster rate. Slow progression of disease is beneficial for both the patient and the healthcare provider because it has a better chance of being detected with the help of a screening test as well as a longer duration of survival regardless of the effectiveness of an intervention. **Length bias** is the overestimation of the survival time of those detected by a screening program (as compared to those diagnosed clinically after the appearance of signs and symptoms) merely because of the overrepresentation of slow-progressing cases among the screened population. Length bias thus gives an exaggerated impression of the success of a screening program or the effectiveness of a treatment.

From an epidemiologic standpoint, the effect of slow progression of a disease can be twofold. One, in a cohort of screened individuals, those with slow progression of disease would be overrepresented as compared with those in whom the disease progresses rapidly. This is because the probability of being identified is directly proportional to the length of time in which cases are detectable and inversely proportional to the rate of progression of disease. Second, the longer duration of survival can be erroneously attributed to the success of a treatment, creating a fallacious impression regarding the effectiveness of a treatment that, in reality, may not be as effective. Depending on the nature of a disease, the range of survival time in screened and unscreened groups can be relatively narrow or quite wide. In practice, of course, rather than using the range of survival time, average survival time for the screened and unscreened groups is reported by pooling the survival time of all individuals in that group.

▶ 12.4 Surveillance

12.4.1 Definition and Distinction from Screening

The World Health Organization (WHO) defines public health surveillance as "the continuous, systematic collection, analysis and interpretation of health-related data needed for the planning, implementation, and evaluation of public health practice."[20] Analysis and interpretation of surveillance data can serve "as an early warning system for impending public health emergencies, document the impact of an intervention, or track progress towards specified goals."[20] Surveillance for specific public health problems also helps policy makers in understanding the epidemiology of those problems, set priorities, and formulate public health policy. [20]

Screening of an individual or a group of individuals is a one-time event that, if necessary, can be repeated after a period of weeks, months, or years, but it is not an ongoing or continuous activity. Surveillance (or monitoring), on the other hand, is an ongoing activity that continues either for a specified length of time or indefinitely and involves ongoing collection, analysis, interpretation, and reporting of data on a specific issue. Depending on the nature of the problem, the period of time for which surveillance is done can vary from a few days or weeks to months or years.

Surveillance provides actionable and timely information to policy makers regarding the need for a specific intervention as well as about the impact of an intervention. Outbreaks of Ebola in West Africa and cholera in Haiti and Yemen in 2014 through 2016 underscore the importance of effective surveillance systems. The most current and pertinent example of surveillance is that for Zika virus transmission and tracking of the cases of microcephaly in the United States by the Centers for Disease Control and Prevention (CDC).[21] Zika virus surveillance is also being done in a number of Latin American countries by each country's public health authorities and by the WHO.[20] Based on the information garnered from this surveillance, the CDC and the WHO, with the help of relevant governmental agencies, have implemented mosquito control programs and issued travel advisories for the general population and especially for women who are either currently pregnant or are trying to get pregnant. The impact of these interventions is also being monitored on an ongoing basis.

Based on the approaches adopted for data collection and the degree of direct involvement of the sponsoring entity in securing data from various sources, surveillance systems are frequently classified into categories such as passive surveillance, active surveillance, sentinel or categorical surveillance, integrated surveillance, and syndromic surveillance. The distinction between these approaches is based only on how engaged the sponsoring agency is in the process of obtaining data. Once the data are collected, there is no difference in the principles and statistical methods applied to the analysis and interpretation of data.

12.4.2 Passive Surveillance

In this approach, as the name suggests, rather than actively soliciting data from various sources by routinely or periodically contacting the sources of information, the sponsoring agency (e.g., local or state public health departments and the CDC) takes a passive role and limits itself to analyzing and interpreting the data and reporting its findings through various channels. Participation of the sources of data is voluntary, and there is no penalty, reward, or other impact on sources for participation or lack thereof. Consequently, there is little, if any, incentive other than a sense of civic or professional obligation on the part of sources of data to make the effort and participate in this kind of surveillance. Inevitably, this means the data are incomplete and may only represent the proverbial tip of the iceberg. Because of the simplicity of this approach and minimal resource commitment on the part of the sponsoring agency, this is the most common form of surveillance. However, from a policy formulation perspective, **passive surveillance** data may not be sufficient to set priorities and devise informed policy.

12.4.3 Active Surveillance

Active surveillance, in contrast with passive surveillance, involves direct solicitation of data and, in many cases, mandates healthcare providers to submit data within a specified length of time and/or provides some incentive, such as regular feedback, to encourage participation. Feedback to participating sources of data includes ways to improve the quality of data when deficiencies are identified. Although more labor-intensive for the sponsoring agency, the information obtained through active surveillance is more complete, and the quality of data is superior to passive surveillance. However, active surveillance is less commonly used than passive surveillance because of the greater need for involvement and commitment of resources, including the need to deploy workers to visit localities to collect data. The use of active surveillance is often related to the seriousness and urgency of the public health problem at hand. Typically, staff members of the agency conducting the surveillance directly contact healthcare practitioners or key individuals in the community to collect information.

The U.S. Behavioral Risk Factor Surveillance System (BRFSS) is an example of an active surveillance system. Established in 1984 with the initial participation of 15 states, BRFSS is the leading health-related telephone survey system in the United States that collects data in all 50 states, the District of Columbia, and three U.S. territories. The data include information regarding health-related risk behaviors, chronic health conditions, and use of preventive services. Every year, about half a million adults complete telephone interviews in this largest continuously conducted surveillance system in the country.[22]

12.4.4 Sentinel or Categorical Surveillance

Sentinel surveillance, or categorical surveillance, is conducted to gather information on a specific event or disease regarding which information may not be ordinarily available through passive surveillance. The agency collecting the information plays an active role, but the distinguishing feature of sentinel surveillance is that it focuses on a small number of carefully selected hospitals, practitioners, or laboratories to gather information on a specific event or disease. The size, location, and characteristics of the settings from which desired information is gathered depend on the nature of the public health problem under investigation. Generally, it may involve a few large facilities that have a high probability of coming across patients with the disease of interest. For example, TropNetEurope, a sentinel surveillance program, has been used in Europe to gather prospective data on imported falciparum malaria.[23] Likewise, sentinel surveillance has been used in Malaysia to collect information on human enterovirus[24] and in Australia to gather data on human papillomavirus and trends in genital warts.[25] Monitoring of crow deaths has been proposed as a sentinel surveillance system for West Nile virus in the United States.[26] Although sentinel surveillance has the benefit of rapidly obtaining high-quality information from a small number of settings at a low cost, it may not be a good strategy to learn about the spread and burden of rare disorders.[20] To gather timely data on relatively uncommon diseases, it is necessary to gather information from a large number of providers or practitioners distributed throughout a country or region.

12.4.5 Syndromic Surveillance

The word *syndrome* derives its origins from the Greek language and generally means "running together." In clinical medicine, it refers to a group of signs and symptoms that are related to one another because of some anatomic, physiologic, or biochemical abnormality. These signs and symptoms may or may not be linked to a specific known disease or a precise diagnosis, but collectively provide a frame of reference for further investigation.[27]

A precise definition of the term **syndromic surveillance** is not available, and the term itself is considered imprecise and lacking in specificity. Generally, the term refers to the monitoring by public health agencies and other public or private sector entities of the frequency of specified sets of clinical features in a population with or without a specific diagnosis. The primary objective of syndromic surveillance is to identify clusters of cases in early symptomatic stage before confirmed diagnoses become available through laboratory testing or other means.[28] According to the CDC,[29] "the term 'Syndromic Surveillance' applies to surveillance using health related data that precede diagnosis and signal a sufficient probability of a case or an outbreak to warrant further public health response." The occurrence of specified sets of signs and symptoms among individuals in a population can indicate the potential occurrence of an infectious disease that poses a serious public health threat and warrants swift action to prevent it from spreading to other individuals. The events of October 2001 involving the malicious mailing of envelopes containing highly potent anthrax spores[30] heightened awareness among policy makers and public health professionals regarding the threat of bioterrorism and gave considerable impetus to syndromic surveillance activities in the United States and other developed countries. Because of the very nature of the threat, syndromic surveillance focuses entirely on gathering, analyzing, and reporting timely information on the occurrence of highly contagious and potentially fatal infectious disorders. The infectious agents that are considered likely to be used in a bioterrorism attack include agents such as anthrax, plague, smallpox, botulism, tularemia, and brucellosis. Most of these organisms, at least in the early stages of the infection, produce nonspecific signs and symptoms such as malaise, fatigue, loss of appetite, fever, and cough.

Syndromic surveillance is intended for early detection of highly contagious infectious disorders in the population being monitored, whether resulting from a bioterrorism attack or through natural occurrence. Public health preparedness and early detection can help in mounting a quick response and effective clinical and public health control measures, including quarantine, chemoprophylaxis, and vaccination of targeted personnel or the general public.[31] Data for syndromic surveillance are gathered by various agencies, including local, state, and federal public health agencies and research centers, including the CDC, through active surveillance or enhanced passive surveillance. Usual sources of data include local health departments and ambulatory and inpatient healthcare providers. Other sources of syndromic data can also include health maintenance organizations (HMOs), 911 call centers, pharmacies, and health information exchanges (HIEs).

In **TABLE 12.10**, agents listed under Category A are deemed to have the greatest potential for large-scale dissemination and adverse public health impact with mass casualties and thus require broad-based public health preparedness. Agents listed under Category B also have potential for large-scale dissemination, but

TABLE 12.10 Critical Biological Agent Categories for Public Health Preparedness

Biological Agent(s)	Disease
Category A	
Variola major	Smallpox
Bacillus anthracis	Anthrax
Yersinia pestis	Plague
Clostridium botulinum (botulinum toxins)	Botulism
Francisella tularensis	Tularemia
Filoviruses and arenaviruses (e.g., *Ebolavirus*, Lassa virus)	Viral hemorrhagic fevers
Category B	
Coxiella burnetii	Q fever
Brucella spp.	Brucellosis
Burkholderia mallei	Glanders
Burkholderia pseudomallei	Melioidosis
Alphaviruses (VEE, EEE, WEE[a])	Encephalitis
Rickettsia prowazekii	Typhus fever
Toxins (e.g., ricin, staphylococcal enterotoxin B)	Toxic syndromes
Chlamydia psittaci	Psittacosis
Food safety threats (e.g., *Salmonella spp., Escherichia coli* O157:H7) Water safety threats (e.g., *Vibrio cholerae, Cryptosporidium parvum*)	
Category C	
Emerging threat agents (e.g., Nipah virus, *Hantavirus*)	

[a]Venezuelan equine encephalitis (VEE), Eastern equine encephalitis (EEE), and Western equine encephalomyelitis (WEE) viruses.

Reproduced from: Rotz LD, Khan AS, Lillibridge SR, Ostroff SM, Hughes JM. Public health assessment of potential biological terrorism agents. Emerg Infect Dis. 2002;8(2):225–230.

cause less-severe illness and pose a lesser risk of mortality. Therefore, these organisms are less likely to have adverse public health impact. Finally, agents listed under Category C do not currently pose a high risk of bioterrorism but have the potential to emerge as a threat to public health in the future.[32]

A 2008 survey of 52 state, territorial, and selected large local jurisdictions in the United States showed that syndromic surveillance programs existed in 83% of these jurisdictions, and emergency department visits were the most commonly used source of information (83%). Many of the programs also collected information from outpatient clinics, pharmacies, and poison control centers.[33] Most of the respondents indicated influenza monitoring to be the most useful outcome of syndromic surveillance. More than half of the systems frequently used BioSense, a biosurveillance system made freely available to health departments by the CDC for early detection and "situation awareness" (www.cdc.gov/nssp/overview.html). The participants in the survey reported mixed experiences with syndromic surveillance to detect "typical community outbreaks due to infectious diseases."[33]

Through legislation and appropriation of funds by the U.S. Congress for an integrated public health surveillance system, the CDC established the National Syndromic Surveillance Program (NSSP) and in 2003 launched the BioSense Platform, a cloud-based secure electronic health information system for users to collect, store, analyze, and share syndromic surveillance data.[34] The advantage of BioSense is that it allows easy access and aggregation of syndromic data from various organizations across the country.

The boundaries between syndromic surveillance and "traditional" public health surveillance are blurring as healthcare providers increasingly adopt electronic medical records and healthcare systems become more linked with public health systems through HIEs. With more timely or even real-time reporting of notifiable diseases, the distinction between syndromic and traditional surveillance is likely to become a moot point in the foreseeable future.[33]

Driven by the threat of infectious disease outbreaks related to bioterrorism, information systems that collect, analyze, and disseminate morbidity, mortality, and other relevant data have proliferated in the United States. A 2004 review of 192 published reports on 115 surveillance systems in the country found 29 systems that were specifically designed to detect bioterrorism-related diseases and 86 systems that were designed for surveillance of naturally occurring illnesses. The review found that few of the systems had been comprehensively evaluated, and only three had both sensitivity and specificity of the reported data evaluated.[35] Given the national and international concern regarding future bioterrorism attacks, the desire to develop efficient and effective response systems is quite appropriate. However, in the absence of empirical evidence in the form of an actual event, a judgment regarding the efficiency and effectiveness of a syndromic surveillance system can only be made through simulations and test exercises. Although a number of computerized algorithms and simulation models of syndromic surveillance offer the promise of detecting a bioterrorism event in a timely fashion, a definitive statement regarding the effectiveness of such a system cannot be made.

The primary purpose of syndromic surveillance is early detection of a bioterrorism event by noting unusually high occurrences and clustering of cases of interest in a community. **FIGURE 12.2** illustrates the rationale for the development and implementation

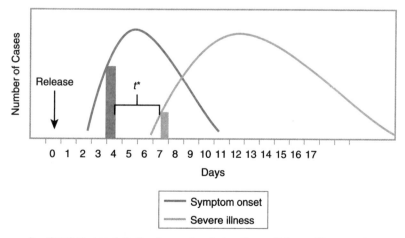

*t = time between detection by syndromic (prediagnostic) surveillance and detection by traditional (diagnosis-based) surveillance.

FIGURE 12.2 Syndromic surveillance—rationale for early detection.

of syndromic surveillance systems. The objective of a syndromic surveillance system is to identify a threshold number of early symptomatic cases and save critical time in launching a response. As shown in the figure, with the intentional release of a potent biologic agent in a population on day 0, the outbreak of severe illness in the population would not begin until about day 6, and the epidemic curve would not reach its peak until day 11 or 12. However, early symptoms and signs would begin to appear in the first wave of exposed individuals by day 2. Identification of these individuals by an effective syndromic surveillance system that could be mobilized by day 3 or 4 would immediately trigger the emergency response system to control the outbreak in a short time with far fewer cases and fatalities. In the figure, the number of days that are saved by an effective syndromic surveillance system, as opposed to a traditional disease notification and epidemic control system, are shown as time interval *t*.

In recent years, the availability of inpatient and ambulatory care electronic health records (EHRs) in many developed countries has created a more favorable environment for the use of clinical data for public health syndromic surveillance. In the United States, Stage 2 of the Centers for Medicare and Medicaid Services (CMS) EHR Meaningful Use Incentives Program would require eligible hospitals and other providers to do ongoing syndromic surveillance reporting. Further refinement and clarifications of requirements and procedures pertaining to syndromic surveillance reporting is slated to take place in Stage 3 of Meaningful Use rules and EHR certification criteria.[36]

Syndromic surveillance based on Internet queries, particularly for diseases such as the flu, has grown since 2004 when it was first attempted by Eysenbach using the Google ad sentinel method to track flu rates in Canada.[37] Based on web searches and Internet queries by the public, "Google Flu Trends" syndromic surveillance system for an influenza-like illness (ILI) was launched by a team of Google researchers in 2008 in the United States and subsequently in 29 other countries to "nowcast" influenza epidemics in various countries. The nowcast results in the United States in the 2010–2011 and 2011–2012 flu seasons initially seemed to match CDC data and preceded CDC findings by 1–2 weeks. However, those estimates were later challenged by other researchers, and Google Flu Trends came under considerable criticism for its gross overestimation of flu cases in the 2012–2013 flu season.[38,39] In the 2013–2014 season as well, Google Flu Trends reportedly overestimated the number of doctor visits for ILI cases in the United States[40] by about 30%. Following the apparent success of Google

Flu Trends, the Intelligent Systems Laboratory in the United Kingdom created Flu Detector, which uses Twitter to track flu rates in the United Kingdom. The main criticism against the use of web-based big data by Google Trends or similar systems is that these data are not generated by research instruments that are specifically designed to produce valid and reliable data suitable for scientific research. Although epidemic tracking techniques based on mining of web data hold considerable future promise, the failure of Google Flu Trends in the 2012–2013 and 2013–2014 seasons served as a stark reminder that web-based large data sets and nowcasting techniques have their greatest utility as complements for rather than substitutes of traditional epidemiologic surveillance systems.[38,39] In the United States, the computerized "traditional" surveillance system overseen by the CDC relies on direct communication with healthcare providers and includes approximately 2,700 healthcare centers in various parts of the country, with more than 30 million patient visits reported annually.

Because of a number of problems identified by researchers in Google's computer models and the resulting overestimation of ILI, in 2015, Google discontinued the use of Google Flu Trends and Google Dengue Trends to report flu and dengue epidemic data in various countries. Google also agreed to pass along its epidemic signal data in the future to the Mailman School of Public Health at Columbia University, Boston Children's Hospital, and the Influenza Division of the CDC.

12.4.6 U.S. National Electronic Disease Surveillance System

With the intent to quickly recognize disease outbreaks and bioterrorism incidents and respond in real time, the CDC has developed and implemented a web-based electronic information sharing platform called the National Electronic Disease Surveillance System (NEDSS). The system is designed to facilitate efficient and secure public health surveillance data transfer from healthcare providers to local and state public health departments and from public health agencies to the CDC. For uniform and consistent data sharing, NEDSS specifications include standards for software, hardware, and data format. The CDC requires that all participating entities use these standards and specifications. Currently, all 50 states and Washington, D.C. use web-based electronic data repository and transfer systems that are compatible with NEDSS and are used to voluntarily submit notifiable disease data to the CDC. These systems allow direct web-based data entry by health systems and laboratories and integration of multiple health information databases for ready use by all stakeholders. The NEDSS Base System provided to reporting jurisdictions by the CDC also helps in data processing, analysis, and transfer.

12.4.7 Triple-S: The European Syndromic Surveillance Project

Triple-S is an inventory of syndromic surveillance systems in Europe that was developed with funding from the European Commission to provide member states and other interested entities an overview of available syndromic surveillance systems in Europe. It also provides comprehensive guidelines for designing and implementing a surveillance system. At the time of its last update in August 2014, the Triple-S consortium included 20 different projects in 13 countries. Through its website (www.syndromicsurveillance.eu/), the Consortium provides information and hyperlinks to the listed systems in various countries. It also includes information on events or incidents in which the syndromic surveillance system provided valuable service through timely information on a disease outbreak or some other emerging public health problem in one country or another. Examples of such events include the H1N1 influenza pandemic, disease outbreaks during the 2012 Olympic Games in London, and the volcanic ash cloud that covered Europe in April 2010.

As an example of the systems listed in the Triple-S inventory, the French SurSaUD syndromic surveillance system was developed by the French National Institute for Public Health Surveillance, in cooperation with emergency health services in 2004 after the 2003 heat wave that resulted in the deaths of more than 15,000 individuals. SurSaUD collects and analyzes on a daily basis morbidity and mortality data from various sources, including general practitioners and hospital emergency departments.

▶ Exercise 12.1

In a population of 17,000, the prevalence of a disease is 18%. A screening test with sensitivity of 83% and specificity of 87% will be used to identify cases of the disease.

Question 1. Construct a 2 × 2 table and calculate the predictive values of positive and negative tests.

Question 2. How many individuals will be falsely labeled as positive and how many will be falsely labeled as negative?

▶ Exercise 12.2

A population of 2,300 individuals was screened to identify cases of disease X. In total, 730 individuals tested positive, of whom 490 were later confirmed with the help of a diagnostic test as actually having the disease. Of the 1,570 whose screening results were negative, 1,190 were later confirmed to be free of disease.

Question 1. Construct a 2 × 2 table and calculate the sensitivity and specificity of the screening test.

Question 2. Also, calculate predictive values of positive and negative screening test results.

Question 3. What were the numbers of false-negative and false-positive individuals?

Question 4. What is the prevalence of disease X in this population?

🔍 *CASE STUDY 12.1: Nosocomial Infection Surveillance*

Modified from: Wisplinghoff H, Bischoff T, Tallent SM, Seifert H, Wenzel R, Edmond MB. Nosocomial bloodstream infections in U.S. hospitals: analysis of 24,179 cases from a prospective nationwide surveillance study. Clin Infect Dis. 2004;39:309–317.

In a prospective nationwide surveillance study published in the *Clinical Infectious Diseases* journal in 2004, Wisplinghoff et al. analyzed 24,179 cases of nosocomial bloodstream infections (BSI) in 49 U.S. hospitals over a 7-year period, from March 1995 through September 2002. In the 49 participating hospitals that were spread out all over the country and ranged in size from 60 to 1,200 beds, infection control personnel prospectively collected bloodstream infection data using a standardized case report form. The authors used data from a concurrent nationwide surveillance study called the Surveillance and Control of Pathogens of Epidemiological Importance (SCOPE) based at Virginia Commonwealth University in Richmond, Virginia, to examine "trends in the epidemiology and microbiology of nosocomial bloodstream infections."

The results showed that of the 24,179 nosocomial BSIs, 87% were caused by a single type of organism (i.e., were monomicrobial), 65% were caused by gram-positive organisms, 25% by gram-negative organisms, and 9.5% by fungi. The mean interval between admission and infection ranged from 16 to 26 days. The overall crude mortality rate was 27%. The most common organisms were coagulase negative (CoN) staphylococci (31%), *Staphylococcus aureus* (20%), enterococci (9%), and *Candida* of various types (9%). Most of the BSIs occurred in internal medicine (37.6%), general surgery (19.8%), and pediatric (13.5%) services. The fewest number of BSIs occurred in pediatric hematology/oncology (1%), urology (1%), and obstetric (0.9%) services. Among the gram-positive organism isolates, 75% of coagulase negative staphylococci and 41% of *S. aureus* were resistant to antimicrobial drugs. Gram-negative organisms were most frequently resistant to Ampicillin (about 98% of *Klebsiella* and 44% of *E. coli*). The percentage of *S. aureus* cultures that were resistant to methicillin increased from 22% in 1995 to 57% in 2001. Resistance to vancomycin varied from 2% to 60% of enterococcus organisms.

Questions

Question 1. What is the importance of nosocomial bloodstream infections in hospitals?

Questions 2. Which hospital units or services would you focus on to address the problem of nosocomial bloodstream infections?

🔍 CASE STUDY 12.2: *Screening for Colorectal Cancer*

Data from: Cubiella J, Salve M, Diaz-Ondina M, et al. Diagnostic accuracy of the faecal immunochemical test for colorectal cancer in symptomatic patients: comparison with NICE and SIGN referral criteria. Colorectal Dis. 2014;16(8):273–282.

The purpose of this study was to compare the accuracy of the fecal immunochemical test (FIT) as a screening tool with that of two separate referral criteria for colorectal cancer (CRC) diagnosis through colonoscopy and to develop a valid CRC predictive index based on available biomarkers. To serve as a screening tool, one of the referral criteria for diagnostic colonoscopy is recommended by the British National Institute for Health and Care Excellence (NICE), while the other one is recommended by the Scottish Intercollegiate Guidelines Network (SIGN). This prospective blinded study was conducted at two tertiary care hospitals in northern Spain in 2012. The study population comprised consecutive patients with gastrointestinal symptoms referred by primary and secondary care providers for a diagnostic colonoscopy. A standard questionnaire was administered by trained nurses to record demographic data and symptoms and to determine if patients met NICE and SIGN referral criteria for CRC. Between April and November 2012, out of 1,179 individuals who were referred for colonoscopy, 787 patients completed the study protocol.

The participants collected a stool sample from one bowel movement without any dietary or medication restrictions and without any visible blood in the stool 1 week before the colonoscopy. FIT was performed on the stool sample using the automated OC-Sensor. A colonoscopy was performed a week later by a colonoscopist who was blind to FIT results. A biopsy was taken if deemed necessary by the colonoscopist, and the specific location of CRC in the rectum, proximal colon, or distal colon was recorded. Staging of cancer was done according to the American Joint Committee on Cancer classification criteria.

Out of the 787 individuals who completed the study protocol, 300 (38.1%) met the NICE screening criteria, 475 (60.4%) met the SIGN screening criteria, and 241 (30.6%) met the FIT screening criterial for CRC. On colonoscopy, 97 patients were found to have colorectal cancer, and 177 were found to have advanced neoplasia (AN). The researchers defined AN as "an advanced adenoma or cancer."**TABLE 12.11** shows some of the results of this study.

Questions

Question 1. Based on the data presented in Table 12.11 and keeping in mind that the total number of participants was 787 (i.e., a total of 787 individuals were screened), construct 2 × 2 tables for NICE and FIT for CRC and AN, and calculate the numbers of false-positive and false-negative test results for NICE and FIT.

Question 2. Based on the data presented in Table 12.11, and keeping in mind that the total number of participants was 787, calculate the prevalence of CRC and AN in the study population.

Question 3. Based on the data presented in Table 12.11, how much better or worse is FIT as a screening tool than NICE and SIGN?

Question 4. Based on the data presented in Table 12.11, between NICE and SIGN, which one is a better screening tool? Explain why and support your argument with data from the table.

TABLE 12.11 Diagnostic Accuracy of FIT, NICE, and SIGN Referral Criteria for Colorectal Cancer and Advanced Neoplasia

	Lesion*	Sensitivity	P‡	Specificity	P§	Positive Predictive Value	Negative Predictive Value
NICE referral criteria (n = 300)	Colorectal cancer (n = 97)	61.9%	<0.001	65.2%	<0.001	20%	92.4%
	AN** (n = 177)	50.8%	<0.001	65.6%	<0.001	30%	82.1%
SIGN referral criteria (n = 475)	Colorectal cancer (n = 97)	82.5%	0.4	42.7%	<0.001	16.8%	94.5%
	AN** (n = 177)	71.2%	1	42.8%	<0.001	26.5%	83.6%
FIT ≥ 100 ng/m; (n = 241)	Colorectal cancer (n = 97)	87.6%		77.4%		35.3%	97.8%
	AN** (n = 177)	71.8%		81.3%		52.7%	90.8%

AN: advanced neoplasia; FIT: fecal immunochemical test; NICE: National Institute for Health and Care Excellence; SIGN: Scottish Intercollegiate Guidelines Network.
*Patients were classified according to the most advanced lesion.
‡Significance of the sensitivity differences when compared with FIT in McNemar's test. Differences with $P < 0.05$ are considered statistically significant.
§Significance of the specificity differences when compared with FIT in McNemar's test. Differences with $P < 0.05$ are considered statistically significant.
**Advanced neoplasia: advanced adenoma (adenoma >1 cm in size, with high grade dysplasia or with villous component >25%) or colorectal cancer.

▶ 12.5 Summary

Screening and surveillance are among the most important preventive activities in a healthcare system. In the United States, active surveillance for notifiable diseases requires healthcare practitioners to report cases of diseases such as cholera, dengue, tuberculosis, and measles to public health authorities within a specified window of time to quickly identify potential outbreaks and take necessary preventive measures. Active surveillance for healthcare-associated infections (HAIs) or nosocomial infections is routinely carried out in hospitals to prevent the spread of serious communicable diseases. Occurrence and reporting of nosocomial infections or HAIs by U.S. hospitals is considered by CMS and by accrediting bodies such as

The Joint Commission to be an important measure of healthcare quality.

As a tool for secondary prevention, screening of newborns for a host of congenital disorders and of adults for malignancies such as cervical, breast, and colorectal cancer is also one of the most important public health activities. Because of their cost-effectiveness in many, if not most, instances, screening services such as periodic mammography and colonoscopy are most times fully covered by insurance companies. In the absence of a definitive diagnosis for a specific condition, syndromic surveillance is employed to identify and prevent the spread of emerging infectious diseases such as sudden acute respiratory syndrome, avian flu, and swine flu, or serious conditions such as anthrax, whose early signs and symptoms may mimic common respiratory disorders. In the wake of serious concerns about bioterrorism, syndromic surveillance has become important to deal with the risk of deliberate spread of conditions such as anthrax that can potentially result in large-scale morbidity, mortality, and societal disruption.

Healthcare managers often need to make decisions about offering community-based screening programs and enhancing the availability and utilization of hospital-based screenings such as mammography and colonoscopy. Implementation of preventive strategies to minimize the occurrence of HAIs is also an important component of managerial responsibilities. Consequently, it is incumbent on healthcare managers to be fully cognizant of the principles and procedures of various public health interventions. To that end, this chapter provides a comprehensive review of primary and secondary prevention strategies, including screening and surveillance.

References

1. Maciosek MV, Coffield AB, Flottemesch TJ, Edwards NM, Solberg LI. Greater use of preventive services in U.S. health care could save lives at little or no cost. Health Aff. 2010;29(9):1656–1660.

2. Cohen JT, Neumann PJ, Weinstein MC. Does preventive care save money? Health economics and the presidential candidates. N Engl J Med. 2008;358:661–663.

3. California Department of Public Health. Newborn Screening Program. September 2017 [cited 2017 Nov 27]. Available from: https://www.cdph.ca.gov/Programs/CFH/DGDS/Pages/nbs/NBS-Disorders-Detectable.aspx

4. Mausner JS, Kramer S. Epidemiology: an introductory text. Philadelphia: W.B. Saunders Company; 1985.

5. Porta M, editor. A dictionary of epidemiology. 6th ed. New York: Oxford University Press; 2014 [cited 2018 May 18]. Available from: http://www.irea.ir/files/site1/pages/dictionary.pdf

6. Wald NJ. Guidance on terminology. J Med Screen. 1004;1:139.

7. Wilson JMG, Jungner G. Principles and practice of screening for disease. Public Health Papers – No. 34. Geneva, Switzerland: World Health Organization; 1968 [cited 2017 Nov 27]. Available from: http://www.who.int/ionizing_radiation/medical_radiation_exposure/munich-WHO-1968-Screening-Disease.pdf

8. Morabia A, Zhang FF. History of medical screening: from concept to action. Postgrad Med J. 2004;80:463–469.

9. LeFevre ML. Screening for abdominal aortic aneurysm: U.S. Preventive Services Task Force Recommendation Statement. Ann Intern Med. 2014;161(4):281–290.

10. Kansagara D, Papak J, Pasha AS, et al. Screening for hepatocellular carcinoma in chronic liver disease: a systematic review. Ann Intern Med. 2014;161(4):261–269.

11. Heidelbaugh JJ. Should family physicians screen for testosterone deficiency in men? Yes, screening for testosterone deficiency is worthwhile for most older men. Am Fam Physician. 2015;91(4):220–221.

12. Fugh-Berman A. Should family physicians screen for testosterone deficiency in men? No, screening may be harmful and benefits are unproven. Am Fam Physician. 2015;91(4):226–228.

13. Obuchowski NA, Graham RJ, Baker ME, Powell KA. Ten criteria for effective screening: their application to multislice CT screening for pulmonary and colorectal cancers. AJR Am J Roentgenol. 2001;176:1357–1362.

14. Kocher MS, Zurakowski D. Clinical epidemiology and biostatistics: a primer for orthopaedic surgeons. J Bone Joint Surg. 2004;86-A(3):607–620.

15. Porta M, editor. A dictionary of epidemiology. 6th ed. New York: Oxford University Press; 2014:288 [cited 2017 Nov 27]. Available from: http://irea.ir/files/site1/pages/dictionary.pdf

16. Kimberlin CL, Winterstein AG. Validity and reliability of measurement instruments used in research. Am J Health Syst Pharm. 2008;65:2276–2284.

17. Gliem JA, Gliem RR. Calculating, interpreting, and reporting Cronbach's alpha reliability coefficient for Likert-type scales. 2003 Midwest Research to Practice Conference in Adult, Continuing, and Community Education. 2003 [cited 2018 May 18]. Available from: https://scholarworks.iupui.edu/bitstream/handle/1805/344/Gliem%20%26%20Gliem.pdf?sequence=1&isAllowed=y

18. Santos JRA. Cronbach's alpha: a tool for assessing the reliability of scales. J Extension. 1999; 37(2).

19. Aschengrau A, Seage GR. Essentials of epidemiology. 2nd ed. Sudbury, MA: Jones and Bartlett Publishers; 2008.

20. World Health Organization. Immunization, vaccines and biologicals: sentinel surveillance. 2016 Oct 17 [cited 2018 May 18]. Available from: http://www.who.int/immunization/monitoring_surveillance/burden/vpd/surveillance_type/sentinel/en/

21. Lee CT, Vora NM, Bajwa W, et al. Zika virus surveillance and preparedness—New York City, 2015–2016. MMWR Morb Mortal Wkly Rep. 2016 Jun 24;65(24) [cited 2018 July 30]. Available from: http://www.cdc.gov/mmwr/volumes/65/wr/mm6524e3.htm

22. Centers for Disease Control and Prevention. At a Glance 2016: Behavioral Risk Factor Surveillance System—monitoring health risks and behaviors among adults. 2016 Aug [cited 2018 May 18]. Available from: https://www.cdc.gov/chronicdisease/resources/publications/aag/brfss.htm

23. Jelinek T, Schulte C, Behrens R, et al. Imported falciparum malaria in Europe: sentinel surveillance data from the European Network on Surveillance of Imported Infectious Diseases. Clin Infect Dis. 2002;34(1):572–576.

24. Podin Y, Gias EL, Ong F, et al. Sentinel surveillance for human enterovirus 71 in Sarawak, Malaysia: lessons from the first 7 years. BMC Public Health. 2006;7(6):180.

25. Donovan B, Franklin N, Guy R, et al. Quadrivalent human papillomavirus vaccination and trends in genital warts in Australia: analysis of national sentinel surveillance data. Lancet Infect Dis. 2011;11:39–44.

26. Edison M, Komar N, Sorhage F, Talbot T, Mostashari F, McLean R. Crow deaths as a sentinel surveillance system for West Nile virus in the northeastern United States, 1999. Emerg Infect Dis. 2001;7(4):615–620.

27. Taber's Cyclopedic Medical Dictionary. 23rd ed. Venes D, editor. Philadelphia: F.A. Davis Company; 2017.

28. Henning KJ. Overview of syndromic surveillance: what is syndromic surveillance? MMWR Morb Mortal Wkly Rep. 2004;53(Suppl.):5–11.

29. Centers for Disease Control and Prevention. Syndromic Surveillance: an Applied Approach to Outbreak Detection. 2006 [cited 2017 Nov 28]. Available from: http://www.webcitation.org/getfile?fileid=cca443e6cd9687d78299ca30ba97e489490af623

30. Centers for Disease Control and Prevention. Update: investigation of anthrax associated with intentional exposure and interim public health guidelines. MMWR Morb Mortal Wkly Rep. 2001;50(41):889–893.

31. Reingold A. If syndromic surveillance is the answer, what is the question? Biosecur Bioterror. 2003;1(2):77–81.

32. Rotz LD, Khan AS, Lillibridge SR, Ostroff SM, Hughes JM. Public health assessment of potential biological terrorism agents. Emerg Infect Dis. 2002;8(2):225–230.

33. Buehler JW, Sonricker A, Paladini M, Soper P, Mostashari F. Syndromic surveillance practice in the United States: findings from a survey of state, territorial, and selected local health departments. Adv Dis Surveill. 2008;6(3):1–8.

34. Centers for Disease Control and Prevention. The National Syndromic Surveillance Program (NSSP). 2016 [cited 2018 May 18]. Available from: http://www.cdc.gov/nssp/overview.html

35. Bravata DM, McDonald KM, Smith WM, et al. Systematic review: surveillance systems for early detection of bioterrorism-related diseases. Ann Intern Med. 2004; 140:910–922.

36. Centers for Disease Control and Prevention. Syndromic surveillance. 2015 [cited 2018 May 18]. Available from: http://www.cdc.gov/ehrmeaningfuluse/syndromic.html

37. Eysenbach G. Infodemiology: tracking flu-related searches on the Web for syndromic surveillance. AMIA Annu Symp Proc. 2006;244–248.

38. Butler D. When Google got flu wrong. Nature. 2013;494: 155–156.

39. Lazer D, Kennedy R, King G, Vespignani A. Google Flu Trends still appears sick: an evaluation of the 2013–2014 flu season. 2014 [cited 2018 May 18]. Available from: http://gking.harvard.edu/publications/google-flu-trends-still-appears-sick%C2%A0-evaluation-2013%E2%80%902014-flu-season

40. Lazer D, Kennedy R, King G, Vespignani A. The parable of Google Flu: traps in big data analysis. Science. 2014; 343:1203–1205.

CHAPTER 13

Basic Statistical Concepts and Tests

LEARNING OBJECTIVES

Having mastered the materials in this chapter, the student will be able to:

1. Comprehend and explain basic statistical concepts and terminology.
2. Interpret the results presented in the case studies reported in this text and commonly reported in published journal articles.
3. Draw reasonable conclusions from the data presented in the case studies in the text and in published journal articles.
4. Calculate measures of central tendency, estimate dispersion of data, and conduct basic statistical tests with the help of commercially available statistical software programs.

CHAPTER OUTLINE

13.1 Introduction
13.2 Examples
    13.2.1 Example 13.1
    13.2.2 Example 13.2
13.3 Basic Statistical Concepts
    13.3.1 Population
    13.3.2 Sample
    13.3.3 Variable
        13.3.3.1 Qualitative or Categorical Variable
        13.3.3.2 Quantitative Variable
        13.3.3.3 Binary Variable
        13.3.3.4 Discrete Variable
        13.3.3.5 Continuous Variable
    13.3.4 Frequency

13.3.5 Percentile
13.3.6 Decile, Quintile, and Quartile
13.3.7 Measures of Central Tendency in Data
    13.3.7.1 Mean
    13.3.7.2 Median
    13.3.7.3 Mode
13.3.8 Measures of Spread or Dispersion of Data
    13.3.8.1 Range
    13.3.8.2 Standard Deviation
13.3.9 Normal Distribution
13.3.10 Confidence Interval
13.3.11 Hypothesis
13.3.12 Significance or P Value
13.3.13 Type I and Type II Errors
13.3.14 Correlation

13.3.15 Regression
13.4 Statistical Tests for Comparison of Groups
    13.4.1 One-Sample z-Test or t-Test
    13.4.2 Two-Sample t-Test for Comparison of
        Independent Means

13.4.3 Test for the Comparison of Independent
    Proportions
Exercise 13.1
Exercise 13.2
13.5 Summary

KEY TERMS

Binary variable	Mean	Range
Categorical variable	Median	Regression
Confidence interval	Mode	Sample
Continuous variables	Normal distribution	Standard deviation
Correlation	Null hypothesis	Type I error
Deciles	Percentile	Type II error
Discrete variables	P values	Variable
Dispersion	Population	t-test
Frequency	Quartiles	z-test
Hypothesis	Quintile	

▶ 13.1 Introduction

Use of epidemiologic evidence for planning, evaluation, and marketing of health services requires mining and interpretation of statistical results presented in research literature. Healthcare managers need to develop sufficient statistical acumen to perform these tasks. Throughout the text, and especially in the case studies, references are made to statistical terms such as standard deviation, 95% confidence interval, and P values, and statistical techniques such as regression models. Descriptive statistics present data in a summary format and allow us to understand the salient features and important characteristics of data. Inferential statistical methods involve exploration of data at more advanced levels and permit us to draw conclusions based on statistical evidence. Most students using this text would have taken an introductory course in biostatistics previously and are expected to have working knowledge of these concepts. This chapter is intended to give students the opportunity to review some of these concepts quickly. For the uninitiated in biostatistics, the chapter serves as a resource to understand the terms and statistical concepts referred to in various case studies.

To demonstrate the application of these concepts and the methods used to derive some of the commonly reported statistics, we begin with two hypothetical examples. Following these examples, we provide definitions and explanations for common statistical concepts. The chapter concludes with two exercises for students to practice basic statistical analysis with the help of a computer.

▶ 13.2 Examples

13.2.1 Example 13.1

A study was conducted at two large Midwestern hospitals in the United States to find answers to the following five questions:

1. To what extent do midlevel managers at these hospitals have good management skills?
2. Is there a significant difference in the management skills of midlevel managers between the two hospitals?
3. To what extent are staff at these hospitals satisfied with their managers?
4. Is there a significant difference in staff satisfaction with managers between the two hospitals?
5. Is there a relationship between midlevel managers' management skills and staff satisfaction?

The researchers administered a standardized test of management skills to 10 randomly selected midlevel managers in each of the two hospitals. The test is known to have high levels of validity and reliability. Possible scores on the test could range from 0 to

100. The researchers also administered a satisfaction survey to 10 randomly selected supervisees of each manager, with a guarantee of participant anonymity. The scale for satisfaction scores on the questionnaire ranged from 0 to 100.

Statistical analyses were conducted to test the following hypotheses:

1. There is a statistically significant difference in the management skills of managers between the two hospitals.

2. There is a statistically significant difference in staff satisfaction with managers between the two hospitals.

3. There is a direct correlation between management skills and staff satisfaction.

TABLE 13.1 shows the data from the two hospitals, and **TABLE 13.2** shows the results of descriptive and inferential statistical analysis of the same data. The results of inferential analyses showed that there was neither a statistically significant difference between the

TABLE 13.1 Management Skills and Staff Satisfaction Scores for 10 Randomly Selected Midlevel Managers at Two Midwestern Hospitals

| | Management Skills Score | | Staff Satisfaction Score | |
No.	Hospital A	Hospital B	Hospital A	Hospital B
1	39	74	410	730
2	58	70	570	785
3	52	30	545	360
4	44	48	635	450
5	65	59	925	525
6	66	61	664	775
7	62	68	690	820
8	46	73	440	830
9	92	88	880	845
10	49	57	460	515

TABLE 13.2 Results of Descriptive and Inferential Statistical Analysis

| | Descriptive Statistics | | | | | |
	Minimum	Maximum	Range	Median	Mean*	Std. Deviation*
Management Skills Scores						
Hospital A	39	92	53	55	57.3	15.3
Hospital B	30	88	58	64.5	62.8	15.9

(continues)

TABLE 13.2   Results of Descriptive and Inferential Statistical Analysis   *(continued)*

Descriptive Statistics						
	Minimum	**Maximum**	**Range**	**Median**	**Mean***	**Std. Deviation***
Staff Satisfaction Scores						
Hospital A	410	925	515	602.5	621.9	175.7
Hospital B	360	845	485	752.5	663.5	181.3
Inferential Statistics						

Comparison of the means of management skills at Hospitals A and B: $p = 0.44$*

Comparison of the means of staff satisfaction scores at Hospitals A and B: $p = 0.61$*

Correlation between management skills of midlevel managers and staff satisfaction: $r = 0.85$*

*Rounded up or down to first or second decimal place.

mean scores for management skills of managers at the two hospitals ($p = 0.44$), nor a difference in mean staff satisfaction scores ($p = 0.61$). The test of statistical correlation between management skills and staff satisfaction showed a moderately strong association ($r = 0.85$, $p = 0.001$) between the two variables. Based on these findings, null hypothesis could not be rejected for Hypotheses 1 and 2 but was rejected for Hypothesis 3.

13.2.2 Example 13.2

In a study to understand the relationship between chief executive officers' (CEOs') experience and midlevel managers' satisfaction with the CEO, the researchers collected data on CEO tenure from 10 acute care hospitals in Arizona and administered a questionnaire to 10 randomly selected midlevel managers at each of the 10 hospitals, with a guarantee of participant anonymity. The standardized questionnaire with 10 questions was known to have high levels of validity and reliability. On each of the 10 questions, the respondent could rate the CEO on a scale of 0 to 5. The total satisfaction score for a CEO could range from 0 to 500.

The researchers wanted answers to the following questions:

1. What is the average tenure of a hospital CEO in Arizona?
2. How satisfied are midlevel managers with their CEOs?
3. Is there a relationship between the length of the CEO's tenure (used as a surrogate for

TABLE 13.3   CEO Length of Tenure and Managers' Satisfaction Data

No.	Tenure (Years)	CEO Satisfaction Scores
1	1	300
2	3	390
3	6	480
4	6	380
5	8	445
6	12	410
7	14	390
8	15	475
9	20	390
10	20	425

experience) and the midlevel manager's satisfaction with the CEO?

The researchers hypothesized that there is a statistically significant positive correlation between CEOs' length of tenure and managers' satisfaction with the CEO. **TABLE 13.3** shows the data collected in the study,

TABLE 13.4 Results of Descriptive and Inferential Statistical Analysis							
Descriptive Statistics							
	N	**Minimum**	**Maximum**	**Range**	**Median**	**Mean***	**Std. Deviation***
CEO Tenure (Years)	10	1	20	19	10	10.5	6.7
CEO Satisfaction Scores	10	300	480	180	400	408.5	52.4
Inferential Statistics							

Correlation between CEO tenure and managers' satisfaction with the CEO[†]: $r^* = 0.35$

[†]Significance $(p) = 0.33$.
*Rounded up or down to first decimal place.

and **TABLE 13.4** shows the results of the descriptive statistical analysis. The results showed that there was no statistical relationship between CEOs' length of tenure and managers' satisfaction with the CEO ($r = 0.35$).

▶ 13.3 Basic Statistical Concepts

13.3.1 Population

In statistical analyses and in epidemiologic investigations, the word **population** refers to a specific group of individuals who are the primary focus of interest, and regarding whom observations can be made and conclusions may be drawn. The size and characteristics of the population of interest depend on the nature and purpose of the investigation. One may be interested in the entire population of a country, state, or county; those belonging to a social class, ethnicity, or profession; all patients of a given disease in a specified geographic area; or those who received care from a specific provider during a given time period.

13.3.2 Sample

Often, it is not practical to study or examine an entire population. However, one can make reasonably good observations about the characteristics of a population by studying a relatively small number of individuals randomly selected, with the assumption that they adequately represent the entire population in terms of the trait or characteristic being investigated. The critical point in obtaining a **sample** is to ensure that every individual in the population has an equal chance of being selected, and the investigator does not influence in any way who

is or is not included in the sample. We can obtain a sample by random-digit telephone dialing, by going to a shopping mall or a train station, or by standing in the lobby of a hospital. Different random sampling methods involve different levels of sophistication and include *systematic*, *stratified*, and *cluster* sampling techniques. For example, a systematic random sample of emergency department patients can be obtained by selecting the fifth patient arriving after 11:00 a.m. in the emergency department of a hospital and thereafter selecting every fifth patient until the desired number of patients to be included in the sample is reached. Cluster sampling, on the other hand, involves first randomly identifying a certain number of clusters and then taking a random sample of subjects within each cluster. For example, to obtain a sample of elementary school children, one might randomly select three elementary schools out of 10 in a geographic area and then obtain a random sample of children in each of the three schools. In this example, each elementary school constitutes a cluster.

13.3.3 Variable

A **variable** is any characteristic, material, or attribute of someone or something that can be measured with or without an instrument or device. The same variable can have different values in different people, in different places, or at different times. Age, race, weight, temperature, calories, IQ, or education level are all examples of different kinds of variables.

13.3.3.1 Qualitative or Categorical Variable

A **categorical variable**, or qualitative variable, is the kind of variable that does not have a numeric value but rather represents an attribute or a characteristic. Breeds of dogs, the color of people's eyes, or religious affiliations of different individuals are all examples of categorical variables. In statistical analysis, these variables cannot be placed on a numeric scale but can be arbitrarily represented by a number, letter, or any other symbol.

13.3.3.2 Quantitative Variable

A quantitative variable is one that can be measured on a numeric scale. Height, weight, and temperature are everyday examples of quantitative variables.

13.3.3.3 Binary Variable

A **binary variable** is any variable that can only be assigned one of two possible values, such as yes or no; present or absent; good or bad; and true or false. In statistical analysis, it is often useful to create binary variables from nonbinary variables, such as designation of rich or poor, based on different income levels. Similarly, we can group people as liberal or conservative based on various other parameters for which the labels "liberal" and "conservative" serve as surrogates.

13.3.3.4 Discrete Variable

Variables that are countable and only take a whole number value rather than fractional values are known as **discrete variables**. Usually, a discrete variable has a finite number of values, such as 1–5, 1–10, or 1–12, but not numerous values. All qualitative variables are discrete variables, but not all discrete variables are qualitative. Each numeric value of a discrete variable represents a different attribute, trait, or entity. The number of books on a shelf, the number of students in a class, or the number of $5 bills in one's wallet are all examples of discrete variables. The number of days a person is absent from work is an example of a discrete quantitative variable, whereas the number of individuals with blue eyes in a group is an example of a qualitative discrete variable.

13.3.3.5 Continuous Variable

Variables such as time or distance that can have an infinite number of fractional values are called **continuous variables**. A line on a chart is a good example of a continuous variable. If necessary, continuous variables can be converted into discrete variables by rounding up or down their fractional values; for example, a value of 2.03 miles can be rounded down to 2 miles.

13.3.4 Frequency

In statistics, **frequency** means the number of times an event, observation, or data value occurs in a data set. *Relative frequency* shows the frequency of occurrence of an event or observation in comparison with the frequency of other events. It is reported as a proportion or a percentage. For example, 60% of students in a class may be women—this percentage is in relation to the frequency of men in the same class. A *frequency table* arranges frequency values or percentages for one or more variables, usually in ascending order, in a tabulated form.

13.3.5 Percentile

Percentile refers to the relative position of a value on a scale of 0 to 100. For example, a Graduate Record Examination (GRE) score that puts a student at the 90th percentile means that 10% of students had a score higher than this student did, and 90% had a lower score. In a numerically arranged, descending-order data set, the 50th percentile represents the midpoint—that is, half of the values in the data set are above and half are below the 50th percentile.

13.3.6 Decile, Quintile, and Quartile

Deciles divide a set of values into 10 equal parts such that each segment or interval is equal to 10%; **quintile** means dividing a set of values into five equal parts, with each part being equal to 20%; and **quartiles** divide a set of values into four equal parts, with each part being equal to 25% of values.

13.3.7 Measures of Central Tendency in Data

13.3.7.1 Mean

The **mean**, commonly known as the *average* and more accurately called the *arithmetic mean*, is one of the measures of the central tendency in a data set, as are *median* and *mode*. It is obtained by adding all the values of a given variable in a data set and dividing the sum of the values by the number of observations in the data set. For example, if the weights of six patients in a clinic were noted as 130, 135, 141, 138, 143, and 136 pounds, the sum total of these weights would be 823 pounds, and the mean would be 823/6 = 137.2 pounds. As long as the values in the data set are within a relatively narrow range, the mean is a reasonably good indicator of the central tendency in the data.

However, if there is a lot of spread or wide variation of values in the data set, then mean becomes somewhat less helpful. Additionally, the mean is strongly affected by even a few extreme values in the data set. Such values can significantly pull the value of the mean in one direction or the other. In our example of the weights of six patients, if a seventh patient with a weight of 320 pounds was added to the group, then the mean weights of seven patients would become 163.3 pounds. Alternatively, if the seventh patient was a child weighing only 37 pounds, the mean weight of the sample of patients would only be 122.9 pounds. In both of these scenarios, the mean is not an accurate reflection of the central tendency of the weights of this group of patients. In these situations, one should either exclude the outlier value(s) from the estimation of the mean or estimate the median value rather than the mean.

Because any measure of central tendency such as mean, median, or mode alone does not provide a full picture of the situation related to a variable, measures of central tendency are best used in combination with some measure of the spread or dispersion of data, such as range, variance, or standard deviation. In notational form, the formula for calculating a sample mean is represented as follows: $\bar{X} = \left(\sum_{i=1}^{n} Xi\right)/n$. In this formula, $\bar{X}$ represents the mean, $\sum_{i=1}^{n} Xi$ represents the sum of all individual observations, and n represents the number of observations in the data set.

13.3.7.2 Median

In statistics, the term **median** refers to the value that is at the midpoint in a data set when data are arranged in a numerically ascending or descending order. In a numerically arranged data set, there is always an equal number of observations or values above and below the median—in other words, the median is the same as 50th percentile. To find the median value in a data set, we use the following formula: median value = $(n + 1)/2$.

For example, let us assume we have a data set with nine values, which, arranged in the increasing order of magnitude, are as follows: 4, 7, 11, 13, 14, 17, 18, 20, 23. Using the formula $(n + 1)/2$, we get $(9 + 1)/2 = 5$. Therefore, the fifth value, 14, is the median value in this data set. If there was an even number of values in the data set instead of an odd number—that is, 10 values rather than 9—the situation would be a little different. For example, if the 10th value was 24 (i.e., 4, 7, 11, 13, 14, 17, 18, 20, 23, 24), then the results will be $(10+1)/2=5.5$.

In such a situation, the median value is derived by averaging the two values immediately above and below the middle point. In our example, the median would be $(14 + 17)/2 = 15.5$.

13.3.7.3 Mode

The statistical term **mode** refers to the most common value in a data set. For example, in a data set including the values 3, 4, 6, 7, 7, 7, 9, 11, 10, the mode is 7. However, in the data set 11, 13, 14, 17, 18, 20, 23, 24, used in the example for calculating the median, there is no mode.

13.3.8 Measures of Spread or Dispersion of Data

13.3.8.1 Range

Range is the difference or interval between the largest and the smallest values in a data set and is the simplest measure of the spread or **dispersion** in the data set. In other words, it sets the upper and lower boundaries of data. In a data set with a minimum value of 10 and the highest value being 90, the range would be $90 - 10 = 80$.

13.3.8.2 Standard Deviation

The **standard deviation** is a statistical measure of the spread or dispersion of the values of a quantitative variable around the mean. For sample data, standard deviation is represented by the notation SD or S, and for population data, it is represented by the Greek letter σ. Standard deviation is derived by taking a square root of the average of squared variations around the mean. In notational format, the formulae for sample and population standard deviations are represented as follows:

$$S = \sqrt{\frac{\sum_{i=1}^{n} (X_i - \bar{X})^2}{n - 1}} \quad \sigma = \sqrt{\frac{\sum_{i=1}^{n} (X_i - \mu)^2}{n - 1}}$$

In the preceding equations, $\bar{X}$ represents the mean of the sample, whereas μ represents the mean for the entire population from which the sample was obtained. As shown in **FIGURE 13.1**, in a normally distributed variable, approximately 68% of values fall within 1 standard deviation, 95% fall within 2 standard deviations, and 99.7% fall within 3 standard deviations around the mean. Therefore, the total spread of data, or the spread of a normal curve, is approximately six standard deviations. That means that the larger the standard deviation, the wider the normal curve, and

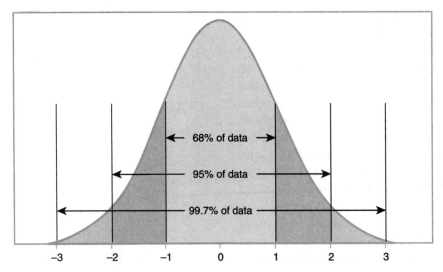

FIGURE 13.1 Example of a typical normal curve.

the greater the dispersion of data around the mean. Typically, standard deviation is reported in conjunction with the mean.

13.3.9 Normal Distribution

The **normal distribution** or *normal curve* is a symmetrical, bell-shaped curve that represents the distribution of a quantitative variable. The fact that the normal curve is symmetrical means that exactly half of the data values are above the mean and half are below the mean. In a normally distributed data set, the midpoint on the *x*-axis represents the mean value of the variable, and the sides represent the spread on either side of the mean. The greater the spread or distribution of values above or below the mean, the wider the curve. Conversely, the greater the proportion of observations close to the mean, the narrower the bell curve. Alternatively, we can say that the size of the standard deviation of data determines the width of the bell or normal curve. Many variables in ordinary life, such as height, weight, or GRE scores of students, and many of the variables encountered in health care, such as blood pressure, fasting serum sugar levels, or waiting time in the doctor's office, are normally distributed. Figure 13.1 provides an example of a typical normal curve.

13.3.10 Confidence Interval

A **confidence interval** can be defined as the interval between two numeric values within which the true value of a variable is expected to lie with a high level of probability. For example, the average weight of women in Mississippi might be estimated by taking a sample of

50 randomly selected women in Mississippi. Because the estimation is based on a sample rather than the entire population of women in Mississippi, there is a possibility that the true average weight of Mississippi is different from the average weight of the sample of women. The estimated confidence interval based on the weights of sampled women would allow us to state the probability of the true average weight of the entire population of women being within the upper and lower boundaries of the confidence interval. The specific level of probability is selected by those doing the estimation. Usually, a probability of 0.95 (i.e., 95% chance) is selected for estimating the confidence interval. In general, the higher the specified probability (i.e., the level of confidence), the wider the statistical interval might be. In our example of the average weight of Mississippi women, 95% confidence interval might be 100–145 lb., and 99% confidence interval might be 93–162 lb. Stated another way, if we took an infinite number of samples of Mississippi women and estimated a confidence interval for each sample, 95% of those confidence intervals would include the true average weight of the entire population of Mississippi women. Confidence intervals can also be used to test hypotheses about differences between two or more populations. For example, we can use a confidence interval to test the hypothesis that French women, on average, weigh 20% less than American women.

13.3.11 Hypothesis

A **hypothesis** is a statistically testable proposition that is based on limited evidence and may or may not be true. For example, one may hypothesize that the average height of Cherokee men (denoted by

A) is greater than the average height of Navajo men (B)—that is, A > B. Another hypothesis can be that the average height of Cherokee men is equal to or less than that of Navajo men—that is, A ≤ B. It is easy to see that only one of these hypotheses can be true; if the second is true, the first must be wrong. In practice, the second hypothesis, which asserts that there is no difference between the heights of men in the two groups or that A might even be less than B, is known as the **null hypothesis** and is, by convention, represented by the notation H_0. The original hypothesis suggesting that A > B is called the *alternative hypothesis* and is given the notation H_1. In practice, statistical tests are conducted to check if the null hypothesis can be accepted or rejected. Based on statistical analysis, if the null hypothesis (H_0) is accepted, then the alternative hypothesis (H_1) must be rejected, and vice versa.

13.3.12 Significance or *P* Value

Reported extensively in inferential statistics, **P values** are used to make assertions about differences or similarities between two or more groups being compared. A *P* value refers to the probability that observed differences between groups or sets of observations may have occurred just by chance. In other words, it is the likelihood of getting a test result as extreme as or more extreme than the one obtained by a statistical test if there truly was no difference between the groups being compared (i.e., if null hypothesis was true). By convention, a *P* value of < 0.05 (i.e., a less than 5% chance) is considered evidence of a real difference between groups. For example, in a comparison of mean GRE scores of students at two different schools, $p < 0.05$ suggests that there is a 95% chance (or 0.95 probability) that there is a real difference in the means of GRE scores at the two schools. Whereas $p < 0.10$ or $p < 0.15$ is interpreted as absence of a real difference between groups, $p < 0.01$ (i.e., less than 1% chance) or $p < 0.001$ (i.e., 1 in a 1,000 chance) is indicative of much stronger evidence of a real difference between groups.

13.3.13 Type I and Type II Errors

In testing a hypothesis, one can make two kinds of errors. If the null hypothesis (H_0) is erroneously rejected, the error is called **Type I error**. This can happen, for example, when statistically significant differences are erroneously discovered between two sets of observations (say, average length of stay at two hospitals) when none really existed. On the other hand, if the null hypothesis is erroneously accepted when it should have been rejected, the error is known as **Type II error**.

For example, in comparing the average length of stay at two hospitals, if a researcher fails to discover a statistically significant difference between the two hospitals when it truly existed—that is, fails to reject the null hypothesis—a Type II error would occur. By convention, the probability of making a Type I error is referred to as alpha (α) and the probability of making a Type II error is denoted as beta (β). It is easy to see that there is an inverse relationship between the likelihood of making a Type I or Type II error—if the probability of Type I error is reduced, the probability of making a Type II error automatically increases. When analyzing data, the level of statistical significance (i.e., the probability of making a Type I error) is usually set at $p = 0.05$. In designing research studies, by convention, the probability of Type II error (β) is set at 0.2, and sample sizes are chosen accordingly so as not to exceed this limit.

13.3.14 Correlation

Statistical analyses often explore the strength of an association between two variables. The term **correlation** only refers to a statistical association between two variables; it does not imply that one of them depends on the other (or is caused by the other). When the values of one variable, however, are believed to depend on the values of another, the statistical exploration of such a relationship is called *regression analysis*. For example, the amount of money people spend on recreational activities may be associated with family income. Likewise, academic performance of students may be associated with the amount of time spent doing homework. In health care, body weight is known to be directly associated with the number of calories consumed on a daily basis. Scatter plots are used to show such paired observations. Each data point on the scatter diagram represents an observed value of the independent variable (say, family income, conventionally shown along the X axis) and its corresponding value for the dependent variable (i.e., the amount of money spent on recreational activities, conventionally shown along the Y axis). The statistical measure of such an association is called the *correlation coefficient* and is denoted by r. Depending on whether the association is positive or negative, the value of the correlation coefficient can vary from +1 to −1. A value of −1 indicates a perfect lock-step negative (or inverse) relationship between an independent variable X and a dependent variable Y. A value of +1, on the other hand, indicates a perfect positive relationship such that a specified amount of increase in the independent variable (say, caloric intake) brings about a fixed amount of increase in the dependent variable.

13.3.15 Regression

Regression analysis examines the simultaneous relationship of one or more independent variables with another variable, with the assumption that the values of the latter depend on the values of the former. When the statistical analysis involves only two variables—an independent and a dependent variable—the analysis is called univariate regression. For example, we may examine whether the amount of money spent on recreational activities depends on household income, or whether student grade point average depends on the number of hours spent doing homework. When two or more independent variables (e.g., X_1, X_2, X_3, and X_4) are included in a statistical model to understand the extent to which each of them affects the value of the dependent variables, the analysis is called *multiple regression* analysis. For example, the outcome of a disease in a given patient or the result of a surgical operation depends on a number of factors, including the age of the patient, severity and duration of disease, existence of comorbid conditions, and the characteristics of the healthcare provider. The general model for multiple regression is represented in the following manner:

$$Y = \beta_0 + \beta_1 X_1 + \beta_2 X_2 + \beta_3 X_3 + \beta_4 X_4 + \varepsilon$$

In the preceding formula, Y represents the value of the dependent variable (say, health outcome), and X represents one or the other independent variable. β represents the amount of change in the dependent variable that occurs with one unit change in the value of the corresponding X variable, and ε represents the error, or the amount of the dependent variable that is not explained by the regression model.

▶ 13.4 Statistical Tests for Comparison of Groups

Note: In current times, it is unrealistic to expect that anyone would manually conduct serious descriptive and inferential statistical analysis. Numerous statistical software packages are available to carry out these tasks in no time at the stroke of a few keys on a computer keyboard, a hand-held calculator, or a mobile/cell phone. The formulae provided in this section are intended only to refresh theoretical understanding of these concepts and to serve as a quick resource for the reader.

13.4.1 One-Sample z-Test or t-Test

A number of statistical tests are available to assess whether data from a sample of the population are similar to those of the overall population. For example, we can measure weights of a random sample of 10-year-old boys in Mississippi and try to assess whether the average weight of our sample ($\bar{X}$) is similar to the average weight of the entire population of 10-year-old boys in the nation (μ). In this situation, the null (H_0) and alternative hypothesis (H_1) would be as follows:

$$H_0: \bar{X} = \mu \,(or\, H_0: \bar{X} - \mu \leq 0)$$

$$H_1: \bar{X} \neq \mu \,(or\, H_1: \bar{X} - \mu > 0)$$

Assuming that the mean weight and standard deviation of the entire population of 10-year-old boys in the nation are known, we can use the following formula (one-sample *z-test*):

$$Z = \frac{\bar{X} - \mu}{\sigma \,/\, \sqrt{n}}$$

In the preceding formula, μ represents the mean weight of 10-year-old boys in the total population, σ represents the standard deviation of the mean weight of 10-year-old boys in the total population, and n represents the sample size.

In the event that the standard deviation σ for the entire population is not known, the alternative formula would be (one-sample *t-test*):

$$t = \frac{\bar{X} - \mu}{\hat{\alpha} \,/\, \sqrt{n}}$$

In this formula, $\hat{\alpha}$ is an estimator of the population standard deviation obtained from the random sample of 10-year-old Mississippi boys.

13.4.2 Two-Sample t-Test for Comparison of Independent Means

If we were interested in comparing the average weight of 10-year-old boys in Mississippi with that of 10-year-old boys in Utah, we could use a slightly different formula, with null hypothesis (H_0) being that there is no significant difference between the average weights of these two populations of 10-year-old boys. In this formula, the average weights and standard deviations of random samples of 10-year-old boys from the two states are used to make the comparison as shown below.

$$t = \frac{\bar{X}_1 - \bar{X}_2}{\sqrt{\left(\dfrac{\hat{\sigma}_1^2}{n_1}\right) + \left(\dfrac{\hat{\sigma}_2^2}{n_2}\right)}}$$

In the preceding formula, $\bar{X}_1$ represents the mean weight of the sample from Mississippi and $\bar{X}_2$

represents the mean weight of the sample from Utah. In the denominator, $\hat{\sigma}_1^2$ represents the square of the standard deviation of the Mississippi sample, whereas $\hat{\sigma}_2^2$ represents the squared standard deviation of the Utah sample.

13.4.3 Test for the Comparison of Independent Proportions

An epidemiologist might be interested in comparing the proportions of children who got the flu in the winter of 2017 at two elementary schools in Baltimore, Maryland. An academic policy maker might want to compare the proportions of African Americans in the 2017 graduating class at Harvard and Yale law schools. In either case, the null hypothesis might be that the two proportions are equal ($H_0: P_1 = P_2; H_1: P_1 \neq P_2$) and may be tested with the following formula.

$$Z = \frac{(\hat{p}_1 - \hat{p}_2)}{\sqrt{(\hat{p}_1\hat{q}_1/n_1) + (\hat{p}_2\hat{q}_2/n_2)}}$$

In this formula, p_1 and p_2 represent the two proportions, q_1 and q_2 represent $(1 - p_1)$ and $(1 - p_2)$, and n_1 and n_2 represent the number of students in each of the samples. The corresponding probability for the Z statistic can be looked up in a Z table in a statistical textbook.

▶ Exercise 13.1

Compare the average length of stay in the first quarter of 2018 at a for-profit acute care community general hospital in Fort Smith, Arkansas, with that of a similar nonprofit local hospital. The length of stay data from 10 randomly selected patient records at each hospital are shown in **TABLE 13.5**. Analyze the data with the help of a statistical software package and answer the following questions.

Questions

Question 1. Calculate the descriptive statistics for the length of stay at each of the two hospitals, including mean, median, and standard deviation.

Question 2. Compare the mean length of stay at the two hospitals and comment whether there is a statistically significant difference between the means.

▶ Exercise 13.2

TABLE 13.6 shows the IQ scores and annual income in 2018 of two random samples of individuals who graduated from the California Institute of Technology (Caltech) and the Massachusetts Institute of Technology (MIT) in 2011. Analyze the data with the help of a statistical software package and answer the following questions.

TABLE 13.5 Length of Stay Data for 10 Randomly Selected Patients During the First Quarter of 2018 at Two Fictitious Hospitals in Fort Smith, Arkansas

Hospital	Length of Stay Data for 10 Patients									
A	8	9	11	5	6	7	10	13	9	8
B	2	6	2	7	4	5	19	4	8	6

TABLE 13.6 Annual Income and IQ Data of Two Randomly Selected Samples of 2011 Graduates of California Institute of Technology and Massachusetts Institute of Technology

Caltech Graduates						MIT Graduates					
No.	IQ	Income	No.	IQ	Income	No.	IQ	Income	No.	IQ	Income
1	123	$168,500	11	128	$391,000	1	141	$261,000	11	127	$190,500
2	119	$143,000	12	138	$171,000	2	115	$239,000	12	129	$397,000
3	133	$171,700	13	117	$217,000	3	138	$198,900	13	136	$244,000

(continues)

TABLE 13.6 Annual Income and IQ Data of Two Randomly Selected Samples of 2011 Graduates of California Institute of Technology and Massachusetts Institute of Technology *(continued)*

Caltech Graduates						MIT Graduates					
No.	IQ	Income	No.	IQ	Income	No.	IQ	Income	No.	IQ	Income
4	114	$195,900	14	118	$176,000	4	119	$247,000	14	124	$183,000
5	129	$247,000	15	121	$163,000	5	125	$393,000	15	136	$249,000
6	120	$181,000	16	140	$144,000	6	138	$345,000	16	123	$203,000
7	136	$347,000	17	131	$243,000	7	118	$238,000	17	131	$171,000
8	128	$211,000	18	122	$187,000	8	129	$184,000	18	124	$233,000
9	109	$157,500	19	126	$191,000	9	120	$219,000	19	128	$167,000
10	121	$193,000	20	134	$139,000	10	135	$188,000	20	115	$378,000

Questions

Question 1. Calculate the descriptive statistics for IQ scores and income for each of the random samples.

Question 2. Is there a statistically significant difference in the mean IQ scores of Caltech graduates as compared with MIT graduates?

Question 3. Is the mean annual income of MIT graduates lower or higher than that of Caltech graduates? Is the difference statistically significant?

Question 4. Is there a statistical correlation between IQ scores and annual income?

▶ 13.5 Summary

To be effective, healthcare managers need to understand basic statistical concepts and use statistical evidence from research literature and published reports.

At times, managers are also called on to conduct their own statistical analysis. This chapter gives future healthcare managers working knowledge of basic statistical concepts, terms, and tests. The chapter begins with introductory ideas about the nature of different kinds of variables and sampling methods. Next, measures of central tendency and dispersion of data are discussed. Concepts related to statistical correlation, hypothesis testing, P values, and errors in hypothesis testing are explained with the help of two hypothetical examples. The chapter includes a compendium of common statistical terms and a brief description of some statistical tests. The formulae given in various sections are designed to give the student some understanding of the underlying principles and rationale for various tests. The two exercises at the end of the chapter provide hands-on opportunities for students to practice basic analytic techniques and develop some degree of confidence in their application.

CHAPTER 14

Observational Studies

LEARNING OBJECTIVES

Having mastered the materials in this chapter, the student will be able to:

1. Explain the difference between ecological, cohort, and case-control studies.
2. Evaluate and critique ecological, cohort, and case-control studies.
3. Apply the findings and results of different types of observational studies to managerial decisions.
4. Contribute effectively to the design and conduct of different types of observational studies.

CHAPTER OUTLINE

14.1 Introduction
14.2 Observational Studies
14.3 Ecological Studies
14.4 Example of an Ecological Study
14.5 Cohort Studies
    14.5.1 Definition of a Cohort
    14.5.2 Cohort Study Design
    14.5.3 Relative Risk
    14.5.4 Risk Ratio
    14.5.5 Rate Ratio
    14.5.6 Considerations in the Selection of a Cohort
    14.5.7 Considerations in the Measurement of Exposure
    14.5.8 Advantages of Cohort Study Design
        14.5.8.1 Scientific Rigor and Quality of Evidence
        14.5.8.2 Estimation of Incidence
    14.5.9 Disadvantages of Cohort Study Design
        14.5.9.1 Complexity of Study Design
        14.5.9.2 Difficulties in the Follow-up of Subjects

        14.5.9.3 Duration of Study
        14.5.9.4 Cost of Study
        14.5.9.5 Size of Cohort
14.6 Example of a Prospective Cohort Study
14.7 Example of a Retrospective Cohort Study
14.8 Case-Control Studies
    14.8.1 Case-Control Study Design
    14.8.2 Definition of a Case
    14.8.3 Definition of a Control
    14.8.4 Sources, Identification, and Recruitment of Cases
    14.8.5 Purpose of Controls
    14.8.6 Sources, Identification, and Recruitment of Controls
    14.8.7 Methods to Obtain Information Regarding Past Exposure
    14.8.8 Considerations in the Measurement of Exposure
    14.8.9 Calculation and Interpretation of Odds Ratio
    14.8.10 Advantages of Case-Control Study Design

14.9   Example of a Case-Control Study
14.10   Risk Factor and Exposure in Cohort and
        Case-Control Studies
14.11   Comparison of Cohort and Case-Control Study
        Design
14.12   Association and Causality
14.13   Bias

14.14   Confounding
Case Study 14.1 – An Ecological Study
Case Study 14.2 – Prospective Cohort Study
Case Study 14.3 – Retrospective Cohort Study
Case Study 14.4 – Case-Control Study
14.15   Summary

KEY TERMS

Ambulatory care sensitive conditions
Bias
Case-control studies
Cohort
Cohort studies
Confounder variables
Cumulative incidence
Ecological bias
Ecological fallacy

Ecological studies
Experimental studies
Exposure
Historical cohort studies
Incidence
Incidence density
Incidence rate
Incidence rate ratio
Multi-group study design

Observational studies
Prospective cohort studies
Relative risk
Retrospective cohort studies
Rate ratio
Risk ratio
Type I error
Type II error

▶ 14.1 Introduction

Every year, thousands of epidemiological studies are published in various journals in the United States alone. These studies address a wide range of biomedical and clinical subjects and belong largely to two categories: observational studies and experimental studies. The purpose of these studies is to test hypotheses, find answers to puzzling questions, provide guidance for policy formulation, and help in clinical decision making. Epidemiological studies help in clinical decision making by not only enhancing our understanding of the frequency and distribution of diseases, but also by providing clues about how and why diseases happen and who gets afflicted with what disease and why. Some studies use existing information available through medical records and patient registries, whereas others involve recruitment of subjects from whom information is directly obtained over a short or long period.

Healthcare managers do not make clinical decisions and may not need to know the etiology or treatment for various diseases. However, they need to have some understanding of how epidemiological investigations are conducted; how one kind of study methodologically differs from another; and the objectives, advantages, and disadvantages of one study design over another. Given the frequency of clinical trials and research studies being conducted in academic and nonacademic healthcare settings and many administrative challenges posed by such undertakings, including potential conflict of interest, patient safety concerns, and logistical challenges, it is imperative for healthcare managers to be familiar with the theoretical and operational framework of such investigations. This chapter is designed to provide necessary information and tools related to one of the two most common categories of epidemiological investigations: the observational studies.

▶ 14.2 Observational Studies

As shown in **FIGURE 14.1**, under the rubric of *analytic* studies, the category of epidemiological investigations known as the **observational studies** is entirely distinct from the category known as the **experimental studies**. Observational studies differ from experimental studies in that the researcher does not manipulate the subjects or attempt to change the health status of participants; alter the natural course of events; or test the effectiveness or safety of a new medication, procedure, or technology. In other words, the role of the researcher in observational studies is merely to be a passive observer of events. However, the researcher makes critical decisions about where, when, and how the observation takes place and who the subject of observation is. Depending on the answers to these questions, observational studies are classified into the following three forms of studies: ecological studies, cohort studies, and case-control studies. In the following sections, we will discuss the theoretical and operational framework of these three

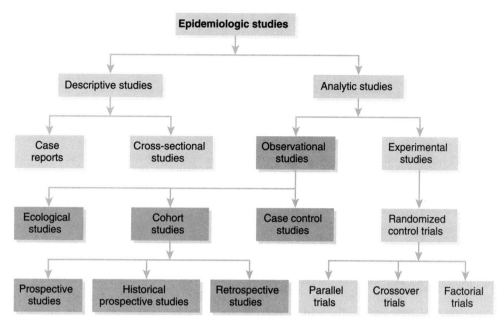

FIGURE 14.1 A schematic diagram of different types of epidemiologic studies.

Data from Friis, 2010; Swallen KC, University of Wisconsin-Madison.

forms of observational studies and provide relevant examples from the current literature.

▶ 14.3 Ecological Studies

Ecological studies investigate the effects of some phenomenon, risk factor, or intervention—whether natural or manmade—in the same population over different periods or in a population in one geographic area as compared with one or more other populations in other areas. For example, an ecological study might investigate the health effects of air pollution in Delhi or Shanghai by examining the **incidence**and prevalence of acute and chronic respiratory diseases in these cities in comparison with London, Paris, or Berlin. Likewise, one might study in children the short- and long-term health effects of exposure to a lead-contaminated municipal water supply system in Flint, Michigan, in 2014 and 2015. One can then compare the occurrence of health outcomes, such as developmental delays, neurologic deficit, and learning disabilities, in this population with the population of children in other towns of similar size and demographic characteristics. Subjects in ecological studies can be grouped by geographic areas such as cities, counties, or ZIP codes (**multi-group study design**) or by time if changes in the same group are investigated longitudinally over time (*time trend studies*). Subjects can also be grouped by both place and time if groups assigned to different geographic areas are studied longitudinally over a period of time (*mixed study design*).[1]

Typically, ecological studies examine the relationship between mean outcomes such as mortality or morbidity rates (e.g., asthma or liver cirrhosis per 100,000 population) and mean levels of exposure (e.g., air pollution or alcohol consumption) across different population groups. Because comparisons have to be made at the population level, ecological studies require aggregated population-level information on risk factors and health outcomes.[2] Because the unit of analysis in these studies is the entire population rather than individuals, usually no individual-level data are sought. For the same reason, no individual-level conclusions are made, nor are inferences drawn regarding the impact of the variable of interest on individuals in the population. Commonly, ecological studies investigate the effect of time and spatial factors on group-level health outcomes or the impact of a health policy on different populations.[1,3,4] These studies can also be used to investigate the impact of population-level interventions such as municipal fluoridation of water, fortification of milk with vitamin D, or levying a heavy tax on cigarettes. Ecological studies are frequently used in occupational epidemiology to understand the relationship of certain occupations with the frequency of one or the other disease.

The advantages of ecological studies, whether cross-sectional or longitudinal, include their simplicity of design and use of existing population-level data from sources such as the Bureau of the Census, disease registries, and local or state health departments. Sources of data for ecological studies in the United States also include the U.S. Centers for Medicare and

Medicaid Services, the U.S. Centers for Disease Control and Prevention, and many other private or public sector national and international agencies.

Despite the advantages of simplicity, convenience, time saving, and low cost, ecological studies are prone to a variety of methodological problems, including the potential for bias, inadequate control of confounders, the use of inappropriate statistical techniques for data analysis, and unwarranted interpretation of results.[1] One limitation of ecological studies, commonly known as the **ecological fallacy** (or **ecological bias**), results from the fact that the unit of analysis is an entire population rather than an individual. Ecological fallacy means that an association observed between a variable of interest and a population does not directly translate into the same association between the risk factor and an individual.[5] The issue of ecological fallacy in ecological studies stems from the underlying reality that individual-level health outcomes or events such as mortality or morbidity are not linked directly with individual-level **exposure** to the risk factor, as they are in individual-level studies such as case-control or cohort studies.[5] For example, a number of "diseases of affluence" (e.g., heart disease) have been shown in the past to be associated at the national level with the sale of television sets.[6] This association, however, does not mean that every individual who owns a television set is at a high risk of, say, heart disease. Despite some methodological issues, well-designed ecological studies play an important role in defining public health problems and in generating causal hypotheses that can be further investigated by cohort or case-control studies. For example, the international comparisons of the incidence of various cancers in different countries in the 1950s and 1960s led to causal hypotheses that were later investigated in depth by other studies.[6]

One recent review[2] of 125 cross-sectional ecological studies found that 16% of the reviewed studies focused on cancer as the primary outcome, while 14% focused on mortality, 13% on chronic diseases, and 10% on cardiovascular disease. In terms of the unit of analysis, 38% of the studies aggregated census tract or neighborhood-level data, 18% aggregated county-level data, 12% used province or state data, and 20% used nations or nation-clusters. The authors of the review concluded that more than half of the studies had some form of ecological fallacy or used inappropriate methodologies in study design or statistical analysis and applied inferences drawn from population-level data to individuals.[2] For example, in 34% of the reviewed studies, hypotheses or conclusions clearly applied to individual-level risk factors or health outcomes.[2]

▶ 14.4 Example of an Ecological Study

Modified from: Rasella D, Harhay MO, Pamponet ML, Aquino R, Barreto ML. Impact of primary health care on mortality from heart and cerebrovascular diseases in Brazil: a nationwide analysis of longitudinal data. BMJ. 2014;349:g4014. doi:10.1136/bmj.g4014

In a recent *mixed study design* ecological study, Rasella et al. (2014) investigated the impact of Brazil's Family Health Program (FHP) on heart and cerebrovascular disease mortality across the country from 2000 to 2009. Brazil's FHP is the largest primary care program in the world and is credited for improved population health outcomes in the country. The FHP program provides health promotion and disease prevention services, including management of cardiovascular disease risk factors, as well as secondary prevention through monitoring and management of hypertension and diabetes. The program relies on domiciliary visits and community-based interventions implemented through community health workers.

The researchers used a *mixed ecological study* model that combines *multi-group'* and longitudinal *time trend* study designs. The unit of analysis in this study was a municipality (county). Using regression models, the researchers analyzed longitudinal vital statistics data from 1,622 Brazilian municipalities (30% of the 5,507 municipalities in Brazil) for the 10-year period. About 75% of the municipalities included in the study had less than 25,000 inhabitants. The annual FHP coverage levels and average FHP coverage level in these municipalities 4, 6, and 8 years after the implementation of the Family Health Program in 2000 were used as the main independent variables. Coverage levels were classified as "None" (0%), "Incipient" (<30%), "Intermediate" (30–69%), and "Consolidated" (≥70%). Age-standardized mortality rates from cerebrovascular diseases, ischemic heart diseases, and other heart diseases that were included in the national list of **ambulatory care sensitive conditions** were calculated for each municipality for each year. Because deaths from accidents are not affected by the availability of primary care in a population, mortality rate from accidents was used as a control variable in these analyses.

The mean population coverage in municipalities with FHP program increased from 21% in 2000 to 68.6% in 2009—an increase of 227%. During the same period, mean cerebrovascular mortality rate in the covered municipalities fell from 40.1 to 27.0 per 100,000 population—a reduction of 32.7%. Heart disease mortality fell by 44.6% from a mean of 23.3 in 2000 to 12.9 per 100,000 in 2009. In comparison, mean mortality rate from accidents, a health status indicator largely outside the influence of access to primary care, actually increased during the same period, from 41.8 to 47.0 per 100,000 inhabitants. This variable was used in the study as a *control variable* to show the contrast between variables expected to be affected by the intervention and those not expected to be influenced by the intervention. Importantly, socioeconomic variables such as monthly per capita income and percentage of population below poverty line (examples of confounding variables) also improved between 2000 and 2009. This observation is important because it demonstrates the role of confounding variables and, in this case, raises the possibility that reduction in cerebrovascular and heart disease mortality may not be attributed entirely or even partially to increased availability of primary care, but may very well have resulted from improved living conditions. The statistical models developed by the researchers adjusted for the potential effects of these confounding variables.

The researchers calculated crude and adjusted ratios of mean mortality rates in municipalities not covered by FHP and those covered at the "Incipient," "Intermediate," or "Consolidated" level. For example, the adjusted cerebrovascular disease mortality rate in municipalities covered at the "Intermediate" level (≥30% to <70% coverage) was found to be 14% lower than those not covered by FHP (adjusted rate ratio = 0.86). Likewise, the adjusted mortality rate related to cerebrovascular disease in municipalities with a "Consolidated" level of coverage (≥70% coverage) was 18% lower than municipalities not covered at all (adjusted rate ratio = 0.82). However, there was no difference in accident-related mortality rates in municipalities with different levels of FHP coverage and those not covered by FHP (adjusted mortality rate ratios of 0.99, 0.97, and 1.02). In other words, the FHP did not have any effect on mortality rates from accidents.

The authors also calculated adjusted ratios of cerebrovascular disease mortality, heart disease mortality, and accident-related mortality in municipalities with no FHP coverage and those with different levels of FHP coverage 4, 6, and 8 years after the onset of the program. The results showed a clear and consistent inverse *dose-response* relationship between the extent of coverage and mortality from cerebrovascular and heart diseases 4, 6, and 8 years after the implementation of the FHP—that is, the greater the average coverage of the population by FHP and the longer the period of coverage, the lower the mortality from cerebrovascular and heart diseases. For example, municipalities that had ≥70% FHP coverage in the past 5 years had 23% lower cerebrovascular disease mortality

(adjusted rate ratio = 0.77) and 25% lower heart disease mortality (adjusted rate ratio = 0.75), but almost the same rate of accident-related mortality (adjusted rate ratio = 1.02) as the municipalities with no coverage. Likewise, in municipalities that had ≥70% FHP coverage in the last 8 years, cerebrovascular disease mortality was 31% lower (adjusted rate ratio = 0.69) and heart disease mortality 36% lower (adjusted rate ratio = 0.64) than municipalities with no coverage in the same period. Again, the accident-related mortality rate in municipalities with 70% or greater coverage in the past 8 years was almost the same (adjusted rate ratio = 1.02) as those with no coverage. This is exactly what the analytical models anticipated from the use of accident-related mortality as the control variable because access to primary care in a community or lack thereof is not expected to have any bearing on mortality from accidents.

The ambulatory care sensitive subgroups of "cerebrovascular," "ischemic heart disease," and "other heart disease" accounted for 40% of all deaths in these categories during the 2000–2009 study period. The researchers reported that FHP coverage in Brazil was negatively associated with mortality rates from the ambulatory care sensitive subgroups of cerebrovascular and heart diseases in analytic models that were adjusted or unadjusted for demographic, social, and economic confounders. They concluded that primary care programs such as Brazil's FHP could help reduce cardiovascular disease morbidity and mortality in developing countries such as Brazil.

The authors also pointed out that the study only provided evidence of an ecological plausibility by establishing an association between the FHP program and municipality-level reduction in cerebrovascular and cardiovascular disease mortality during the study period. As the study investigated the effectiveness of the FHP program only at the aggregated (municipality) level, no assertion can be made about the positive impact of the FHP program at the individual level. In fact, the study cannot determine whether individuals who experienced the intended impact of the FHP program (i.e., survival from cerebrovascular and cardiovascular disease) were even covered by the program or received any services.

▶ 14.5 Cohort Studies

14.5.1 Definition of a Cohort

The word *cohort* is derived from Latin and traces its origin to the legions of Roman soldiers who shared the experience of staying together in an army camps and fighting together in a battle. Strictly speaking, it referred to one of the 10 divisions of a Roman legion. In common usage, the word simply refers to a group of individuals (or animals) who share an experience or effort over time. The duration of time over which the experience or effort happens is unrestricted and may vary from one cohort to another. One example might be a cohort of students at a college or university, such as the "cohort of 2018" (i.e., the class of students who graduated in 2018). Another example might be the cohort of astronauts who went on the successful Apollo 11 mission to the moon. In epidemiologic investigations, the word **cohort** refers to a group of participants who are collectively exposed to a risk factor, substance, drug, or event and are observed over time to examine the effects, if any, of such exposure. Because of the shared experience of having been exposed to such a factor, the group of participants in the study constitutes a cohort.

14.5.2 Cohort Study Design

Typically, the cohort study design involves identification and recruitment of two groups of participants. One group comprises individuals who are or were in the past exposed to the risk factor being investigated; the other group consists of individuals not exposed to the risk factor. Both groups are then prospectively followed or observed for a duration of time to see whether they acquire the disease of interest. Because subjects are prospectively followed over time, these studies are also commonly referred to as *prospective studies*. By their very nature, **cohort studies** attempt to test a hypothesis regarding the etiology of a disease. However, because of the difficulties in establishing a causal relationship between a disease and a risk factor, the goals of such a study are limited only to revealing or refuting a positive or negative statistical association between a risk factor and the disease of interest. Depending on the nature of exposure and the disease, the period of observation or follow-up can be relatively short or long. It is not uncommon for the follow-up period to span years or even decades.

There are many variations in cohort study design. In one variation, known as the *open or dynamic cohort design*, the study begins with a cohort of participants to which new recruits are added on an ongoing basis along the way. In this kind of study, the follow-up period for all participants is not exactly the same, but differs from one subject to another. Even without the addition of new participants along the way, which is the case in typical *closed cohort study design*, the period of observation for subjects who were all recruited at the same time at the onset of the study

can be different. This can happen because some of the participants later opt out of the study or discontinue for one or the other reason, whereas others may be lost to follow-up because of death or migration. In another variation of cohort study design, a group of individuals (a cohort) is identified from historical record of one kind or another. Historical records can include medical records, employment records, medical claims data, or reimbursement records. In such a study, subjects are followed in time through their medical records to understand how their health status changed going forward from a point in time in the past. Such cohort studies are known as **retrospective cohort studies** or **historical cohort studies**.

Regardless of whether the study is based on a historical cohort or a prospective cohort, one feature common to all cohort studies is that study participants consist of two subgroups: One subgroup comprises those who are exposed to a risk factor that is suspected to have a causal (or protective) role in the occurrence of disease, whereas the second subgroup consists of those who are not exposed to that risk factor. The ratio of those in the cohort who are exposed to the risk factor to those who are not exposed can be predetermined to a specific level, such as one exposed participant for one unexposed individual (ratio of 1:1), or some other level, such as a ratio of 1:2 or 1:3. The ratio of exposed individuals to unexposed individuals in the study depends on several factors, including the availability of participants as well as the nature and frequency of the risk factor.

Ideally, the exposed and unexposed members of the cohort are matched for age, race, sex, education, geographic area, and other factors to minimize the differences between the two groups. Sex-matched pairs of twins in which one of the twins is exposed to the risk factor while the other is not make the best matches. Other good matches include unexposed siblings or age- and sex-matched friends. **TABLE 14.1** shows the conceptual framework of a cohort study.

14.5.3 Relative Risk

Relative risk, which is also known as *risk ratio*, *rate ratio*, or, more precisely, **incidence rate ratio**,[7] is a measure of the strength of association between a risk factor and a disease and is obtained by deriving the ratio of incidence rate in the exposed population and in the unexposed population. In cohort studies, because the population of both groups—those exposed to a risk factor and those not exposed—is known and the incidence rate can be directly calculated for both groups, it is possible to derive relative risk. Essentially, relative risk indicates the excess risk

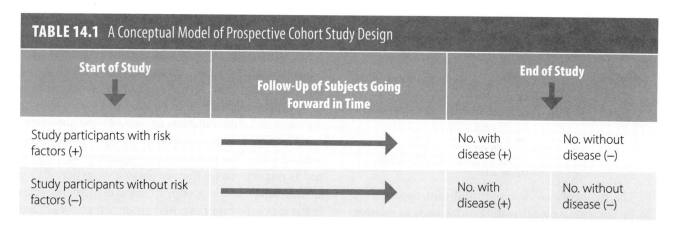

TABLE 14.1 A Conceptual Model of Prospective Cohort Study Design

Start of Study	Follow-Up of Subjects Going Forward in Time	End of Study	
Study participants with risk factors (+)	→	No. with disease (+)	No. without disease (−)
Study participants without risk factors (−)	→	No. with disease (+)	No. without disease (−)

TABLE 14.2 Relative Risk Derivation – Notational Example

		Disease		
		Yes	No	Total
Exposure	Yes	*a*	*b*	*a + b*
	No	*c*	*d*	*c + d*
	Total	*a + c*	*b + d*	*a + b + c + d*

TABLE 14.3 Relative Risk Derivation – Numeric Example

		Disease		
		Yes	No	Total
Exposure	Yes	40	460	500
	No	15	485	500
	Total	55	945	1,000

of disease in the exposed group as compared with the unexposed group. In other words, relative risk is the proportion of cases in the exposed population that can be attributed to the risk factor. **TABLES 14.2** and **14.3** are designed to demonstrate how relative risk is derived.

In Table 14.2, *a* represents the number of cases of disease in the group exposed to the risk factor in a cohort study, and *c* represents the number of cases in the unexposed group.

Thus, incidence rate or risk of disease among the exposed is represented by = *(a) / (a + b)*.

The incidence rate or risk of disease among the unexposed is represented by = *(c) / (c + d)*.

Relative risk is the ratio of the risk of disease among the exposed and the risk of disease among the unexposed. Alternatively, it is the ratio of incidence rate in the exposed group and incidence rate in the unexposed group. Therefore,

$$\text{Relative Risk} = \frac{(a \,/\, a + b)}{(c \,/\, c + d)}$$

Table 14.3 shows data from a hypothetical prospective cohort study in which 500 individuals who were exposed to a risk factor and 500 who were not exposed to the risk factor were followed over a period of time.

As shown, the incidence of disease in the exposed group was 40, and in the unexposed group it was 15. The relative risk of disease in the two groups was:

$$\text{Relative Risk} = \frac{(40 / 500)}{(15 / 500)}$$

$$\text{or} = \frac{0.08}{0.03}$$

$$\text{or} = 2.67$$

The frequency of disease in different populations can be compared by calculating ratios such as relative risk, relative rate, risk ratio, and rate ratio. We have discussed relative risk in the preceding paragraphs in some detail because it is frequently used as an umbrella term for relative rate, risk ratio, and rate ratio. In the interest of clarity, definitions for these terms are provided below.

14.5.4 Rate Ratio or Incidence Rate Ratio

Typically, in a cohort study, all participants join the study at the same time, although they are not all followed for the full duration of the study for reasons such as death, willful discontinuation of participation, relocation, or being "lost to follow-up" for other reasons. In some variations of cohort study design, subjects can join the study at different times during the course of the study and also leave the study at different times for various reasons (such a cohort is called an *open* or *dynamic* cohort). In these situations, because different subjects are followed for different periods of time, the **incidence rate** (IR) in each group is referred to as **incidence density** and incidence rate is calculated in terms of person-years (PYs) of follow-up by using the aggregated follow-up time contributed by all subjects combined in that group as the denominator. For example, IR in the exposed group might be expressed as 105 per 1,000 PYs of follow-up. The 2015 prospective cohort study by Falade-Nwulia et al. discussed in section 14.6 is an example of an open cohort study in which incidence rates in the exposed and unexposed groups were calculated in PYs. As shown in **TABLE 14.4**, the IR in the exposed group may be represented by the expression $IR_e = a / K$ and the IR in the unexposed group may be represented by the notation $IR_u = c / L$. The subscripts e and u in these expressions refer to *exposed* and *unexposed* groups. The denominator in each group (i.e., K and L, respectively) is the sum of follow-up periods for all individuals in that group. The ratio of incidence rates in the exposed and unexposed group is therefore called a **rate ratio** or, more accurately, incidence rate ratio.

Incidence rate ratio, therefore, would be represented by the following expression:

$$\text{Incidence Rate Ratio} = \frac{IR_e}{IR_u}\left(i.e., \frac{(a / K)}{(c / L)}\right)$$

A rate ratio of 1 in a cohort study suggests that there is no difference in the frequency or rate of the disease per period between the exposed group and the unexposed group. In other words, exposure to the risk factor did not increase the rate of the disease among those who were exposed to the risk factor. On the other hand, a rate ratio of greater than 1 (rate ratio >1) indicates that the frequency or rate of the disease per period was higher in the exposed group as compared with the unexposed group. Likewise, a rate ratio of less than 1 (rate ratio <1) suggests that those exposed to the risk factor (e.g., red wine or a Mediterranean diet) got the disease less frequently than those who were not exposed to the risk factor. Alternatively, we can say that exposure (e.g., to red wine) conferred some protection from the disease or reduced the likelihood of disease in the exposed group as compared with the unexposed group.

TABLE 14.5 provides a numeric example of the estimation of incidence rate ratio in a prospective

TABLE 14.4 Incidence Rate Ratio Derivation – Notational Example

		Disease			
		Yes	No	Total Follow-Up in PYs	Incidence Rate per 1,000 Person-Years
Exposure	Yes	a	b	K	$IR_e = a / K$
	No	c	d	L	$IR_u = c / L$
	Total	$a+c$	$b+d$	$K+L$	

Incidence Rate Ratio $= IR_e / IR_u = (a/K) / (c/L)$

cohort study in which 1,400 exposed individuals were enrolled in a study that lasted 10 years. The aggregated follow-up time for the 1,400 individuals totaled 12,000 PYs. The unexposed group consisted of 1,600 hundred individuals whose combined follow-up time over the 10-year period totaled 13,000 PYs. Thus, incidence rate per 1,000 PYs in the exposed group was:

$$\left(\frac{400}{12,000}\right) \times 1,000 = 33.3 \text{ per 1,000 person-years}$$

Likewise, incidence rate in the unexposed group was:

$$\left(\frac{100}{13,000}\right) \times 1,000 = 7.7 \text{ per 1,000 person-years}$$

The incidence rate ratio of the exposed group with the unexposed group, therefore, was:

$$\text{Incidence Rate Ratio} = \frac{33.3}{7.7} = 4.3$$

$$\left(\begin{array}{l}\text{i.e., the incidence rate in the exposed group}\\\text{was 4.3 times of that in the unexposed group}\end{array}\right)$$

A rate ratio of 4.3 in this example suggests that those exposed to the risk factor of interest got the disease 4.3 times more per 1,000 PYs of follow-up as those in the unexposed group.

14.5.5 Risk Ratio

Conceptually, a **risk ratio** (RR) is slightly different from a *rate ratio* (or *incidence rate ratio*) because there is no mention of time in estimating the risk of disease in the exposed and unexposed groups. In terms of data collection and analysis, it simply means that researchers choose to disregard the issue of dropouts and "lost to follow-up" and assume that all participants were engaged for the full duration of the study. The mathematical operations for deriving a *risk ratio* or a rate ratio are practically the same. The difference lies in the fact that in risk ratio, the incidence merely represents the proportion of those in the exposed or unexposed group who got the disease. Thus, it involves a comparison of proportions rather than rates of disease in the two groups. As such, in risk ratio, the incidence of disease in the two groups is compared on the bases of **cumulative incidence** (CI) over a period of time. Identical to Table 14.4 in the previous section, **TABLE 14.6** uses

TABLE 14.5 Incidence Rate Ratio Derivation – Numeric Example

		Disease			
		Yes	No	Total Follow-Up in Person-Years	Incidence Rate per 1,000 PYs
Exposure	Yes	400	1,000	12,000	$IR_e = (400 / 12,000) \times 1,000 = 33.3$
	No	100	1,500	13,000	$IR_u = (100 / 13,000) \times 1,000 = 7.7$

Incidence Rate Ratio $= IR_e / IR_u = 33.3 / 7.7 = 4.3$.

TABLE 14.6 Cumulative Incidence Derivation – Notational Example

		Disease			
		Yes	No	Total	Cumulative Incidence
Exposure	Yes	a	b	$a+b$	$CI_e = a/a+b$
	No	c	d	$c+d$	$CI_u = c/c+d$
	Total	$a+c$	$b+d$	$a+b+c+d$	

Risk Ratio or Cumulative Incidence Ratio $= CI_e / CI_u = (a/a+b) / (c/c+d)$.

TABLE 14.7 Cumulative Incidence Derivation – Numeric Example

		Disease			
		Yes	No	Total	Cumulative Incidence
Exposure	Yes	20	100	120	$CI_e = (20 / 120) = 0.17$
	No	15	150	165	$CI_u = (15 / 165) = 0.09$

Risk Ratio or Cumulative Incidence Ratio = $CI_e / CI_u = 0.17 / 0.09 = 1.89$.

the same notations and the same mathematical formulas to calculate the risk of disease (or CI) in the exposed (CI_e) and unexposed (CI_u) groups. Likewise, **TABLE 14.7** provides a numeric example of the estimation of risk of disease or cumulative incidence in the exposed and unexposed groups and its use to derive a risk ratio. The most important point to understand about a risk ratio is that it is based on a comparison of the proportions of exposed and unexposed individuals who got the disease in an entire period and is indicative of the comparative risk of disease in the two groups. For example, the risk ratio of 1.89 shown in Table 14.7 ($CI_e / CI_u = 0.17 / 0.09 = 1.89$) means that the risk of disease in the exposed group was 1.89 times that of risk in the unexposed group in the same period. Note that in this example, we refer to the risk of disease, rather than the rate of disease.

14.5.6 Considerations in the Selection of a Cohort

There are several important considerations in the selection of subjects for *exposed* and *unexposed* groups or *index* and *comparison* groups in a cohort study. Clearly, the availability and willingness of potential subjects to participate in a study as well as their commitment to providing or allowing researchers access to necessary information in accordance with the study protocol are the basic requirements. Beyond these basic considerations, however, many other factors also determine the suitability of individuals as potential study participants. For example, individuals whose jobs involve extensive travel or posting in different cities or states may not be suitable candidates to participate in a longitudinal cohort study either as exposed or unexposed individuals.[7] One of the most important aspects of selecting study participants is the

degree of similarity between those in the exposed group and those in the unexposed group. Except for exposure to the factor whose effects are being investigated (e.g., hypertension, alcohol, obesity), the researchers must make every effort to have subjects in the exposed and unexposed groups be as similar as possible in all other respects. This can be achieved either by matching subjects in both groups on as many demographic and socioeconomic variables as possible or by recruiting subjects from the same settings, environment, and communities. Siblings, friends, neighbors, teammates, or classmates of subjects in the exposed group can make good candidates for the unexposed group as long as they are not exposed to the variable under investigation. In these respects, both cohort and case-control studies are similar to experimental studies in which subjects being exposed to an intervention are similar to those not being exposed to the intervention whose effects are being studied. It is also important to have a sufficient number of participants in both groups to ensure adequate statistical power of the study and having approximately equal numbers of subjects in both exposed and unexposed groups. To ensure equally rigorous efforts in following subjects during the course of a prospective cohort study, at times it is useful to mask from those responsible for follow-up and continued data gathering the information as to which subjects are in the exposed group and which are in the comparison group.

14.5.7 Considerations in the Measurement of Exposure

The term *exposure* refers to a factor, behavior, or agent that plays a role in the occurrence of a disease, in preventing a disease, or in the amelioration of a disease.[7] When the relationship of an extraneous factor or agent with a disease is causal in nature or that of facilitation, such a factor is also referred to as a *risk factor*. In a cohort or case-control study, it is important to define carefully the *exposure* or *risk factor* being investigated and deciding before the onset of the study how exposure will be assessed.

The characterization and assessment of the intensity and duration of exposure are important in both cohort and case-control studies. It is not sufficient to ask whether exposure to a particular factor or noxious agent occurred; it is necessary to fully understand the circumstances of such exposure. To make a definitive statement about an association between exposure and outcome, one must be able to develop measures of different levels of exposure and consistently apply the same definition of exposure to all subjects throughout the duration of a study.

Often the presumed or hypothesized relationship between disease and exposure requires exploration of dose–response relations—that is, it is essential to know how much exposure occurred on an hourly, daily, or weekly basis and for how long. For example, a study on the hazardous impact of radiation must determine the intensity (dose) of radiation; its frequency (hourly, daily, or weekly exposure); and its duration in weeks, months, or years. Similarly, a cohort study on the presumed protective effect of lactation on diabetes in women (see Case Study 14.2 at the end of this chapter) must carefully establish whether lactation was combined or supplemented with formula milk, as well as the frequency and duration of lactation. In **prospective cohort studies**, variations and changes in exposure over a period of months or years must also be carefully monitored, and analysis of data must adjust for such variations and difference in the level of exposure among different subjects.

It is also important to be clear about what sources of information will be used to ascertain exposure and how information about exposure will be verified or validated. If exposure information is based on interviews and personal reports, there can be potential for bias either because of poor recall or purposeful over- or underreporting of the intensity, frequency, and duration of exposure. For example, cases of lung cancer may underreport frequency and duration of cigarette smoking because of a "guilt complex" or "shame complex," or possibly to hold a cigarette manufacturer liable. Alternatively, they may overreport the intensity and duration of smoking for the same ulterior motive. If medical records are used to assess exposure, there might be underestimation of exposure because of incomplete or missing information in patients' history and physicians' notes.

14.5.8 Advantages of Cohort Study Design

Cohort study design has several advantages over other studies such as cross-sectional studies and case-control studies. Some of these advantages are briefly discussed next.

14.5.8.1 Scientific Rigor and Quality of Evidence

As long as a study is properly designed and implemented, cohort study design is more robust in elucidating an association or the absence of an association between a risk factor of interest and a disease. This study design allows more rigorous and direct investigation of the strength of association of a disease with different levels of exposure to a risk factor as well as different durations of exposure to the same risk factor. For example, one can study the differential effects of smoking one, two, or three packs of cigarettes for 5 years, 10 years, or 20 years.

14.5.8.2 Estimation of Incidence

Cohort study design allows direct estimation of the incidence of disease in the population at risk that cannot be done with case-control studies, in which the total number of individuals exposed to the risk factor (i.e., population at risk or the denominator) is not known. Moreover, cohort study design allows estimation of incidence density in terms of the occurrence of disease per 1,000, per 10,000, or per 100,000 PYs of exposure to the risk factor or *cumulative incidence rate* in terms of the number of new cases of disease per year in the population at risk.

14.5.9 Disadvantages of Cohort Study Design

14.5.9.1 Complexity of Study Design

The design of a cohort study is complex because of the challenges involved in conceptualizing or hypothesizing a scientifically plausible and logical relationship between risk factors and the disease being investigated. These challenges increase if several different risk factors are to be explored simultaneously. A number of *a priori* procedural decisions must be made regarding the specific characteristics of individuals who will be eligible to participate in the study. Other questions that must be settled before the onset of the study include the following: (1) How will recruitment of subjects be carried out? (2) How will operational and ethical issues related to the methods of collecting data, self-selection bias, and confidentiality be handled? (3) How will a potential *Hawthorne effect* (alteration of behavior by the subjects because of their awareness of being observed or followed) be assessed and adjusted for in the final analysis? (4) How long will the follow-up period be? (5) How will a "case" be defined? (6) What clinical and laboratory tests will be done to diagnose and confirm the occurrence of disease?

14.5.9.2 Difficulties in the Follow-up of Subjects

Some degree of attrition in the number of subjects in exposed and unexposed groups is almost inevitable in all cohort studies, with the exception of historical or retrospective cohort studies that rely on previously existing historical data. The degree of attrition can be related to a number of factors, including the nature of exposure, expected duration of the study, demographic characteristics of the study population, and procedures adopted for follow-up of participants. Whether attrition happens because of migration, death, or lack of motivation on the part of subjects or failure to communicate with subjects for other reasons, it presents serious problems for the validity of study results. A bias can be introduced if participants with certain characteristics selectively discontinue their participation or attrition rates are differentially distributed between the exposed and unexposed groups or within different categories of the exposed group.

14.5.9.3 Duration of Study

For diseases that develop slowly, it can take a long time before signs and symptoms of the disease become clinically noticeable and before a definitive diagnosis can be made. Therefore, the follow-up period must be long enough for a sufficient number of new cases of disease to develop in the exposed and unexposed groups. A long follow-up period not only poses many operational challenges and increases the cost of the study, but also increases the likelihood of biased results because less-motivated individuals may drop out of the study in high numbers, leaving more motivated people in the study who may be systematically different from the less-motivated group. For example, highly motivated individuals who continue to participate in the study might be more educated, more conscientious about their health, or sicker than less-motivated subjects who dropped out of the study.

14.5.9.4 Cost of Study

Cost considerations play a major role in the design and implementation of any project. As compared with cross-sectional studies or other types of observational studies, cohort studies in general and prospective studies in particular can incur much higher costs. These costs are largely associated with the logistics of subject recruitment and ongoing follow-up. Clearly, these costs are directly proportional to the size of the cohort and the duration of follow-up, which in turn are related to the power of the study and the nature of the disease under investigation. Multicenter studies also cost more than single-center studies. The higher costs and longer time to get study results act as a counterpoint to the argument that cohort studies have greater scientific rigor and results that are more valid. Given the stiff competition for research funding and the desire on the part of researchers and funding agencies alike to see results more quickly, the issue of higher costs demands a careful consideration of alternative study designs such as case-control studies.

14.5.9.5 Size of Cohort

In the case of rare or uncommon diseases, the size of the cohort must be large enough to yield a sufficient number of cases in both exposed and unexposed groups to allow a meaningful statistical comparison. A large number of participants not only increases administrative difficulties of managing the project, but also proportionately increases the cost of the study.

▶ 14.6 Example of a Prospective Cohort Study

Modified from: Falade-Nwulia O, Seaberg EC, Snider AE, et al. Incident hepatitis B virus infection in HIV-infected and HIV-uninfected men who have sex with men from pre-HAART to HAART period. Ann Intern Med. 2015;163(9):673–680.

Men who have sex with men (MSM) are at high risk of hepatitis B virus (HBV) infection. The purpose of this prospective cohort study was to identify risk factors of HBV infection among HIV-infected and HIV-uninfected MSM. Researchers used data from a multicenter (Baltimore, Chicago, Los Angeles, and Pittsburgh) AIDS longitudinal study (MAC) that had followed a cohort of MSM since 1984. The MAC included men who either already had HIV or were at risk for HIV. The participants in MAC were initially recruited from 1984 to 1985 and then again from 1987 to 1991 and from 2001 to 2003. These individuals were interviewed and tested for HIV every 6 months. At the time of enrollment into MAC, they were also tested for hepatitis B.

The eligibility criteria for the present study that was nested in the MAC and was started in January 1985 included negative hepatitis B test results at the time of enrollment in the MAC and availability of one or more blood samples from subsequent visits to be tested for hepatitis B.

The incidence of hepatitis B was defined as seroconversion of a previously negative individual to a positive HBsAg (hepatitis B surface antigen) or anti HBc (antibody to hepatitis B core antigen) test result. The participating men in the study were followed until December 31, 2013, or the last follow-up visit or the date of incident HBV infection—whichever happened first. Data on a number of variables, including age, race, number of sexual partners, injection-drug use, and alcohol use, were abstracted at each semiannual visit.

The results of the hepatitis B cohort study showed that out of the 6,972 men enrolled in the MAC until the end of 2003, a total of 2,375 had negative test results for hepatitis B virus at the first study visit on or after January 1, 1985. Of these, 1,784 were HIV-uninfected

(75%) and 591 (25%) were HIV infected. Of the 1,784 HIV-uninfected MSM at the onset of the study in January 1985, 151 (8.5%) became HIV infected (i.e., had seroconversion) during the course of the study. The 2,375 HBV-negative men accrued 25,322 PYs of follow-up period. During this time, 244 cases of HBV infection occurred in this group, resulting in an overall unadjusted HBV incidence rate of 9.6 per 1,000 PYs (95% confidence interval [CI], 8.5 to 11.0). Among the HIV-infected men, 94 cases of HBV infection occurred during the 6,301 PYs of the follow-up period, yielding an incidence rate of 14.9 per 1,000 PYs (95% CI, 12.2 to 18.3). Among the HIV-uninfected men, 150 cases of HBV infection occurred during a total follow-up period of 19,020 PYs, with an incidence rate of 7.8 per 1,000 PYs (95% CI, 6.7 to 9.3). Thus, HBV incidence rate in the HIV-infected group was significantly higher than the HIV-uninfected group with an incidence rate ratio (IRR) of 1.9 (95% CI, 1.5 to 2.4).

TABLE 14.8 shows the incidence and IRR of HBV infection in HIV-infected and HIV-uninfected men

TABLE 14.8 Univariate Analysis of Risk Factors Associated with HBV Infection by HIV Infection Status

Variable	HIV Uninfected			HIV Infected		
	IR*/1,000 PYs***	IRR** (95% CI†)	P Value	IR*/1,000 PYs***	IRR** (95% CI†)	P Value
Age						
≥40 years	4.0	1		7.4	1	
<40 years	12.4	3.1 (2.2–4.5)	<0.001	22.8	3.1 (1.9–4.9)	<0.001
Race						
Nonwhite	7.5	1		11.8	1	
White	8.0	1.1 (0.7–1.6)	0.81	16.5	1.4 (0.9–2.2)	0.150
Alcohol						
≤13 drinks/wk	8.1	1		14.0	1	
>13 drinks/wk	8.8	1.1 (0.6–1.9)	0.75	36.0	2.6 (1.4–4.8)	0.003
Ever Injection Drug Use						
No	7.7	1		14.4	1	
Yes	14.0	1.8 (0.9–3.7)	0.100	21.2	1.5 (0.8–2.8)	0.25

(continues)

Variable	HIV Uninfected			HIV Infected		
TABLE 14.8 Univariate Analysis of Risk Factors Associated with HBV Infection by HIV Infection Status *(continued)*						
Sexual Exposure in Previous 6 Months						
0–1 partners	3.4	1		8.0	1	
≥2 partners	12.2	3.6 (2.4–5.2)	<0.001	21.8	2.7 (1.7–4.3)	<0.001

*Incidence rate.
**Incidence rate ratio.
***Person-years (PYs).
†Confidence interval.

Modified from: Falade-Nwulia O, Seaberg EC, Snider AE, Rinaldo CR, Phair J, Witt MD, Thio CL. Incident hepatitis B virus infection in HIV-infected and HIV-uninfected men who have sex with men from pre-HAART to HAART period. Ann Intern Med, 163(9):673–680. Copyright © 2015 American College of Physicians. All rights reserved. Reprinted with permission of American College of Physicians, Inc.

stratified by various risk factors such as age, race, use of alcohol, injection-drug use, and the number of sexual partners during the last 6 months. Note that in both HIV-infected and HIV-uninfected participants, the incidence rate of HBV infection was much higher in individuals who were younger than 40 years, consumed more than 13 drinks of alcohol per week, were injection-drug users, and had two or more sexual partners in the last 6 months.

The results of multivariate analysis of the independent relationship of factors such as age, race, injection-drug use, and the number of sexual partners with the risk of HBV infection in all MSM participating in the study and HIV-infected MSM in the study showed that MSM were more likely to have HBV infection if they were younger than 40 years, had more than one sexual partner in the last 6 months, and were HIV infected. Conversely, all MSM who had had one or more than one dose of HBV vaccine, regardless of whether they were HIV infected or HIV uninfected, were significantly less likely to get HBV infection as compared to those who had had none.

▶ **14.7 Example of a Retrospective Cohort Study**

Modified from: Kelley AS, McGarry K, Gorges R, Skinner JS. The burden of health care costs for patients with dementia in the last 5 years of life. Ann Intern Med. 2015;163(10):729–736.

In a 2015 retrospective cohort study in the United States, the researchers examined the end-of-life costs of dementia for Medicare beneficiaries during the 5-year period preceding death. The data for the retrospective study were obtained from a national longitudinal (prospective) cohort study called the Health

and Retirement Study, which involves interviewing every 2 years a nationally representative sample of U.S. adults older than 50 years. The participants were interviewed regarding their health status and healthcare expenses paid through Medicare, Medicaid, private health insurance, and out-of-pocket, as well as an estimation of the cost of informal care provided by family members and others.

The subjects in this retrospective study were 1,702 deceased individuals 70 years or older who had died of dementia ($n = 555$), cancer ($n = 279$), heart disease ($n = 431$), and other conditions ($n = 437$) between 2005 and 2010. Longitudinal interview data from these subjects were available because, as a part of the Health and Retirement Study, they had been interviewed every 2 years prior to their death. Postdeath interviews regarding healthcare expenses before the death of each of these subjects were conducted with a spouse or some other proxy individual.

The results showed that average total costs from all sources and costs to different entities such as Medicare, Medicaid, and out-of-pocket expenses for end-of-life care for patients who had dementia were much higher than end-of-life care costs for patients who had heart disease, cancer, or some other condition. For example, average total payment from all sources combined for dementia patients was $287,038, whereas for cancer patients it was $173,383 and for heart disease patients it was $175,136. Total government payment for dementia patients on average was $121,776, but for cancer and heart disease patients it was $102,486 and $96,514, respectively. Out-of-pocket expenses for dementia patients on average were $61,522, whereas for cancer and heart disease patients, respectively, they were $28,818 and $35,294. The difference in informal care costs was even more pronounced. The authors concluded that the cost of end-of-life care is disproportionately high for families of patients with dementia as compared to patients of heart disease, cancer, and other diseases.

▶ 14.8 Case-Control Studies

At the onset, it is important to clarify that all **case-control studies** are retrospective, but not all retrospective studies are case-control studies. Cohort studies that use historical records of a cohort beginning at some specific point in the past and track changes in the health status of the cohort going forward in time are also (erroneously) considered retrospective in design but are not case-control studies; they are called retrospective cohort studies. To illustrate the point that case-control study design is the opposite of prospective cohort study design, the made-up word *trohoc* (*cohort* spelled backwards) is sometimes used for case-control studies.

As illustrated in **TABLE 14.9**, case-control studies are retrospective because each of these studies begins with a group of people who already have the disease (cases) and another group of people who do not have the disease (controls), and compares the two groups regarding their odds of having been exposed to a potential risk factor in the past. The question being investigated in these studies is whether cases differ from control in terms of past exposure to a given risk factor. As the name suggests, the cases of a disease are identified first and then their history is traced back to discover whether these individuals had been exposed in the past to the risk factor(s) of interest and, if so, what the circumstances, intensity, and duration of such exposure were. If the history of these individuals—whether discovered through direct personal communication, an examination of past medical records, or some other means such as employment records—provides evidence of past exposure to the risk factor(s) of interest, then the strength of association between the disease and the risk factor(s) being investigated is assessed through appropriate statistical analysis.

In this study design, one, two, or several hypothesized risk factors can be investigated simultaneously as potential contributors or causal factors for the disease of interest as long as sources of past information or historical records provide valid and reliable information regarding exposure to such risk factors. To examine the possibility that exposure to the hypothesized risk factor(s) may have no relationship with the occurrence of the disease of interest, a parallel group of individuals who do not have the specific disease are also included in the study. The history of this group of disease-free subjects is also examined through the same mechanisms as those of the diseased individuals to discover whether these individuals too had been exposed in the past to the risk factor(s) being investigated. In conducting a case-control study, careful attention is paid to the accuracy of medical diagnosis of diseased individuals labeled as *cases*. The sources and quality of information regarding past exposure to risk factors(s) and similarities of cases with nondiseased *controls* must be carefully examined. Other than the absence of disease, controls must, as much as possible, resemble cases in terms of age, race, sex, education, and other personal characteristics. The eligibility criteria for cases and controls, such as specification of age, race, sex, education, and potential for exposure to the suspected risk factor, must be established before the onset of the study and must be applied consistently and uniformly to both groups. Some of these issues are further discussed in the following sections.

14.8.1 Case-Control Study Design

A case-control study begins with the identification and recruitment of cases of the disease of interest. The identification and recruitment of cases can occur in a healthcare setting, such as a hospital or a nursing

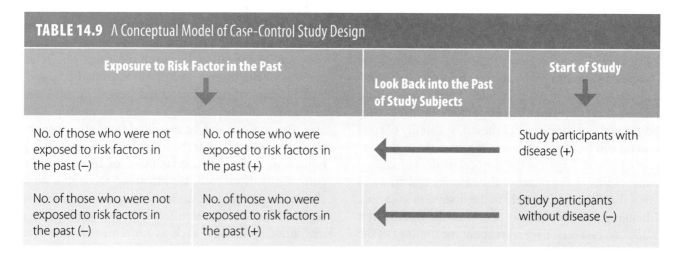

TABLE 14.9 A Conceptual Model of Case-Control Study Design

Exposure to Risk Factor in the Past		Look Back into the Past of Study Subjects	Start of Study
No. of those who were not exposed to risk factors in the past (−)	No. of those who were exposed to risk factors in the past (+)	←	Study participants with disease (+)
No. of those who were not exposed to risk factors in the past (−)	No. of those who were exposed to risk factors in the past (+)	←	Study participants without disease (−)

home, or even at the individuals' homes. It can also be done merely through medical records without ever being actually in contact with the patient. When a study is based entirely on medical, billing, employment, and other relevant records of cases and controls, no recruitment or direct communication with individuals, whether cases or controls, is needed. As long as study protocols regarding accessing and protecting confidential medical and personal records are followed, the entire study can be conducted on the bases of paper or electronic records from various sources. For each case of the disease under investigation, one or more matched controls are also included in the study. Inclusion or recruitment of cases and controls can take place over time as patients with the disease or records of patients with said disease become available. The number of cases and controls to be included in the study is specified and predetermined at the conceptual stages of the study, but can be changed as the study progresses. Typically, for common diseases, the number of cases may be large, but in the case of a rare disease, the researcher may have no choice but to limit the study to a small number of patients. However, to have a reasonable degree of confidence in the findings of the study, the number of cases and controls also depends on the desired statistical power of the study.

14.8.2 Definition of a Case

The word *case* refers to a person who had already been diagnosed with the disease whose relationship with a suspected risk factor is being investigated. The diagnostic criteria on which the determination is made regarding whether a person has the disease in question must be established carefully and explicitly before the onset of the study. The decision to include or exclude individuals in a case-control study depends on such criteria. The definition of a case must be developed on the bases of established clinical guidelines and standard laboratory tests that provide the grounds for diagnosing and treating patients of the disease. In the event there is confusion, controversy, or ambiguity in published literature regarding the criteria for diagnosing cases of a disease, researchers must establish explicit evidence-based criteria from the existing body of literature and diligently adhere to these criteria throughout the course of the study. Validity of such criteria can be tested on a few known cases of the disease or checked against the medical records of known patients before the onset of the case-control study to see if the criteria accurately fit the disease in question. Changing the definition of a case in the middle of a study can cast serious doubts about the findings of the

study because not all the cases included in the study were based consistently and uniformly on the same criteria.

What follows is an example of a precise definition of a case in a case-control study. In a study to investigate the potential risk of pituitary tumor associated with cellphone use, Shrestha et al.[8] defined a case as "an individual between 20 to 69 years of age with either a histologically confirmed pituitary tumor (ICD oncology code C75.1) or unequivocal brain scan-based identification of a space occupying lesion during the study period."

14.8.3 Definition of a Control

The criteria to define a control must also be carefully developed before the onset of the study and then consistently applied throughout the study. The number of controls for each case, whether one, two, or three, can be altered during the course of the study without compromising the findings of the study as long as each control meets the same uniform definition and eligibility criteria. For example, if the criteria for recruiting controls in the study state that same-sex siblings will be used as controls, then using same-sex neighbors or schoolmates of the opposite sex as controls would violate the study protocol.

As an example of selecting case-matched controls, in a study to understand risk factors for ischemic and intracerebral hemorrhagic stroke,[9] age-, sex-, and ethnicity-matched hospitalized individuals, outpatient clinic patients, or relatives of hospitalized individuals with no previous history of stroke were recruited as controls. One control was recruited for each case of ischemic stroke and one for each case of hemorrhagic stroke.

14.8.4 Sources, Identification, and Recruitment of Cases

The setting or geographic location for recruiting cases should also be determined and specified before the onset of the study. For example, cases can be all patients of the disease of interest admitted to a specific hospital during a specified period or admitted to a group of hospitals in a county or metropolitan area. Patients can also be recruited from other healthcare settings, such as ambulatory care clinics, nursing homes, or assisted living facilities, or from within a community. If subjects are identified through a nonclinical setting such as an insurance plan or a disease registry, they can be recruited directly from homes or institutional settings, such as retirement homes and assisted living facilities, in a predefined geographic area. Whether all or some of the eligible individuals are recruited depends on the nature of the disease as well as the sampling methodology employed in the study. In the case of a commonly occurring disease, a random or systematic sample of cases identified in a clinical setting or reported at a registry during a given period may be used. On the other hand, if the disease being investigated is rare, then all diagnosed or reported cases in the past can be recruited.

14.8.5 Purpose of Controls

The purpose of controls is to provide a comparison group for cases in the study and to shed light on the frequency of exposure to a given risk factor in the entire population from which cases emerged. For that reason, it is important that controls should be representative in their characteristics of the general population from which they are drawn. Having a control group in the study is of critical importance because many diseases have a multifactorial etiology. A given chemical, physical, or biologic agent may be just one of the factors that contribute to the development and occurrence of a disease. If such is the case, then estimation of exposure to a given risk factor can provide only limited information regarding the underlying causes of a disease. It is worth noting that a vast majority of noninfectious diseases cannot be attributed to a single causal agent, as is the case with infectious disease such as HIV, tuberculosis, or malaria. For such diseases, exposure to a risk factor does not always lead to disease (i.e., the disease does not occur despite exposure). On the other hand, a multifactorial disease can occur in the absence of a given risk factor—in other words, exposure to a risk factor may be neither necessary nor a sufficient condition for the disease of interest to occur. Whereas cases in a case-control study provide information about the extent to which a disease occurred with or without exposure to a given risk factor, controls allow researchers to understand the extent to which a disease may not occur despite exposure.

14.8.6 Sources, Identification, and Recruitment of Controls

Controls in a case-control study are usually recruited from the same source population from which the cases emerged. For example, if cases of a cancer are identified and recruited through a statewide cancer registry, the controls should also be from the same state and should be as similar to the cases as possible in terms

of demographic and socioeconomic characteristics. If cases are recruited throughout the state or from specific ZIP codes, counties, or neighborhoods, so should be the controls. The controls should also be similar to cases in terms of the potential for past exposure in the same period as the cases. However, researchers should have no knowledge of the history and potential past exposure of controls to the risk factor, and selection of controls should be strictly without any reference to past risk exposure. Likewise, if any exclusionary criteria are applied to cases, the same criteria must also be applied to the controls.

If recruited from the general population, the controls should be selected through a random sampling protocol. However, controls can also be selected from the same clinical settings as cases, such as patients in the same hospital admitted for reasons unrelated to the disease being studied. In such an instance, care must be taken to ensure that the condition or malady for which controls are admitted to the hospital is unrelated to the disease for which cases are admitted. This would also mean exclusion of individuals admitted to the hospital for diseases etiologically related to the risk factor being investigated. Further, the referral and admission process for controls and their medical conditions should be the same as cases in the study. The diagnoses or list of medical conditions for which controls are admitted to the hospital need not be limited to only one or two as long as they are unrelated to the disease for which cases are admitted in the same facility.

14.8.7 Methods to Obtain Information Regarding Past Exposure

A variety of methods, such as personal interviews; abstraction of data from medical, employment, pharmaceutical, or laboratory records; or direct measurement of the variable of interest, can be used to obtain information regarding past exposure to a risk factor and the current health status of both cases and controls. The suitability and availability of any of these sources of data can vary from one study to another and depend entirely on the circumstances and nature of the specific case-control study. As much as possible, it is paramount that the validity and reliability of data regarding the current medical diagnosis and past exposure to the risk factor are carefully established and cross-checked from various sources. None of the mentioned methods of information gathering can be guaranteed to be 100% accurate. Each can pose its own challenges, and each is vulnerable to contamination from a variety of sources. For example, information obtained through personal interviews may be impossible to verify and can suffer from problems related to poor memory (*recall bias*) or deliberate over- or underreporting by the subject (errors of omission and commission). Likewise, data obtained from medical records can pose difficulties such as incomplete or unavailable medical records, lack of clarity regarding primary or secondary diagnoses, verification of the date of diagnosis, and the timing of the first appearance of signs and symptoms.

14.8.8 Considerations in the Measurement of Exposure

For both cases and controls, several important points should be considered in the assessment of exposure to the risk factor. The timing, duration, and degree of exposure should be carefully established and, for cases, it must precede the occurrence or manifestation of disease—that is, the temporal sequence of events should be logical for an assertion to be made that the risk factor played a role in the occurrence of the disease. The question that must be clearly answered in a case-control study is: When did exposure occur in relation to the appearance of signs and symptoms or diagnosis of the disease? For controls, an arbitrary but carefully thought out reference date in the past can be used to discover whether they had been exposed to the risk factor before that date and what the duration and level of exposure were. The quantification of exposure in terms of both duration and level of exposure is necessary to assess a dose–response relationship between exposure and the disease.

14.8.9 Calculation and Interpretation of Odds Ratio

In cohort studies, the relative risk (also known as risk ratio, rate ratio, or incidence rate ratio) of disease associated with exposure to a risk factor is calculated by directly comparing the proportions of new cases of a disease in the exposed and unexposed groups of people. Because the total number of exposed and unexposed people from which new cases of disease emerged is not known in case-control studies, direct estimation of relative risk is not possible. Consequently, case-control studies are limited to an indirect estimation of relative risk by comparing the odds of past exposure in diseased and disease-free individuals. Estimation of the odds of past exposure in the diseased and disease-free individuals and calculation of relative odds of exposure in the two groups (*odds ratio*) provides an acceptable measure of the strength of association between a disease and the risk factor being examined.

TABLE 14.10 Odds Ratio Derivation – Notational Example

		Disease		
		Yes	No	Total
Exposure	Yes	a	b	a+b
	No	c	d	c+d
	Total	a+c	b+d	a+b+c+d

In **TABLE 14.10**, the odds of exposure among the cases can be obtained by dividing the number of cases of disease with past exposure (*a*) by the number of cases without a history of past exposure (*c*). So, the odds of exposure among the cases can be represented as follows:

$$\text{Odds of exposure among the cases} = \frac{a}{c}$$

Similarly, the odds of past exposure among the controls are obtained by dividing the number of controls with a history of past exposure to the risk factor (*b*) by the number of controls who did not have a history of past exposure to the risk factor (*d*). Again, the odds of exposure among the controls can be represented as:

$$\text{Odds of exposure among the controls} = \frac{b}{d}$$

The ratio between the odds in the two groups (odds ratio) is obtained simply by dividing the odds of exposure among the cases (*a* / *c*) by the odds of exposure among the controls (*b* / *d*).

Thus,

$$\text{Odds Ratio (OR)} = \frac{(a / c)}{(b / d)}$$

$$or = \frac{ad}{bc}$$

An odds ratio of 1.0 means that the odds of having been exposed to a risk factor in the past are equal for both groups—cases and controls. In other words, it is likely that there is no association between the risk factor and the disease in question. An odds ratio of greater than 1.0 (i.e., >1.0) suggests a positive link between a risk factor and a disease (i.e., a possible causal link), whereas an odds ratio of less than 1.0 (i.e., <1.0) suggests a negative association (i.e., a possible protective

TABLE 14.11 Odds Ratio Derivation – Numeric Example

		Disease		
		Yes	No	Total
Exposure	Yes	80	70	150
	No	220	530	750
	Total	300	600	900

effect conferred by the risk factor). **TABLE 14.11** shows the results of a hypothetical case-control study. The estimation of odds ratio in this case would be as follows:

$$\text{Odds Ratio (OR)} = \frac{(80 \times 530)}{(70 \times 220)}$$
$$\text{or} = \frac{42,400}{15,400}$$
$$\text{or} = 2.75$$

The results of this hypothetical study would indicate that the cases of disease were 2.75 times more likely than the controls to have been exposed to the risk factor in the past.

14.8.10 Advantages of Case-Control Study Design

Case-control studies have several advantages over cohort studies, including the fact that they are relatively easier to conduct and require less time, money, and other resources to complete. Because there is no long-term follow up of subjects, they are not prone to attrition of study participants over time and potential self-selection bias resulting from the possibility that those who continue to participate in a cohort study over a period of time might be more motivated or different in some other ways from those who decide to drop out. For the same reason, case-control studies can be completed with relatively small numbers of subjects and do not require participant samples as large as those for cohort studies. Case-control studies also allow the opportunity to simultaneously explore the relationship of several different risk factors with the disease being investigated. Therefore, multiple etiologic hypotheses can be tested in the same study, and the interaction of several risk factors with one another can be conveniently explored. Finally, an important

advantage of case-control studies is their suitability to investigating the etiology of relatively uncommon or rare diseases as well as those disorders that have a long latent period. Data on rare diseases can be found from national or regional registries, large medical centers, or insurance companies. Suitable historical controls can also be found through the same sources. In a case-control study, even with a few cases of a rare disease, meaningful results can be obtained with the help of advanced statistical techniques.

▶ 14.9 Example of a Case-Control Study

Modified from: Friis S, Riis AH, Erichsen R, Baron JA, Sorensen HT. Low-dose aspirin or nonsteroidal anti-inflammatory drug use and colorectal cancer risk: a population-based case-control study. Ann Intern Med. 2015;163(5):347–355.

This 2015 population-based case-control study used data from northern Denmark to assess whether there was an association between past use of low-dose aspirin or other nonsteroidal anti-inflammatory drugs (NSAIDs) and subsequent risk of colorectal cancer (CRC). Some studies in the past have shown a lower risk of colorectal cancer associated with at least 5 years' use of low to moderate doses of aspirin or use of nonaspirin NSAIDs. Data on drug use, comorbid conditions, and history of colonoscopy for 10,280 patients (cases) with colorectal cancer and 102,800 controls were obtained from a prescription database and three patient registries.

Data from these four sources were linked by using the unique identification number assigned to each Danish resident by the government. In Denmark, low-dose aspirin (75 mg, 100 mg, or 150 mg tablets) is almost exclusively (>90%) sold with a prescription, whereas high-dose aspirin (500 mg tablets or more) is largely sold over the counter. All nonaspirin NSAIDs, with the exception of 200 mg tablets of ibuprofen, are sold only with a prescription. Therefore, data on over-the-counter purchase of high-dose (500 mg) aspirin and low-dose (200 mg) ibuprofen were not available. Cases comprised all individuals in northern Denmark with a histologically verified first diagnosis of CRC between 1994 and 2011 and at least 5 years of prescription drug coverage before diagnosis of CRC ($n = 10,280$). All cases were between 30 to 85 years of age at the time of CRC diagnosis and lived in one of the four counties in northern Denmark. The case definition also excluded all individuals with previous history of cancer (other than nonmelanoma skin cancer), inflammatory bowel disease, or history of familial adenomatous polyposis before being diagnosed with

CRC. For each case of CRC, 10 controls matched for birth year, sex, and county of residence were included in the study ($n = 102,800$).

The researchers used logistic regression analysis to estimate age-, sex-, and area-matched odds ratios (ORs) as well as multivariable (e.g., high-dose aspirin, hormone replacement therapy, antidepressants, and statin drugs, plus a number of other variables) adjusted ORs and 95% CIs for the association of CRC with use of low-dose aspirin or nonaspirin NSAIDs such as ibuprofen. They created multiple statistical models to estimate ORs based on the dose, frequency, duration, and continuity of use of low-dose aspirin. For example, they estimated adjusted ORs for CRC among "ever users," "recent users," and "former users" of low-dose aspirin and nonaspirin NSAIDs (see TABLE 14.12). In all analyses, nonuse of aspirin or nonuse of nonaspirin NSAIDs was used as the reference category.

The results showed that ORs for colon cancer associated with ever using aspirin (≥ 2 prescriptions) and nonaspirin NSAIDs were 1.03 (95% CI 0.98–1.09) and 0.94 (95% CI 0.90–0.98). Continued long-term use (≥ 5 years) of 75 mg to 150 mg of aspirin (Model 4 in Table 14.12) was associated with a 27% reduction in the risk of CRC (OR 0.73; 95% CI 0.54–0.99). On the other hand, no reduction of CRC risk was observed with overall long-term use of low-dose aspirin. Five years or longer high-intensity use of nonaspirin NSAIDs was associated with 30% to 38% reduced risk of colorectal cancer. The possibility of confounding factors such as diet and physical activity affecting the results of the study could not be completely ruled out because the authors did not look into those factors. Overall, the authors concluded that unless taken regularly, low-dose aspirin did not seem to confer protection consistently against colorectal cancer.

TABLE 14.12 Use of Low-Dose Aspirin or Nonaspirin NSAIDs and Risk of Colorectal Cancer			
NSAID Use	**Case Patients**	**Control Patients**	**Multivariate-Adjusted OR (95% CI)†**
Low-Dose Aspirin			
Nonuse‡	7,984	79,807	Reference
Ever use§	2,296	22,993	1.03 (0.98–1.09)
Recent use[	2,058	20,652	1.03 (0.97–1.09)
Former use¶	238	2,341	1.06 (0.92–1.22)
Model 2: Cumulative Duration of Use**††			
<5 years	1,321	13,133	1.04 (0.97–1.11)
5 to <10 years	595	6,187	1.00 (0.91–1.10)
≥10 years	142	1,332	1.13 (0.94–1.35)
Model 3: Tablet Dose With Cumulative Duration of Use ≥ 5 Years**††‡‡			
75–100 mg	243	2,450	1.03 (0.90–1.19)
150 mg	200	2,085	0.99 (0.85–1.15)
Model 4: Continuous Use**§§			
Continuous use ≤5 years	45	634	0.73 (0.54–0.99)

Nonaspirin NSAIDs			
Nonuse[‡]	5,647	54,748	Reference
Ever use[§]	4,633	48,052	0.94 (0.90–0.98)
Model 2: Duration of Use[‖]			
<5 years	2,331	22,935	0.99 (0.94–1.04)
5 to <10 years	1,414	15,590	0.89 (0.83–0.94)
≥10 years	888	9,527	0.90 (0.83–0.98)
Model 3: Intensity of Use with Duration of Use ≥ 5 Years[‖]			
<0.1 DDD[¶]	1,459	14,836	0.96 (0.90–1.02)
0.1 to <0.3 DDD[¶]	505	5,515	0.89 (0.81–0.98)
>0.3 DDD[¶]	338	4,766	0.70 (0.62–0.78)
Model 4: Consistent Use			
Consistent use ≥5 years[***]	93	1,426	0.64 (0.52–0.80)

NSAID: nonsteroidal anti-inflammatory drug; OR: odds ratio; DDD: defined daily dose.

[†]In addition to age, sex, and area; adjusted for a number of additional variables, such as use of high-dose aspirin, hormone replacement therapy, use of antidepressants, statins, plus other variables.

[‡]<2 prescriptions, more than 1 year before the date of CRC diagnosis (index date).

[§]≥2 prescriptions, more than 1 year before the date of CRC diagnosis (index date).

[‖]≥2 prescriptions for low-dose aspirin and ≥ 1 prescription within 1 to <3 years before the index date.

[¶]≥2 prescriptions for low-dose aspirin but no prescription within 1 to <3 years before the index date.

[**]Analysis restricted to recent users and nonusers of low-dose aspirin.

[††]Cumulative treatment periods were defined according to the number of dispensed tablets and grace periods of 30 days.

[‡‡]Exclusive use of 75–100 mg or 150 mg. Mixed use not included.

[§§]One continuous treatment period defined according to the number of dispensed tablets and grace periods of 30 days.

[‖‖]Time period between the first and last filled prescriptions (disregarding the last year before the index date).

[¶¶]Cutoff values of estimated average dose per day in DDDs, defined by approximate tertiles of estimated average dose per day among control participants.

[***]≥2 prescriptions per consecutive years of nonaspirin NSAID use until 1 year before the index date.

Modified from: Friis S, Riis AH, Erichsen R, Baron JA, Sorensen HT. Low-dose aspirin or nonsteroidal anti-inflammatory drug use and colorectal cancer risk: a population-based case-control study. Ann Intern Med, 163(5):347–355. Copyright © 2015 American College of Physicians. All rights reserved. Reprinted with permission of American College of Physicians, Inc.

▶ 14.10 Risk Factor and Exposure in Cohort and Case-Control Studies

In epidemiology, the term *risk factor* refers to any factor, whether external or intrinsic to the subject, that directly or indirectly increases or decreases the likelihood of death, disease, or disability in a person. External factors can include chemical, physical, or biologic agents. Internal factors can be related to genetic makeup and personal characteristics, including age, race, sex, or behavioral characteristics. The term *risk factor* generally implies a causal relationship of one or more such factors with a disease. Because a cause-and-effect relationship is difficult to prove, evidence of a statistically significant association between a risk factor and a disease can be considered an appropriate objective for an epidemiological study. In other words, based on the strength of statistical association, both cohort and case-control studies provide an estimation of the risk of disease associated with a given factor. Alternatively, we can state that cohort and case-control studies are *risk assessment* studies.

It is not sufficient to make a claim of exposure to a risk factor in a cohort or case-control study; rather, it is necessary to substantiate and report the exact circumstances, nature, degree, and duration of exposure. Exposure to a factor that has a positive or negative effect on the likelihood of getting a disease in the future can be short or long in duration and mild or severe in intensity. Exposure to a risk factor, whether malicious or protective in nature, can occur in the following three forms: (1) exposure occurs in the form of a bolus (i.e., large amount of exposure as a single event of a short duration), (2) continued low-dose exposure over an extended period of time with cumulative effects, and (3) intermittent or sustained high-level exposure over a period of time. Naturally, the effects of exposure to a risk factor depend not only on the amount and duration of exposure but also, and most important, on the nature of the risk factor itself. It is also important to point out that not all individuals exposed to a risk factor will necessarily respond in the same manner and may or may not develop disease. Even with the same dose and duration of exposure, some individuals will develop the associated disease (or immunity if exposure confers protection), whereas others may show little or no effect at all. Likewise, because of the multifactorial etiology of many diseases, some individuals who have had no exposure whatsoever may still develop a disease frequently associated with a risk factor. In other words, absence of disease does not rule out past exposure, and absence of exposure does not rule out the occurrence of disease. Of course, evidence of a dose–response relationship between exposure to a risk factor and a disease adds exponentially to the credibility of both case-control and cohort studies.

A dose–response relationship means that there is a direct statistical correlation between the amount, duration, and intensity of exposure and the intensity of disease or the degree of protection against the disease conferred by the exposure to a risk factor. Although the term *risk factor* has a negative connation, it also refers to a factor, such as a vaccine, that has a protective effect against a disease. The term *dose–response relationship* in the context of a vaccine or a therapeutic agent refers to the efficacy of such an agent in generating antibodies or mounting resistance against disease.

The term *exposure assessment* refers to the steps, procedures, and protocols by which the level, frequency, and duration of exposure to a risk factor are estimated. In both cohort and case-control studies, it is necessary to carry out exposure assessment in a careful manner to determine who was exposed to the risk factor. Therefore, exposure assessment must clarify as to when, where, how, and how much exposure occurred.

▶ 14.11 Comparison of Cohort and Case-Control Study Design

Cohort and case-control studies are sometimes referred to as the studies of "natural experiments" because, in both kinds of studies, individuals are "naturally" exposed to some risk factor(s) rather than being deliberately or intentionally exposed by the researcher to a chemical, physical, biologic, or psychological agent or stressor. The use of the word *natural* is intended to be in contrast with *intentional*, *deliberate*, or *manipulative*, in which case the researcher selectively introduces, controls, and manipulates the nature, amount, and duration of exposure to one or more risk factors for one or more groups of individuals (or laboratory animals).

Although both kinds of studies are valuable epidemiologic tools, each has its advantages or disadvantages. **TABLE 14.13** is designed to help the reader understand these advantages or disadvantages in a comparative context only. To test a hypothesis about the association of a risk factor with a disease, researchers can begin by first conducting a case-control study. If the results of the case-control study support their hypothesis, they may choose to invest further time and resources in conducting a cohort study to see if the results of the case-control study are validated.

▶ 14.12 Association and Causality

Our thinking about the causation of diseases has evolved since the time of Hippocrates in the 4th century BCE, and especially since the identification of *Mycobacterium tuberculosis* by Koch in 1882 and the identification between 1897 and 1900 of microbial organisms responsible for 22 different infectious diseases. Before the identification of microbial organisms in the second half of the 19th century, diseases such as tuberculosis (also called "consumption" or "phthisis" in older literature), malaria, and cholera were not seen as specific and separate diseases distinct from one another. Rather, they were all seen as the health effects of poor environmental and sanitary conditions lumped under the title "miasmas." The identification of microbial organisms such as tubercle bacillus and *Vibrio cholerae* led to the belief that every disease is caused by one and only one specific causative agent or substance. This belief in the existence of a single underlying causative agent is known as the theory of

TABLE 14.13 Comparison of Case-Control and Prospective Cohort Study Design

Consideration*	Case-Control Study	Prospective Cohort Study
Duration of study	Relatively short (months)	Much longer (years)
Number of participants	Relatively smaller	Much larger
Cost of study	Relatively inexpensive	Much more expensive
Need for other resources	Relatively less	Much greater
Logistics and organization	Less complicated	Complicated or challenging
Study design	More straightforward	Complex
Potential for bias	Possibly greater	Somewhat easier to avoid
Quality of data	May be less than optimal	Usually superior
Confidence in results	Relatively less	Much greater
Scientific rigor	Somewhat lesser	Much greater

*The considerations listed are only in comparative and relative terms between the two study designs rather than absolute.

mono-causal etiology of diseases. The implications of this theory were that each disease is caused by a single underlying factor that does not cause any other disease, and a particular disease cannot be caused by any other agent or factor.[10] Consequently, the theory ruled out the possibility that diseases can result from a complex interaction of multiple biologic and socioeconomic factors—that is, diseases can have a *multifactorial* etiology or can be *multicausal* in nature. The monocausal theory of disease etiology is clearly reflected in Koch's postulates formulated in the late 19th century that have fallen out of favor in modern times.

Recognition of the fact that not all individuals exposed to a microbial agent such as *Vibrio cholerae* contract acute symptomatic disease and that not all those exposed to the microbe *Salmonella typhi* suffer from typhoid fever led to the concept of an *epidemiologic triangle*. The idea of an epidemiologic triangle suggested that diseases result from a dynamic interaction among the causative agent, the host, and the environment in which both the agent and the host exist. The causative agent can be a specific biologic, chemical, or physical entity whose presence is necessary to produce the disease. However, the presence of such an agent may not be a sufficient condition to produce the disease of interest. Favorable host characteristics such as suscep-

tibility or weak constitution, and environmental conditions such as appropriate temperature and humidity may be essential for the agent to cause disease.

In addition to the role of a specific causal agent, the epidemiologic triangle model explicitly recognizes the role of the environment in which the agent and host interact. The presence of an agent such as a microbe, a chemical agent, or a physical factor is necessary but not always sufficient for a disease to occur.

With new developments in science and increasing incidence and prevalence of noninfectious chronic disorders, such as a variety of cancers, hypertension, and diabetes, it was recognized that the epidemiologic triangle model applies predominantly, if not exclusively, to infectious diseases. The epidemiologic triangle fails to incorporate the role played by coexisting multiple factors—such as age, race, gender, diet, occupation, and lifestyle—in determining whether an illness occurs and the extent, severity, and course of disease.

In the last 50 years or so, there has been a growing emphasis on multifactorial etiology of diseases. In recognition of the fact that chronic disorders such as coronary artery disease, stroke, cancer, and arthritis result from a complex interplay of a number of different factors, a new etiologic model called the *web of causation* has emerged with widespread acceptance. The web of causation explicitly recognizes that the occurrence and severity of a disease is a function of a complex interaction among biologic, social, and environmental factors such as genetic predisposition, employment, social support, and access to various services to support a healthy lifestyle. While the web of causation emphasizes the role that multiple intrinsic and extrinsic variables play to affect the probability of a disease occurring in an individual or groups of people, it does not address the fact that certain social, racial, or ethnic groups may be inherently at a higher or lower risk of a disease.

A number of philosophic and conceptual objections have been leveled against both the mono-causal and web of causation perspectives. The criticism of the web of causation model is largely on the grounds that it assigns a causal role to one or more factors based on a statistical association with the disease. The critics argue that statistical association of factors such as marital status, poverty, unemployment, or housing with a disease (e.g., diabetes or hypertension) merely constitutes identification of risk factors or increased probability of the occurrence of disease rather than a causal relationship. The critics also object to the interchangeable use of the terms *exposure* and *risk factor*. They argue that the term *exposure* should be reserved for factors or agents that have a clearly causal relationship with a disease, whereas *risk factors* merely increase the probability of acquiring a disease but are not a part of the causal pathway. They point out that factors such as age, poverty, or low levels of immunity, as implied by the word *risk*, only increase the likelihood of getting a disease but, in and of themselves, have no pathophysiologic role in causing the disease. Frequently, these factors are associated with both the causal factor(s) and the disease and therefore, as discussed later in this chapter, are referred to as **confounder variables**.

The theory of *general susceptibility*, which has gained some ground in the last two or three decades, specifically makes the point that, all else being equal, certain ethnic or demographic groups, per se, are more prone to some diseases than other groups. Rather than focusing on causality, the theory of general susceptibility emphasizes the role of socioenvironmental factors. Before the theory of general susceptibility, most medical thinkers and social scientists believed in the principles of necessary cause and disease specificity. Necessary cause meant that a particular disease could not occur in the absence of a particular agent or factor; disease specificity meant that each disease is unique in being caused by a specific agent and none other, and the causative agent of one disease could not cause another disease.[10]

The theory of general susceptibility is rooted in the idea that each individual is an open system that survives only through adaptation to the changes taking place in its surroundings or external environment. This also means that to cope with the changes taking place in the external environment, the individual should maintain a stable internal environment. Therefore, the occurrence of a disease is viewed as a failure of the individual's adaptive struggle to cope with the changes taking place in his/her physical and social environment.[10] Conversely, healthy individuals are seen as those who have successfully adapted to their external environment. The ability to adapt successfully to changes in one's physical and social environment is a function of the individual's own constitution as well as the severity and nature of changes occurring in the external environment.[10]

The theory of general susceptibility draws support from examples of infectious diseases caused by opportunistic organisms that are ubiquitous in our surroundings or exist in the body but do not cause harm under ordinary circumstances, only when the individual is exposed to physical and social stressors.[10] For example, studies[11-13] have shown that stressful experiences or events increase the risk of streptococcal infections. Similarly, a strong association of stressful life events is observed with mental disorders such as depression and suicide.

In contrast to the theory of general susceptibility, the necessary cause and disease specificity beliefs couched in the mono-causal model of disease etiology view the individual as a closed system impervious to, immune to, or isolated from the effects of the stressors in the physical and social environment. Viewing the individual as a closed system was useful to understanding the interaction between agent and host in the context of infectious diseases. For contemporary multiple-cause chronic diseases such as hypertension, stroke, and diabetes, the open system perspective is much more useful. An important aspect of the open system perspective is its recognition of the fact that a stressful life event, such as divorce or loss of employment, can have a variety of health effects. Conversely, a health outcome may have multiple stressful stimuli as its antecedents.[10]

▶ 14.13 Bias

The Dictionary of Epidemiology[14] provides the following definition of **bias**:

> Systematic deviation of results or inferences from truth. Processes leading to such deviation. An error in the conception and design of a

study—or in the collection, analysis, interpretation, reporting, publication, or review of data—leading to results or conclusions that are systematically (as opposed to randomly) different from truth.

The dictionary lists dozens of different forms and sources of conscious or unconscious bias in epidemiologic research. As indicated by the preceding definition, bias can get introduced in a study through multiple sources, including (1) flaws in study design, (2) procedures and criteria for selection of subjects, and (3) inadequate methods of data collection and analysis.[14,16]

The impact of a bias in epidemiologic studies can be overestimation or underestimation of whatever is being measured and unwarranted conclusion based on the findings of the study. For example, in case-control studies, erroneous conclusions regarding a statistical association between a risk factor and a disease can be drawn and causal assertions can be made because of a bias in the selection of subjects or poor recall of participants regarding past exposure to a risk factor. Conversely, a valid association between a risk factor and disease can be missed because of an underestimation resulting from biased study design, data collection, or statistical analysis. Put another way, biased results of a study can lead to either a **Type I error** or a **Type II error** (i.e., erroneous rejection of a null hypothesis or erroneous acceptance of a null hypothesis). It is useful to recall that, in statistics, a null hypothesis states that there is no statistical relationship between the two variables being examined (i.e., risk factor and disease). In case-control studies, Type I and Type II errors can occur because of erroneous assignment of cases and controls to the wrong group—that is, misclassification of cases to the control group and vice versa, or erroneous assignment of exposure (i.e., assignment to the exposed group when there was no exposure to the risk factor, or to the unexposed group when there had been exposure). Likewise, in screening programs discussed elsewhere in this text, bias associated with the administration of a test or interpretation of test results can lead to erroneous assignment of many individuals to the disease-positive group or the disease-negative group. Such a situation can result in over- or underestimation of the magnitude of the problem and cause unnecessary confusion, concern, and avoidable follow-up investigations.

Case-control studies are more prone to interviewer bias, observation bias, recall bias, or misclassification bias because of the methods used for selecting cases and controls and for collecting necessary information. For example, bias can be introduced if individuals with certain characteristics (e.g., age, sex, ethnicity, and income) are over- or under-selected or excluded altogether. In case-control studies, bias can also be introduced because of a difficulty in establishing an appropriate temporal relationship between the alleged causal factor and the disease being studied. A causal relationship can only be alleged if exposure to the risk factor can be shown to have preceded the occurrence of disease. If exposure to the risk factor occurred after the appearance of disease, then clearly the risk factor being examined could not have contributed to the development of the disease. For example, if someone starts drinking heavily because he or she is depressed, then occurrence of depression cannot be attributed to the consumption of alcohol.

It is critically important to avoid any sources of bias in study design and data collection because such problems are difficult to detect and nearly impossible to correct after the completion of data collection. To avoid the possibility of bias or systematic error in an epidemiologic study, researchers must understand potential sources of bias, such as those related to the selection of participants and collection of data, whether in the form of direct observation, personal interviews, or administration of surveys. To address the issue of bias after the conclusion of a study, researchers not only need to look into the sources of bias but also must assess the degree or seriousness and the direction of bias to determine its impact in terms of over- or underestimation of the strength of association between variables. A small degree of bias may not seriously affect an observed association between variables, but a strong bias can totally invalidate the findings of a study.

▶ 14.14 Confounding

The word *confound*, derived from the Latin word *confundere*, means to cause confusion or to mix up one thing with something else.[15] In any observational study, whether case control or cohort, the operative assumption is that there is a direct cause-and-effect relationship between Risk Factor A (or exposure, such as smoking) and the Disease of Interest B. The situation, however, can be muddied if a third variable or factor exists, such that it is related to both—the risk factor and the disease. This third variable or factor is called a confounder variable. The relationship of the confounder variable with the risk factor and with the disease is independent of the relationship

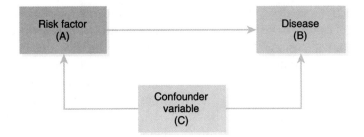

FIGURE 14.2 Illustration of the relationship of a confounder variable with the risk factor and the disease or health outcome.

between the risk factor and the disease. The value of the risk factor can increase or decrease as the value of the confounder increases or decreases. Similarly, the occurrence and intensity of the disease also varies with a change in the value of the confounder variable. Thus, a confounder variable can account for, partly or fully, an apparent relationship between exposure and disease.

Many authors consider confounding to be a form of bias because it systematically distorts the measurement or assessment of the relationship between exposure to a risk factor and disease.[17,18] To be a confounder, a variable must fulfill the following three conditions: (1) it must be associated with the disease of interest; (2) it must be associated with the risk factor and should be unequally distributed between the exposed and unexposed groups or between different levels of exposure; and (3) it should not be the result or effect of the risk factor—that is, it should not be a part or intermediate step in the causal pathway between exposure and disease.[17,18] **FIGURE 14.2** illustrates the relationship of a confounder variable with the risk factor (exposure) and the disease or health outcome.

In both observational and experimental studies (i.e., cohort and case-control studies and clinical trials), researchers employ various techniques during planning, implementation, and analytic stages to prevent or control the effects of confounder variables. These techniques include matching of exposed and unexposed subjects or cases and controls on potentially confounding variables such as age, race, sex, ethnicity, and other demographic and socioeconomic variables. In experimental studies, random assignment of subjects to experimental and control groups is also done to avoid the distortion

of study results by various confounding variables. During analyses, data can be stratified, for example, by age groups to deal with the effect of age on the degree of exposure (e.g., hypertension) and the disease (e.g., stroke).

FIGURE 14.3 provides an example of a confounder variable in a case-control study by O'Donnell et al.[9] The study, described more in detail later in this chapter, was conducted to investigate the relationship of a number of risk factors with stroke. During the design stage, cases were matched with controls on age, sex, and ethnicity. The multivariate analysis to examine the relationship of a given risk factor with stroke also adjusted for a number of confounder variables. For example, the multivariate model for the relationship of hypertension with stroke was adjusted for age, race, sex, diet, smoking, alcohol intake, and several other variables. Figure 14.3 shows the relationship of hypertension with stroke. In this case, stress is shown as a confounder variable that, unless adjusted for in statistical analysis, could have distorted the estimation of the role hypertension plays as a causal factor in the occurrence of stroke.

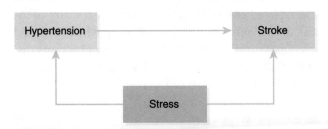

FIGURE 14.3 An example of a confounder variable in a case-control study (See Case Study 14.4 at the end of the chapter).

🔎 *CASE STUDY 14.1: An Ecological Study*

Modified from: Molina G, Weiser TG, Lipsitz SR, et al. Relationship between cesarean delivery rate and maternal and neonatal mortality. JAMA. 2015;314(21):2263–2270.

Cesarean delivery is an important lifesaving procedure for both mother and child in obstructed labor and other complicated obstetric situations. However, as a surgical procedure, it is also associated with potential complications. The overuse of this procedure can expose women and babies to unwarranted risk. Based on the findings of previous studies, the World Health Organization (WHO) recommends that national cesarean delivery rates should not exceed 10 to 15 cesarean deliveries per 100 live births. Notwithstanding these recommendations, cesarean delivery rates in many countries have remained considerably higher.

The purpose of this cross-sectional ecological study was to better understand the relationship between national cesarean delivery rates and maternal and neonatal mortality and provide estimates of national cesarean delivery rates that are associated with minimal maternal and neonatal mortality. Data on total population, life expectancy at birth, percent urban population, gross domestic product per capita, total health expenditure per capita, total fertility rate, and national birth rate were obtained for the 194 member states of the WHO from the World Bank's World Development Indicators. Additional data were also obtained from the United Nations, the WHO, and the U.S. Central Intelligence Agency. Data on all of these indicators were obtained for the year 2012. When data for 2012 were not available, data for the years 2005 through 2011 were collected.

Annual cesarean delivery rates were estimated from data collected for the period 2005 through 2012. Data on cesarean delivery rates in 2012 were available for only 54 countries. For 118 of the 140 countries for which 2012 data were not available, cesarean delivery rates were imputed from other years. For each of the remaining 22 countries for which no cesarean delivery data were available, these rates were imputed from total health expenditure per capita, fertility rate, life expectancy, percent of urban population, and geographic region. The 172 countries for which cesarean delivery data were available represented 97.6% of all live births in the world. Among these countries, South Sudan had the lowest cesarean delivery rate, 0.6%, and Brazil had the highest rate, 55.6%.

The risk factor of interest in this study was the cesarean delivery rate, and the main outcomes were maternal mortality ratio or neonatal mortality rate. The overall estimated number of cesarean deliveries in the 194 countries in 2012 was 22.9 million (95% CI, 22.5 million to 23.2 million). 45 countries that accounted for 12.9% of the global population and 25.7% of global live births in 2012 had estimated cesarean delivery rates of ≤7.2 per 100 live births. Fifty-three countries that accounted for 22.4% of the global population and 15.9% of global live births in 2012 had estimated cesarean delivery rates of >27.3 per 100 live births. The 48 countries that were within the range of >7.2 to 19.1 cesarean sections per 100 live births accounted for 38.0% of the global live births in 2012.

The group of countries that were in the highest mean cesarean delivery rate of ≥27.3 per 100 live births collectively represented only 15.9% of global live births in 2012, but 35.7% (95% CI 34.3% to 37.2%) of global cesarean deliveries in the same year. On average, these countries had a cesarean delivery rate of 35.3 per 100 live births (95% CI 33.1 to 37.5) and accounted for approximately 8.2 million cesarean deliveries (95% CI 8.0 million to 8.4 million) in 2012. Altogether, these countries had a maternal mortality ratio of only 36.7 maternal deaths per 100,000 live births (95% CI 27.7 to 45.8) in 2013, a neonatal mortality rate of 6.3 neonatal deaths per 1,000 live births (95% CI 5.3 to 7.3), and on average spent $1,509 per capita on healthcare (95% CI $1,031 to $1,987) in 2012.

In contrast, the group of countries that were in the lowest mean cesarean delivery rate of ≤7.2 per 100 live births collectively represented 25.7% of global live births, but only 6% of global cesarean deliveries in 2012. On average, these countries had a cesarean delivery rate of 4.4 per 100 live births (95% CI 3.8 to 5.1) and accounted for only 1.4 million (95% CI 1.3 to 1.4) cesarean deliveries in 2012. However, these countries had a high maternal mortality ratio of 463.3 maternal deaths per 100,000 live births (95% CI 393.6 to 533.1) in 2013, a neonatal mortality rate of 30.2 neonatal deaths per 1,000 live births (95% CI 27.6 to 32.7), and on average spent only $86 per capita (95% CI $36 to $136) on healthcare in 2012.

The group of countries that had a mean cesarean delivery rate of >7.2 to 19.1 per 100 live births had a maternal mortality ratio of 137 maternal deaths per 100,000 live births (95% CI 100.4 to 173.5) in 2013, a neonatal mortality rate of 17.3 per 1,000 live births (95% CI 14.1 to 20.5), and on average spent $722 per capita (95% CI $314 to $1,131) on healthcare in 2012.

Questions

Question 1. What research question was addressed in this study?

Question 2. Does there seem to be a relationship between cesarean delivery rate and maternal mortality ratio? Explain your answer with the help of data reported in the study.

(continues)

Question 3. Does there seem to be a relationship between cesarean delivery rate and neonatal mortality rate? Explain your answer with the help of data reported in the study.

Question 4. Does there seem to be a relationship between cesarean delivery rate and per capita healthcare spending? Explain your answer with the help of data from reported in the study.

Question 5. Does there seem to be a relationship between neonatal mortality rate and per capita healthcare spending? Explain your answer with the help of data from reported in the study.

🔍 *CASE STUDY 14.2: Prospective Cohort Study*

Modified from: Gunderson EP, Hurston SR, Ning X, et al. Lactation and progression of type 2 diabetes mellitus after gestational diabetes mellitus: a prospective cohort study. Ann Intern Med. 2015; 163(12):889–898.

Gestational diabetes mellitus (GDM) is a disorder of glucose tolerance that affects 5%–9% of all U.S. pregnancies (approximately 250,000 pregnant women). Women who experience GDM have a 7 times greater risk of subsequent diabetes mellitus (DM) than women who do not. Breastfeeding or lactation is a modifiable postpartum behavior that improves glucose and lipid metabolism and has favorable metabolic effects that persist after weaning.

The purpose of this study was to examine whether breastfeeding had any effect on or a relationship with the occurrence of DM in the 2-year period following delivery among women who had GDM during pregnancy. A total of 1,035 pregnant women who had been diagnosed with GDM and who delivered a baby after 35 weeks or more of pregnancy were enrolled and followed from August 2008 to December 2011. Three in-person examinations of these women from 6 to 9 weeks after delivery were conducted to collect baseline data. Thereafter, annual follow-ups included anthropometric measurements, personal interviews, and glucose tolerance testing 2 hours after oral administration of 75 grams of glucose.

Of the 1,035 women initially enrolled, 25 were excluded from the study because they either had DM 6–9 weeks after delivery or delivered a baby before 35 weeks of pregnancy. Out of the remaining 1,010 women who delivered a baby after 35 or more weeks of pregnancy and did not have DM 6–9 weeks after delivery, the researchers were able to follow 959 (95%) for up to 2 years, and 113 (11.8%) of them were noted to have developed DM during the course of this time.

Data were analyzed using advanced statistical methods, including regression analysis, to examine the independent association of different levels and durations of breastfeeding with the incidence of DM after adjusting for potential confounding factors such as age, race, and weight.

Crude incidence rate of Type 2 DM within 2 years of follow-up of women with GDM by lactation intensity groups at 6 to 9 weeks after delivery showed that women in the "exclusively formula milk" group had an incidence rate of 8.79 per 1,000 person-months of follow-up, those in the "mostly formula milk" group had an incidence rate of 6.47, those in "mostly lactation" group had an incidence rate of 4.88, and those in the "exclusively lactation" group had an incidence rate of 3.95 per 1,000 person-months of follow-up. **TABLE 14.14** shows lactation intensity groups 6–9 weeks after delivery and adjusted hazard ratios (representing the risk of DM) of the incidence of DM within the 2-year follow-up period among women who had GDM during pregnancy.

Questions

Question 1. What research question was addressed in this study, or what hypothesis was tested?

Question 2. Why are incidence rates of DM in this study reported per 1,000 person-months rather than per 100 or per 1,000 women, and what does person-months mean?

Question 3. What do hazard ratios in Table 14.14 indicate? Are these results statistically significant? Explain your answer with the help of data from the table.

Question 4. Why in this study were the estimates of the health outcome (DM) statistically adjusted for variables such as age, maternal risk factors, neonatal outcomes, and postpartum maternal lifestyle?

TABLE 14.14 Lactation Intensity Groups 6–9 Weeks After Delivery and Adjusted Hazard Ratios of the Incidence of Diabetes Mellitus Within the 2-Year Follow-Up Period Among Women Who Had Gestational Diabetes During Pregnancy

Type of Regression Model	Adjusted Hazard Ratio of Incidence of Diabetes Mellitus Within 2 Years of Follow-Up by Lactation Intensity			
	Exclusively Formula n = 153, (95% CI*)	Mostly Formula & Inconsistent Lactation n = 214, (95% CI*)	Mostly Lactation n = 387, (95% CI*)	Exclusively Lactation n = 205, (95% CI*)
Age-adjusted	1.00 (reference group)	0.72 (0.43–1.23)	0.54 (0.33–0.89)	0.43 (0.23–0.82)
Maternal risk factors (**A**)	1.00 (reference group)	0.64 (0.37–1.12)	0.54 (0.32–0.92)	0.46 (0.24–0.88)
A + newborn outcomes (**B**)	1.00 (reference group)	0.65 (0.37–1.13)	0.53 (0.31–0.91)	0.47 (0.25–0.91)
A + **B** + postpartum lifestyle	1.00 (reference group)	0.66 (0.38–1.14)	0.56 (0.32–0.95)	0.48 (0.25–0.92)

*95% confidence interval.

Modified from: Gunderson EP, Hurston SR, Ning X, Lo JC, Crites Y, Walton D, Dewey KG, Azevedo RA, Young S, Fox G, Elmasian CC, Salvador N, Lum M, Sternfeld B, Quesenberry CP. Lactation and progression of type 2 diabetes mellitus after gestational diabetes mellitus: a prospective cohort study. Ann Intern Med, 163(12):889–898. Copyright © 2015 American College of Physicians. All rights reserved. Reprinted with permission of American College of Physicians, Inc.

🔍 CASE STUDY 14.3: Retrospective Cohort Study

Modified from: Hansen KW, Sorensen R, Madsen M, et al. Effectiveness of an early versus a conservative invasive treatment strategy in acute coronary syndromes. Ann Intern Med. 2015; 163(10):737–746.

This retrospective cohort study investigated the adverse cardiovascular outcomes of an *early invasive treatment strategy* (EITS) in comparison with a *conservative invasive treatment strategy* (CITS) in a national cohort of patients who had been diagnosed with acute coronary syndrome (ACS). EITS was defined as diagnostic coronary angiography within 72 hours of the index hospitalization and cardiac catheterization. The rationale for the study was that randomized clinical trials (RCTs) in the past have reported that, in patients with ACS, EITS has lower mortality and fewer rehospitalizations due to myocardial infarction (MI) than CITS.

The researchers abstracted data on all acute invasive procedures, hospitalizations, and outcomes in patients with ACS from the Danish national registries that hold data on all 5.6 million residents of Denmark. The study included 19,704 patients who were hospitalized with a diagnosis of ACS for the first time between January 1, 2005, and December 31, 2011. Patients in the EITS ($n = 9,852$) and CITS ($n = 9,852$) groups were matched for other variables that could have affected their likelihood of being treated for ACS (propensity score matching). These patients were retrospectively tracked in the data set for rehospitalization due to MI within 60 days of the index hospitalization for ACS, death, or emigration—whichever of the three happened first. The results showed that acute coronary syndrome patients who were subjected to EITS experienced 25% fewer cardiac deaths (hazard ratio = 0.75, $P<0.001$), 33% fewer myocardial infarction–related rehospitalizations (hazard ratio = 0.67, $P<0.001$) and 35% fewer all-cause deaths (hazard ratio = 0.65, $P<0.001$) than those subjected to CITS.

Questions

Question 1. What research question was addressed in this study, or what hypothesis was tested?

Question 2. Who were the study subjects, and how were they identified and followed?

Question 3. What do the results of the study indicate?

Question 4. How much confidence can one have in the results of the study?

⌕ *CASE STUDY 14.4: Case-Control Study*

Modified from: O'Donnell MJ, Zavier D, Liu L, et al. Risk factors for ischaemic and intracerebral haemorrhagic stroke in 22 countries (the INTERSTROKE study): a case-control study. Lancet. 2010; 376:112–123.

Stroke is one of the leading causes of death and disability worldwide. However, the role of various risk factors in contributing to the overall burden of stroke, especially in many low- and middle-income countries, is not understood. The researchers conducted this standardized case-control study in 22 countries between March 1, 2007 and April 23, 2010 to examine the association of known and newly emerging risk factors with stroke and its primary subtypes and to understand the difference between risk factors for stroke and myocardial infarction. This study constituted phase 1 of the INTERSTROKE multicenter international study and included 3,000 cases and 3,000 controls from 84 centers in 22 countries.

Cases were defined as patients who had their first acute stroke and were identified within 5 days of onset of symptoms and within 72 hours of hospital admission. *Stroke* was defined as "a clinical syndrome characterized by rapidly developing clinical symptoms and/or signs, and at times global loss of cerebral function, with symptoms lasting more than 24 hours or leading to death, with no apparent cause other than a vascular one." Controls were hospital- (admitted or outpatient) or community-based individuals who had no previous history of stroke. One control was matched with one case within 5 years of age and for sex. In some countries with multiple ethnic groups, controls were also matched with cases for ethnicity. All participants completed a structured questionnaire and went through a physical examination. For those patients who were unable to communicate sufficiently to complete the questionnaire, proxy respondents were used. Most participants also provided blood and urine samples. Neuroimaging and electrocardiography (ECG) were done at baseline for all cases.

Risk factor assessment was done on the bases of hypertension, diabetes, anthropometric measurements (height, weight, and waist and hip circumference), physical activity, diet, alcohol intake, smoking status, and psychosocial factors. Blood pressure and heart rate for cases and controls were also recorded. Hypertension was defined on the basis of self-reported history and/or blood pressure of 160/90 mm Hg. Diabetes was defined on the basis of self-report. Alcohol intake was classified into: (a) never or former drinker, (b) moderate drinker [1–30 drinks per month], (c) more than 30 drinks per month, and (d) binge drinkers [>5 drinks per day at least once a month]. Smoking status was categorized as: (a) never, (b) former, and (c) current [any tobacco in the past 12 months]. The researchers calculated odds ratios (ORs) and population attributable risk (PARs) to understand the relationship of selected risk factors with *all stroke, ischemic stroke*, and *intracerebral hemorrhagic stroke*.

Logistic regression analysis of data was carried out adjusting for age, sex, and region. Multiple logistic regression models were developed for various risk factors and adjusted ORs were estimated. Partial results of statistical analyses are presented in **TABLE 14.15**.

Questions

Question 1. What research question was addressed in this study, or what hypothesis was tested?

Question 2. Which risk factors were significantly associated with *all stroke, ischemic stroke*, and *intracerebral hemorrhagic stroke*?

Question 3. Which two risk factors were associated with the highest risk of *all stroke* and with *intracerebral hemorrhagic stroke*?

Question 4. What relationship did alcohol intake have with *all stroke* and with *ischemic stroke*?

Question 5. What relationship did regular physical activity have with *all stroke* and with *ischemic stroke*?

TABLE 14.15 Risk of Stroke Associated with Risk Factors in the Overall Population (Multivariate Analysis)

		Prevalence		All Stroke[†]	Ischemic Stroke[†]	Intracerebral Hemorrhagic Stroke
	Control (*n* = 3,000)	Ischemic Stroke (*n* = 2,337)	Intracerebral Hemorrhagic Stroke (*n* = 663)	Odds Ratio (99% CI)	Odds Ratio (99% CI)	Odds Ratio (99% CI)
Variable 1: Hypertension						
A: Self-reported history of hypertension	954/2,996 (32%)	1,277/2,335 (55%)	399/662 (60%)	2.64 (2.26–3.08)	2.37 (2.00–2.79)	3.80 (2.96–4.78)
B: Self-reported history of hypertension or blood pressure >160/90 mm Hg	1,109/3,000 (37%)	1,550/2,337 (66%)	551/663 (83%)	3.89 (3.33–4.54)	3.14 (2.67–3.71)	9.18 (6.80–12.39)
Variable 2: Smoking Status						
Current smoker[‡]	732/2,994 (24%)	868/2,333 (37%)	207/662 (31%)	2.09 (1.75–2.51)	2.32 (1.91–2.81)	1.45 (1.07–1.96)
Variable 3: Waist-to-Hip Ratio						
Tertile 2 vs. Tertile 1	989/2,960 (33%)	768/2,303 (33%)	266/655 (41%)	1.42 (1.18–1.71)	1.34 (1.10–1.64)	1.65 (1.22–2.23)
Tertile 3 vs. Tertile 1	984/2,960 (33%)	987/2,303 (43%)	231/655 (35%)	1.65 (1.36–1.99)	1.69 (1.38–2.07)	1.41 (1.02–1.93)
Variable 4: Diet Risk Score						
Tertile 2 vs. Tertile 1	1,064/2,982 (36%)	842/2,303 (37%)	271/658 (41%)	1.35 (1.12–1.61)	1.29 (1.06–1.57)	1.53 (1.13–2.08)
Tertile 3 vs. Tertile1	904/2,982 (30%)	807/2,303 (35%)	221/658 (34%)	1.35 (1.11–1.64)	1.34 (1.09–1.65)	1.41 (1.01–1.97)
Variable 5: Physical Activity						
Regular physical activity[¶]	362/2,994 (12%)	193/2,334 (8%)	45/662 (7%)	0.69 (0.53–0.90)	0.68 (0.51–0.91)	0.70 (0.44–1.13)
Variable 6: Diabetes						
Diabetes mellitus	350/2,999 (12%)	495/2,336 (21%)	68/662 (10%)	1.36 (1.10–1.68)	1.60 (1.29–1.99)	‖

(continues)

TABLE 14.15 Risk of Stroke Associated with Risk Factors in the Overall Population (Multivariate Analysis)						
	Prevalence			**All Stroke[†]**	**Ischemic Stroke[†]**	**Intracerebral Hemorrhagic Stroke**
	Control (*n* = 3,000)	**Ischemic Stroke** (*n* = 2,337)	**Intracerebral Hemorrhagic Stroke** (*n* = 663)	**Odds Ratio** (99% CI)	**Odds Ratio** (99% CI)	**Odds Ratio** (99% CI)
Variable 7: Alcohol Intake[‡]						
1–30 drinks per month	524/2,989 (18%)	338/2,326 (15%)	121/660 (18%)	0.90 (0.72–1.11)	0.79 (0.63–1.00)	1.52 (1.07–2.16)
>30 drinks per month or binge drinker	324/2,989 (11%)	383/2,326 (16%)	108/660 (16%)	1.51 (1.18–1.92)	1.41 (1.09–1.82)	2.01 (1.35–2.99)
Variable 8: Psychosocial Factors						
A: Psychosocial stress	440/2,987 (15%)	465/2,324 (20%)	124/654 (19%)	1.30 (1.06–1.60)	1.30 (1.04–1.62)	1.23 (0.89–1.69)
B: Depression	424/2,995 (14%)	489/2,320 (21%)	100/645 (16%)	1.35 (1.10–1.66)	1.47 (1.19–1.83)	‖
Variable 9: Cardiac Causes						
Cardiac causes**	140/3,000 (5%)	321/2,337 (14%)	28/662 (4%)	2.38 (1.77–3.20)	2.74 (2.03–3.72)	‖
Variable 10: Ratio of ApoB to Apo1[††]						
Tertile 2 vs. Tertile 1	695/2,091 (33%)	501/1,698 (30%)	136/468 (29%)	1.13 (0.90–1.42)	1.30 (1.01–1.67)	‖
Tertile 3 vs. Tertile 1	696/2,091 (33%)	825/1,698 (49%)	165/468 (35%)	1.89 (1.49–2.40)	2.40 (1.86–3.11)	‖

All models were adjusted for age, sex, and region. T: tertile; Apo: apolipoprotein.

*Data were missing for some individuals: 7 for self-reported history of hypertension, 11 for smoking status, 82 for waist-to-hip ratio, 57 for diet risk score, 10 for physical activity, 3 for diabetes mellitus, 25 for alcohol intake, 35 for psychosocial stress, 40 for depression, 1 for cardiac causes, and 1,743 for apolipoprotein concentrations. These individuals were excluded from the denominator in percentage calculations.

[†]Individual risk factor estimates for variables 1–9 are derived from the multivariable model, including all variables (1A and 2–9). For intracerebral hemorrhagic stroke, the multivariate model included variables 1A, 2–5, 7, and 8A.

[‡]Comparator for current smoker and alcohol intake is never or former.

[§]For variables expressed in tertiles, population-attributable risk was calculated from T2 plus T3 versus T1.

[¶]For the protective factor of physical activity, population-attributable risks are provided for the group without this factor.

[‖]Odds ratio and population-attributable risk was not calculated because the variable was not significant in univariate analyses and so was excluded from multivariate analyses.

**Includes atrial fibrillation or flutter, previous myocardial infarction, rheumatic valve disease, or prosthetic heart valve.

[††]Estimate derived from multivariable model, including all variables (1A and 2–10; *n* = 4,257).

Reprinted from: O'Donnell MJ, Zavier D, Liu L, et al. Risk factors for ischaemic and intracerebral haemorrhagic stroke in 22 countries (the INTERSTROKE study): a case-control study. Lancet. 2010;376:112–123. Copyright © 2010 with permission from Elsevier.

▶ 14.15 Summary

The purpose of observational studies is to examine the likelihood of a potentially causal relationship between exposure to a risk factor and a disease. Because of the multifactorial etiology of most diseases and difficulties in demonstrating a causal relationship, observational studies only strive to demonstrate a statistical relationship between exposure and disease. If an observational study can demonstrate the strength and consistency of association, dose–response relationship, and temporally correct relationship between exposure and disease, then a strong argument can be made that a cause-and-effect relationship exists between exposure and the disease. Through appropriate study design, researchers also attempt to keep these studies as free of bias and contaminating effects of confounding variables that can result in over- or underestimation of the strength of association between exposure and disease. This chapter gives the reader necessary tools to develop a good understanding of the conceptual framework, complexities of appropriate study design, and the strengths and weaknesses of various kinds of observational studies. With the help of several recently published observational studies in medical literature and hypothetical data used to calculate relative risk, risk difference, and odds ratios, the chapter provides an overview of ecological, cohort, and case-control studies. The chapter also sheds light on issues that can compromise the validity of findings reported by these studies.

References

1. Morgenstern H. Ecologic studies in epidemiology: concepts, principles, and methods. Ann Rev Public Health. 1995;16: 61–81.
2. Dufault B, Klar N. The quality of modern cross-sectional studies: a bibliometric review. Am J Epidemiol. 2011;174(10):1101–1107.
3. Tu JV, Ko DT. Ecological studies and cardiovascular outcomes research. Circulation. 2008;9:2588–2593.
4. Wakefield J. Ecological studies revisited. Ann Rev Public Health. 2008;29:75–90.
5. Greenland S, Robins J. Ecologic studies–biases, misconceptions, and counterexamples. Am J Epidemiol. 1994;139:747–760.
6. Pearce N. The ecological fallacy strikes back. J Epidemiol Community Health. 2000;54:326–327.
7. Aschengrau A, Seage GR. Essentials of epidemiology in public health. Sudbury, MA: Jones and Bartlett Publishers; 2008.
8. Shrestha M, Raitanen J, Salminen T, Lahkola A, Auvinen A. Pituitary tumor risk in relation to mobile phone use: a case-control study. Acta Oncol. 2015;54:1159–1165.
9. O'Donnell MJ, Zavier D, Liu L, et al. Risk factors for ischaemic and intracerebral haemorrhagic stroke in 22 countries (the INTERSTROKE study): a case-control study. Lancet. 2010;376:112–123.
10. Kunitz SJ. Holism and the idea of general susceptibility to disease. Int J Epidemiol. 2002;31:722–729.
11. Haggerty RJ. Stress and illness in children. Bull N Y Acad Med. 1986;62(7):707–718.
12. Friedman SB, Glasgow LA. Psychologic factors and resistance to infectious disease. Pediatr Clin North Am. 1966; 13(2):315–335.
13. Marsland AL, Bachen EA, Cohen S, Rabin B, Manuck SB. Stress, immune reactivity and susceptibility to infectious disease. Physiol Behav. 2002;77:711–716.
14. Porta M. Bias. A dictionary of epidemiology. 6th ed. New York: Oxford University Press; 2014 [cited 2017 Dec 11], p. 21. http://irea.ir/files/site1/pages/dictionary.pdf
15. Porta M. Confounding. A dictionary of epidemiology. 6th ed. New York: Oxford University Press; 2014 [cited 2018 June 1], p. 55. http://irea.ir/files/site1/pages/dictionary.pdf
16. Mausner JS, Kramer S. Epidemiology—an introductory text. Philadelphia, PA: W.B. Saunders Company; 1985.
17. Jager KJ, Zoccali C, MacLeod A, Dekker FW. Confounding: what it is and how to deal with it. Kidney Int. 2008;73: 256–260.
18. Braga LH, Farrokhyar F, Bhandari M. Practical tips for surgical research. Confounding: what is it and how do we deal with it? Can J Surg. 2012;55(2):132–138.

CHAPTER 15

Experimental Studies

LEARNING OBJECTIVES

Having mastered the materials in this chapter, the student will be able to:

1. Evaluate the design, conduct, and findings of randomized clinical trials (RCTs) reported in literature.
2. Compare and contrast the strengths and weaknesses in the design, conduct, and findings of RCTs that used the same intervention.
3. Participate in the design and conduct of an RCT as a competent member of a team.
4. Distinguish between different kinds of RCTs and assess their suitability in a given situation.

CHAPTER OUTLINE

15.1   Introduction
15.2   Experimental or Interventional Study Design
15.3   Categorization of Experimental Studies
15.4   Randomized Controlled Trials or Clinical Trials
    15.4.1   Phases of Randomized Clinical Trials
    15.4.2   Eligibility Criteria
    15.4.3   Sample Size and Power of Study
15.5   Example of a Randomized Clinical Trial

15.6   Community Trials
15.7   Example of a Community Trial
15.8   Natural Experiments
15.9   Factorial Trials
Case Study 15.1 – Randomized Control Trial –
                Chlorhexidine Bathing in ICUs to
                Prevent HAIs
15.10 Summary

KEY TERMS

Community trials
Comparison group
Control group
Crossover trials
Experimental group
Factorial trials
Natural experiment

Null hypothesis
Parallel trials
Phase I clinical trials
Phase II clinical trials
Phase III clinical trials
Preventive trials
Prophylactic trials

Randomized clinical trials
Study group
Therapeutic trials
Type I error
Type II error

▶ 15.1 Introduction

Many healthcare providers, including academic and nonacademic medical centers, participate in experimental studies of new biomedical and pharmaceutical products. They also receive significant amounts of research funding from the pharmaceutical industry and entities such as the U.S. National Institutes of Health (NIH) to conduct or participate in these studies. Experimental research, although critically important for the advancement of knowledge and development of new products, involves potential risks for participants. It also raises the prospect of administrative challenges and ethical considerations for healthcare providers and administrators. The institutional review boards (IRBs) of host sites play an important role in assessing and monitoring these challenges through their approval and monitoring processes for research protocols. Although healthcare mangers are usually not involved in the implementation and conduct of experimental studies, as members of the administrative staff at host sites, they have a stake in understanding the fundamental principles and operational framework of these activities.

Between October 18, 2016, and November 8, 2016, out of the 15 studies published in the Original Investigation section of the four consecutive issues of the *Journal of the American Medical Association (JAMA)*, 60% (9/15) were randomized clinical trials (RCTs). Although it is quite likely that, from the thousands of Original Investigation manuscripts submitted to the journal every year, *JAMA* preferentially publishes RCTs, this example is only meant to underscore the importance of experimental studies in clinical medicine. **FIGURE 15.1** shows the yearly increase in the number of clinical trials registered with the U.S. ClinicalTrials.gov (https://clinicaltrials.gov/) web resource, a registry of clinical trials maintained by the U.S. National Library of Congress. According to the website, as of November 11, 2016, close to 230,000 studies with locations in all 50 U.S. states and in 193 other countries were registered with this resource. The purpose of this and other registries is to disseminate information from clinical trials worldwide in an efficient and timely manner. The U.S. Department of Health and Human Services (DHHS) requires that every clinical trial partly or fully funded by the NIH be registered with ClinicalTrials.gov and summary information from such studies be posted in a timely manner.[1] Since 2004, the International Committee of Medical Journal Editors has also required registration of clinical trials with the International Clinical Trials Registry Platform (ICTRP) as a condition of publication. A recent study by Viergever and Li[2] reported that as of 2013, the ICTRP database contained information on more than 186,000 interventional clinical trials. The yearly number of clinical trials registered with the ICTRP increased from

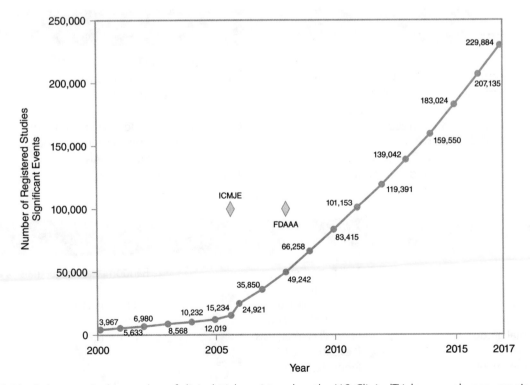

FIGURE 15.1 Yearly increase in the number of clinical trials registered on the U.S. ClinicalTrials.gov web resource since 2000.

approximately 3,300 in 2004 to nearly 23,500 in 2013. **FIGURE 15.2** shows the number and percentage of registered studies on ClinicalTrials.gov by location as of November 9, 2016.

As the most valuable epidemiologic tool to investigate the effectiveness of new pharmaceutical products and other therapeutic modalities, the importance of experimental studies (or RCTs) cannot be overstated. While RCTs generate the highest-quality evidence related to the safety and effectiveness of the products being investigated, they are also the most difficult, complex, and expensive form of epidemiologic investigations. Every drug approved for human use goes through a multistage rigorous testing process

that includes RCTs. The process of assessing the safety and effectiveness of a medicinal product or technology through experimental studies often continues for many years after the product has been approved and put to common use. This chapter provides a comprehensive overview of different forms of experimental studies that are also known as **randomized clinical trials** or randomized controlled trials. **FIGURE 15.3** shows the place of RCTs in the scheme of all epidemiologic investigations.

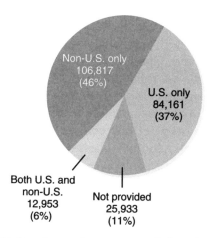

FIGURE 15.2 Number and percentage of all studies registered on ClinicalTrials.gov by location (as of November 9, 2016): total 229,864 studies.

Reproduced from: ClinicalTrials.gov. Available at: https://clinicaltrials.gov/ct2/resources/trends#RegisteredStudiesOverTime

▶ 15.2 Experimental or Interventional Study Design

Experimental studies are typically designed to generate evidence regarding the safety and efficacy, or lack thereof, of a new product or intervention intended to prevent, treat, or manage a health problem. To generate such evidence, investigators test a hypotheses or supposition regarding the safety and efficacy of the product by conducting a carefully designed scientific investigation. As suggested by the words *experimental* or *interventional*, these kinds of studies involve intentional exposure of a group of human or animal subjects, the **study group**, to some newly developed intervention to test its success or failure in achieving specific health outcomes. To demonstrate that the observed positive or negative outcomes in subjects exposed to the intervention are not merely the result of a chance occurrence, a **comparison group** or **control group** is used, and subjects are randomly assigned between

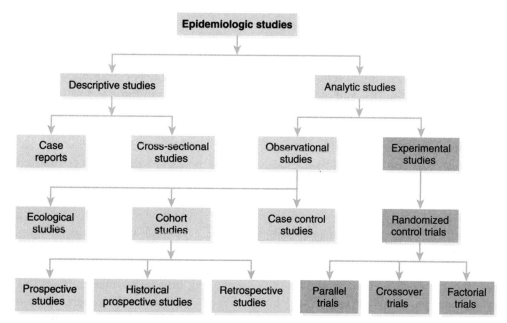

FIGURE 15.3 A schematic diagram of different types of epidemiologic studies.

Data from Friis, 2010; Swallen KC, University of Wisconsin-Madison.

the two groups. The control group comprises subjects who are not exposed to the intervention but in all other respects are similar to the study group. In some experimental studies, the control group may be exposed to another previously developed intervention whose effects in subjects similar to the study group are already known. The intervention being investigated in an experimental study can be a biologic or chemical agent designed to render future protection from a disease (for example, a new vaccine for polio) or to treat an existing disease such as hypertension or diabetes.

It is important to note that there is a fundamental difference between the objectives of observational studies, such as cohort or case-control studies, and the objectives of experimental studies. Observational studies are designed to find evidence in support of or against a hypothesis related to the etiology of a disease or to understand the role a particular factor plays in the occurrence of a disease. In contrast, experimental studies are designed to find evidence in support of or against a hypothesis related to the protective, therapeutic, or deleterious effects of a new drug, procedure, or technology. Therefore, although experimental studies are of little use in understanding the etiology of diseases, they are critically important in finding preventive or therapeutic modalities to combat diseases.

As compared with observational studies, the quality of evidence generated by experimental studies is superior. In fact, experimental studies are widely considered to be the most complex and most rigorous of all epidemiologic investigations. The random allocation of subjects to the study and control groups allows for more reliable results and more valid claims about the success or failure of the intervention. Because of concerns regarding the protection of study participants, experimental studies are subjected to a rigorous approval process and are closely monitored for adherence to the study protocol by the IRB and other regulatory or funding agencies. Despite some concerns regarding the ethics of intentional exposure of subjects to a potentially harmful substance or of withholding a potentially lifesaving intervention for a length of time from subjects who may critically need it, there is little disagreement regarding the value and scientific merits of experimental studies.

The length of time for which subjects are exposed to an intervention depends on the nature of the study and differs from one experimental study to the next. In some studies, the follow-up period might be in weeks or months, whereas in others, it may be longer. Having an adequate sample size is essential for obtaining results that are valid and generalizable to the larger population. Calculations of sample size must also take into consideration attrition of subjects or potential losses to follow-up because some of the participants, for one reason or another, may discontinue their participation before the completion of the study.

Typically, before the onset of an experimental study, a study protocol describing all operational details of the proposed study is developed and submitted to the IRB for approval. The study protocol not only provides a detailed road map for researchers to conduct the study, but also serves as a monitoring tool to assess progress and adherence to ethical standards required to protect all participants. Routinely, a study protocol should include the following details.

1. The specification and articulation of the research question or hypothesis being tested. For example, the test question might be that the newly developed drug X is successful in treating disease Y. In this case, of course, it would be imperative to define carefully the measure of "success," whether it is the normalization of a measurable factor, such as serum sugar level, or elimination of a pathogen, such as the hepatitis B virus.

2. Procedures for the identification and selection of study participants and specification of criteria based on which subject may be included or excluded from the study. This might include specification of age, race, sex, or other characteristics of individuals as well as specification of diagnostic criteria to establish the presence of the disease of interest in alleged patients. The protocol might also specify conditions under which participation of existing subjects can be terminated. For example, rapid deterioration of the condition of a patient might preclude his or her continued participation in the study.

3. Details about the total population of interest, known as the *reference population*, from which a representative sample will be drawn and how participation of identified individuals from the reference population will be sought through informed consent. It should also describe sampling procedures, anticipated sample size, and desired power of the study. The description of randomization techniques employed to assign participants to the experimental or study group and control group must be included in the research protocol.

4. Specification of whether the study is *single blind*, *double blind*, or *triple blind*—meaning whether subjects, investigators, and/or analysts—are prevented from knowing which group is the **experimental group** (receiving the intervention or experimental drug) and which one is the control group (receiving a placebo or standard treatment). The placebo is usually an inert or harmless substance that may be administered in the form of a pill, capsule, or liquid. In single blind trials, the subjects do not know, but investigators and data analysts know, which subjects are assigned to the study group and which ones are assigned to the control group. In double blind trials, both subjects and investigators do not know which subjects are assigned to which group. Finally, in triple blind studies, neither subjects, nor investigators, nor data analysts know which group is the treatment group and which one is the control group. Blinding of subjects, researchers, and analysts is done to avoid bias in the findings of the study that might be introduced through altered behavior or perceptions of one, two, or all three of these players in the study.

5. A detailed description of the procedures for administering the intervention to the study group and placebo to the control group as well as appropriate tracking procedures, while keeping the identity of each group masked for blinding purposes.

6. Specification of parameters to assess the clinical impact, efficacy, and health outcomes resulting from the intervention (including changes in signs, symptoms, laboratory findings, and other measurements) and methods to consistently apply these parameters during the course of the study.

7. The specific *end point* of the study, at which time the study would be completed, terminated, or aborted.

▶ 15.3 Categorization of Experimental Studies

Because experimental studies typically involve random assignment of subjects to two or more groups to avoid selection bias and to make the groups similar in their demographic and socioeconomic characteristics, the word *randomized* almost always appears in any classification or categorization of experimental studies. For example, if a study is conducted to examine the safety and effectiveness of a new drug, the study would be called a *randomized clinical trial* or a *randomized controlled trial*—especially if participants and investigators are blinded regarding which subjects are assigned to which group.

There are multiple ways to classify experimental studies. One way to categorize experimental studies is based on the unit of participation or analysis, that is, whether the unit of analysis is an individual (*individual trial*) or an entire community (*community trial*). If an experimental study is conducted to investigate the prophylactic or preventive potential of a new drug or technology, the study is correspondingly called a **prophylactic trial** or a **preventive trial**. Likewise, if the purpose of the study is to assess the therapeutic potential of a new modality of treatment or pharmaceutical product, it might be called a **therapeutic trial**. Another way of categorizing experimental studies is based on whether assignment of subjects to one group or another remains unchanged throughout the course of the study. The studies in which subjects randomly assigned to the experimental and comparison groups are given their respective interventions concomitantly and are followed for a period of time without being exposed to the alternative intervention are called **parallel trials**. Alternatively, if interventions are switched between the two groups after an initial period of exposure and follow-up is continued further into the future, such trials are called **crossover trials**. **TABLES 15.1** and **15.2** present conceptual models of parallel and crossover study designs. Finally, in contrast to the classic *one-arm* experimental study, in which

TABLE 15.1 Conceptual Model of a Parallel Trial		
Exposure to Intervention	**Parallel Follow-Up**	**Study Endpoint**
Group A – Intervention A	⟶	Results of Group A – Intervention A
Group B – Intervention B	⟶	Results of Group B – Intervention B

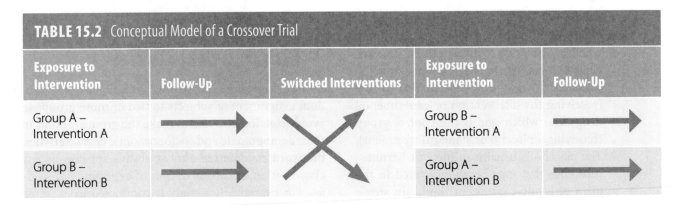

TABLE 15.2 Conceptual Model of a Crossover Trial

Exposure to Intervention	Follow-Up	Switched Interventions	Exposure to Intervention	Follow-Up
Group A – Intervention A			Group B – Intervention A	
Group B – Intervention B			Group A – Intervention B	

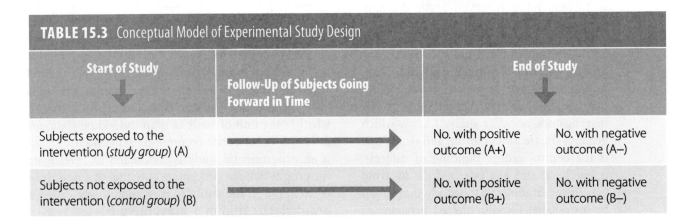

TABLE 15.3 Conceptual Model of Experimental Study Design

Start of Study	Follow-Up of Subjects Going Forward in Time	End of Study	
Subjects exposed to the intervention (*study group*) (A)		No. with positive outcome (A+)	No. with negative outcome (A−)
Subjects not exposed to the intervention (*control group*) (B)		No. with positive outcome (B+)	No. with negative outcome (B−)

the effects of only one intervention are investigated, researchers may concurrently implement two or more unrelated interventions on the same group of participants. This strategy may be adopted in the interest of efficiency and cost savings. Studies in which participants are simultaneously exposed to entirely different multiple interventions whose outcomes do not affect one another are called *factorial trials*.

▶ 15.4 Randomized Controlled Trials or Clinical Trials

It should be noted that some authors limit the use of the term *controlled trial* to only those experimental studies in which the control group only receives a placebo (an inert substance with no pharmacological effect or properties) rather than a real drug or an active agent. In the following discussion, we will use the term *randomized controlled trial* interchangeably with *randomized clinical trial*.

In a randomized clinical trial or a randomized controlled trial, study participants are randomly assigned to two or more groups. If only one intervention (for example, a new drug) is being tested, subjects would be randomly divided into a study group and a control group. However, if two or more interventions are being tested in the same study, or different levels of exposure to the same intervention are involved, then subjects would be randomly divided into as many groups as necessary. At the end of the study period, data from these groups are compared for differences in expected outcomes, such as improvement in health, duration of survival, mortality rates, or recovery from disease. Ethical considerations prevent researchers from purposefully exposing subjects to potentially harmful organisms, chemicals, or devices to understand the etiology of a disease. For that purpose, observational studies, such as case-control or cohort studies, are clearly more suited. RCTs are designed only to examine the preventive and therapeutic potential of interventional tools, such as new technologies and drugs. **TABLE 15.3** shows a conceptual model of experimental study design.

In an RCT, randomization of participants is carried out to achieve the following goals:

1. To have intervention and control groups that are similar in demographic, socioeconomic, and clinical characteristics. Whether the groups were truly alike and comparable must be verified at the time of the analysis of study results.

2. To avoid the possibility of bias introduced by self-selection of participants into one or the other group or by preferential assignment of some participants into the treatment or control group by the investigator.

3. To have study results that are valid in terms of findings or conclusions and reliable or reproducible by other investigators through similar studies.

Depending on study design and the unit of analysis, randomization can be done at the level of an individual, a household, a school or hospital, or a ZIP code. Before or after randomized selection, the sample can also be stratified by gender, age, education, or income.[3]

15.4.1 Phases of Randomized Clinical Trials

Clinical trials of new drugs are conducted in multiple phases; the first three phases are completed before the marketing and use of the new product, while the fourth phase of an RCT happens after the drug has been marketed and its use begun at the population level. **Phase I clinical trials** are the initial human safety studies involving small numbers (usually between 20 and 100) of nonrandomized healthy volunteers to assess the safety, side effects, and safe dose range of the new product. These studies also help in understanding the metabolic and pharmacological properties of the *investigational new drug* (IND). **Phase II clinical trials** are controlled efficacy studies done with larger numbers of volunteer participants, mostly patients suffering from the targeted disease, to assess the efficacy of the product and to further evaluate its safe short-term use in humans. Phase II clinical trials may or may not be randomized. When randomized, they can be done in the form of double blind studies—meaning that neither the researchers nor the subjects know who is in the study group (receiving the experimental drug or treatment) or in the control group (receiving a placebo or standard treatment). This procedure is intended to eliminate bias. Depending on the clinical end point of the study, Phase II randomized clinical trials can take one or more years to complete. Only after the safety and efficacy of the new drug have been reasonably established, **Phase III clinical trials** are conducted with much larger numbers of patients with the disease in question (as many as 2,000 or 3,000 patients) and randomized assignment to study and control groups. Phase III trials are usually double or even triple blind (i.e., data analysts also do not know which group is the study or control group). The control group is either given a placebo or a previously established standard treatment. Phase III clinical trials are designed to understand the long-term safety, toxicity, and efficacy of the new drug. Finally, Phase IV happens over the life of the drug after it has been put to common clinical use. Phase IV of the study process helps all stakeholders in understanding the long-term efficacy and toxicity of the drug, including adverse reactions in some patients.

15.4.2 Eligibility Criteria

Eligibility criteria or *inclusion/exclusion criteria* determine whether a person, group, or entity (such as a school or hospital) can participate in a research study. Inclusion criteria specify the conditions or characteristics that must be met in order to be included in the study, whereas exclusion criteria define the characteristics that prevent a person, group, or entity from participating in a study. For example, a study may seek to enroll only women of childbearing age, while another study may focus only on men and women diagnosed with Alzheimer's disease. These criteria must be explicitly and clearly established during the planning stages of a study. By definition, the eligibility criteria for enrollment in a study depend on the purpose of the study and the research question being addressed. In addition to the specified purpose and needs of the study, these criteria are also guided by concerns for the safety and well-being of participants. Depending on study design, healthy, sick, or at-risk individuals of specific demographic and social characteristics, including age, gender, ethnicity, and educational status, might be invited to participate voluntarily in a study, with the freedom to drop out at any time.

15.4.3 Sample Size and Power of Study

Before the onset of the study, it is necessary to calculate the appropriate sample size or the number of subjects to be recruited in the study. To answer the question being pursued by the study, it is essential to have an appropriate number of subjects. With an insufficient number of participants, a study can easily fail to answer the question being addressed. These calculations depend on the investigator's preference regarding the size of the difference between the experimental and comparison groups that the study should be able to detect. In general, to detect a small difference between groups, sample size needs to be large. However, a relatively small sample in a well-designed study can adequately detect a difference in the outcome of interest between the experimental and control groups if such a difference truly exists. During preparatory stages, the investigator must specify the acceptable level of statistical significance, or alpha (α). In statistical terms, α represents the probability of finding a difference between groups just by chance when none really existed. This is also known as the probability of **Type I error** (erroneously rejecting the null hypothesis). At the onset of any observational or experimental study, the investigator makes a supposition or hypothesizes that there is no difference in the outcome of interest between the *exposed* and *nonexposed* groups or *experimental* and *comparison* groups, and any difference discovered by the study is due to a chance occurrence. In the language of statistics, this is known as the **null hypothesis**. In most instances, the hope of an observational or experimental study is to reject the null hypothesis. Rejection of the null hypothesis indicates that a meaningful or statistically "significant" difference in the outcome of interest (for example, mortality rate) truly exists between the groups being compared. In statistical terms, a meaningful or significant difference implies a small probability ($\alpha = 0.05$, or $\alpha = 0.01$, i.e., 5 or 1 in a 100 chance) that the observed difference between groups was just a chance occurrence. By convention, α is usually set at 0.05, which means that the probability is 0.95 that the observed difference between the two groups is real rather than a chance occurrence. If a study erroneously rejects the null hypothesis and makes a claim of a true difference between the groups being compared, the error is known as a Type I error. If the investigator specifies α to be 0.05, the probability of making a Type I error is 0.05, or 5%. On the other hand, if a study erroneously fails to reject the null hypothesis (i.e., fails to detect a difference between groups when such a difference truly existed), the error is called a **Type II error**. Denoted by the symbol β (beta), the probability of making a Type II error depends on a number of factors, including the sample size. By convention, the acceptable probability of making a Type II error is set at 0.2 (4 times the level of α). The probability of correctly rejecting the null hypothesis ($1 - \beta$) is known as the *power* of the study and is usually set at 0.8 (or 80%).

Unfortunately, it is not possible to minimize simultaneously the probabilities of both Type I and Type II errors. There is an inverse relationship between the values of α and β—as one goes down, the other goes up. Clearly, rejecting the null hypothesis when it is true or failing to reject it when it is false are both problematic situations. For example, erroneous rejection of the null hypothesis (Type I error) can result in fruitless continuation of research into the efficacy of a drug that may eventually prove to be of no value. Failing to reject the null hypothesis (Type II error), on the other hand, can lead to premature discontinuation of research into a drug that could have been a lifesaving product. The researchers therefore must carefully assess and compare the disadvantages of erroneously rejecting or failing to reject the null hypothesis. One way of reducing the likelihood of a Type I error is to use 0.01 or even 0.001 level of α.

▶ 15.5 Example of a Randomized Clinical Trial

Modified from: MacPherson H, Tilbrook H, Richmond S, et al. Alexander Technique lessons or acupuncture sessions for persons with chronic neck pain. Ann Intern Med. 2015;163(9):653–662.

In a three-group parallel RCT, the researchers were interested in evaluating the clinical effectiveness of acupuncture and a method of self-care for neck pain known as the *Alexander Technique* as compared with usual care at a primary care physician's office. The usual care at a doctor's office involved treatment of chronic neck pain with prescription medication and physical therapy. Acupuncture is a form of Chinese traditional medicine that involves insertion of needles into the skin of the patient at various points, plus diagnosis-specific advice and counseling. The Alexander Technique is a method of self-care that helps patients increase their control of reaction to pain and improve the way they carry on with their daily activities.

Persons who had had neck pain lasting 3 months or longer and had a score of at least 28% on the Northwick Park Questionnaire (NPQ) for neck pain and associated disability without any serious underlying pathology were eligible to participate in the study. Patients who consented to participate were recruited from a number of primary care physicians' offices and were randomly and equally assigned to the two intervention groups and the usual care group. The two interventions involved (1) 12 acupuncture sessions of 50 minutes' duration plus usual care at a primary care physician's office, and (2) 20 one-on-one Alexander Technique lessons of 30 minutes' duration plus usual care at a primary care physician's office. Each intervention totaled 600 minutes.

The primary clinical outcome in all three groups was the NPQ score at 0, 3, 6, and 12 months, with 12 months being the primary endpoint of the clinical trial. The study also involved the following three secondary outcomes: (1) chronic pain self-efficacy score on the 5-question Pain Management subscale of the Chronic Pain Self-Efficacy scale (scored 0 to 8, with higher scores indicating better self-efficacy) reported by patients through text messaging to researchers on a monthly basis; (2) self-reported quality of life score on Short Form 12 version 2 (SF12v2); and (3) adverse events reported by physicians and patients directly to researchers regardless of whether the adverse event was related to either of the two interventions.

A total of 517 patients were enrolled in the study, with 173 in the acupuncture intervention group, 172 in the Alexander Technique lessons intervention group, and 172 in the usual care group (one was excluded from the final analysis of usual care because of missing baseline data).

The results for the acupuncture group in comparison with the usual care group showed a 3.92% lower NPQ score after 12 months (95% CI, 0.97–6.87). The results for the Alexander Technique lessons group showed a 3.79% lower NPQ score after 12 months than the usual care group (95% CI, 0.91–6.66). As compared with the baseline, the reduction in NPQ score in the acupuncture group after 12 months was 32%, with 31% in the Alexander lessons group. Self-efficacy of patients in the acupuncture group was associated with a 3.34% lower NPQ score as compared with the usual care group (95% CI, 2.31%–4.38%). In the Alexander lessons group, self-efficacy was associated with a 3.33% lower NPQ score in comparison with the usual care group.

The researchers concluded that both acupuncture and Alexander Technique lessons resulted in significantly greater improvement in patients with chronic neck pain after 12 months as compared with usual care.

▶ 15.6 Community Trials

At times, investigators can conduct experimental trials at a community level by exposing an entire community to an intervention for a period of time and comparing the frequency of specific health outcomes in the community with those in similar communities where the intervention had not been implemented. The intervention of interest can be a potentially protective substance, such as small quantities of fluoride in drinking water, or an educational activity such as sex education in schools, or availability of a resources such as swimming pools or exercise facilities in a community. Such trials are important to formulate public health policies such as routine fluoridation of a municipal water supply system or removal of soda vending machines from schools.

As compared with experimental studies that target a relatively small number of high-risk individuals in a population, **community trials** have several advantages. For example, community trials affect a much larger number of individuals to prevent disease and promote health. Further, it is easier to implement interventions

through policy formulation and environmental change, such as fluoridation of the municipal water supply or requiring children to be vaccinated for certain diseases before they are allowed to attend school. Examples of community trials vary, from smoking cessation education to weight loss programs, and from vitamin A supplemental use or fortification of milk with vitamin D to family planning promotion.[4]

▶ 15.7 Example of a Community Trial

Modified from: Marino R, Villa A, Guerrero S. A community trial of fluoridated powdered milk in Chile. Community Dent Oral Epidemiol. 2001;29:435–442.

This community trial was conducted in two rural communities in central Chile between 1994 and 1999. The researchers wanted to investigate the effectiveness of fluoridated milk and milk products in preventing dental caries by comparing the baseline and 5-years' postintervention data from the experimental and control populations. Using the National Complementary Feeding Program, the researchers gave fluoridated milk and milk-cereal to 1,000 preschool children in Codegua, a rural community in the 6th Region of Chile with low fluoride concentration in its drinking water. The population of Codegua in 1994 was 10,567. La Punta, a community of similar oral health conditions, demographic, and socioeconomic characteristics about 10 km north of Codegua, was used as the control population. In the experimental group, the estimated daily fluoride dose from fluoridated powdered milk varied from 0.25 mg to 0.75 mg for age groups 0–<2 years, ≥2–<3 years and ≥3–6 years. In Codegua, 2 kg of fluoridated milk powder per month was given to children up to 23 months of age, and 1 kg of fluoridated milk-cereal per month was given to children aged 2–6 years. During the study years, data from both communities were gathered through multiple cross-sectional samples. Baseline dental examinations were conducted in Codegua in 1994, and follow-up examinations were conducted every year thereafter until 1999. In the control community of La Punta, dental examinations were conducted from 1997 through 1999. Data for decayed, missing, and filled dental surfaces (DMFS) from the two groups of children were compared at baseline. The 1994 data from Codegua and 1999 data from La Punta were used as baseline data. Data from Codegua (the experimental group) for the year 1994 were compared with 1999 data for DMFS. For La Punta (the control group), data from 1997 were compared with 1998 and 1999 data. Cross-sectional sample data from the two groups were compared for the year 1999.

TABLE 15.4 Age-Specific Mean Number of Decayed, Missing, and Filled Primary Tooth Surfaces and Standard Deviations (shown in parentheses) in 3- to 6-Year-Old Children Living in Codegua (Central Chile) by Year of Data Collection

Age (Years)	1994	1999	Reduction[a]	P[b]
3	3.11 (5.07)	1.52 (2.48)	51%	<0.06
4	5.40 (8.10)	3.18 (7.27)	41%	<0.05
5	13.75 (16.12)	3.03 (4.83)	78%	<0.01
6	19.21 (12.94)	5.63 (6.23)	71%	<0.01
3–6	11.78 (13.69)	3.35 (5.68)	72%	<0.01

[a]Percentage changes in indices.
[b]Mann-Whitney test.

Reprinted with permission from: Marino R, Villa A, Guerrero S. A community trial of fluoridated powdered milk in Chile. Community Dent Oral Epidemiol. 2011;29:435–442.

Baseline data for the two communities (Codegua 1994 and La Punta 1997) in terms of the mean number of DMFS were statistically similar. For the experimental group (Codegua) there was a clear pattern of improving situation between 1994 and 1999, whereas the situation in the control group (La Punta) remained unchanged. In Codegua, the mean number of DMFS in 3-year-old children decreased from 3.11 (Sd = 5.07) in 1994 to 1.52 (Sd = 2.48) in 1999, and in 6-year-old children it decreased from 19.21 (Sd = 12.94) in 1994 to 5.63 (Sd = 6.23) in 1999. In contrast, the mean number of DMFS in 3-year-old children in La Punta in 1997 was 2.25 (Sd = 3.05) and in 1999 it was 3.85 (Sd = 5.67). In 6-year-old La Punta children it was 8.67 (Sd = 8.57) in 1997 and 8.79 (Sd = 8.89) in 1999. Partial results of the study are presented in **TABLE 15.4**.

▶ **15.8 Natural Experiments**

Natural events or disasters, such as an earthquake, or the consequences of a manmade event, such as building a dam or a highway, can create the situation of a natural experiment. The effects of such an event or *natural intervention* can be studied by following the affected individuals over a period of time. Those affected by such events become the unwitting random *participants* in a natural experiment. In these situations, other populations that are similar in socioeconomic, demographic, and health characteristics to the study group but unexposed to the events in

question can be used as a control group. Examples of such events include the April 16, 2016 earthquake in Ecuador; the 2015 outbreak of Zika virus in Latin America and the United States; the April 26, 1986 Chernobyl nuclear power plant disaster in Ukraine; and the March 12, 2011 Fukushima Daiichi nuclear power plant disaster in Japan. Another large-scale example of a natural experiment is the December 26, 2004 Indian Ocean earthquake and tsunami that killed about 230,000 people in 14 countries, with more than 131,000 killed in Indonesia alone—the country most affected by the tsunami. These events have created large cohorts of individuals who were exposed to a natural intervention and could subsequently be studied in comparison with nonexposed populations. In the United States, lead contamination of the water supply system in Flint, Michigan, in 2014–2015 also created an unfortunate natural experiment. The long-term effects of exposure to lead in the residents of Flint in comparison with the populations of other similar towns with uncontaminated water supply systems may be studied in the coming years.

John Snow's investigation of cholera outbreaks in London in the early 1850s in communities supplied water by different companies provides a classic example of investigating the effects of a natural experiment. Longitudinal studies of the effects of radiation exposure in the populations of Hiroshima and Nagasaki compared with populations in other Japanese cities in the years following the dropping of atomic bombs near the end of World War II are also examples of natural experiment studies.[5,6]

▶ 15.9 Factorial Trials

RCTs are costly and technically challenging undertakings. Investigators can make the most of such opportunities by simultaneously testing more than one intervention. Experimental studies that involve exposure of the same study population to more than one intervention—say, two different drugs—are known as **factorial trials**.[7] Essentially, in a factorial trial, two or more RCTs are conducted on the same population at the same time.[8] For the same reason, recruitment of participants in factorial trials can be more challenging because participants have to meet the eligibility criteria for not just one intervention, but each of the interventions. The simultaneous exposure of subjects to multiple interventions also raises concerns about the safety of participants and the ethics of such exposure. **FIGURE 15.4** shows a conceptual model of a factorial trial with two interventions. In this scenario, the study population is randomly divided into the following four groups: (1) those who receive only the first intervention, (2) those who receive only the second intervention, (3) those who receive both interventions, and (4) those who do not receive any intervention.

Factorial trials are particularly advantageous as an efficient study design when the sample size is quite large because the effects of interventions are relatively more discernable and statistically more likely to be significant. This kind of study can be conducted either to investigate the independent (non-interactive) effects of two or more entirely different interventions if the outcomes of one intervention do not affect the outcomes of the other intervention, or to understand the interaction, positive or negative, between two or more interventions.[9] Because of the ability to investigate the interactive effects of two or more drugs when used simultaneously, factorial study design is particularly valuable in developing combination therapies when monotherapy with one or the other drug alone at a nontoxic dose is ineffective. A hypothetical example of drugs suitable for a factorial trial can be when one of the drugs is designed to lower blood cholesterol, and the other is intended to reduce prostatic enlargement in men. Often, the interventions or *factors* employed in factorial trials have only two levels—that is, they are binary variables of the intervention/no intervention (yes/no or positive/negative) variety. If a factorial trial involves only two interventions and both interventions are binary in nature (i.e., yes/no or positive/negative), then such a trial is called a 2 × 2 factorial trial because the study participants can only be divided into four possible groups.[8] **TABLE 15.5** illustrates this point with hypothetical data.

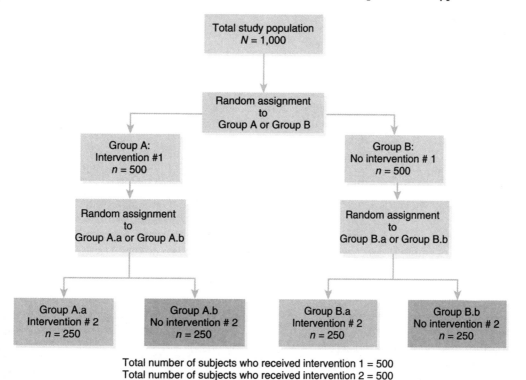

Total number of subjects who received intervention 1 = 500
Total number of subjects who received intervention 2 = 500
Subjects who received only intervention 1 = 250
Subjects who received only intervention 2 = 250
Subjects who received both interventions 1 & 2 = 250
Subjects who did not receive any intervention = 250

FIGURE 15.4 Conceptual model of a factorial trial with two interventions.
Modified from: Aschengrau A, Seage GR. Essentials of epidemiology in public health. 2nd ed. Boston, MA: Jones and Bartlett Publishers;2008.

TABLE 15.5 A Hypothetical Example of a 2 × 2 Factorial Trial with Four Possible Combinations of Subjects

		Intervention A		Total
		+	**−**	
Intervention B	**+**	**Group 1** A+ & B+ 30	**Group 2** A− & B+ 20	50
	−	**Group 3** A+ & B− 25	**Group 4** A− & B− 125	150
Total		55	145	200

🔎 *CASE STUDY 15.1: Randomized Control Trial – Chlorhexidine Bathing in ICUs to Prevent HAIs*

Modified from: Noto MJ, Domenico HJ, Byrne DW, Talbot T, Rice TW, Bernard GR, Wheeler AP. Chlorhexidine bathing and health care-associated infections: a randomized clinical trial. JAMA. 2015;313(4):369–378.

Infections acquired during a hospital stay result in a longer hospital stay, increased mortality, and higher costs of health care. Human skin is a large reservoir of microorganisms that can gain access to the bloodstream, urinary tract, and lungs through venous central lines, urinary catheters, and ventilator-connected tracheal tubes in seriously ill patients. Bathing intensive care unit (ICU) patients with broad-spectrum antimicrobial agents (i.e., disinfectants) such as chlorhexidine can reduce bacterial skin colonization and possibly provide some protection against nosocomial (healthcare-associated) infections. Once-daily bathing of patients with chlorhexidine is commonly done in U.S. hospitals with the intent to reduce the incidence of healthcare-associated infections (HAIs).

In this single-center, multiple-crossover, cluster RCT involving 9,340 patients in five ICUs at Vanderbilt University Medical Center in Nashville, Tennessee, Noto et al. investigated the effect of once-daily bathing of patients with chlorhexidine, a topical broad-spectrum antimicrobial (disinfectant) agent, in preventing HAIs. From July 2012 through July 2013, a total of 9,340 patients who were admitted to five adult ICUs participated in the study. Each of the five ICUs was treated as a cluster. In all five ICUs, the study started with a 2-week washout period during which all patients received a once-daily bath with a nonantimicrobial cloth.

For the purpose of assignment to the treatment (i.e., experimental) or control (i.e., comparison) group, each ICU was randomly designated as number 1 or 2. The ICUs designated number 1 started as treatment clusters (chlorhexidine), while those designated 2 started as comparison clusters (nonantimicrobial bathing). Within each cluster (i.e., ICU), all eligible patients were assigned to the same bathing regimen (chlorhexidine or nonantimicrobial). In the experimental clusters, all patients were given a once-daily bath with disposable cloths impregnated with 2% chlorhexidine, whereas patients in the control clusters were given a once-daily bath with disposable nonantimicrobial cloths. In the experimental clusters, bathing with chlorhexidine-impregnated cloths was continued for 10 weeks, followed by a 2-week washout period in which daily bathing was done with disposable nonantimicrobial cloths. In the control clusters, patients were given 10 weeks of nonantimicrobial bathing followed by 2-week washout period before switching over to chlorhexidine bathing for the next 10 weeks. At the completion of the 2-week washout period, the experimental cluster patients were switched over to the alternate bathing regimen with nonantimicrobial cloths. During the 1-year study period, each ICU switched three times between experimental and alternate bathing regimens.

Because of the different scent and color of chlorhexidine-impregnated and nonantimicrobial cloths, patients, physicians, and nurses could not be blinded regarding which patients were being given chlorhexidine baths (i.e., which were in the treatment group) and which were being given nonantimicrobial baths (i.e., which were in the control group). However, infection control staff who make the determination regarding the presence or absence of infection (based on a standard protocol) were blinded to the identity of patients in the treatment and control groups.

The prespecified primary outcome was the composite number of (1) central line-associated bloodstream infections (CLABSIs), (2) catheter-associated urinary tract infections (CAUTIs), (3) ventilator-associated pneumonia (VAP), and

(4) *Clostridium difficile* infections (CDIs). Outcomes of secondary interest included (1) rates of clinical cultures that tested positive for multidrug-resistant organisms, (2) contaminated blood cultures, (3) healthcare-associated bloodstream infections, (4) rates of primary outcome in each of the five ICUs, (5) in-hospital mortality, and (6) hospital and ICU length of stay. A total of 10,783 patients were admitted to the five ICUs during the study period, of which 1,443 were excluded from analysis because they were admitted during washout periods. Of the 9,340 patients included in the study, 4,488 were in the chlorhexidine bathing periods, and 4,852 were in control bathing periods. The results were compiled in terms of number of infections per 1,000 patient-days of treatment or alternate regimen. Data analysis were conducted on the basis of *intention-to-treat*, which means that patients were included in the analyses regardless of whether they completed the entire period of exposure to their assigned bathing regimen or, for whatever reason (e.g. death or discharge), participated only for a part of the duration. The demographic characteristics of patients in terms of median age, sex, and race; their distribution in different ICUs; and the clinical characteristics of the patients in the treatment and control groups were statistically quite comparable (i.e., differences were statistically not significant at $P = 0.05$). Infection rates of different types per 1,000 patients-days including CLABSI, CAUTI, CDI, and VAP in the two groups were also statistically comparable as was mean ICU and hospital length of stay. A total of 55 infections at a rate of 2.86 infections per 1,000 patient-days occurred during the chlorhexidine bathing period and 60 infections at a rate of 2.90 infections per 1,000 patient-days occurred during the control bathing period ($P = 0.95$). The researchers concluded that daily bathing of ICU patients with chlorhexidine did not reduce the incidence of HAIs and the study results do not support this practice.

Questions

Question 1. What were the primary and secondary outcomes in this study, and how were they measured in comparison with the control group?

Question 2. What differences in primary and secondary outcomes of treatment with 2% chlorhexidine as compared with nonantimicrobial cloth bathing were found by the study?

Question 3. Did chlorhexidine reduce the rate of HAIs? Was there any difference between the treatment and control groups regarding HAIs? If so, was the difference statistically significant?

Question 4. What were the overall findings of the study, and what are the implications of those findings?

Question 5. Why were the results presented in the form of (infections per 1,000 patient-days) rather than (infections per 100 or per 1,000 patients)?

Question 6. What is the purpose of blinding? Was this study blinded? If not, why not?

▶ 15.10 Summary

Because of their scientific rigor and application in testing new treatment modalities, randomized clinical trials are among the most commonly conducted epidemiologic investigations. However, because a new drug or technology is tested on a select group of individuals, investigators have to be careful about generalizing the findings of the study to the overall population of similar subjects. Additionally, the scientific rigor of experimental studies comes with the challenges of stringent application of eligibility criteria, difficulties in recruiting subjects, logistical challenges in follow-up, and potential for a bias introduced by a high proportion of intentional dropouts from the study or those lost to follow-up for other reasons. Experimental studies also pose ethical questions about exposing subjects to the risks of unknown adverse reactions to an experimental drug or a new technology, or withholding a potentially lifesaving remedy from the larger population of patients for a period of time during which the study is being conducted or its results are being evaluated. Many trials are terminated early because either too many subjects develop serious adverse reactions to the intervention being tested, or overwhelmingly positive results make it unethical to any longer withhold the benefits of a new drug from patients who may die in the interim.

Various forms of experimental studies discussed in this chapter have their own advantages and disadvantages. For example, community trials are somewhat easier to implement and offer the advantage of affecting the lives of many more individuals than typical RCTs, in which relatively smaller numbers of individuals are recruited. Crossover trials can be done with the participation of a relatively small group of individuals because the same individuals, at different times in the course of the trial, serve as both the experimental group and the control group. Likewise, factorial trials offer the benefit of testing two or more interventions in the same study without having to find different groups of eligible participants and spending more resources on conducting separate trials.

Over the years, industry-sponsored experimental studies became increasingly common, raising questions about potential conflict of interest on the part of investigators and the use of sound research methods in the design and conduct of these studies. However, during the last decade or two, IRBs, journal editors, academic medical centers, and federal regulatory authorities took notice of these issues and have taken steps, such as requiring a disclosure of funding sources on the part of researchers and a declaration of potential conflict of interest by authors submitting research manuscripts for publication. These steps have helped to restore the integrity of experimental research and to alleviate concerns about conflict of interest and intrinsic bias on the part of investigators.

References

1. Department of Health and Human Services. Clinical trials registration and results information submission: 42 CFR Part 11 [Docket Number NIH-2011-0003] RIN: 0925-AA55. 2016. Available from: https://s3.amazonaws.com/public-inspection.federalregister.gov/2016-22129.pdf
2. Viergever RF, Li K. Trends in global clinical trial registration: an analysis of number of registered clinical trials in different parts of the world from 2004 to 2013. BMJ. 2015;5(9):e008932.
3. Mausner JS, Kramer S. Epidemiology: an introductory text. London: W.B. Saunders Company; 1985.
4. Lutalo T, Kigozi G, Kimera E, et al. A randomized community trial of enhanced family planning outreach in Rakai, Uganda. Stud Fam Plann. 2010;41(1):55–61.
5. Boice JD. Studies of atomic bomb survivors: understanding radiation effects. JAMA. 1990;264(5):622–623.
6. Beebe GW, Hamilton HB. Review of thirty years study of Hiroshima and Nagasaki atomic bomb survivors. J Radiat Res. 1975; Sep. (Suppl.):149–164.
7. Piantadosi S. Factorial design in clinical trials. Encyclopedia of biostatistics. John Wiley & Sons; 2005 [cited 2018 June 4]. Available from: http://onlinelibrary.wiley.com/doi/10.1002/0470011815.b2a01025/pdf
8. Evans SR. Clinical trial structures. J Exp Stroke Transl Med. 2010;3(1):8–18.
9. Collins LM, Dziak JJ, Kugler KC, Trail JB. Factorial experiments: efficient tools for evaluation of intervention components. Am J Prev Med. 2014;47:498–504.

List of Acronyms

A

ABA	American Burn Association
ACHE	American College of Healthcare Executives
ACHI	Association for Community Health Improvement
ACS	Ambulatory Care Sensitive Condition
ACS	American College of Surgeons
ADA	Americans with Disabilities Act
ADL	Activities of Daily Living
AHA	American Hospital Association
AHRQ	Agency for Healthcare Research and Quality
AJCC	American Joint Committee on Cancer
AN	Advanced Neoplasia
APACHE	Acute Physiology and Chronic Health Evaluation
APS	Acute Physiologic Score
APS-DRG	All Payer Severity Adjusted Diagnosis Related Group
ASA	American Society of Anesthesiology
ASDR	Age-Specific Death Rate
ARI	Acute Respiratory Infection
ARDI	Alcohol-Related Disease Impact
ART	Antiretroviral Treatment
ART	Assisted Reproductive Technology

B

BASS	Bay Area Solvent Study
BMI	Body Mass Index
BMJ	British Medical Journal
BSI	Bloodstream Infection

C

CASPER	Community Assessment for Public Health Emergency Response
CAUTI	Catheter Associated Urinary Tract Infection
CBR	Crude Birth Rate
CDC	Centers for Disease Control and Prevention
CDI	Clostridium Difficile Infection
CDPH	California Department of Public Health
CDR	Crude Death Rate
CEA	Cost-Effectiveness Analysis
CEO	Chief Executive Officer
CFR	Case Fatality Rate
CHA	Community Health Assessment
CHA	Catholic Health Association
CHAMPUS	Civilian Health and Medical Program of the Uniformed Services
CHAT	County Health Assessment Team
CHC	Community Health Center
CHF	Congestive Heart Failure
CHIP	Children's Health Insurance Program
CHNA	Community Health Needs Assessment
CI	Confidence Interval
CIA	Central Intelligence Agency
CLABSI	Central Line Associated Bloodstream Infection
CLT	Cohort Life Table
CMS	Centers for Medicare and Medicaid Services
CON	Certificate of Need
COPD	Chronic Obstructive Pulmonary Disease
CPT	Current Procedural Terminology
CPSC	Consumer Products Safety Commission
CRC	Colorectal Cancer
CSDR	Cause-Specific Death Rate
CSR	Crude Survival Rate
CTG	Community Transformation Grant

D

DALY	Disability-Adjusted Life Year
DAWN	Drug Abuse Warning Network

DBCI	Digital Behavior Change Interventions
DHHS	Department of Health and Human Services
DMFS	Decayed, Missing, and Filled Dental Surfaces
DOJ	Department of Justice
DPCP	Detectable Preclinical Phase
DRG	Diagnosis Related Group
DUI	Driving Under the Influence

E

EBP	Evidence-Based Practice
EBM	Evidence-Based Management
ECDC	European Center for Disease Control and Prevention
ED	Emergency Department
EHR	Electronic Health Record
EHT	Elzinga-Hogarty Test
EID	Emerging Infectious Disease
EMO	Emergency Medical Officer
EMUP	Exceptional Medically Underserved Population
ENDS	Electronic Nicotine Delivery Systems
EPA	Environmental Protection Agency
ERR	Excess Readmission Ratio
ESI	Emergency Severity Index
EU	European Union
EVD	Ebola Virus Disease

F

FBI	Federal Bureau of Investigations
FCA	Floating Catchment Area
FDA	Food and Drug Administration
FHP	Family Health Program
FHWA	Federal Highway Administration
FIT	Fecal Immunochemical Test
FMR	Fetal Mortality Rate
FQHC	Federally Qualified Health Center
FTC	Federal Trade Commission
FTE	Fulltime Equivalent

G

GBD	Global Burden of Disease
GDM	Gestational Diabetes Mellitus
GDP	Gross Domestic Product
GIS	Geographic Information System

H

HAI	Healthcare Associated Infection
HALY	Health-Adjusted Life Year
HBV	Hepatitis B Virus
HCFA	Health Care Financing Administration
HCH	Health Care for the Homeless
HCUP	Healthcare Cost and Utilization Project
HEV	Human Entero Virus
HFMD	Hand, Foot, and Mouth Disease
HHI	Herfindahl-Hirsman Index
HHS	Health and Human Services
HIA	Health Impact Assessment
HICPAC	Healthcare Infection Control Practices Advisory Committee
HIE	Health Information Exchange
HIPAA	Health Insurance Portability and Accountability Act
HIV	Human Immunodeficiency Virus
HMO	Health Maintenance Organization
HP	Healthy People
HPSA	Health Professional Shortage Area
HPV	Human Papilloma Virus
HRA	Health Risk Appraisal
HRQOL	Health Related Quality of Life
HRR	Hospital Referral Region
HRRP	Hospital Readmission Reduction Program
HRS	Health and Retirement Study
HRSA	Health Resources and Services Administration
HSA	Hospital Service Area
HVBP	Hospital Value-Based Purchasing
HVBPS	Hospital Value-Based Purchasing Scorecard

I

IADL	Instrumental Activities of Daily Living
ICD	International Classification of Diseases
ICF	International Classification of Functioning, Disability and Health
ICMJE	International Committee of Medical Journal Editors
ICTRP	International Clinical Trials Registry Platform
ICU	Intensive Care Unit
IHI	Institute for Healthcare Improvement

ILI	Influenza-Like Illness
ILO	International Labor Organization
IMR	Infant Mortality Rate
IMU	Index of Medical Underservice
IND	Investigational New Drug
INICC	International Nosocomial Infection Control Consortium
IOM	Institute of Medicine
IOM	International Organization for Migration
IPPS	Inpatient Prospective Payment System
IQR	Inpatient Quality Reporting
IRB	Institutional Review Board
IRS	Internal Revenue Service
IVF	In-Vitro Fertilization

J

JAMA	Journal of the American Medical Association

K

KID	Kid's Inpatient Database
KP CHNA	Kaiser Permanente Community Health Needs Assessment

L

LEO	Law Enforcement Officer
LEOKA	Law Enforcement Officers Killed and Assaulted
LHI	Leading Health Indicators
LIFO	Little In From Outside
LOFI	Little Out From Inside
LOS	Length of Stay

M

MCH	Maternal and Child Health
MCD	Minor Civil Division
MERS	Middle East Respiratory Syndrome
MMR	Maternal Mortality Rate
MMWR	Morbidity and Mortality Weekly Report
MODS	Multiple Organ Dysfunction Score
MPFS	Medicare Physician Fee Schedule
MPM	Mortality Prediction Model
MRSA	Methicillin Resistant Staphylococcus Aureus

MUA	Medically Underserved Area
MUP	Medically Underserved Population

N

NCHS	National Center for Health Statistics
NEDS	National Emergency Department Sample
NEDSS	National Electronic Disease Surveillance System
NEISS	National Electronic Injury Surveillance System
NHANES	National Health and Nutrition Examination Survey
NHIS	National Health Interview Survey
NHS	National Health Service
NHSN	National Healthcare Safety Network
NHTSA	National Highway Traffic Safety Administration
NICE	National Institute for Health and Care Excellence
NIDA	National Institute on Drug Abuse
NIH	National Institutes of Health
NIS	Nationwide Inpatient Sample
NLMS	National Longitudinal Mortality Study
NMR	Neonatal Mortality Rate
NNDSS	National Notifiable Disease Surveillance System
NPSG	National Patient Safety Goal
NQF	National Quality Forum
NSAID	Nonsteroidal Anti-Inflammatory Drug
NSCH	National Survey of Children's Health
NSDUH	National Survey on Drug Use and Health
NSSP	National Syndromic Surveillance Program
NTD	Neglected Tropical Disease
NTI	National Trauma Institute
NVDRS	National Violent Death Reporting System

O

OECD	Organization for Economic Cooperation and Development
ODH	Ohio Department of Health
OMB	Office of Management and Budget
OR	Odds Ratio

P

P4P	Pay-For-Performance
PAE	Preventable Adverse Event
PCS	Procedure Coding System
PHAB	Public Health Accreditation Board
PKU	Phenylketonuria
PMR	Postneonatal Mortality Rate
PMR	Proportional Mortality Ratio
PPH	Potentially Preventable Hospitalization
PPO	Preferred Provider Organization
PPR	Potentially Preventable Readmission
PQRS	Physician Quality Reporting System
PY	Person Year

Q

QALY	Quality-Adjusted Life Year
QOF	Quality Outcomes Framework

R

RCT	Randomized Controlled Trial
RCT	Randomized Clinical Trial
RHC	Rural Health Clinic
RNA	Rapid Needs Assessment
RR	Relative Risk
RRS	Rapid Response System
RTCDA	Real-Time Clinical Deterioration Alert
RTI	Research Triangle Institute

S

SAPS	Simplified Acute Physiology Score
SARS	Sudden Acute Respiratory Syndrome
SASD	State Ambulatory Surgery and Services Databases
SCOPE	Surveillance and Control of Pathogens of Epidemiological Importance
SE	Standard Error
SEDD	State Emergency Department Databases
SEI	Socioeconomic Index
SHARE	Survey of Health, Aging, and Retirement in Europe
SID	State Inpatient Databases
SIGN	Scottish Intercollegiate Guidelines Network
SIM	Society, The Individual, and Medicine

SMR	Standardized Mortality Ratio
SMSA	Standard Metropolitan Statistical Areas
SNAP	Supplemental Nutrition Assistance Program
SOFA	Sepsis-Related Organ Failure Assessment
SRC	State Reportable Condition
SRE	Serious Reportable Events
SSI	Surgical Site Infection
STD	Sexually Transmitted Disease
STRIVE	Sierra Leone Trial to Introduce a Vaccine
SUD	Substance Use Disorder

T

TBI	Traumatic Brain Injury
TBSA	Total Body Surface Area

U

USPSTF	United States Preventive Services Taskforce
UTI	Urinary Tract Infection

V

VA	Veterans Affairs
VAP	Ventilator Associated Pneumonia
VHA	Veterans Health Administration
VMT	Vehicle-Miles Traveled

W

WC	Waist Circumference
WDI	World Development Indicators
WHO	World Health Organization
WHR	Waist-to-Hip Ratio
WISQARS	Web-based Injury Statistics Query and Reporting System

Y

YLD	Years Lived with Disability
YLL	Years of Life Lost
YPLL	Years of Potential Life Lost

Z

ZKV	Zika Virus

Glossary of Terms

Access The ability to make timely use of healthcare resources. Various dimensions of access include financial, geographic, and sociocultural.

Accountable care Coordinated and consolidated care in which healthcare providers are held accountable by tying payment for services to the quality of care.

Active errors Medical errors whose effects appear immediately or in a short time.

Active surveillance Surveillance that requires direct communication and solicitation of information from healthcare providers by the agency responsible for gathering data and monitoring the incidence and prevalence of diseases.

Acute A disease or exposure with sudden onset and short duration.

Adverse event A negative health-related development or outcome that occurred during or after the process of care and that may have resulted from the process of care rather than the underlying problem for which care was being given.

Agent A physical, chemical, or biologic entity that can cause disease in an animal or a person.

Age-specific death rate The number of deaths of people in a given age group in a given year per 1,000 or per 100,000 population in that age group. Also referred to as the *age-specific mortality rate.*

Allostatic load The cumulative effect of multiple interactive factors that affect the overall health of a person.

Ambulatory care sensitive conditions Medical conditions for which there should be no need to hospitalize patients if the condition is appropriately managed in outpatient settings.

Attack rate The proportion of individuals or subjects who got sick after being exposed to an infectious agent.

Behavioral epidemiology The investigation of the distribution and determinants of health-related behaviors in populations.

Bias An intentional or unintentional prejudice against or in favor of someone or something; a prejudice introduced into the findings of a study because of a flaw in study design.

Binary variable A variable that can have only two possible values.

Body mass index A measure of body fat in adult men and women age ≥20 years, derived by dividing body weight in kilograms by the height of the person in meters squared (i.e., kg/m^2).

Brain injury An injury that disrupts the normal function of the brain.

Burden of disease The overall impact of a disease or a group of diseases in a population. It is estimated by counting the number of existing or new cases of a disease during a specified period or the number of deaths resulting from the disease, or by estimating the overall economic loss resulting from the disease in terms of years of potential life lost (YPLL) or health-adjusted life-years (HALYs) lost.

Burn Injury caused by too much exposure to thermal, electrical, chemical, or radioactive agents. Most burns result from fire and scalding.

Carrier A person or animal that does not show the signs and symptoms of a disease but harbors the infectious agent and acts as a vehicle of transmission.

Case-control studies Observational epidemiologic investigations that compare past exposure to a risk factor in those with the disease and those without.

Case fatality rate/ratio The proportion of cases of a disease that result in death. It is an indicator of the virulence of a disease.

Case mix The unique mix of the variety and severity of patients who receive care from a given provider or constitute a specific patient population. The mix represents the demographic and socioeconomic characteristics of patients as well as the variety and severity of medical conditions they present with.

Case mix index An index derived by aggregating the relative weights assigned to the diagnosis-related groups (DRGs) of patients treated at a hospital as a measure of the total resources required to treat those patients. The index serves as an overall measure of the complexity of patients treated at a healthcare facility (hospital). Higher indexes are linked to higher reimbursement rates from Medicare and private insurance companies.

Case report A descriptive account of the clinical presentation and demographic characteristics of patients of a previously unknown disease or an unusual presentation of a known disease, including the circumstances in which the disease may have been acquired.

Community Assessment for Public Health Emergency Response (CASPER) A toolkit developed by the U.S. Centers for Disease Control and Prevention to assist public health officials in assessing the healthcare needs of a population after a disaster.

Categorical surveillance Also called *sentinel surveillance*, categorical surveillance involves collection of information on a specific event or disease regarding which information may not be ordinarily available through routine passive surveillance.

Categorical variable A variable that represents an attribute or a characteristic of someone or something.

Cause-specific death rate The total number of deaths in a population attributed to a specific cause in a given year. Also referred to as the *cause-specific mortality rate*.

Chronic A disease or exposure that lasts from weeks to years. The U.S. National Center for Health Statistics defines a chronic condition as one that lasts 3 months or longer.

Cohort A group of people who have some shared experience in common.

Cohort life table A life table that starts at birth and follows the mortality experience of a group of individuals in consecutive calendar years until the last person in the cohort dies.

Cohort studies Observational epidemiologic investigations that compare the frequency of disease in those exposed to a risk factor and those not exposed.

Confidence interval A range of data or values that has a specified probability that a given value lies within that range or interval.

Commitment index Out of the total number of patients admitted to or discharged from a hospital, the proportion that originated from a given geographic area.

Common source exposure Exposure of a number of individuals to a chemical or biologic agent from the same source or place, but not necessarily at the same time.

Common source outbreak An outbreak of an infectious disease resulting from the exposure of multiple individuals to a biologic agent from the same place, experience, or event.

Community A group of people living in the same geographic area who have some common characteristics or interests, and is perceived or perceives itself as distinct in some respect from the larger society in which it exists.

Community trials Randomized clinical trials in which the unit of analysis is entire communities rather than individuals.

Comorbidities Simultaneous presence of two or more chronic conditions in a patient. Diseases that exist simultaneously in a patient in addition to the index condition that is the focus of treatment or the subject of a study.

Comorbidity measures Comorbidity measures were developed by the U.S. Agency for Healthcare Research and Quality (AHRQ) and identify coexisting medical conditions that are likely to have existed prior to the hospital stay and are not directly related to the principal diagnosis or the main reason for hospital admission.

Comparison group Also known as the *control group*, the group of participants in an experimental study not exposed to the intervention whose effects are being investigated.

Confounder variable A third variable that can lead to erroneous conclusions about an association or a "cause-and-effect" relationship between two other variables because it is related to both of those variables.

Continuous variable A variable that can potentially have an infinite number of fractional values.

Control charts Graphs in which data points are plotted to understand how a process changes over time.

Control group Also known as the *comparison group*, the group of participants in an experimental study who are not exposed to the intervention whose effects are being investigated.

Convalescent period The period of recovery from a disease.

Correlation A relationship between two variables such that the value of one is affected positively or negatively by a change in the value of the other.

Critical point A point in the natural history of a disease after which the onset of treatment cannot attain full recovery and total avoidance of complications or long-term disability.

Cross-sectional study Epidemiologic investigations usually conducted in the form of population surveys to give a snapshot of information regarding participant characteristics, exposure to risk factors, and health conditions in a population.

Crossover trials Randomized clinical trials in which, after a period of initial exposure and follow up, interventions are switched between the experimental and comparison groups.

Crude birth rate The total number of live births per 1,000 population in a given year.

Crude death (mortality) rate The total number of deaths from all causes per 100,000 population in a given year. Also referred to as the *crude mortality rate*.

Crude survival rate The proportion or percentage of cases of a disease that survive for a specified period regardless of the cause of death.

Cumulative incidence Also known as *incidence risk* or *incidence proportion*, it is a measure of the probability of getting a disease during a specified period. Alternatively, it is the proportion of the at-risk population who got the disease during a specified period.

Current Procedural Terminology A nationwide system of numeric codes used in the United States to bill insurance companies and the Centers for Medicare and Medicaid Services for procedures carried out by healthcare providers in outpatient or ambulatory care settings.

Death Permanent and irreversible cessation of all vital functions, including those of the heart, lungs, and brain.

Decile Each of the parts when a rank-ordered set of values or observations is divided into 10 equal parts.

Demand An insistent and urgent request made as if by right. In economics, it means the consumer's willingness to pay a price for a good or service, or the amount of a good or service that can be sold fully without any left over.

Determinants of disease All the intrinsic factors, such as genetic mutations, or extrinsic factors, such as microorganisms and chemicals in the environment, whose presence or absence can make individuals or groups of individuals sick.

Determinants of health All the genetic, socioeconomic, racial, behavioral, and environmental factors that make a person more or less vulnerable to disease or illness and affect the overall health of a person.

Direct standardization Derivation of comparable overall morbidity or mortality rates in two or more populations by applying age-, race-, or sex-stratified rates of such populations to a reference population. This is done to adjust for differences in the age, race, or sex composition of different populations.

Disability A partial or complete physical or mental impairment that limits the ability to perform normal tasks and activities of life and work.

Disability-adjusted life years Based on the time before death lived in a state of less than full health, it is an overall measure of the burden of a disease or a group of diseases and is reported as the number of years lost due to poor health, disability, or early death.

Discrete variable A numeric variable that can only have nonfractional values.

Dispersion In statistics, dispersion refers to the spread of a data set. It is a measure of the degree to which values of a variable differ from a fixed value such as the mean.

Ebola virus disease A relatively rare but frequently fatal disease caused in humans by four of the five strains of *Ebolavirus* genus of the family *Filoviridae*.

E-cigarette Battery-operated electronic cigarettes that deliver vapors of nicotine by heating liquid nicotine.

Ecological bias Also known as *ecological fallacy*, the mistake of extrapolating to individual members of the population the findings of an ecological study and the risk of population-level health outcomes associated with exposure to a risk factor.

Ecological fallacy Also known as *ecological bias*, the mistake of extrapolating to individual members of the population the findings of an ecological study and the risk of population-level health outcomes associated with exposure to a risk factor.

Ecological studies Population studies that investigate the effects of some phenomenon or intervention in a population over time or compare such effects across different populations.

Electronic nicotine delivery systems Battery-operated devices in the form of electronic cigarettes, pipes, and hookahs that heat and deliver flavored or nonflavored aerosolized vapors of e-liquid nicotine and other chemicals.

Elzinga–Hogarty test A test to determine the geographic boundaries of a market based on the principles of *Little In From Outside* (LIFO) and *Little Out From Inside* (LOFI).

Endemic The constant and continuous presence of a disease, particularly an infectious disease, in a geographic area.

Environment (physical environment) The physical conditions, including air, temperature, light, humidity, water, and other conditions that play a role in the transmission of an infectious disease.

Environmental heterogeneity Variation in the nature, duration, and intensity of exposure to environmental factors across individuals and populations.

Epidemic The occurrence of new cases of a disease in a population during a specified period clearly in excess of its usual occurrence.

Epidemiology The study of the distribution and determinants of diseases and injuries in human populations.

Evidence-based management Making managerial decisions that are based on the best available qualitative and quantitative evidence.

Evidence-based practice Making decisions through explicit use of the best available evidence from multiple sources.

Excess readmission ratio A ratio of a hospital's actual readmission rate and its expected readmission rate as an indicator of the quality of care provided by the hospital.

Experimental group In an experimental study such as a randomized clinical/controlled trial, the group that is exposed to the intervention whose effects are being investigated.

Experimental studies Studies in which one or more groups of subjects are intentionally exposed to a risk factor, treatment, or some other intervention to investigate the beneficial or harmful effects of such exposure.

Exposure Intentional or accidental subjection of humans or other animals to a physical, biologic, chemical, or psychological factor that can produce harmful or beneficial health effects in the subject.

Factorial trials Randomized clinical/controlled trials in which the health effects of two or more interventions are simultaneously investigated by exposing the participants to entirely different interventions whose clinical effects are expected not to influence one another.

Fatality A death, especially when it is caused by an accident, infection, occupational disorder, or a large-scale disaster.

Fecal transplant Rectal administration of diluted liquefied feces from a healthy donor into the colon of the patient to restore populations of normal intestinal microorganisms.

Fetal mortality rate The number of fetal deaths in a population in a given year per 1,000 live births and fetal deaths.

Firearm A handheld weapon that uses explosive materials to propel at high speed an object toward a person, place, or target.

Frequency A measure of how often something happens during a specified period of time in a given population, sample of population, or a geographic area.

Garbage can model A theory of organizational choice and decision making suggesting that the decision-making process in organizations is disorganized, chaotic, and irrational, with disconnect between problems and proposed solutions.

Genetic heterogeneity Variation in the genetic makeup of individuals and populations.

Geographic information systems Computer systems designed to integrate and analyze spatially or geographically referenced data in relation to the surface of the Earth.

Geographic market A geographic area, whether defined by a commonly recognized administrative boundary such as county line or zip code, a specified radius around an organization, or some other parameter such as population density, in which an organization does business and draws clientele from. The delineation or demarcation of a geographic market is important in consideration of merger proposals and potential violation of antitrust laws.

Gestational diabetes mellitus Diabetes diagnosed during pregnancy; often a precursor of type 2 diabetes later in life and a risk factor for pregnancy-related hypertension in women and birth defects in newborns.

Health A state of physical, mental, and social well-being in which all functions of the body and mind are performing normally.

Health geography Also known as *medical geography*, it is the branch of epidemiology that investigates the impact of geography and climate on population health.

Health index A numeric measure of the overall health of a person or a population based on aggregated scores for survey responses to a battery of questions or a composite of scores on various parameters of population health. Examples of different kinds of health indices include urban health index and community health index.

Health outcome Change in the health of an individual, group of people, or population that is attributable to an intervention or series of interventions (regardless of whether such an intervention was intended to change health status).

Health Professional Shortage Areas Urban and rural counties or ZIP codes in the United States designated by the U.S. Health Resources and Services Administration as shortage areas for doctors and other healthcare professionals.

Healthcare-associated infection Also known as a hospital-acquired infection or a nosocomial infection. An infection originating in a medical facility and affecting a patient or staff member in whom the infection was not present at the time of arrival at the facility, including infections that are acquired in a medical facility but are manifested after discharge.

Herfindahl–Hirschman index An index to assess the level of competition among healthcare providers in a geographic area.

Historical cohort studies Also known as *retrospective cohort studies*, epidemiologic investigations that use past medical, demographic, and other records to understand changes in the health status of participants going forward from a time in the past.

Homicide The legal, technical, or journalistic term for murder.

Hospital readmission The return and admission of a patient to a hospital (or some other inpatient care facility) shortly after discharge—usually defined as within 30 days of discharge.

Hospital service area The geographic area or collection of ZIP codes whose residents receive most of their inpatient care from a given hospital or the hospitals in that area.

Host An animal or person in which an infectious agent harbors, grows, and multiplies.

Hypothesis A statistically testable proposition that may or may not be true.

Incidence The occurrence of new cases of a disease in a population.

Incidence density Also known as *incidence rate*, it is the number of new cases of a disease (usually an uncommon or rare disease) in at-risk populations in a defined period in an "open cohort" or "dynamic cohort study" in which the duration of follow-up varies from one subject to another and is reported as the number of new cases of a disease per 1,000 or per 100,000 person-years (PYs) of follow-up.

Incidence rate A measure of the occurrence or frequency of a disease reported in terms of the number of new cases of a disease in at-risk populations per unit of time. In an "open cohort" or "dynamic cohort" study, incidence rate is called *incidence density* and is reported in terms of follow-up period such as per 1,000 or per 100,000 person-years (PYs). In such studies, the denominator can also be expressed in other units such as person-miles traveled.

Incidence rate ratio Also known as *relative risk* or *rate ratio*, it is the ratio of the incidence of disease in subjects exposed and not exposed to a risk factor in a study when all subjects are not followed for the same length of time and the rate of occurrence of new cases or incidence rate is expressed in person-years. Alternatively, it is the ratio of incidence rate in two different populations.

Incubation period The time elapsed from the moment of exposure to a pathogenic organism to the first appearance of the sign and/or symptoms of a disease.

Indirect standardization Derivation of comparable overall morbidity or mortality rates in two or more populations by applying age-, race-, or sex-stratified rates of a reference population to those stratifications in each of the populations being compared. This is done to adjust for differences in the age, race, or sex composition of different populations.

Infant mortality rate The number of deaths of children before 1 year of life per 1,000 live births.

Infection A disease caused by a microorganism.

Infectious A microorganism capable of being transmitted from one host to another and producing disease.

Infectivity The ability of a microorganism to invade and multiply in the body of a host.

Infestation The lodgment and reproduction of parasites, such as worms or arthropods, on the skin of an animal or person.

Integrated healthcare delivery Delivery of a comprehensive menu or full spectrum of services under one umbrella organization comprising a network of multiple organizations or providers.

International Classification of Diseases A standardized system of assigning codes to diseases, injuries, abnormalities, and various signs and symptoms for the purpose of classification, reimbursement, and statistical analysis. It also facilitates comparison of morbidity and mortality data within and across countries.

Invasiveness The ability of a microorganism to invade and multiply in the body of a host.

Latent errors Medical errors whose effects can remain dormant for a relatively long time.

Lead-time The length of time from disease detection through screening to the first appearance of signs and symptoms.

Lead-time bias The bias introduced in the estimation of survival time because of the overestimation of survival time in patients of a disease when the disease is detected earlier than usual (and prior to the appearance of sign and symptoms) with the help of a screening test, as compared to those in whom the disease is clinically diagnosed after the appearance of signs and symptoms.

Length bias A bias introduced in the estimation of survival time of patients of a disease; length bias is attributed to a treatment or to the benefits of a screening program because of the naturally slower progression of disease in some individuals as compared with others.

Length of stay Time spent in an inpatient facility from the time of admission to the time of discharge.

Level I trauma center A tertiary care medical center in the United States that meets specific local or state criteria to provide optimal advanced care for trauma patients.

Life expectancy at birth The average number of years that children born in a particular year in a given population are expected to live.

Life's Simple 7 Seven behavioral health factors targeted by the American Heart Association to achieve its goal of 20%

improvement in the cardiovascular health of all Americans by 2020.

Little In From Outside (LIFO) A measure of the size of a geographic market based on the proportion of hospitalized patients at local hospitals who came from outside the geographic area.

Little Out From Inside (LOFI) A measure of the size of a geographic market based on the proportion of patients from an area who receive inpatient care at hospitals outside the geographic area.

Management The act, manner, or practice of managing, supervising, or controlling.

Managerial epidemiology The use of epidemiologic tools in making decisions, designing health services, and formulating health policy to meet the needs of target populations.

Marital status A person's state of being single, married, separated, divorced, or widowed.

Market share The proportion of all hospitalizations or discharges from a geographic area that occurred at a particular hospital.

Maternal mortality rate/ratio The total number of deaths of women due to pregnancy-related causes per 100,000 live births in a population during a given period.

Mean A measure of the central tendency of a data set obtained by dividing the sum of the values of a variable by the number of observations in the data set.

Median The value at the midpoint of a data set that is arranged in a numerically ascending or descending order.

Medical care model A model of healthcare delivery that puts a greater premium on health recovery through treatment and rehabilitation rather than preventing disease and promoting health by focusing on behavioral and socioeconomic determinants of health.

Medical error An act of commission or omission that results in the failure of a planned activity to be completed in the manner it was intended or the use of a wrong activity to achieve an objective.

Medical geography Also known as *health geography*, it is the branch of epidemiology that investigates the impact of geography and climate on population health.

Medically Underserved Areas Geographic areas or markets in the United States designated by the U.S. Health Resources and Services Administration as medically underserved and eligible for some federal grants.

Medically Underserved Populations Population groups such as an ethnic or racial minority within a specified geographic area in the United States designated by the U.S. Health Resources and Services Administration as medically underserved and eligible for special considerations and incentives to enhance the number of healthcare providers or some federal grants.

Mental health The psychological well-being or condition of a person.

Metabolic equivalent An indicator of the functional capacity of a person assessed by measuring the amount of oxygen consumed per minute.

mHealth The use of mobile health technologies to monitor and improve health outcomes.

Microbe Also known as a *microorganism*, it is a minute living body not perceptible to the naked eye, such as bacteria, fungi, and viruses.

Microbiome The mix of microorganisms unique to an individual or an environment.

Microorganism Also known as a *microbe*, it is a minute living body not perceptible to the naked eye, such as bacteria, fungi, and viruses.

Mode The most common value in a data set.

Multi-group study design Ecological studies in which populations in different ZIP codes, counties, cities, or other geographic districts are studied and compared.

My Life Check An online self-assessment tool developed by the American Heart Association for individuals to enter demographic and lifestyle data to receive instantly a cardiovascular health status report.

National Electronic Injury Surveillance System A national probability sample of hospitals in the United States and its territories from which information for all emergency hospital visits involving an injury associated with consumer products is collected by the U.S. Consumer Products Safety Commission. The total number of product-related injuries treated in hospital emergency rooms nationwide can be estimated from this sample.

National Healthcare Safety Network A commonly used healthcare-associated infection tracking system established by the U.S. Centers for Disease Control and Prevention.

National Violent Death Reporting System A state level data collection system developed, sponsored, and supported by the U.S. Centers for Disease Control and Prevention to collects data on all violence-related deaths, including homicides, suicides, unintentional firearms deaths, legal deaths (those resulting from the use of deadly force by law enforcement authorities but excluding executions), and deaths from undetermined intent.

Natural experiment A natural event or phenomenon, such as an earthquake or flood, whose health effects can subsequently be studied in individuals and populations.

Need Something that is necessary but lacking or is required because it is important.

Needs assessment A systematic process of assessing the prevailing situation, setting priorities, and allocating resources.

Neonatal mortality rate The number of deaths of children during the first 28 days after birth per 1,000 live births in a given period.

Never event Medical errors that are clearly identifiable, preventable, and serious in their consequences for patients.

Nonprogrammed decisions Decisions for problems that are unprecedented and demand innovative solutions.

Normal distribution A symmetrical bell-shaped curve that represents the distribution of a quantitative variable such that exactly half of the data values are above the mean and half are below the mean.

Null hypothesis A supposition that there is no statistically significant difference in the outcome of interest in the groups being compared, and any observed difference is due to a chance occurrence.

Observational studies Studies in which subjects are not manipulated or exposed to an intervention in an attempt to alter the natural course of events or to test the effectiveness or safety of a new medication, procedure, or technology.

Observed survival rate The proportion or percentage of patients still alive at a specified time after the diagnosis of a disease.

Outbreak A rapidly spreading and relatively short-lived infectious disease epidemic in a well-defined population.

Outcome (health outcome) A change in the health status of an individual or a population that can be attributed to one or more interventions regardless of whether such an intervention was intended to affect the health status of that individual or population.

Parallel trials Randomized clinical/controlled trials in which subjects assigned to the experimental and comparison groups are given their respective interventions and followed over time without being exposed to the other intervention.

Passive surveillance Surveillance that involves voluntary reporting of information to local or state public health agencies by healthcare providers without any penalties for failing to provide information.

Pathogen A microorganism that can cause disease in humans or other animals.

Pathogenesis The biologic mechanisms or processes through which a microorganism causes disease.

Pathogenicity The ability of an organism to cause damage or disease in the host.

Patient-centered care Coordinated, integrated, and responsive care that is focused entirely on the needs of patients and their families by respecting their values and concerns and by informing, educating, and involving them in decisions related to their care.

Patient Protection and Affordable Care Act The U.S. healthcare reform law, also known as Obamacare, enacted in 2010 primarily to increase health insurance coverage for the uninsured.

Pay for Performance (P4P) Financial incentives given to healthcare providers to improve the quality of care and health outcomes.

Percentile The relative position of a value, such as height or weight of a person, on a scale of 0 to 100.

Period life table A life table that is based on a hypothetical cohort of newborns to whom age-specific mortality rates of a known population are applied to derive the expected number of deaths and survivorship at each age interval.

Phase I clinical trials Initial human safety studies involving small numbers of nonrandomized healthy volunteers to assess the safety, side effects, and safe dose range of a new drug or technology.

Phase II clinical trials Randomized or nonrandomized studies conducted to assess the efficacy of a new drug or technology and to further evaluate its safe short-term use in humans.

Phase III clinical trials Double- or triple-blind randomized clinical trials with relatively large numbers of patients of a disease to understand the long-term safety, toxicity, and efficacy of a new drug.

Planning The process by which a course of action is selected to achieve specific outcomes.

Point source Exposure of a group of individuals to a common source of infection at a specific point in time. The resulting outbreak is referred to as a point source outbreak.

Population All individuals living in a specific geographic area or a group of individuals who share a common characteristic and from which a sample of individuals can be drawn.

Population health A field of study that examines the health-related characteristics, health status, and distribution of health outcomes in a population.

Population health model A model of organizing and delivering services that focuses on the well-being of the entire person in the context of one's existence as a social animal rather than dealing with an episode of illness or disease in an isolated manner.

Postneonatal mortality rate The number of deaths of children from the 29th day after birth to 1 year of age per 1,000 live births in a given year.

Potentially preventable hospitalizations Those admissions to hospitals for acute or chronic conditions that, if adequately managed in ambulatory care settings, including primary care, should not result in a hospital admission.

Predictive value negative The probability that a person with a negative screening test truly does not have the disease for which he or she was tested—that is, the proportion of individuals who, among all those who tested negative, actually do not have the disease.

Predictive value positive The probability that a person with a positive screening test truly has the disease for which the person was tested—that is, the proportion of individuals who, among all those who tested positive, actually have the disease.

Prevalence The total number of cases of a disease in a population at a specific point in time or during a specified period.

Preventable hospitalization A hospital admission that could have been avoided if the medical condition(s) had been appropriately treated in outpatient settings.

Preventive trials Randomized clinical trials conducted to investigate the preventive ability of a new drug, vaccine, or technology.

Primary prevention Activities designed to prevent the occurrence or development of a disease.

Process Sequential steps taken or activities carried out to achieve a particular objective.

Prodromal stage The early stage of a disease in which nonspecific symptoms such as malaise, aches, and fatigue appear before full-blown specific symptoms and signs appear.

Programmed decisions Decisions that address problems that are repetitive in nature and encountered frequently in organizations.

Propagated outbreak An outbreak that occurs as a result of continued or sequential exposure of susceptible healthy individuals to sick or apparently healthy germ-carrying individuals.

Prophylactic trials Randomized clinical trials conducted to investigate the prophylactic potential of a new drug or technology.

Proportion A proportion or fraction is the magnitude or quantity of something in relation to the whole.

Proportional mortality The proportion of all deaths in a population that occurred from a particular disease or condition during a specified period.

Proportional mortality ratio A ratio or comparison of the proportional mortality from a specific cause in an occupational or other group with the proportional mortality from the same cause in the general population.

Prospective cohort studies Longitudinal observational studies in which subjects exposed and not exposed to a risk factor are followed over time to see if there are statistically significant differences in the health outcomes of the two groups.

P **value** The probability that observed statistical differences between two or more groups or sets of observations may have occurred just by chance.

Quality-adjusted life years An overall measure of the burden of disease that combines the quality and duration of life lived. It is commonly used to assess the comparative advantage of medical technologies and public health interventions in terms of health improvement resulting from each intervention.

Quartile Each of the parts when a rank-ordered set of observations is divided into four equal parts, with each part being equal to 25% of values.

Quintile Each of the parts when a rank-ordered set of observations is divided into five equal parts, with each part being equal to 20% of values.

Race A construct based on different morphological characteristics to distinguish between populations, which also implies genetic differences between populations within a species. Many scientists believe that meaningful or significant genetic differences between racial groups do not exist.

Randomized clinical trials Experimental studies in which participants are randomly assigned to two or more groups and exposed to some newly developed drug or technology to assess its safety and efficacy.

Range The interval between the largest and the smallest values in a data set representing the spread or dispersion of the data set.

Rate The number of times an event occurs in a population during a defined period.

Rate ratio Also known as *relative risk*, or *incidence rate ratio*, it is the ratio of the incidence rate in the exposed with the incidence rate in the unexposed.

Ratio A comparison of the magnitude of two different numbers or indication of the number of times one quantity is contained in another.

Regression A statistical technique to examine the relationship of one or more *independent* variables with a *dependent* variable, with the assumption that the values of the latter depend on the values of the former.

Relative risk Also known as *rate ratio*, *risk ratio*, or *incidence rate ratio*, it is the ratio of the incidence or risk of disease in a given period in subjects exposed and not exposed to a risk factor.

Relevance index The proportion of patients from a geographic area who use a particular hospital.

Reliability The ability of a test or survey instrument to produce the same results when administered again to the same subject at another occasion.

Retrospective cohort studies Also known as *historical cohort studies*, epidemiologic investigations in which past medical, demographic, and other types of records are used to understand how the health status of participants changed going forward from a point in time in the past.

Risk management The process of monitoring, assessing, and avoiding medical errors and adverse medical events.

Risk ratio Also known as *relative risk*, it is the ratio of the incidence or risk of disease in a given period in subjects exposed and not exposed to a risk factor in cohort studies in which the follow-up period for all participants is assumed to be the same.

Run charts Line graphs of data plotted over time to monitor quality and to understand how it changes over time.

Sample A subset of observations selected from a data set or a population to show what the entire data set or population looks like.

Screening The identification of a disease in a preclinical stage by the application of tests or procedures that are relatively simple, inexpensive, and quick.

Secondary prevention Activities designed to alter the course of a disease through early detection and intervention.

Sensitivity The ability of a screening test to correctly identify those with asymptomatic preclinical disease (i.e., the proportion of those with asymptomatic disease who are correctly labeled as such by the test). In other words, it is the probability that the screening test will be positive if asymptomatic preclinical disease is present.

Sentinel event A patient safety event that calls for immediate investigation and response because of the potential for death, disability, or permanent harm to the patient.

Sentinel surveillance Involves collection of information on a specific event or disease regarding which information may not be ordinarily available through passive surveillance; also called *categorical surveillance*.

Service area A specified geographic area or locality in which a healthcare organization provides services or from which a health insurance plan accepts potential enrollees.

Severity of disease The seriousness of a disease or medical condition in terms of the risk of complications, death, and disability.

Socioeconomic determinants of health Socioeconomic factors such as education, income, ethnicity, and social class that affect the health of individuals and populations.

Socioeconomic status A descriptive term for a person's place in society based on such criteria as income, occupation, level of education, or place of residence.

Specificity The ability of a screening test to rule out correctly those without a detectable disease for which screening is being done. In other words, it is the probability that the screening test will be negative if the disease is not present.

Standard deviation A statistical measure of the dispersion of values of a quantitative variable around the mean.

Structure The arrangement and interaction of the multiple components or parts of a complex system.

Study group The group of participants in an experimental study who are exposed to the intervention whose effects are being studied.

Syndromic surveillance Monitoring the frequency of specified sets of clinical features in a population with or without a specific diagnosis.

***t*-test** A statistical test to compare the mean of a sample with the mean of the entire population (1 sample *t*-test) or to compare the means of two independent samples from two different populations (two-samples *t*-test).

Tertiary prevention Activities designed to restore function and avoid complications or permanent disability resulting from a disease.

Therapeutic trials Randomized clinical trials conducted to assess the therapeutic potential of a new modality of treatment or pharmaceutical product.

Total service area The geographic district or the collection of ZIP codes that produce most—between 80% and 90%—of a hospital's admissions or discharges.

Transmission The mechanisms through which an infectious agent is passed from a carrier or sick animal or person to another host.

Trauma A physical injury caused by an external force or an emotional or psychological shock that may disturb feelings or behavior of a person.

Type I error Erroneous rejection of the null hypothesis when it is true.

Type II error Erroneous acceptance of the null hypothesis when it is false.

Unmet need The gap between the type and amount of goods and services needed and what is currently available.

Validity The accuracy of a test (i.e., the ability of a test to identify correctly a person who does or does not have the disease of interest). The term encompasses both sensitivity and specificity of a test.

Variable A measurable factor or characteristic that can have more than one value.

Vector An insect such as a mosquito or a flea that passes the infectious organism from one host to another.

Virulence The severity or intensity of disease caused by a pathogen. Case fatality ratio is a good indicator of the virulence of a disease.

Waist circumference A measurement taken around the abdomen at the level of the superior iliac crest to assess the level of abdominal obesity as an indicator of potential health problems including the risk of heart disease.

Years of potential life lost Based on average life expectancy in a population, an estimate of the number of years not lived by those in a population who died prematurely. It is commonly used to rank-order leading causes of death in a population.

z-test A statistical test to assess whether data from a sample of the population are similar to those for the overall population. It is used when the standard deviation of data for the entire population is not known.

Zika virus An arbovirus that is transmitted from one person to another by the bite of an infected *Aedes aegypti* mosquito and causes the Zika virus disease.

Index

Note: Page numbers followed by *f* or *t* refer to figures or tables, respectively.

A

acceptability, measurement of quality, 175
access to health services, 201, 232*t*
    determinants, 237–238
accessibility, measurement of quality, 175
accountable care, 16
active errors, 177
active medical errors, 177
active surveillance, 266–267
acute diseases or conditions, 131
adjustment of rates, 75–77
administrative decisions, patient
        outcomes, 7–9
adverse events, 177
age, demographic characteristic, 86–87
agents, 131
age-specific death {mortality} rate
        (ASDR), 67
    population health, 67
alcohol abuse, behavioral epidemiology,
        112–114
allostatic loads, 20
alternative hypothesis, 285
Altschuld, J.W., 205
Alzheimer, Alois, 97
ambulatory care sensitive conditions,
        179, 180*t*, 199*f*, 292
ASDR (age-specific death {mortality}
        rate), population health, 67
attack rate, 131

B

basic statistical concepts
    confidence interval, 284
    correlation, 285
    deciles, 282
    frequency, 282
    hypothesis, 284
    measures of central tendency in data,
        282–283
    measures of spread or dispersion of
        data, 283
    normal distribution, 283–284
    P values, 285
    percentile, 282
    population, 281
    quartiles, 282

    quintiles, 282
    regression, 285–286
    sample, 281
    Type I and II errors, 285
    variable, 281–282
Bayesian probabilities, 4
behavioral epidemiology, 106–107
    alcohol and substance abuse, 112–114
    BMI (body mass index), 107, 110,
        111*f*, 118, 119*t*, 120*t*
    cardiovascular disease, 114–115
    diabetes, 115–118
    incentives for providers, 116–117
    obesity and poor nutrition, 110–112
    patient incentives to promote healthy
        behavior, 115–116
    physical activity, 107–108
    risk of mortality, 118–120
    smoking, 108–110
    waist circumference, 118–120
Bertillon, Jacques, 51
bias, 312–313
    observational studies, 312–313
big data, 241
"Bills of Mortality" (Graunt), 51
binary variable, 282
Blue Sky scenario, managerial
        epidemiology, 6–7
BMI (body mass index), 107, 110,
        118–120, 335
body mass index (BMI), 107, 110, 111*f*,
        118, 119*t*, 120*t*
brain injuries, 64*t*, 151–153
burden of disease, 48
    assessment, 48
burns, 153, 154*t*
    epidemiology, 153–155

C

cancer, sex distribution, 89–90, 89*t*
candidates, screening tests, 256, 256*t*
cardiovascular disease, behavioral
        epidemiology, 114–115
carriers, 131
case fatality rate (CFR), 71, 131
case fatality ratio, 62
case management events, 182
case mix, 183
case mix index, 183

case reports, 97–98
case series reports, 97, 98
case studies
    Assessment of Burden of Disease, 54
    Behavioral Factors and Risk of
        Gestational Diabetes, 117–118
    Body Mass Index, Waist
        Circumference, and Risk of
        Mortality, 118–120
    California Measles Outbreak, 141
    Case Series Report, 97, 98
    Case-Control Study, 318
    Cross-Sectional Study, 100, 101–102
    Cumulative Incidence, 80, 81*t*
    Ecological Study, 315
    Effect of Education on Health, 28–31
    Effect of Scoioeconomic Status on
        Health, 31–33
    Epidemiologic Patterns That Can
        Guide Policy Decisions, 10–12
    Healthcare Needs of the
        Homeless, 214–217
    Hospital-Based Injury Surveillance,
        167–168
    Impact of a Rapid Response System
        on Inpatient Mortality and
        Length of Stay, 189–190
    Impact of Administrative Decisions
        on Patient Outcomes, 7–9
    Impact of Unmet Healthcare Needs,
        217–219
    Influence of Gender and Age on
        Disability After Stroke, 55
    Nosocomial Infection Surveillance, 271
    Ohio Botulism Outbreak, 142
    Planning for Mental Health
        Services, 244–246
    Prevalence Study, 81–82
    Prospective Cohort Study, 316–317
    Randomized Control Trial-
        Chlorhexidine Bathing in ICUs
        to Prevent HAIs, 334–335
    Reasons for Postsurgical Hospital
        Readmissions, 189
    Regional Market Analysis, 242–243
    Retrospective Cohort Study, 317
    Screening for Colorectal
        Cancer, 272–273
    Unintentional Firearm Deaths, 168–169
case-control studies, 303–307, 318–319
    versus cohort, 310

risk factors, 307–310
cases, 303
case-specific death {mortality} rate
        (CSDR), population health,
        67–68
CASPER (Community Assessment
        Health Emergency Response
        (CASPER), 209, 210*f*
categorical surveillance, 267
categorical variable, 281–282
causality, 310
cause-specific death rate, 67
CBR (crude birth rate), 71
CDR (crude death {mortality} rate), 66
    population health, 66–67
Certificate of Need (CON)
        programs, 234
CFR (case fatality rate), 71, 131
*Checklist Manifesto: How to Get Things
        Right, The* (Gawande), 184
Chetty, R., 92
CHNA (community health needs
        assessment). *See* community
        health needs assessment
chronic diseases/conditions, 131
CI (cumulative incidence), 297
cigarette smoking, epidemiology,
        108–109
codes, CPT (Current Procedural
        Terminology), 51–52
cohort, 293–294
cohort life table, 72–73
cohort studies, 293–302
    versus case-control, 310
    prospective, 300–302, 316–317
    retrospective, 302, 317
    risk factors, 307–310
colorectal cancer, screening tests,
        272–273
commitment index, 226
common source exposure, 136
common source outbreaks, 135, 336
community, 197
Community Assessment for Public
        Health Emergency Response
        (CASPER), 209
community health, assessment, 46–47
community health needs assessment,
        195–196, 202–205, 220
    data nature and type, 205–208
    data sources, 208–209
    definition and scope of a community
        health needs assessment,
        201–202
    determinants of healthcare needs,
        196–200
    estimation of future healthcare needs,
        210–211
    forecasting methods, 211–214
    health status of the population, 197
    impact of unmet healthcare needs,
        217–219
    methods and process, 202–205

metrics, 207*t*
need versus demand, 200–201
Patient Protection and Affordable
        Care Act, 202
planning, 205
post-disaster, 209
priority setting, 209
size and demographic characteristics
        of population, 197
unmet need, 209–210
community trials, 331
comorbidity, 183
comorbidity measures, 183
comparison groups, 298
comparison of independent proportions,
        286–287
CON (Certificate of Need) programs, 234
confidence interval, 284
confounder variable, 312
confounding, observational studies,
        313–314
continuity care, 7–8
continuous variables, 282
control charts, 175
control groups, 305, 325
controls, 304
convalescent period, 132
correlation, 285
County Health Rankings & Roadmap, 17
CPT (Current Procedural Terminology),
        51–52
criminal events, 182
critical point, 263
    diseases, 263
crossover trials, 327
cross-sectional studies, 99–100, 100–102
crude birth rate (CBR), 71
crude death {mortality} rate (CDR), 336
    population health, 66–67
crude survival rate, 73–74
CSDR (case-specific death {mortality}
        rate), population health, 66
cumulative incidence, 80
    population health, 64–65
cumulative incidence (CI), 296
Current Procedural Terminology (CPT),
        51–52
cycstic fibrosis, benefit of drug Kalydeco
        for, 21

D

DALYs (disability-adjusted life years),
        48–50
DBCIs (digital behavior change
        interventions), 106–107
death, 38–42
deciles, 282
    statistical concepts, 282
decision-making process, 3–4
demand, 200

demand versus need, 200–201
Deming, Edward, 175
demographics, 17
descriptive epidemiology
    case reports, 97–98
    case series reports, 98–99
    cross-sectional studies, 99–102
    epidemiologic investigations, 96–97
    medical geography
        GISs (Geographic Information
                Systems), 93–95
        place, 92–93
    person, 86
        age, 86–87
        marital status, 92
        occupation, 90–91
        race, 87–89
        sex, 89–90
        socioeconomic status, 92
    time, 95–96
detectable preclinical phase (DPCP),
        264–265
determinants of disease, 19
determinants of health, 19–20, 201
    education, 24–31
    genetic makeup, 20–22
    socioeconomic, 22–27, 31–33
determinants of healthcare quality,
        175–176, 196–200
device events, 182
diabetes, behavioral epidemiology,
        115, 117–118
diagnostic medical errors, 178
digital behavior change interventions
        (DBCIs), 106–107
digital marketing, 240–241
direct standardization, 77–78
disability, 38–42
    assessment, 44–45
    influence of gender and age after
        stroke, 55
disability-adjusted life years (DALYs),
        48–50
discrete variables, 282
disease, definition of, 38–42
disease frequency, population health,
        62–63
diseases. *See also* screening tests
    assessment, 53–54
    classification, 50–52
    critical point, 263
    DPCP (detectable preclinical phase),
        264–265
    prevalence, 257
    reportable/notifiable, 52–53
    severity, assessment of quality,
        183–184
dispersion of data, 283
distribution of healthcare quality,
        176–182
Donabedian, Avedis, 175
DPCP (detectable preclinical phase),
        264–265

E

EBM (evidence-based management), 2, 4–5, 12, 337
    EBP (evidence-based practice), 4–5
Ebola virus, 130*t*, 133, 140
EBP (evidence-based practice), 4–5
e-cigarettes, 109
    epidemiology, 109–110
ecological bias, 292
ecological fallacy, 292
ecological studies, 291–294, 314–315
economic impact, injury epidemiology, 155–157
education as a determinant of health, 24–26, 28–31
effectiveness, measurement of quality, 175
efficiency, measurement of quality, 175
EHT (Elzinga-Hogarty Test), geographic market estimation, 228–229
electronic nicotine delivery systems, 109
eligibility criteria, 329
Elzinga-Hogarty Test (EHT), 228
    geographic market estimation, 228–229
endemic, 132
environment, 132
    infectious disease epidemiology, 132
environmental events, 182
environmental heterogeneity, 21
epidemics, 132–135
epidemiologic investigations, 96–97
epidemiologic patterns, policy decisions, 10–12
Epidemiologic Patterns That Can Guide Policy Decisions case study, 10–12
epidemiology, definition of, 2
    EBM (evidence-based management), 5
equitability, measurement of quality, 175
ERR (excess readmission ratio), 185–186
estimation of incidence, cohort studies, 299
European Syndromic Surveillance Project, 271
evidence-based management (EBM). *See* EBM (evidence-based management)
evidence-based practice (EBP). *see* EBP (evidence-based practice)
excess readmission ratio, 185–186
exercises, YPLL and DALYs, 53, 53*t*, 54, 55*f*
experimental groups, 327
experimental studies, 323–336. *See also* experimental studies; observational studies
    categorization, 327–328
    community trials, 331–332
    factorial trials, 333–334
    interventional study design, 325–327

    natural, 332
    randomized controlled trials (RCTs), 328–331, 334–335
exposed groups, 296, 298
exposure, 292, 295*t*, 296*t*, 297*t*

F

facility location planning, 233
factorial trials, 333–334
Farr, William, 51
fatality rates, 147
fecal transplant, 126
fetal mortality rate (FMR), 69–70
firearm-related injuries, 147
Fleming, S.T., 5
FMR (fetal mortality rate), 69–70
forecasting methods, community health needs assessment, 211–214
frequency, 282
    statistical concepts, 282
functioning and disability, assessment, 44–45

G

Gawande, Atul, 184
GDM (gestational diabetes mellitus), 117–118
genetic heterogeneity, 21
genetic makeup, determinants of health, 20–22
Geographic Information Systems (GISs), 93–95
geographic markets, 225
    determinants, 225–226
    estimation, 226–230
    measuring competition, 230
geopolitical boundaries, geographic market estimation, 228
gestational diabetes mellitus (GDM), 117–118
Gillam, S., 202
GISs (Geographic Information Systems), 93–95
global burden, infectious disease epidemiology, 127–129
global epidemiology of burns, 158–161
global epidemiology of drowning, 161
global epidemiology of injury, 157–158
global epidemiology of road traffic injuries, 161–163
grabage can model, 4
Graunt, John, 51

H

HAIs (healthcare-associated infections), 174
HALYs (health-adjusted life years), 48

health, 16
    World Health Organization definition, 16
health and well-being, self-assessment, 45–46
health geography. *See* medical geography
health index, 46
health professional shortage areas, 234
    designation of, 234–237
health-adjusted life years (HALYs), 48
healthcare needs, estimation of future, 210–211
healthcare planning and marketing, 223–247
    CON (Certificate of Need) programs, 234
    data sources, 238–239
    designation of health professional shortage areas, 234–237
    determinants of access of health services, 237–238
    determinants of geographic markets and service areas, 225–226
    estimation of geographic and service areas, 226–230
    facility location planning, 233
    geographic market competition level, 230
    hospital clustering based on patient origin data, 229–230
    marketing definition, scope, and purpose, 239–241
    planning, 225
    priority setting, 230–231
    small area health planning, 231–233
healthcare-associated infections (HAIs), 174
health-related quality of life (HRQOL), 48
Herfindahl–Hirschman index, 230
historical cohort studies, 294
homeless, healthcare needs, 214–217
homicide rates, 147
hospital clustering based on patient origin data, 229–230
Hospital Compare, 185
hospital quality reporting system, 185
hospital readmission rates, 174
    measurement of quality, 179–180
Hospital Readmission Reduction Program (HRRP), 185–186
hospital service areas, 242
hospital-based injury surveillance, 167–168
hosts, 132
HPSAs (Health Professional Shortage Areas), 234
HRQOL (health-related quality of life), 48
HRRP (Hospital Readmission Reduction Program), 185–186
hypothesis, 284–285

I

ICD (International Classification of Diseases), 50–52
IHI (Institute for Healthcare Improvement), 186
Impact of Administrative Decisions on Patient Outcomes case study, 7–9
IMR (infant mortality rate), 68–69
incidence, 63
incidence density, 296
    population health, 64
incidence rate, 63
    population health, 63–64
    relationship between prevalence, 66
incidence rate ratio, 294–296
inclusion/exclusion criteria, 329
income as a determinant of health, 23–24
incubation period, 132
indirect standardization, 78–79
individual-level exposure, 292
infant mortality rate, 62
infant mortality rate (IMR), 68–69
infection, 132
infectious, 132–133
infectious disease epidemiology, 126, 135–140
    acute diseases or conditions, 131
    agents, 131
    attack rate, 131
    carriers, 131
    case fatality rate (CFR), 131
    chronic diseases/conditions, 131–132
    convalescent period, 132
    emergence of new and resurgence of previously infectious diseases, 129–130
    endemic, 132
    environment, 132
    epidemic, 132
    epidemics, 132, 134–135
    fecal transplant, 126
    global burden, 127–129
    hosts, 132
    incubation period, 132
    infection, 132
    infectious, 132–133
    infectious disease triad, 130–131
    infectivity, 132
    infestation, 132–133
    microbe, 133
    microbial organism, 133
    microbiome, 126
    microorganism, 133
    outbreak, 133
    outbreaks, 134–135
        investigation, 135–140
    pathogen, 133
    pathogenesis, 133
    prodromal stage, 133–134

    transmission, 134
    United States, 127
    vector, 134
    virulence, 134
infectivity, 132
infestation, 132–133
injury epidemiology, 146, 161–167
    burns, 153–155
    economic impact, 155–157
    global epidemiology of burns, 158–161
    global epidemiology of drowning, 161
    global epidemiology of injury, 157–158
    global epidemiology of road traffic injuries, 161–163
    hospital-based injury surveillance, 167–168
    intentional injuries, 147–150
    nature, distribution, and impact of injuries, 146–147
    NEISS (National Electronic Injury Surveillance System), 157
    NVDRS (National Violent Death Reporting System), 155–157
    road traffic injuries and death, 150–151
    TBI (traumatic brain injury), 151–153
    unintentional firearm deaths, 168–169
Institute for Healthcare Improvement (IHI), 186
integrated healthcare delivery, 16
intentional injuries, 147–150
International Classification of Diseases (ICD), 50–52
interventional study design, 325–327
invasive procedure events, 182
invasiveness, 132
investigations
    epidemiologic patterns, 96–97
    outbreaks, 135–140

J

Juran, Joseph, 175

K

Kalydeco, as benefit for cystic fibrosis, 21
KID (Kids' Inpatient Database), 239
Kids' Inpatient Database (KID), 239
Kovner, A.R., 4

L

latent medical errors, 177
lead time, 264
leading causes of death, United States, 148t

lead-time bias, 264
    screening tests, 264–265
length bias, 265
    screening tests, 265–266
length of stay data, 287
length of stay (LOS), 174
Level I trauma centers, 146
life expectancy at birth, 71–72
life expectancy at specific age intervals, 72–73, 76
life tables at specific age intervals, 72–73
LIFE's Simple 7, 114–115
LIFO (Little In From Outside), 228–229
Little In From Outside (LIFO), 228–229
Little Out From Inside (LOFI), 228–229
LOFI (Little Out From Inside), 228–229
LOS (length of stay), 174

M

management, 2
    purpose, 3
management skills standardized test, 278–280
managerial epidemiology, 2, 5–6
    Blue Sky scenario, 6–7
marital status, 92
    demographic characteristic, 92
market analysis
    community health needs assessment, 209–210
    regional, 242–243
market share, 227
    estimation, 227
marketing. See healthcare planning and marketing
maternal mortality rate (MMR), 70–71
McAlearney, A.S., 4
McVey, L., 5
mean, 282–283
measurement of quality, 174, 191
    acceptability, 175
    accessibility, 175
    definition and goals, 174–175
    determinants of healthcare quality, 175–176
    distribution of healthcare quality, 176–182
    effectiveness, 175
    efficiency, 175
    equitability, 175
    hospital quality reporting system, 185
    hospital readmissions, 179–180
    HRRP (Hospital Readmission Reduction Program), 185–186
    medical errors, 177–179
    patient safety, 180–182
    PPHs (potentially preventable hospitalizations), 179

PQRS (Physician Quality Reporting System), 184–185
quality assessment study, 186–188
quality improvement checklists, 184
rapid response system on inpatient mortality, 189–190
safety, 175
sentinel events, 180–182
severity of disease, 183
Triple Aim, 186–187
measures of population health, summary of, 48–49
median, 283
medical care model, 18
versus population health model, 18
medical errors, 177–179
medical geography, 92–93
GISs (Geographic Information Systems), 93–95
Medically Underserved Areas (MUAs), 234
Medically Underserved Populations (MUPs), 234
mental health, 43
assessment, 43–44
link between physical health, 18–19
metabolic equivalent, 107
mHealth, 106
microbe, 133
microbial organism, 133
microbiome, 126
microorganism, 133
Mintzberg, H., 3
mixed study design, 292
MMR (maternal mortality rate), 70–71
mode, 283
MUAs (Medically Underserved Areas), 234
multi-group study design, 291
multiple regression analysis, 285–286
MUPs (Medically Underserved Populations), 234
My Life Check, 115

N

National Electronic Disease Surveillance System (NEDSS), 270–271
National Electronic Injury Surveillance System (NEISS), 157
National Healthcare Safety Network (NHSN), 176
National Inpatient Sample (NIS), 239
National Quality Forum
never events, 179
serious reportable events, 182
National Violent Death Reporting System (NVDRS), 155–157

Nationwide Emergency Department Sample (NEDS), 239
natural experiments, 332
NEDS (Nationwide Emergency Department Sample), 239
NEDSS (National Electronic Disease Surveillance System), 270–271
need, 200
need versus demand, 200–201
needs assessment, 201
NEISS (National Electronic Injury Surveillance System), 157
neonatal mortality rate (NMR), 68
never events, 178
new infectious diseases, emergence of, 129–130
NHSN (National Healthcare Safety Network), 176
NIS (National Inpatient Sample), 239
NMR (neonatal mortality rate), 68
nonprogrammed decisions, 3–4
normal distribution, 284
nosocomial infection surveillance, 271
notifiable diseases, 52–53
null hypothesis, 284, 330
NVDRS (National Violent Death Reporting System), 155–157

O

obesity, behavioral epidemiology, 110–112
observational studies, 289–321. *See also* experimental studies
association and causality, 310–312
bias, 312–313
case-control, 302–307, 317–319
versus cohort, 310
risk factors, 307–310
cohort, 293–302, 315–317
versus case-control, 310
risk factors, 307–310
confounding, 313–314
ecological, 291–294
ecological studies, 315–316
observed survival rates, 73–74
occupation, demographic characteristic, 90–91
occupational status as a determinant of health, 26–27
Ohio botulism outbreak, 142
one-sample *t*-test, 286
one-sample *z*-test, 286
outbreak, definition of, 133
outbreaks, 134–135
California measles, 141

common source, 135
Ebola virus, 138–139
investigation, 135–140
Ohio botulism, 142
propagated, 135
Zika, 138–139
outcome, 176
healthcare quality, 176

P

P values, 278, 284–285
P4P (pay-for-performance), 116
parallel trials, 327
Paré, Ambroise, 38
passive surveillance, 266
pathogen, 133
pathogenesis, 133
pathogenicity, 133
pathogens, 130
patient incentives to promote healthy behavior, 115–116
patient outcomes, administrative decisions, 7–9
Patient Protection and Affordable Care Act, 202
patient protection events, 182
patient safety, measurement of quality, 180–182
patient-centered care, 16, 175
pay-for-performance (P4P), 116
percentile, 282
statistical concepts, 282
period life table, 73
period prevalence, population health, 65
person (demographic characteristic), 86
age, 86–87
marital status, 92
occupation, 90–91
race, 87–89
sex, 89–90
socioeconomic status, 92
personal health, assessment, 42
phantom limb/phantom pain, 38
phase I clinical trials, 140, 329
phase II clinical trials, 140, 329
phase III clinical trials, 140, 329
phases, RCTs (randomized controlled trials), 328–329
physical activity, behavioral epidemiology, 107–108
physical health, link between mental health, 18–19
Physician Quality Reporting System (PQRS), 184–185
physician sustainability, 7
physiologic health, assessment of, 43
place (medical geography), 92–93

planning, 5, 6, 225
  healthcare, 225
Plato, Mark, 6
PNMR (postneonatal mortality
    rate), 68
point source, 135
policy decisions, epidemiologic patterns,
    10–12
poor nutrition, behavioral epidemiology,
    110–112
population, definition of, 17
  statistical concepts, 280–281
population health, 17, 60, 78–79
  adjustment of rates, 75–77
  ASDR (age-specific death {mortality}
      rate), 67
  CBR (crude birth rate), 71
  CDR (crude death {mortality} rate),
      66–67
  CFR (case fatality rate), 71
  CSDR (case-specific death {mortality}
      rate), 67–68
  cumulative incidence, 64–65
  direct standardization, 77–78
  FMR (fetal mortality rate), 69–70
  IMR (infant mortality rate), 68–69
  incidence density, 64
  incidence rate, 63–64
  indirect standardization, 78–79
  life expectancy at birth, 71–72
  life expectancy at specific age
      intervals, 72–73
  life tables at specific age intervals,
      72–73
  measures of disease frequency, 62–63
  MMR (maternal mortality rate),
      70–71
  NMR (neonatal mortality rate), 68
  observed survival rates, 73–74
  PNMR (postneonatal mortality
      rate), 68
  population health model versus
      medical care model, 18
  prevalence, 65–66
  proportional mortality, 71
  proportional statistics, 61
  rate statistics, 61–62
  ratio stats, 60
  relationship between incidence rate
      and prevalence, 66
  relative survival rates, 73–74
  SMR (standardized mortality ratio),
      80
  standardization of rates, 75–77
  summary measures of, 47–48
population health model, 18
postneonatal mortality rate
    (PNMR), 68
potential criminal events, 182
potentially preventable hospitalizations
    (PPHs), 179
power of study, 329–330

PPHs (potentially preventable
    hospitalizations), 179
PQRS (Physician Quality Reporting
    System), 184–185
predictive value negative, 263
predictive value positive, 263
prevalence, 81–82
  diseases, 257
  population health, 65–66
  relationship between incidence
      rate, 66
preventable adverse events, 177–179
preventable hospitalization, 179
prevention
  nature, scope, and levels of
      proportion, 250–255
  primary, 251–252
  screening, 255–266
  secondary, 252–254
  tertiary, 254–255
preventive medical errors, 178
previously known infectious
    diseases, reemergence
    of, 129–130
primary prevention, 251–252
priority setting, role of "Health People"
    (HR) reports, 230–231
probability, 62
process of care, 175
  healthcare quality, 175
prodromal stage, 133–134
product events, 182
programmed decisions, 3–4
Pronovost, Peter, 184
propagated outbreaks, 135
prophylactic trial, 327
proportion, 61
  population health statistics, 61
proportional mortality, 71
proportional mortality ratio, 71
prospective cohort studies, 300–302,
    315–316
psychosocial development, assessment,
    43–44

Q

QALYs (quality-adjusted life years),
    48, 50
quality assessment study, 186–188
quality improvement checklists, 184
quality of evidence, cohort studies, 299
quality-adjusted life years (QALYs),
    48, 50
quantitative analysis, 3
quantitative variable, 282
quartiles, 282
  statistical concepts, 282
quintiles, 282
  statistical concepts, 282

R

race, 27
  demographic characteristic, 87–89
race as a determinant of health, 27
radiologic events, 182
radius method, geographic market
    estimation, 227
randomized controlled trials (RCTs), 99,
    328–331, 334–335
range, definition of, 283
rate, population health
    statistics, 61–62
rate ratio, 294–295
ratio, 60
  population health
      statistics, 60–61
RCTs (randomized controlled trials), 99,
    328–331, 334–335
reasons for postsurgical hospital
    readmissions, 189
regional market analysis, 242–243
regression, 286
relative frequency, 282
relative risk, 294–295
relative survival rates, 73–74
relevance index, 226
reliability, 261
  screening tests, 261–262
reportable diseases, 52–53
reportable events, 182
reporting criteria, 52
retrospective cohort studies, 294, 302,
    317–318
risk factors, 298
  case-control studies, 307–310
  cohort studies, 309–312
risk management, 174
risk of mortality, 118–120
risk ratio (RR), 297
road traffic injuries and death, 150–151
Robert Wood Johnson Foundation, 17
Rohrer, J.E., 5
run charts, 175

S

safety, measurement of quality, 175
sample, 281
  statistical concepts, 281
sample sizes, RCTs (randomized
    controlled trials), 329–330
SASD (State Ambulatory Surgery
    and Services Databases),
    238–239
scientific rigor, cohort studies, 299
scope of community health needs
    assessment, 201–202
screening tests, 255–266
  candidates, 256–257

colorectal cancer, 272–273
criteria of effective, 256
detection of disease before reaching
    critical point, 263
high accuracy for detectable
    preclinical phase, 258
lead-time bias, 264–265
length bias, 265–266
morbidity, invasiveness, and
    inconvenience, 263
predictive value negative, 263
predictive value positive, 263
relationship between sensitivity and
    specificity, 261–262
reliability, 261–262
sensitivity, 259
specificity, 259–261
validity, 258–259
seatbelt usage rate, 151
secondary prevention, 252–254
SEDD (State Emergency Department
    Databases), 238
SEI (Socioeconomic Index), 26–27
self-assessment, health and well-being,
    45–46
sensitivity, 259
    screening tests, 259, 261–262
sentinel surveillance, 267
sentinel events, 178
    measurement of quality, 180–182
serious reportable events, 182
service areas, 225
    determinants, 225–226
    estimation, 226–230
severity of disease, 183
    assessment of quality, 183–184
sex, demographic characteristic, 89–90
Shewhart, Walter, 175
SID (State Inpatient Databases), 238
small area health planning, 231–233
smoking, epidemiology, 108–110
SMR (standardized mortality
    ratio), 80
social media marketing, 240–241
socioeconomic determinants of health,
    22–27, 31–33
socioeconomic status, demographic
    characteristic, 92
specificity, 342
    screening tests, 259–262
spread of data, 283
SRCs (State Reportable Conditions), 52
standard deviation, 283
standardization of rates, 75–77
standardized mortality ratio (SMR), 80

State Ambulatory Surgery and Services
    Databases (SASD), 238–239
State Emergency Department Databases
    (SEDD), 238
State Inpatient Databases (SID), 238
State Reportable Conditions (SRCs), 52
statistical concepts
    confidence interval, 284
    correlation, 285
    deciles, 282
    frequency, 282
    hypothesis, 284
    measures of central tendency in data,
        282–283
    measures of spread or dispersion of
        data, 283
    normal distribution, 283–284
    P values, 284–285
    percentile, 282
    population, 280–281
    quartiles, 282
    quintiles, 282
    regression, 285–286
    sample, 281
    Type I and II errors, 285
    variable, 281–282
statistical tests, 286–288
statistics, population health. *See*
    population health
stroke, influence of gender and age on
    disability, 55
structure, 175
    healthcare quality, 175
study groups, 325
substance abuse, behavioral
    epidemiology, 112–114
surgical procedure events, 182
surveillance, 266
    active, 266–267
    NEDSS (National Electronic Disease
        Surveillance System), 270–271
    nosocomial infection, 271
    passive, 266
    sentinel, 267
    syndromic, 267–270
    Triple-S, 271
syndromic surveillance, 267–270

T

Taber's Cyclopedic Medical Dictionary,
    16–17
TBI (traumatic brain injury), 151–153
tertiary prevention, 252–255, 342

therapeutic trial, 327
total service area, 226
traffic injuries and death, 150–151
transmission, definition of, 134
trauma, 146
traumatic brain injury (TBI), 151–153
treatment medical errors, 178
Triple Aim, 186
Triple-S, 271
t-test, 286
two-sample *t*-test, 286
Type I and II errors, 285, 313

U

under-5 mortality rate, 62
unintentional firearm deaths, 168–169
unmet healthcare needs
    assessment, 209–210
    impact, 217–219
unmet need, 209

V

validity, 258
    screening tests, 258–259
variables, 281
    statistical concepts, 281–282
vector, 134
virulence, 134

W

waist circumference, 107, 118–120
Witkin, B.R., 205

Y

Yarnell, C.J., 12
years of potential life lost (YPLL), 5, 48

Z

Zika virus outbreak investigation,
    138–139
Zika virus, 343
z-test, 286